YOWAMUSHI PEDAL

WATARU WATANABE

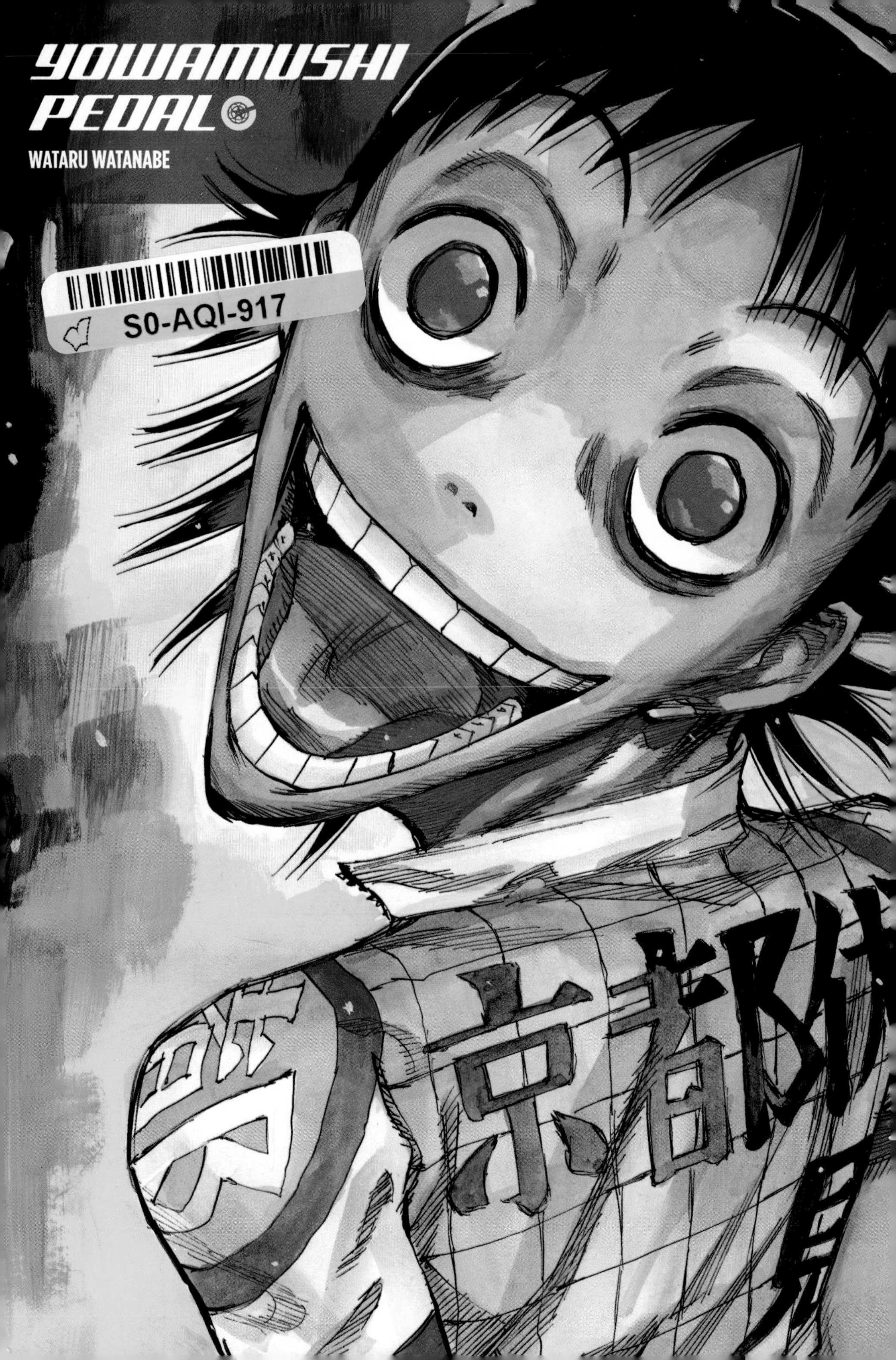
京都

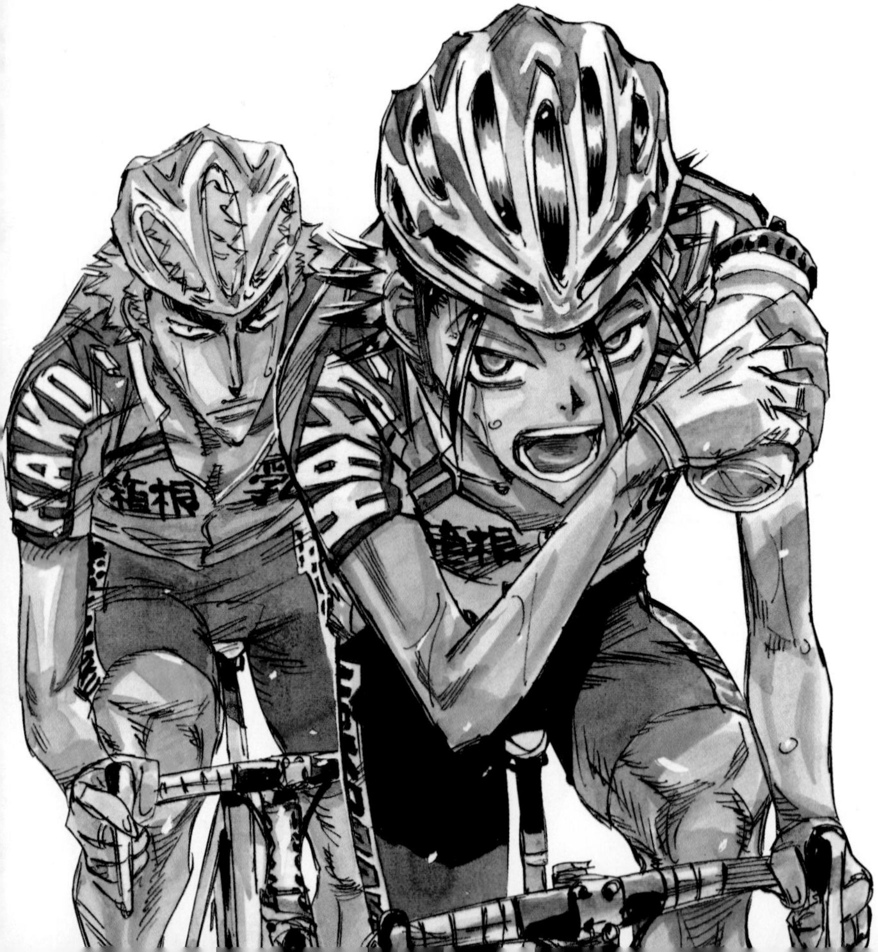
箱根
箱根

YOWAMUSHI PEDAL

WATARU WATANABE

8

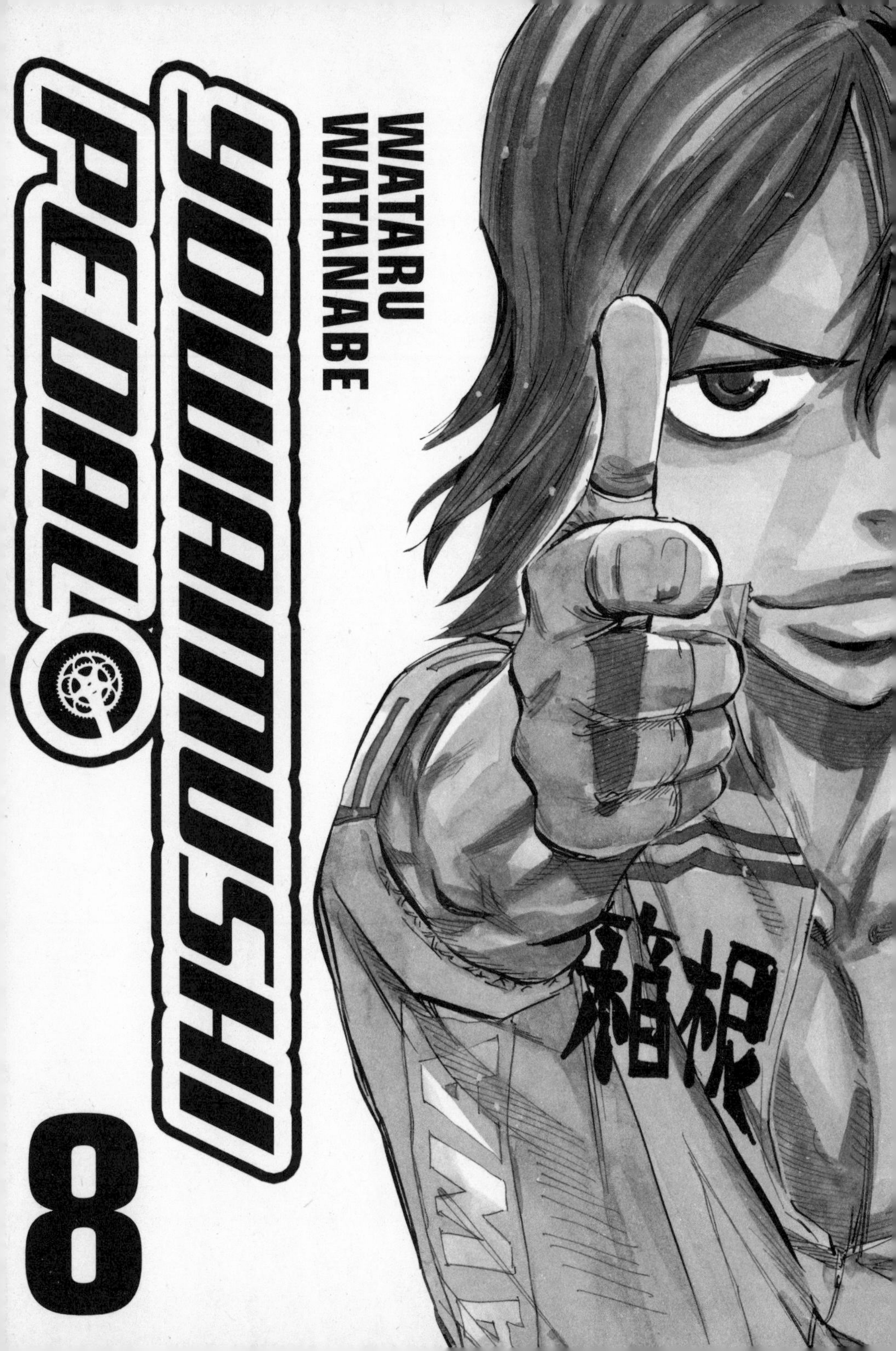
箱根

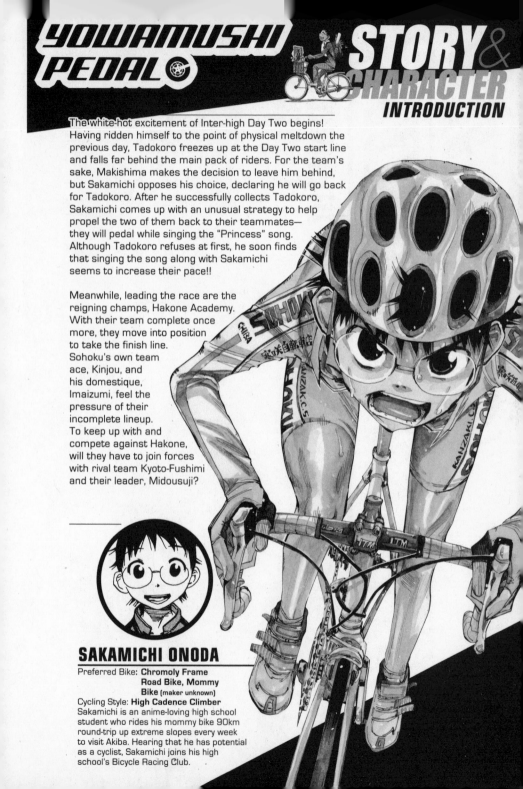

YOWAMUSHI PEDAL

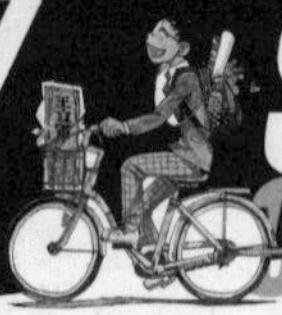

STORY & CHARACTER INTRODUCTION

The white-hot excitement of Inter-high Day Two begins! Having ridden himself to the point of physical meltdown the previous day, Tadokoro freezes up at the Day Two start line and falls far behind the main pack of riders. For the team's sake, Makishima makes the decision to leave him behind, but Sakamichi opposes his choice, declaring he will go back for Tadokoro. After he successfully collects Tadokoro, Sakamichi comes up with an unusual strategy to help propel the two of them back to their teammates—they will pedal while singing the "Princess" song. Although Tadokoro refuses at first, he soon finds that singing the song along with Sakamichi seems to increase their pace!!

Meanwhile, leading the race are the reigning champs, Hakone Academy. With their team complete once more, they move into position to take the finish line. Sohoku's own team ace, Kinjou, and his domestique, Imaizumi, feel the pressure of their incomplete lineup. To keep up with and compete against Hakone, will they have to join forces with rival team Kyoto-Fushimi and their leader, Midousuji?

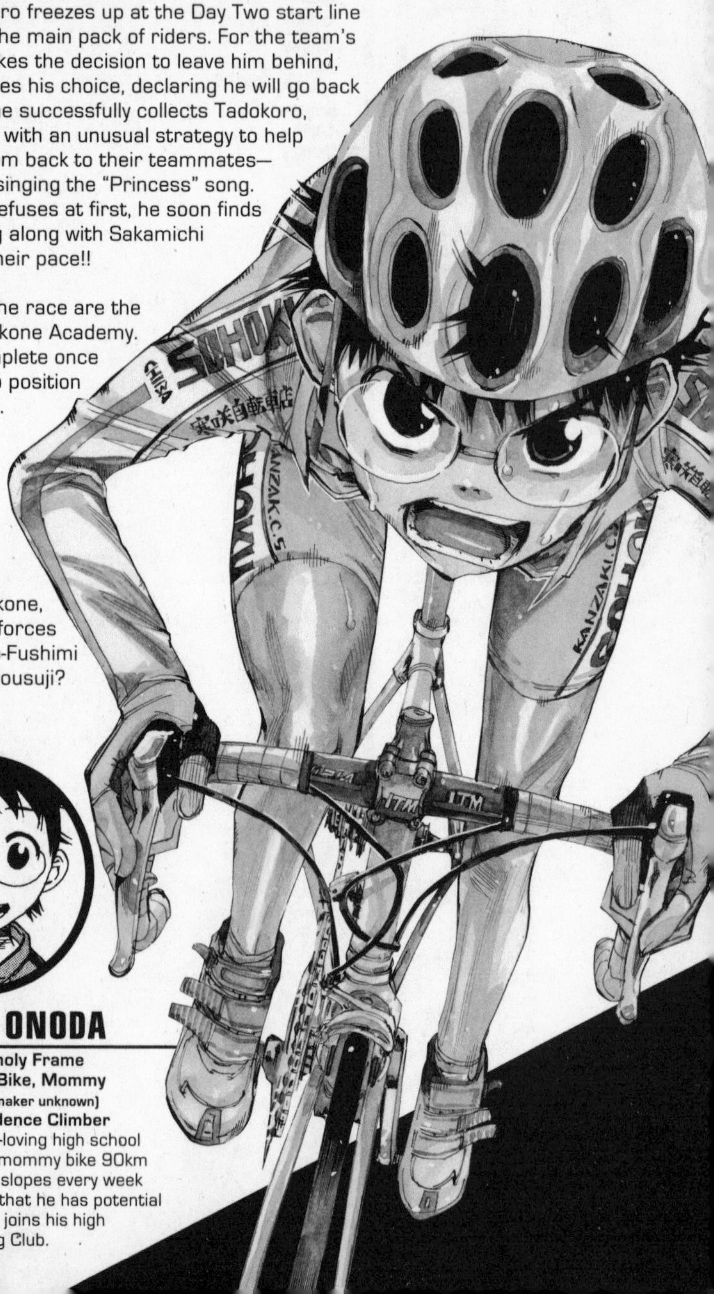
CHIBA
KANZAKI.C.S

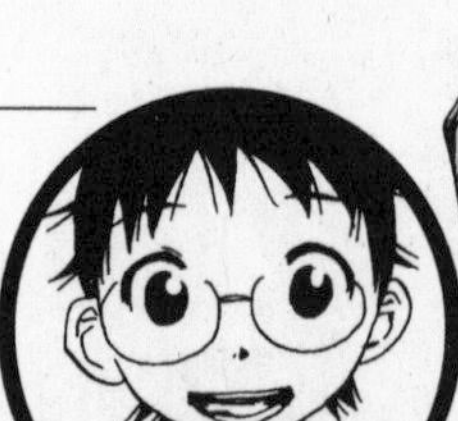

SAKAMICHI ONODA

Preferred Bike: **Chromoly Frame Road Bike, Mommy Bike** (maker unknown)

Cycling Style: **High Cadence Climber**

Sakamichi is an anime-loving high school student who rides his mommy bike 90km round-trip up extreme slopes every week to visit Akiba. Hearing that he has potential as a cyclist, Sakamichi joins his high school's Bicycle Racing Club.

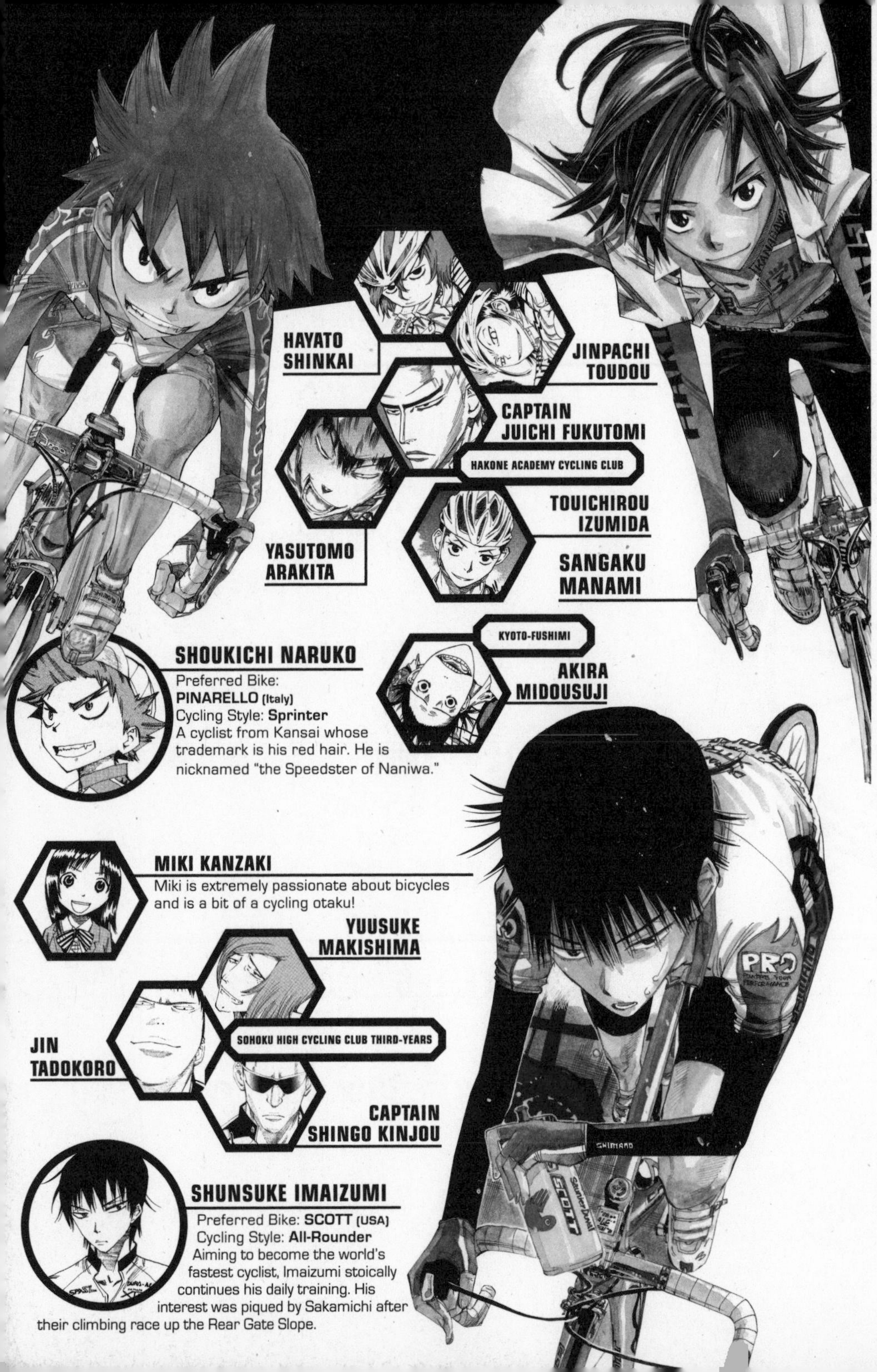

HAKONE ACADEMY CYCLING CLUB

HAYATO SHINKAI

JINPACHI TOUDOU

CAPTAIN JUICHI FUKUTOMI

TOUICHIROU IZUMIDA

YASUTOMO ARAKITA

SANGAKU MANAMI

SHOUKICHI NARUKO

Preferred Bike: **PINARELLO (Italy)**
Cycling Style: **Sprinter**
A cyclist from Kansai whose trademark is his red hair. He is nicknamed "the Speedster of Naniwa."

KYOTO-FUSHIMI

AKIRA MIDOUSUJI

MIKI KANZAKI

Miki is extremely passionate about bicycles and is a bit of a cycling otaku!

SOHOKU HIGH CYCLING CLUB THIRD-YEARS

YUUSUKE MAKISHIMA

JIN TADOKORO

CAPTAIN SHINGO KINJOU

SHUNSUKE IMAIZUMI

Preferred Bike: **SCOTT (USA)**
Cycling Style: **All-Rounder**
Aiming to become the world's fastest cyclist, Imaizumi stoically continues his daily training. His interest was piqued by Sakamichi after their climbing race up the Rear Gate Slope.

VOL.8 *YOWAMUSHI PEDAL* CONTENTS

RIDE.120 KYOTO-FUSHIMI LAUNCHES — 09

RIDE.121 PROVOCATION — 29

RIDE.122 HAKONE'S #4 — 49

RIDE.123 SHINKAI — 69

RIDE.124 SOHOKU, DISADVANTAGED — 89

RIDE.125 RAH, RAH, RAH — 109

RIDE.126 SHINKAI, HOUNDED — 129

RIDE.127 DEMON — 149

RIDE.128 THE TRIUMPHANT MAN — 171

197 **RIDE.129** THE FASTEST AND THE STRONGEST

217 **RIDE.130** THE SECOND HALF

237 **RIDE.131** ONODA'S RIDE

257 **RIDE.132** SOHOKU UNITE!!

277 **RIDE.133** THE SPRINTERS' END

297 **RIDE.134** DEAD WEIGHT DISCARDED

317 **RIDE.135** TRANSFER OF THE CROWN

337 **RIDE.136** THE CHAMPIONS' END

357 **RIDE.137** SINGLE-DIGIT NUMBER TAGS

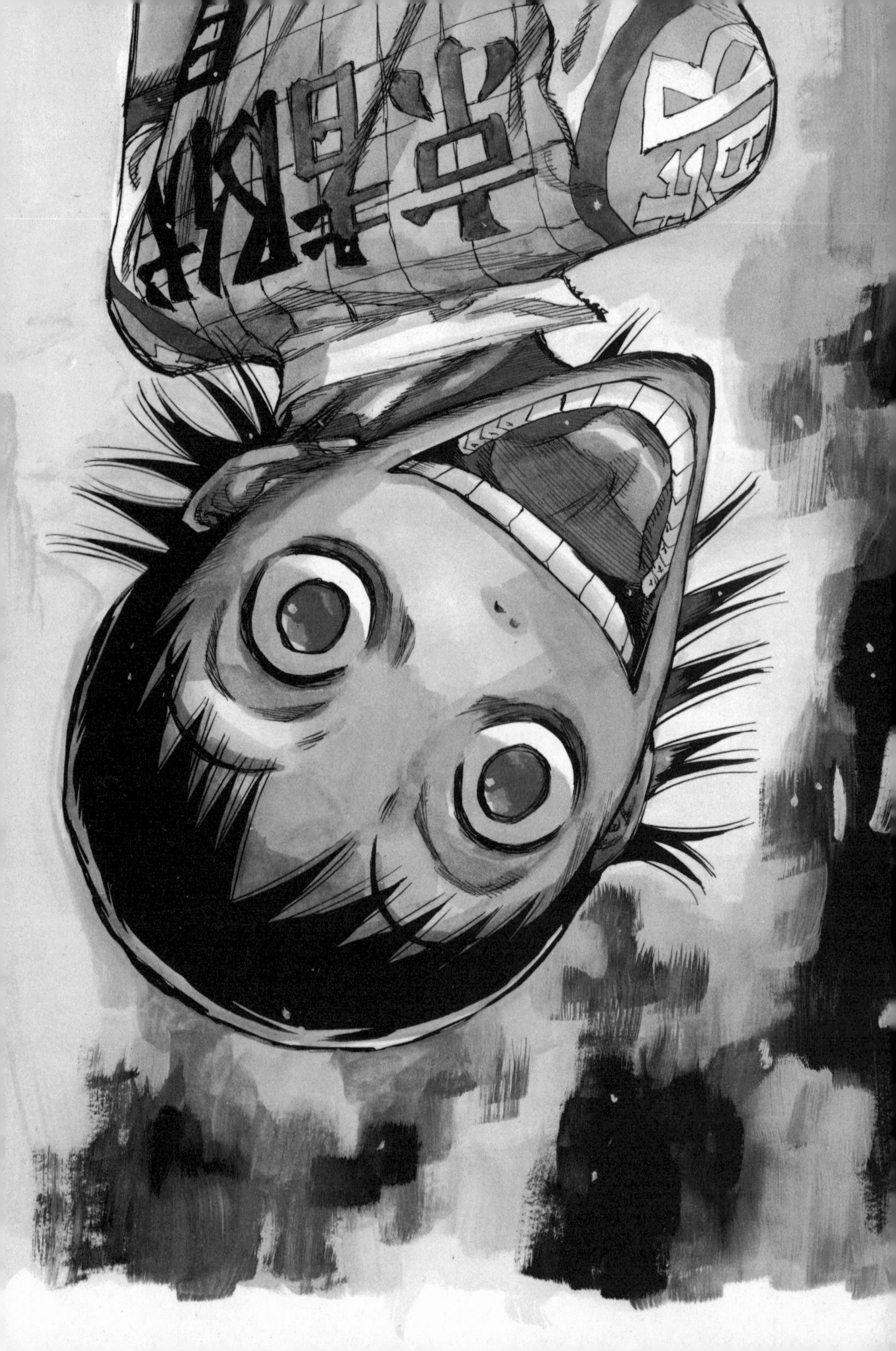

RIDE.120 KYOTO-FUSHIMI LAUNCHES

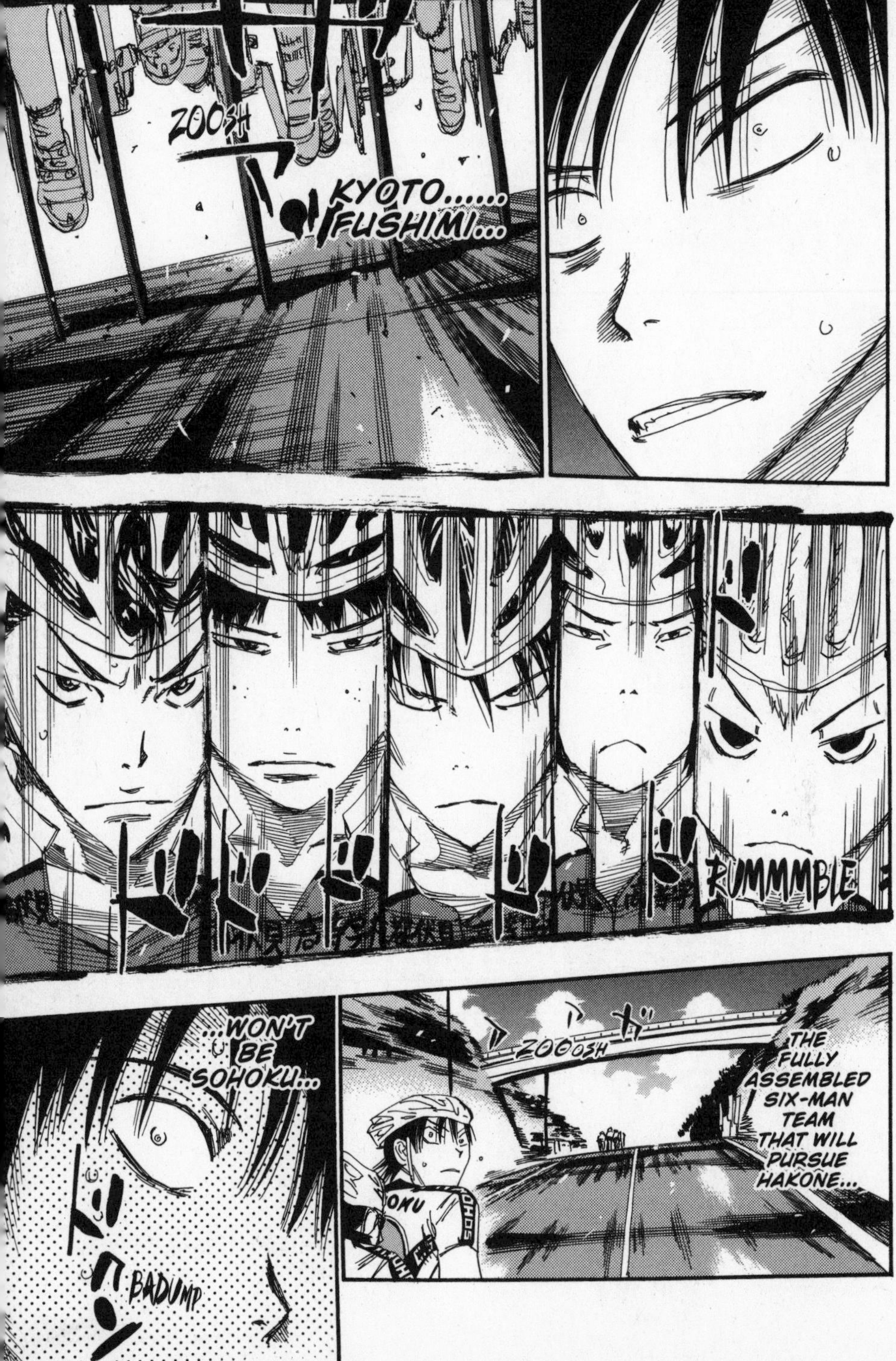
ZOOSH
KYOTO...... FUSHIMI...
RUMMMBLE
ZOOOSH
THE FULLY ASSEMBLED SIX-MAN TEAM THAT WILL PURSUE HAKONE...
...WON'T BE SOHOKU...
BADUMP

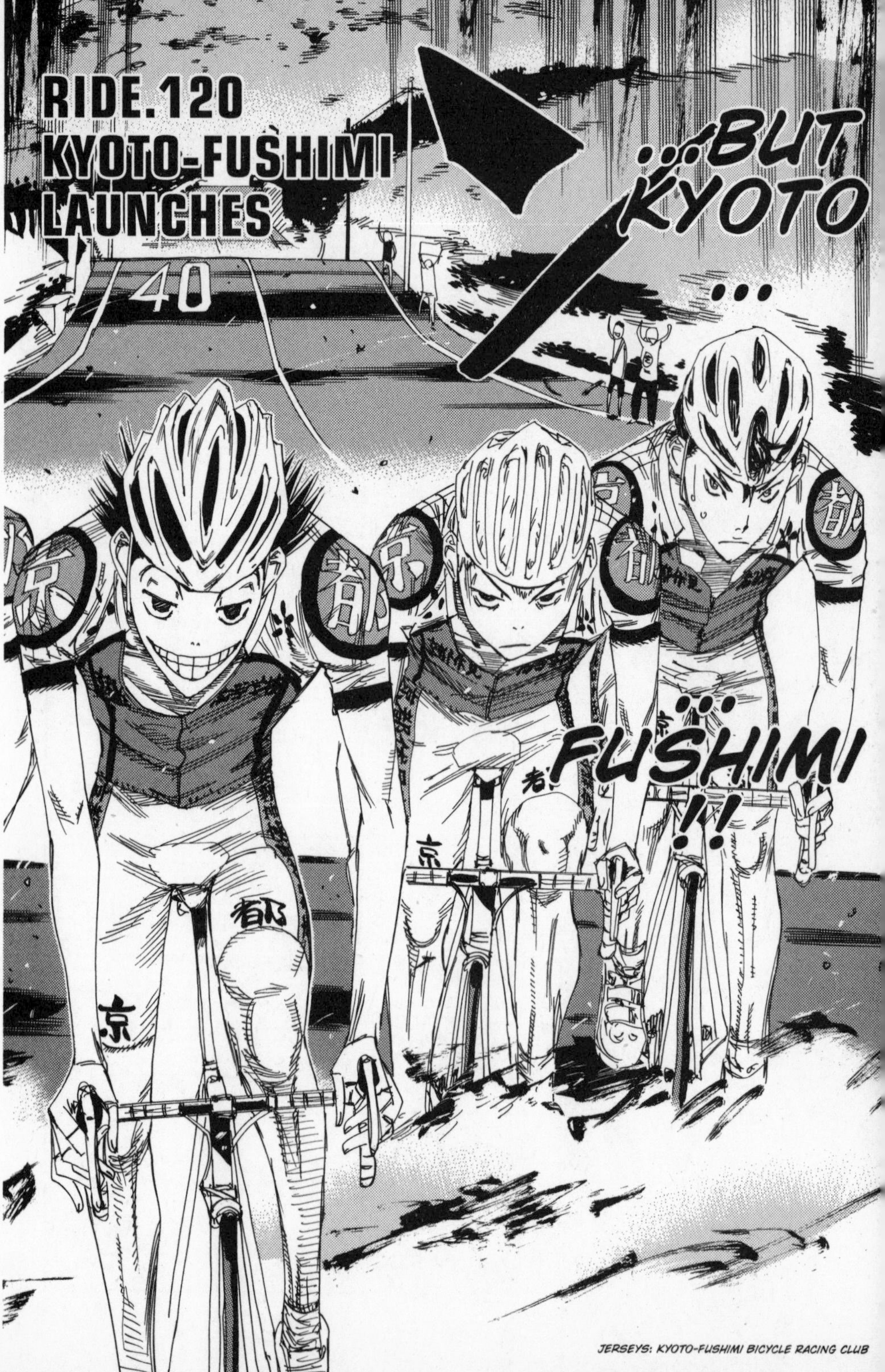
...BUT KYOTO...
RIDE.120
KYOTO-FUSHIMI
LAUNCHES
40
...FUSHIMI!!

JERSEYS: KYOTO-FUSHIMI BICYCLE RACING CLUB

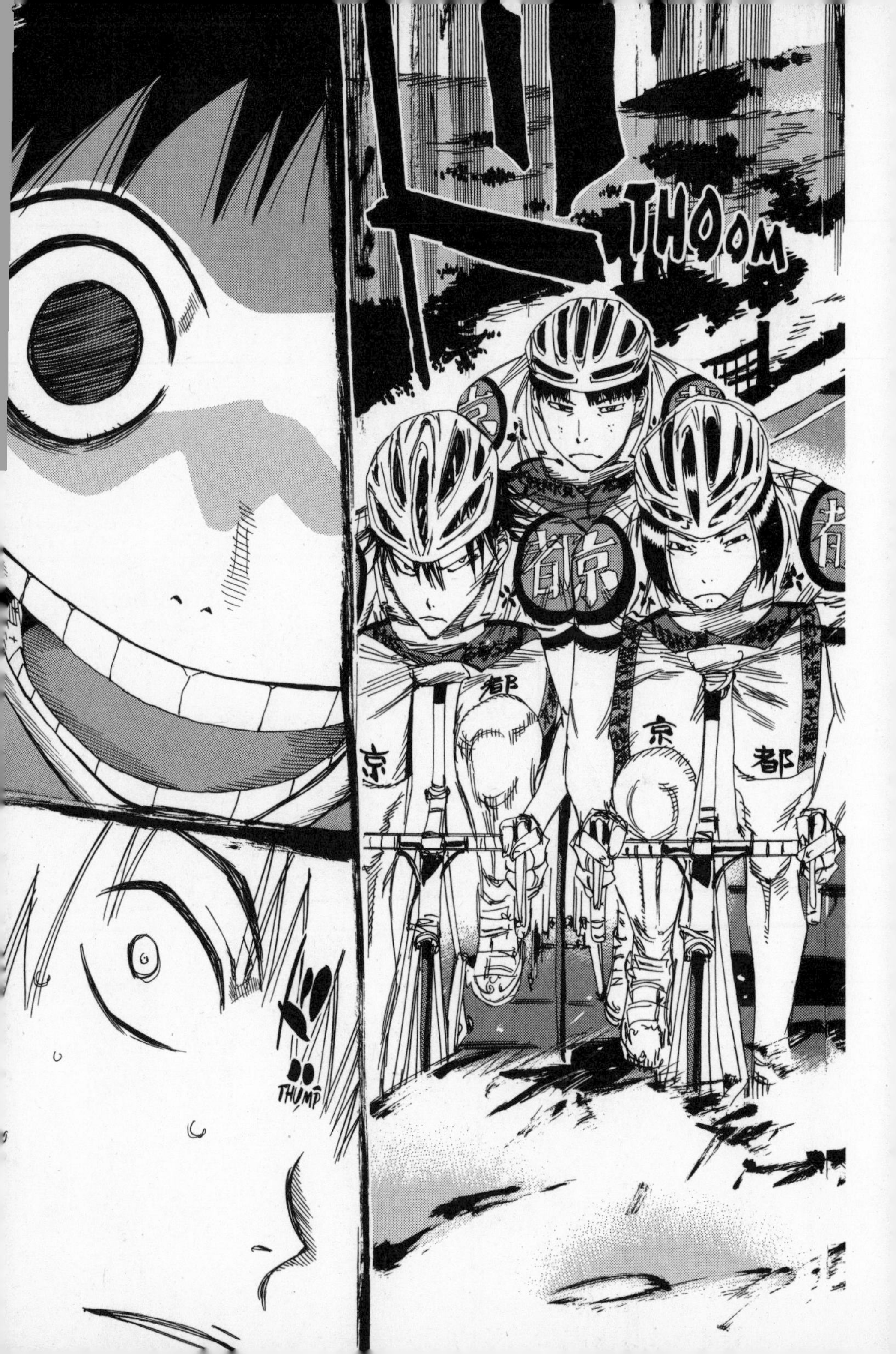
THOOM
DO THUMP

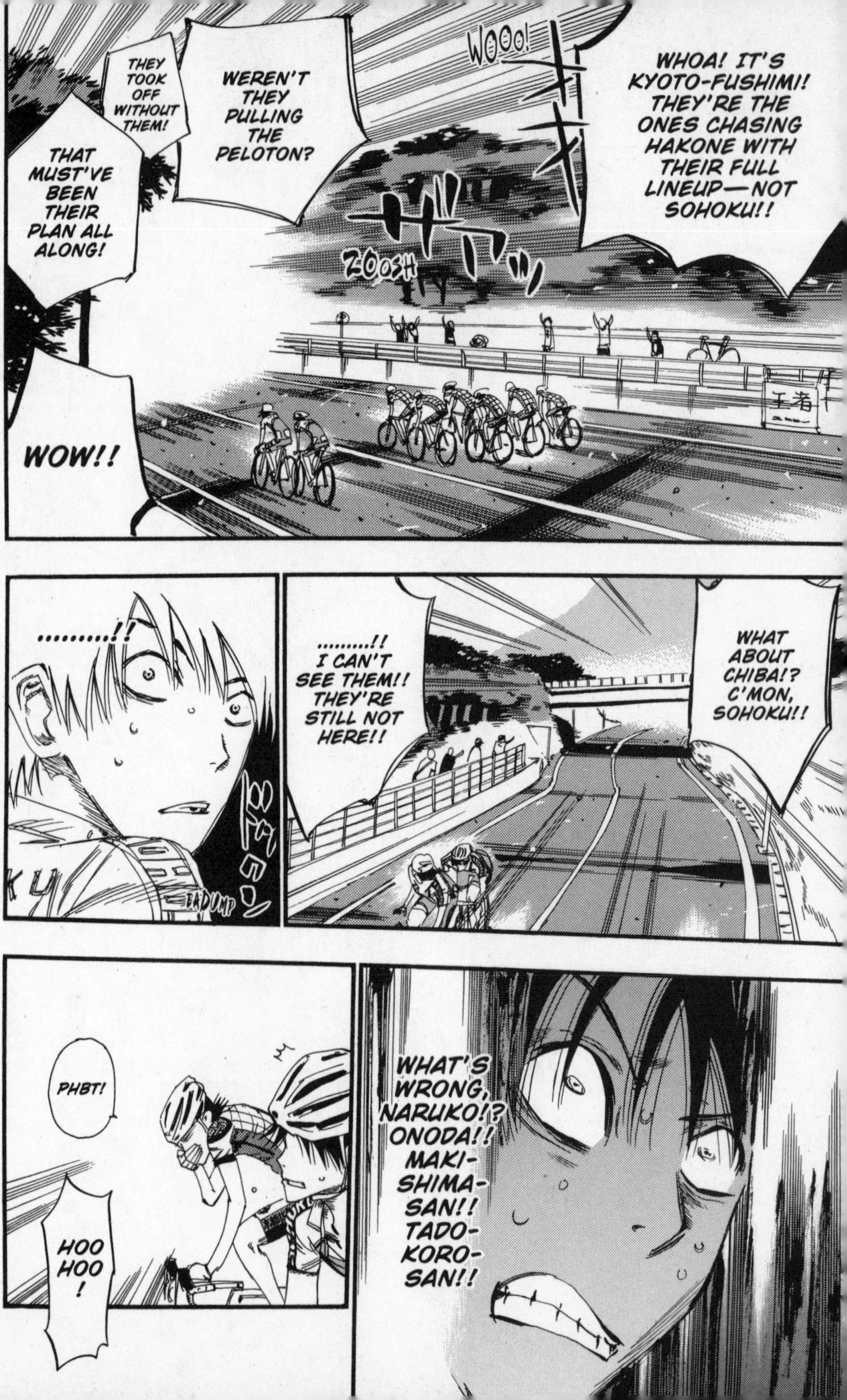
WHOA! IT'S KYOTO-FUSHIMI!! THEY'RE THE ONES CHASING HAKONE WITH THEIR FULL LINEUP—NOT SOHOKU!!
WOOO!
WEREN'T THEY PULLING THE PELOTON?
THEY TOOK OFF WITHOUT THEM!
THAT MUST'VE BEEN THEIR PLAN ALL ALONG!
ZOOSH
WOW!!
WHAT ABOUT CHIBA!? C'MON, SOHOKU!!
.........!! I CAN'T SEE THEM!! THEY'RE STILL NOT HERE!!
.........!!
BADUMP
WHAT'S WRONG, NARUKO!? ONODA!! MAKI-SHIMA-SAN!! TADO-KORO-SAN!!
PHBT!
HOO HOO!

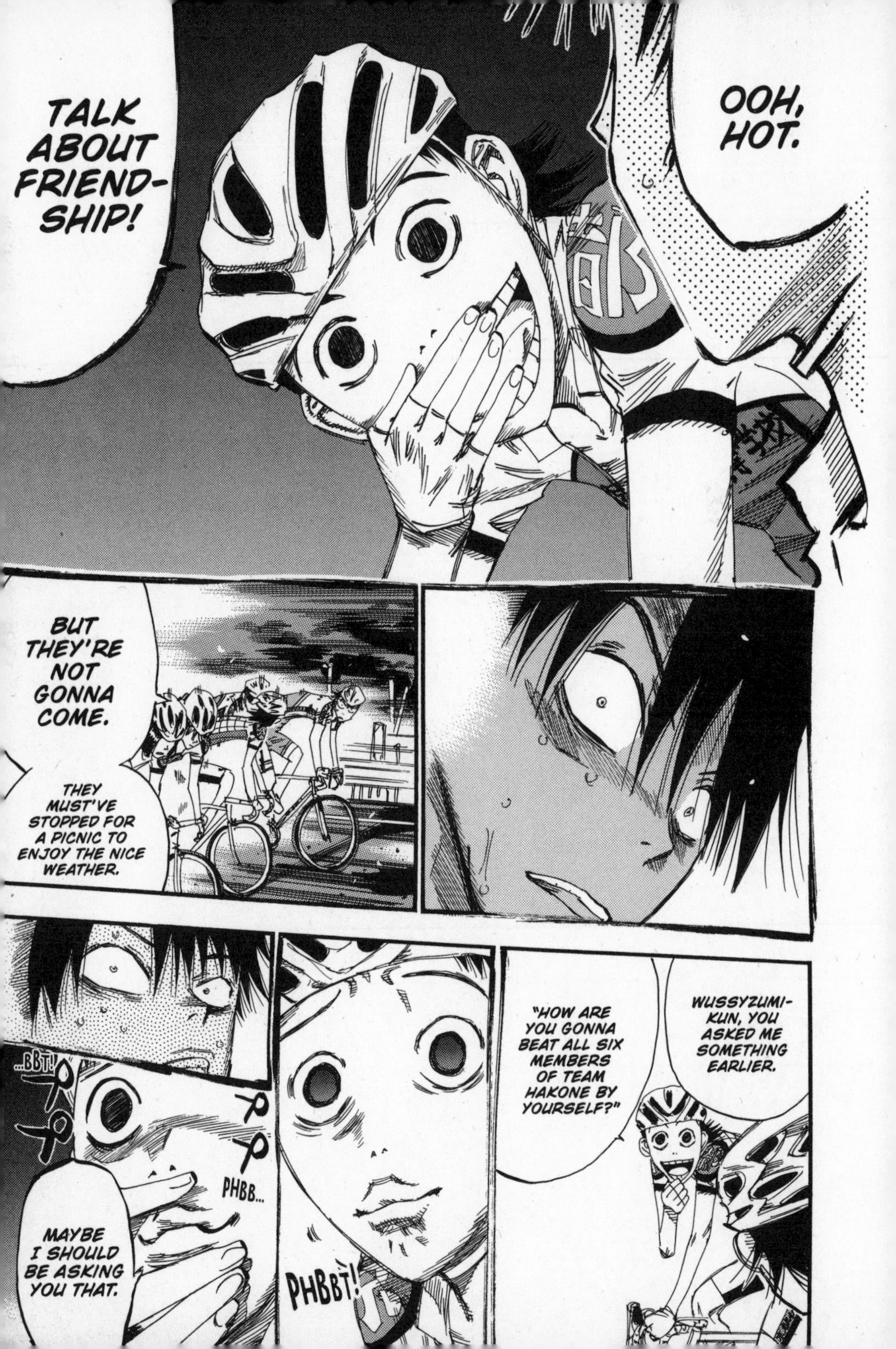
OOH, HOT.
TALK ABOUT FRIEND-SHIP!
BUT THEY'RE NOT GONNA COME.
THEY MUST'VE STOPPED FOR A PICNIC TO ENJOY THE NICE WEATHER.
WUSSYZUMI-KUN, YOU ASKED ME SOMETHING EARLIER.
"HOW ARE YOU GONNA BEAT ALL SIX MEMBERS OF TEAM HAKONE BY YOURSELF?"
PHBBT!
...BBT!
PHBB...
MAYBE I SHOULD BE ASKING YOU THAT.

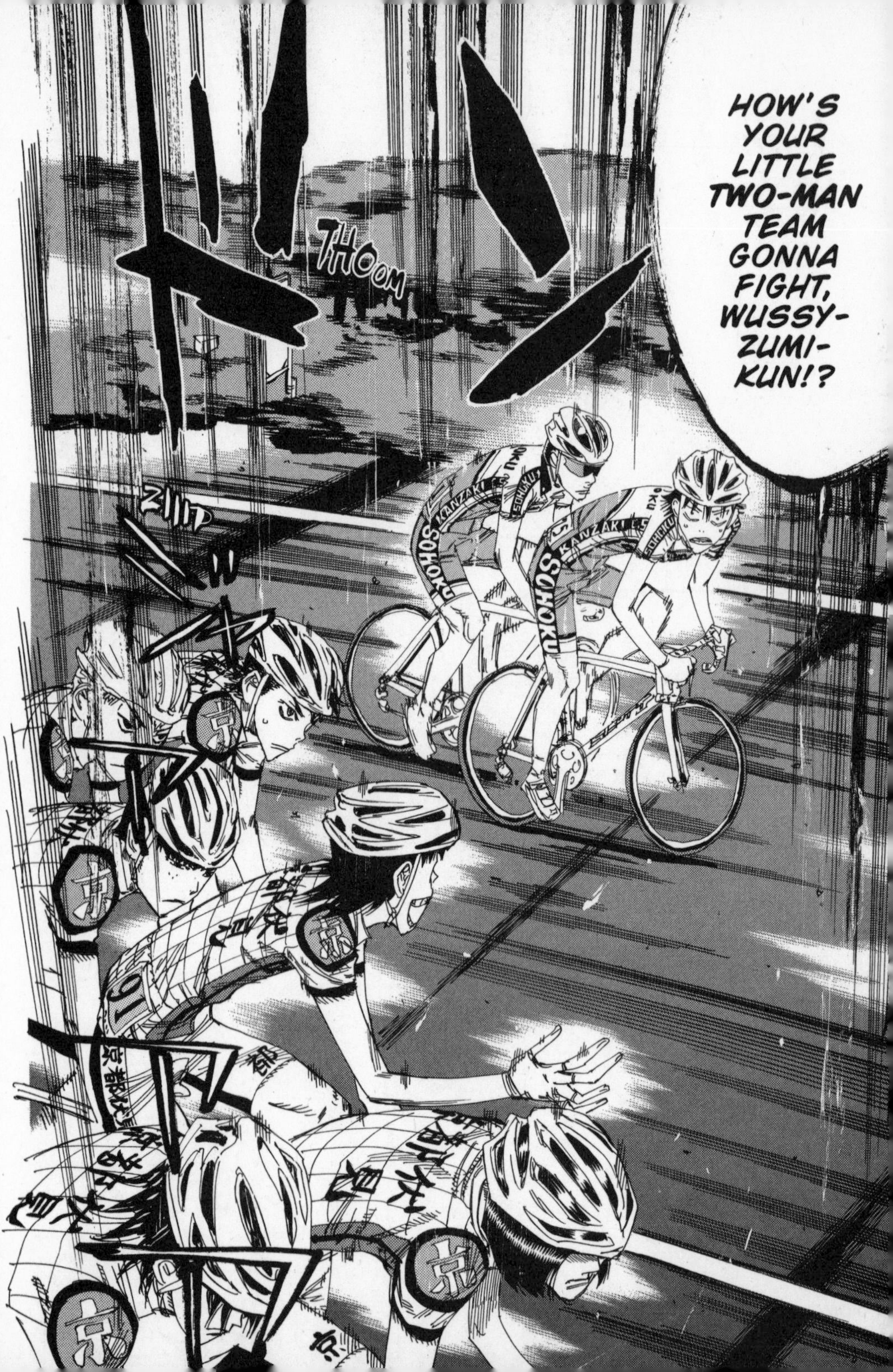
HOW'S YOUR LITTLE TWO-MAN TEAM GONNA FIGHT, WUSSY-ZUMI-KUN!?
THOOM
ZIIIP

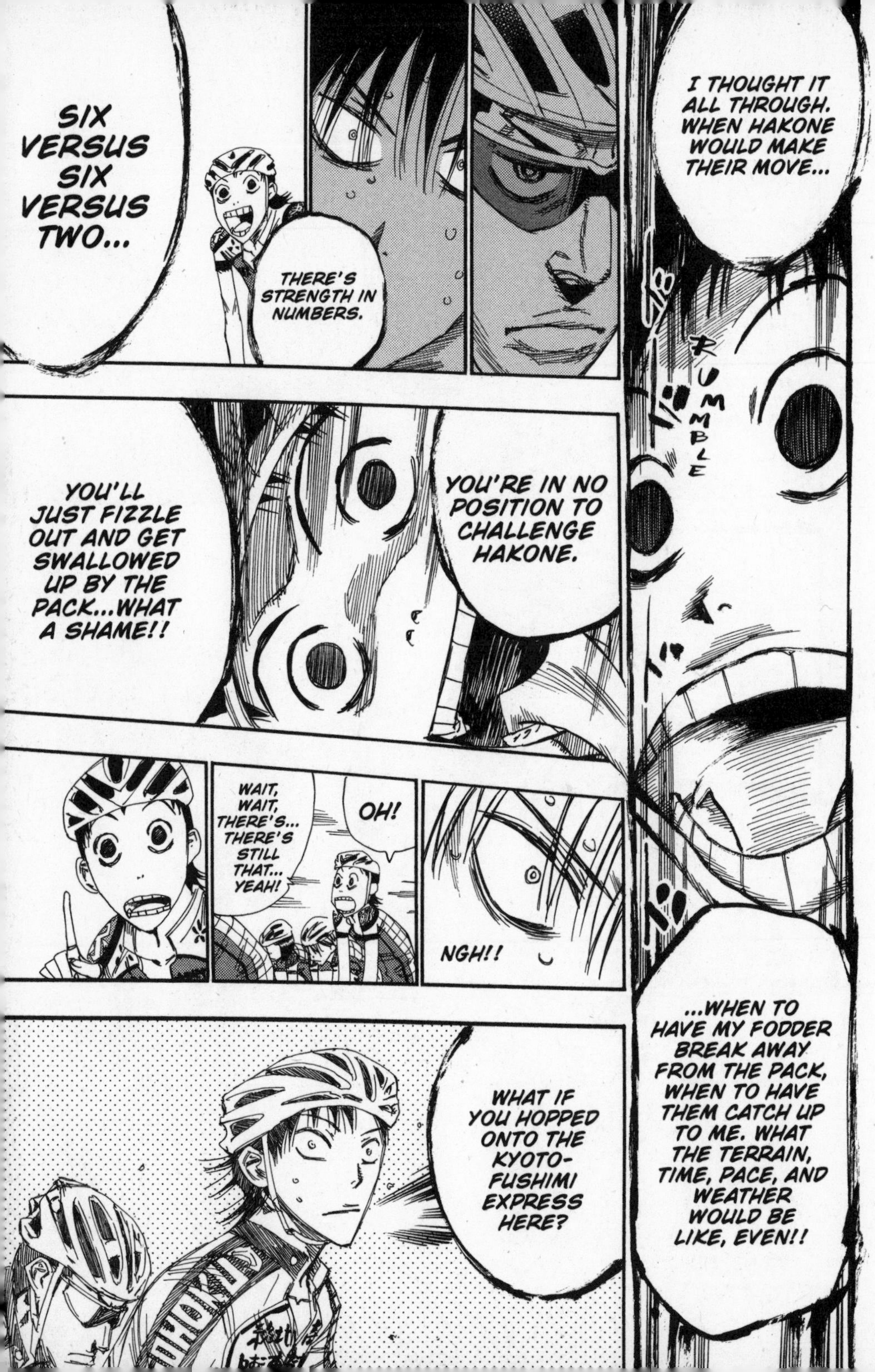
I THOUGHT IT ALL THROUGH. WHEN HAKONE WOULD MAKE THEIR MOVE...
RUMMBLE
...WHEN TO HAVE MY FODDER BREAK AWAY FROM THE PACK, WHEN TO HAVE THEM CATCH UP TO ME. WHAT THE TERRAIN, TIME, PACE, AND WEATHER WOULD BE LIKE, EVEN!!
SIX VERSUS SIX VERSUS TWO...
THERE'S STRENGTH IN NUMBERS.
YOU'RE IN NO POSITION TO CHALLENGE HAKONE.
YOU'LL JUST FIZZLE OUT AND GET SWALLOWED UP BY THE PACK...WHAT A SHAME!!
NGH!!
OH!
WAIT, WAIT, THERE'S... THERE'S STILL THAT... YEAH!
WHAT IF YOU HOPPED ONTO THE KYOTO-FUSHIMI EXPRESS HERE?

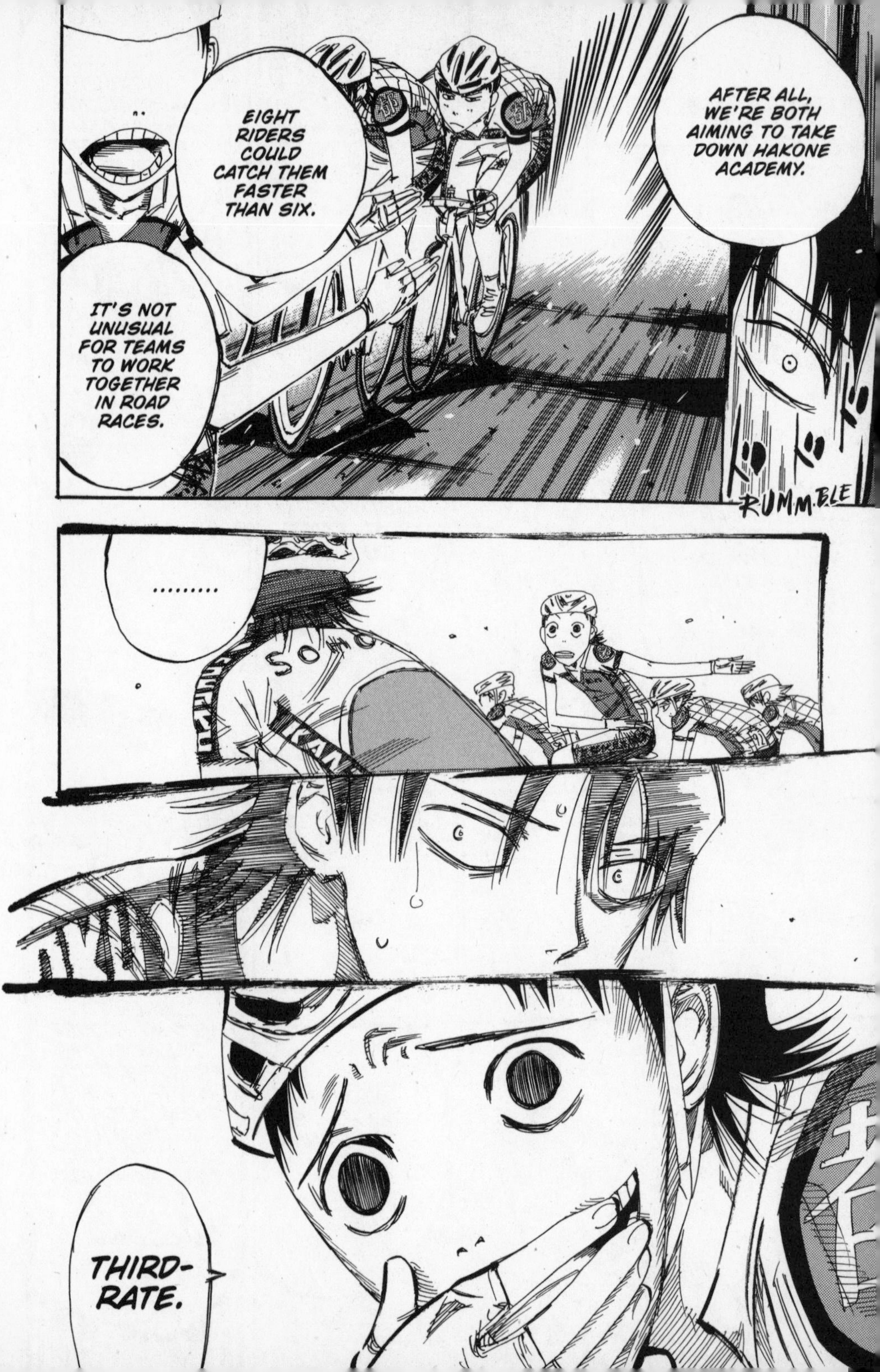
AFTER ALL, WE'RE BOTH AIMING TO TAKE DOWN HAKONE ACADEMY.
EIGHT RIDERS COULD CATCH THEM FASTER THAN SIX.
IT'S NOT UNUSUAL FOR TEAMS TO WORK TOGETHER IN ROAD RACES.
RUMMBLE
....
THIRD-RATE.

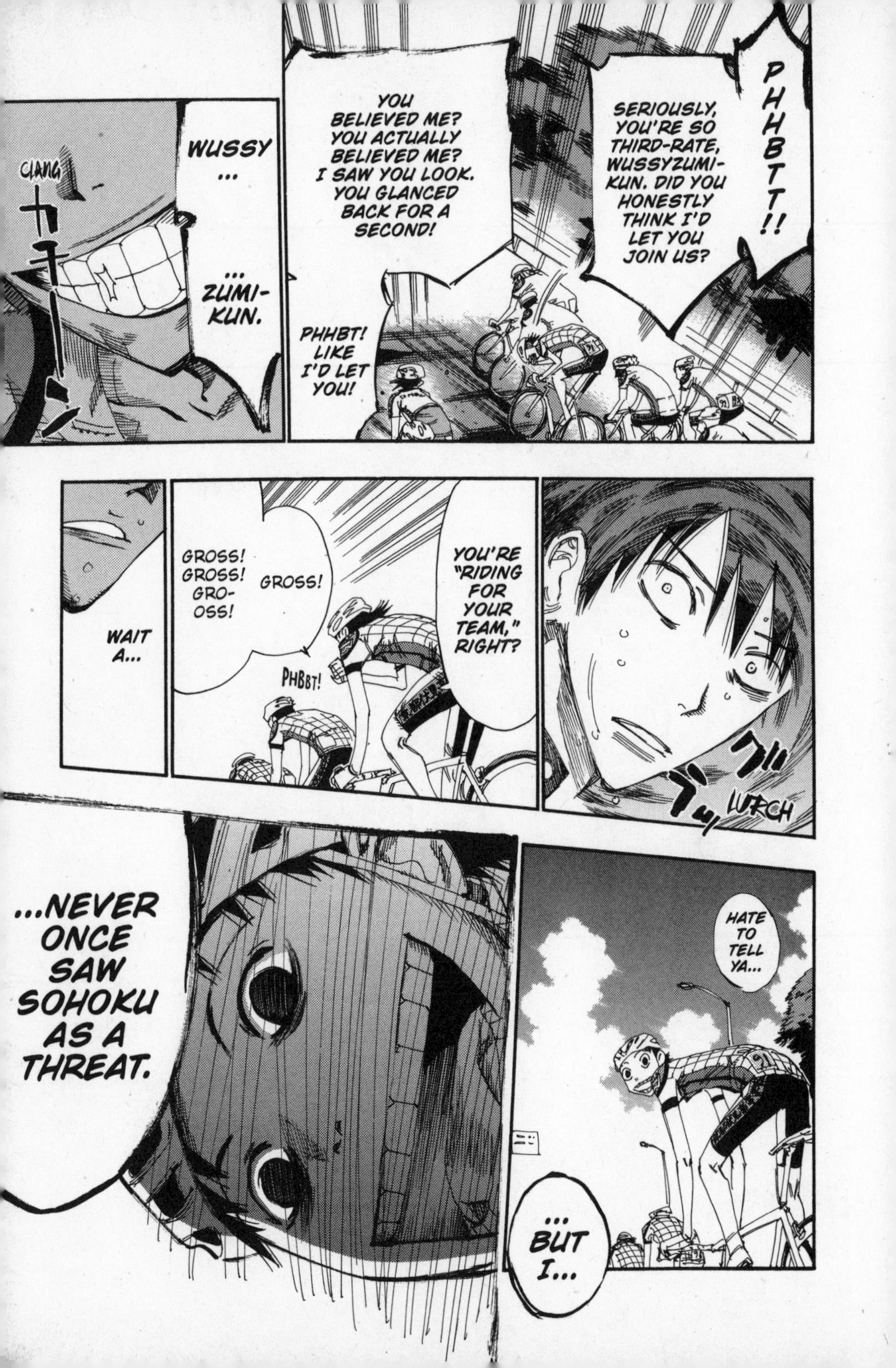
PHHBTT!!
SERIOUSLY, YOU'RE SO THIRD-RATE, WUSSYZUMI-KUN. DID YOU HONESTLY THINK I'D LET YOU JOIN US?
YOU BELIEVED ME? YOU ACTUALLY BELIEVED ME? I SAW YOU LOOK. YOU GLANCED BACK FOR A SECOND!
PHHBT! LIKE I'D LET YOU!
WUSSY...
...ZUMI-KUN.
CLANG
YOU'RE "RIDING FOR YOUR TEAM," RIGHT?
LURCH
GROSS!
GROSS! GROSS! GRO-OSS!
PHBBT!
WAIT A...
HATE TO TELL YA...
...BUT I...
...NEVER ONCE SAW SOHOKU AS A THREAT.

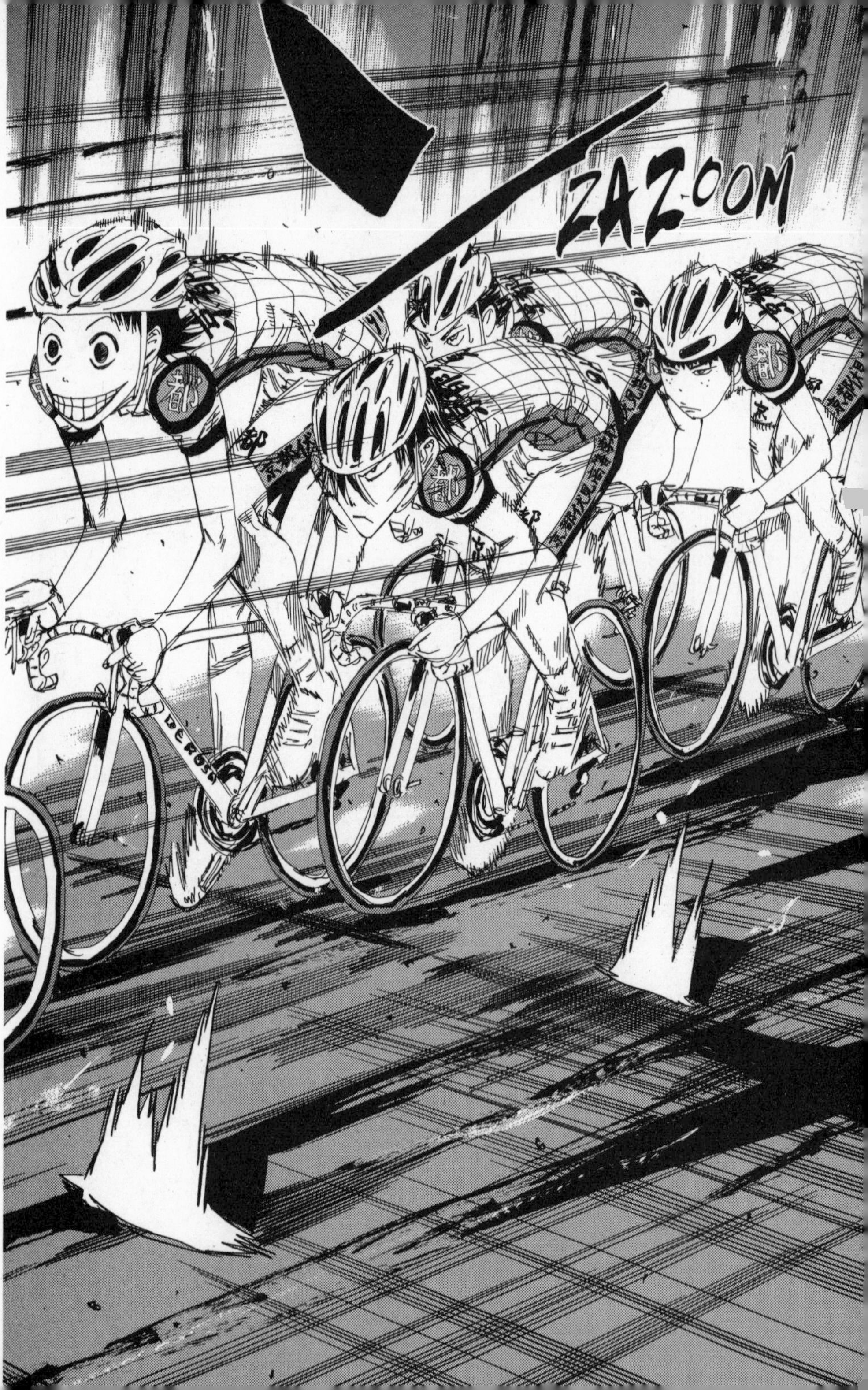
ZAZOOM

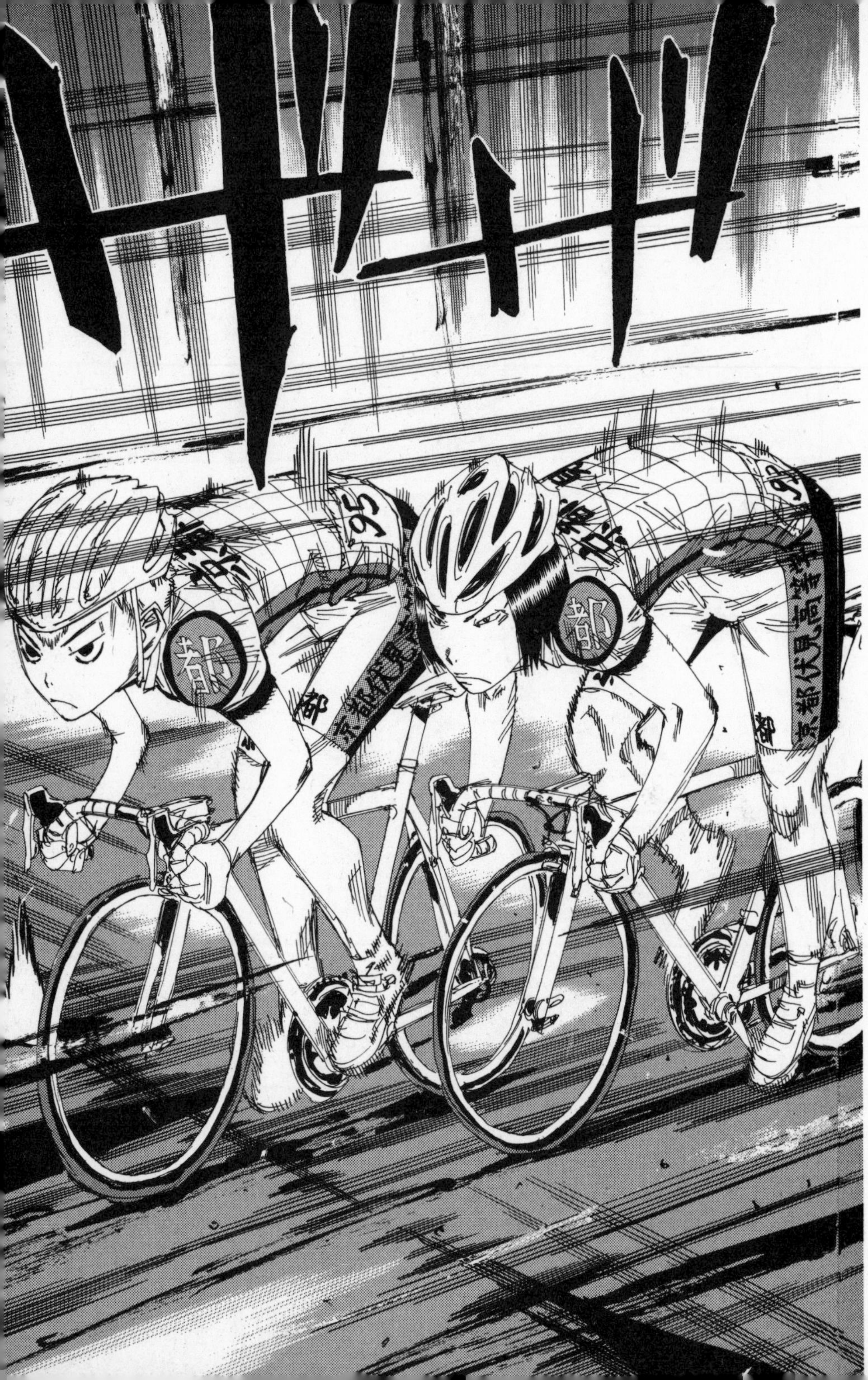
95
都
京都伏見
都
京都伏見高

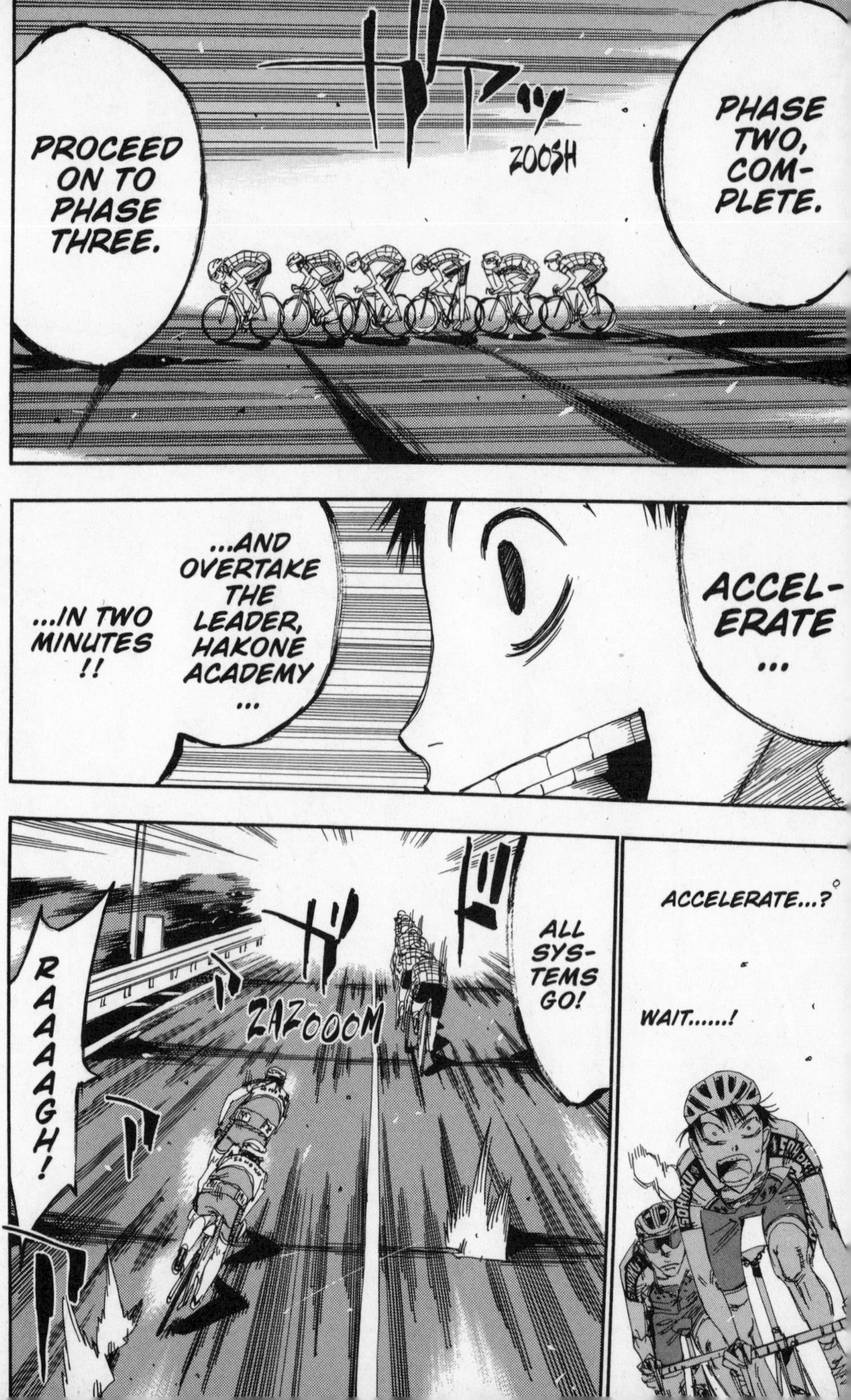
PHASE TWO, COMPLETE.
ZOOSH
PROCEED ON TO PHASE THREE.
ACCELERATE...
...AND OVERTAKE THE LEADER, HAKONE ACADEMY...
...IN TWO MINUTES!!
ACCELERATE...?
WAIT......!
ALL SYSTEMS GO!
ZAZOOOM
RAAAAAGH!

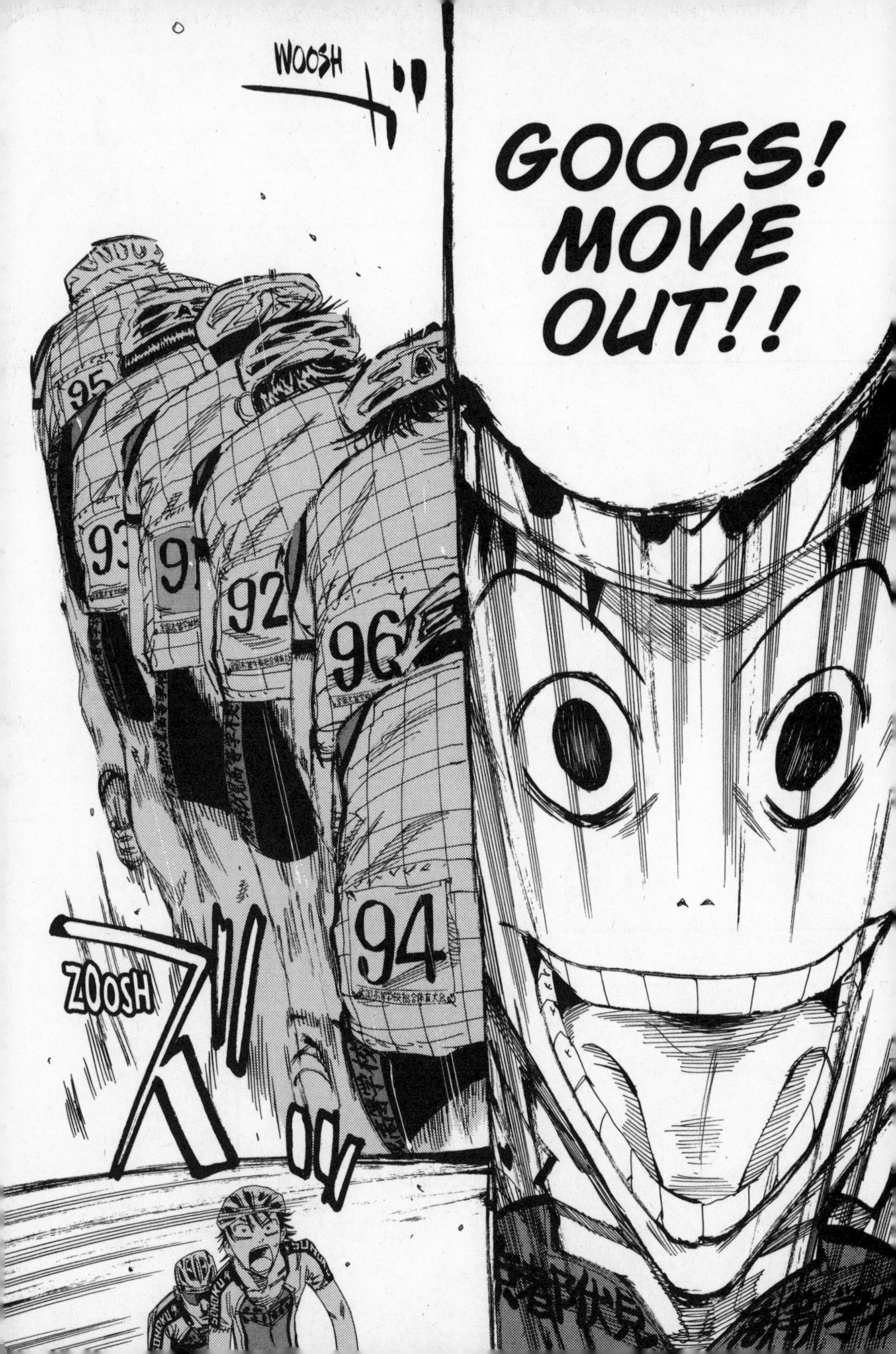
GOOFS! MOVE OUT!!
WOOSH
ZOOSH

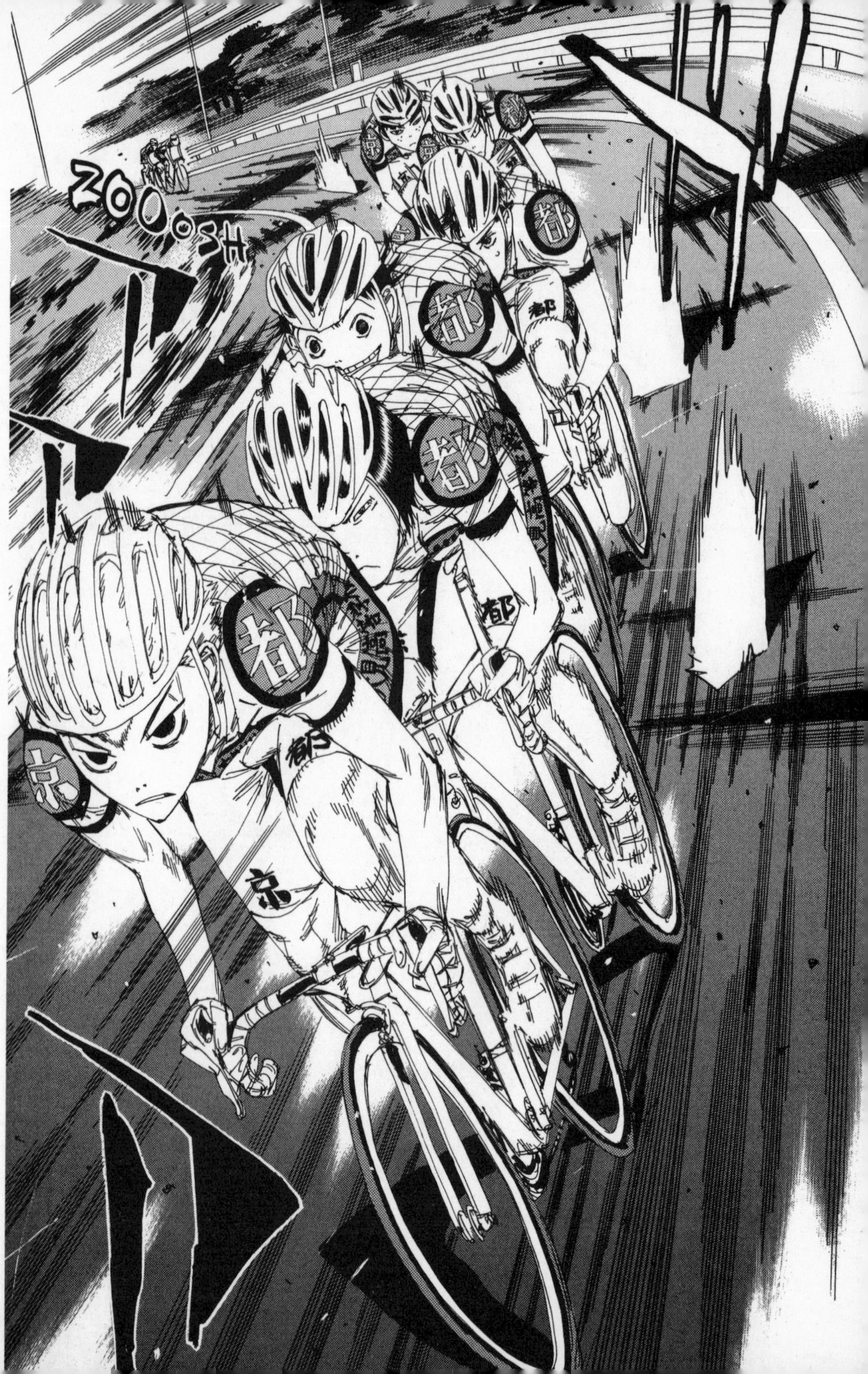
ZOOOSH

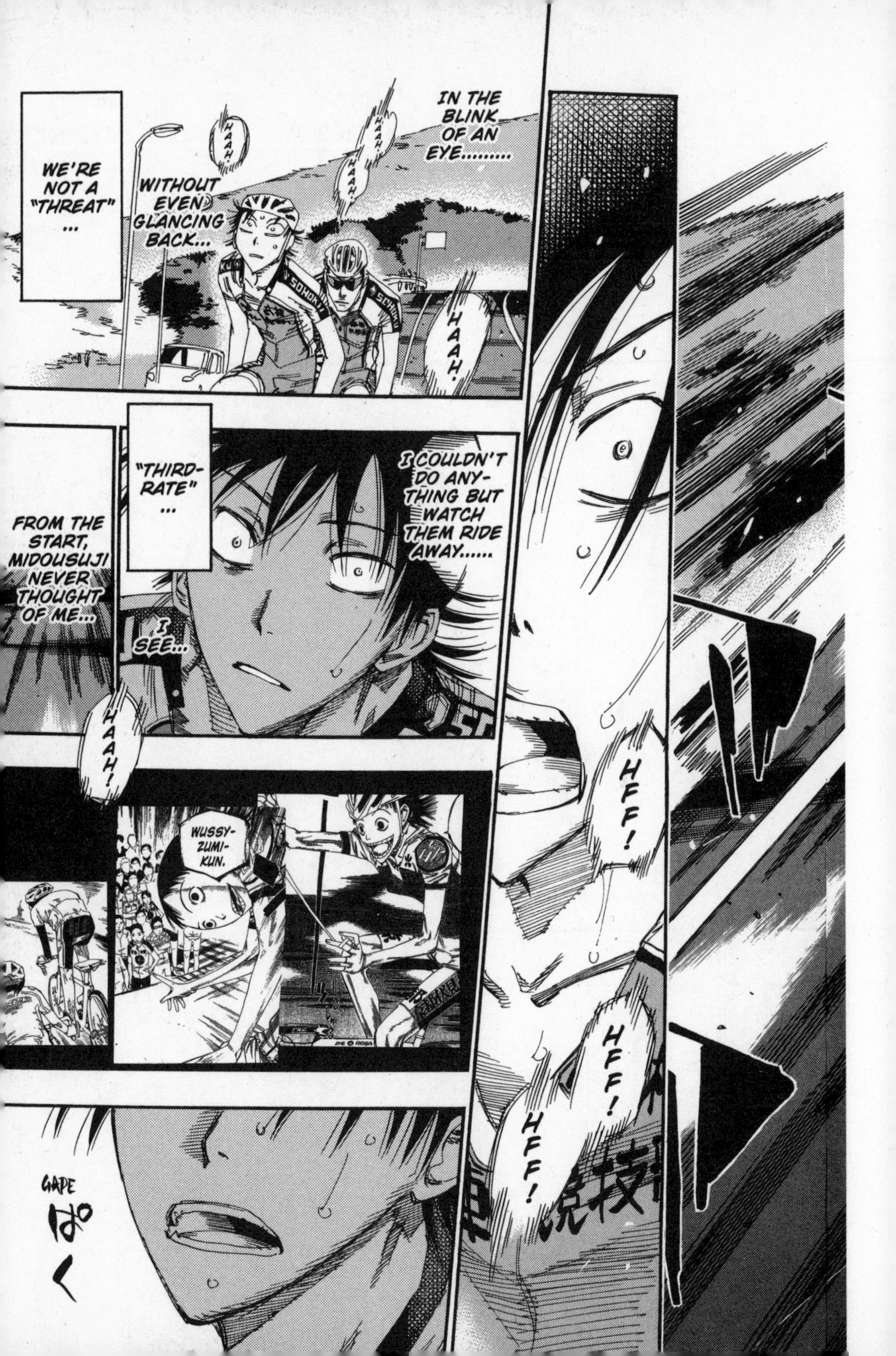
HFF!
HFF!
HFF!
IN THE BLINK OF AN EYE........
HAAH. HAAH.
HAAAH.
HAAH!
WITHOUT EVEN GLANCING BACK...
WE'RE NOT A "THREAT" ...
I COULDN'T DO ANYTHING BUT WATCH THEM RIDE AWAY......
"THIRD-RATE" ...
I SEE...
FROM THE START, MIDOUSUJI NEVER THOUGHT OF ME...
HAAAH!
WUSSY-ZUMI-KUN.
GAPE
ぱく

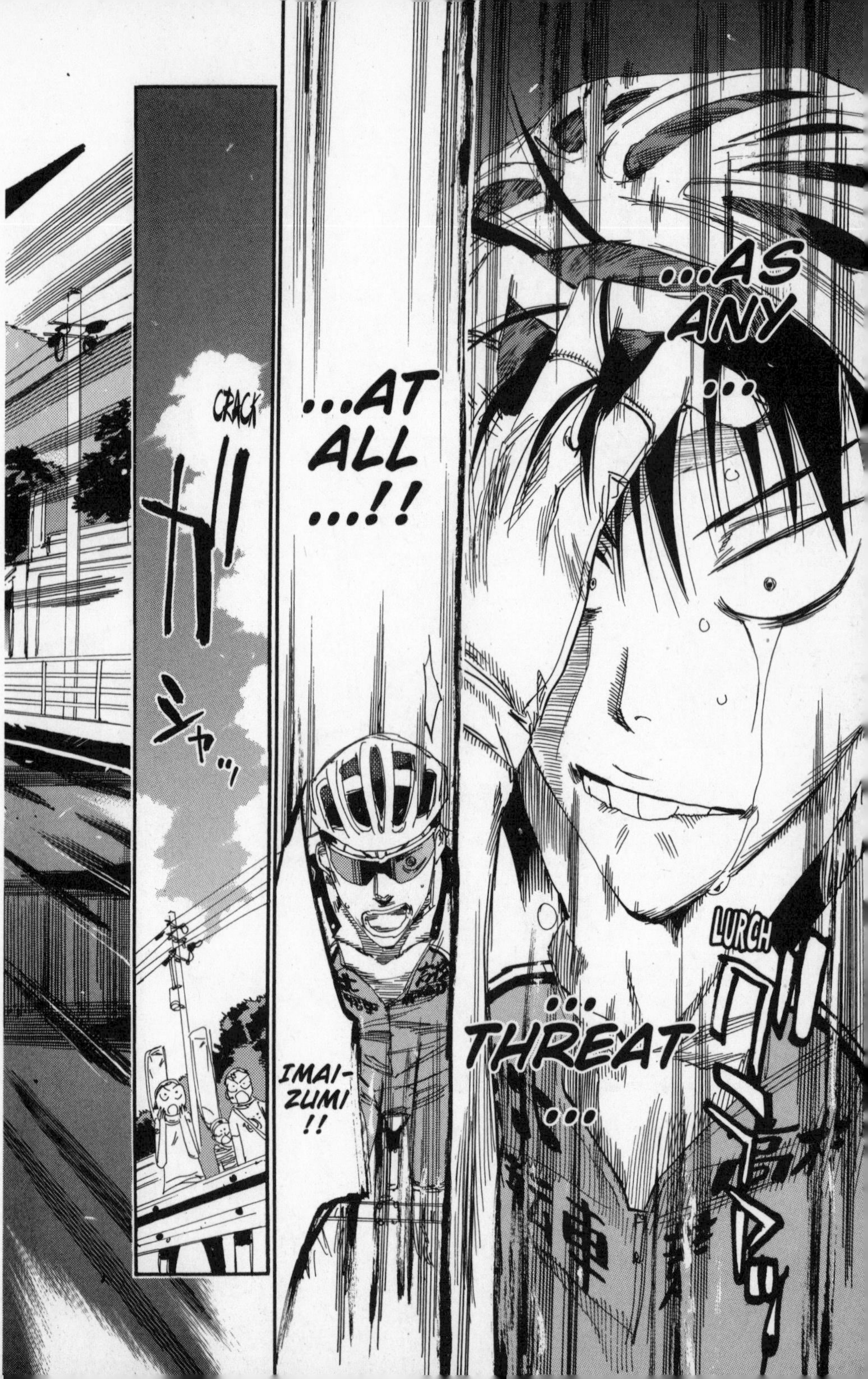
...AS ANY ...
LURCH
...THREAT ...
...AT ALL ...!!
IMAI-ZUMI!!
CRACK

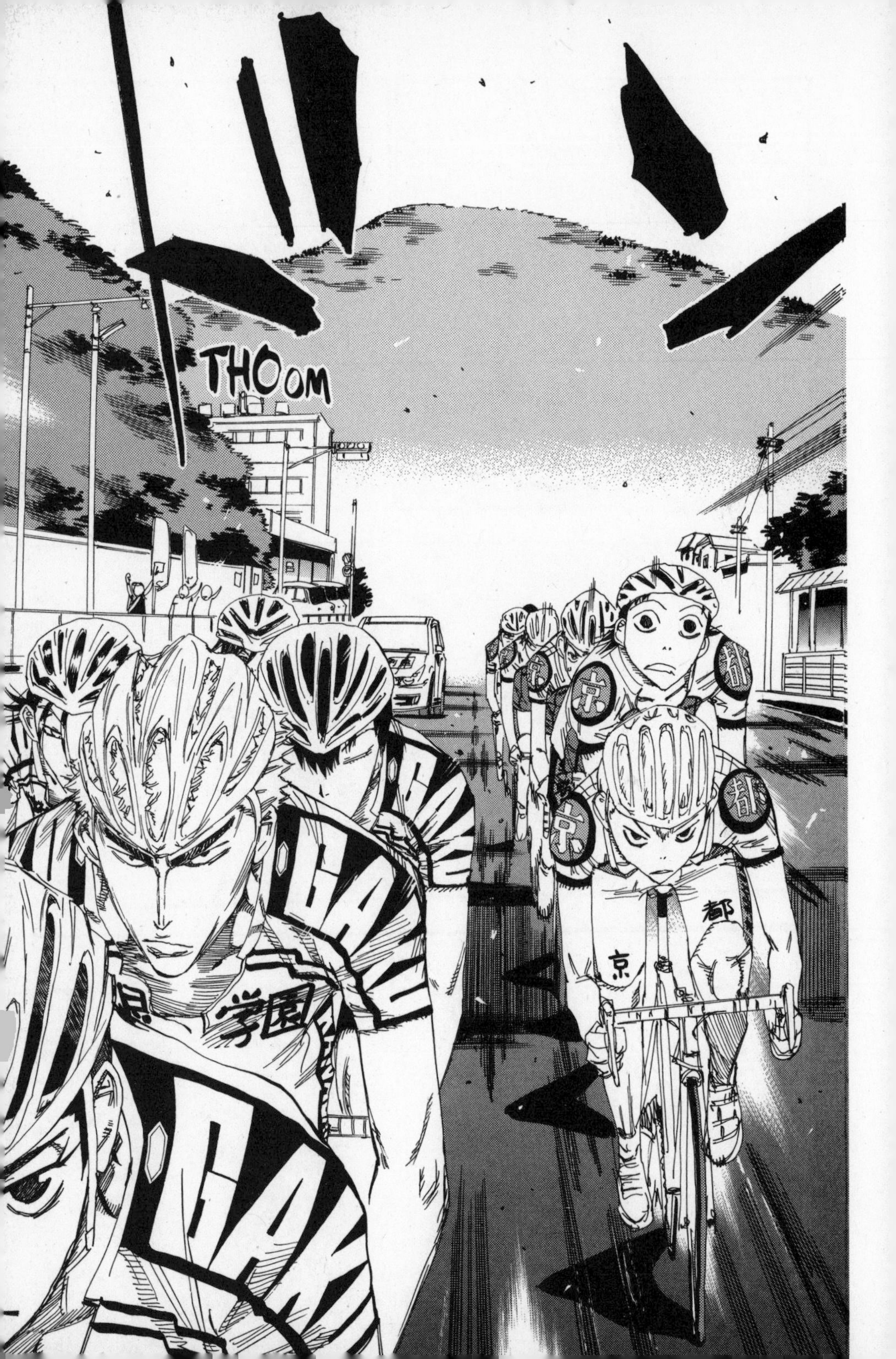
THOOM

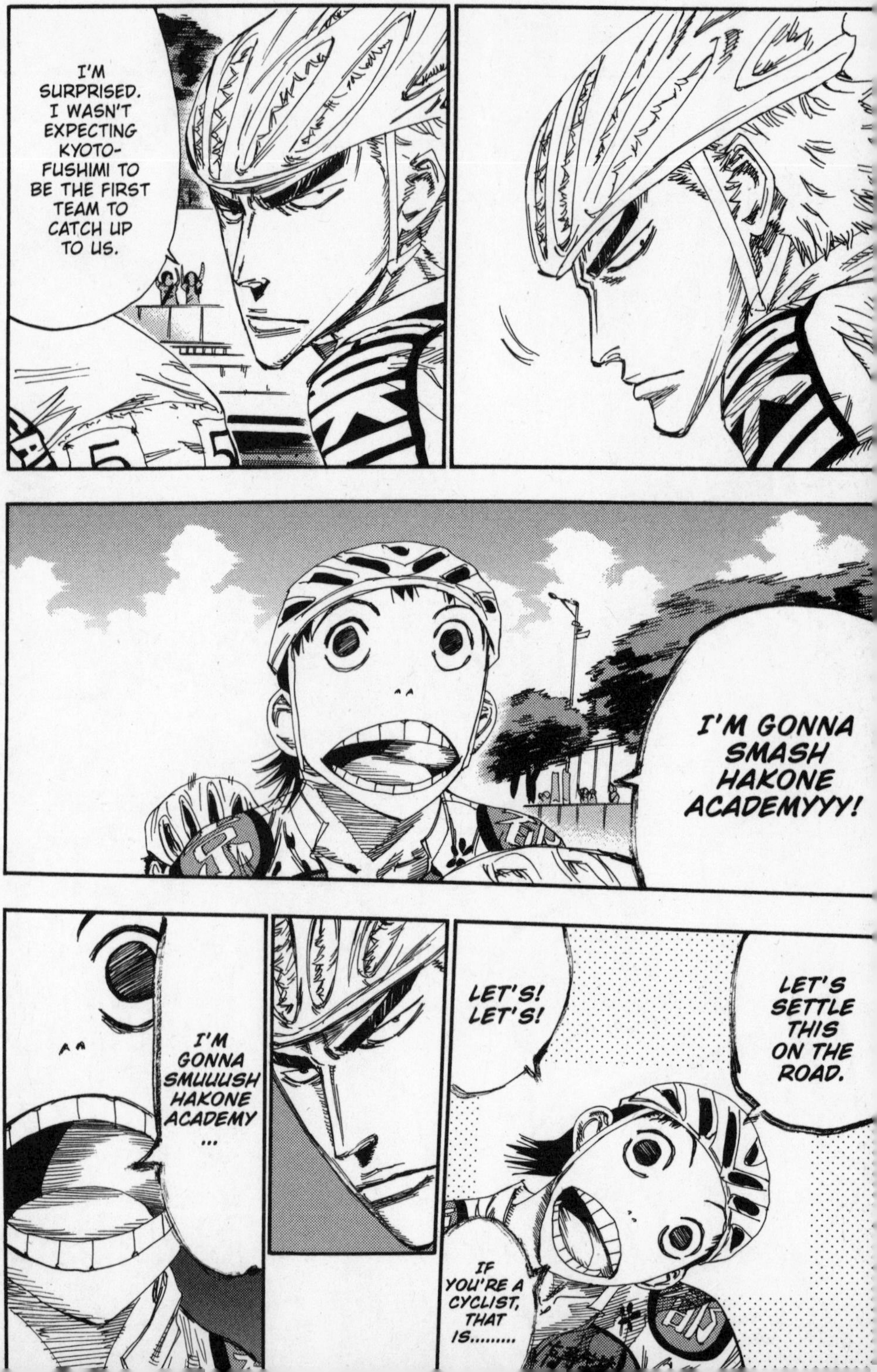
I'M SURPRISED. I WASN'T EXPECTING KYOTO-FUSHIMI TO BE THE FIRST TEAM TO CATCH UP TO US.
I'M GONNA SMASH HAKONE ACADEMYYY!
LET'S SETTLE THIS ON THE ROAD.
LET'S! LET'S!
IF YOU'RE A CYCLIST, THAT IS.........
I'M GONNA SMUUUSH HAKONE ACADEMY ...

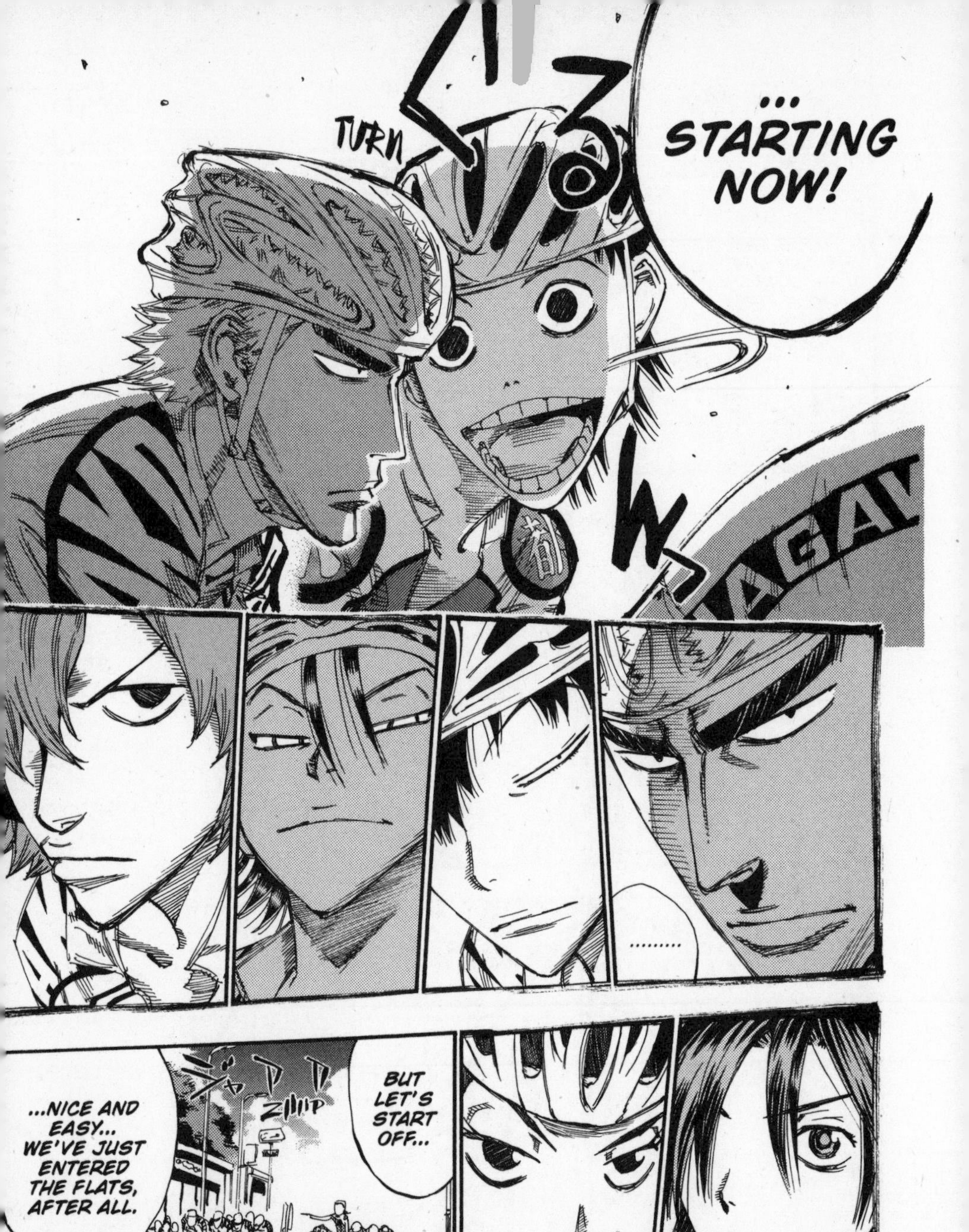
...STARTING NOW!
TURN
....
BUT LET'S START OFF...
ZIIIIP
...NICE AND EASY... WE'VE JUST ENTERED THE FLATS, AFTER ALL.

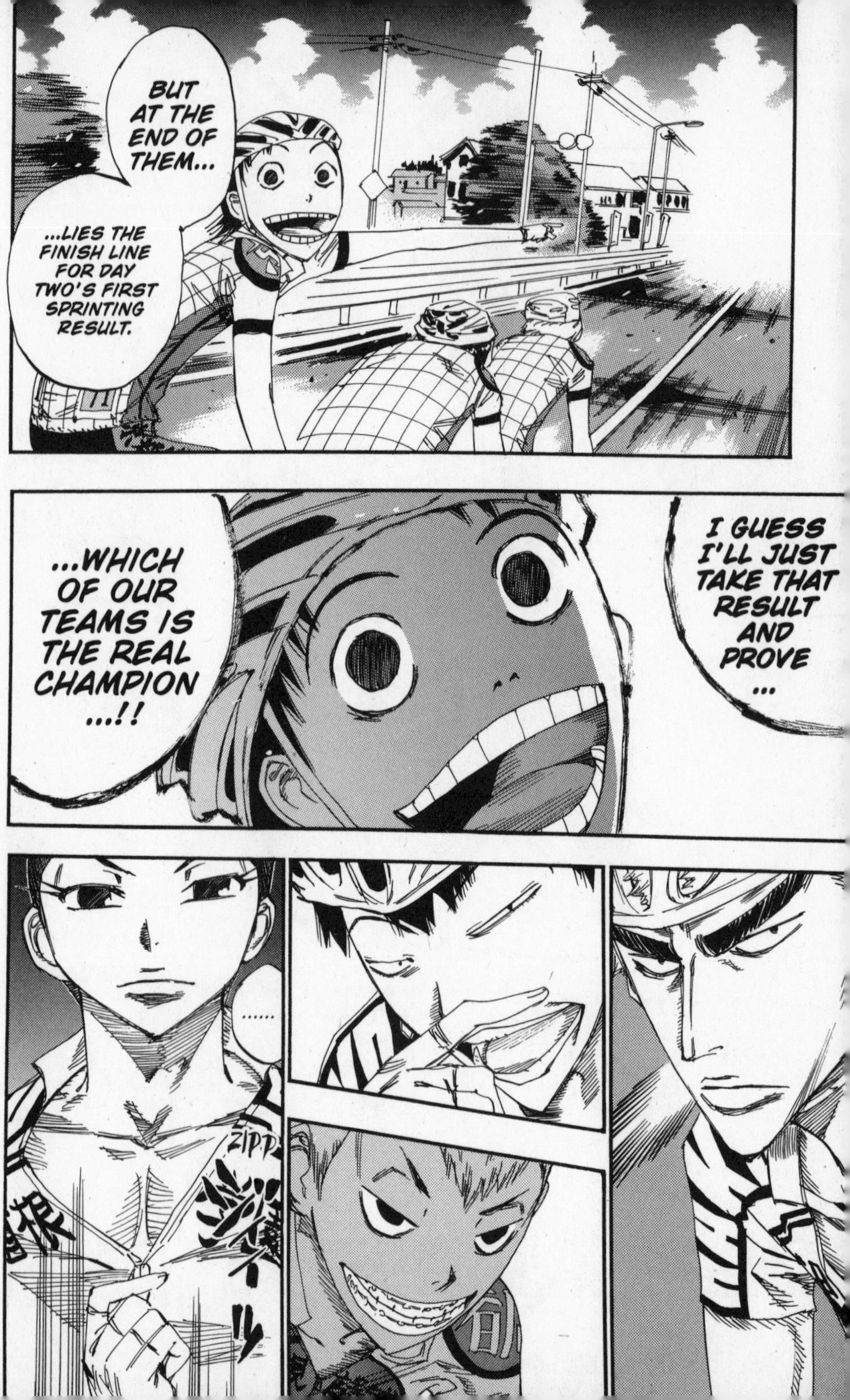
BUT AT THE END OF THEM...
...LIES THE FINISH LINE FOR DAY TWO'S FIRST SPRINTING RESULT.
I GUESS I'LL JUST TAKE THAT RESULT AND PROVE ...
...WHICH OF OUR TEAMS IS THE REAL CHAMPION ...!!
......
ZIPP
!!

RIDE.121 PROVOCATION

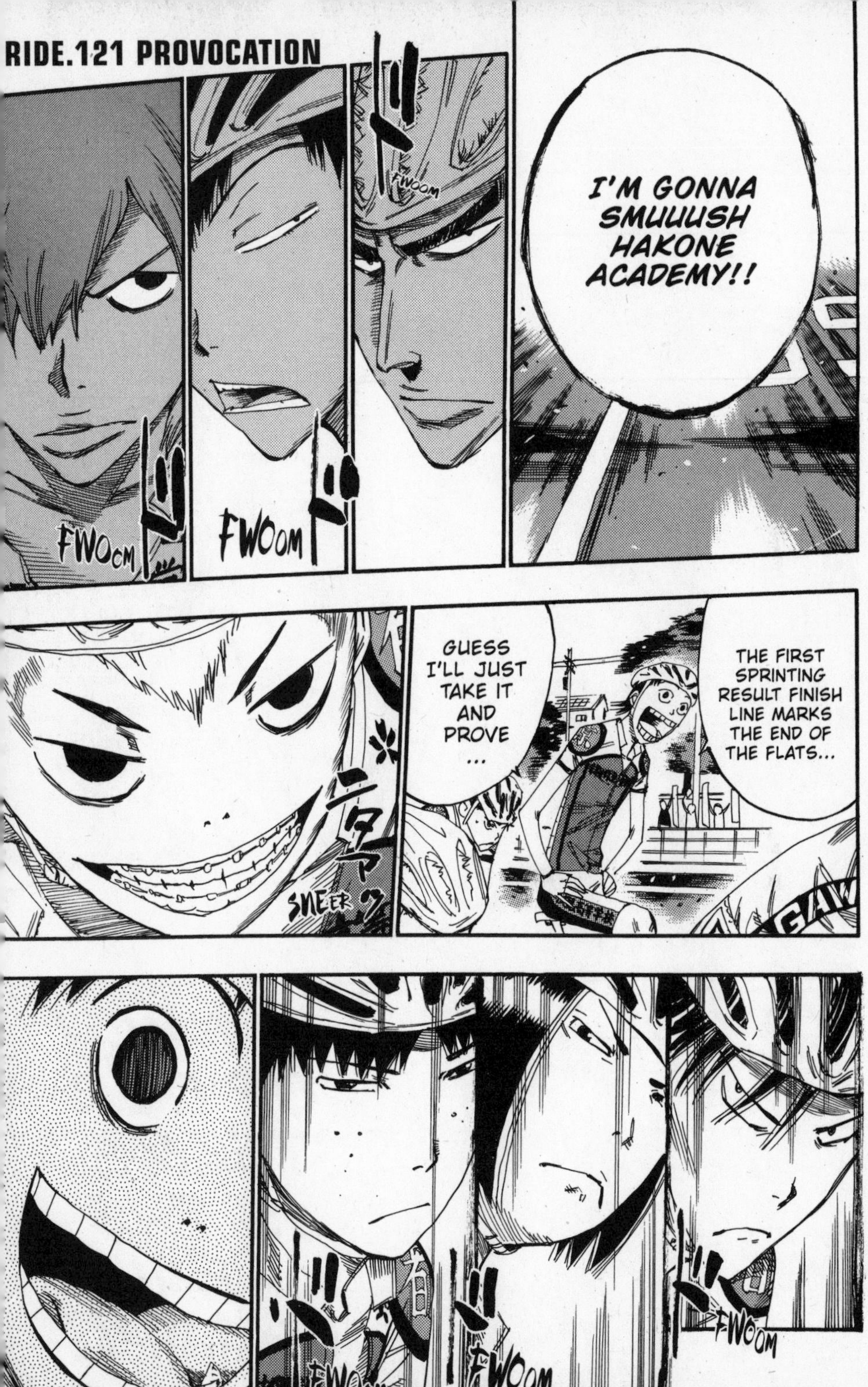
I'M GONNA SMUUUSH HAKONE ACADEMY!!
FWOOM
FWOOM
FWOOM
THE FIRST SPRINTING RESULT FINISH LINE MARKS THE END OF THE FLATS...
GUESS I'LL JUST TAKE IT AND PROVE ...
SNEER
FWOOM
FWOOM
FWOOM

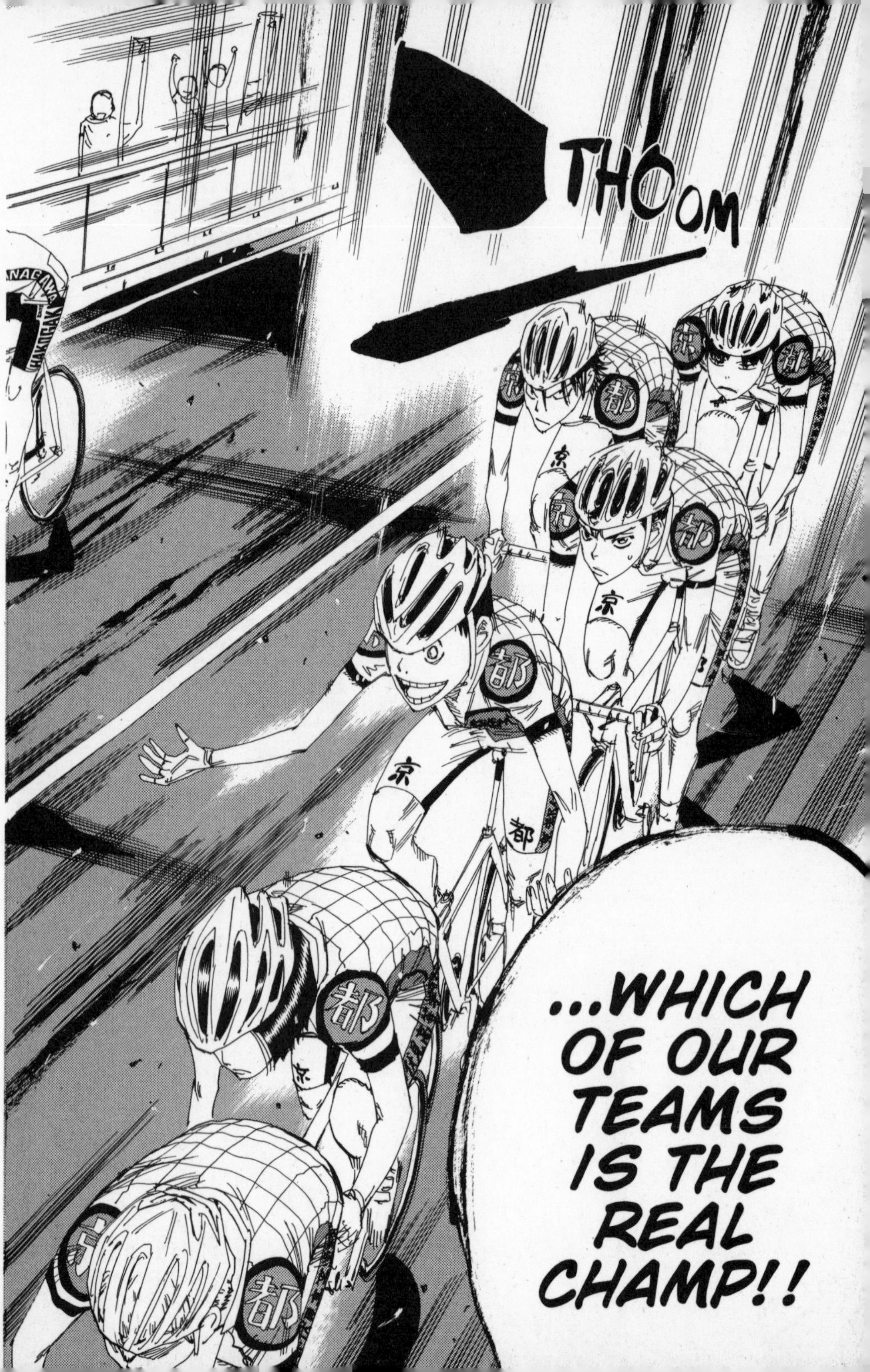
THOOM
...WHICH OF OUR TEAMS IS THE REAL CHAMP!!

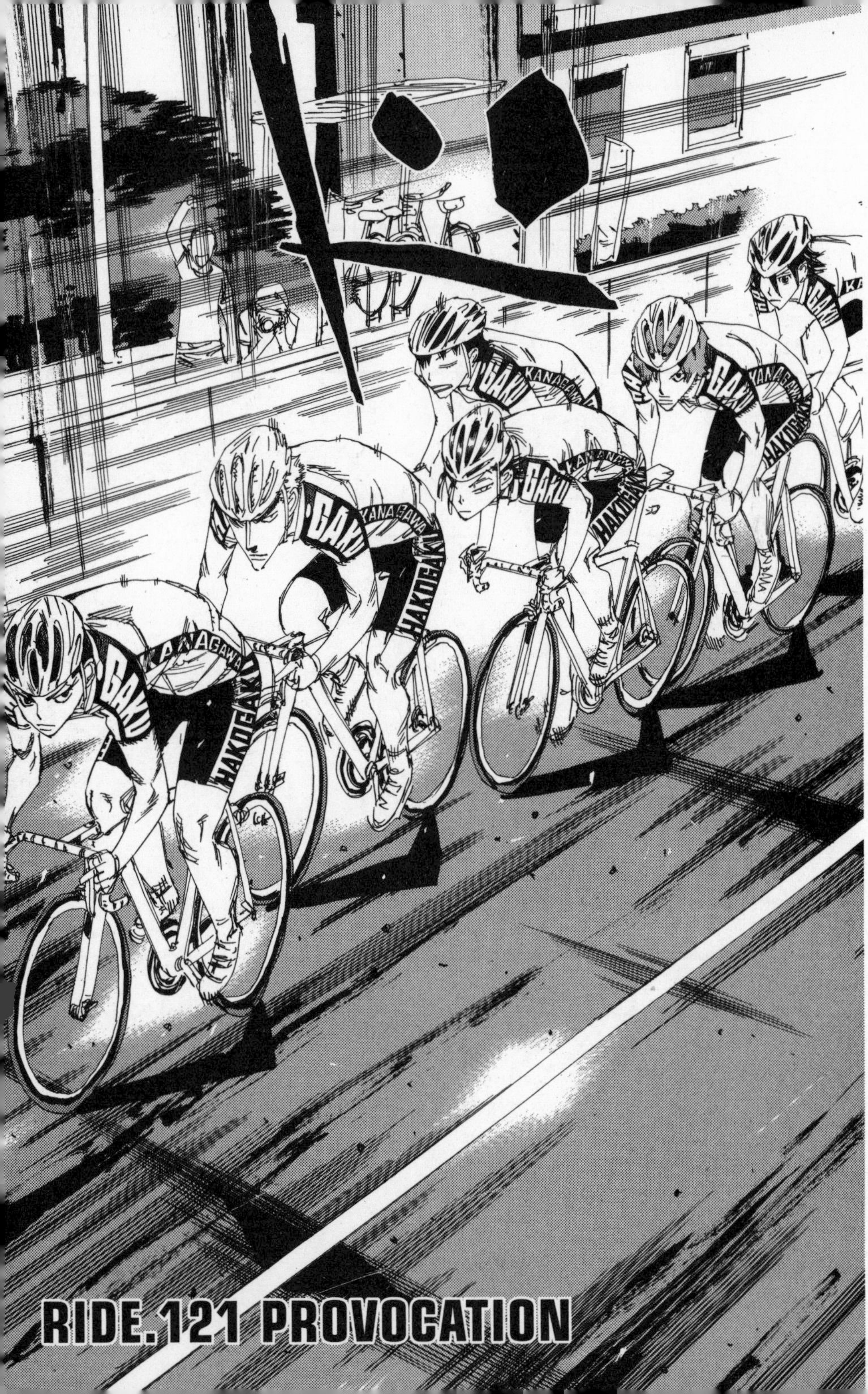
KANAGAWA
GAKU
HAKOGAKU

RIDE. 121 PROVOCATION

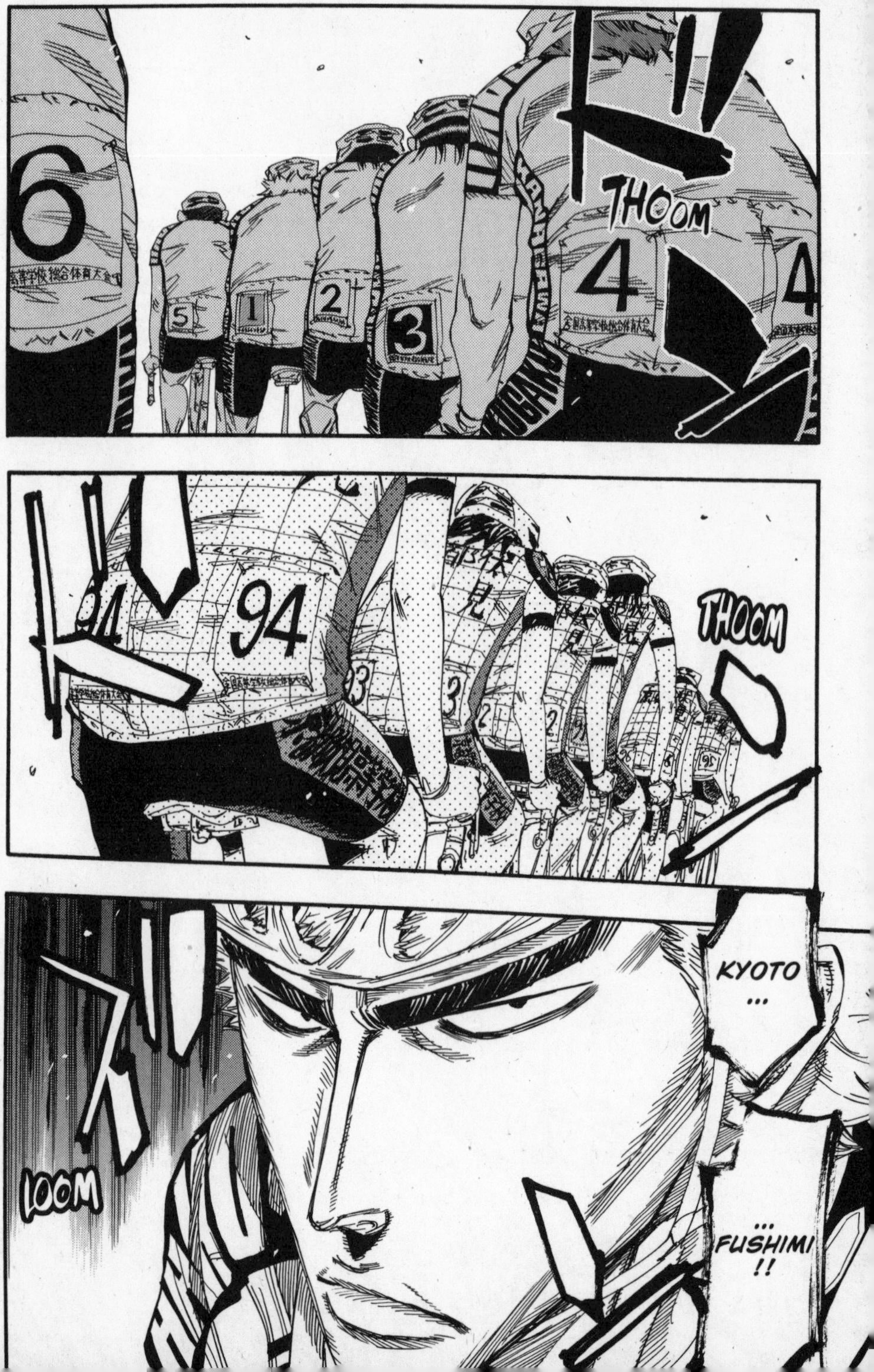
THOOM
THOOM
KYOTO ...
... FUSHIMI !!
IOOM

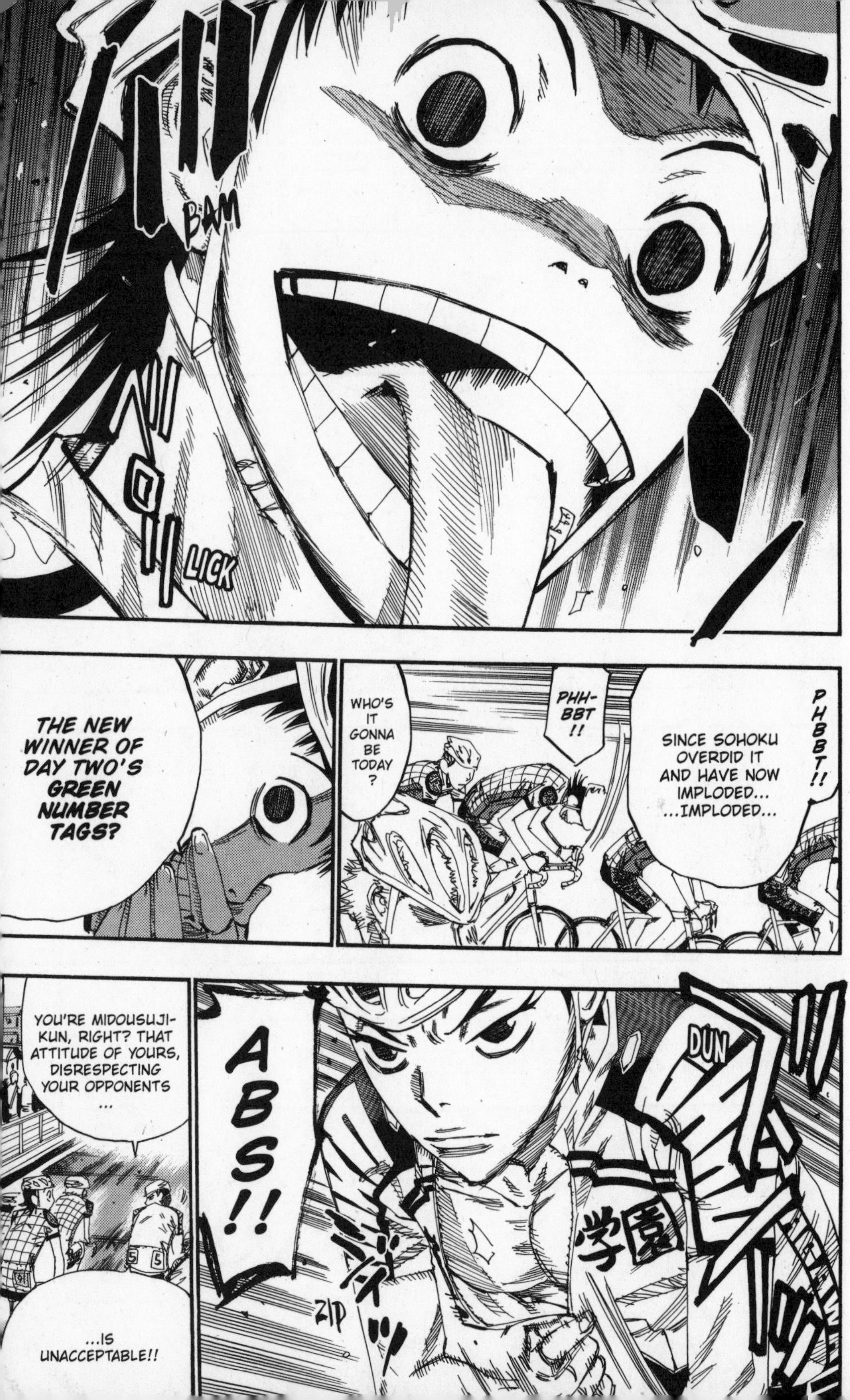
BAM
LICK
PHBBT!!
SINCE SOHOKU OVERDID IT AND HAVE NOW IMPLODED... ...IMPLODED...
PHH-BBT!!
WHO'S IT GONNA BE TODAY?
THE NEW WINNER OF DAY TWO'S GREEN NUMBER TAGS?
DUN
ABS!!
学園
ZIP
YOU'RE MIDOUSUJI-KUN, RIGHT? THAT ATTITUDE OF YOURS, DISRESPECTING YOUR OPPONENTS ...
...IS UNACCEPTABLE!!

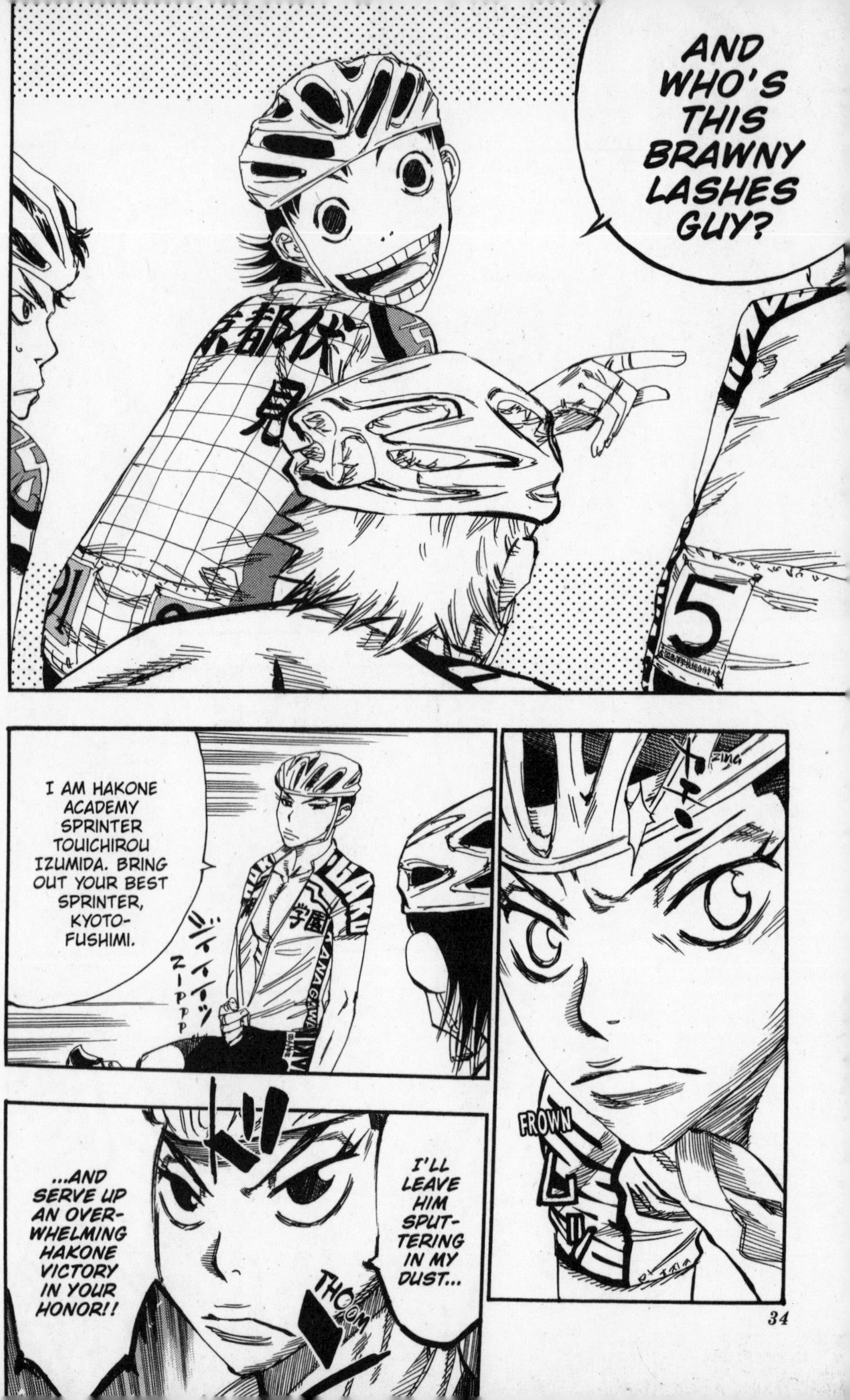
AND WHO'S THIS BRAWNY LASHES GUY?
ZING
FROWN
I AM HAKONE ACADEMY SPRINTER TOUICHIROU IZUMIDA. BRING OUT YOUR BEST SPRINTER, KYOTO-FUSHIMI.
Z-IPPP
I'LL LEAVE HIM SPUT-TERING IN MY DUST...
...AND SERVE UP AN OVER-WHELMING HAKONE VICTORY IN YOUR HONOR!!
THOOM

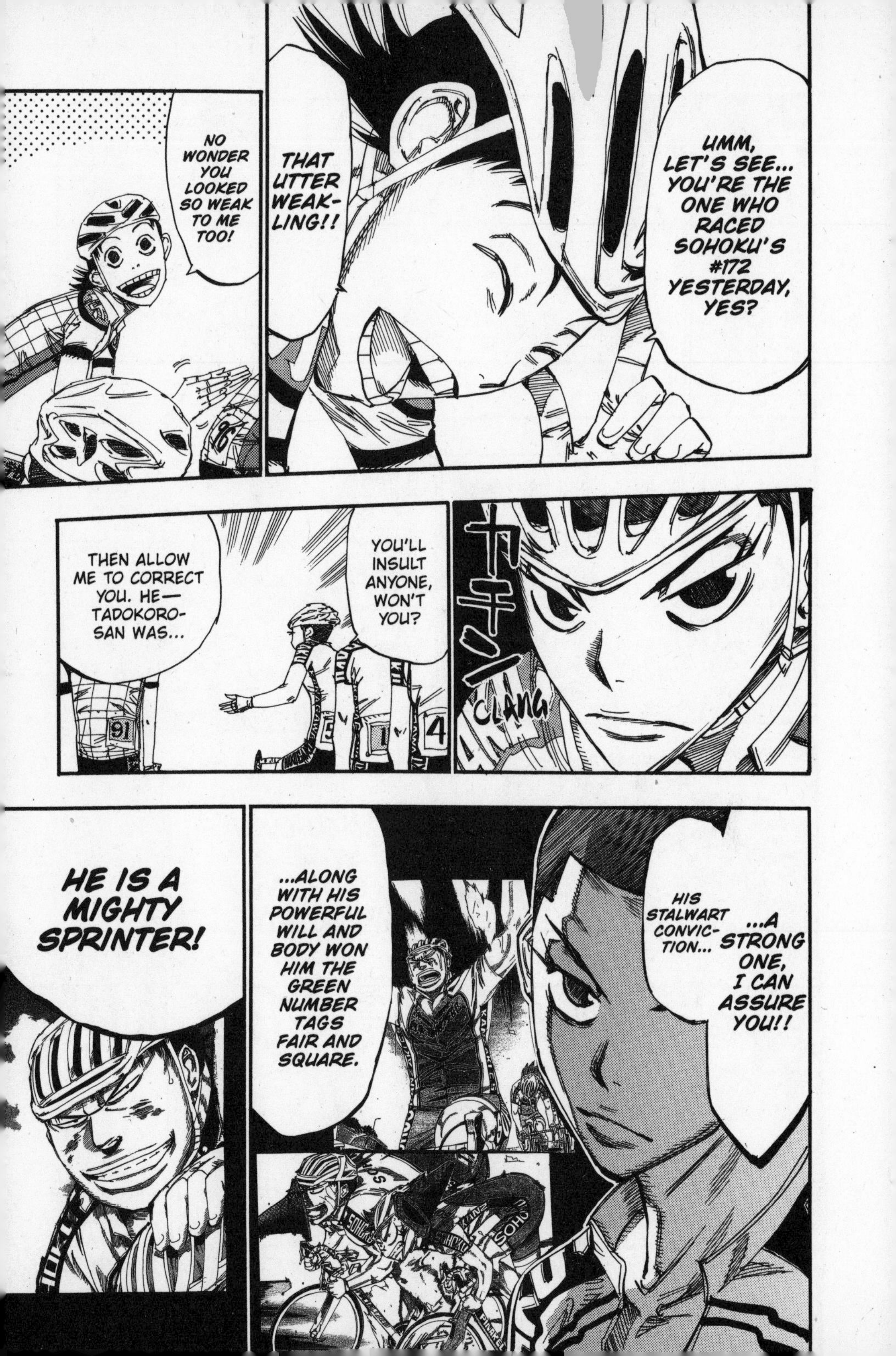
UMM, LET'S SEE... YOU'RE THE ONE WHO RACED SOHOKU'S #172 YESTERDAY, YES?
THAT UTTER WEAK-LING!!
NO WONDER YOU LOOKED SO WEAK TO ME TOO!
CLANG
YOU'LL INSULT ANYONE, WON'T YOU?
THEN ALLOW ME TO CORRECT YOU. HE—TADOKORO-SAN WAS...
HIS STALWART CONVIC-TION...
...A STRONG ONE, I CAN ASSURE YOU!!
...ALONG WITH HIS POWERFUL WILL AND BODY WON HIM THE GREEN NUMBER TAGS FAIR AND SQUARE.
HE IS A MIGHTY SPRINTER!

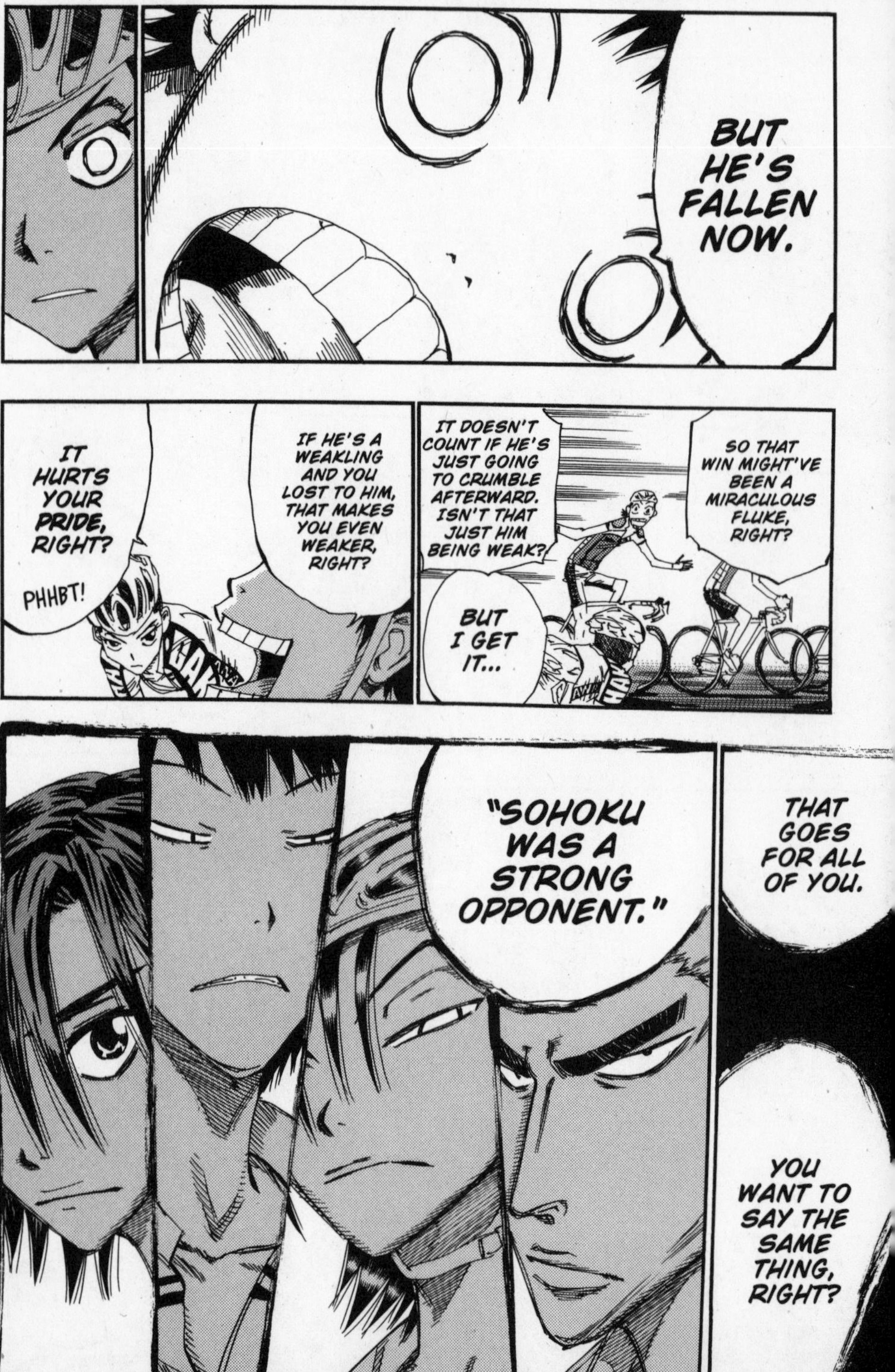
BUT HE'S FALLEN NOW.
SO THAT WIN MIGHT'VE BEEN A MIRACULOUS FLUKE, RIGHT?
IT DOESN'T COUNT IF HE'S JUST GOING TO CRUMBLE AFTERWARD. ISN'T THAT JUST HIM BEING WEAK?
BUT I GET IT...
IF HE'S A WEAKLING AND YOU LOST TO HIM, THAT MAKES YOU EVEN WEAKER, RIGHT?
IT HURTS YOUR PRIDE, RIGHT?
PHHBT!
THAT GOES FOR ALL OF YOU.
YOU WANT TO SAY THE SAME THING, RIGHT?
"SOHOKU WAS A STRONG OPPONENT."

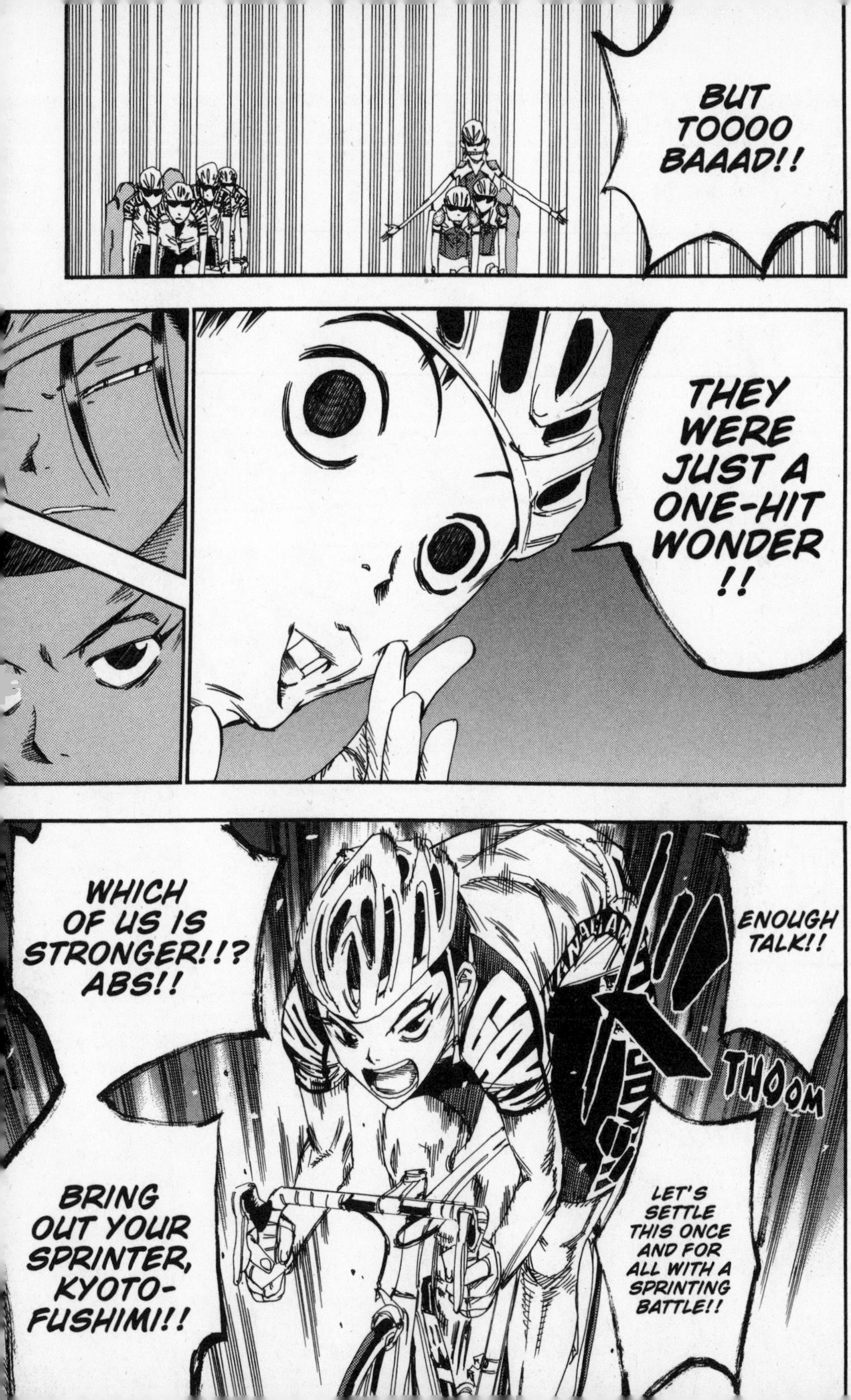
BUT TOOOO BAAAD!!
THEY WERE JUST A ONE-HIT WONDER!!
ENOUGH TALK!!
WHICH OF US IS STRONGER!!? ABS!!
THOOM
LET'S SETTLE THIS ONCE AND FOR ALL WITH A SPRINTING BATTLE!!
BRING OUT YOUR SPRINTER, KYOTO-FUSHIMI!!

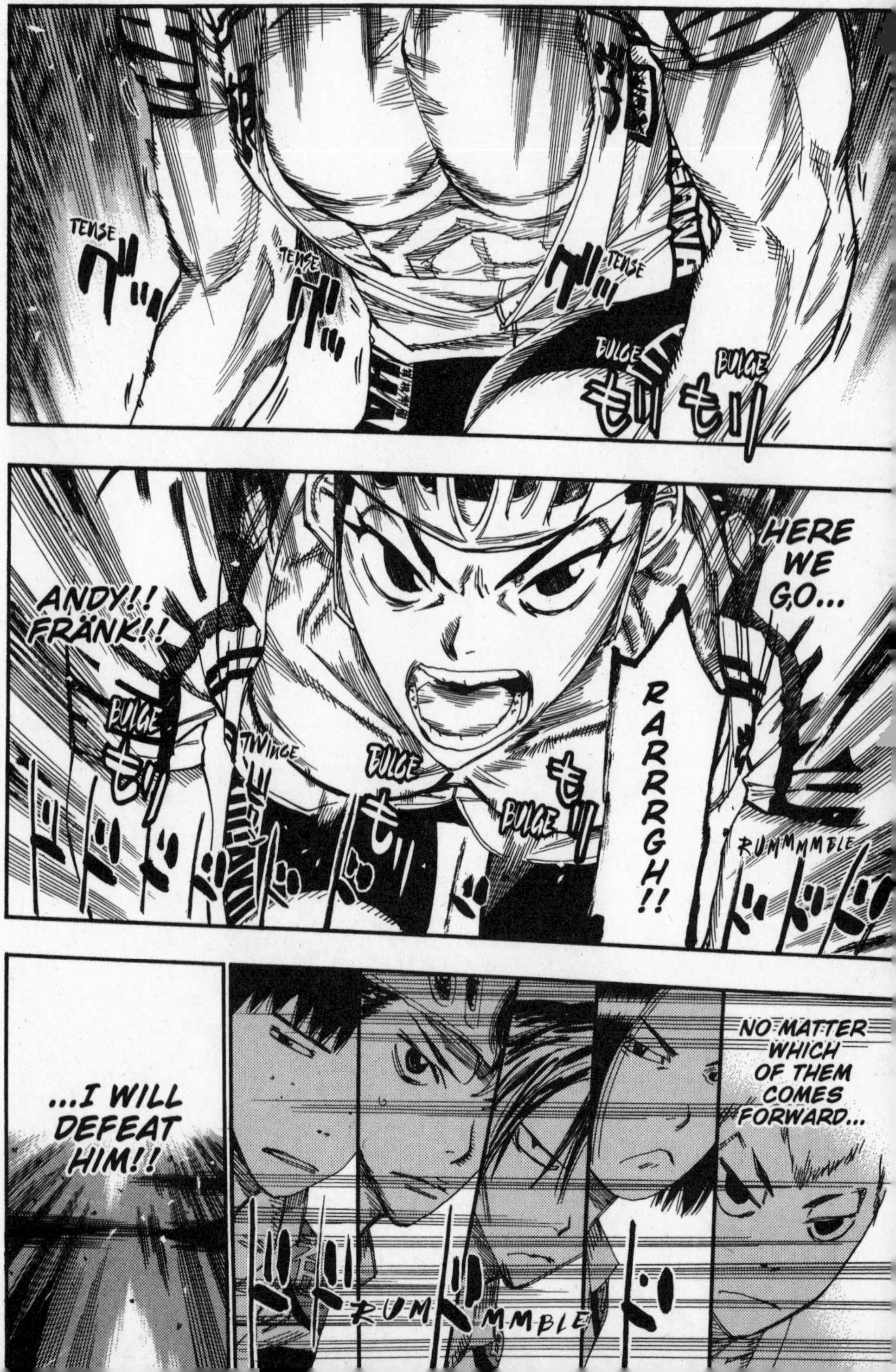
TENSE
TENSE
TENSE
BULGE
BULGE
HERE WE GO...
RARRRGH!!
ANDY!! FRÄNK!!
BULGE
BULGE
TWINGE
BULGE
BULGE
RUMMMMBLE
NO MATTER WHICH OF THEM COMES FORWARD...
RUMMMMBLE
...I WILL DEFEAT HIM!!

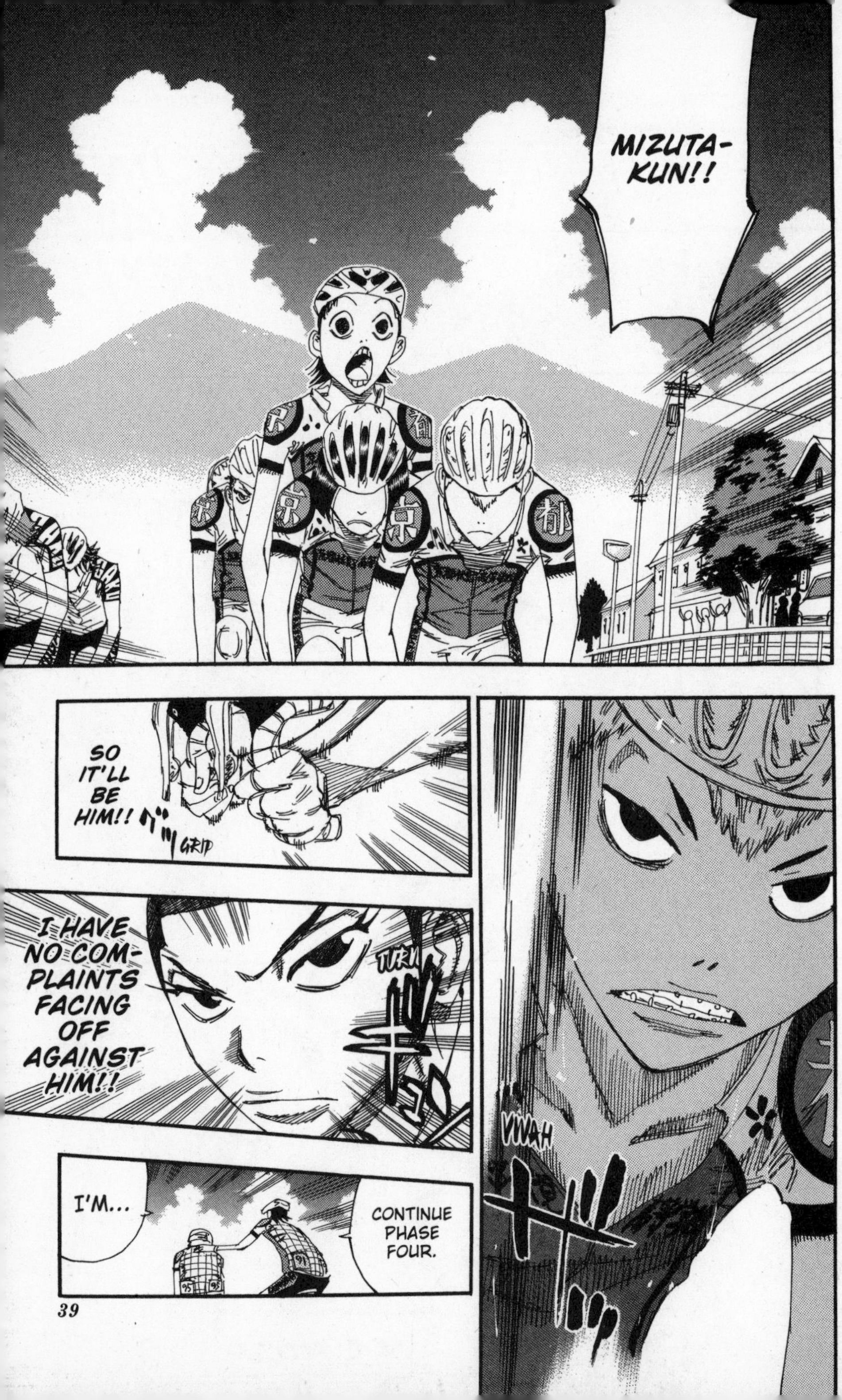
MIZUTA-KUN!!
VWAH
SO IT'LL BE HIM!!
GRIP
I HAVE NO COMPLAINTS FACING OFF AGAINST HIM!!
TURN
CONTINUE PHASE FOUR.
I'M...

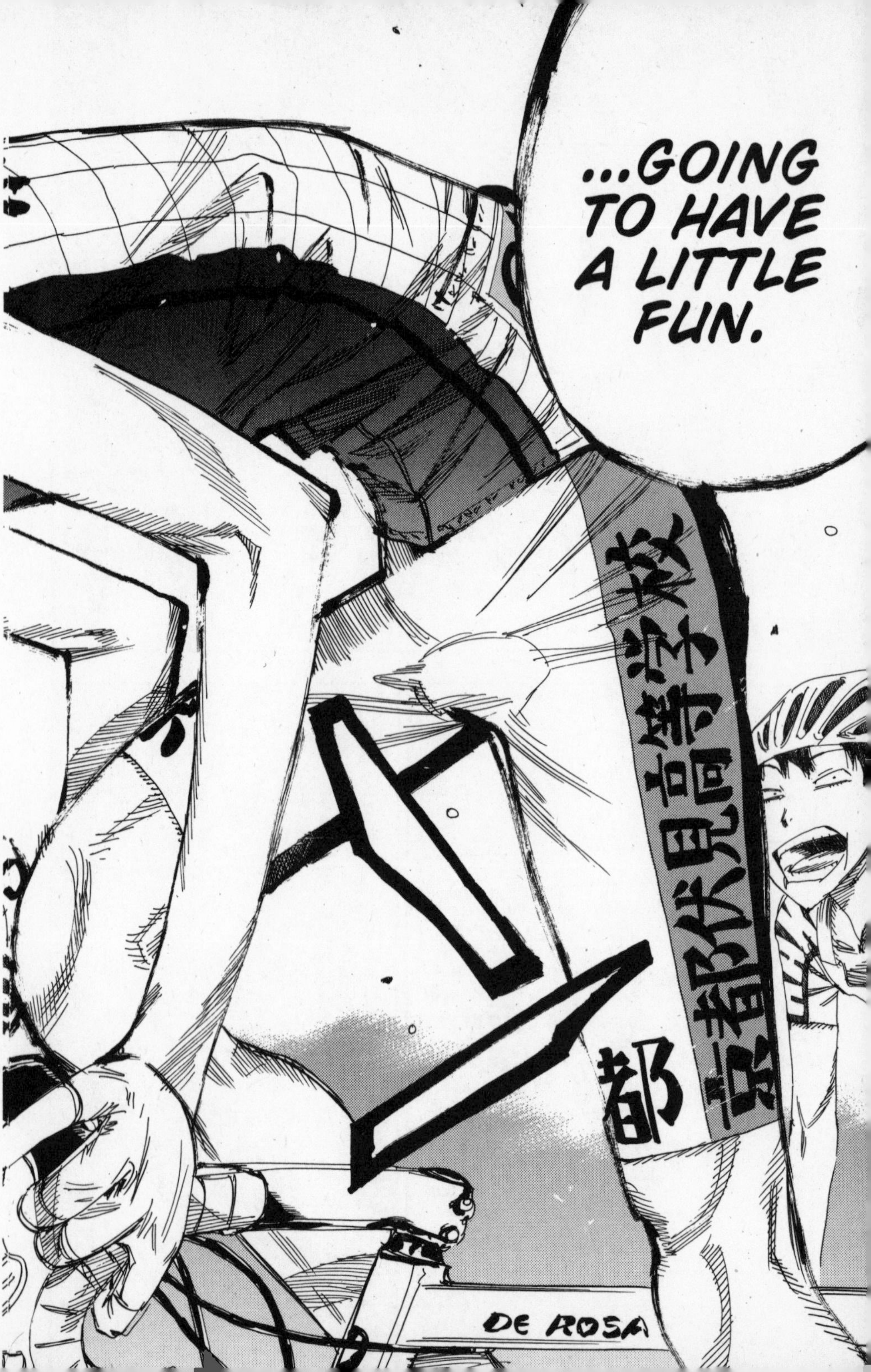
...GOING TO HAVE A LITTLE FUN.
京都伏見高等学校
都
DE ROSA

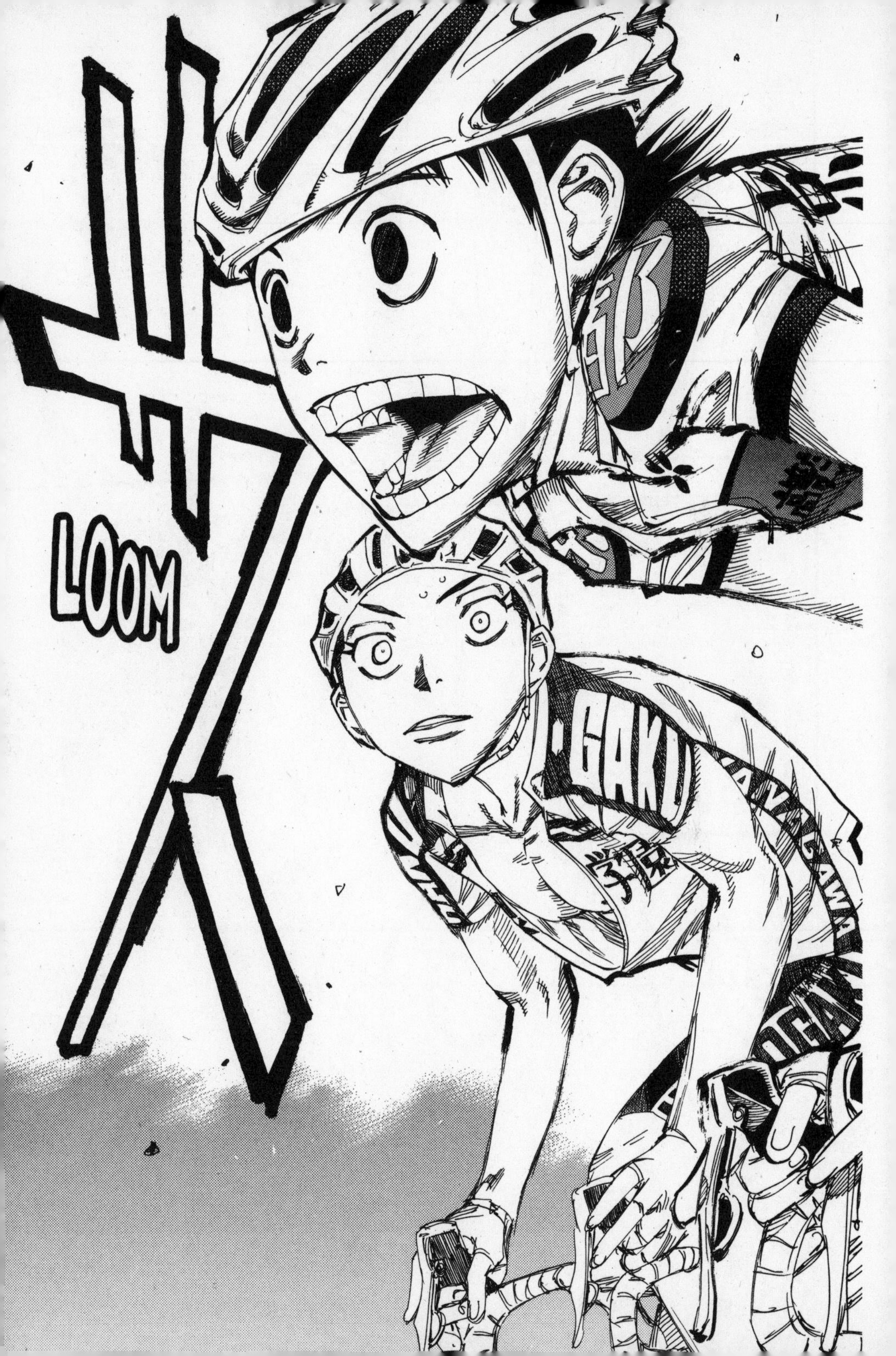
LOOM

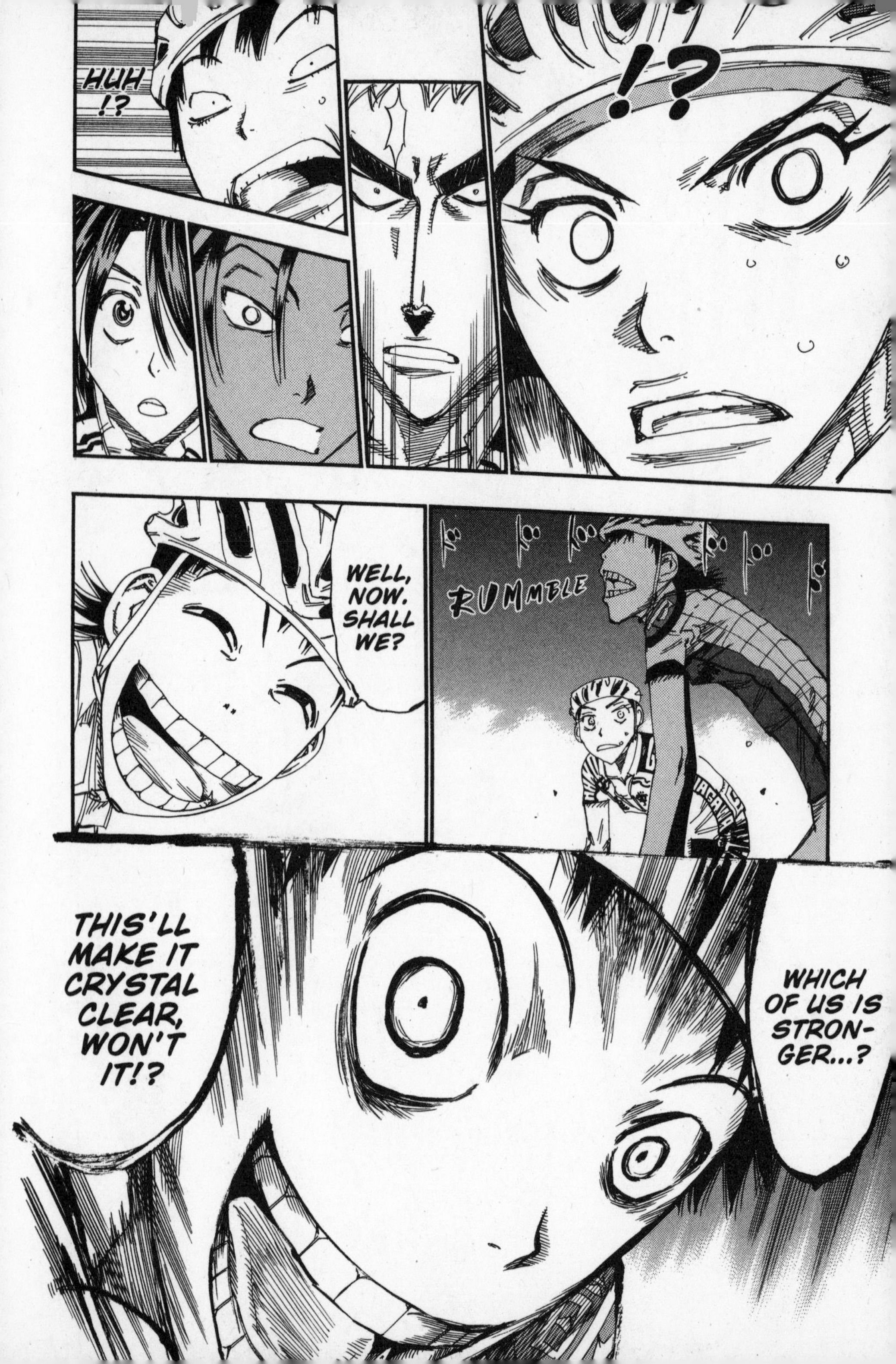
!?
HUH!?
RUMMBLE
WELL, NOW. SHALL WE?
WHICH OF US IS STRONGER...?
THIS'LL MAKE IT CRYSTAL CLEAR, WON'T IT!?

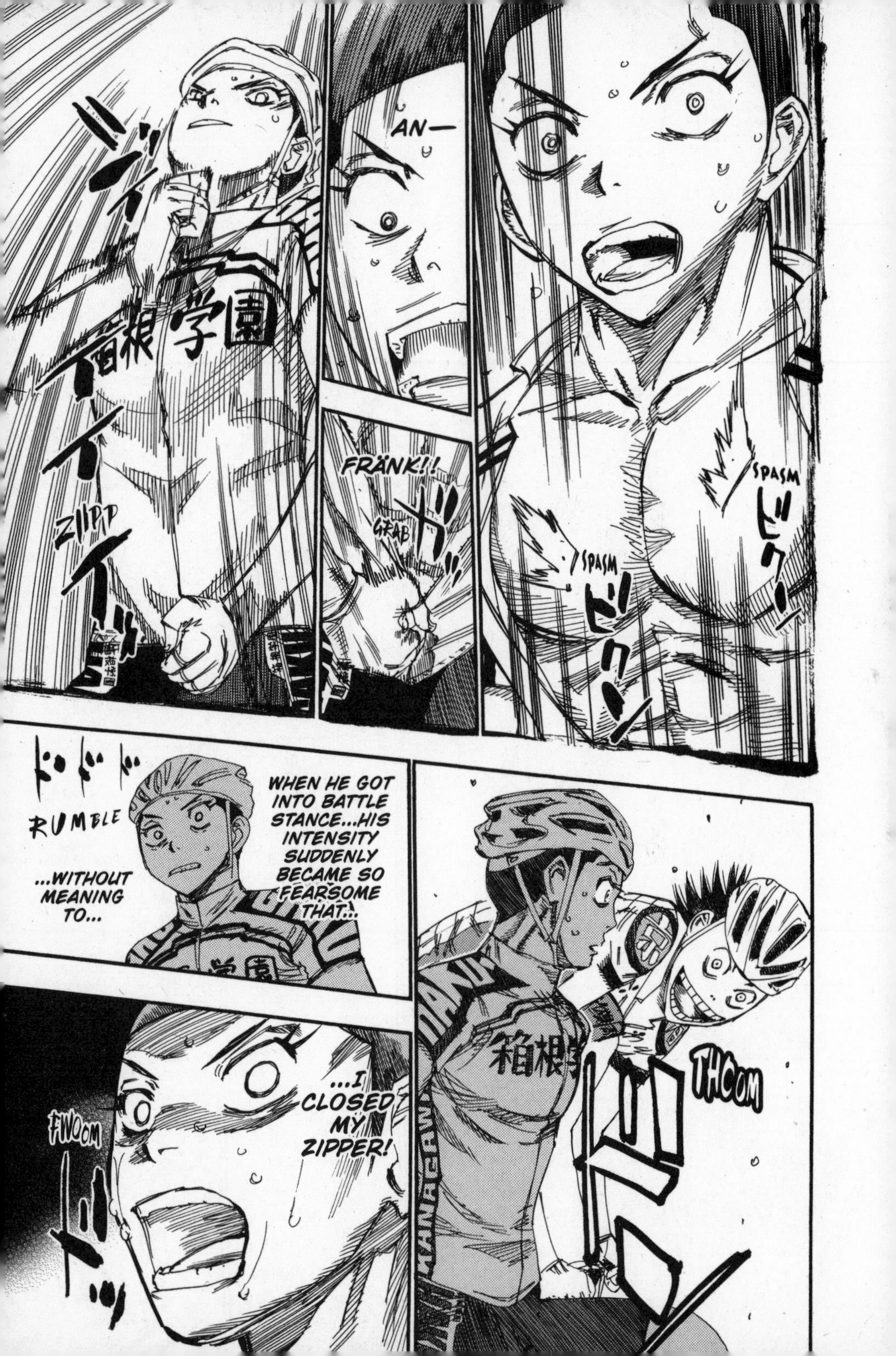
SPASM
SPASM
AN—
FRÄNK!!
GRAB
ZIIPP
THOOM
WHEN HE GOT INTO BATTLE STANCE...HIS INTENSITY SUDDENLY BECAME SO FEARSOME THAT...
RUMBLE
...WITHOUT MEANING TO...
...I CLOSED MY ZIPPER!
FWOOM

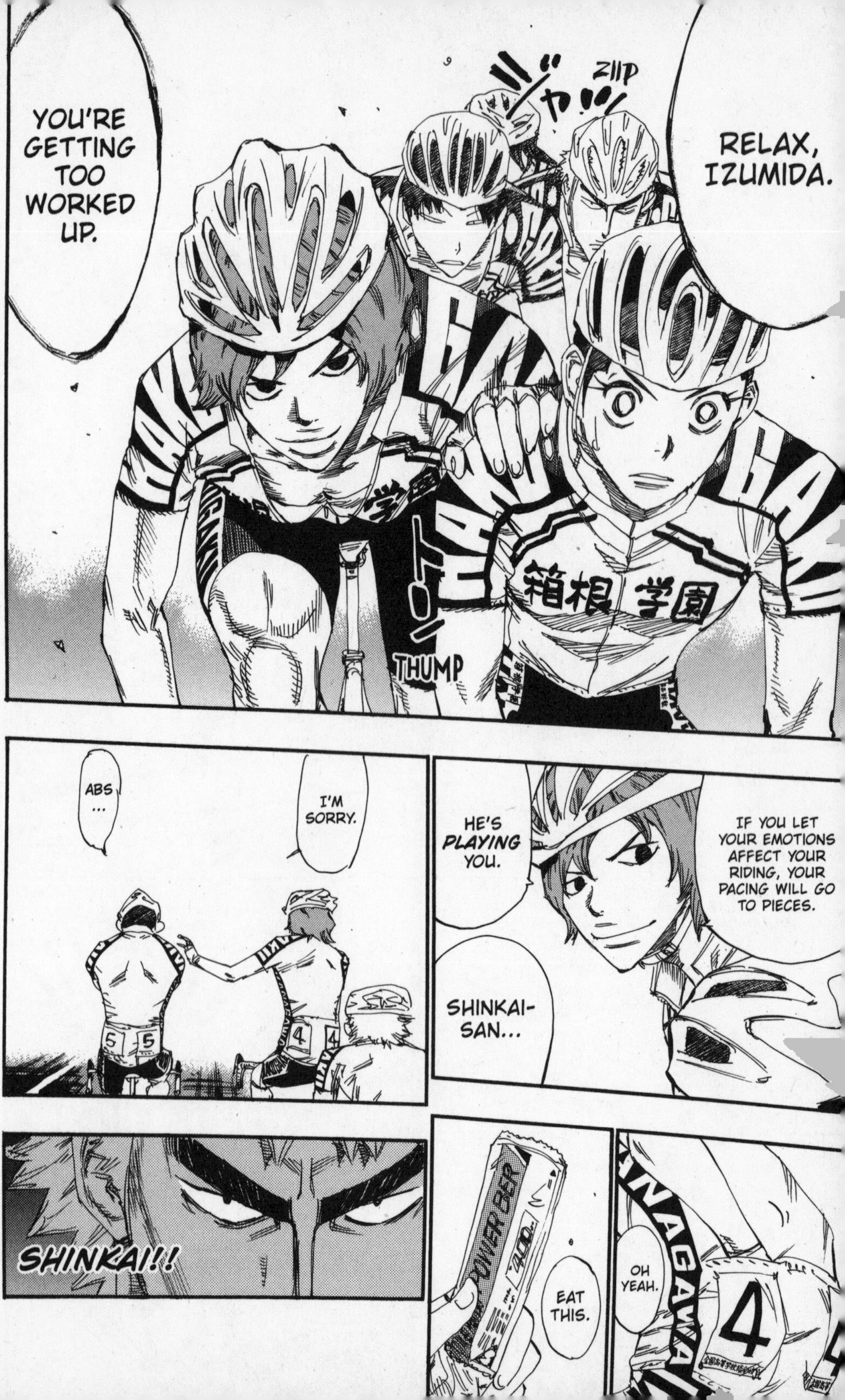
ZIIP
RELAX, IZUMIDA.
YOU'RE GETTING TOO WORKED UP.
THUMP
IF YOU LET YOUR EMOTIONS AFFECT YOUR RIDING, YOUR PACING WILL GO TO PIECES.
HE'S *PLAYING* YOU.
SHINKAI-SAN...
I'M SORRY.
ABS ...
OH YEAH.
EAT THIS.
SHINKAI!!

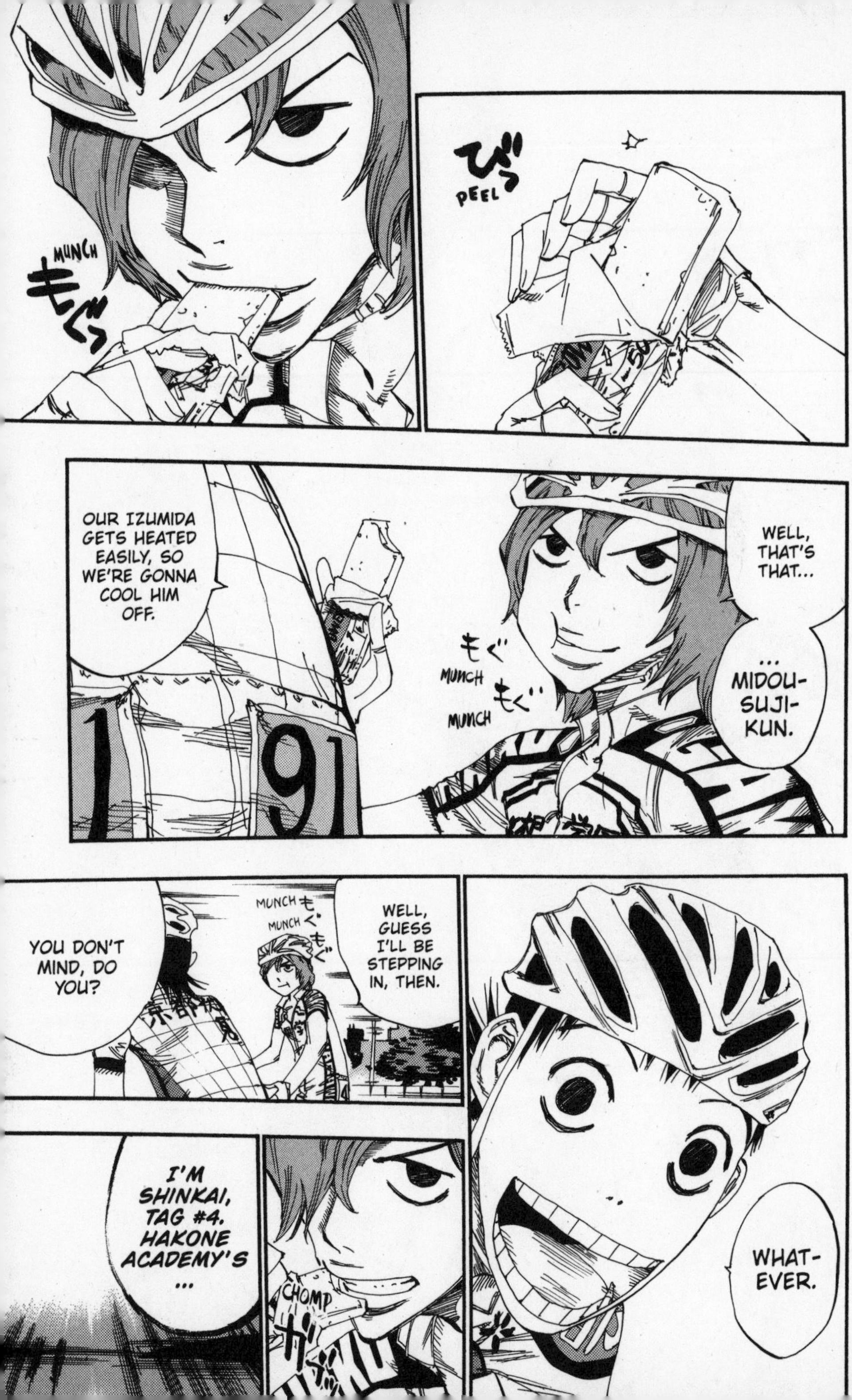

びっ
PEEL
MUNCH
もぐっ
WELL, THAT'S THAT...
... MIDOUSUJI-KUN.
もぐ MUNCH もぐ MUNCH
OUR IZUMIDA GETS HEATED EASILY, SO WE'RE GONNA COOL HIM OFF.
WHAT-EVER.
WELL, GUESS I'LL BE STEPPING IN, THEN.
MUNCH もぐ MUNCH もぐ
YOU DON'T MIND, DO YOU?
CHOMP
I'M SHINKAI, TAG #4. HAKONE ACADEMY'S ...

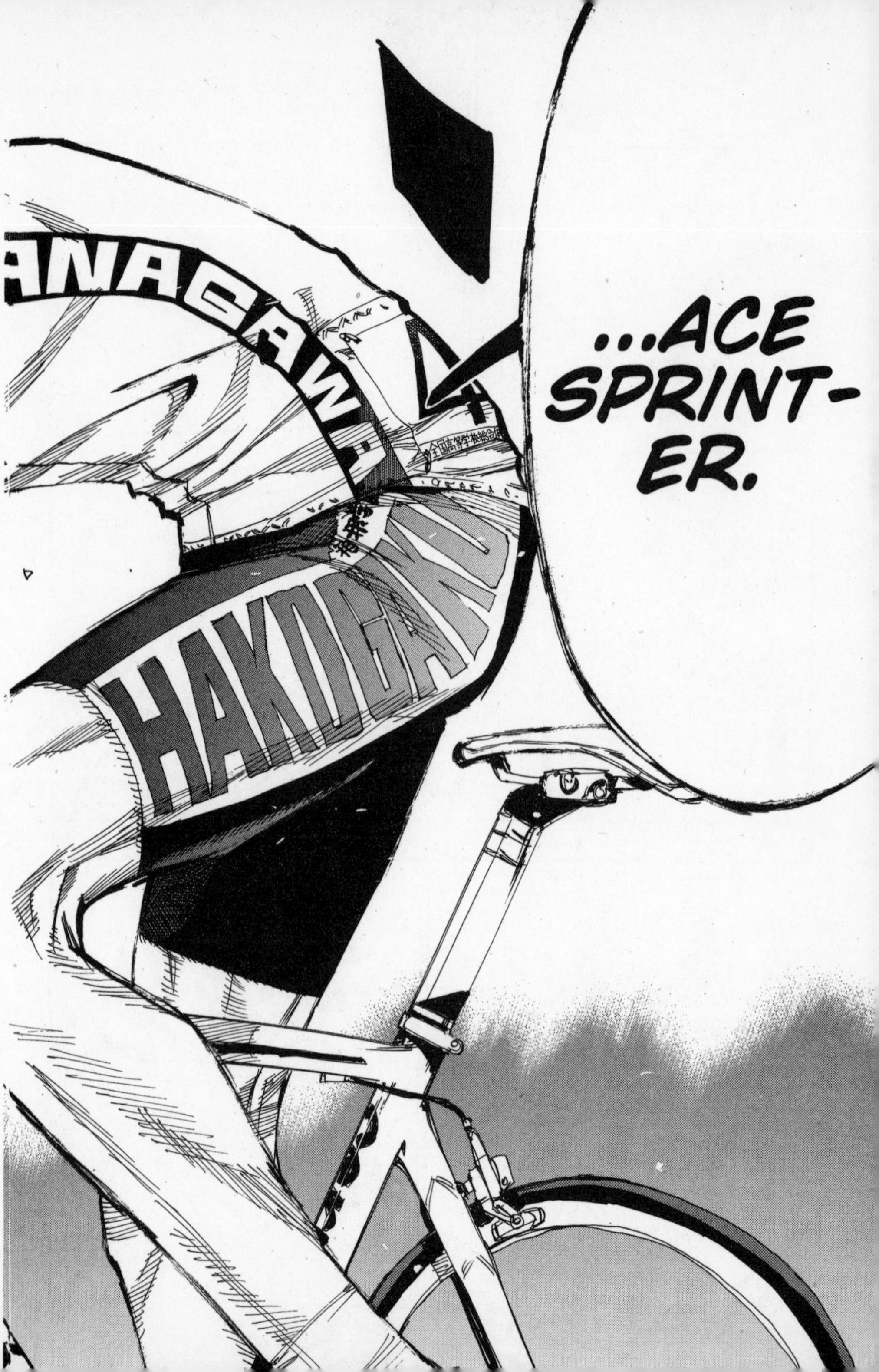
...ACE SPRINTER.
HAKOGAKU

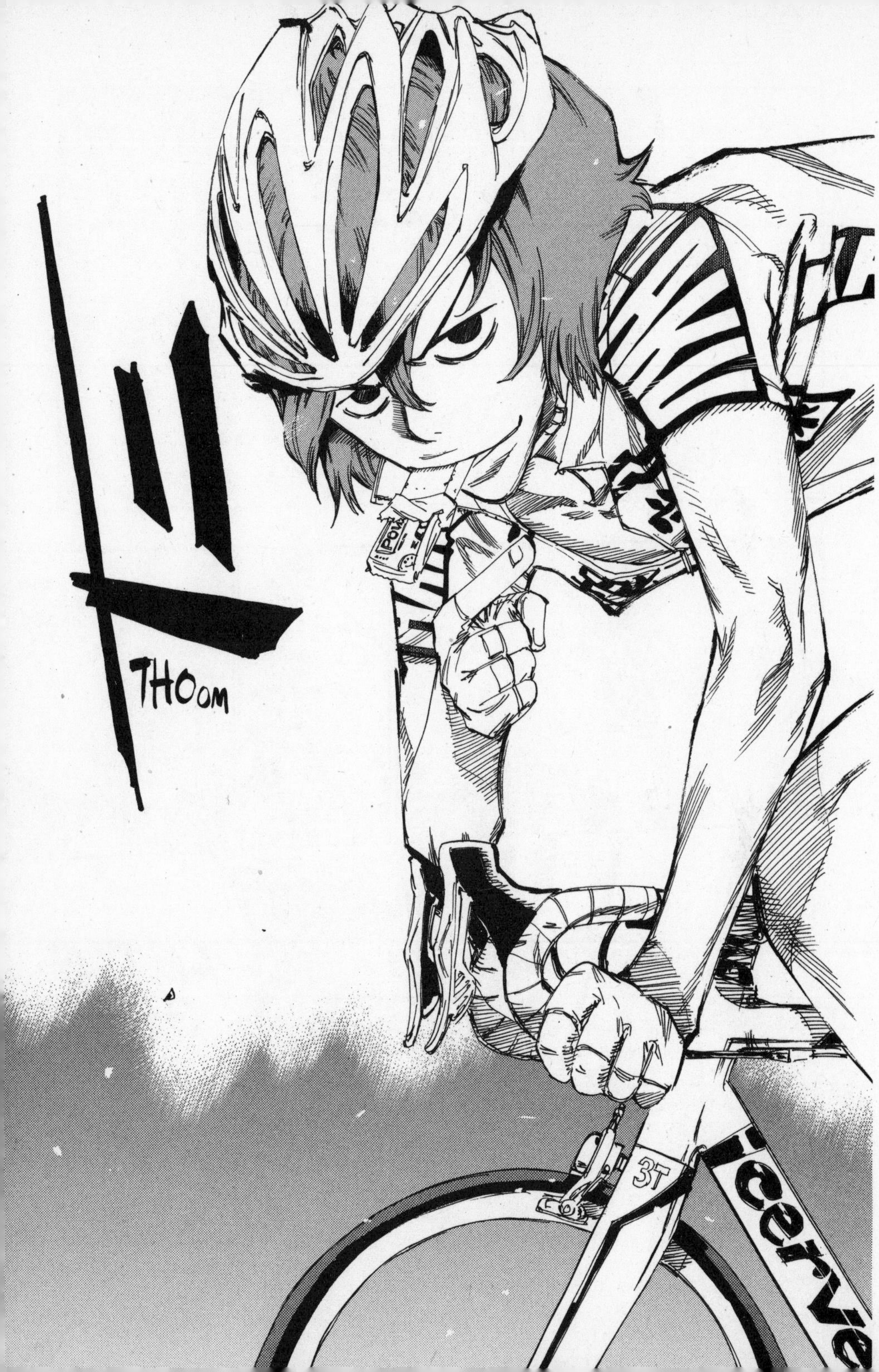
THOom
3T

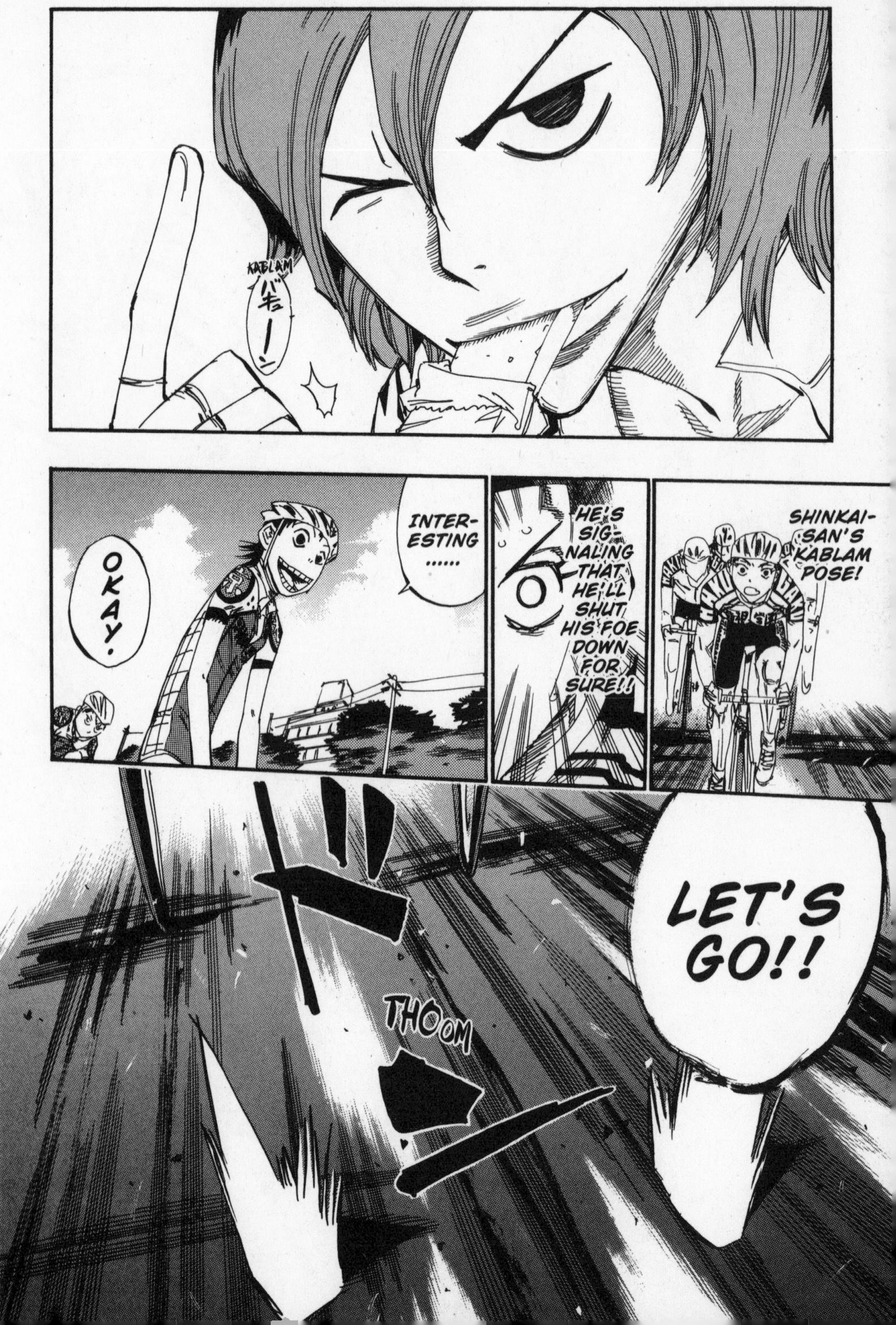
KABLAM
バキューン
SHINKAI-SAN'S KABLAM POSE!
HE'S SIG-NALING THAT HE'LL SHUT HIS FOE DOWN FOR SURE!!
INTER-ESTING......
OKAY.
LET'S GO!!
THOOM

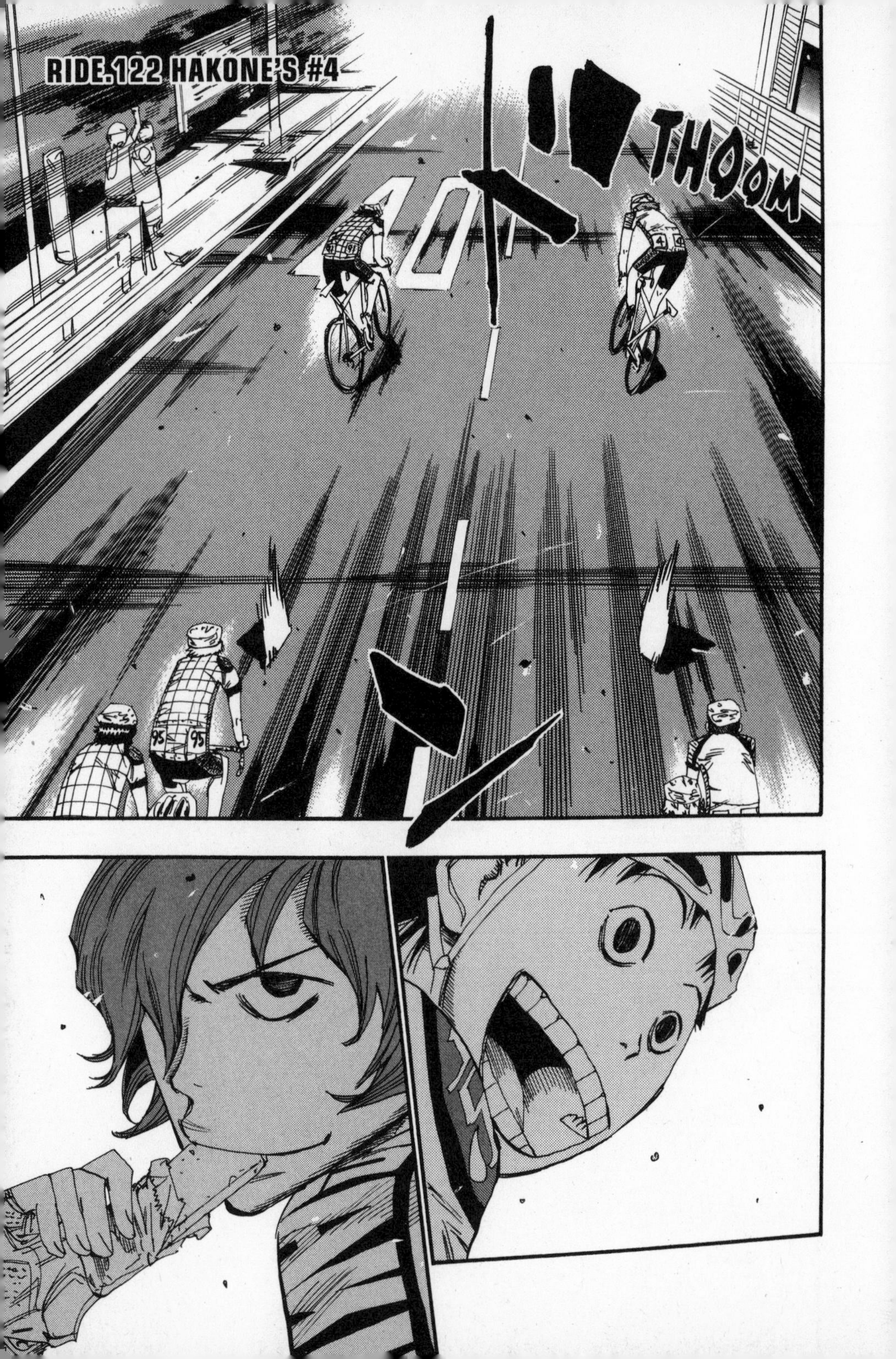
RIDE.122 HAKONE'S #4
THOOM

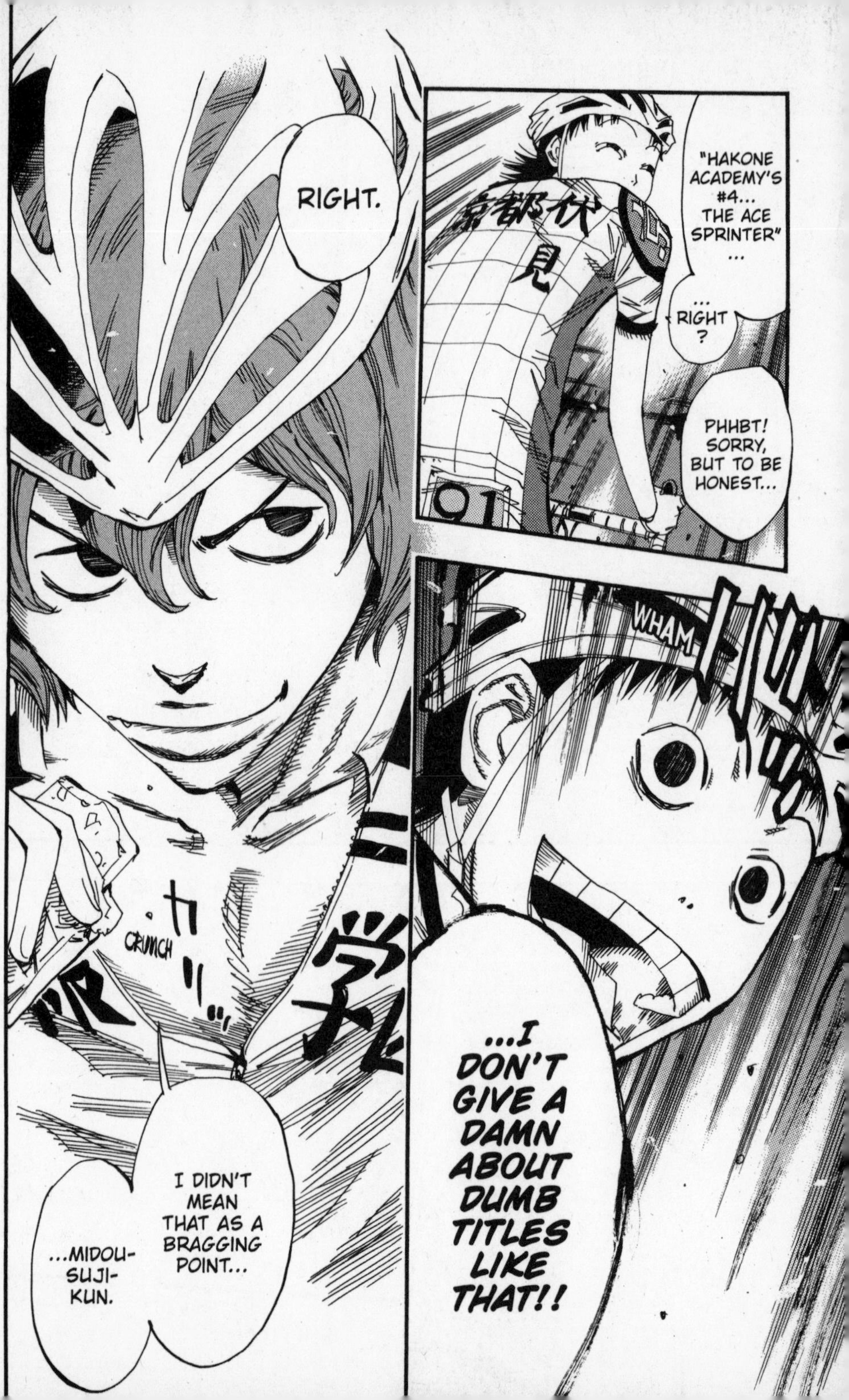
"HAKONE ACADEMY'S #4... THE ACE SPRINTER" ...
... RIGHT ?
京都伏見
PHHBT! SORRY, BUT TO BE HONEST...
WHAM
...I DON'T GIVE A DAMN ABOUT DUMB TITLES LIKE THAT!!
RIGHT.
CRUNCH
I DIDN'T MEAN THAT AS A BRAGGING POINT...
...MIDOUSUJI-KUN.

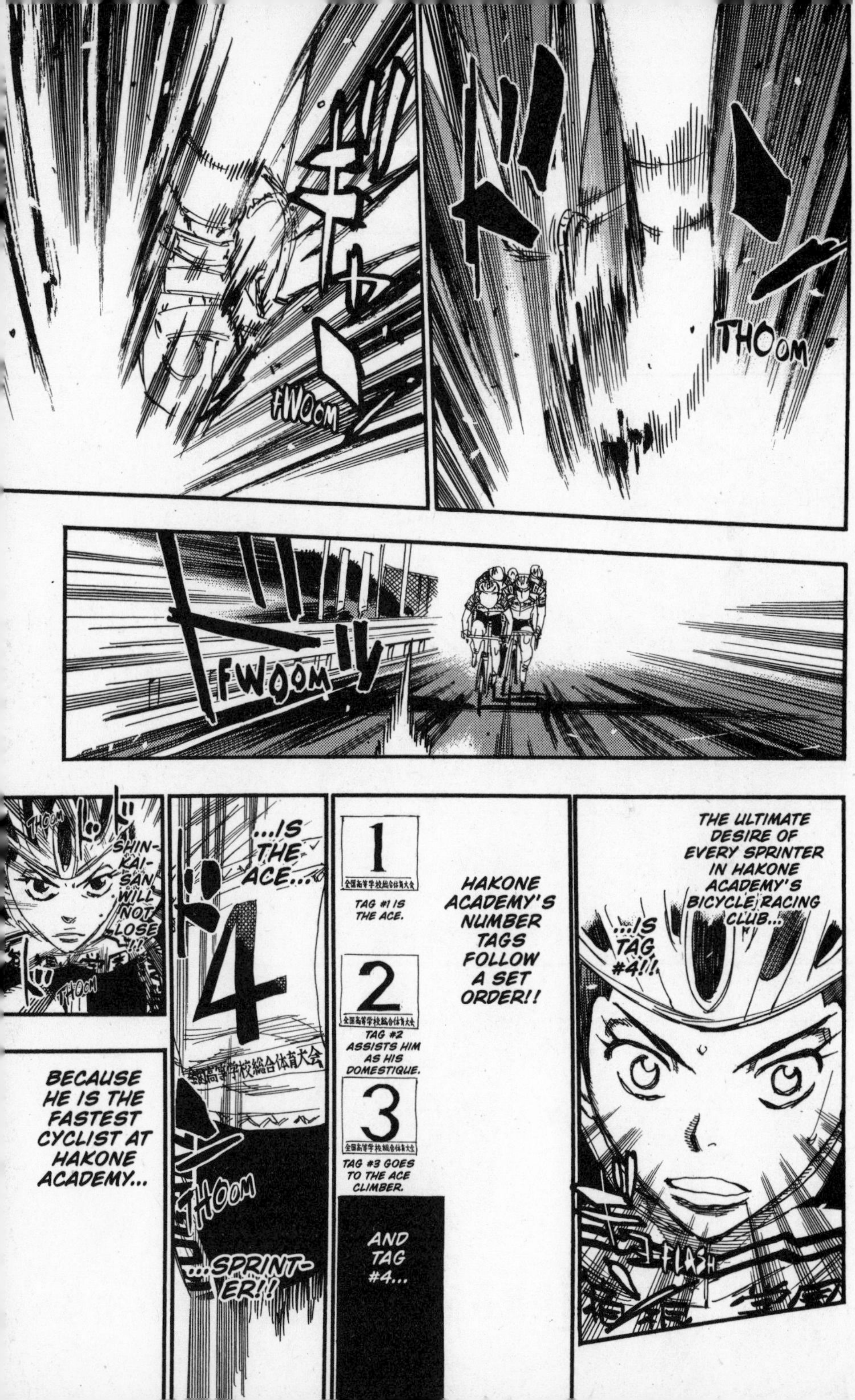

THOOM
FWOOM
FWOOM
THE ULTIMATE DESIRE OF EVERY SPRINTER IN HAKONE ACADEMY'S BICYCLE RACING CLUB...
...IS TAG #4!!
FLASH
HAKONE ACADEMY'S NUMBER TAGS FOLLOW A SET ORDER!!
1
TAG #1 IS THE ACE.
2
TAG #2 ASSISTS HIM AS HIS DOMESTIQUE.
3
TAG #3 GOES TO THE ACE CLIMBER.
AND TAG #4...
...IS THE ACE...
4
THOOM
...SPRINTER!!
THOOM
SHINKAI-SAN WILL NOT LOSE!!
THOOM
BECAUSE HE IS THE FASTEST CYCLIST AT HAKONE ACADEMY...

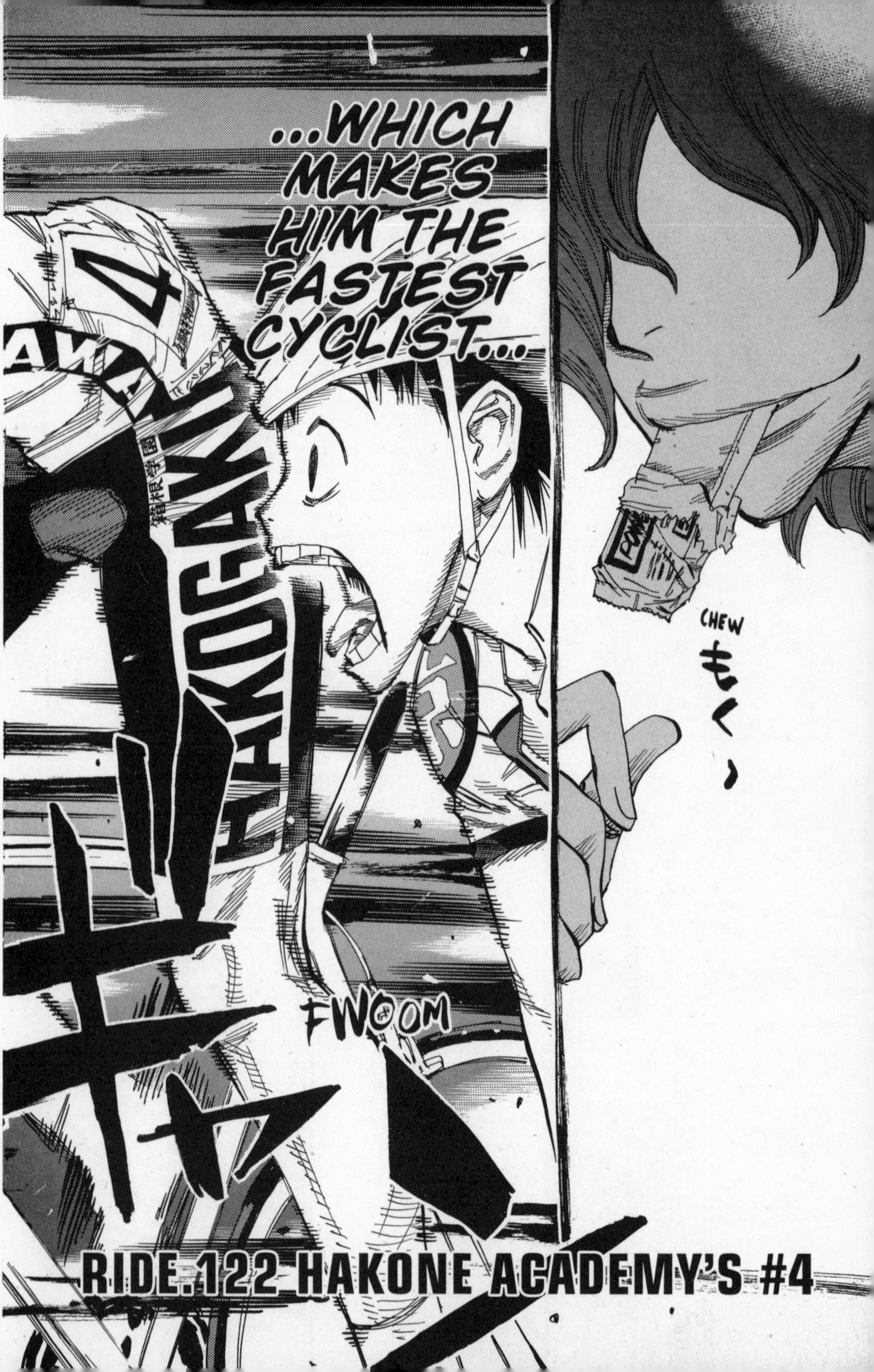
CHEW
もく
...WHICH MAKES HIM THE FASTEST CYCLIST...
FWOOM

RIDE.122 HAKONE ACADEMY'S #4

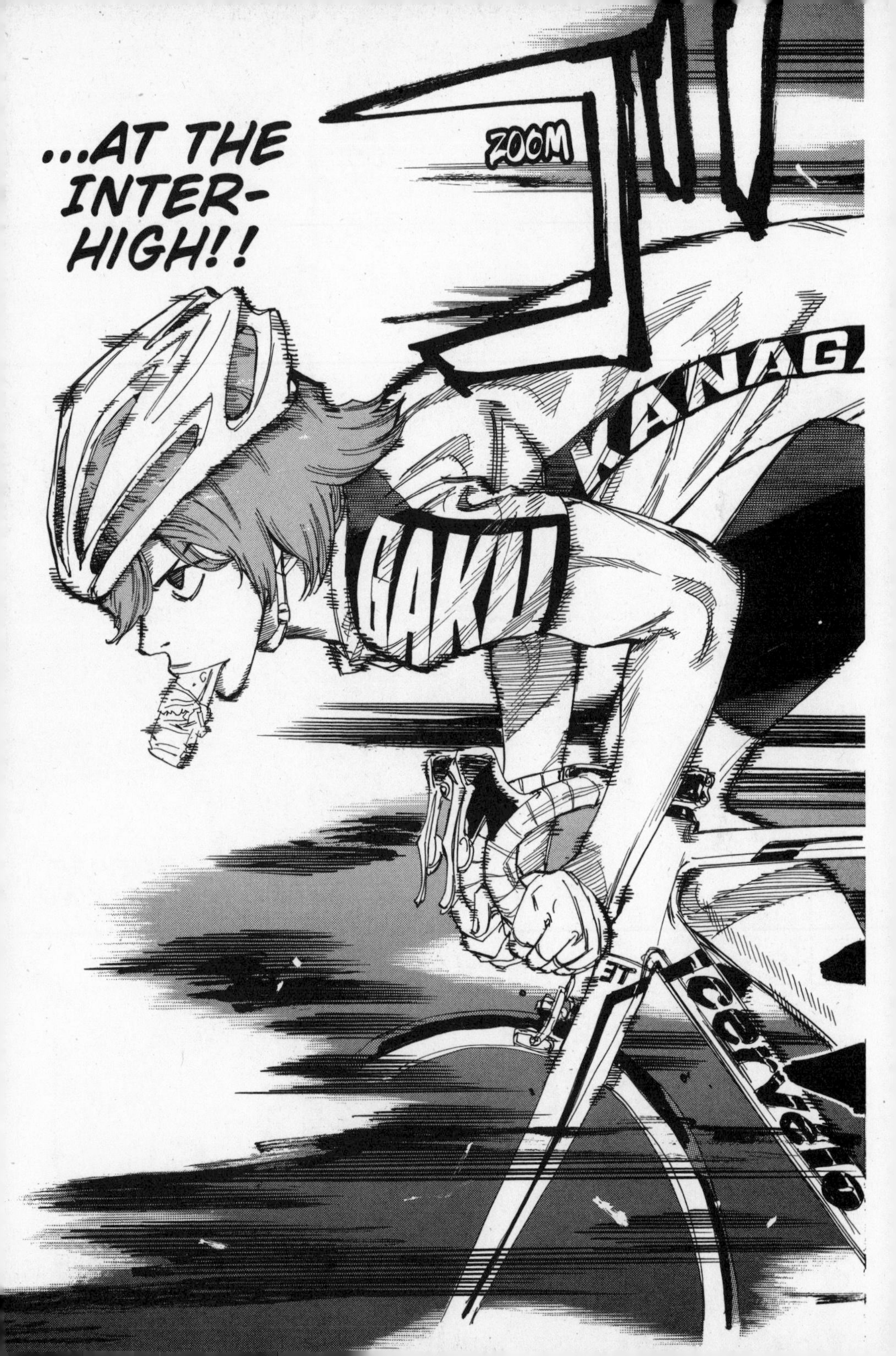
...AT THE INTER-HIGH!!
ZOOM
KANAG
GAKU

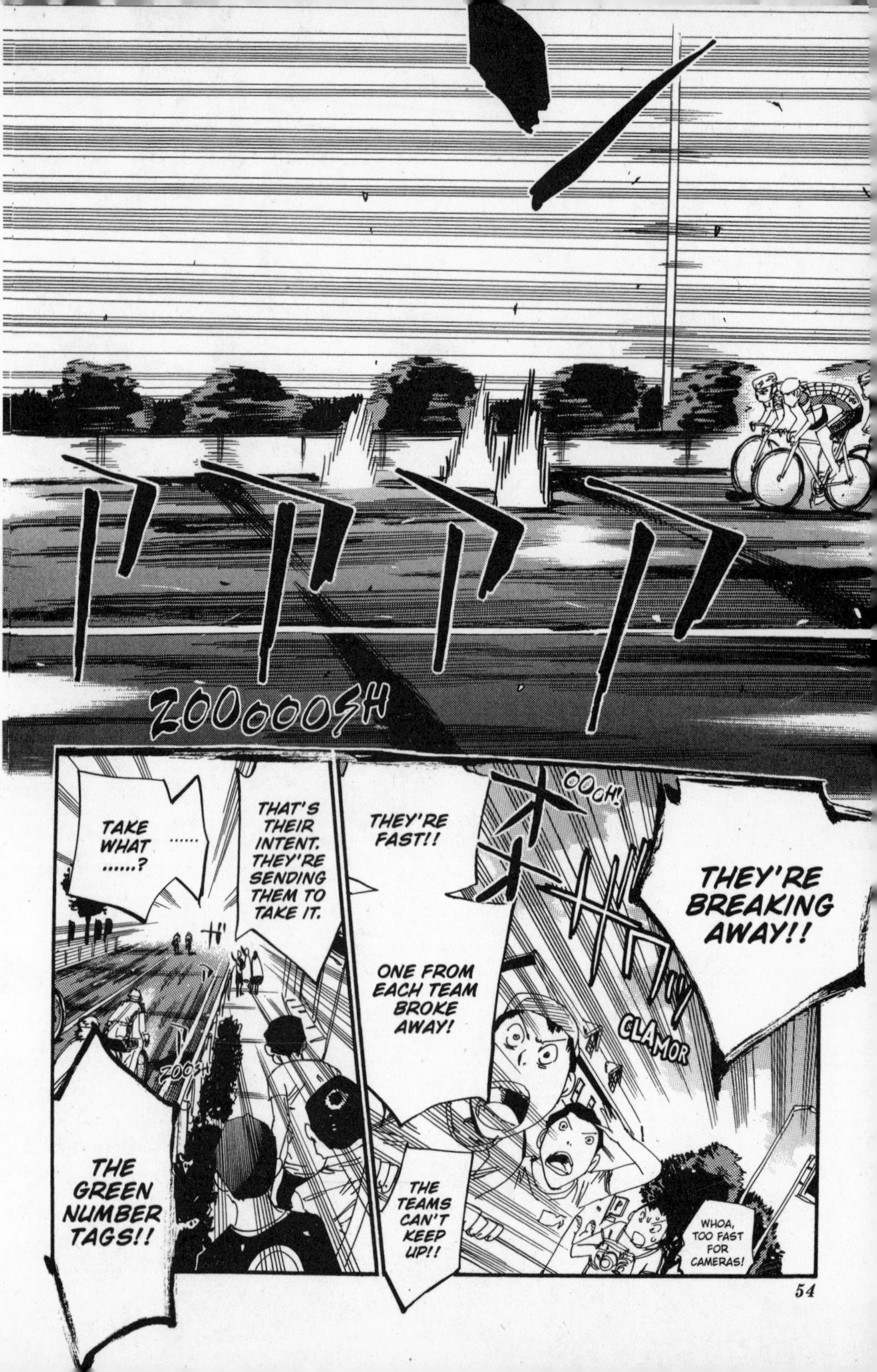
ZOOOOOSH
OOOH!
THEY'RE BREAKING AWAY!!
CLAMOR
WHOA, TOO FAST FOR CAMERAS!
THEY'RE FAST!!
ONE FROM EACH TEAM BROKE AWAY!
THE TEAMS CAN'T KEEP UP!!
THAT'S THEIR INTENT. THEY'RE SENDING THEM TO TAKE IT.
TAKE WHAT ......?
......
ZOOSH
THE GREEN NUMBER TAGS!!

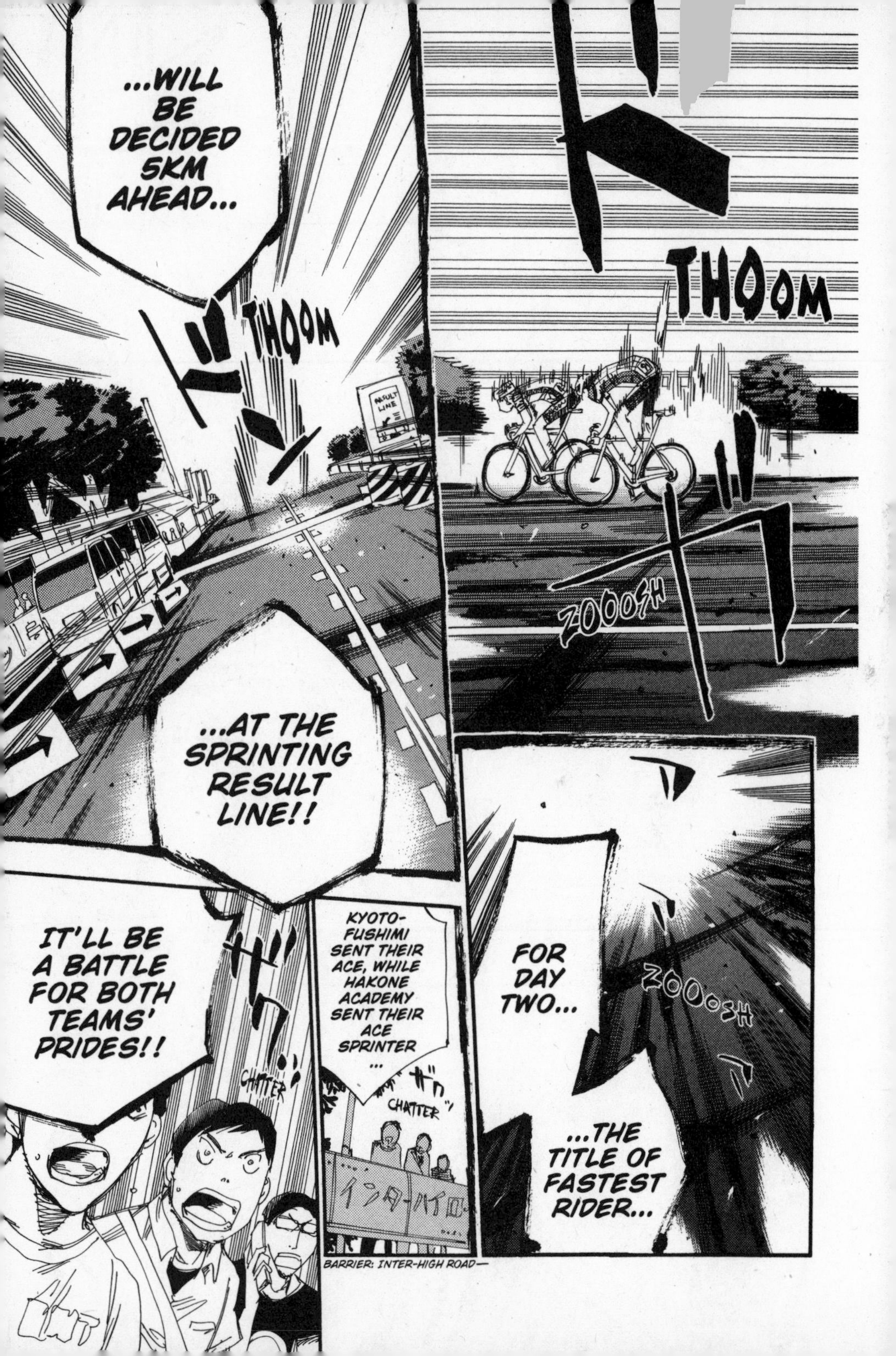
THOOM
ZOOOSH
FOR DAY TWO...
ZOOOSH
...THE TITLE OF FASTEST RIDER...
...WILL BE DECIDED 5KM AHEAD...
THOOM
RESULT LINE
...AT THE SPRINTING RESULT LINE!!
KYOTO-FUSHIMI SENT THEIR ACE, WHILE HAKONE ACADEMY SENT THEIR ACE SPRINTER...
CHATTER
BARRIER: INTER-HIGH ROAD—
IT'LL BE A BATTLE FOR BOTH TEAMS' PRIDES!!
CHATTER

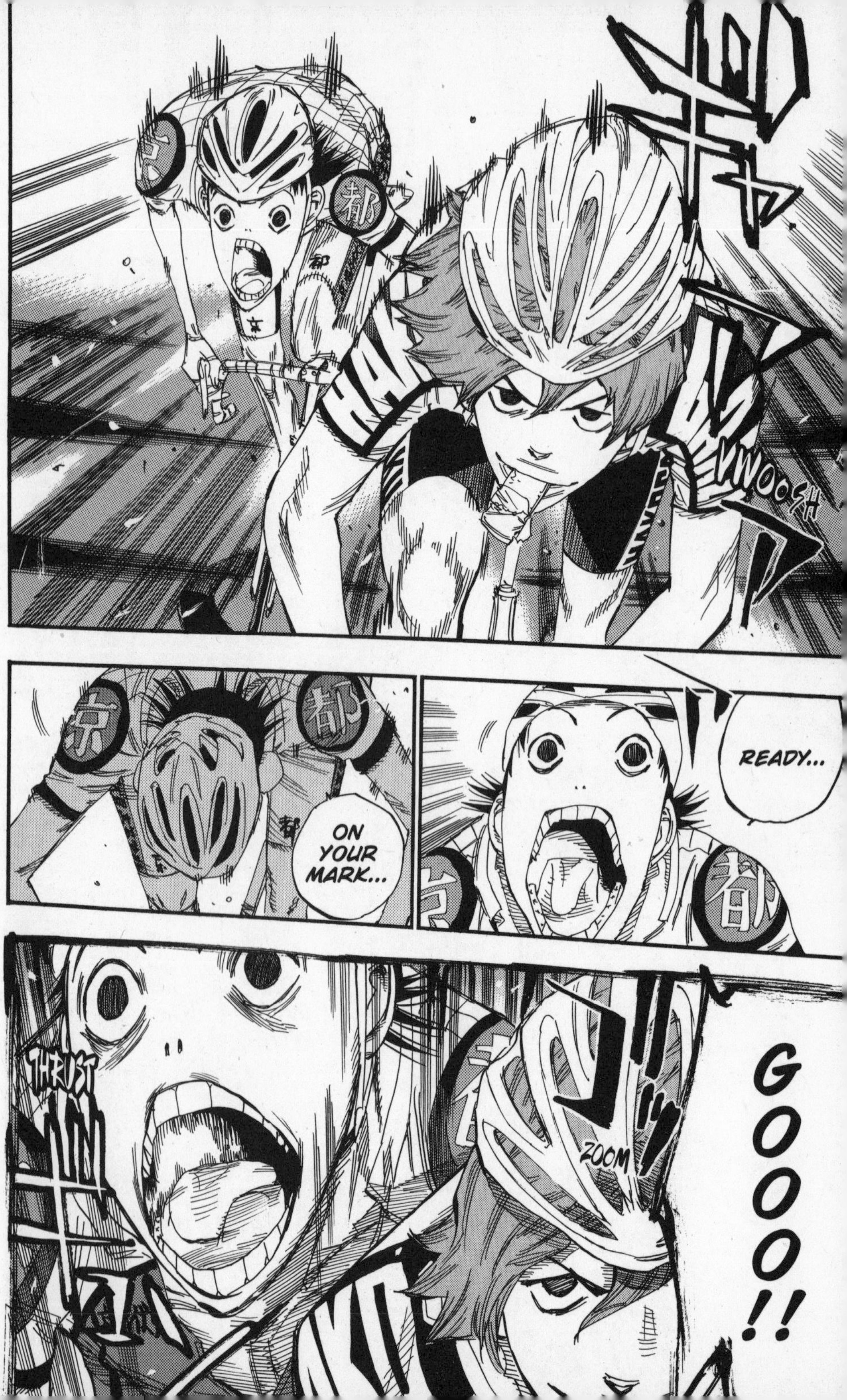
VWOOSH
READY...
ON YOUR MARK...
GOOOO!!
ZOOM
THRUST

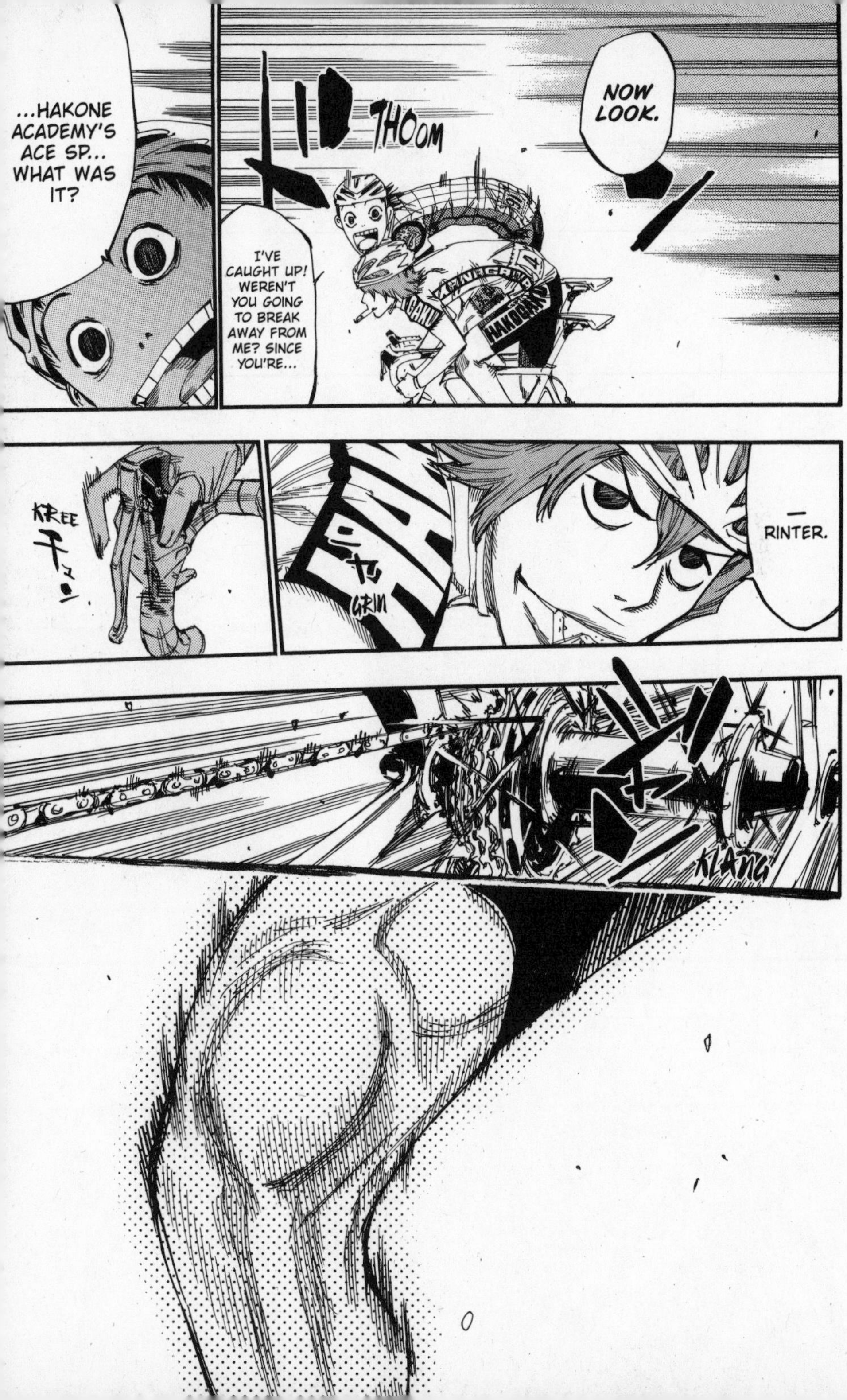
NOW LOOK.
THOOM
I'VE CAUGHT UP! WEREN'T YOU GOING TO BREAK AWAY FROM ME? SINCE YOU'RE...
...HAKONE ACADEMY'S ACE SP... WHAT WAS IT?
—RINTER.
GRIN
KREE
KLANG

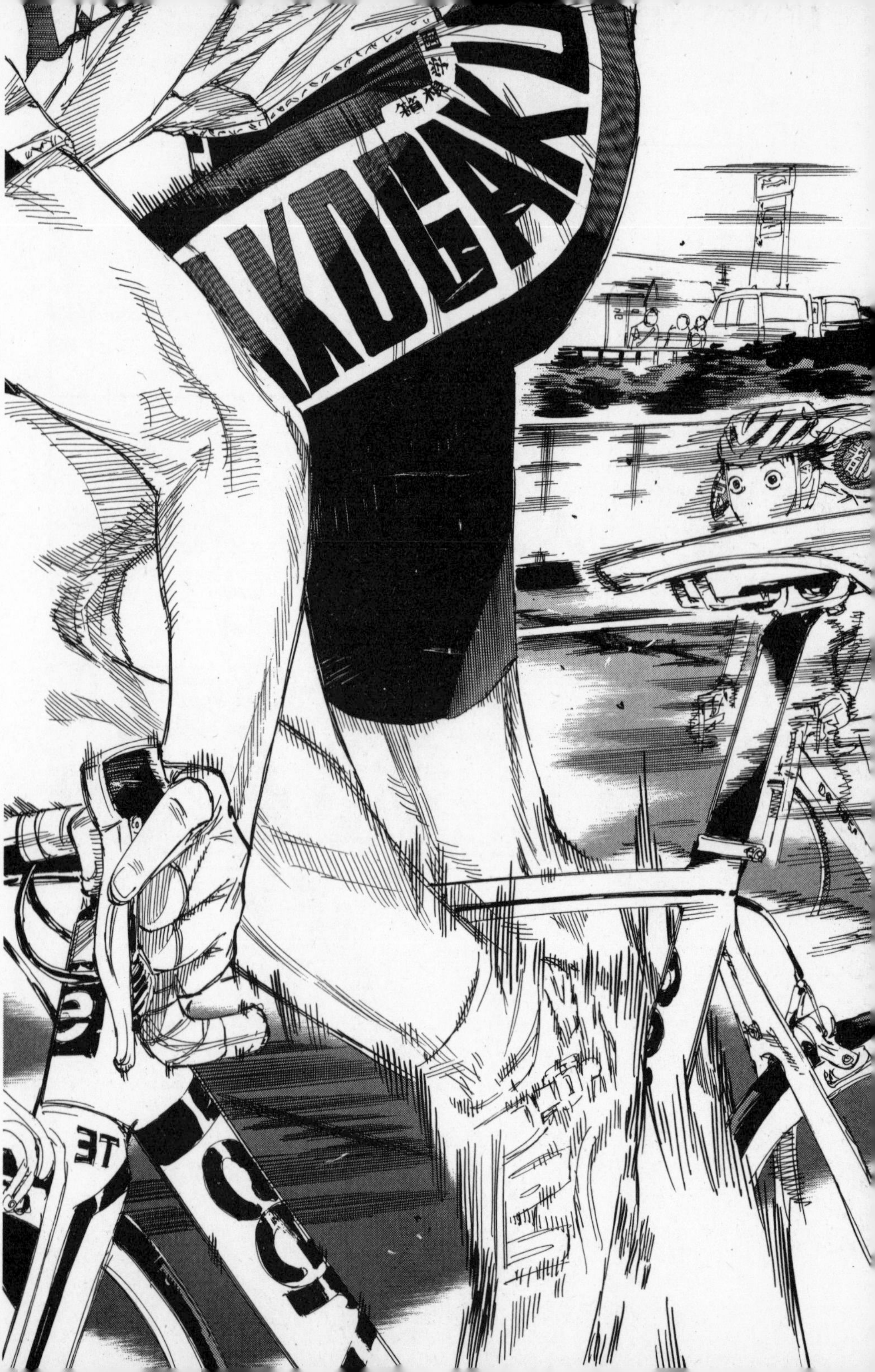

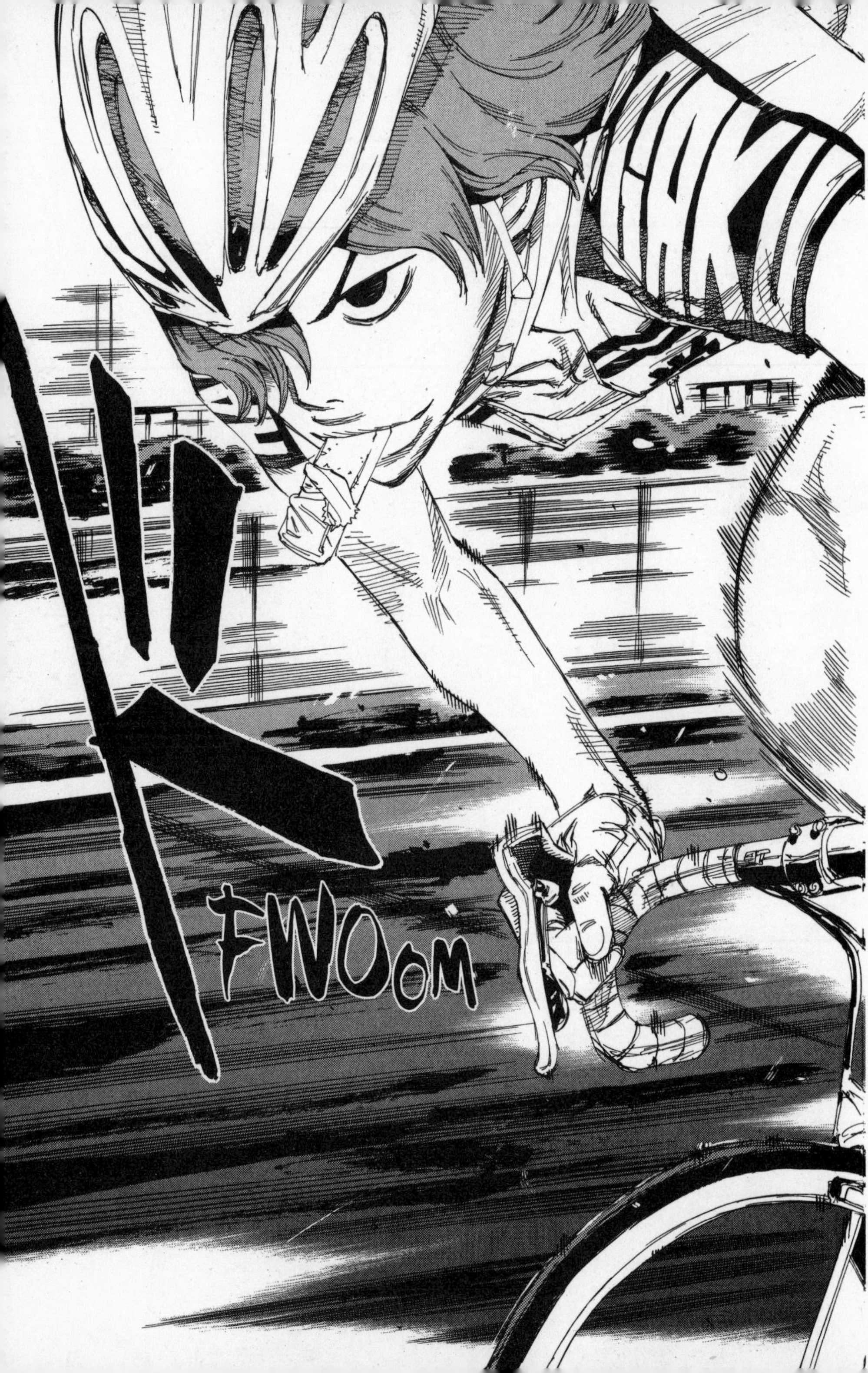
FWOOM

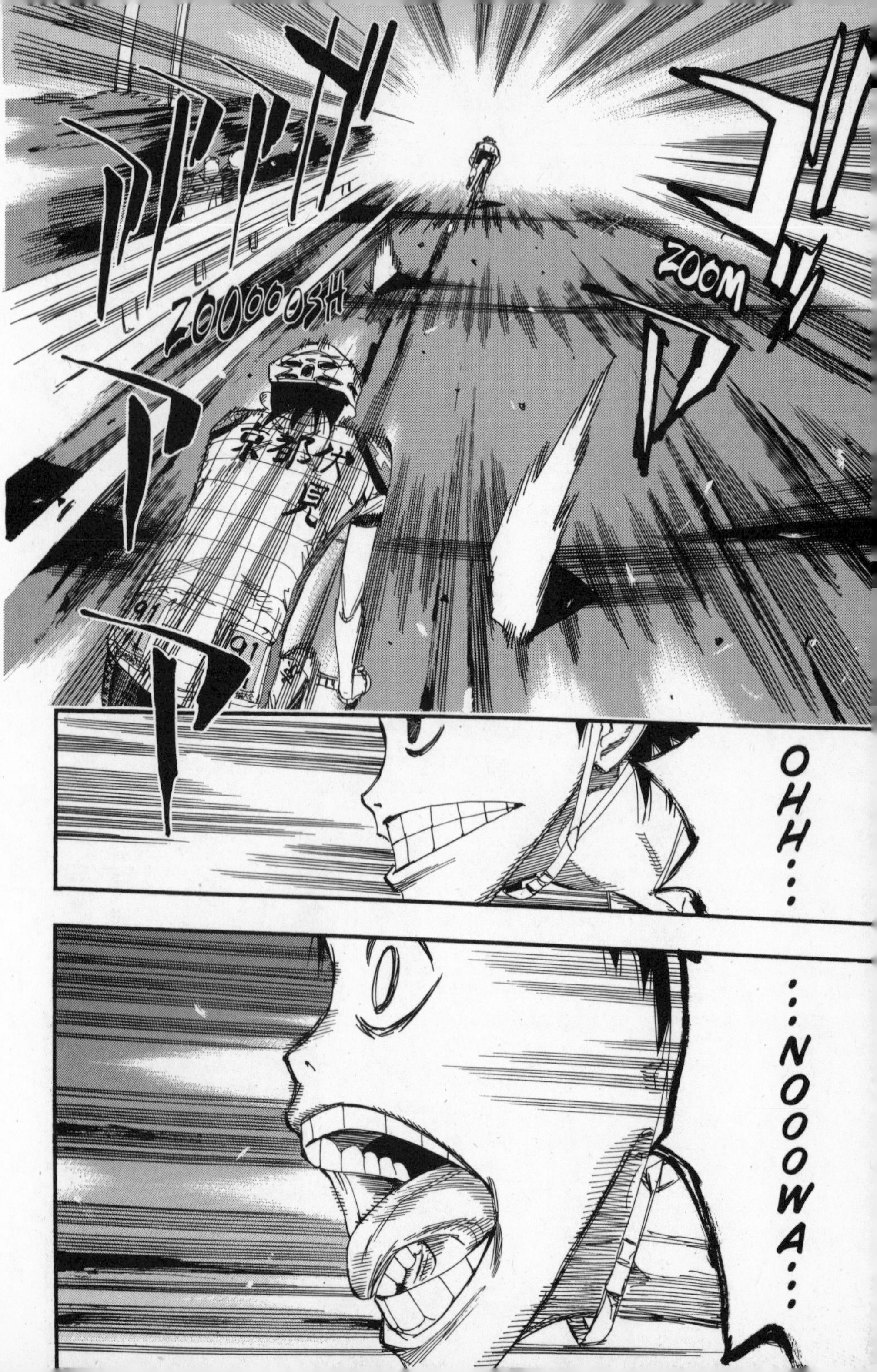
ZOOM
ZOOOOOSH
OHH...
...NOOOOWA...

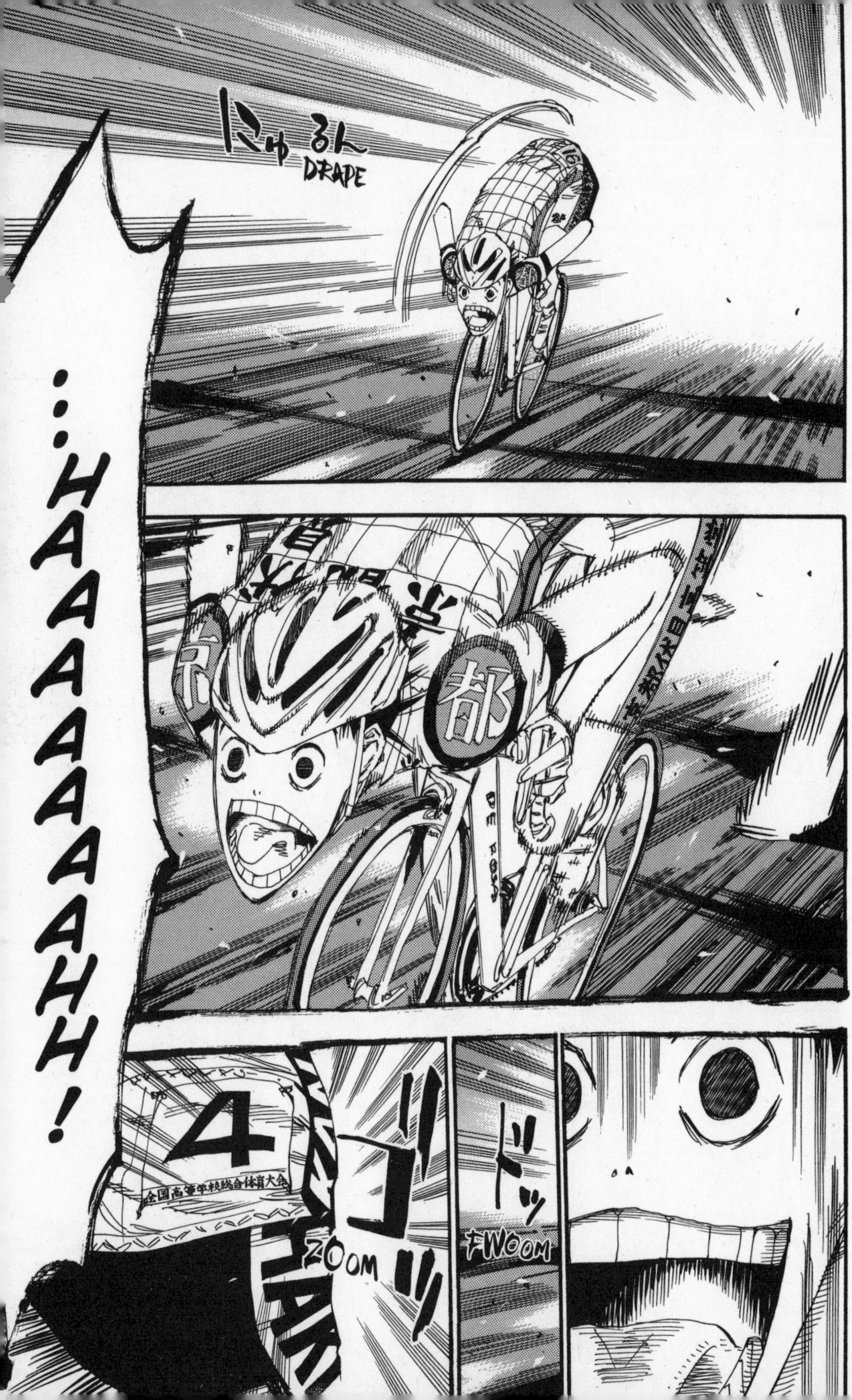
にゅるん
DRAPE
ドッ
FWOOM
ゴッ
ZOOM
4
全国高等学校総合体育大会
...HAAAAAAAAAAHH!

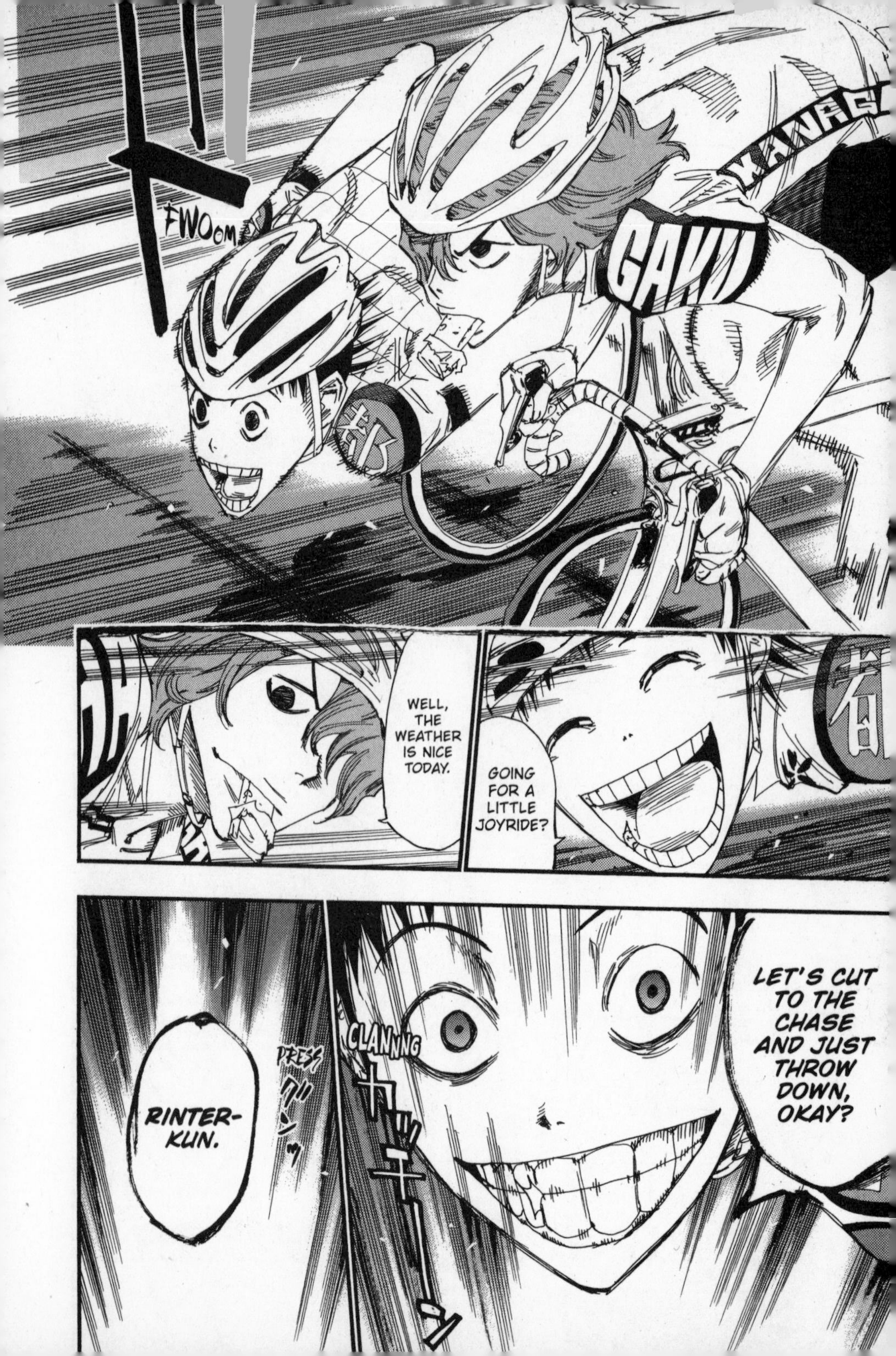
FWOOM
GOING FOR A LITTLE JOYRIDE?
WELL, THE WEATHER IS NICE TODAY.
LET'S CUT TO THE CHASE AND JUST THROW DOWN, OKAY?
CLANNNG
PRESS
RINTER-KUN.

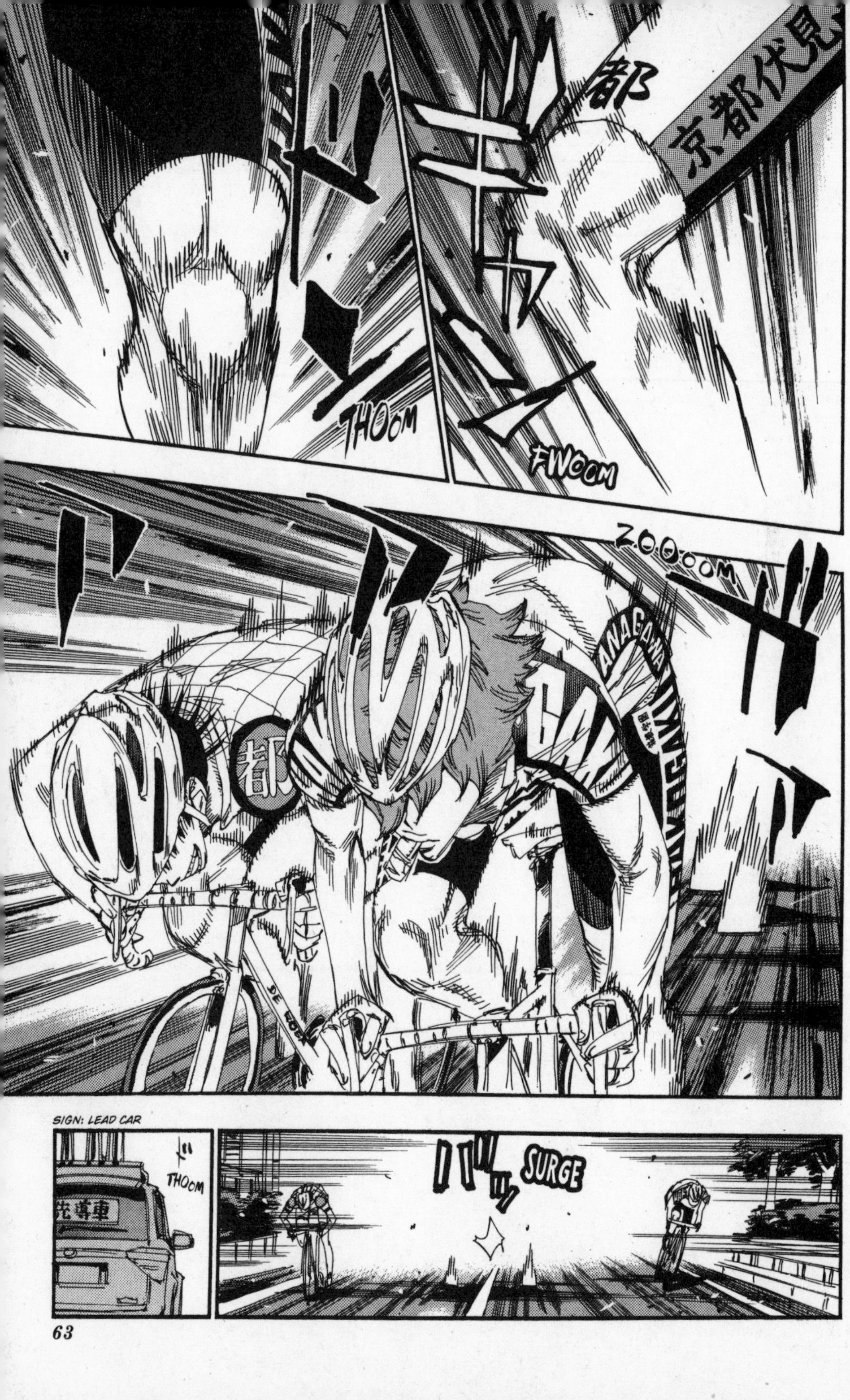
京都伏見
都
FWOOM
THOOM
ZOOOOM
SIGN: LEAD CAR
SURGE
先導車
THOOM

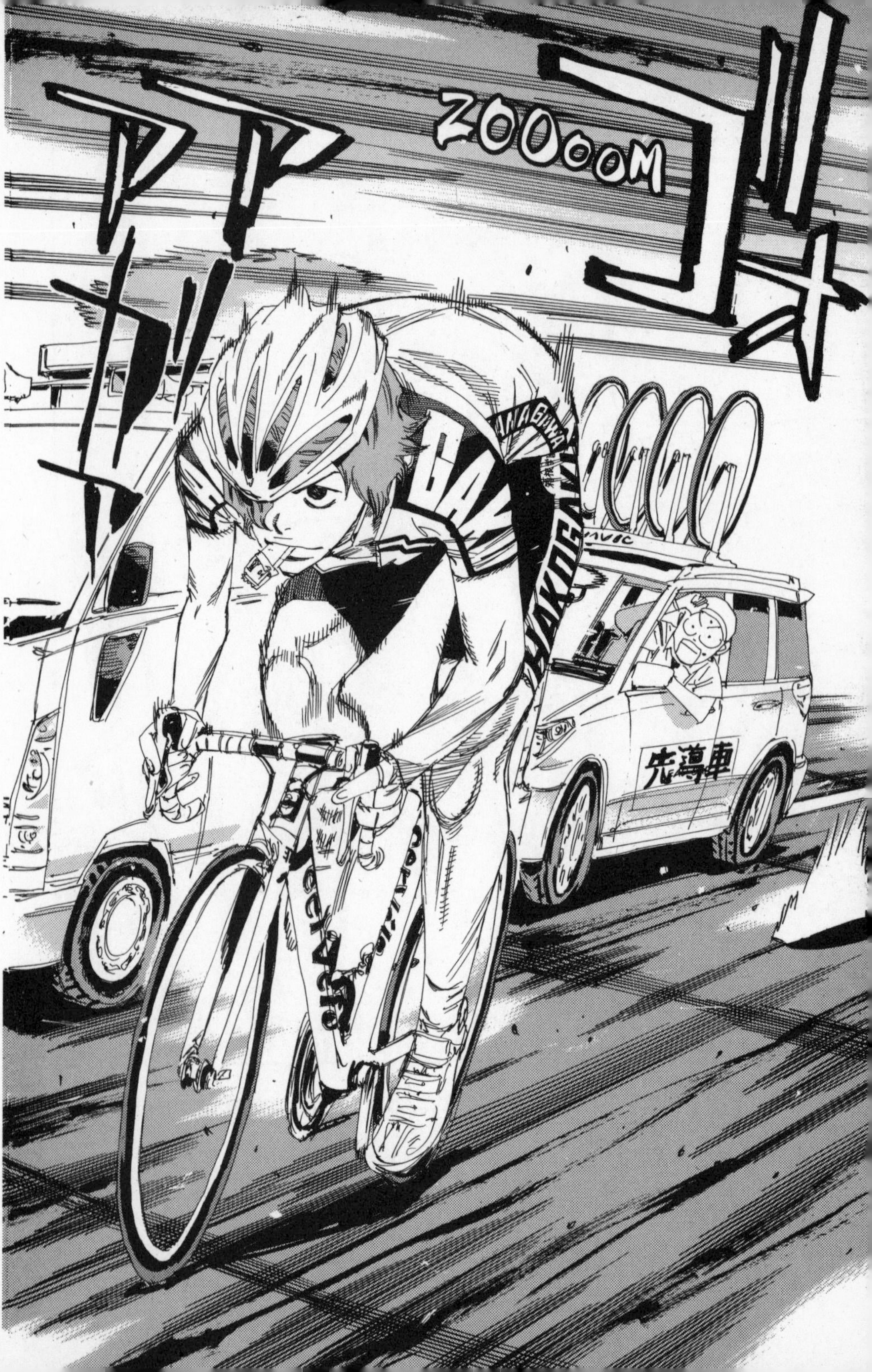
ZOOooOM
先導車

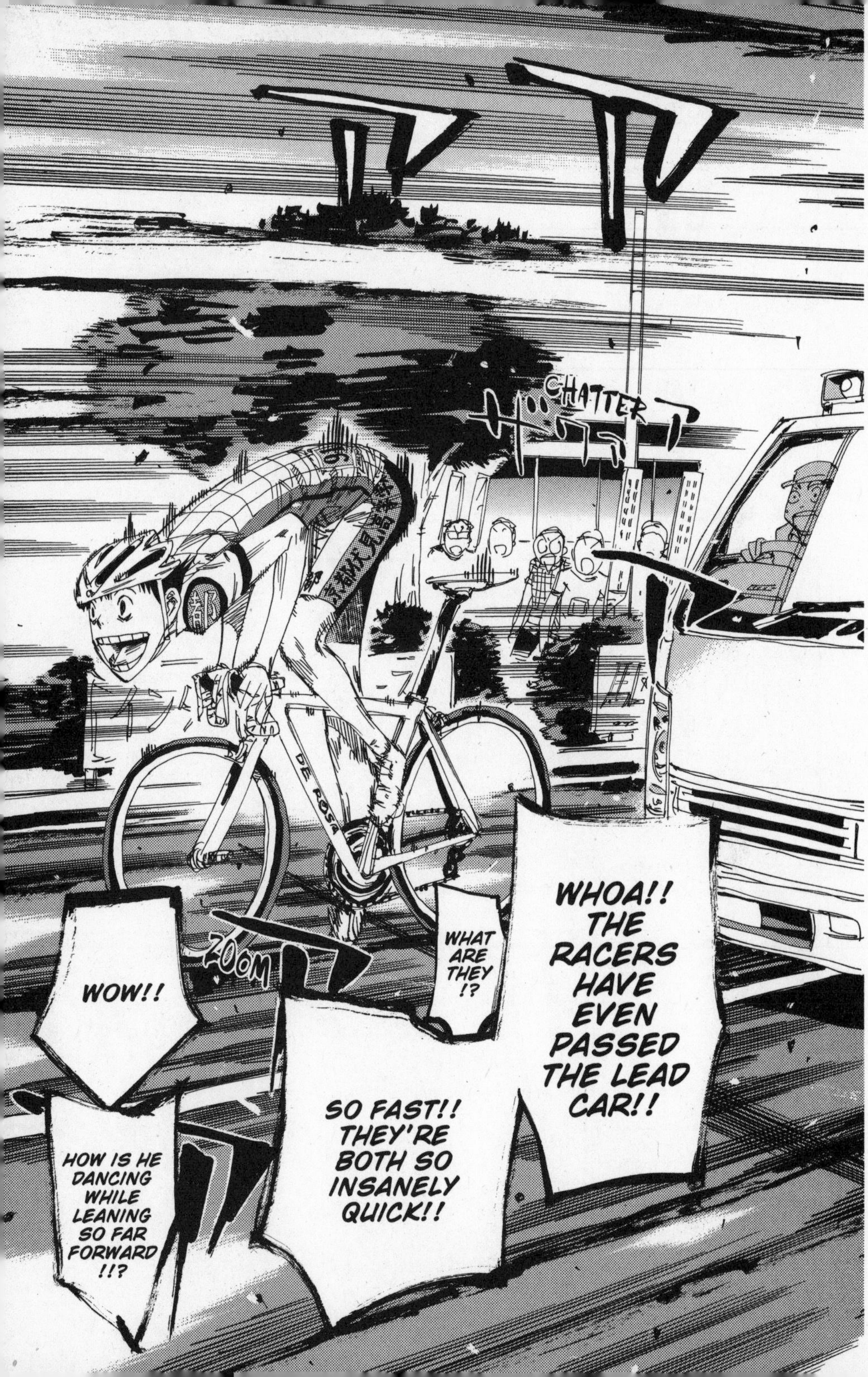
CHATTER
WHOA!! THE RACERS HAVE EVEN PASSED THE LEAD CAR!!
WHAT ARE THEY !?
SO FAST!! THEY'RE BOTH SO INSANELY QUICK!!
ZOOM
WOW!!
HOW IS HE DANCING WHILE LEANING SO FAR FORWARD !!?

FWOOM

ZOOOOM

HOW—
AFTER
THEM!

Y-
YES,
SIR!

ZOOOSH

!?

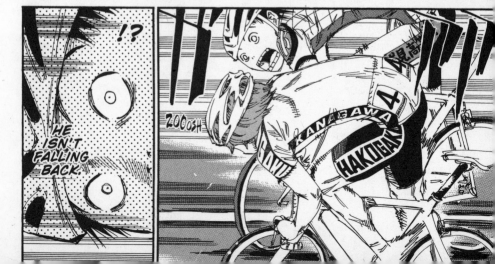

!?

HE
ISN'T
FALLING
BACK.

ZOOOSH

KANAGAWA
HAKOGA
4

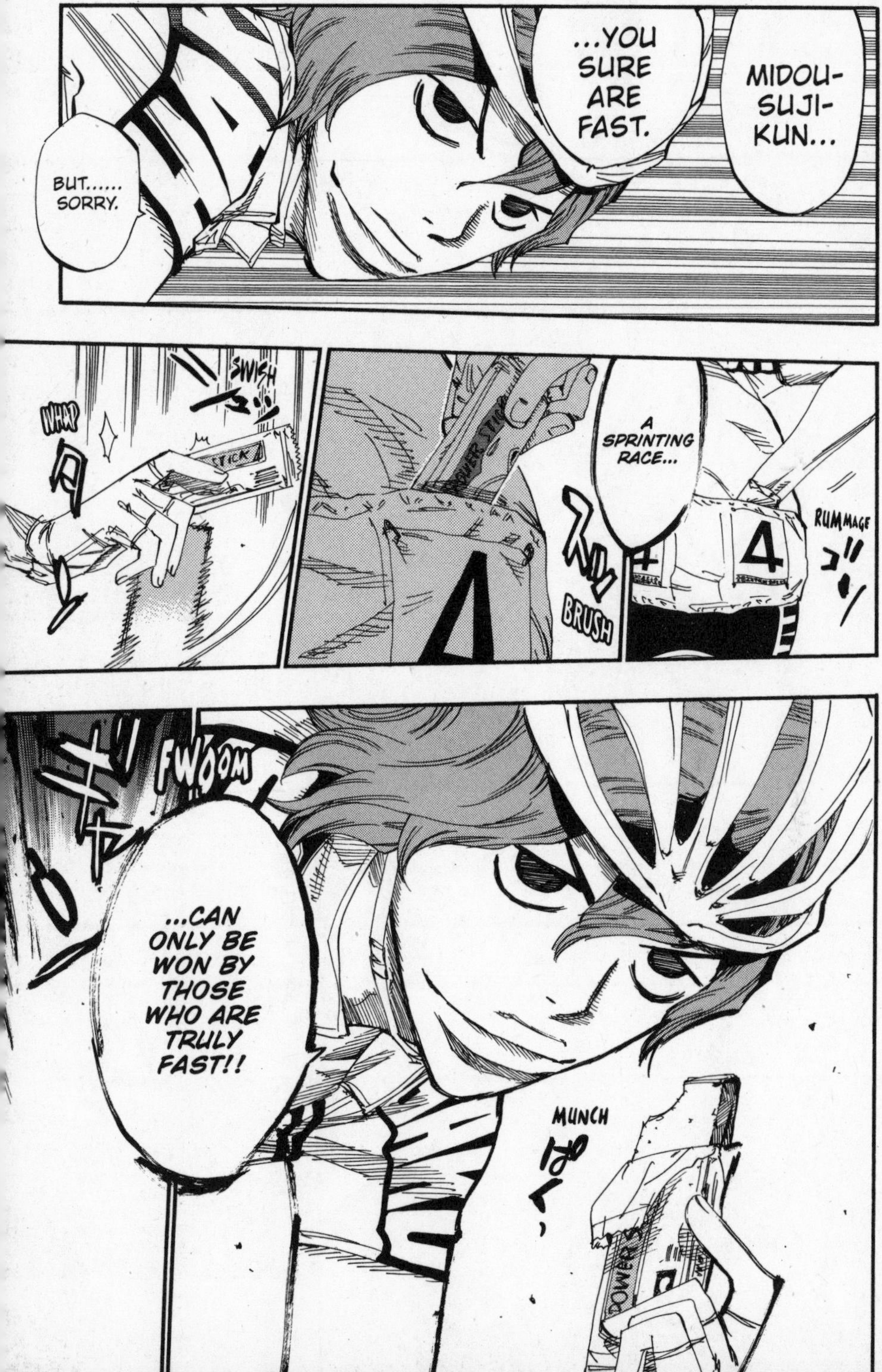
MIDOU-SUJI-KUN...
...YOU SURE ARE FAST.
BUT...... SORRY.
A SPRINTING RACE...
RUMMAGE
BRUSH
SWISH
WHAP
FWOOM
...CAN ONLY BE WON BY THOSE WHO ARE TRULY FAST!!
MUNCH

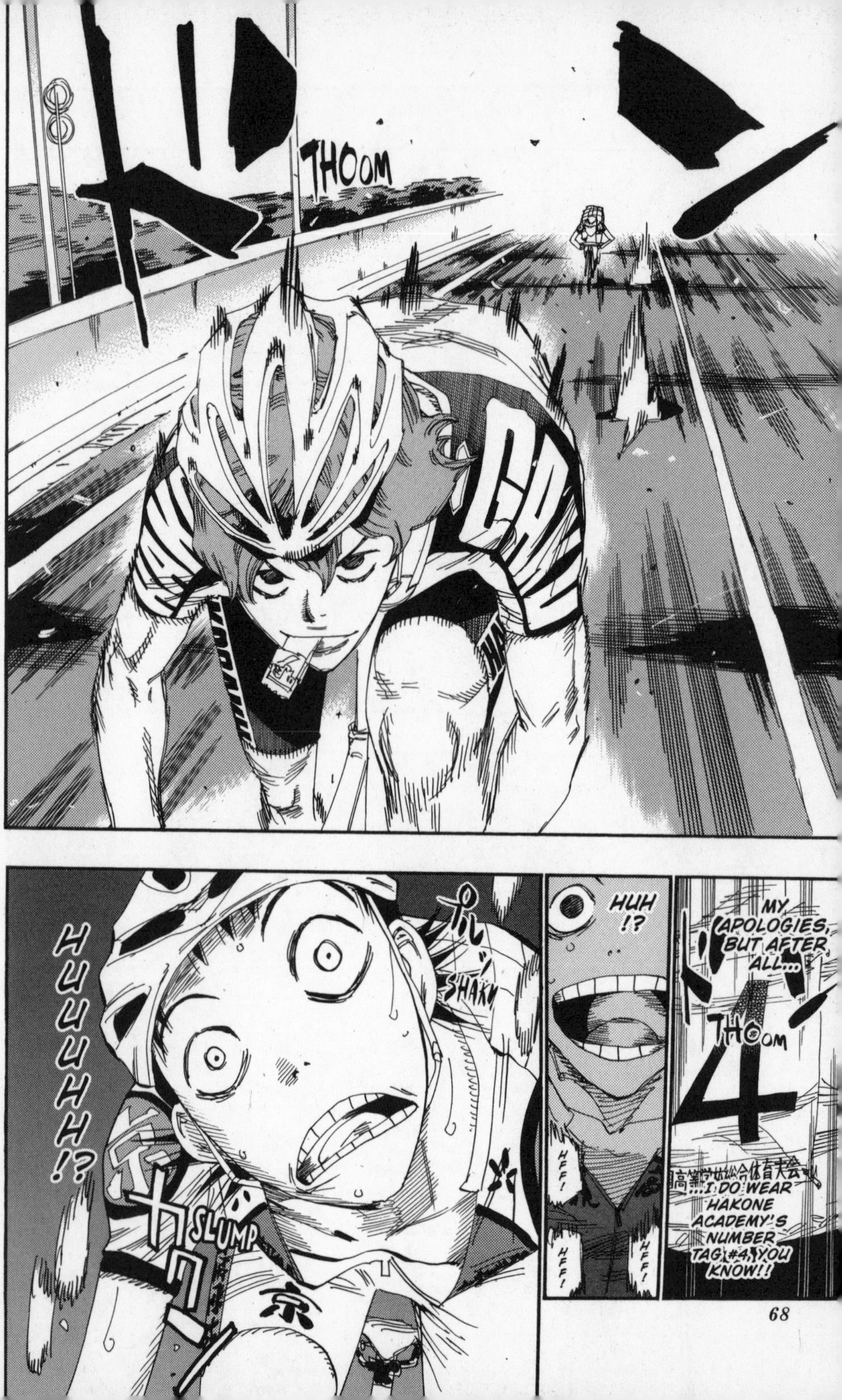
THOOM
MY APOLOGIES, BUT AFTER ALL...
THOOM
...I DO WEAR HAKONE ACADEMY'S NUMBER TAG #4, YOU KNOW!!
HUH!?
HFF!
HFF!
HFF!
SHAKU
HUUUUHH!?
SLUMP

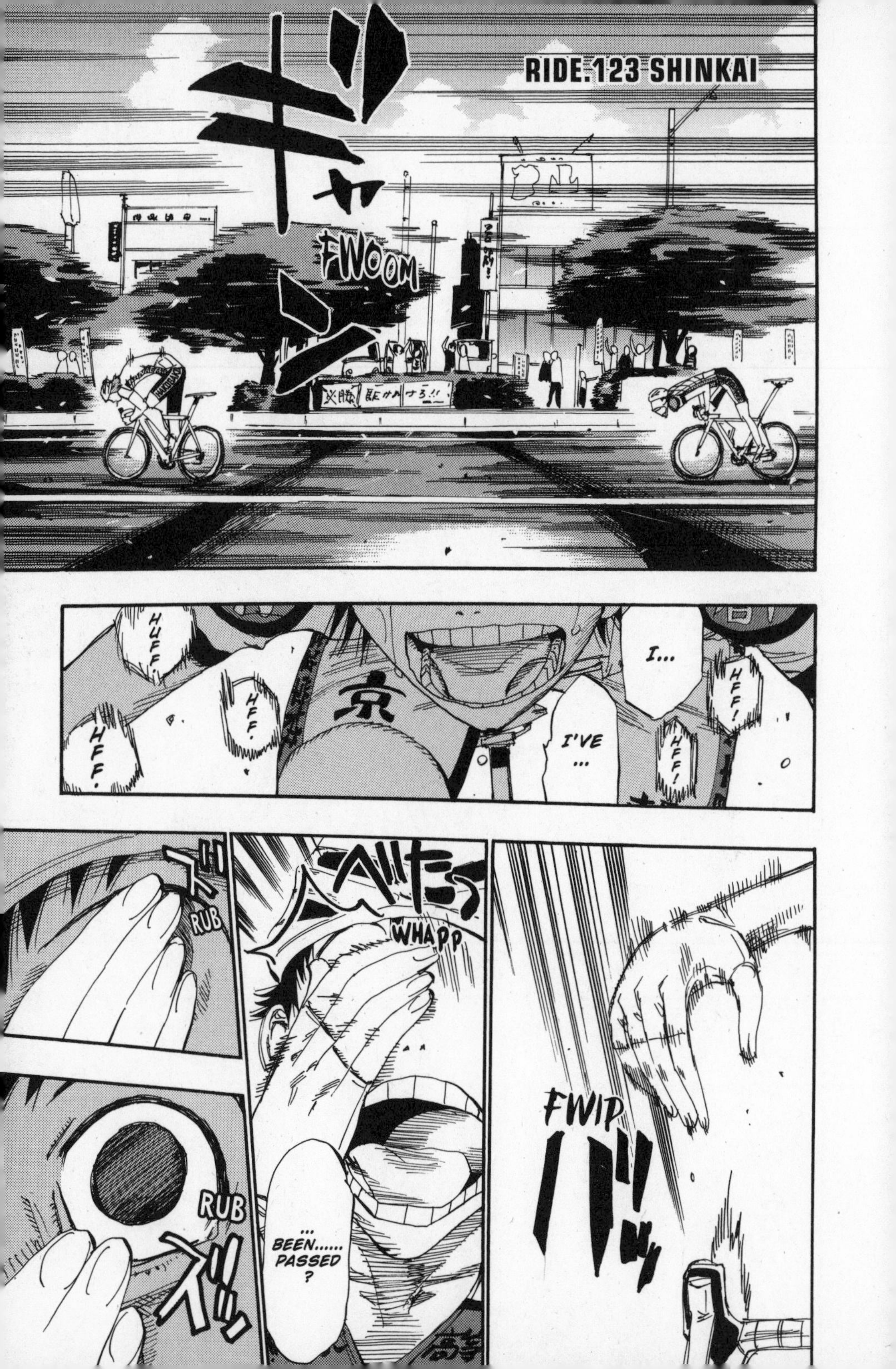
RIDE.123 SHINKAI
FWOOM
HFF!
HFF!
I...
I'VE ...
HFF.
HFF.
HUFF.
FWIP
WHAPP
... BEEN...... PASSED ?
RUB
RUB

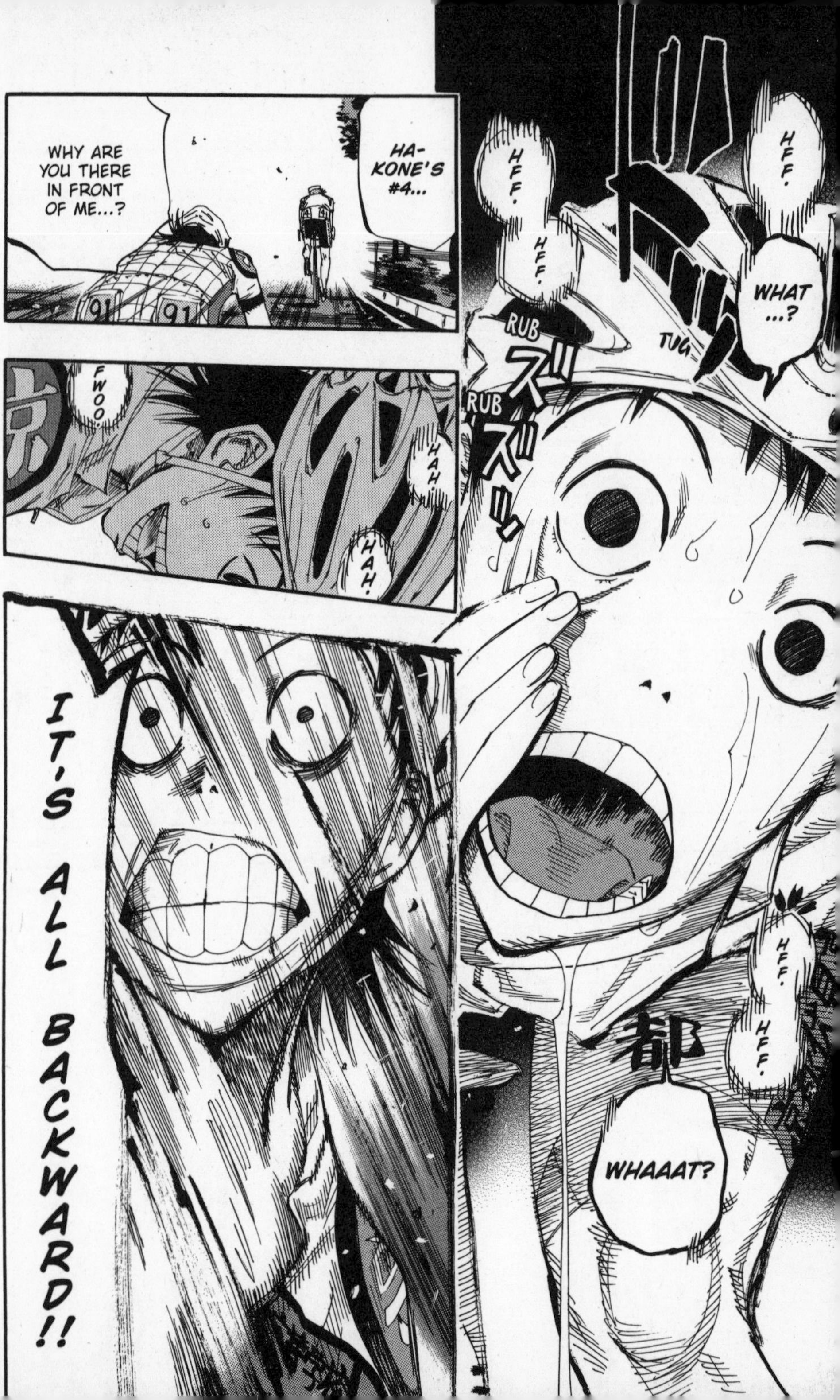
HFF.
HFF.
HFF.
WHAT ...?
TUG
RUB
RUB
HFF.
HFF.
WHAAAT?
HA-KONE'S #4...
WHY ARE YOU THERE IN FRONT OF ME...?
HAH.
HAH.
FWOO.
IT'S ALL BACKWARD!!

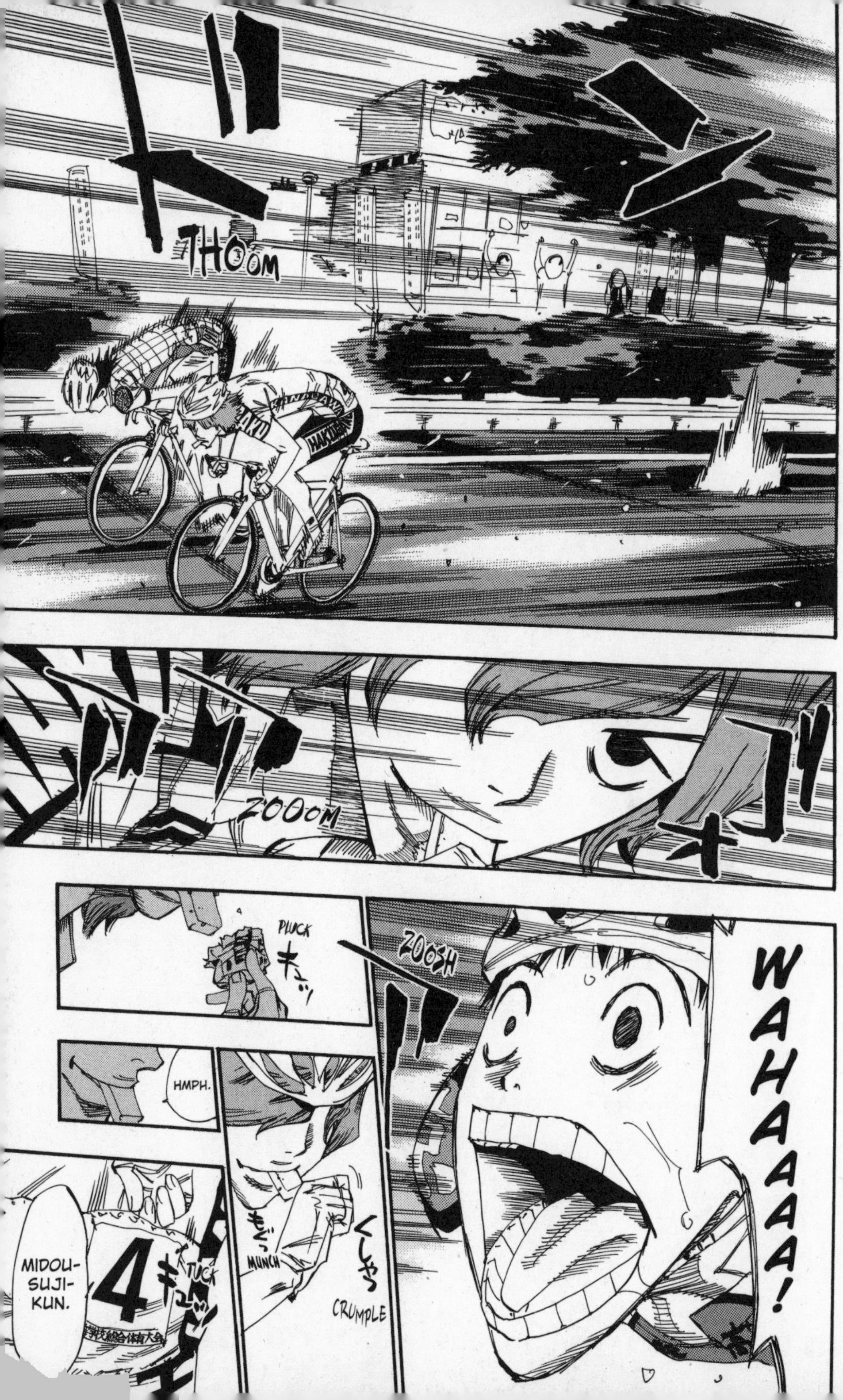
THOOM
ZOOOM
ZOOSH
WAHAAAAA!
PLUCK
キュッ
MUNCH
もぐっ
CRUMPLE
HMPH.
MIDOUSUJI-KUN.
TUCK
4

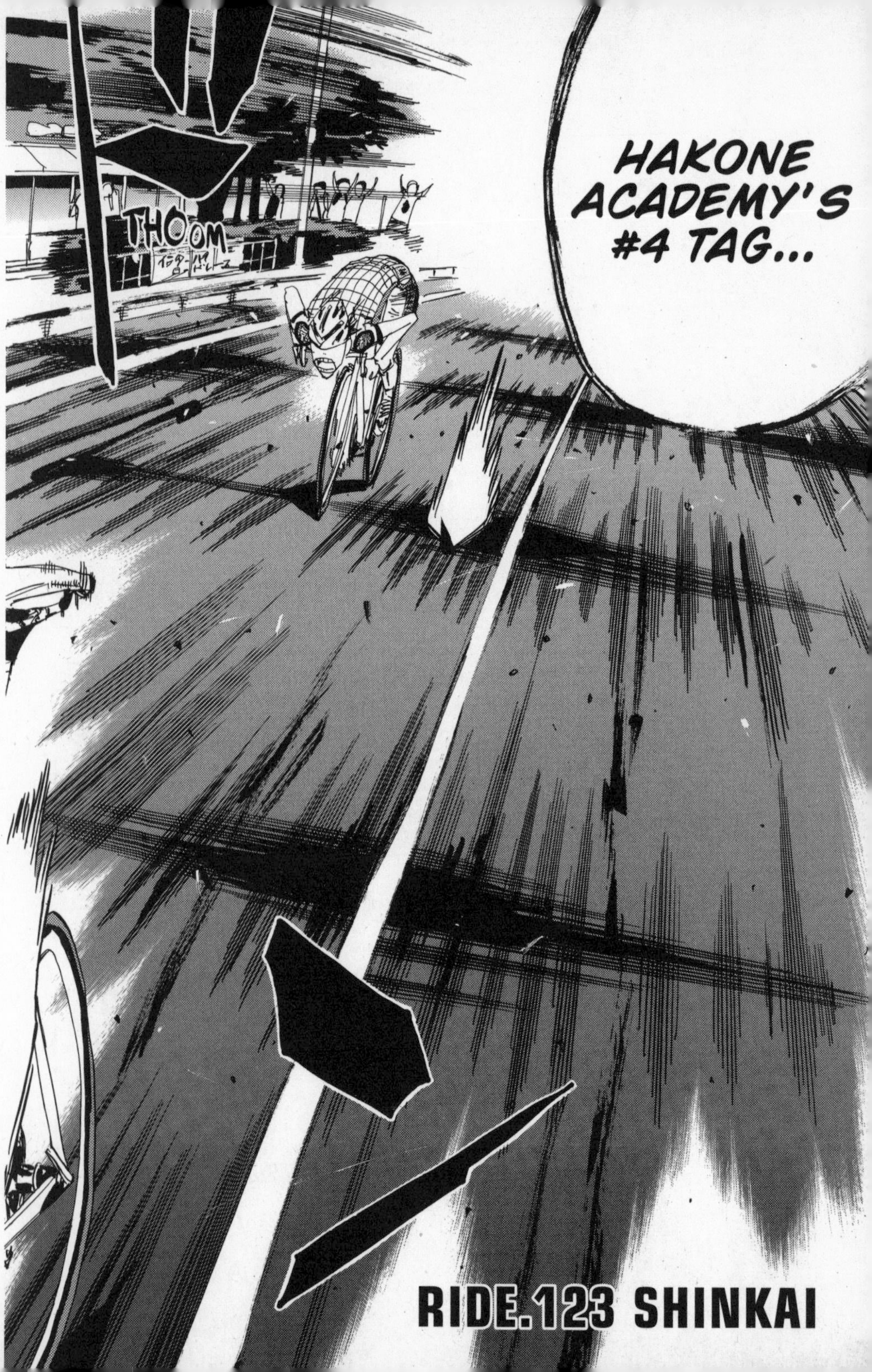
HAKONE ACADEMY'S #4 TAG...
THOOM
RIDE.123 SHINKAI

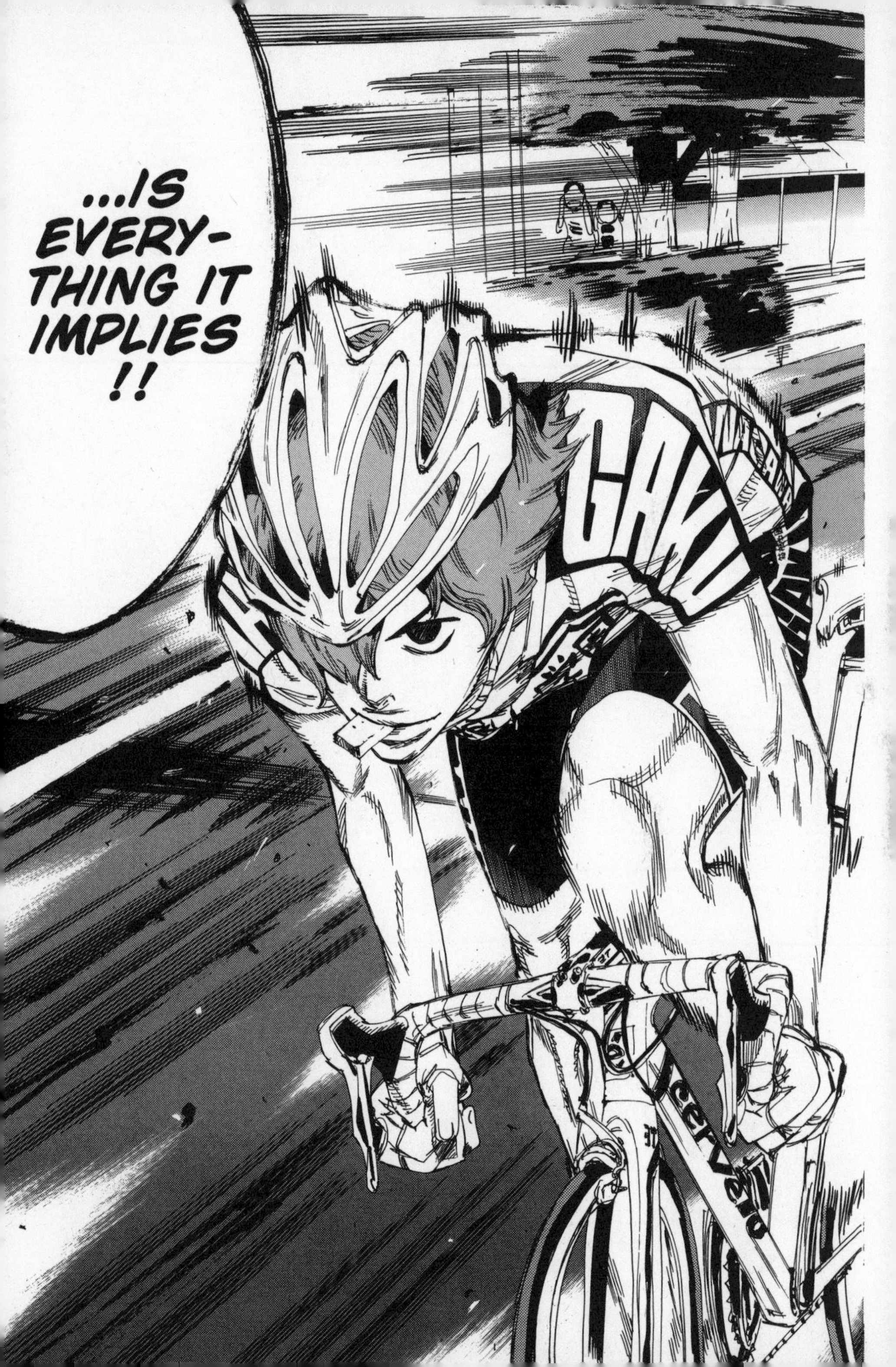
...IS EVERY-THING IT IMPLIES !!

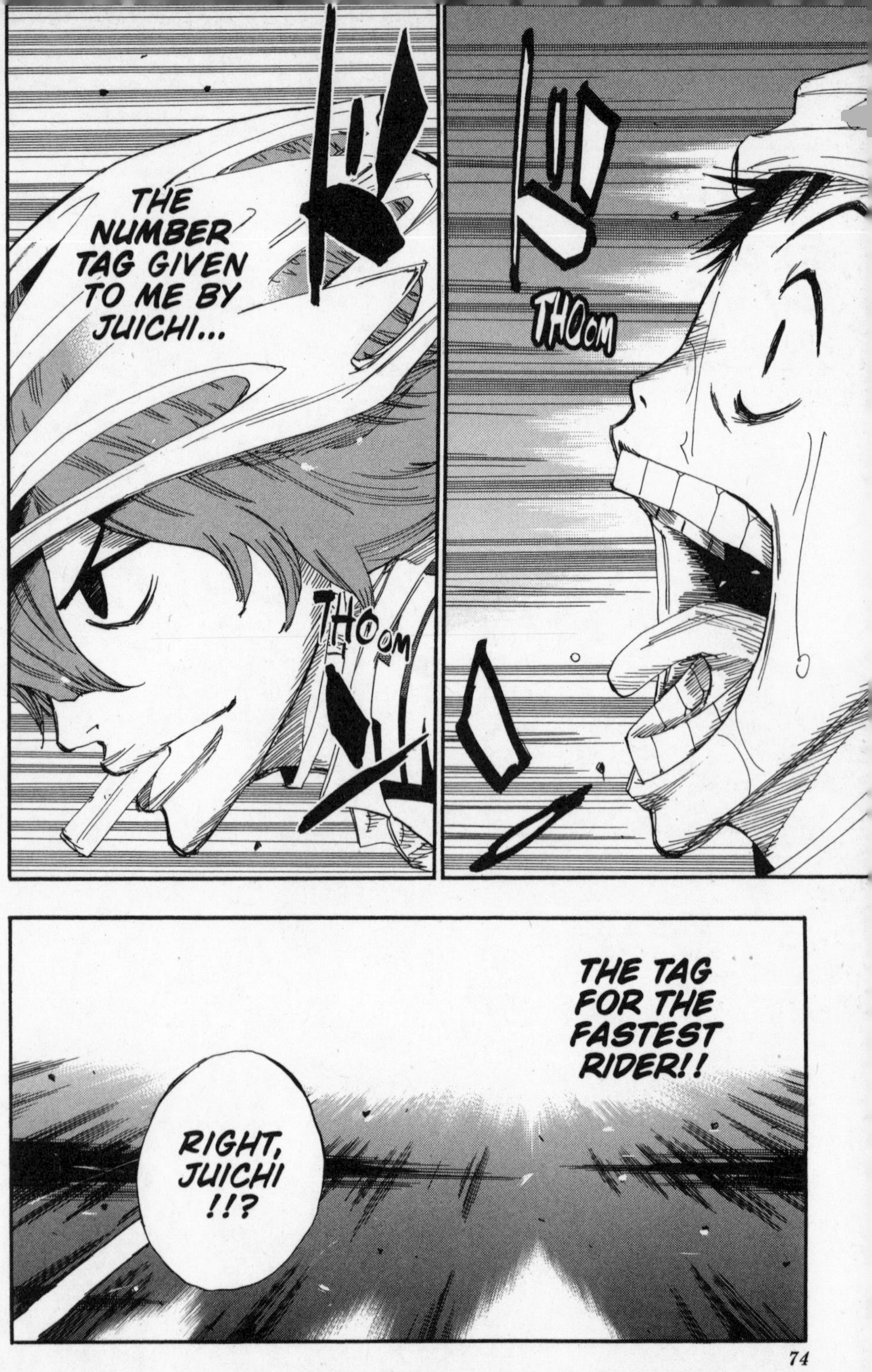
THOOM
THE NUMBER TAG GIVEN TO ME BY JUICHI...
THOOM
THE TAG FOR THE FASTEST RIDER!!
RIGHT, JUICHI !!?

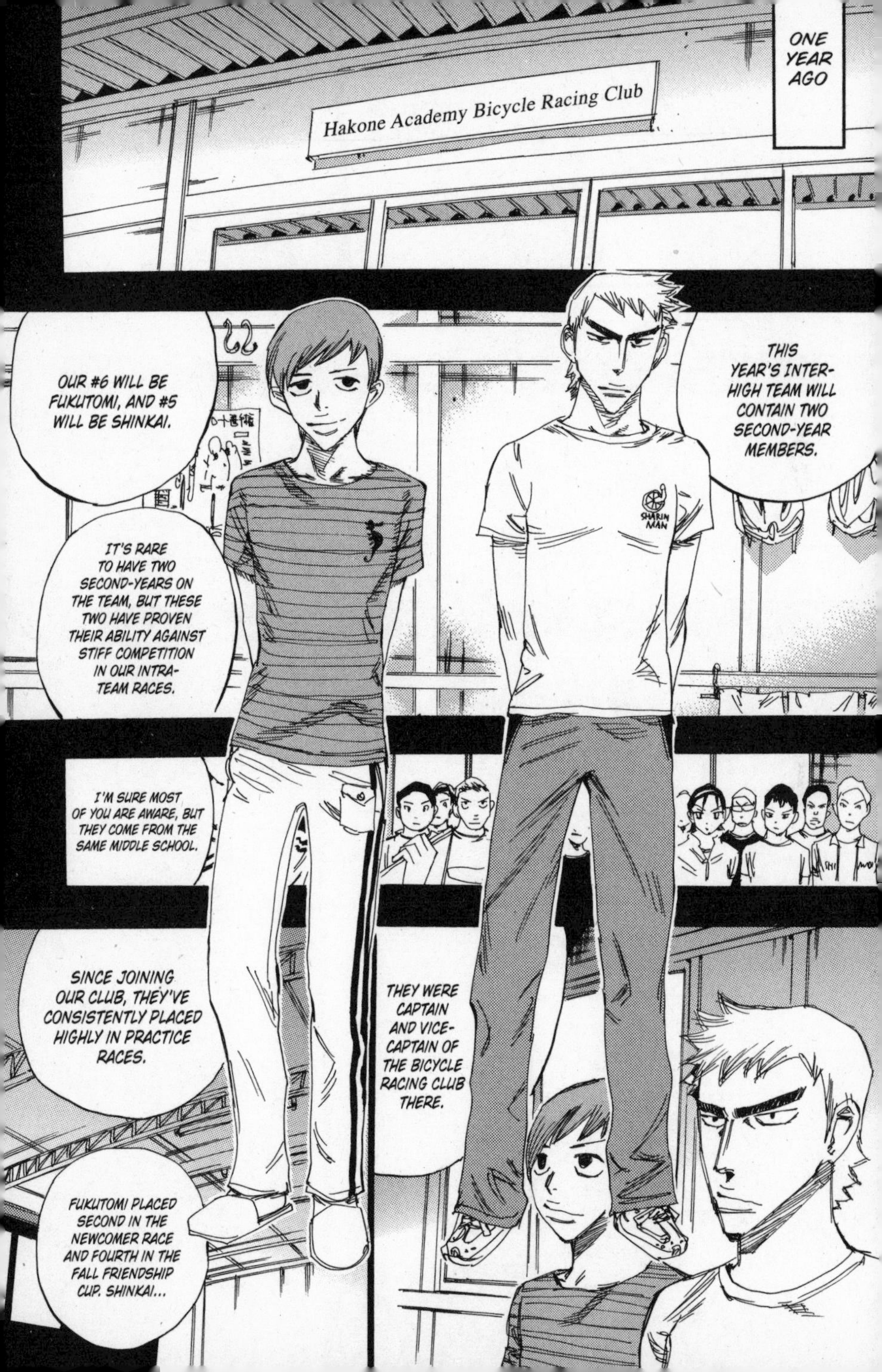
ONE YEAR AGO
Hakone Academy Bicycle Racing Club
THIS YEAR'S INTER-HIGH TEAM WILL CONTAIN TWO SECOND-YEAR MEMBERS.
OUR #6 WILL BE FUKUTOMI, AND #5 WILL BE SHINKAI.
SHARIN MAN
IT'S RARE TO HAVE TWO SECOND-YEARS ON THE TEAM, BUT THESE TWO HAVE PROVEN THEIR ABILITY AGAINST STIFF COMPETITION IN OUR INTRA-TEAM RACES.
I'M SURE MOST OF YOU ARE AWARE, BUT THEY COME FROM THE SAME MIDDLE SCHOOL.
THEY WERE CAPTAIN AND VICE-CAPTAIN OF THE BICYCLE RACING CLUB THERE.
SINCE JOINING OUR CLUB, THEY'VE CONSISTENTLY PLACED HIGHLY IN PRACTICE RACES.
FUKUTOMI PLACED SECOND IN THE NEWCOMER RACE AND FOURTH IN THE FALL FRIENDSHIP CUP. SHINKAI...

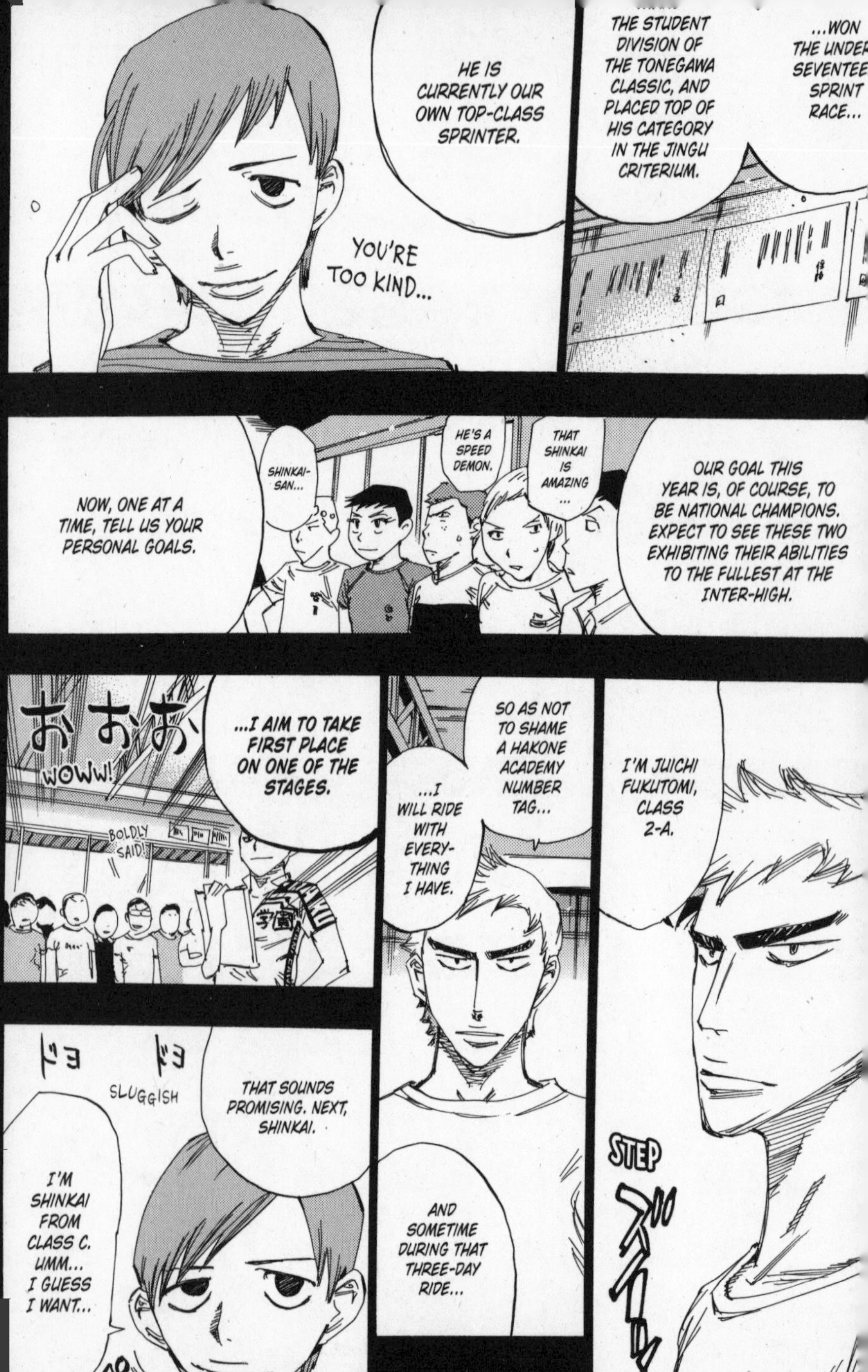
...WON THE UNDER SEVENTEE SPRINT RACE...
THE STUDENT DIVISION OF THE TONEGAWA CLASSIC, AND PLACED TOP OF HIS CATEGORY IN THE JINGU CRITERIUM.
HE IS CURRENTLY OUR OWN TOP-CLASS SPRINTER.
YOU'RE TOO KIND...
OUR GOAL THIS YEAR IS, OF COURSE, TO BE NATIONAL CHAMPIONS. EXPECT TO SEE THESE TWO EXHIBITING THEIR ABILITIES TO THE FULLEST AT THE INTER-HIGH.
THAT SHINKAI IS AMAZING...
HE'S A SPEED DEMON.
SHINKAI-SAN...
NOW, ONE AT A TIME, TELL US YOUR PERSONAL GOALS.
I'M JUICHI FUKUTOMI, CLASS 2-A.
STEP
SO AS NOT TO SHAME A HAKONE ACADEMY NUMBER TAG...
...I WILL RIDE WITH EVERYTHING I HAVE.
AND SOMETIME DURING THAT THREE-DAY RIDE...
...I AIM TO TAKE FIRST PLACE ON ONE OF THE STAGES.
おおお
WOWW!
BOLDLY SAID!
THAT SOUNDS PROMISING. NEXT, SHINKAI.
ドヨ ドヨ
SLUGGISH
I'M SHINKAI FROM CLASS C. UMM... I GUESS I WANT...
ペコ
BOW

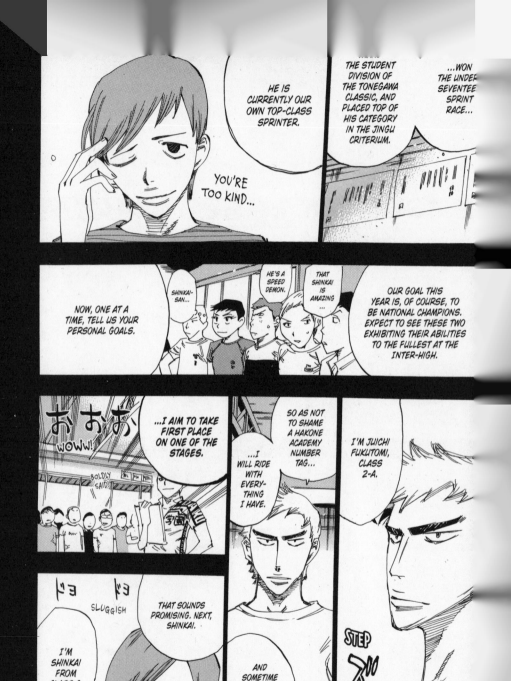

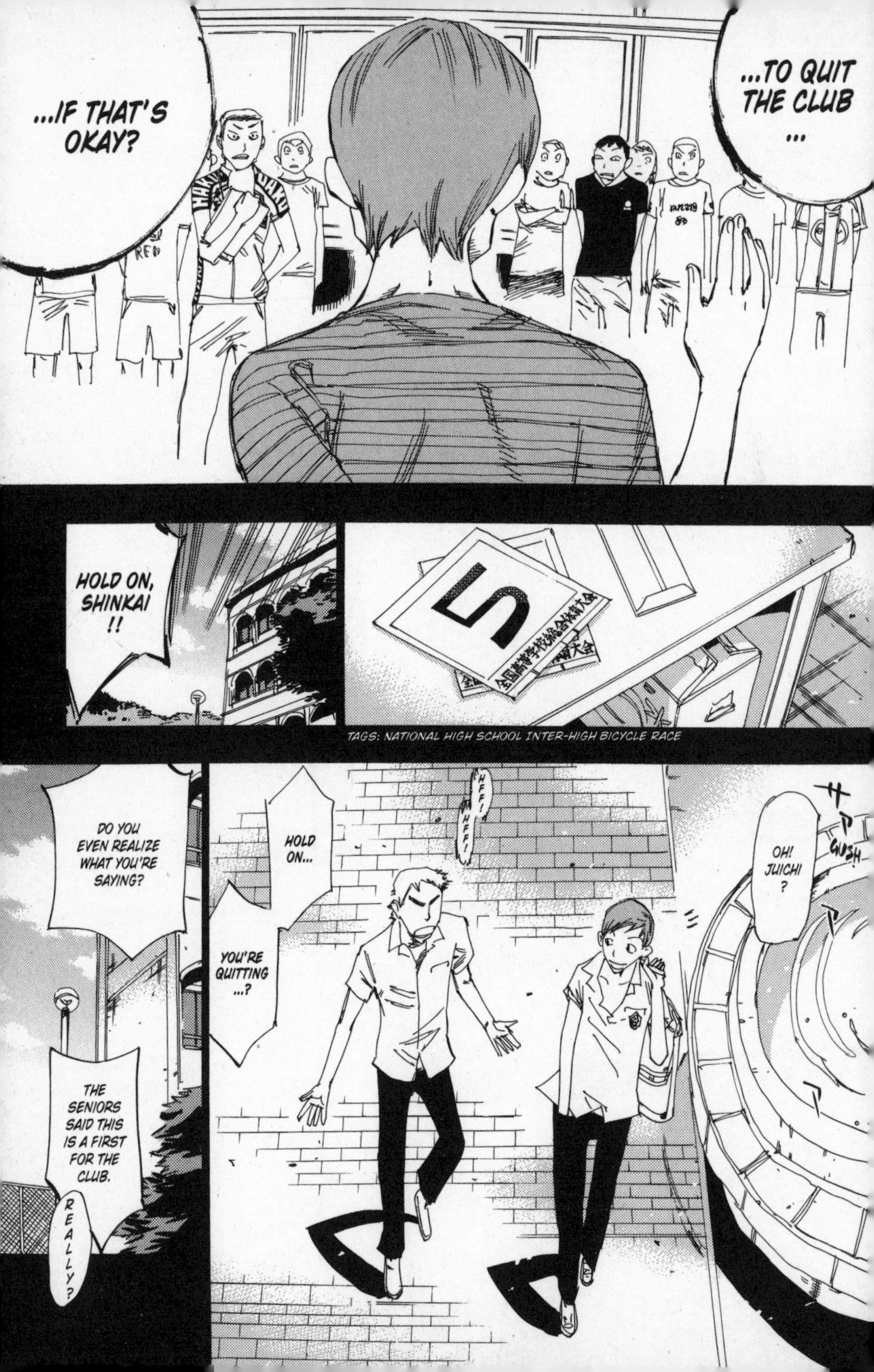
...TO QUIT THE CLUB ...
...IF THAT'S OKAY?
HOLD ON, SHINKAI !!
TAGS: NATIONAL HIGH SCHOOL INTER-HIGH BICYCLE RACE
GUSH
OH! JUICHI ?
HFF! HFF!
HOLD ON...
YOU'RE QUITTING ...?
DO YOU EVEN REALIZE WHAT YOU'RE SAYING?
THE SENIORS SAID THIS IS A FIRST FOR THE CLUB.
REALLY?

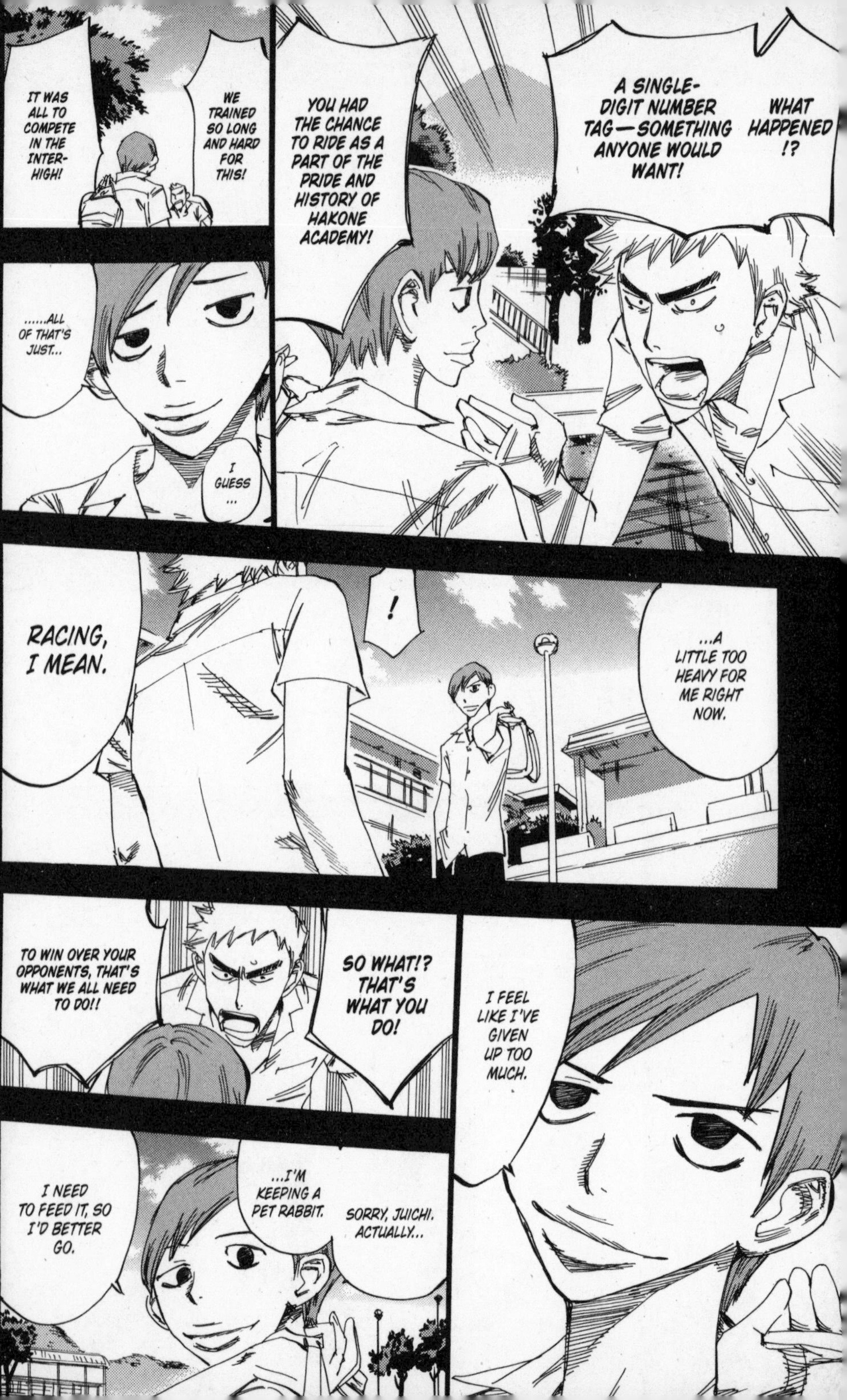
WHAT HAPPENED!?
A SINGLE-DIGIT NUMBER TAG—SOMETHING ANYONE WOULD WANT!
YOU HAD THE CHANCE TO RIDE AS A PART OF THE PRIDE AND HISTORY OF HAKONE ACADEMY!
WE TRAINED SO LONG AND HARD FOR THIS!
IT WAS ALL TO COMPETE IN THE INTER-HIGH!
......ALL OF THAT'S JUST...
I GUESS...
...A LITTLE TOO HEAVY FOR ME RIGHT NOW.
!
RACING, I MEAN.
I FEEL LIKE I'VE GIVEN UP TOO MUCH.
SO WHAT!? THAT'S WHAT YOU DO!
TO WIN OVER YOUR OPPONENTS, THAT'S WHAT WE ALL NEED TO DO!!
SORRY, JUICHI. ACTUALLY...
...I'M KEEPING A PET RABBIT.
I NEED TO FEED IT, SO I'D BETTER GO.

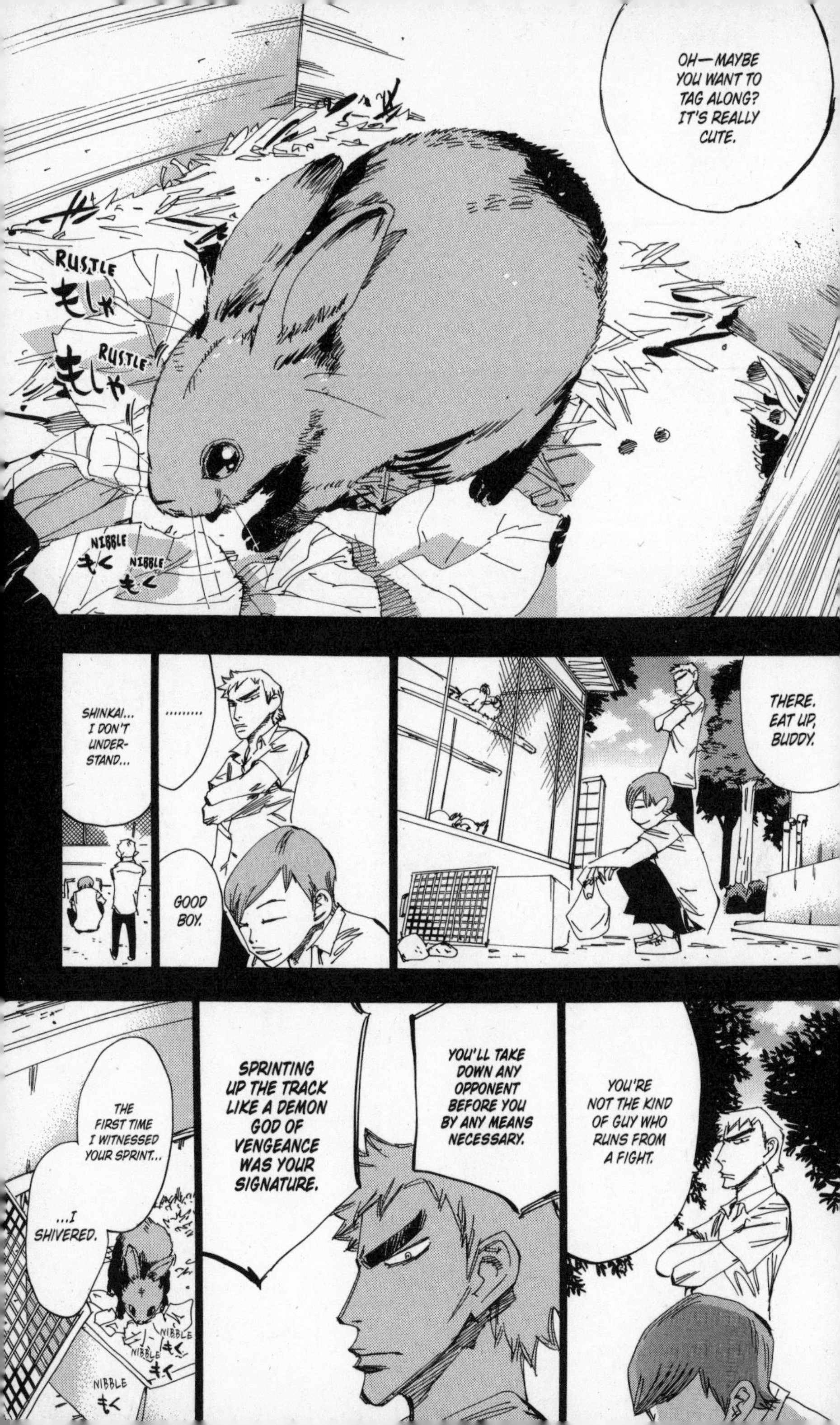
OH— MAYBE YOU WANT TO TAG ALONG? IT'S REALLY CUTE.
RUSTLE もしゃ
RUSTLE もしゃ
NIBBLE もく
NIBBLE もく
THERE. EAT UP, BUDDY.
....
GOOD BOY.
SHINKAI... I DON'T UNDER-STAND...
YOU'RE NOT THE KIND OF GUY WHO RUNS FROM A FIGHT.
YOU'LL TAKE DOWN ANY OPPONENT BEFORE YOU BY ANY MEANS NECESSARY.
SPRINTING UP THE TRACK LIKE A DEMON GOD OF VENGEANCE WAS YOUR SIGNATURE.
THE FIRST TIME I WITNESSED YOUR SPRINT...
...I SHIVERED.
NIBBLE もく
NIBBLE もく
NIBBLE もく

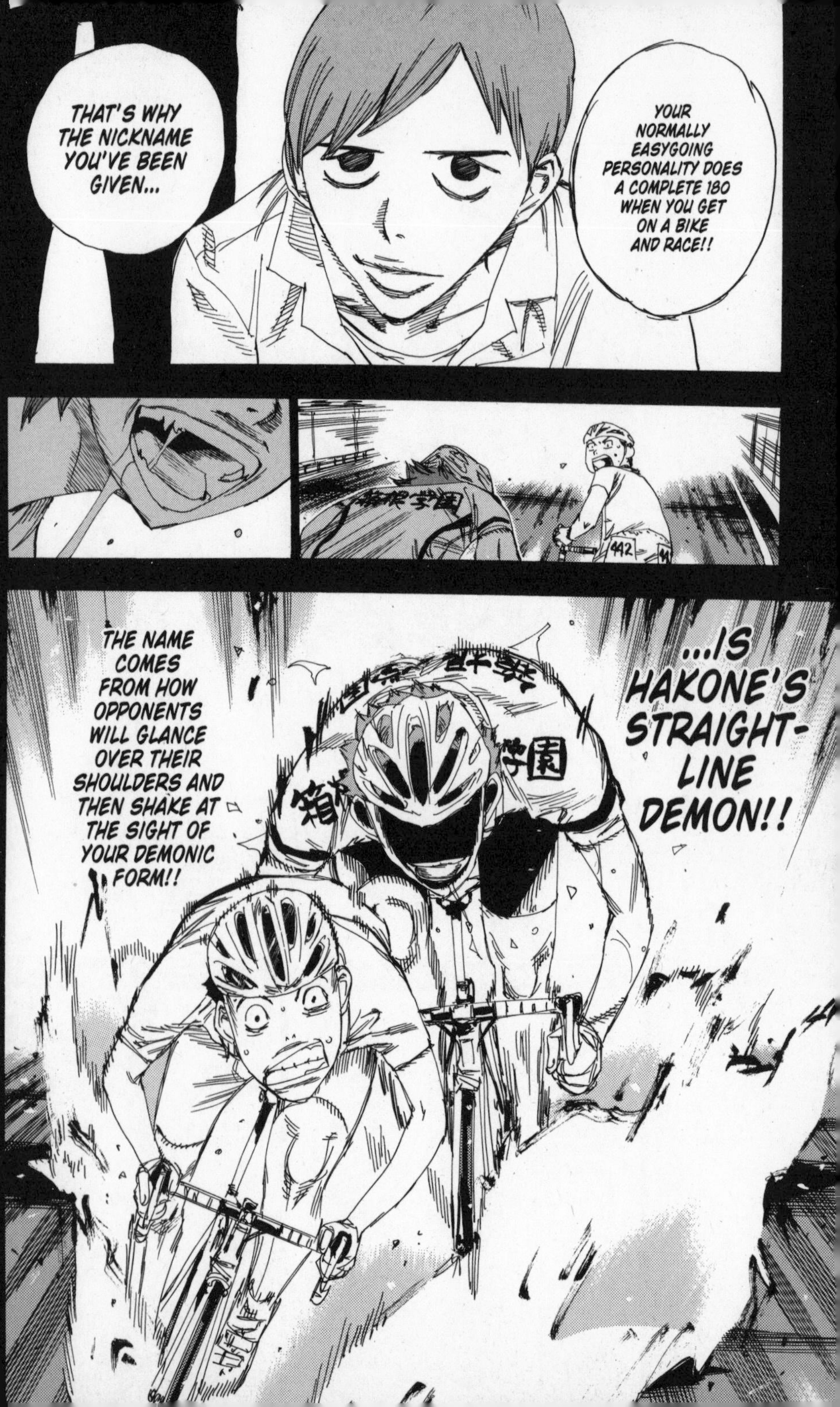
YOUR NORMALLY EASYGOING PERSONALITY DOES A COMPLETE 180 WHEN YOU GET ON A BIKE AND RACE!!
THAT'S WHY THE NICKNAME YOU'VE BEEN GIVEN...
...IS HAKONE'S STRAIGHT-LINE DEMON!!
THE NAME COMES FROM HOW OPPONENTS WILL GLANCE OVER THEIR SHOULDERS AND THEN SHAKE AT THE SIGHT OF YOUR DEMONIC FORM!!

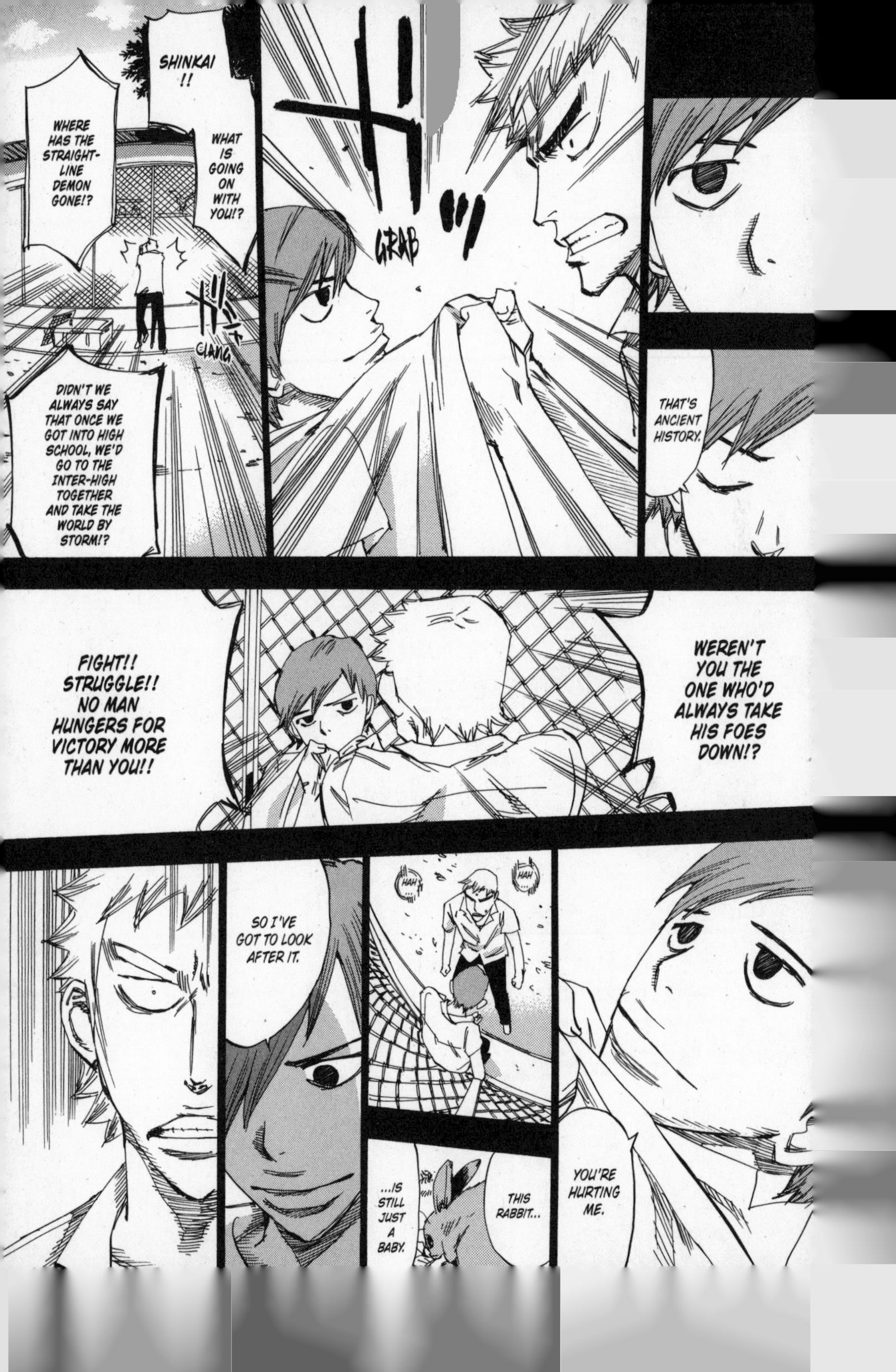
THAT'S ANCIENT HISTORY.
GRAB
SHINKAI!!
WHAT IS GOING ON WITH YOU!?
WHERE HAS THE STRAIGHT-LINE DEMON GONE!?
CLANG
DIDN'T WE ALWAYS SAY THAT ONCE WE GOT INTO HIGH SCHOOL, WE'D GO TO THE INTER-HIGH TOGETHER AND TAKE THE WORLD BY STORM!?
WEREN'T YOU THE ONE WHO'D ALWAYS TAKE HIS FOES DOWN!?
FIGHT!! STRUGGLE!! NO MAN HUNGERS FOR VICTORY MORE THAN YOU!!
YOU'RE HURTING ME.
HAH
HAH
THIS RABBIT...
...IS STILL JUST A BABY.
SO I'VE GOT TO LOOK AFTER IT.

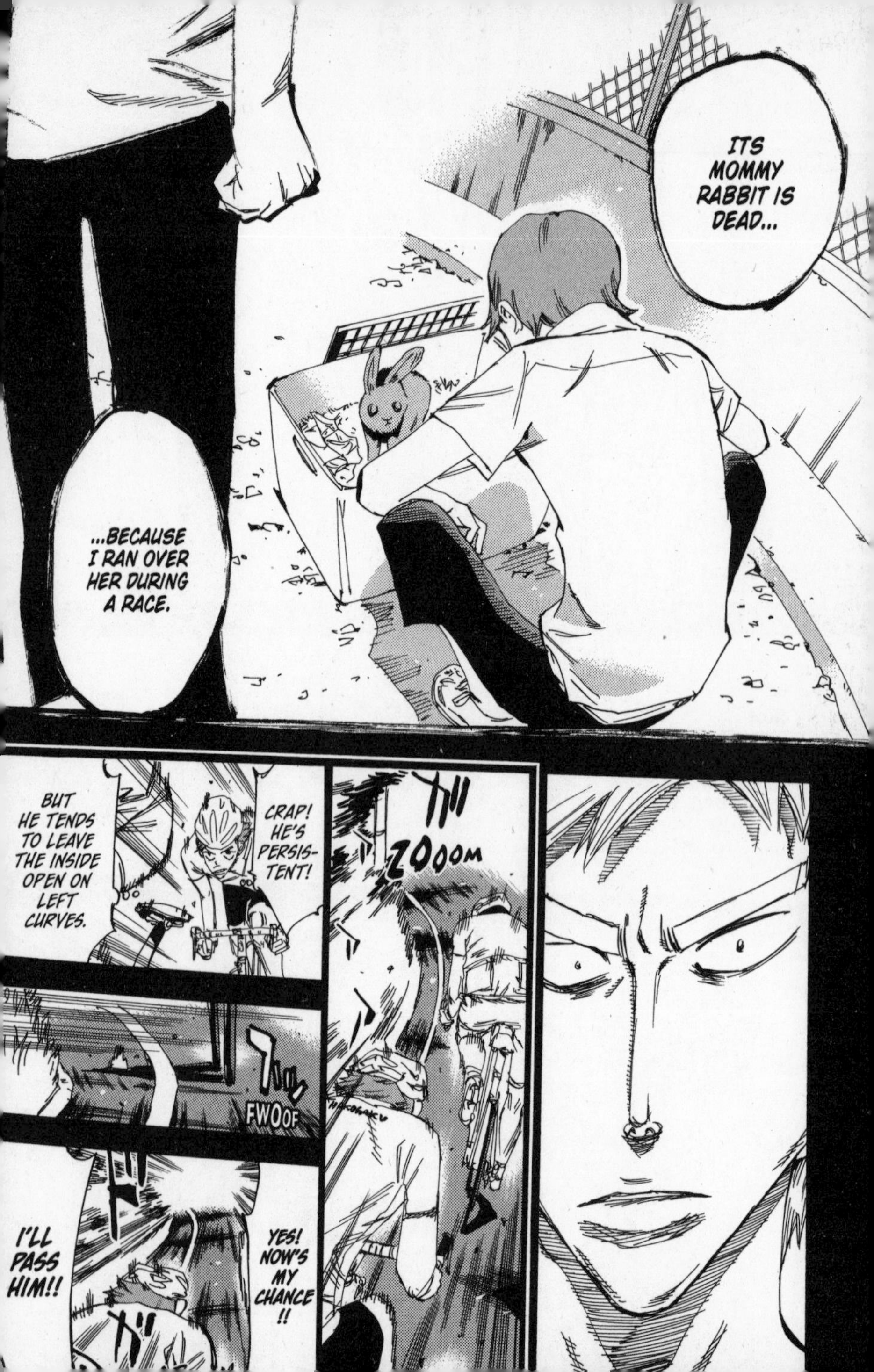
ITS MOMMY RABBIT IS DEAD...
...BECAUSE I RAN OVER HER DURING A RACE.
ZOOOM
CRAP! HE'S PERSIS-TENT!
BUT HE TENDS TO LEAVE THE INSIDE OPEN ON LEFT CURVES.
FWOOF
YES! NOW'S MY CHANCE!!
I'LL PASS HIM!!

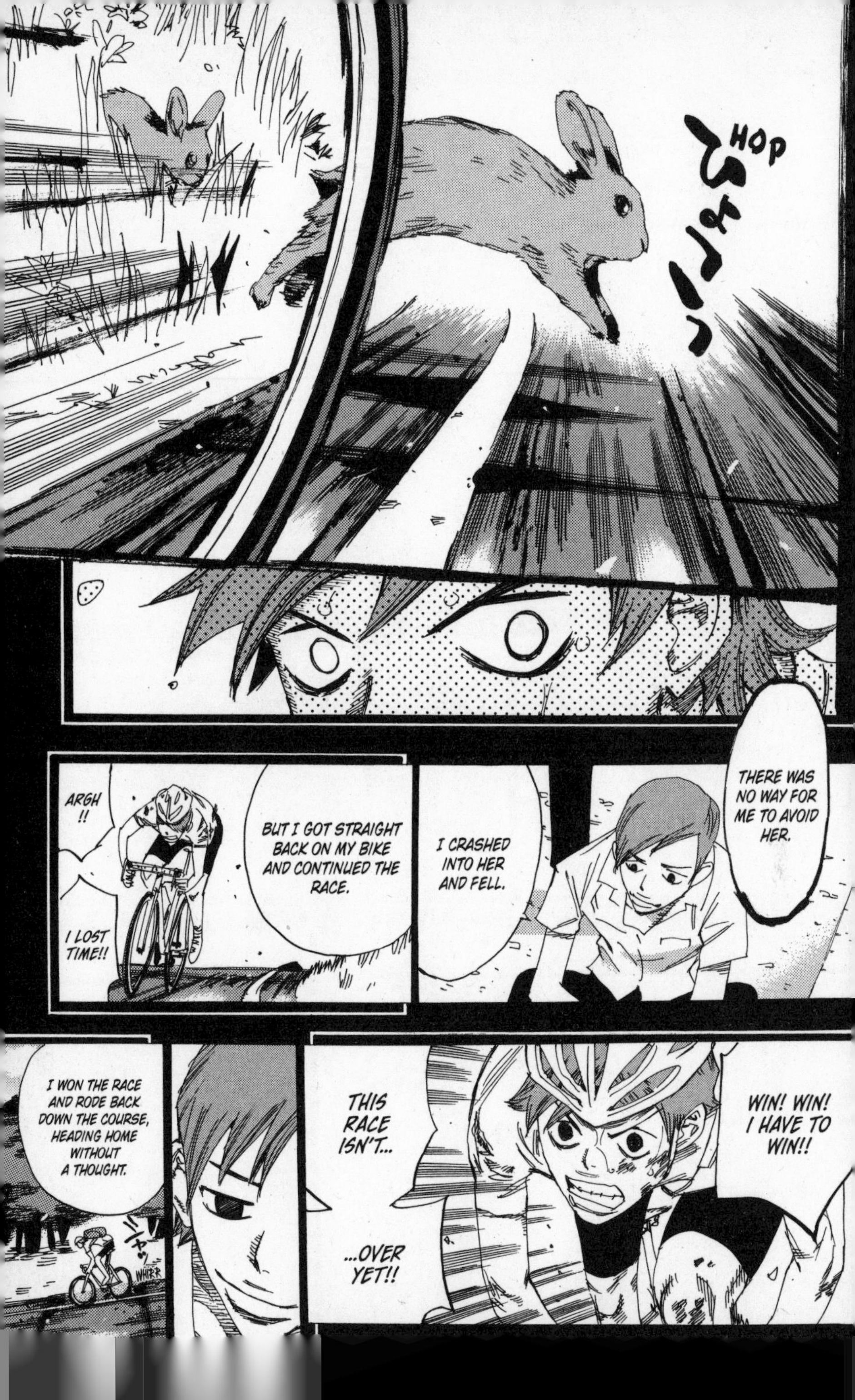
HOP
ぴょこっ
THERE WAS NO WAY FOR ME TO AVOID HER.
I CRASHED INTO HER AND FELL.
BUT I GOT STRAIGHT BACK ON MY BIKE AND CONTINUED THE RACE.
ARGH!!
I LOST TIME!!
WIN! WIN! I HAVE TO WIN!!
THIS RACE ISN'T...
...OVER YET!!
I WON THE RACE AND RODE BACK DOWN THE COURSE, HEADING HOME WITHOUT A THOUGHT.
WHIRR

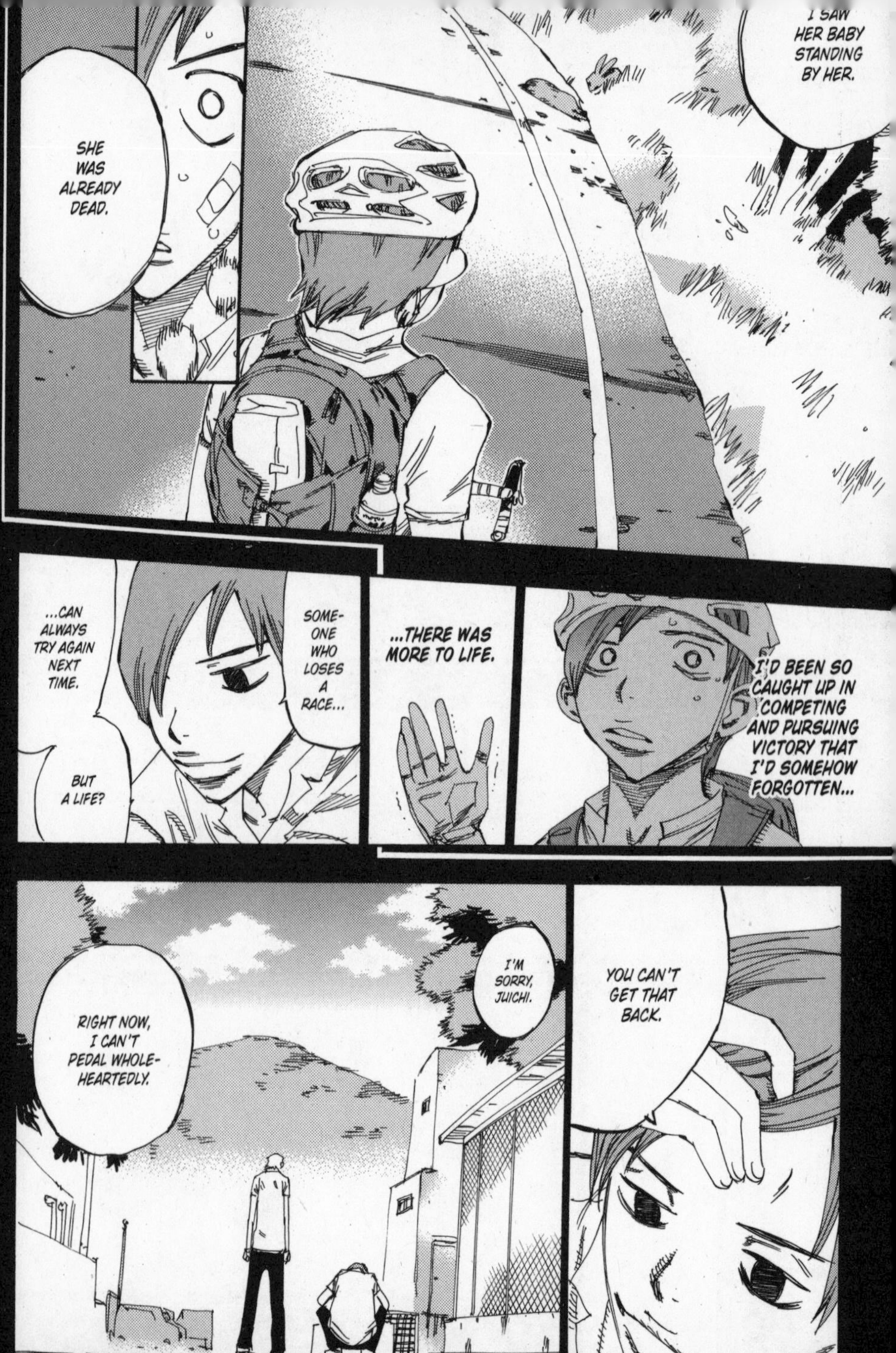
I SAW HER BABY STANDING BY HER.
SHE WAS ALREADY DEAD.
I'D BEEN SO CAUGHT UP IN COMPETING AND PURSUING VICTORY THAT I'D SOMEHOW FORGOTTEN...
...THERE WAS MORE TO LIFE.
SOME-ONE WHO LOSES A RACE...
...CAN ALWAYS TRY AGAIN NEXT TIME.
BUT A LIFE?
YOU CAN'T GET THAT BACK.
I'M SORRY, JUICHI.
RIGHT NOW, I CAN'T PEDAL WHOLE-HEARTEDLY.

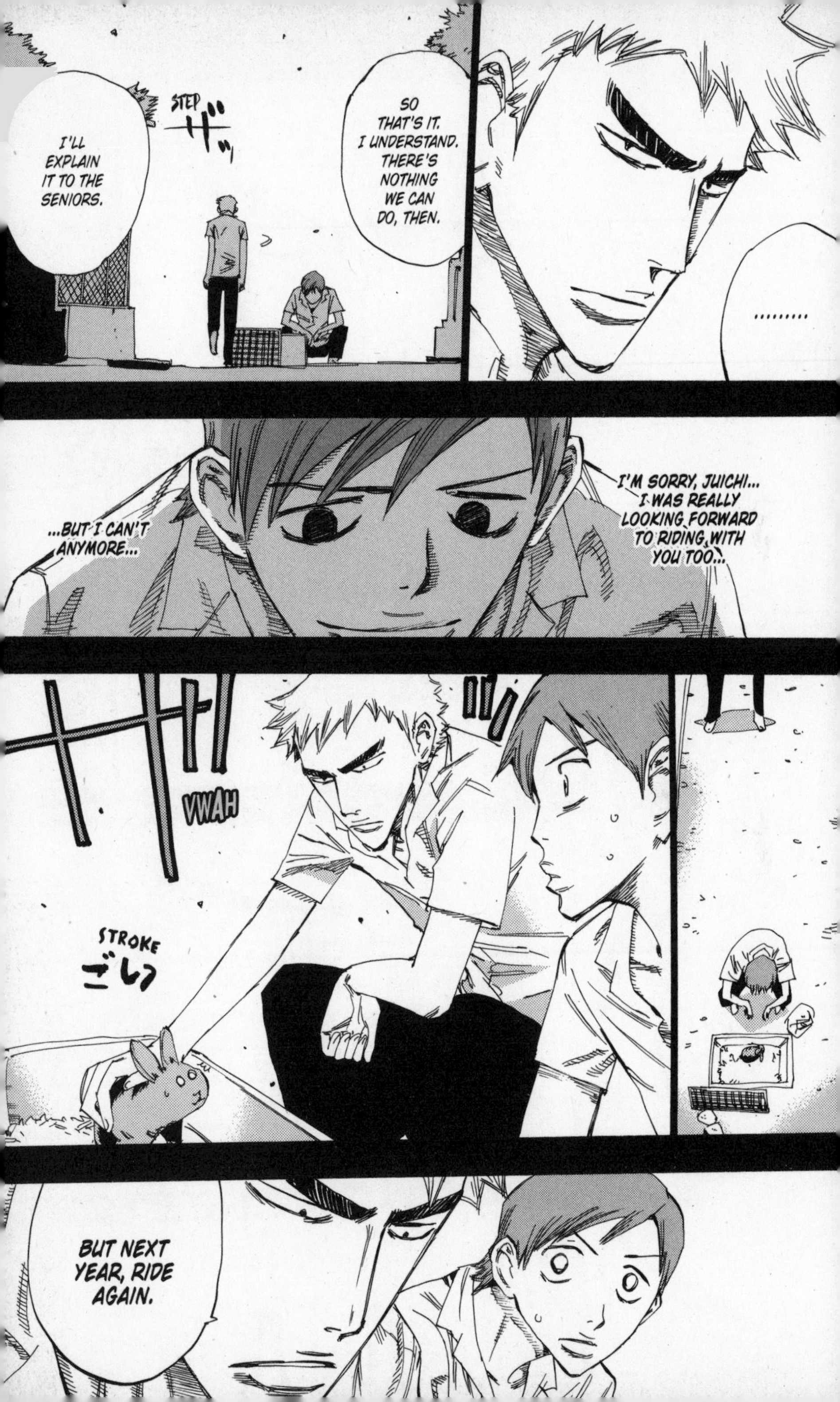

....
SO THAT'S IT. I UNDERSTAND. THERE'S NOTHING WE CAN DO, THEN.
STEP
I'LL EXPLAIN IT TO THE SENIORS.
I'M SORRY, JUICHI... I WAS REALLY LOOKING FORWARD TO RIDING WITH YOU TOO...
...BUT I CAN'T ANYMORE...
VWAH
STROKE
BUT NEXT YEAR, RIDE AGAIN.

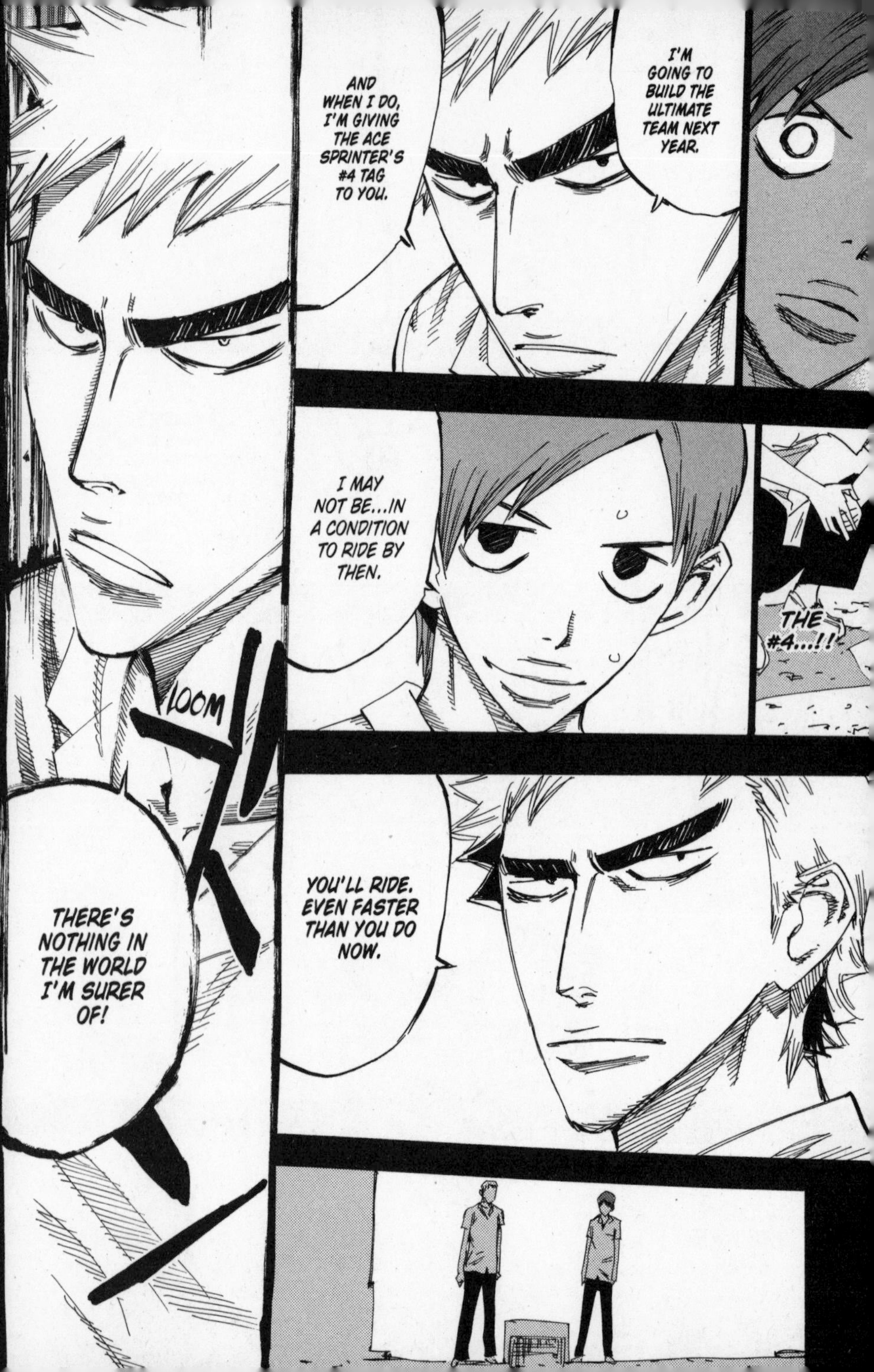
I'M GOING TO BUILD THE ULTIMATE TEAM NEXT YEAR.
AND WHEN I DO, I'M GIVING THE ACE SPRINTER'S #4 TAG TO YOU.
THE #4...!!
I MAY NOT BE...IN A CONDITION TO RIDE BY THEN.
YOU'LL RIDE. EVEN FASTER THAN YOU DO NOW.
LOOM
THERE'S NOTHING IN THE WORLD I'M SURER OF!

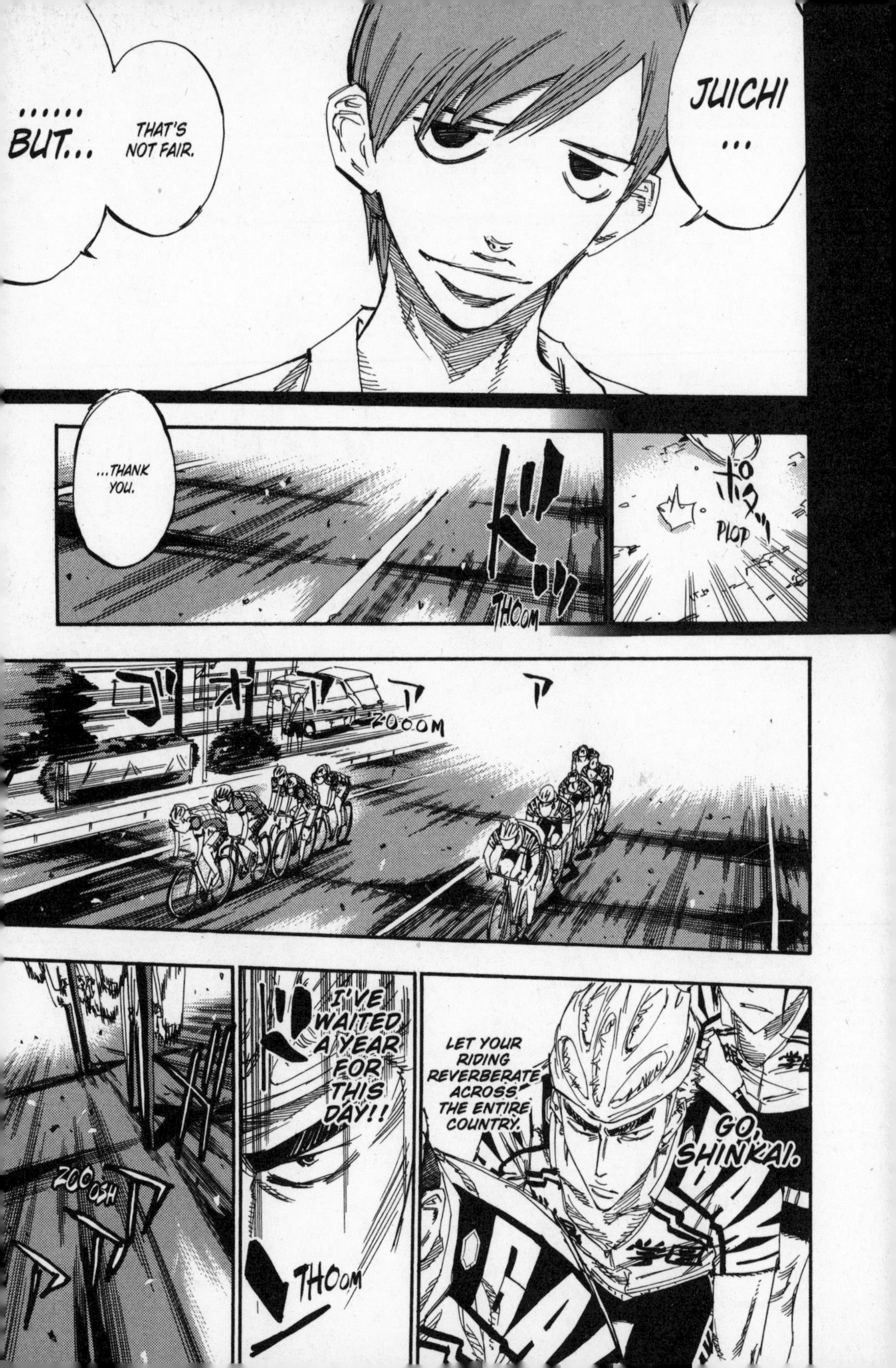

JUICHI ...
...... BUT...
THAT'S NOT FAIR.
PLOP
...THANK YOU.
THOOM
ZOOOM
GO, SHINKAI.
LET YOUR RIDING REVERBERATE ACROSS THE ENTIRE COUNTRY.
I'VE WAITED A YEAR FOR THIS DAY!!
THOOM
ZOOOSH

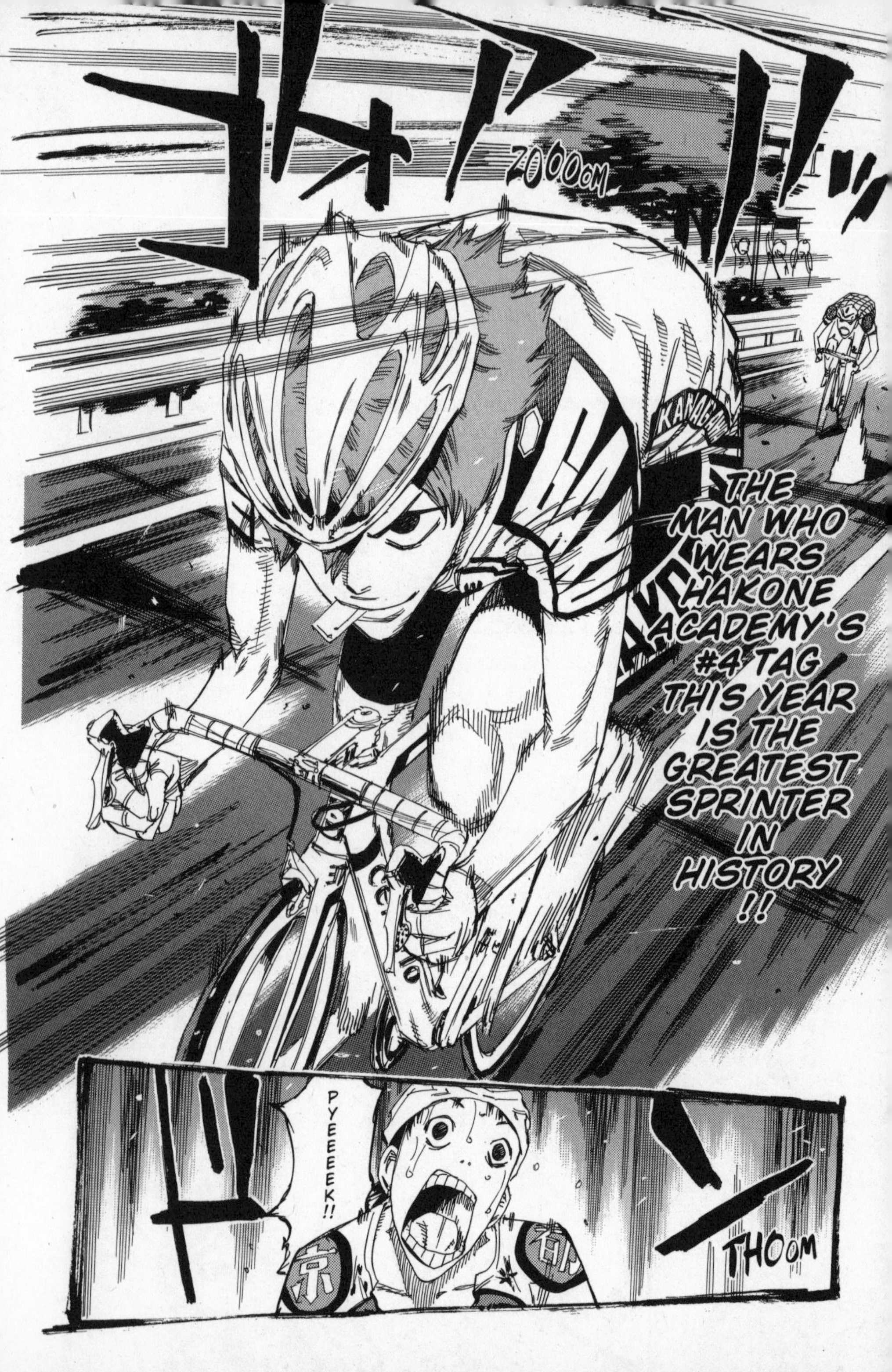
ZOOOOM
THE MAN WHO WEARS HAKONE ACADEMY'S #4 TAG THIS YEAR IS THE GREATEST SPRINTER IN HISTORY!!
THOOM
PYEEEEK!!

RIDE.124 SOHOKU, DISADVANTAGED

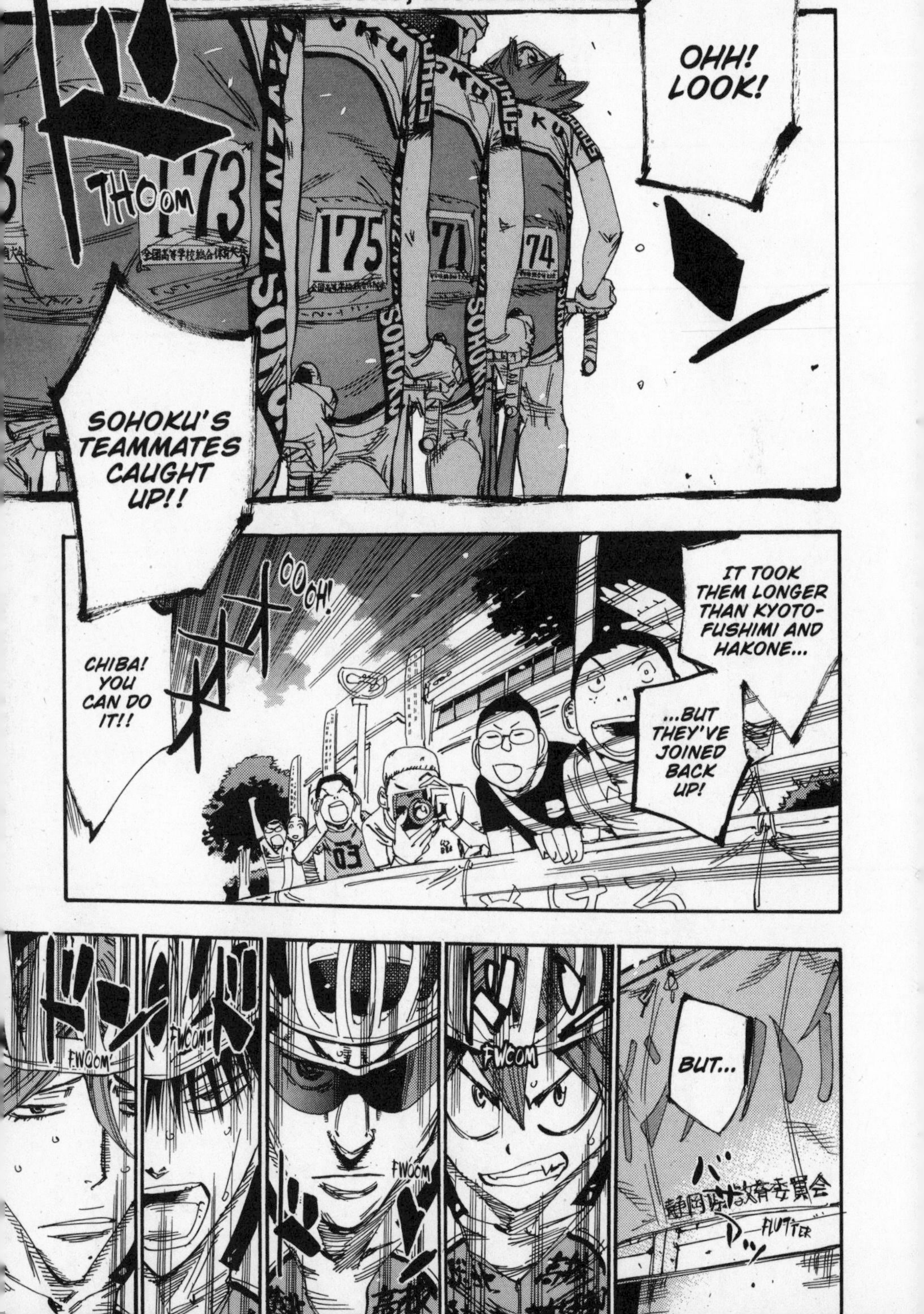
OHH! LOOK!
THOOM
SOHOKU'S TEAMMATES CAUGHT UP!!
IT TOOK THEM LONGER THAN KYOTO-FUSHIMI AND HAKONE...
...BUT THEY'VE JOINED BACK UP!
OOOH!
CHIBA! YOU CAN DO IT!!
BUT...
FLUTTER
FWCOM
FWOOM
FWCOM
FWOOM

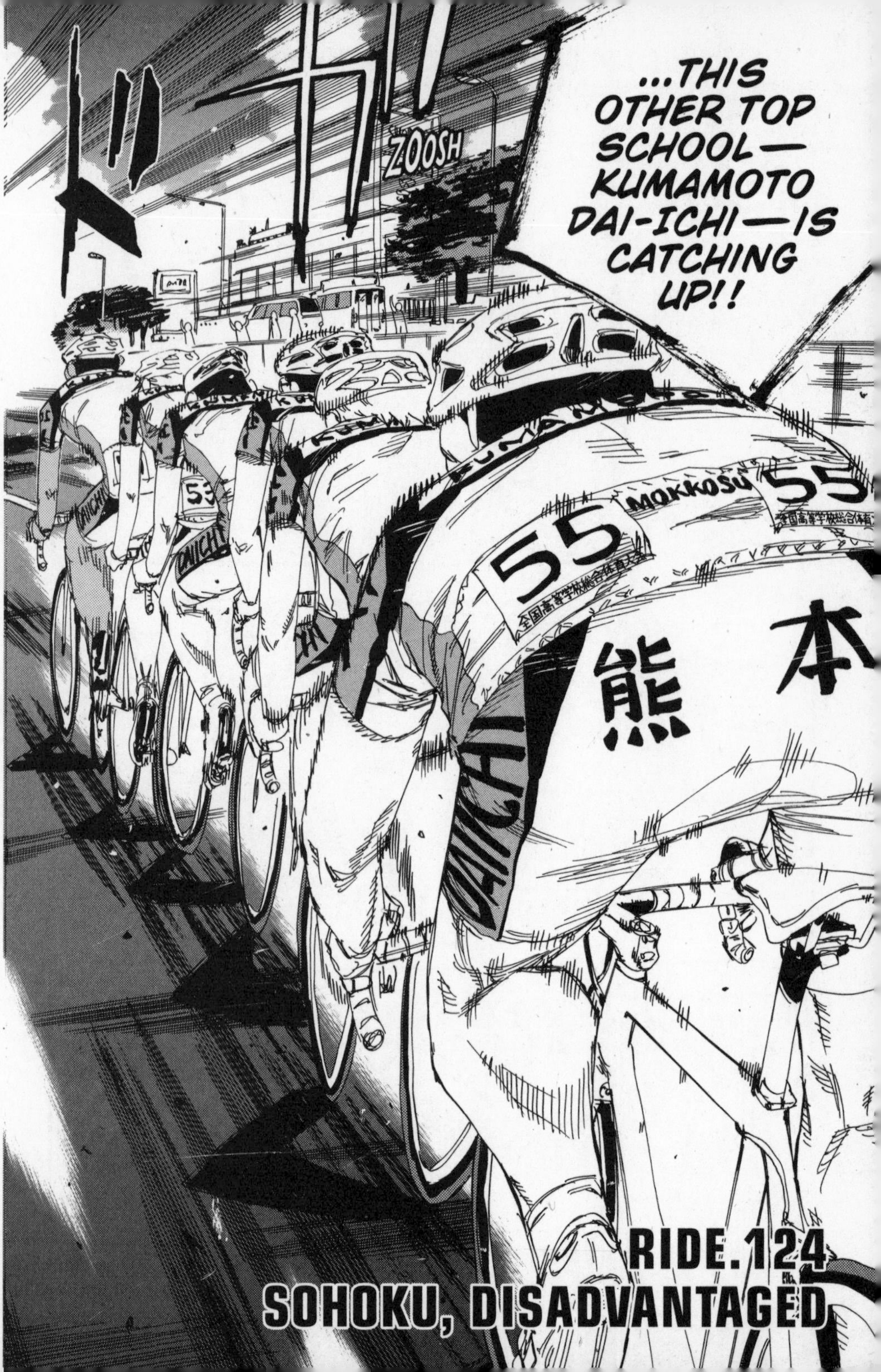
...THIS OTHER TOP SCHOOL—KUMAMOTO DAI-ICHI—IS CATCHING UP!!
ZOOSH

RIDE.124 SOHOKU, DISADVANTAGED

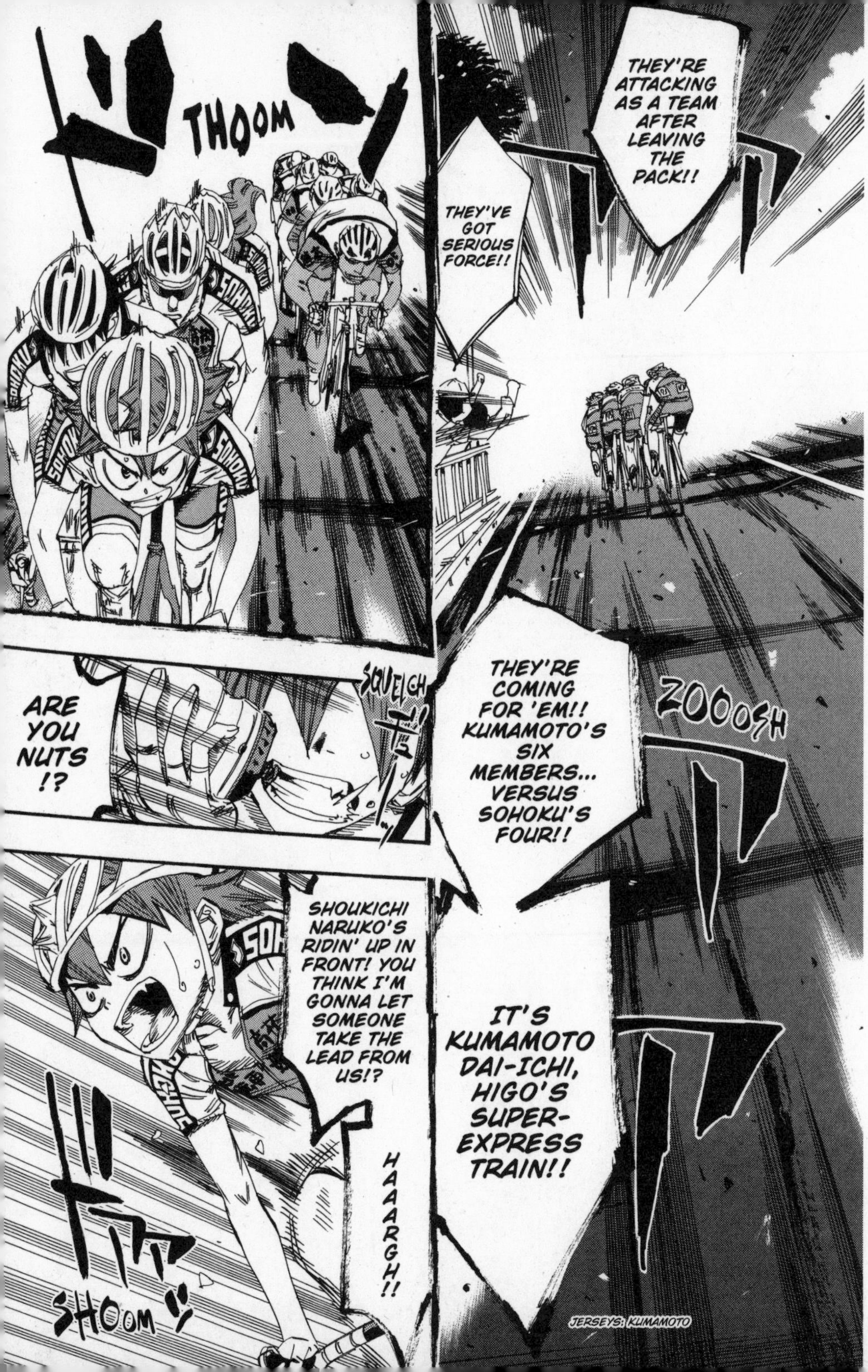

THEY'RE ATTACKING AS A TEAM AFTER LEAVING THE PACK!!
THEY'VE GOT SERIOUS FORCE!!
ZOOOSH
THEY'RE COMING FOR 'EM!! KUMAMOTO'S SIX MEMBERS... VERSUS SOHOKU'S FOUR!!
IT'S KUMAMOTO DAI-ICHI, HIGO'S SUPER-EXPRESS TRAIN!!
JERSEYS: KUMAMOTO
THOOM
SQUELCH
ARE YOU NUTS!?
SHOUKICHI NARUKO'S RIDIN' UP IN FRONT! YOU THINK I'M GONNA LET SOMEONE TAKE THE LEAD FROM US!?
HAAARGH!!
SHOOM

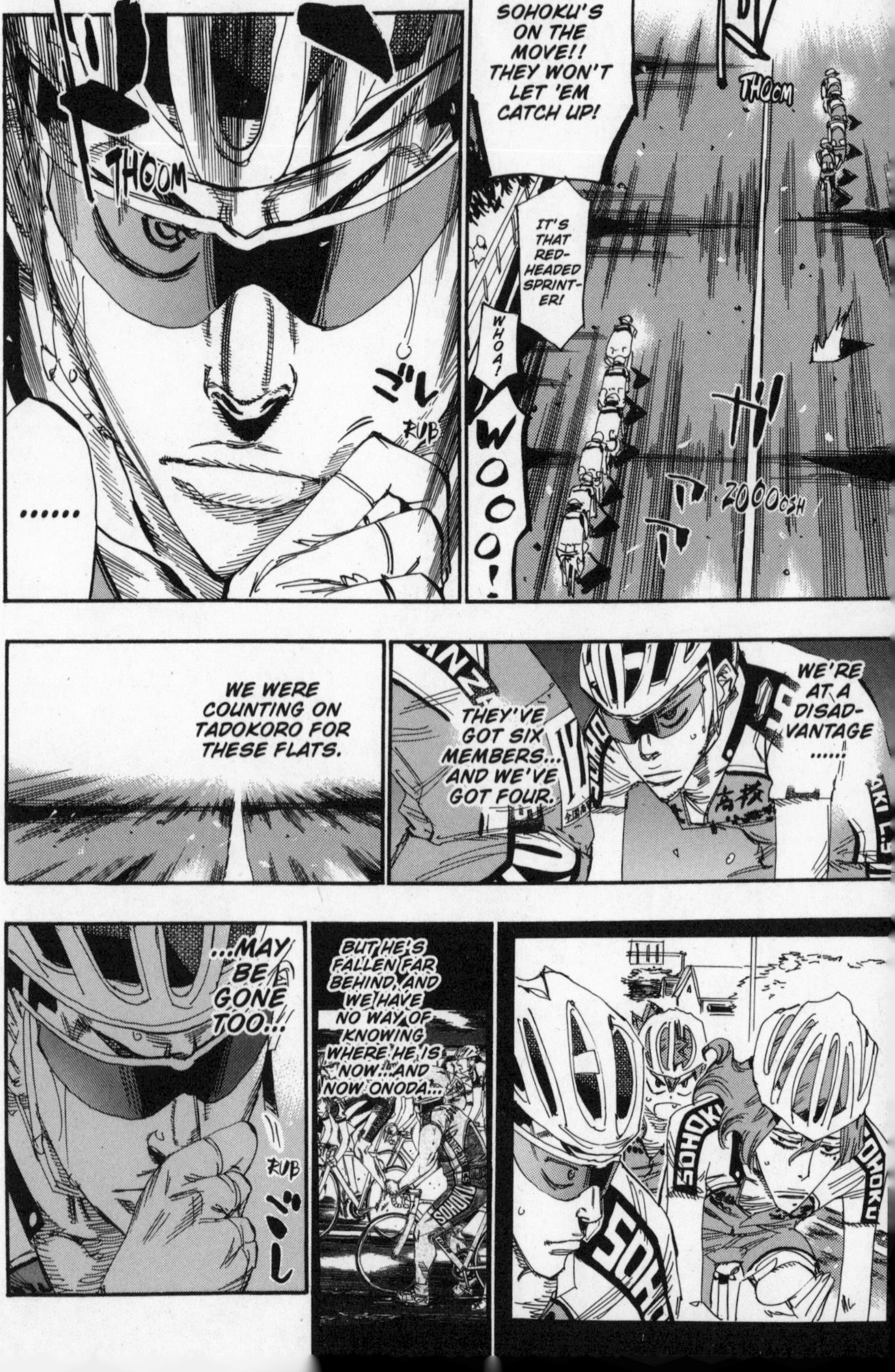
SOHOKU'S ON THE MOVE!! THEY WON'T LET 'EM CATCH UP!
THOOM
IT'S THAT RED-HEADED SPRINTER!
WHOA!
WOOOO!
ZOOOOSH
THOOM
RUB
......
WE'RE AT A DISADVANTAGE......
THEY'VE GOT SIX MEMBERS... AND WE'VE GOT FOUR.
WE WERE COUNTING ON TADOKORO FOR THESE FLATS.
BUT HE'S FALLEN FAR BEHIND, AND WE HAVE NO WAY OF KNOWING WHERE HE IS NOW... AND NOW ONODA...
...MAY BE GONE TOO...
RUB

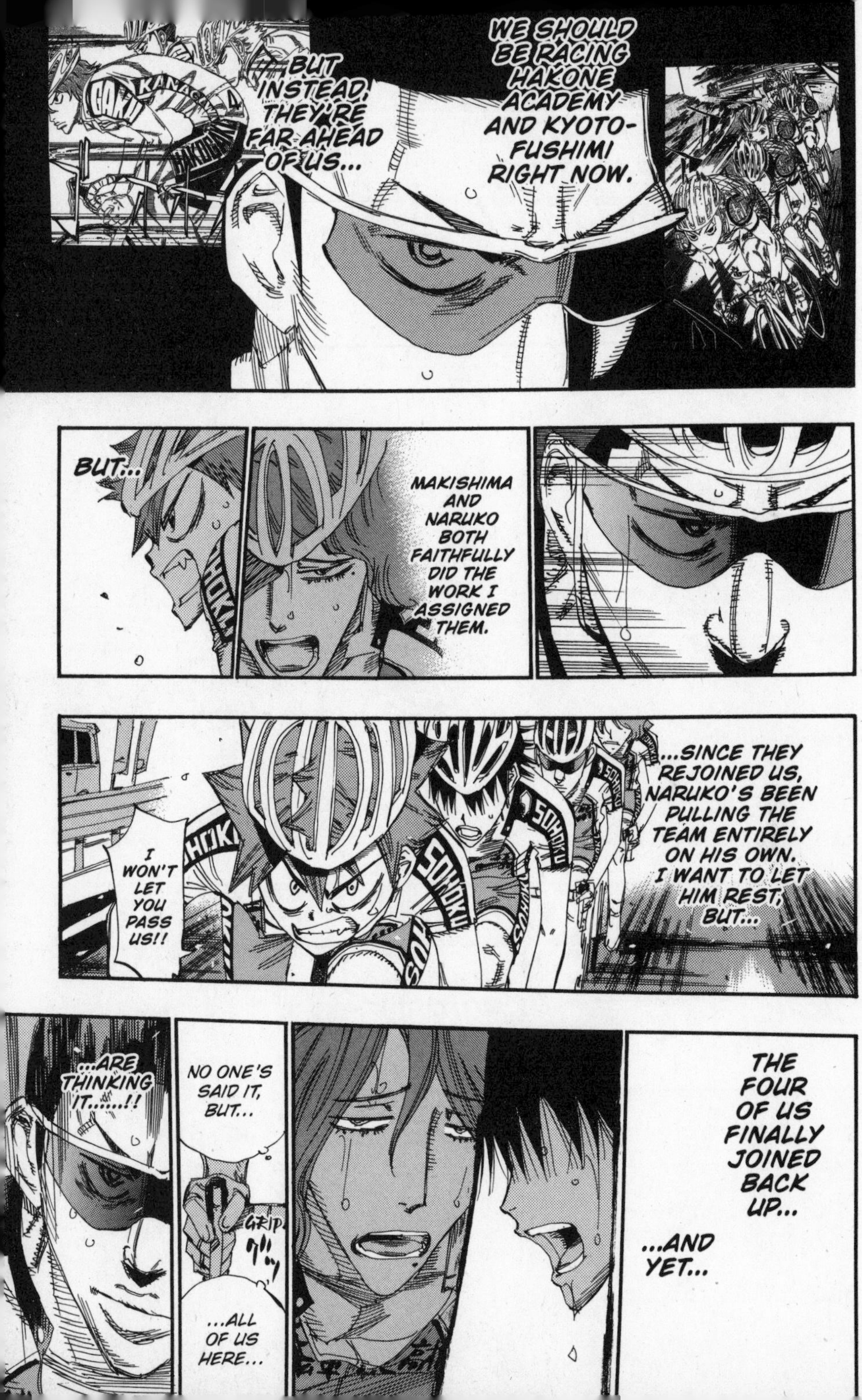
WE SHOULD BE RACING HAKONE ACADEMY AND KYOTO-FUSHIMI RIGHT NOW.
BUT INSTEAD, THEY'RE FAR AHEAD OF US...
MAKISHIMA AND NARUKO BOTH FAITHFULLY DID THE WORK I ASSIGNED THEM.
BUT...
...SINCE THEY REJOINED US, NARUKO'S BEEN PULLING THE TEAM ENTIRELY ON HIS OWN. I WANT TO LET HIM REST, BUT...
I WON'T LET YOU PASS US!!
THE FOUR OF US FINALLY JOINED BACK UP...
...AND YET...
NO ONE'S SAID IT, BUT...
GRIP
...ALL OF US HERE...
...ARE THINKING IT......!!

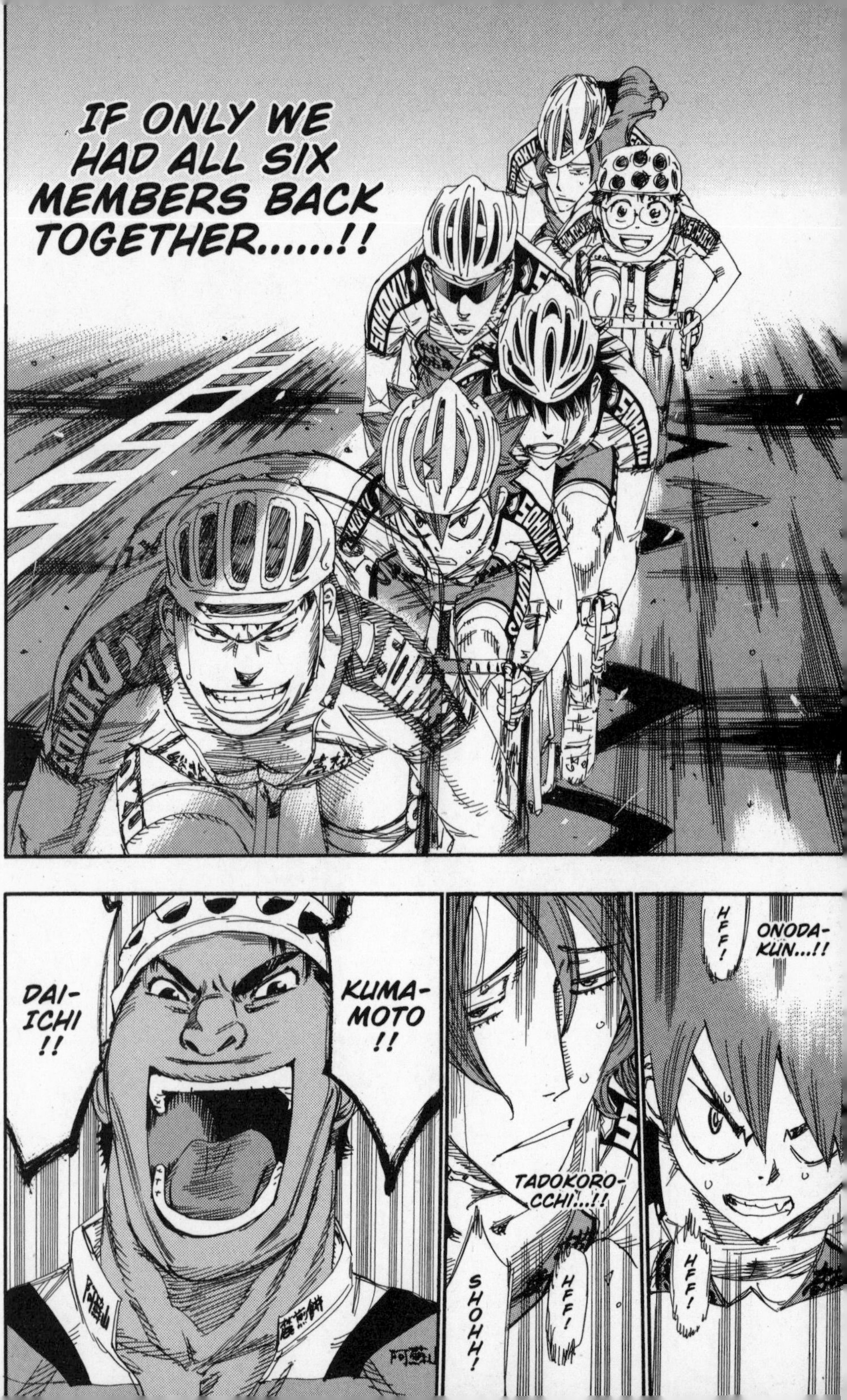
IF ONLY WE HAD ALL SIX MEMBERS BACK TOGETHER......!!
ONODA-KUN...!!
HFF!
HFF!
TADOKORO-CCHI...!!
HFF!
SHOHH!
KUMAMOTO!!
DAICHI!!

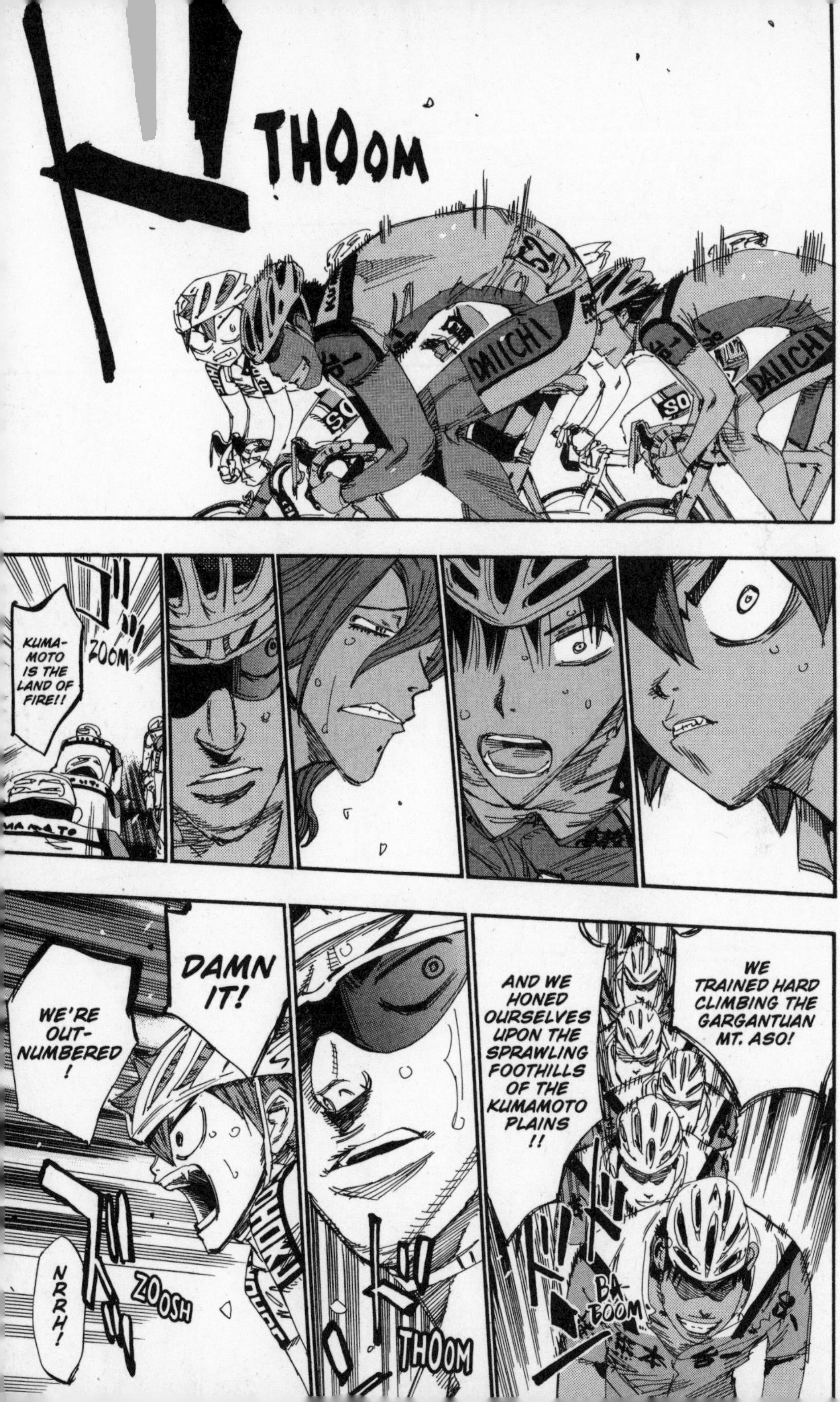
THOOM
KUMAMOTO IS THE LAND OF FIRE!!
ZOOM
WE TRAINED HARD CLIMBING THE GARGANTUAN MT. ASO!
AND WE HONED OURSELVES UPON THE SPRAWLING FOOTHILLS OF THE KUMAMOTO PLAINS!!
BA-BOOM
THOOM
DAMN IT!
WE'RE OUTNUMBERED!
NRRH!
ZOOSH

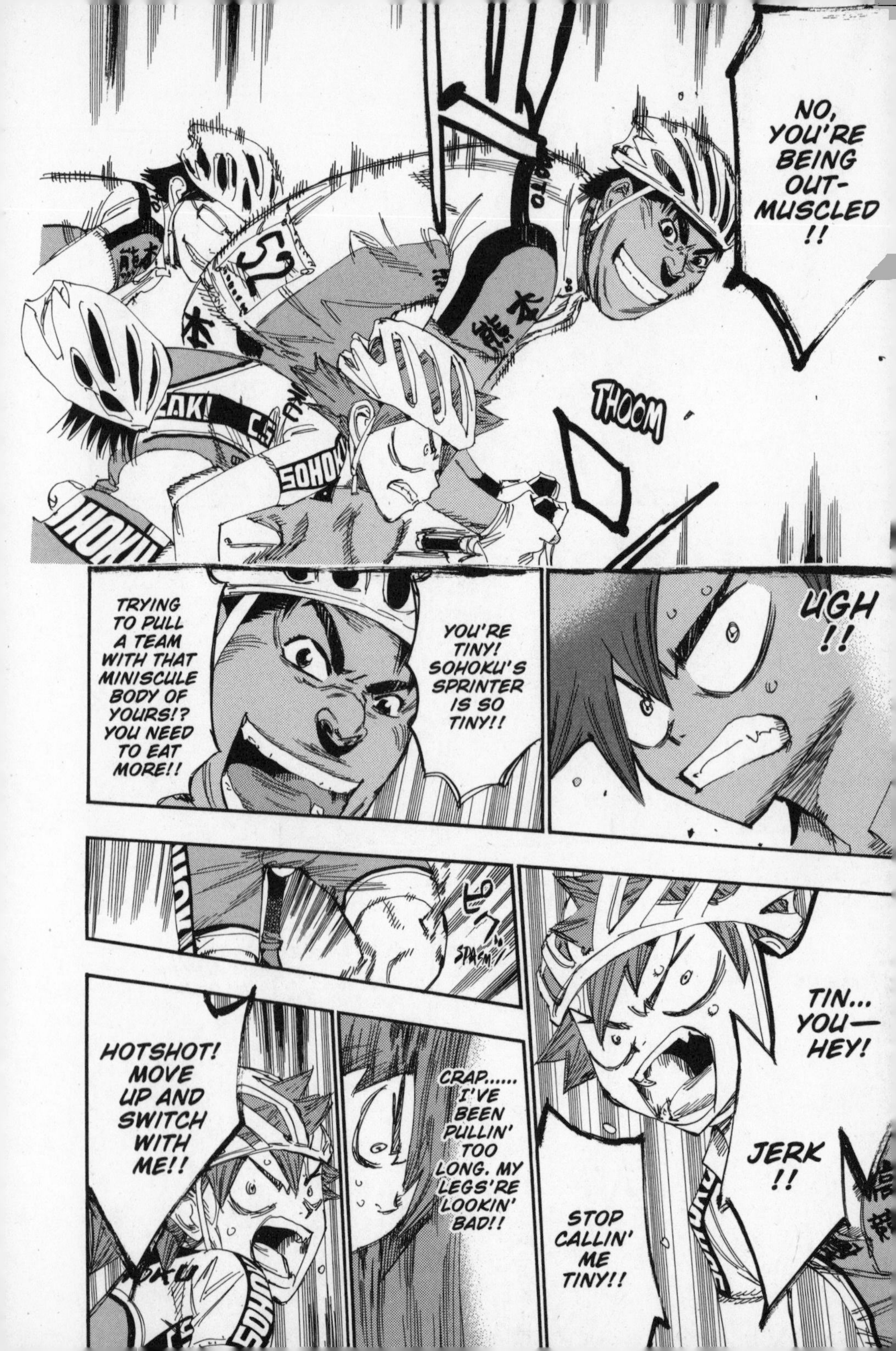
NO, YOU'RE BEING OUT-MUSCLED!!
THOOM
UGH!!
YOU'RE TINY! SOHOKU'S SPRINTER IS SO TINY!!
TRYING TO PULL A TEAM WITH THAT MINISCULE BODY OF YOURS!? YOU NEED TO EAT MORE!!
TIN... YOU— HEY!
JERK!!
STOP CALLIN' ME TINY!!
SPASM
CRAP...... I'VE BEEN PULLIN' TOO LONG. MY LEGS'RE LOOKIN' BAD!!
HOTSHOT! MOVE UP AND SWITCH WITH ME!!

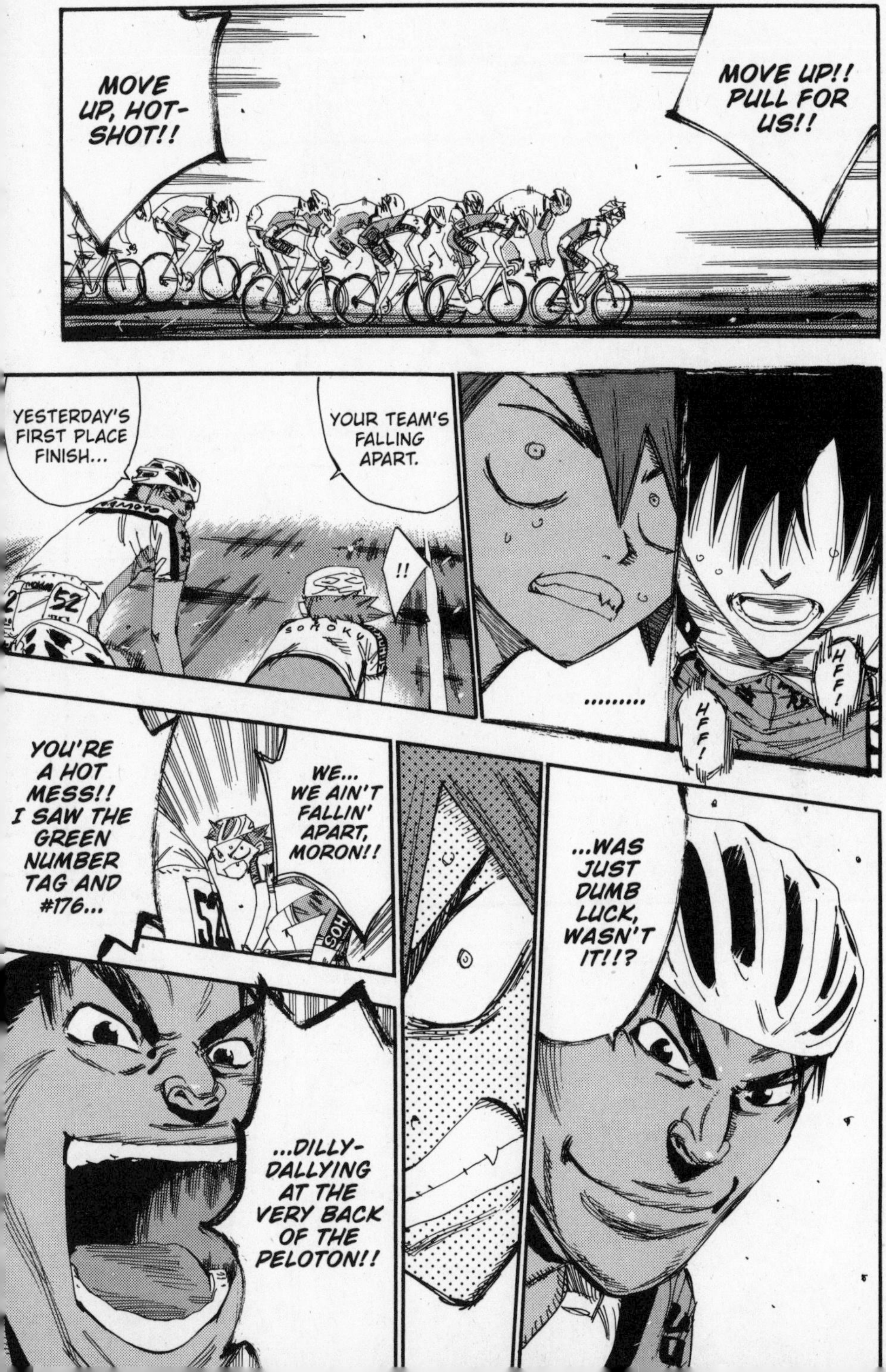

MOVE UP!! PULL FOR US!!
MOVE UP, HOT-SHOT!!
HFF! HFF!
....
YOUR TEAM'S FALLING APART.
YESTERDAY'S FIRST PLACE FINISH...
!!
...WAS JUST DUMB LUCK, WASN'T IT!!?
WE... WE AIN'T FALLIN' APART, MORON!!
YOU'RE A HOT MESS!! I SAW THE GREEN NUMBER TAG AND #176...
...DILLY-DALLYING AT THE VERY BACK OF THE PELOTON!!

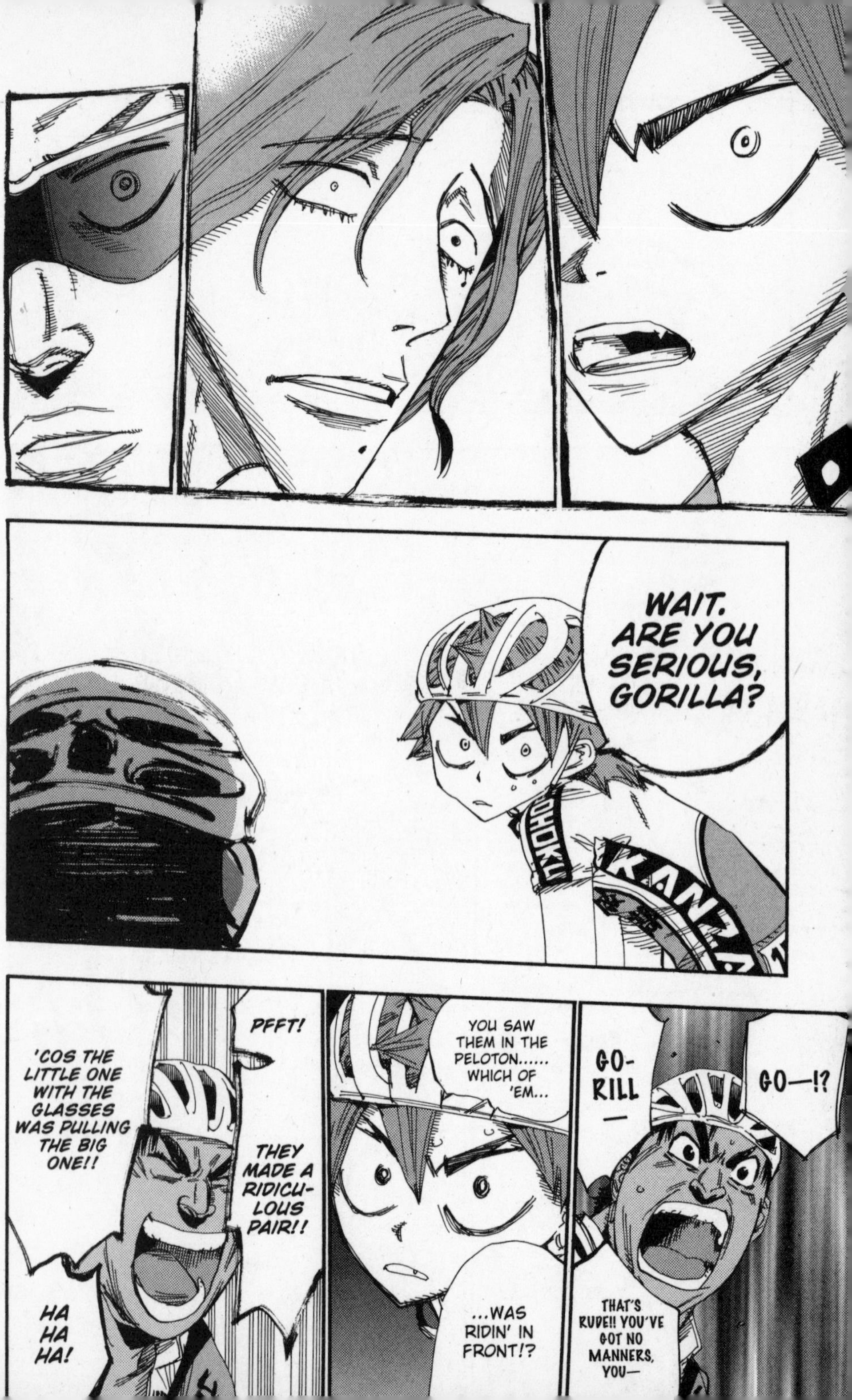
WAIT. ARE YOU SERIOUS, GORILLA?
GO—!?
GO-RILL—
THAT'S RUDE!! YOU'VE GOT NO MANNERS, YOU—
YOU SAW THEM IN THE PELOTON...... WHICH OF 'EM...
...WAS RIDIN' IN FRONT!?
PFFT!
'COS THE LITTLE ONE WITH THE GLASSES WAS PULLING THE BIG ONE!!
THEY MADE A RIDICULOUS PAIR!!
HA HA HA!

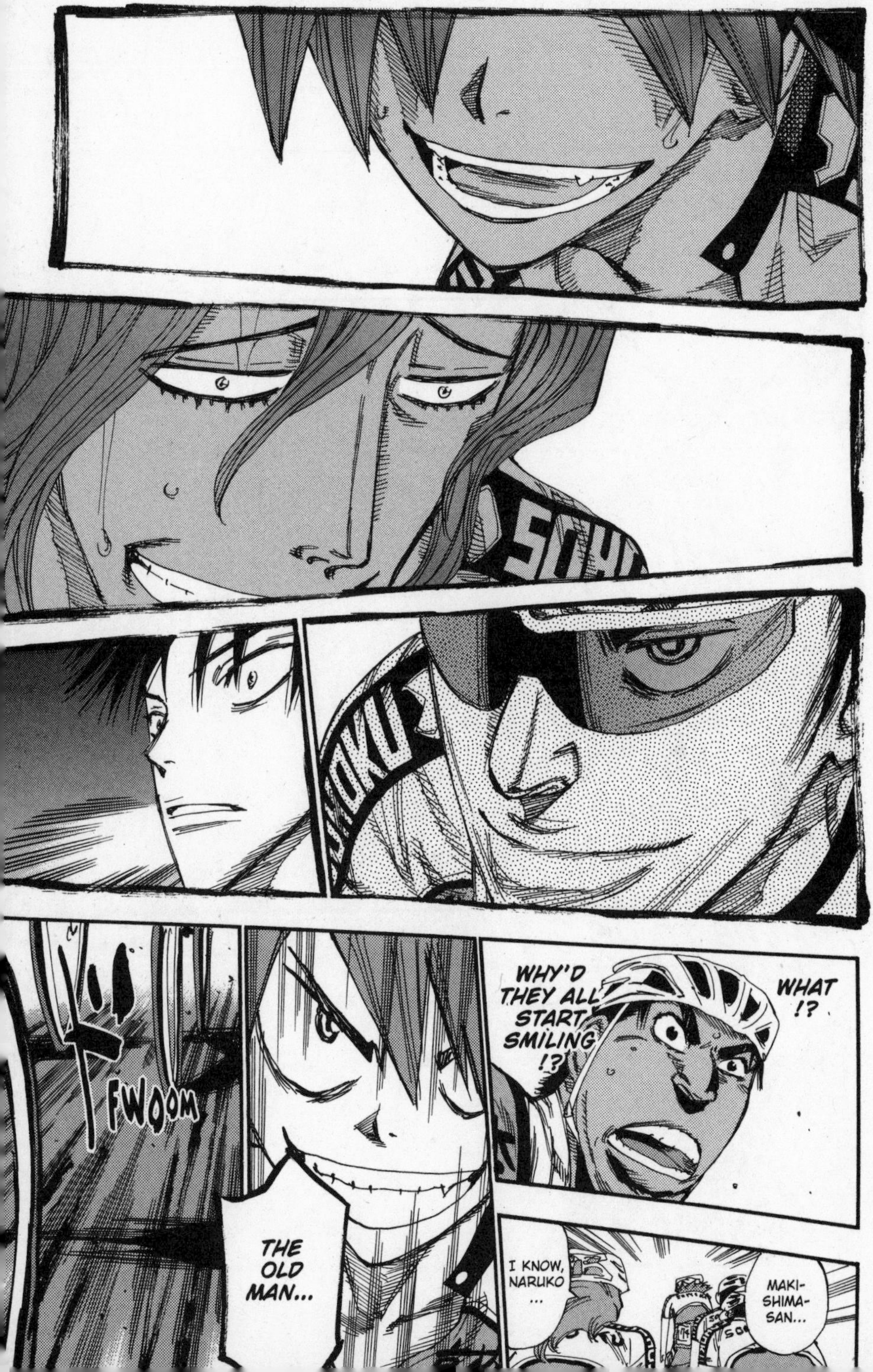
WHAT!?
WHY'D THEY ALL START SMILING!?
MAKI-SHIMA-SAN...
I KNOW, NARUKO...
THE OLD MAN...
FWOOM

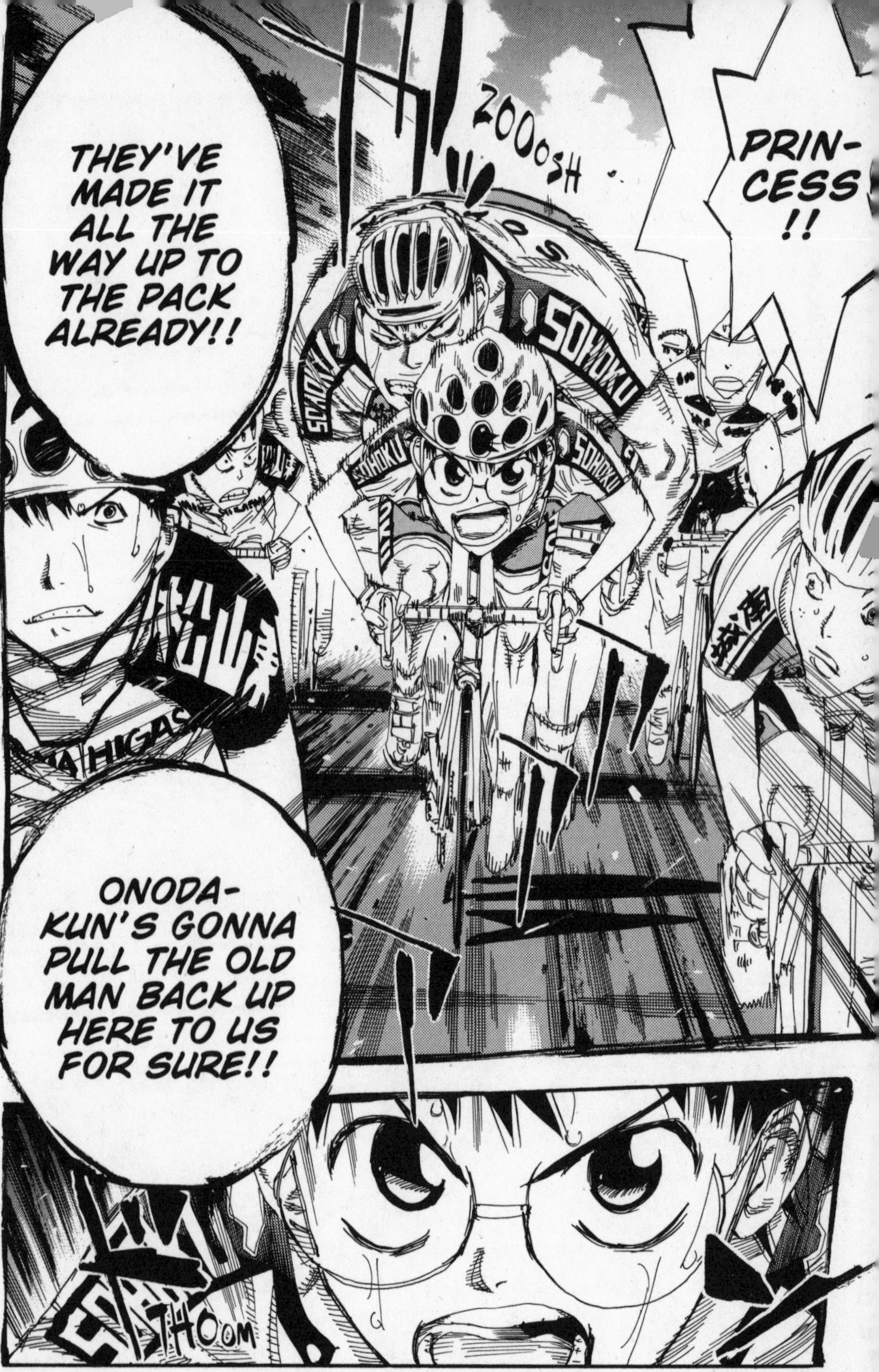
PRIN-CESS!!
ZOOOSH
THEY'VE MADE IT ALL THE WAY UP TO THE PACK ALREADY!!
ONODA-KUN'S GONNA PULL THE OLD MAN BACK UP HERE TO US FOR SURE!!
THOOM

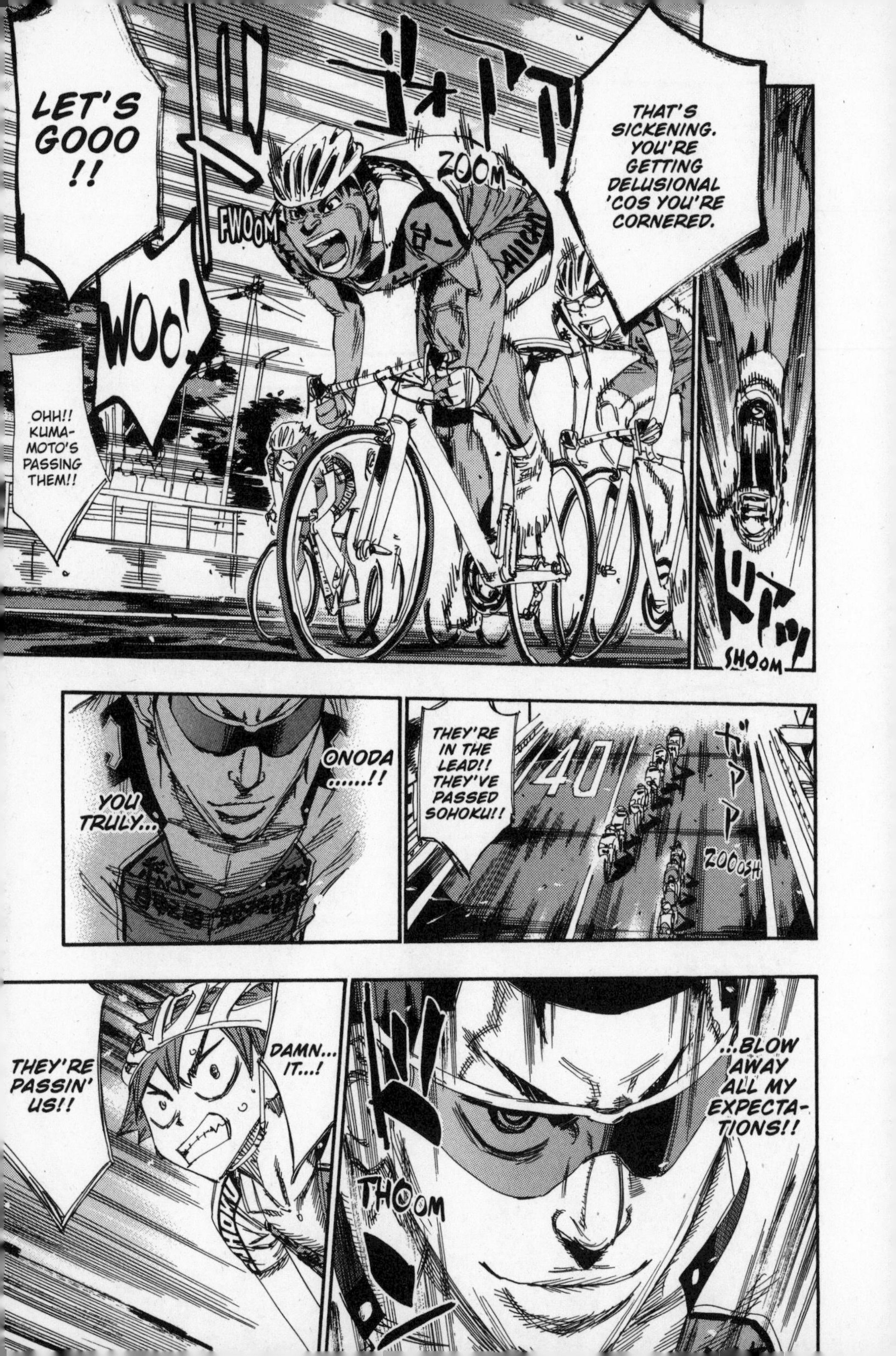

SHOOM
THAT'S SICKENING. YOU'RE GETTING DELUSIONAL 'COS YOU'RE CORNERED.
ZOOM
LET'S GOOO!!
FWOOM
WOO!
OHH!! KUMAMOTO'S PASSING THEM!!
THEY'RE IN THE LEAD!! THEY'VE PASSED SOHOKU!!
ZOOOSH
ONODA......!!
YOU TRULY...
...BLOW AWAY ALL MY EXPECTATIONS!!
THOOM
DAMN... IT...!
THEY'RE PASSIN' US!!

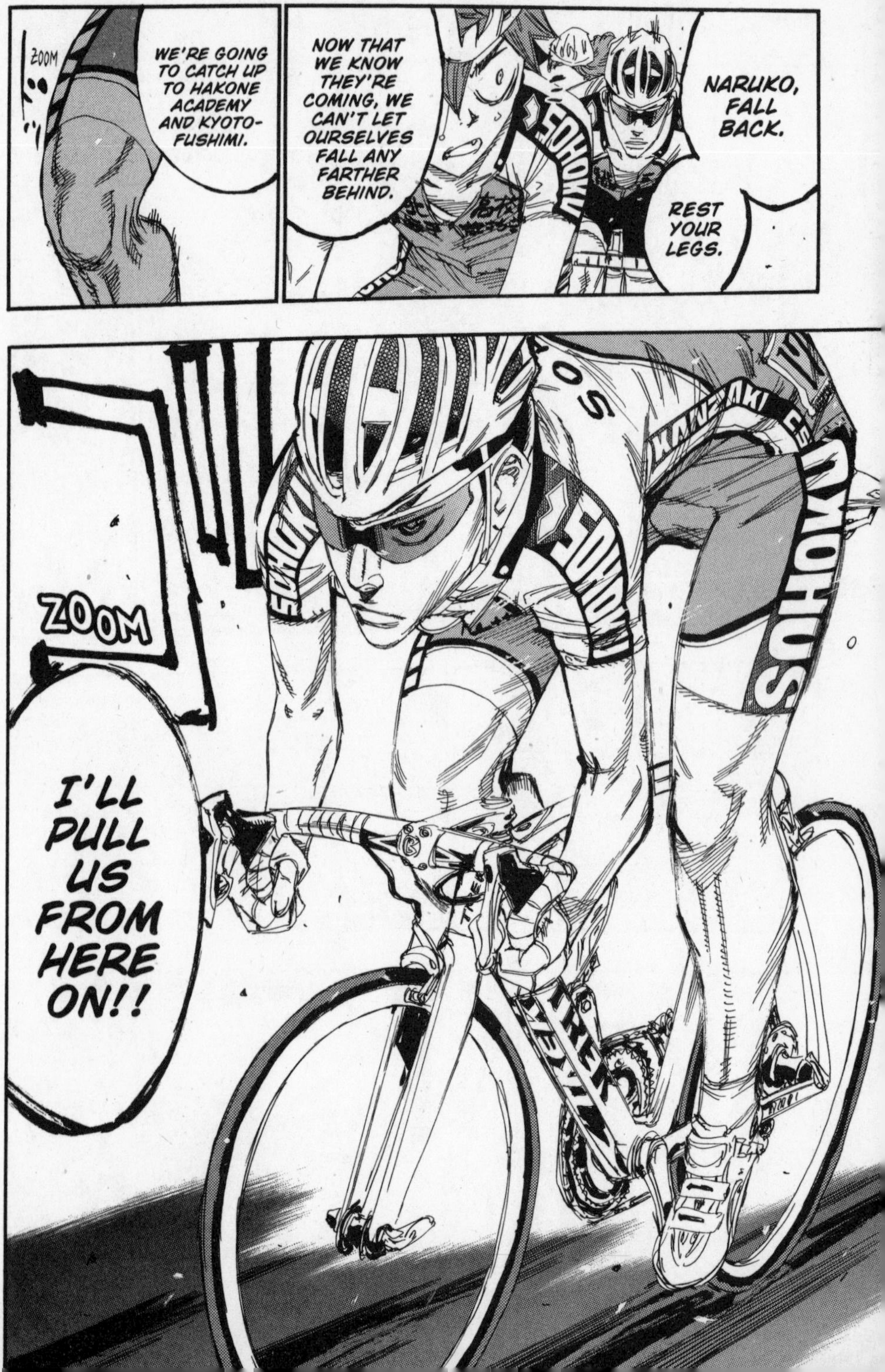
NARUKO, FALL BACK.
REST YOUR LEGS.
NOW THAT WE KNOW THEY'RE COMING, WE CAN'T LET OURSELVES FALL ANY FARTHER BEHIND.
WE'RE GOING TO CATCH UP TO HAKONE ACADEMY AND KYOTO-FUSHIMI.
ZOOM
ZOOM
I'LL PULL US FROM HERE ON!!

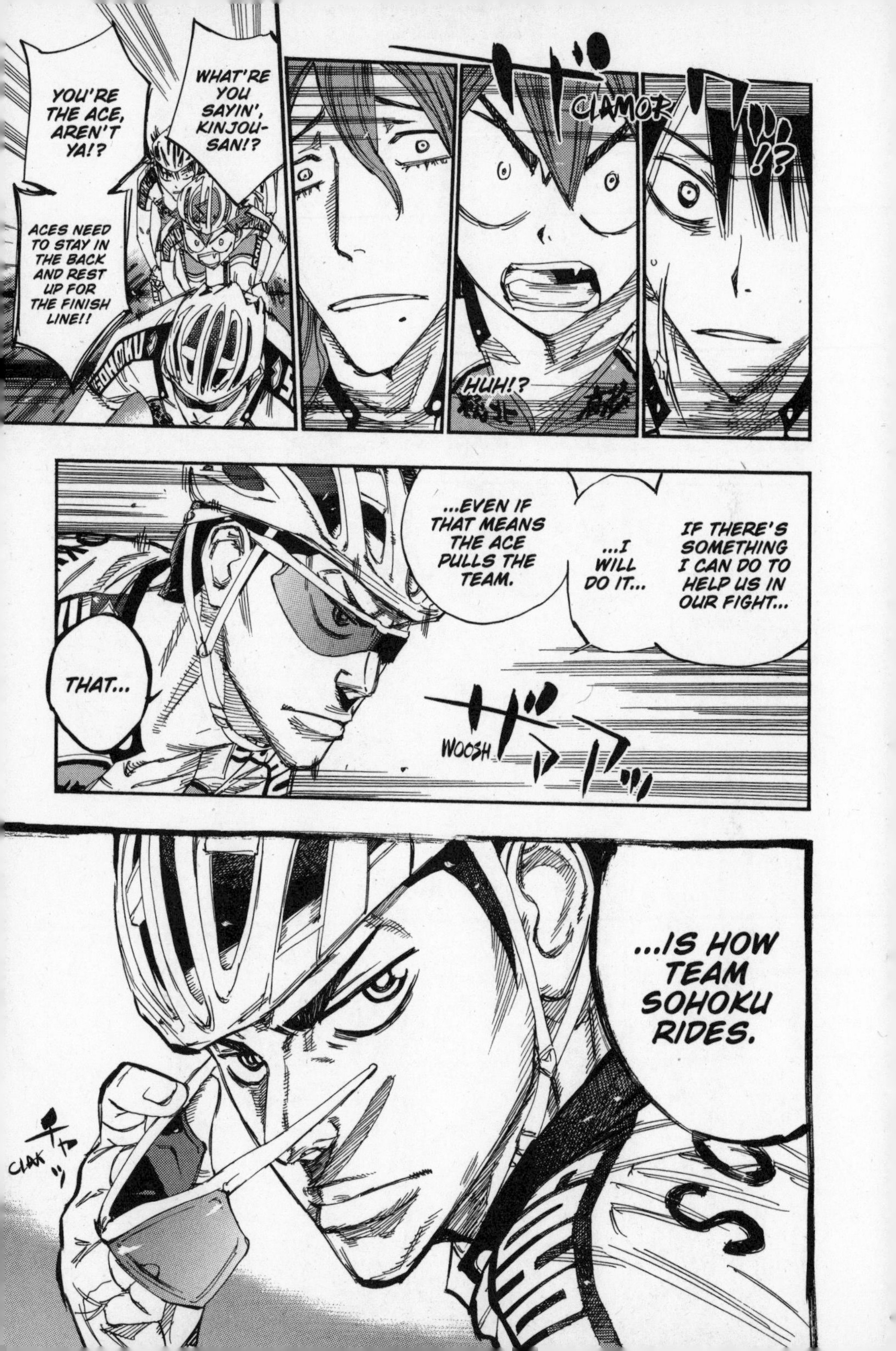
CLAMOR
!?
HUH!?
WHAT'RE YOU SAYIN', KINJOU-SAN!?
YOU'RE THE ACE, AREN'T YA!?
ACES NEED TO STAY IN THE BACK AND REST UP FOR THE FINISH LINE!!
IF THERE'S SOMETHING I CAN DO TO HELP US IN OUR FIGHT...
...I WILL DO IT...
...EVEN IF THAT MEANS THE ACE PULLS THE TEAM.
WOOSH
THAT...
...IS HOW TEAM SOHOKU RIDES.
CLAK

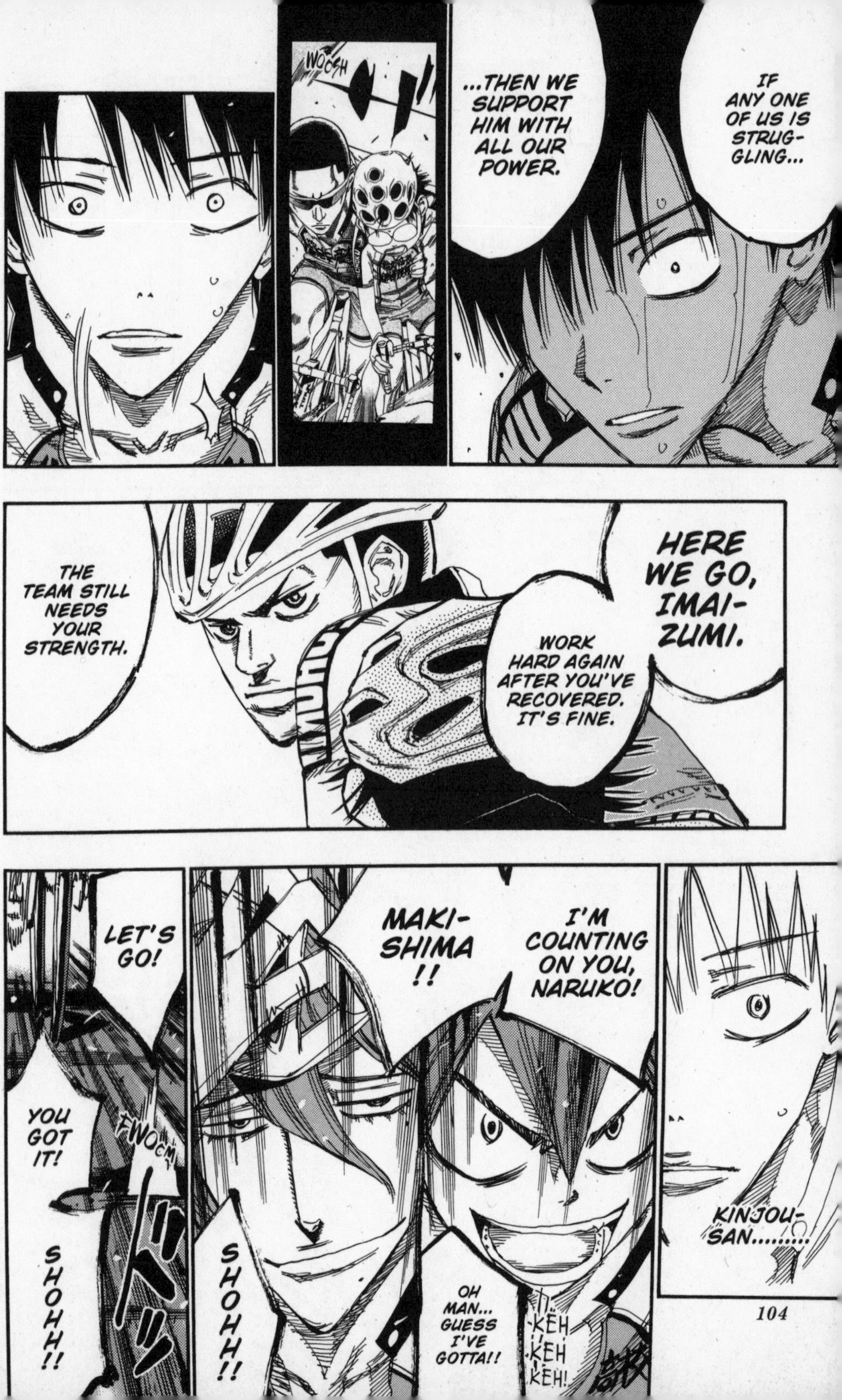
IF ANY ONE OF US IS STRUG-GLING...
...THEN WE SUPPORT HIM WITH ALL OUR POWER.
WOOSH
HERE WE GO, IMAI-ZUMI.
WORK HARD AGAIN AFTER YOU'VE RECOVERED. IT'S FINE.
THE TEAM STILL NEEDS YOUR STRENGTH.
KINJOU-SAN.........
I'M COUNTING ON YOU, NARUKO!
MAKI-SHIMA!!
KEH KEH KEH!
OH MAN... GUESS I'VE GOTTA!!
SHOHH!!
LET'S GO!
YOU GOT IT!
SHOHH!!

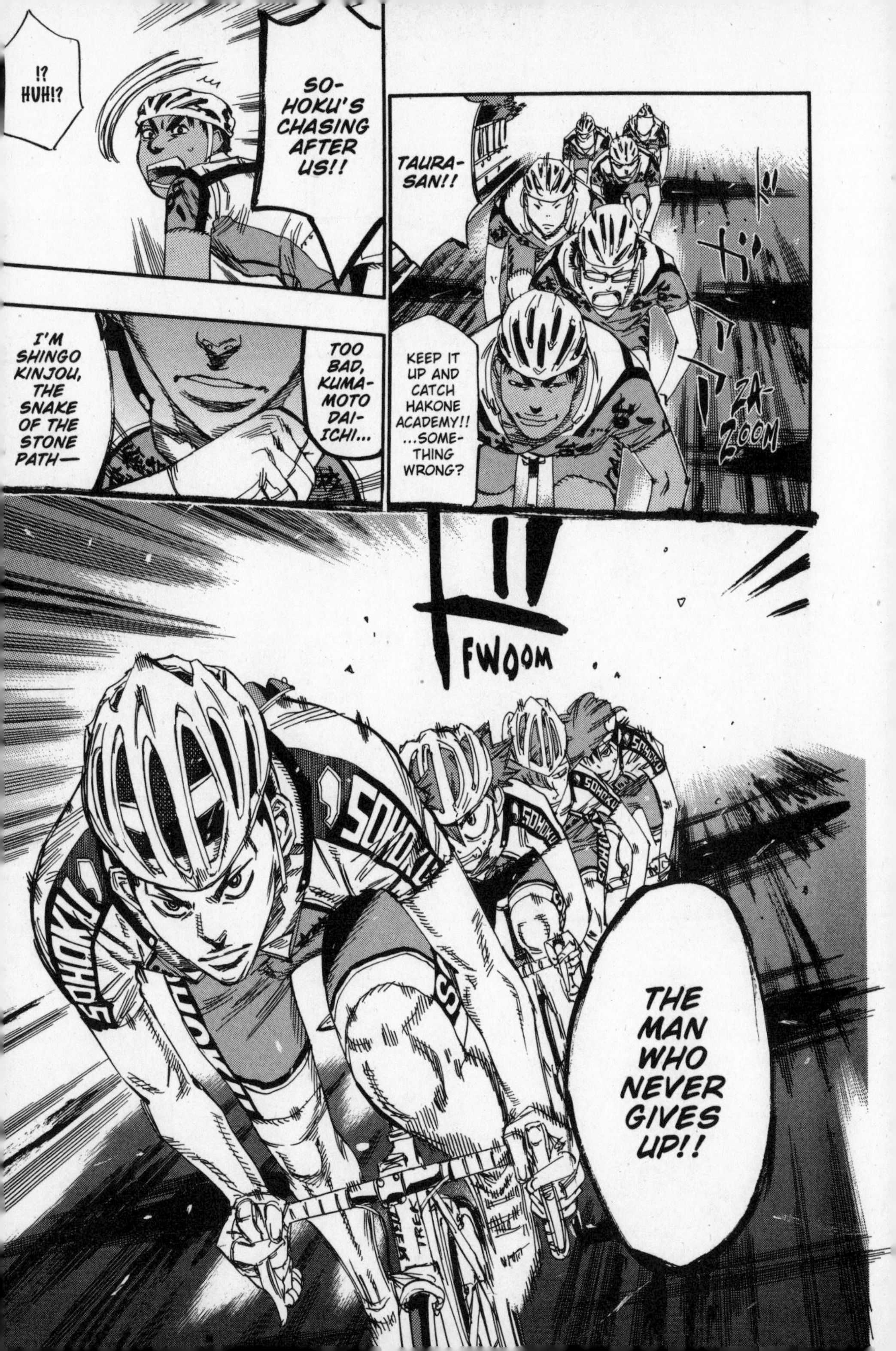

TAURA-SAN!!
KEEP IT UP AND CATCH HAKONE ACADEMY!! ...SOMETHING WRONG?
ZA-ZOOM
SO-HOKU'S CHASING AFTER US!!
!? HUH!?
TOO BAD, KUMAMOTO DAICHI...
I'M SHINGO KINJOU, THE SNAKE OF THE STONE PATH—
FWOOM
THE MAN WHO NEVER GIVES UP!!

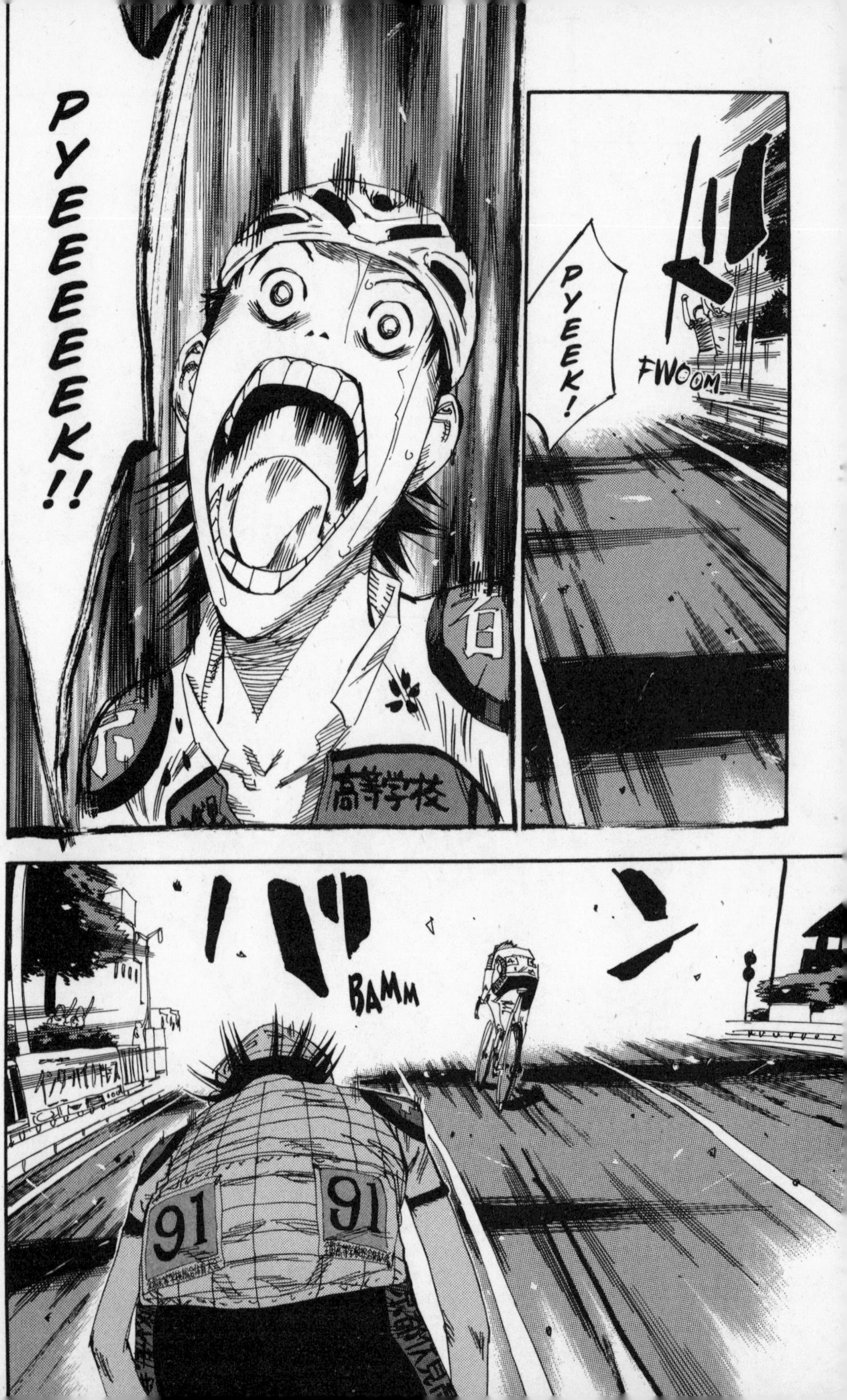
PYEEEK!
FWOOM
PYEEEEEEEK!!
高等学校
BAMM

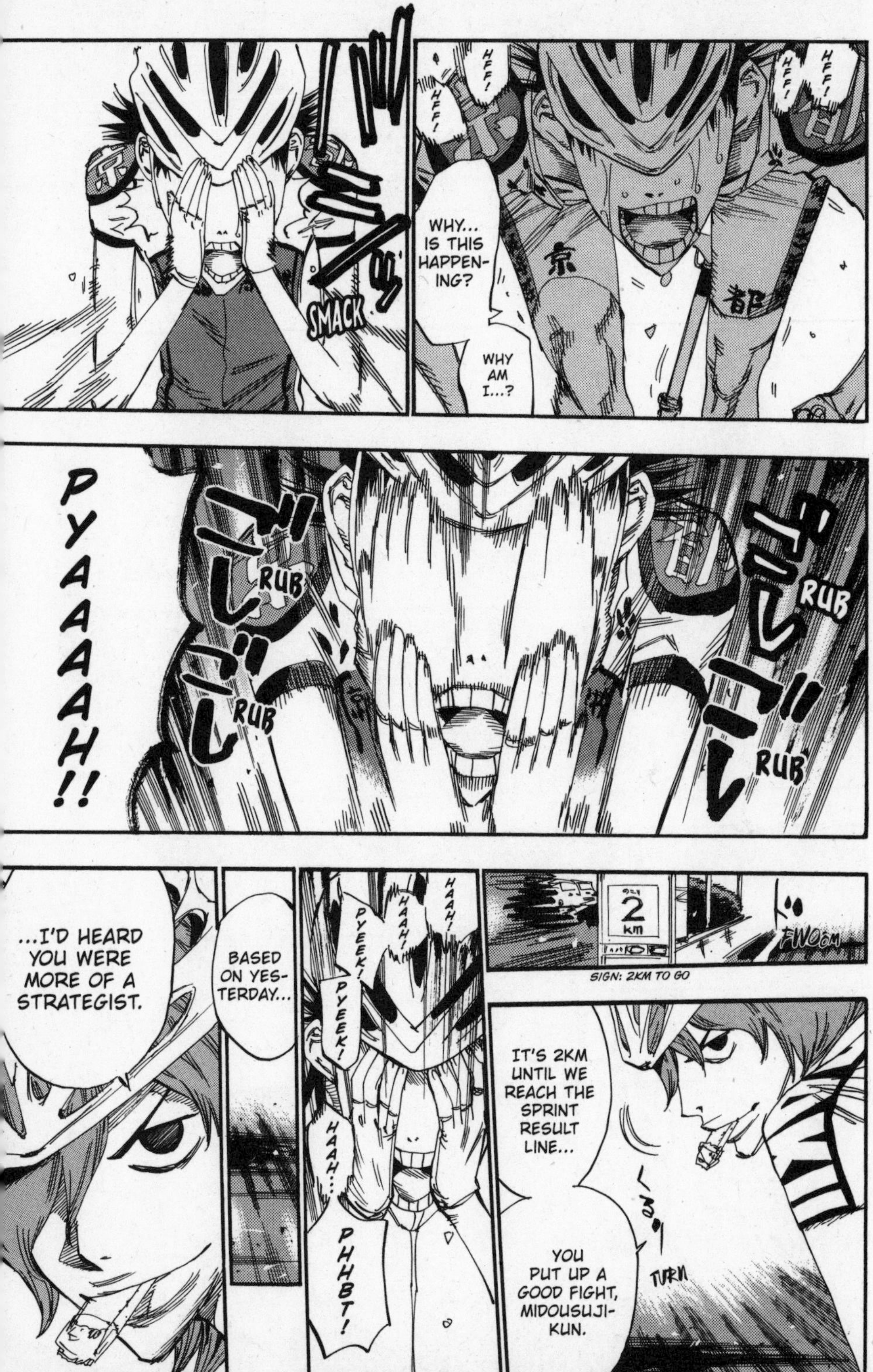
HFF! HFF!
HFF! HFF!
WHY... IS THIS HAPPEN-ING?
WHY AM I...?
SMACK
RUB
RUB
RUB
RUB
PYAAAAAH!!
2 km
FWOOM
SIGN: 2KM TO GO
IT'S 2KM UNTIL WE REACH THE SPRINT RESULT LINE...
TURN
YOU PUT UP A GOOD FIGHT, MIDOUSUJI-KUN.
HAAH! HAAH!
PYEEK! PYEEK!
HAAH...
PHHBT!
BASED ON YES-TERDAY...
...I'D HEARD YOU WERE MORE OF A STRATEGIST.

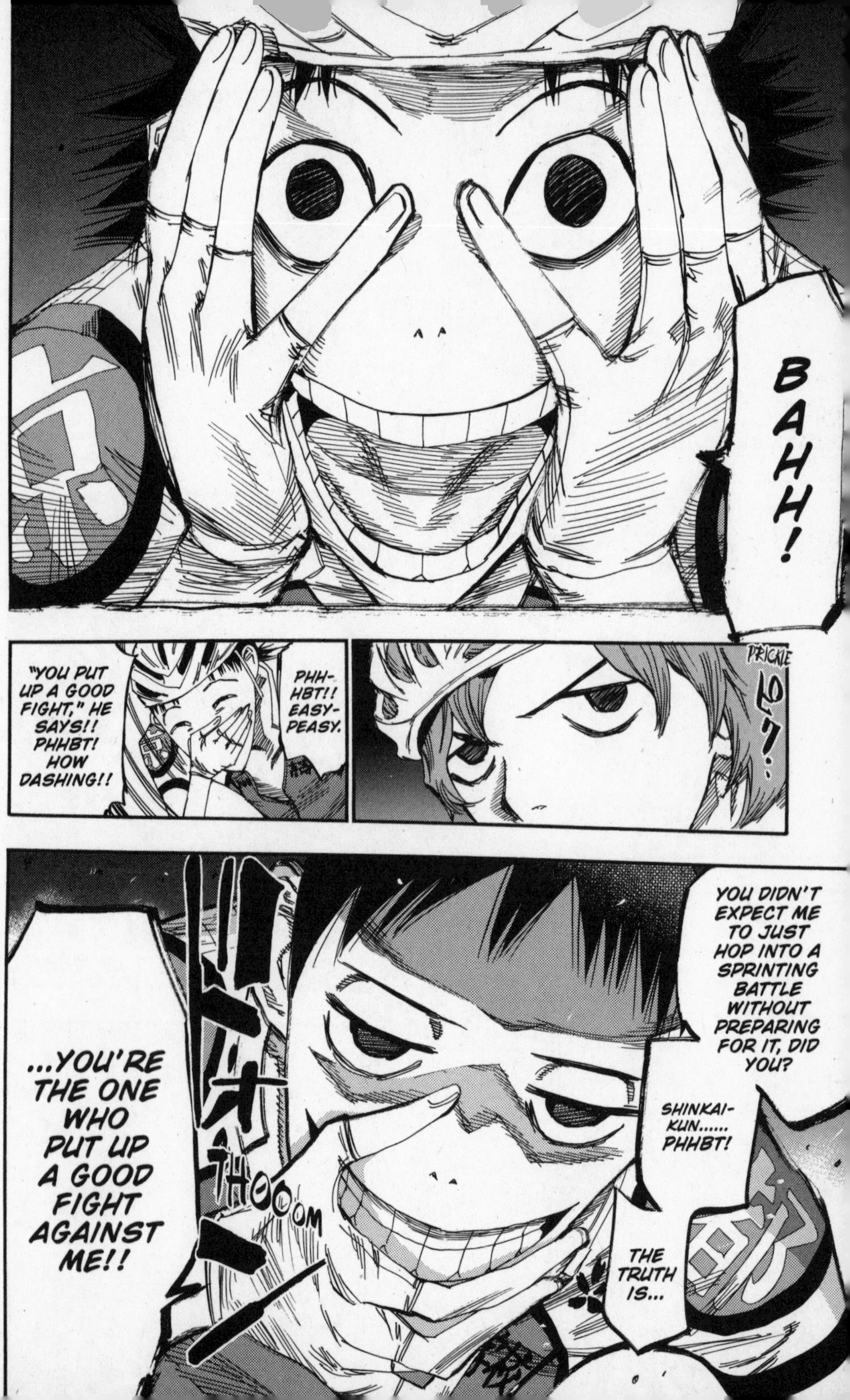
BAHH!
PRICKLE
PHH-HBT!! EASY-PEASY.
"YOU PUT UP A GOOD FIGHT," HE SAYS!! PHHBT! HOW DASHING!!
YOU DIDN'T EXPECT ME TO JUST HOP INTO A SPRINTING BATTLE WITHOUT PREPARING FOR IT, DID YOU?
SHINKAI-KUN...... PHHBT!
THE TRUTH IS...
THOOOM
...YOU'RE THE ONE WHO PUT UP A GOOD FIGHT AGAINST ME!!

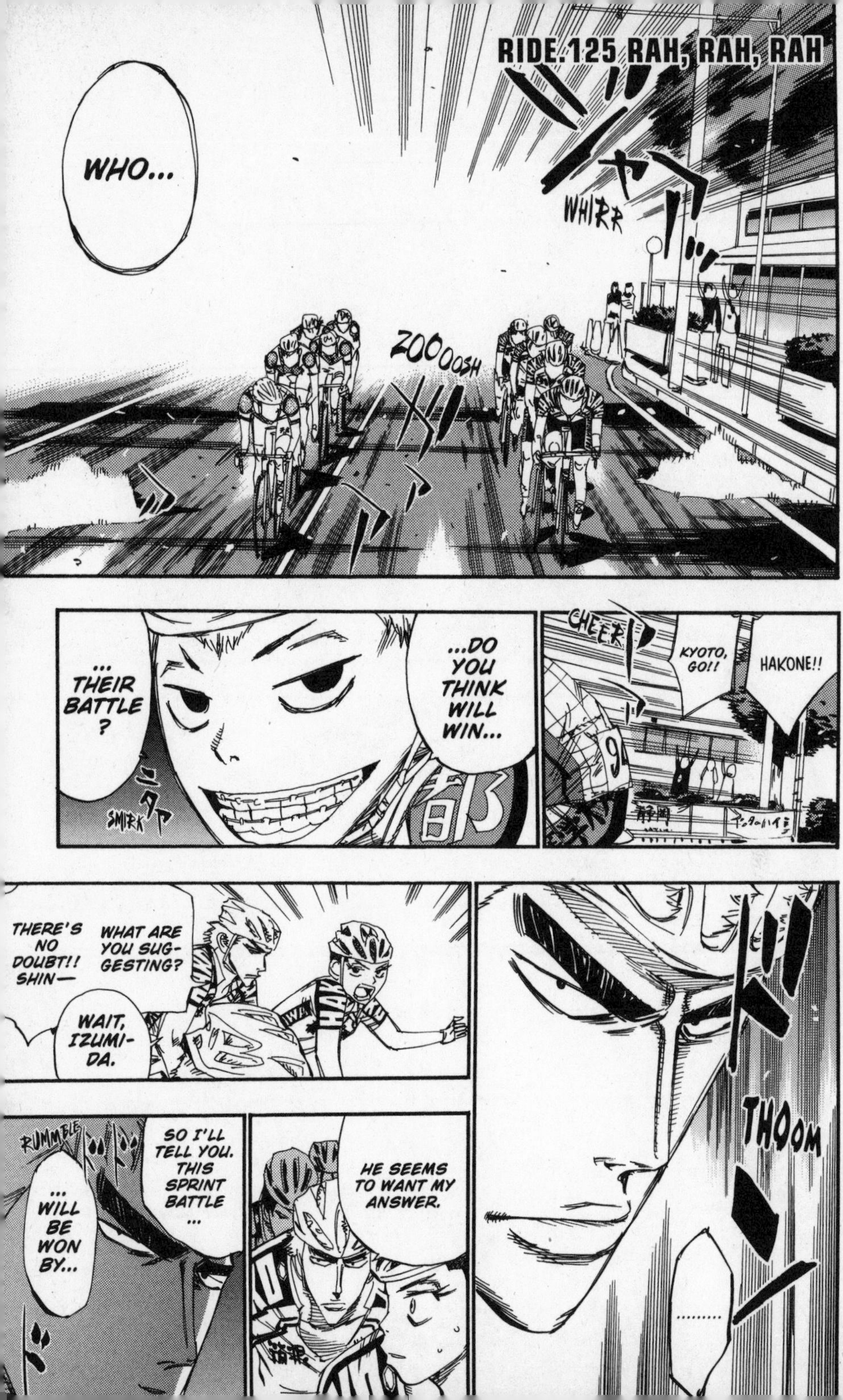
RIDE.125 RAH, RAH, RAH
WHIRR
WHO...
ZOOOOSH
CHEER
HAKONE!!
KYOTO, GO!!
...DO YOU THINK WILL WIN...
...THEIR BATTLE?
SMIRK
THOOM
....
WHAT ARE YOU SUG-GESTING?
THERE'S NO DOUBT!! SHIN—
WAIT, IZUMI-DA.
HE SEEMS TO WANT MY ANSWER.
SO I'LL TELL YOU. THIS SPRINT BATTLE...
...WILL BE WON BY...
RUMMBLE

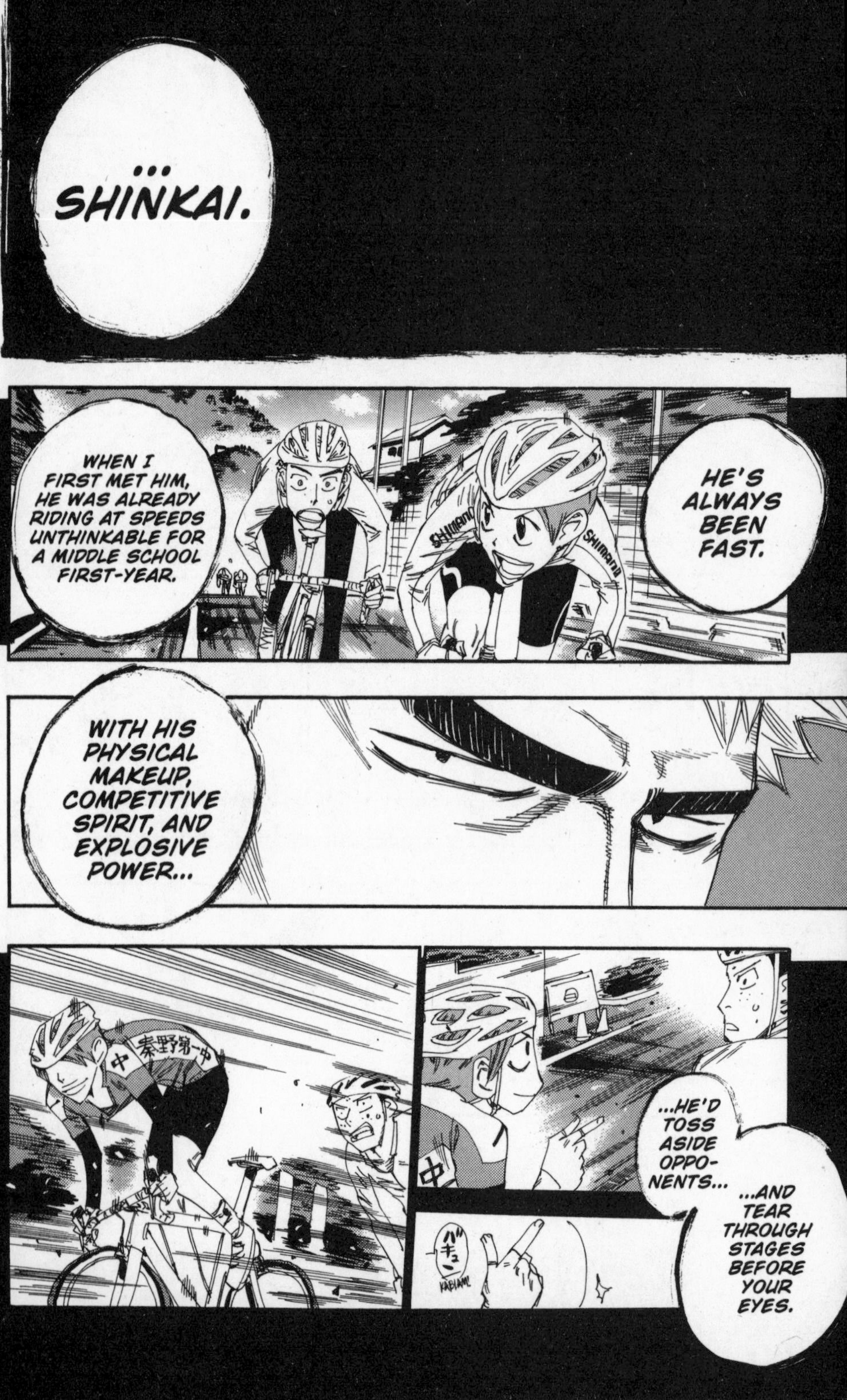
...SHINKAI.
HE'S ALWAYS BEEN FAST.
WHEN I FIRST MET HIM, HE WAS ALREADY RIDING AT SPEEDS UNTHINKABLE FOR A MIDDLE SCHOOL FIRST-YEAR.
WITH HIS PHYSICAL MAKEUP, COMPETITIVE SPIRIT, AND EXPLOSIVE POWER...
...HE'D TOSS ASIDE OPPO-NENTS...
KABLAM!
...AND TEAR THROUGH STAGES BEFORE YOUR EYES.

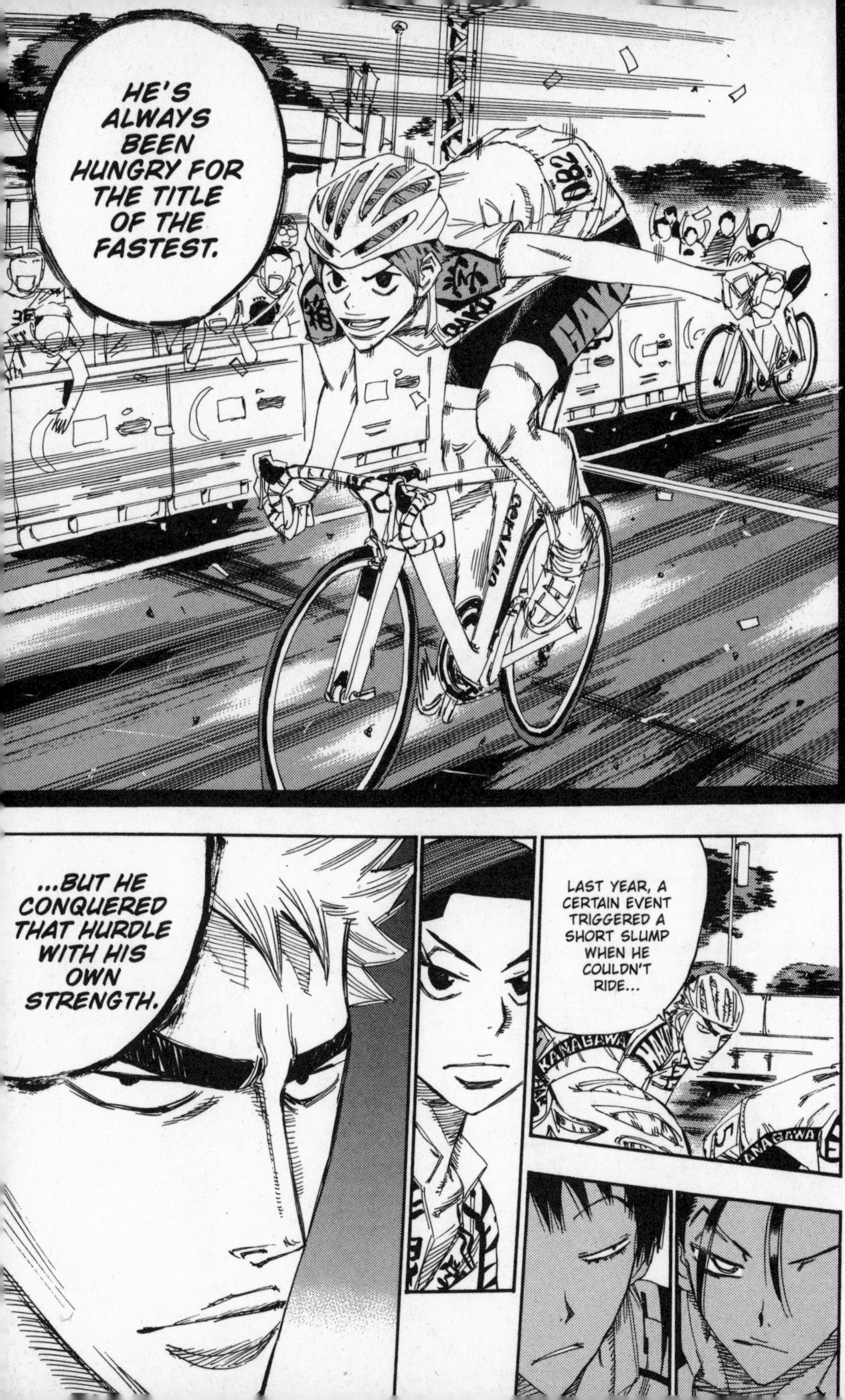
HE'S ALWAYS BEEN HUNGRY FOR THE TITLE OF THE FASTEST.
280
LAST YEAR, A CERTAIN EVENT TRIGGERED A SHORT SLUMP WHEN HE COULDN'T RIDE...
KANAGAWA
...BUT HE CONQUERED THAT HURDLE WITH HIS OWN STRENGTH.

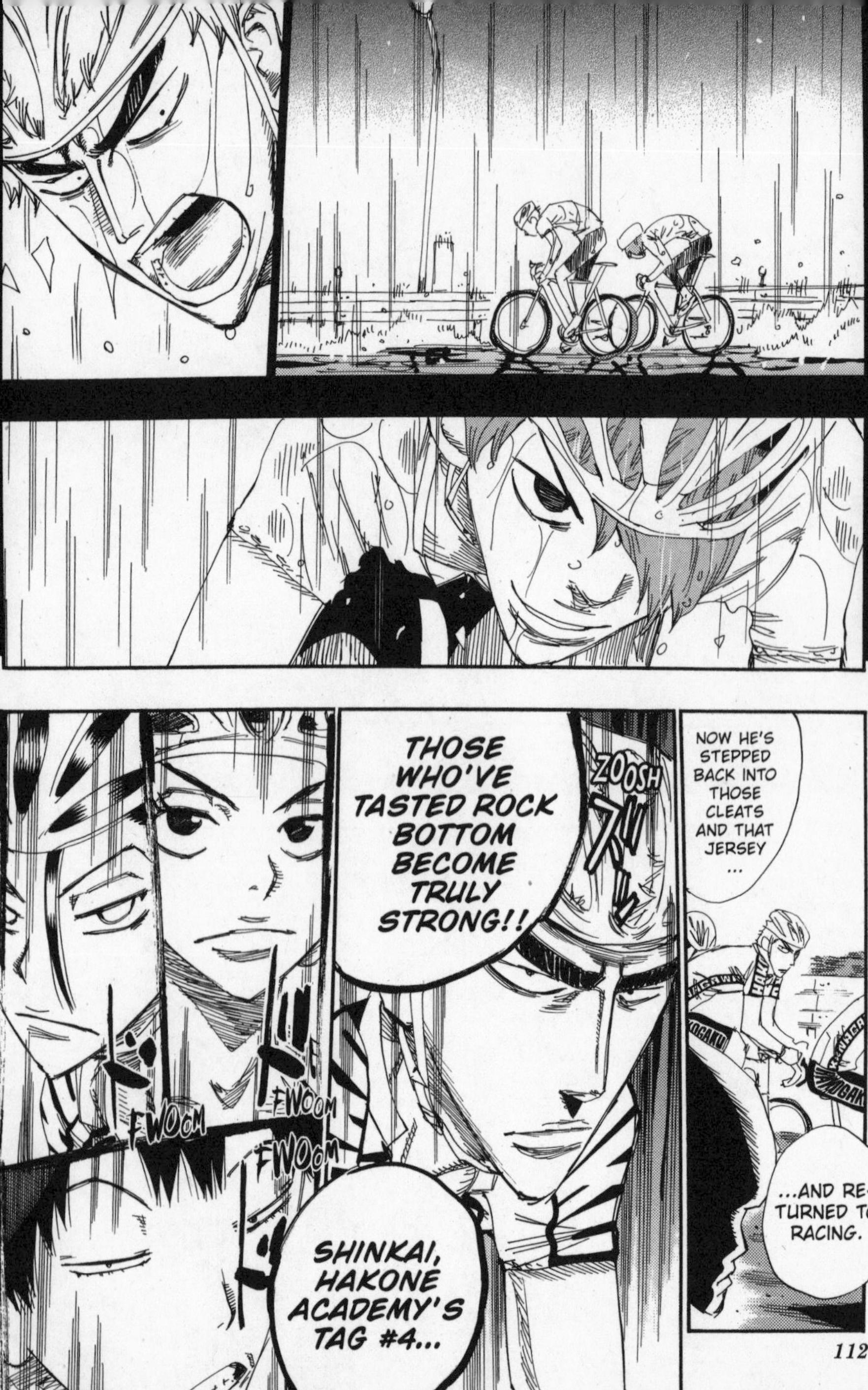
NOW HE'S STEPPED BACK INTO THOSE CLEATS AND THAT JERSEY...
...AND RE-TURNED TO RACING.
ZOOSH
THOSE WHO'VE TASTED ROCK BOTTOM BECOME TRULY STRONG!!
SHINKAI, HAKONE ACADEMY'S TAG #4...
FWOOM
FWOOM
FWOOM

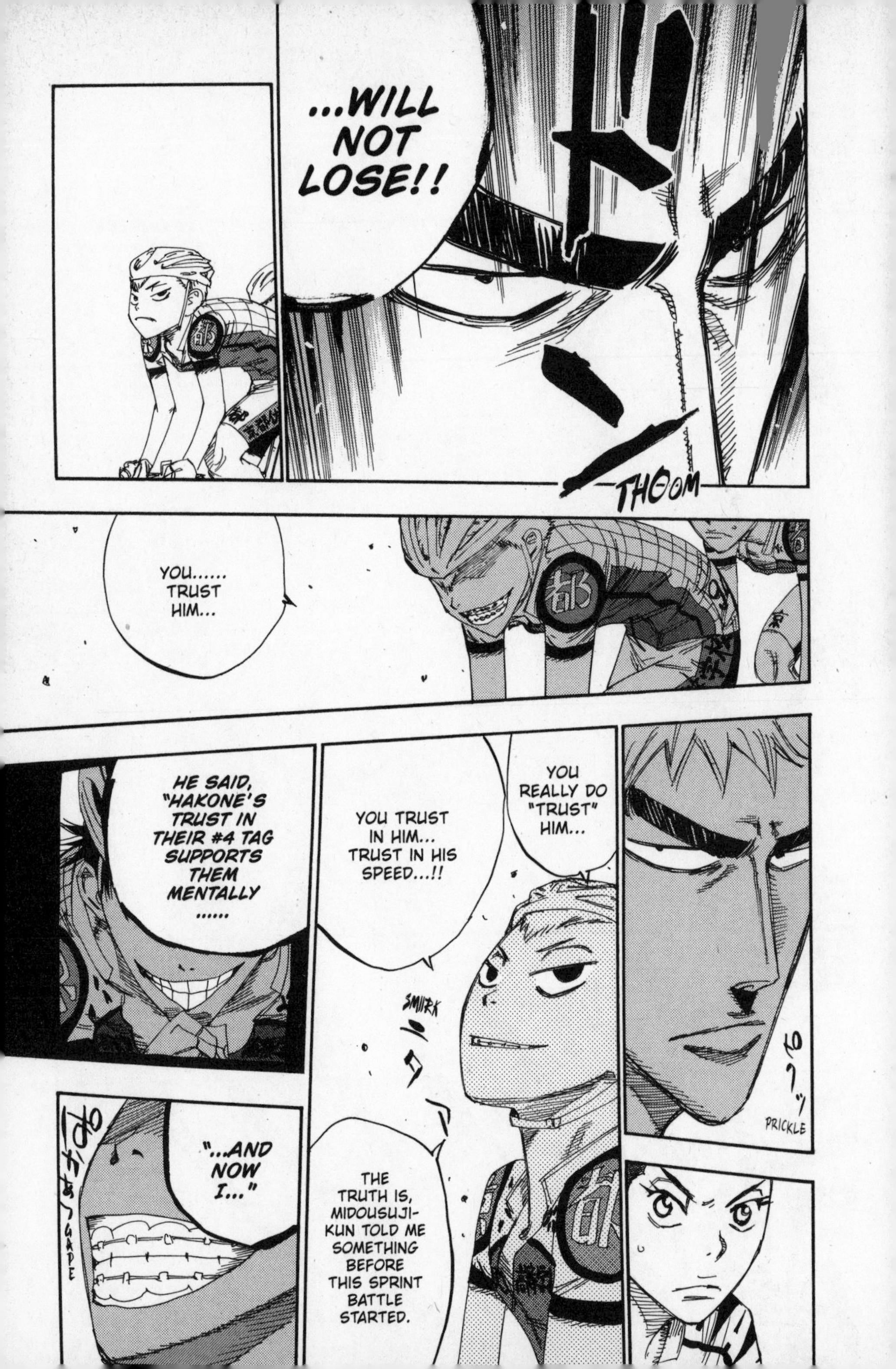

...WILL NOT LOSE!!
THOOM
YOU...... TRUST HIM...
PRICKLE
YOU REALLY DO "TRUST" HIM...
YOU TRUST IN HIM... TRUST IN HIS SPEED...!!
SMIRK
THE TRUTH IS, MIDOUSUJI-KUN TOLD ME SOMETHING BEFORE THIS SPRINT BATTLE STARTED.
HE SAID, "HAKONE'S TRUST IN THEIR #4 TAG SUPPORTS THEM MENTALLY ......
"...AND NOW I..."
GAPE

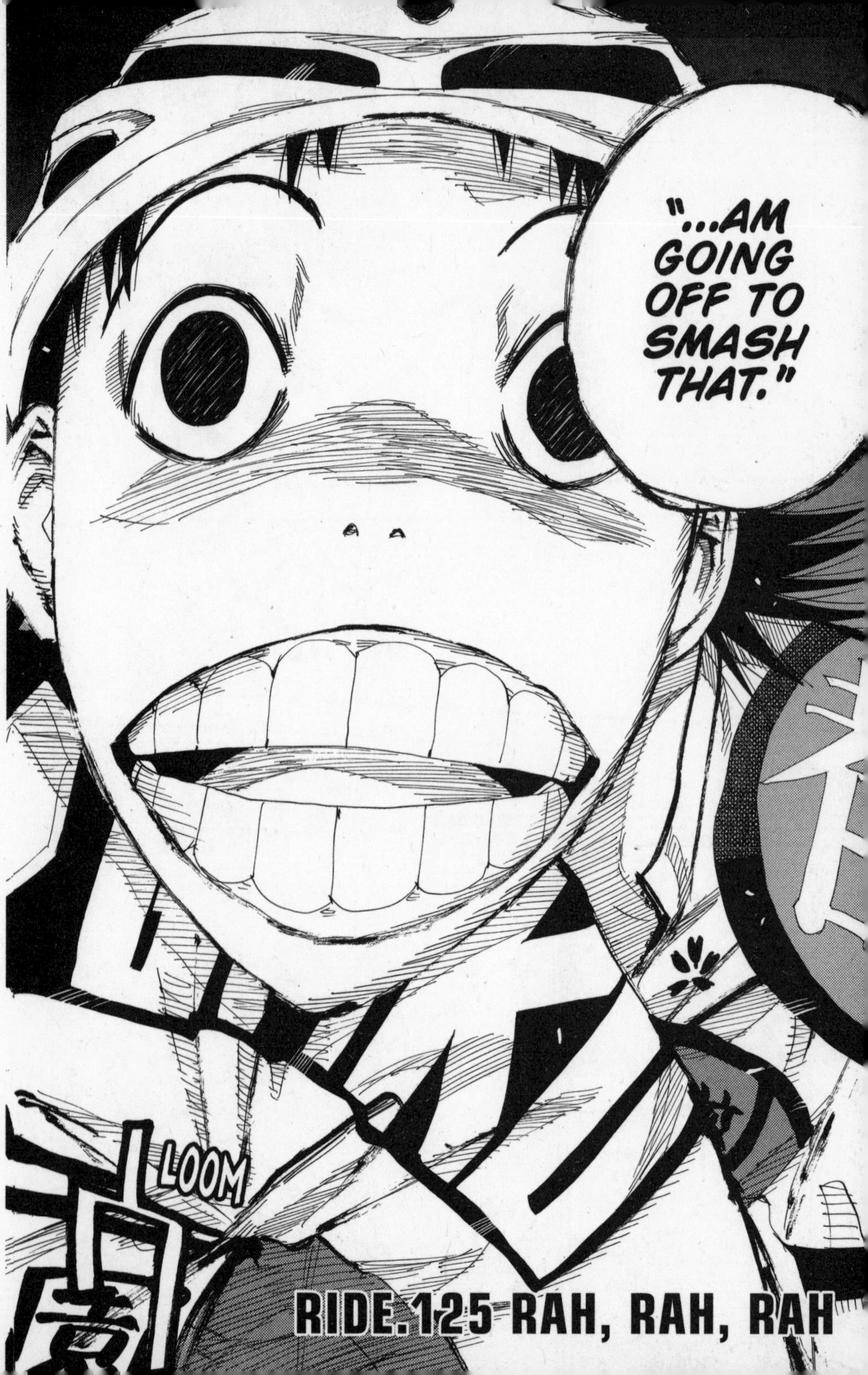
"...AM GOING OFF TO SMASH THAT."
LOOM
RIDE.125 RAH, RAH, RAH

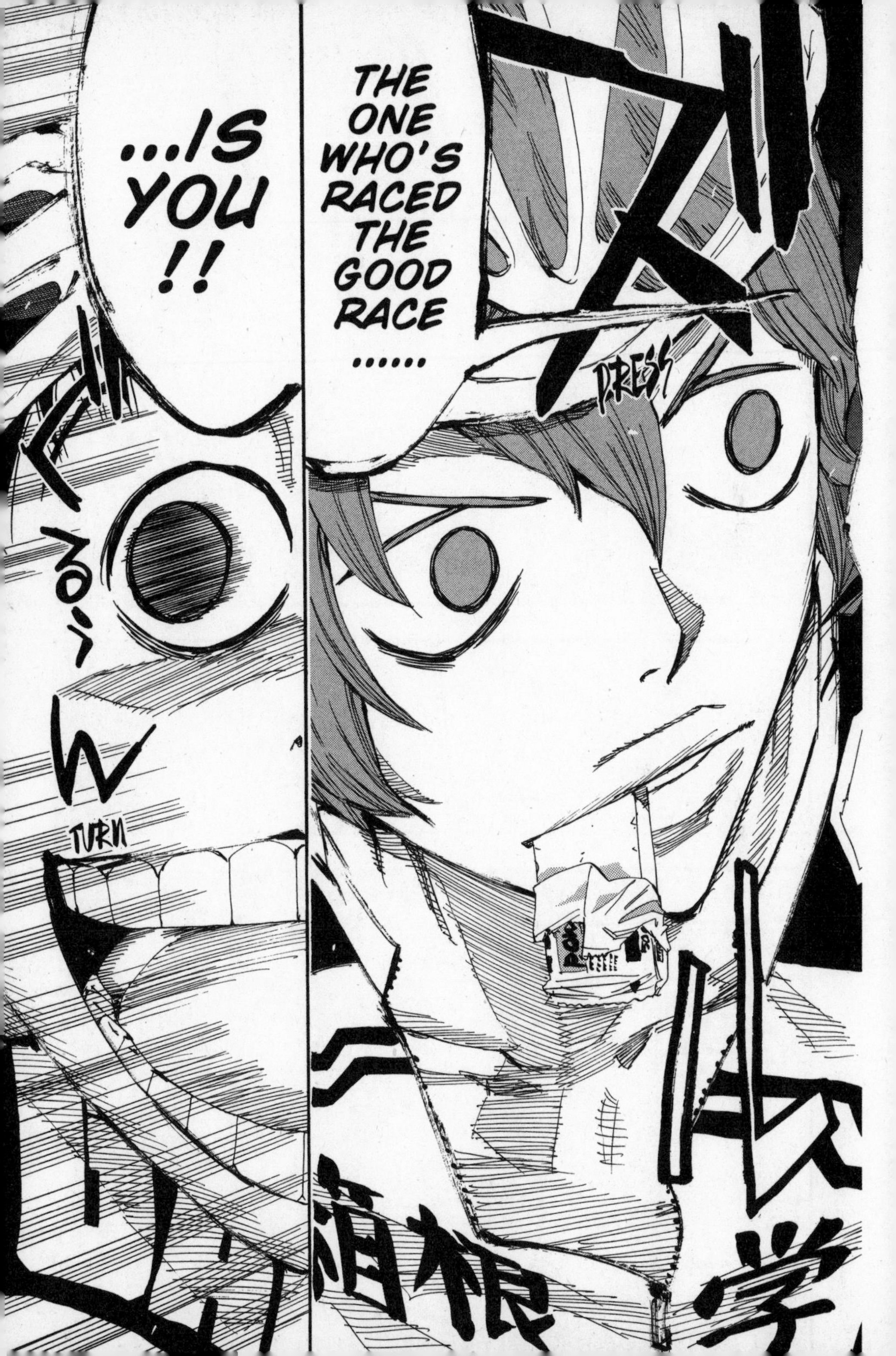
THE ONE WHO'S RACED THE GOOD RACE ......
PRESS
箱根学
...IS YOU!!
TURN

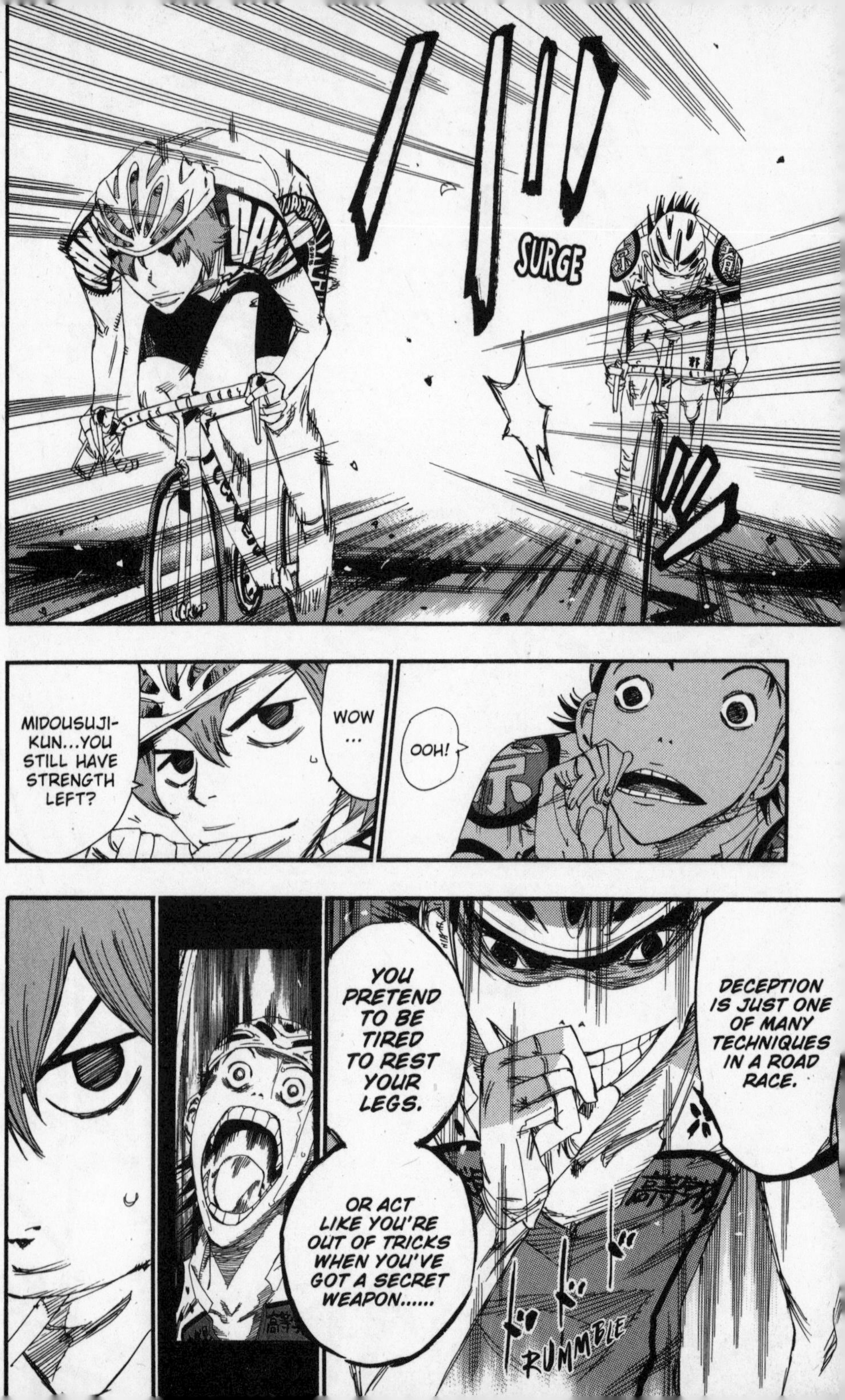
SURGE
OOH!
WOW ...
MIDOUSUJI-KUN...YOU STILL HAVE STRENGTH LEFT?
DECEPTION IS JUST ONE OF MANY TECHNIQUES IN A ROAD RACE.
YOU PRETEND TO BE TIRED TO REST YOUR LEGS.
OR ACT LIKE YOU'RE OUT OF TRICKS WHEN YOU'VE GOT A SECRET WEAPON......
RUMMBLE

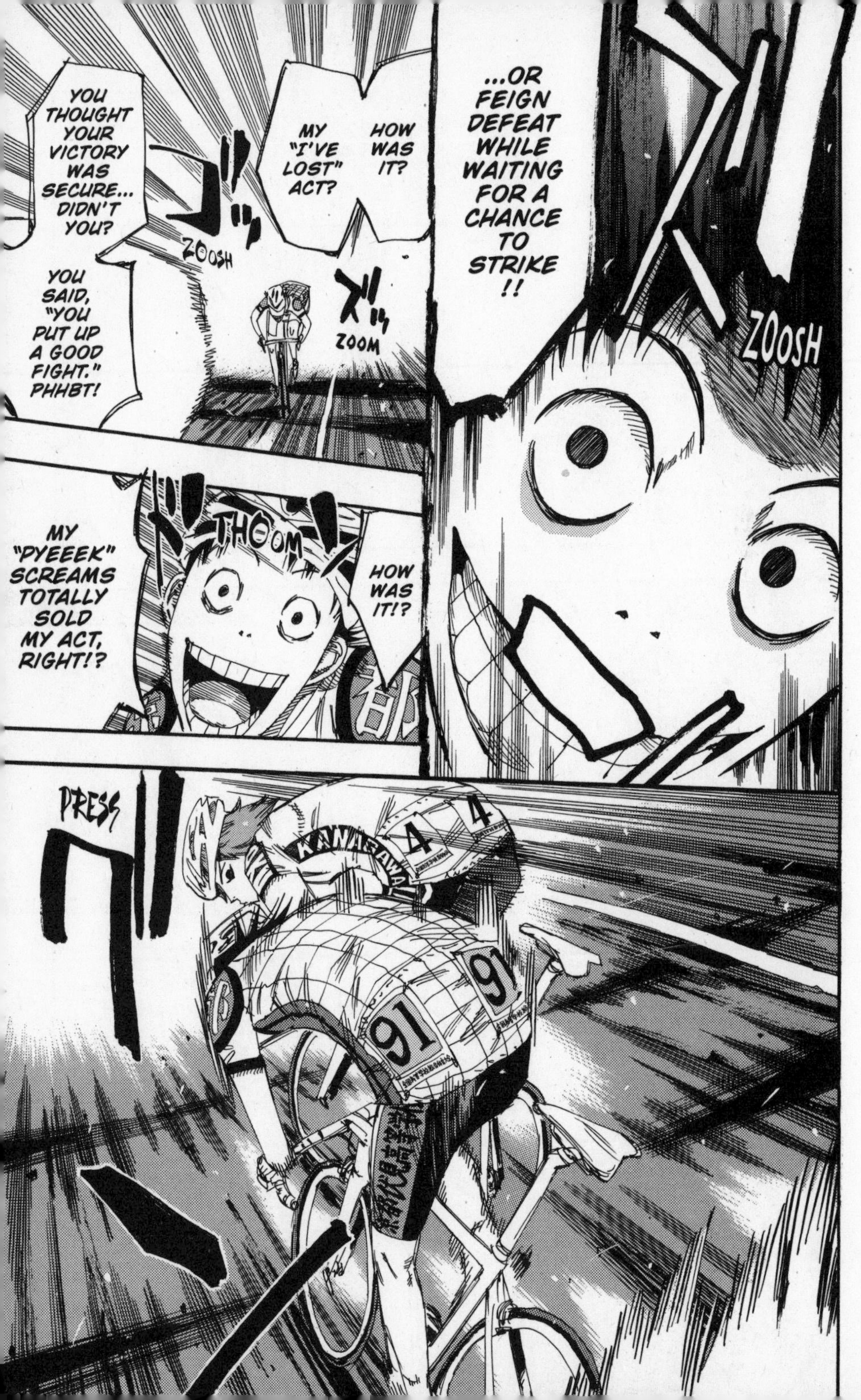
...OR FEIGN DEFEAT WHILE WAITING FOR A CHANCE TO STRIKE!!
ZOOSH
HOW WAS IT?
MY "I'VE LOST" ACT?
YOU THOUGHT YOUR VICTORY WAS SECURE... DIDN'T YOU?
ZOOSH
ZOOM
YOU SAID, "YOU PUT UP A GOOD FIGHT." PHHBT!
THOOM
HOW WAS IT!?
MY "PYEEEK" SCREAMS TOTALLY SOLD MY ACT, RIGHT!?
PRESS

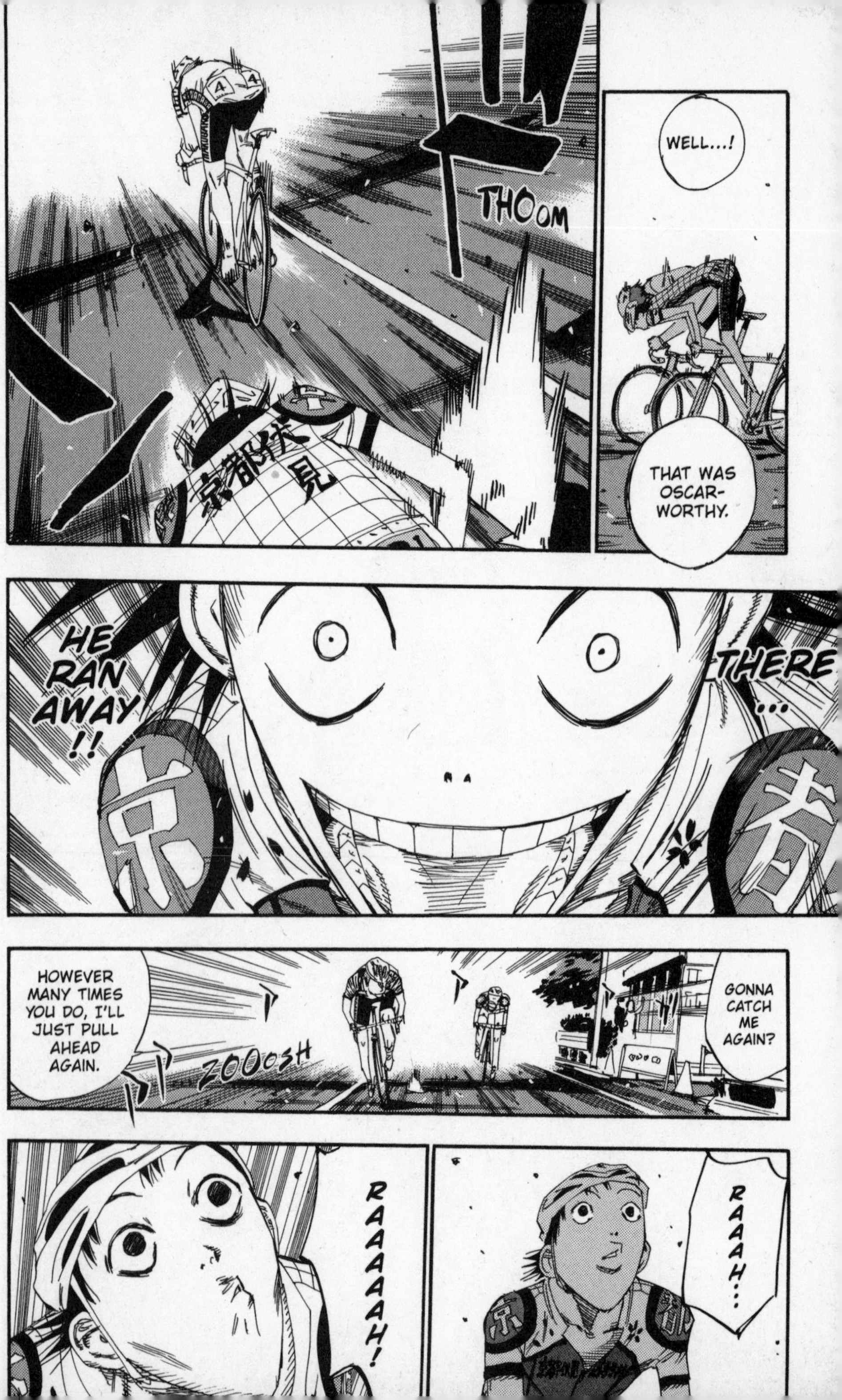
WELL...!
THAT WAS OSCAR-WORTHY.
THOOM
京都伏見
THERE...
HE RAN AWAY!!
GONNA CATCH ME AGAIN?
HOWEVER MANY TIMES YOU DO, I'LL JUST PULL AHEAD AGAIN.
ZOOOSH
RAAAH...
RAAAAAAH!

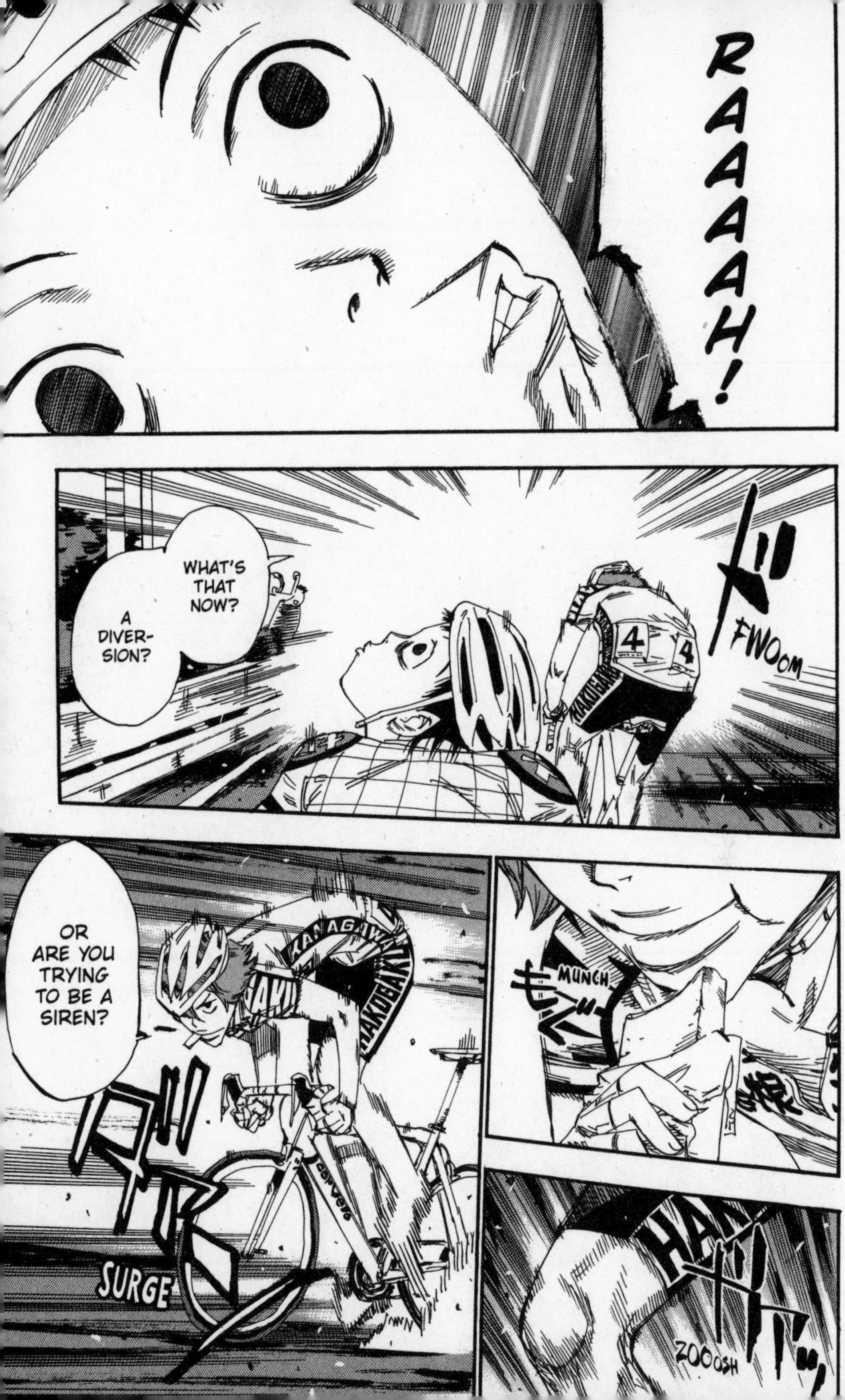
RAAAAAH!
WHAT'S THAT NOW?
A DIVERSION?
FWOOM
MUNCH
ZOOOSH
OR ARE YOU TRYING TO BE A SIREN?
SURGE

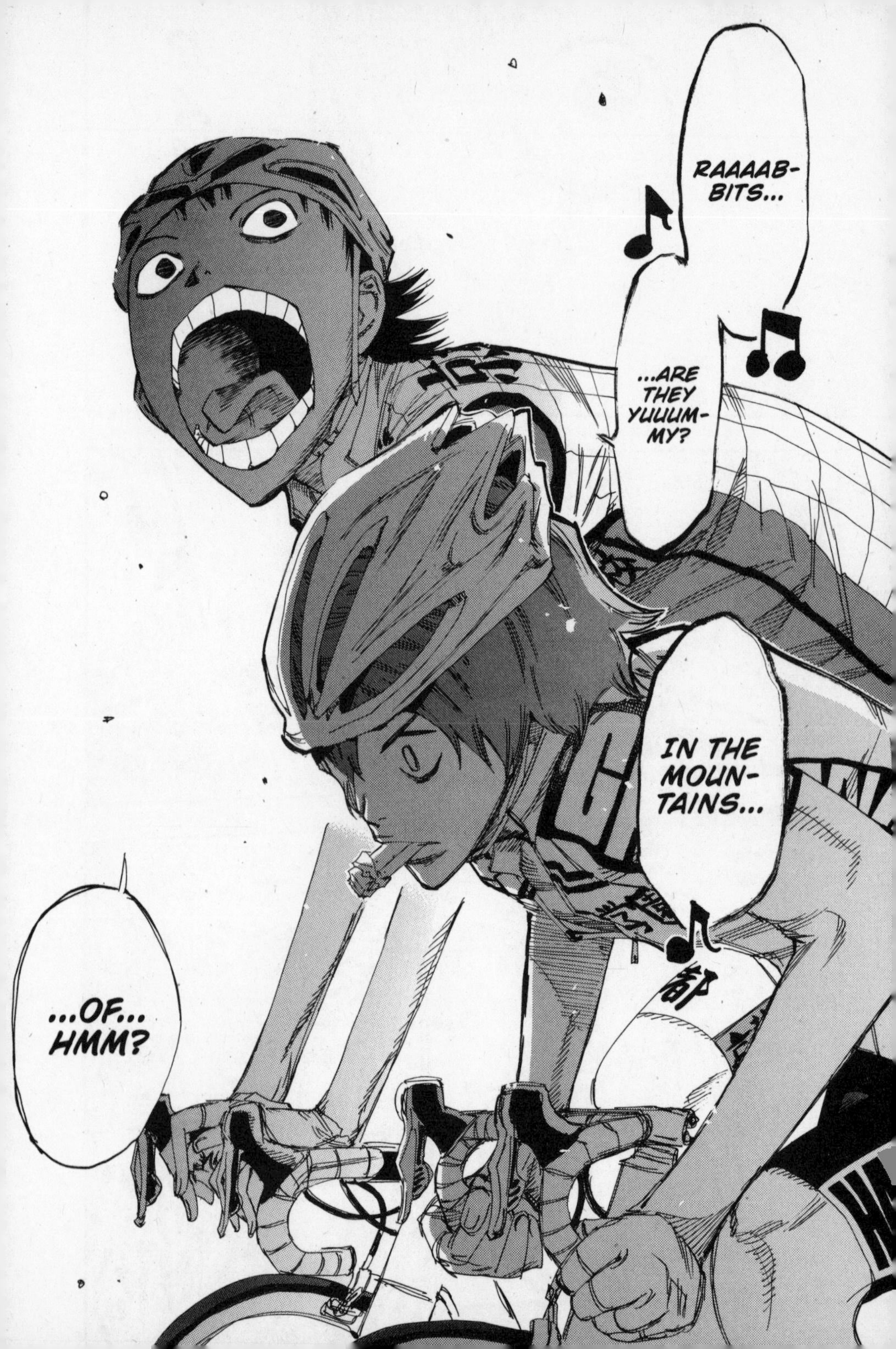
RAAAAB-BITS...
...ARE THEY YUUUM-MY?
IN THE MOUN-TAINS...
...OF... HMM?

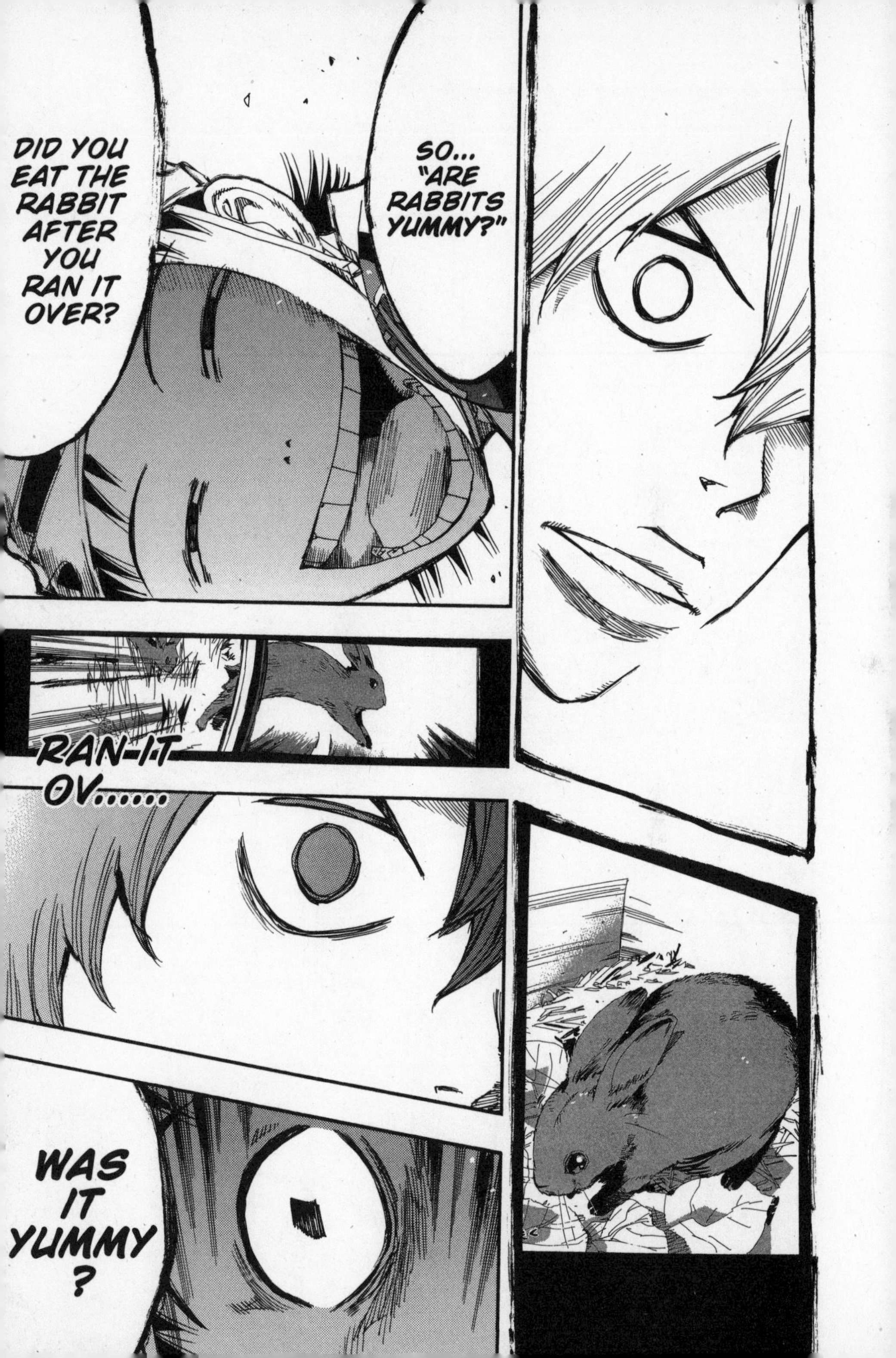
SO... "ARE RABBITS YUMMY?"
DID YOU EAT THE RABBIT AFTER YOU RAN IT OVER?
RAN-IT OV......
WAS IT YUMMY?

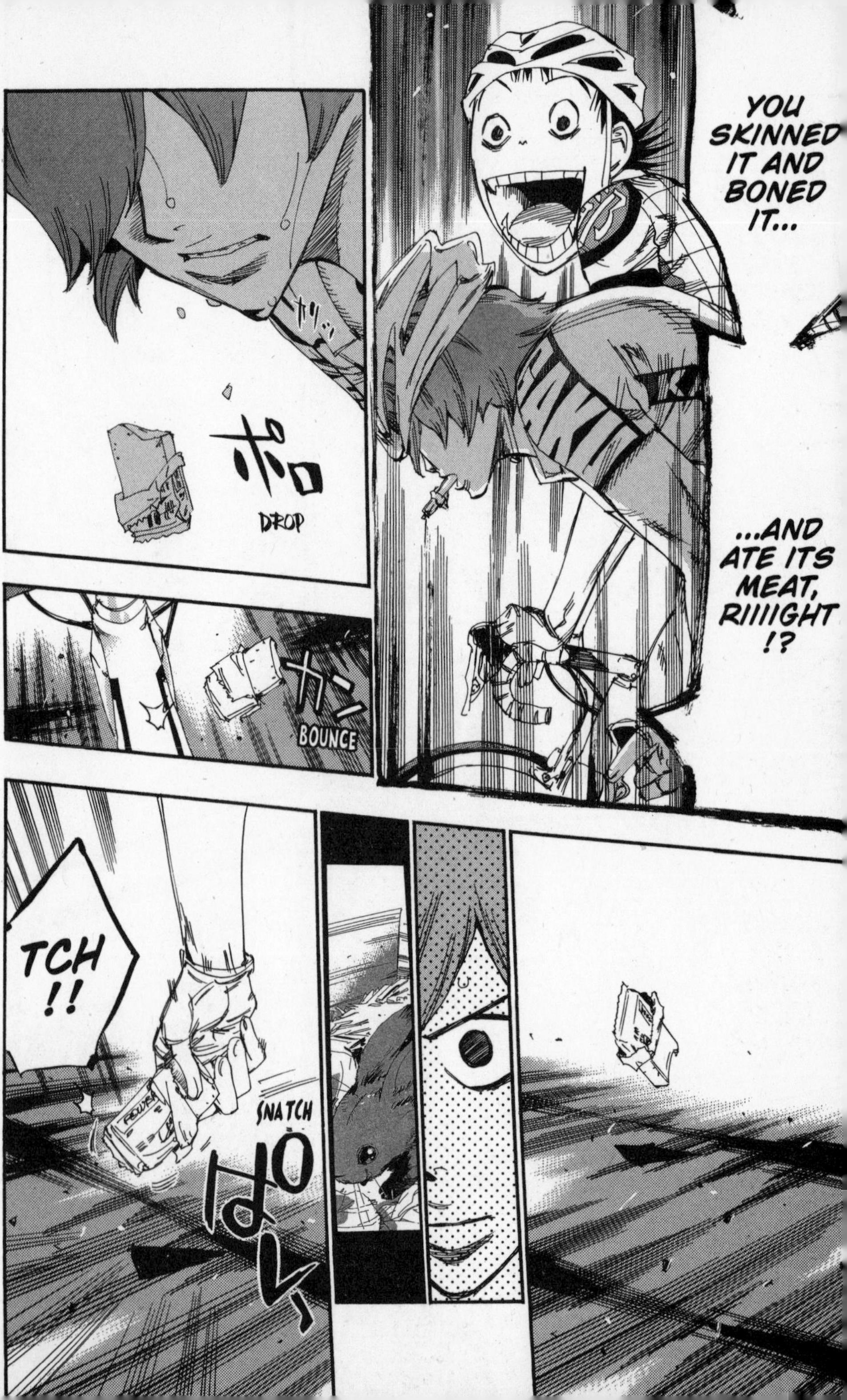
YOU SKINNED IT AND BONED IT...
...AND ATE ITS MEAT, RIIIIGHT !?
ポロ
DROP
カン
BOUNCE
TCH !!
SNATCH

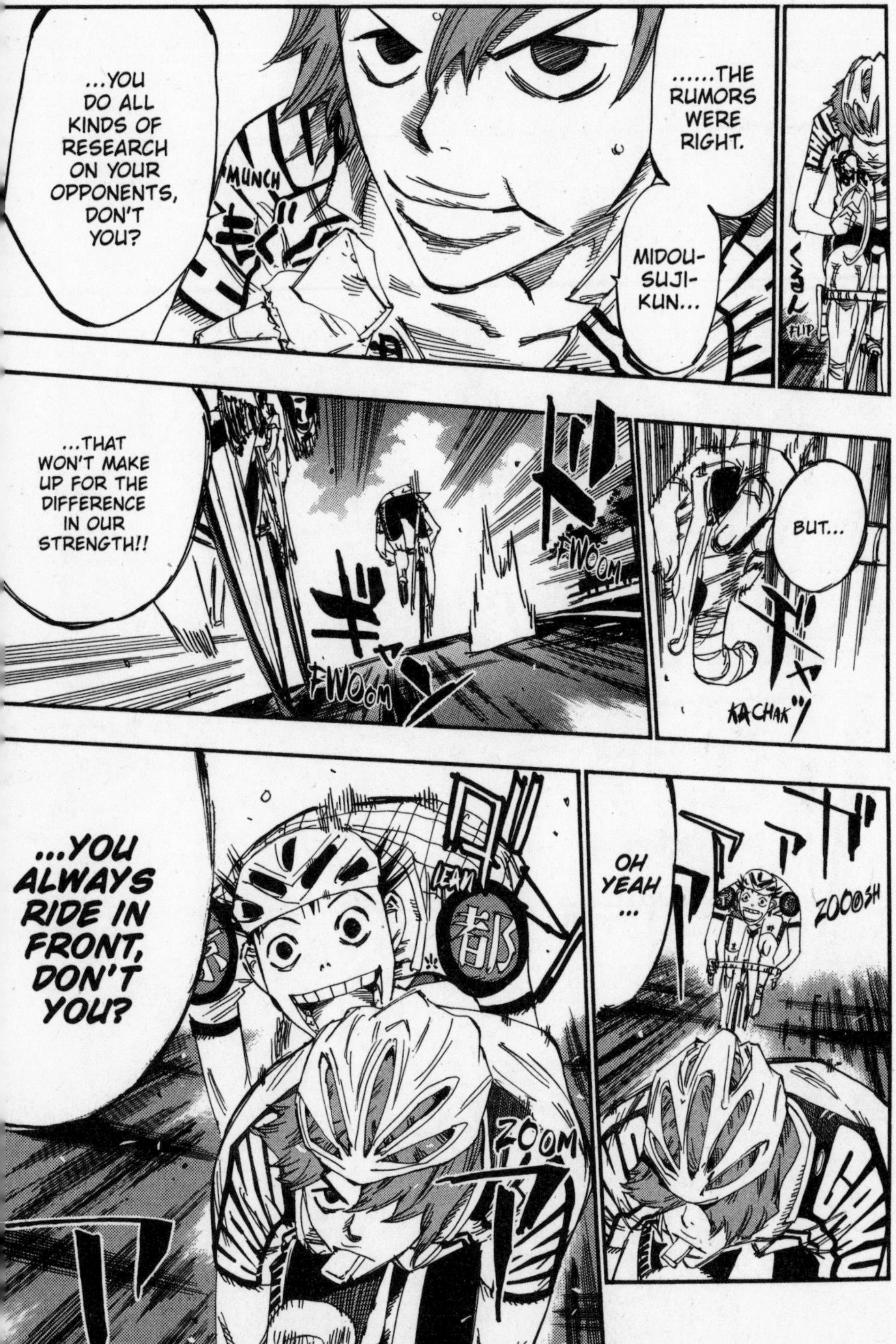
FLIP
......THE RUMORS WERE RIGHT.
MIDOU-SUJI-KUN...
...YOU DO ALL KINDS OF RESEARCH ON YOUR OPPONENTS, DON'T YOU?
MUNCH
BUT...
KACHAK
...THAT WON'T MAKE UP FOR THE DIFFERENCE IN OUR STRENGTH!!
FWOOM
FWOOM
OH YEAH ...
ZOOOSH
...YOU ALWAYS RIDE IN FRONT, DON'T YOU?
LEAN
ZOOM

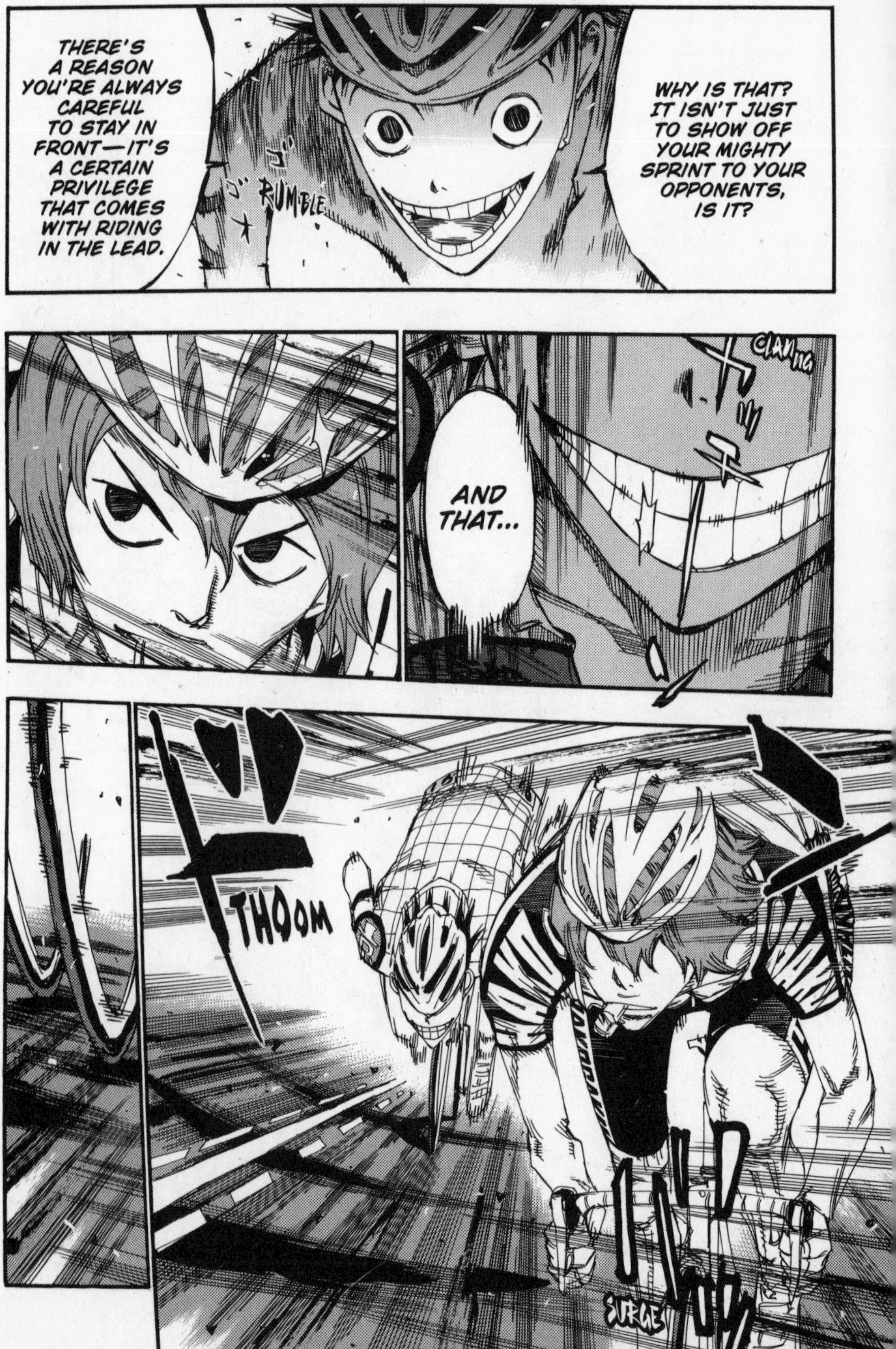
WHY IS THAT? IT ISN'T JUST TO SHOW OFF YOUR MIGHTY SPRINT TO YOUR OPPONENTS, IS IT?
THERE'S A REASON YOU'RE ALWAYS CAREFUL TO STAY IN FRONT—IT'S A CERTAIN PRIVILEGE THAT COMES WITH RIDING IN THE LEAD.
RUMBLE
CLANNG
AND THAT...
THOOM
SURGE

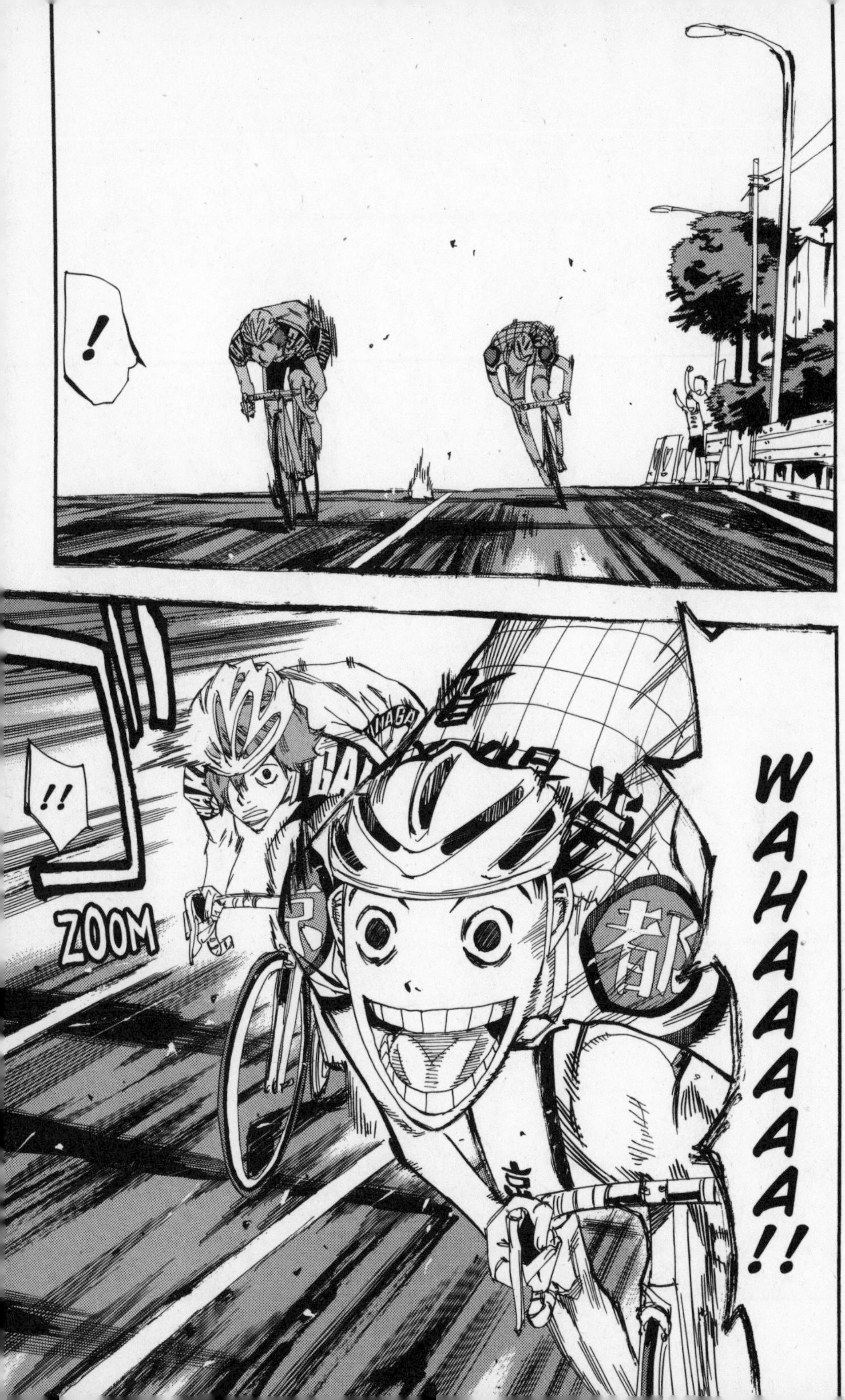
!
WAHAAAAAA!!
!!
ZOOM

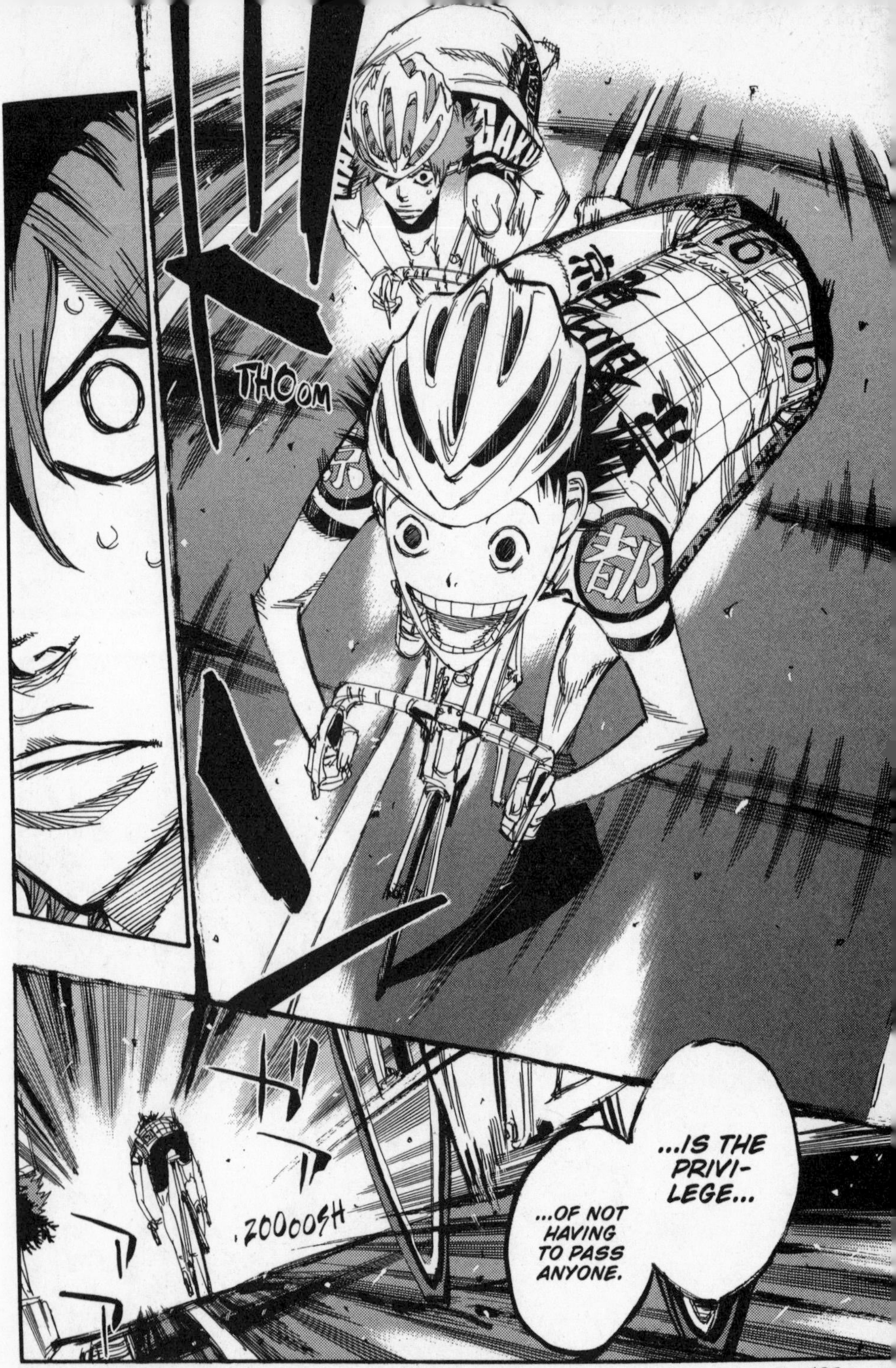
THOOM
...IS THE PRIVI-LEGE...
...OF NOT HAVING TO PASS ANYONE.
ZOOOOSH

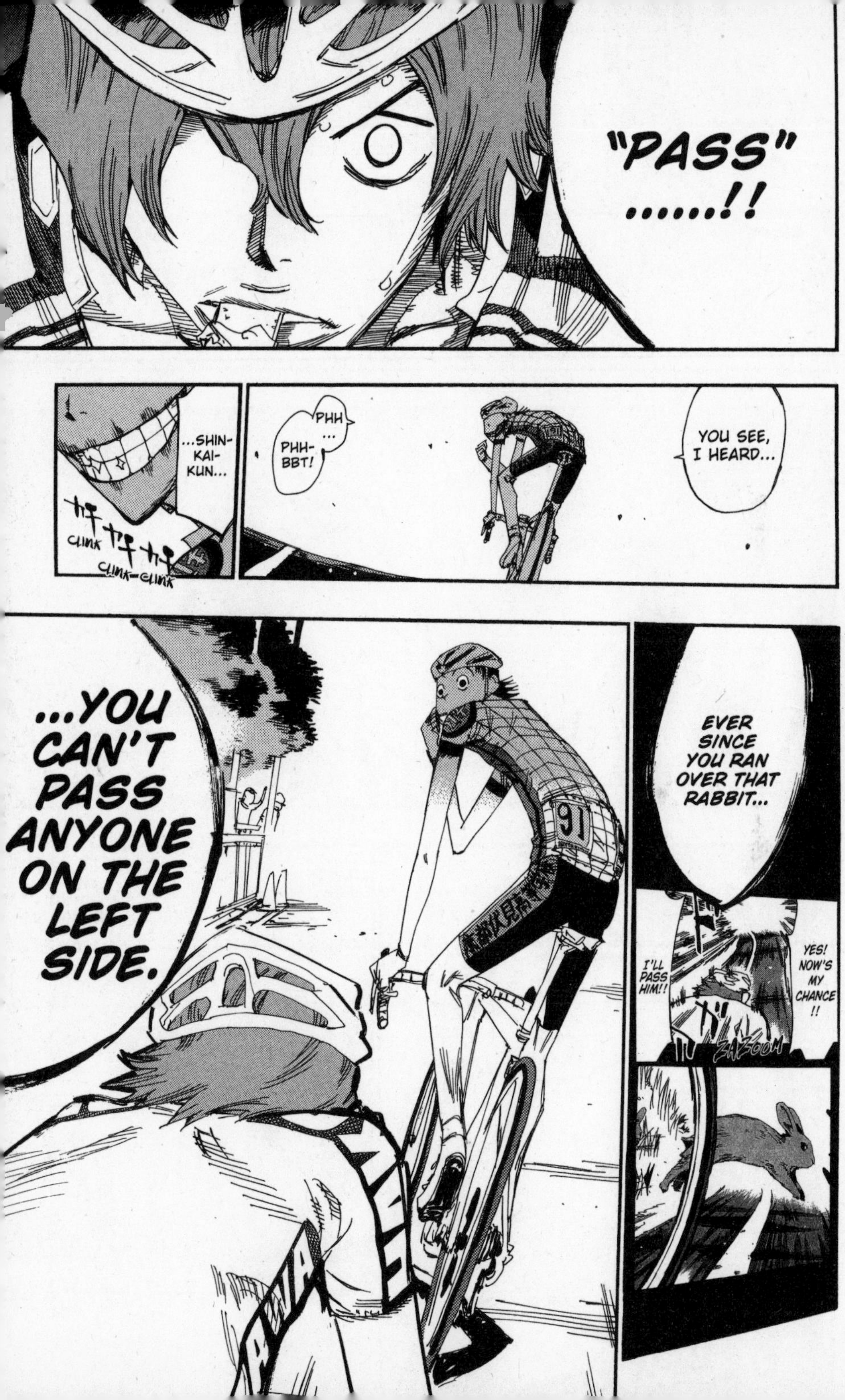

"PASS" ......!!
YOU SEE, I HEARD...
PHH ... PHH-BBT!
...SHIN-KAI-KUN...
CLINK
CLINK-CLINK
EVER SINCE YOU RAN OVER THAT RABBIT...
YES! NOW'S MY CHANCE !!
I'LL PASS HIM!!
ZAZOOM
...YOU CAN'T PASS ANYONE ON THE LEFT SIDE.

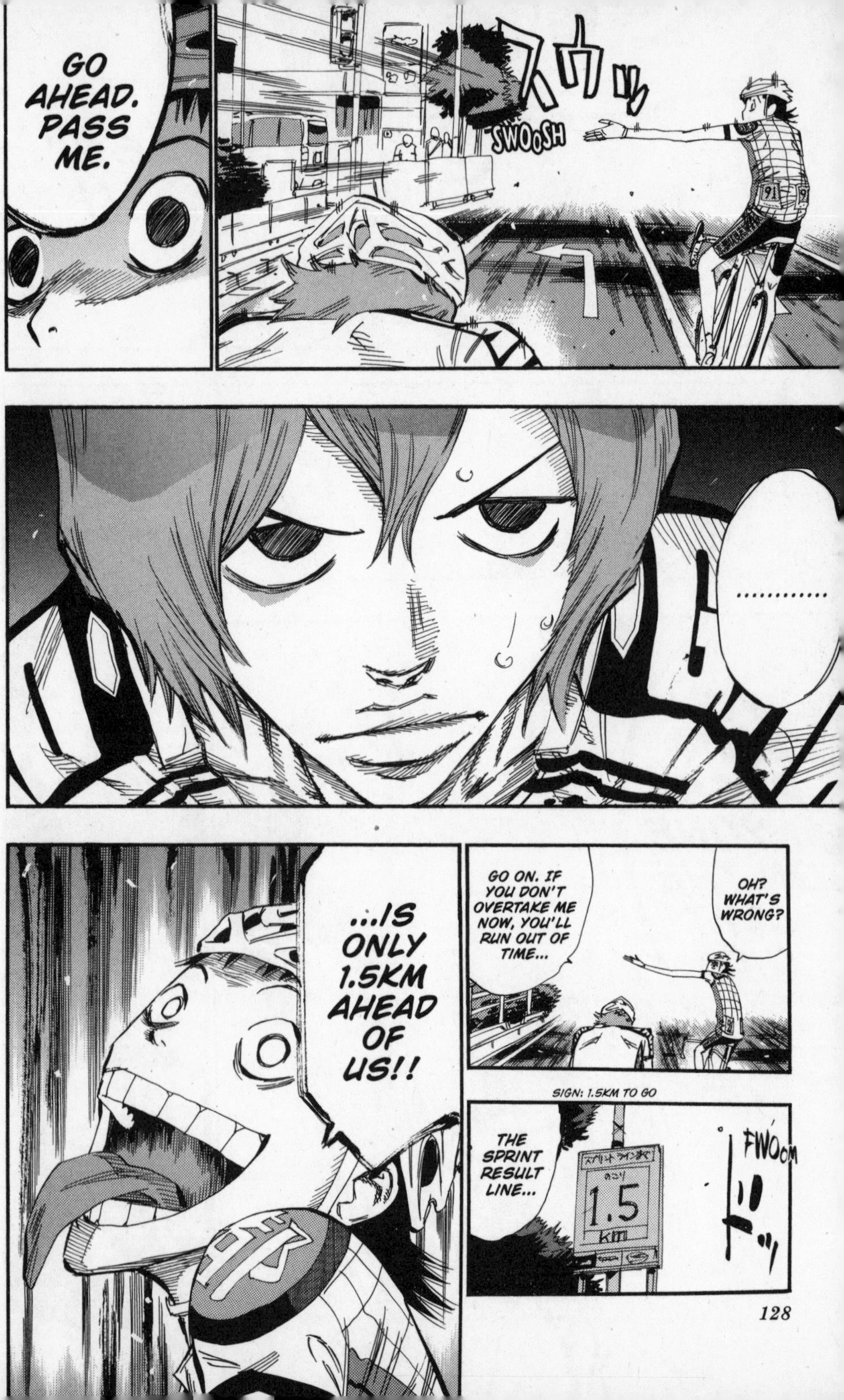
SWOOSH
GO AHEAD. PASS ME.
....
OH? WHAT'S WRONG?
GO ON. IF YOU DON'T OVERTAKE ME NOW, YOU'LL RUN OUT OF TIME...
SIGN: 1.5KM TO GO
FWOOM
THE SPRINT RESULT LINE...
1.5
km
...IS ONLY 1.5KM AHEAD OF US!!

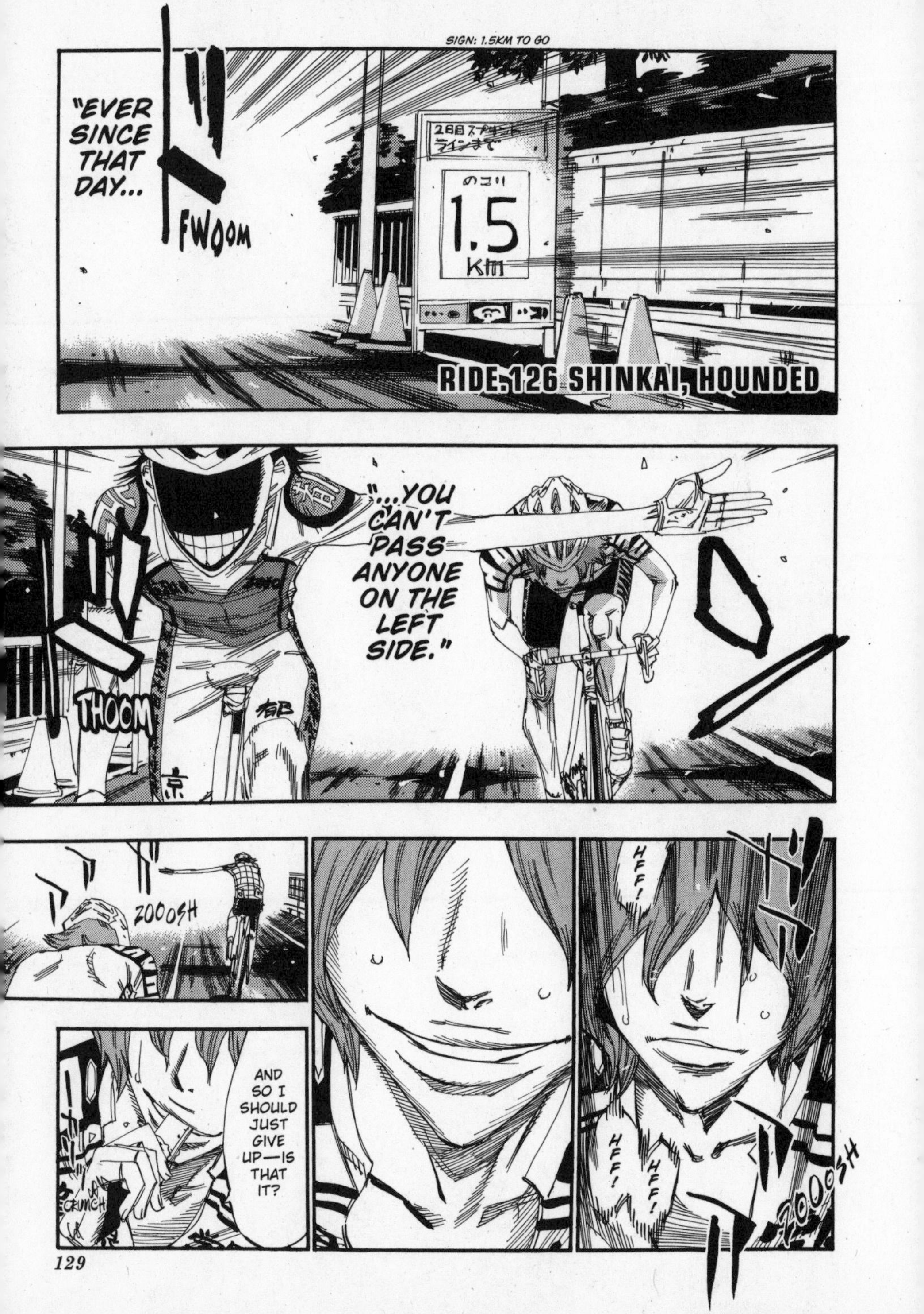
SIGN: 1.5KM TO GO
"EVER SINCE THAT DAY...
FWOOM
のこり
1.5
Km
RIDE.126 SHINKAI, HOUNDED
"...YOU CAN'T PASS ANYONE ON THE LEFT SIDE."
THOOM
HFF!
HFF!
HFF!
ZOOOSH
ZOOOSH
AND SO I SHOULD JUST GIVE UP—IS THAT IT?
CRUNCH

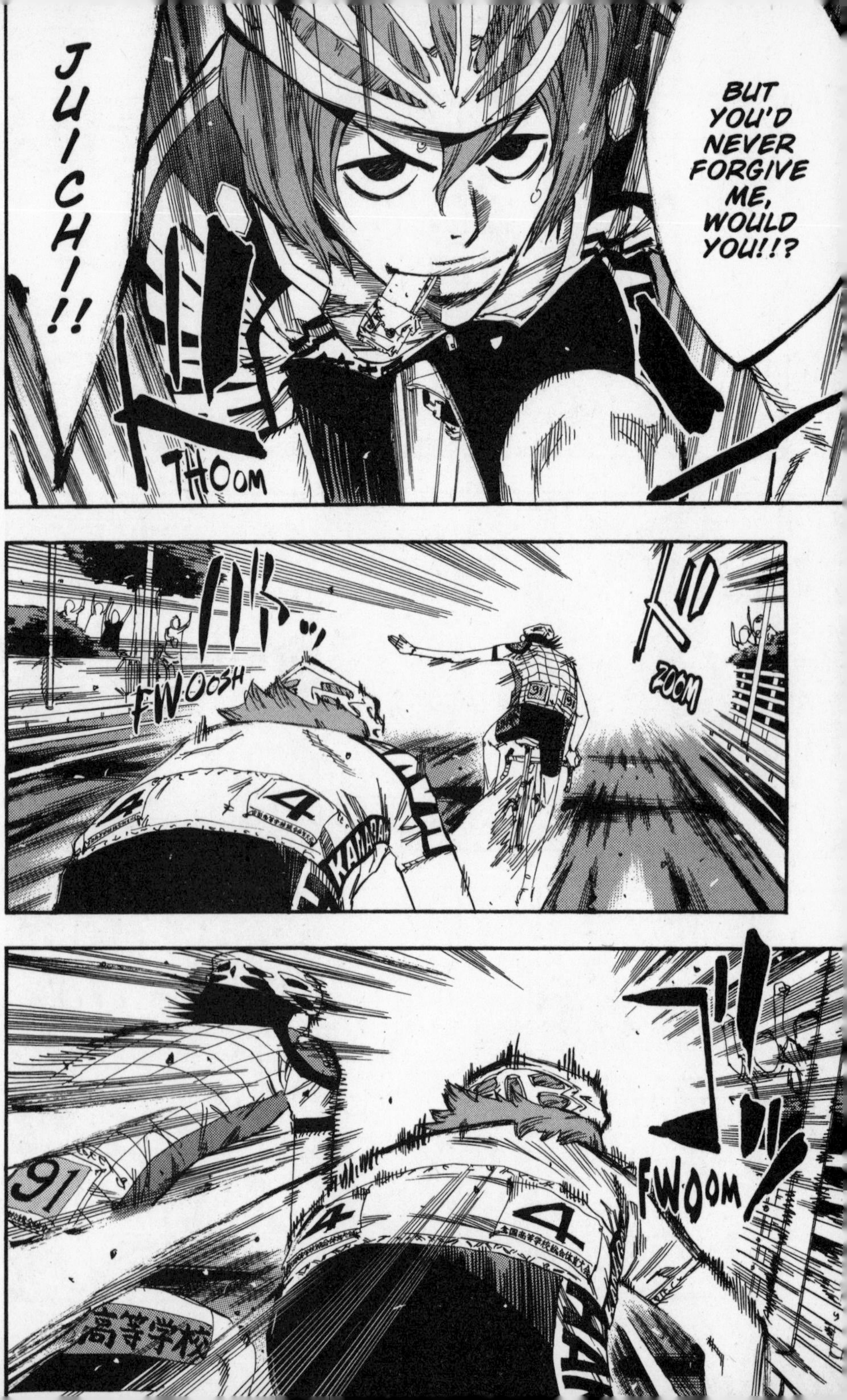
BUT YOU'D NEVER FORGIVE ME, WOULD YOU!!?
JUICHI!!
THOOM
ZOOM
FWOOSH
FWOOM
高等学校

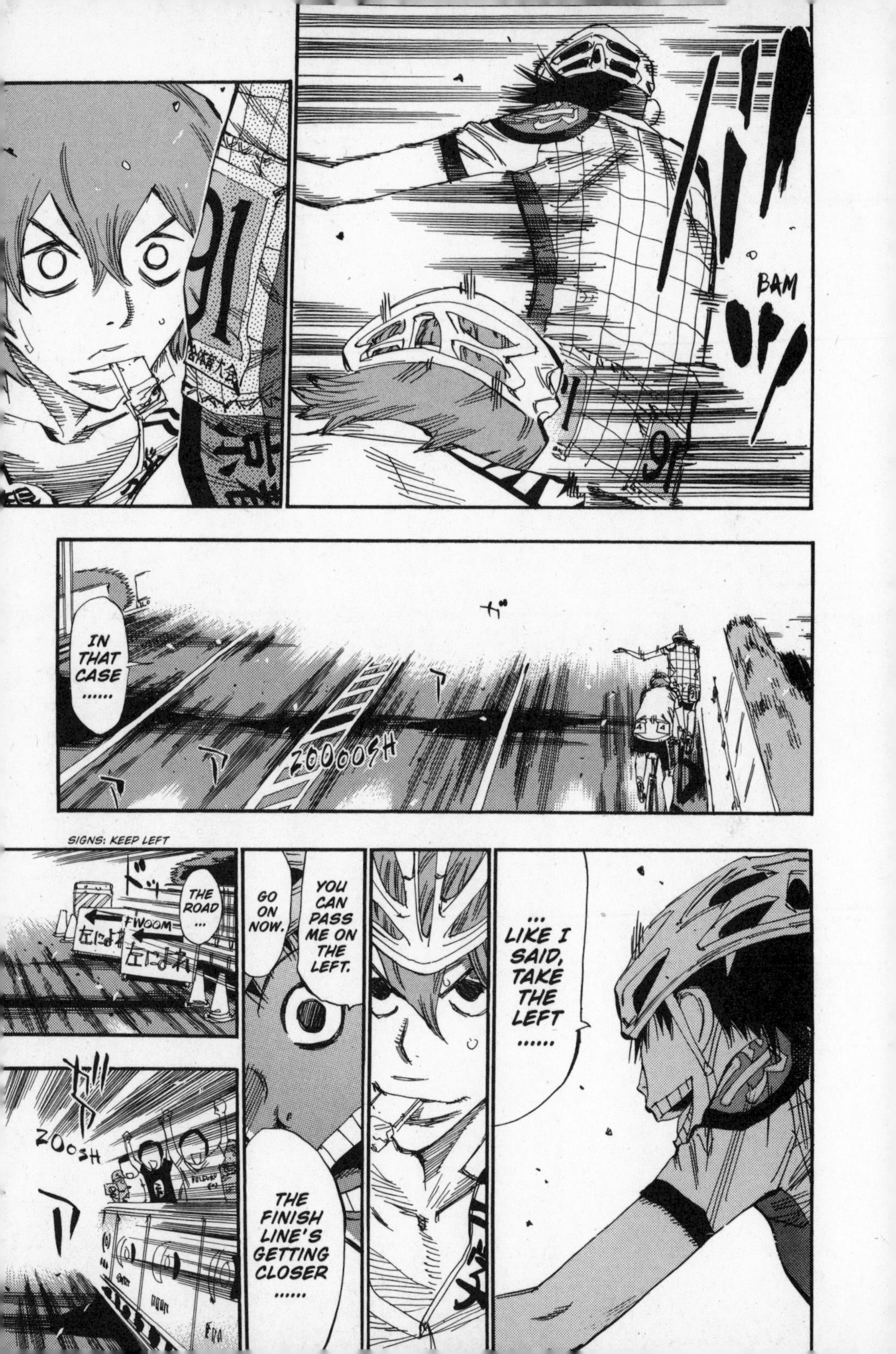
BAM
IN THAT CASE ......
ZOOOOOSH
SIGNS: KEEP LEFT
... LIKE I SAID, TAKE THE LEFT ......
YOU CAN PASS ME ON THE LEFT.
GO ON NOW.
THE FINISH LINE'S GETTING CLOSER ......
THE ROAD ...
FWOOM
左によれ
左によれ
ZOOSH

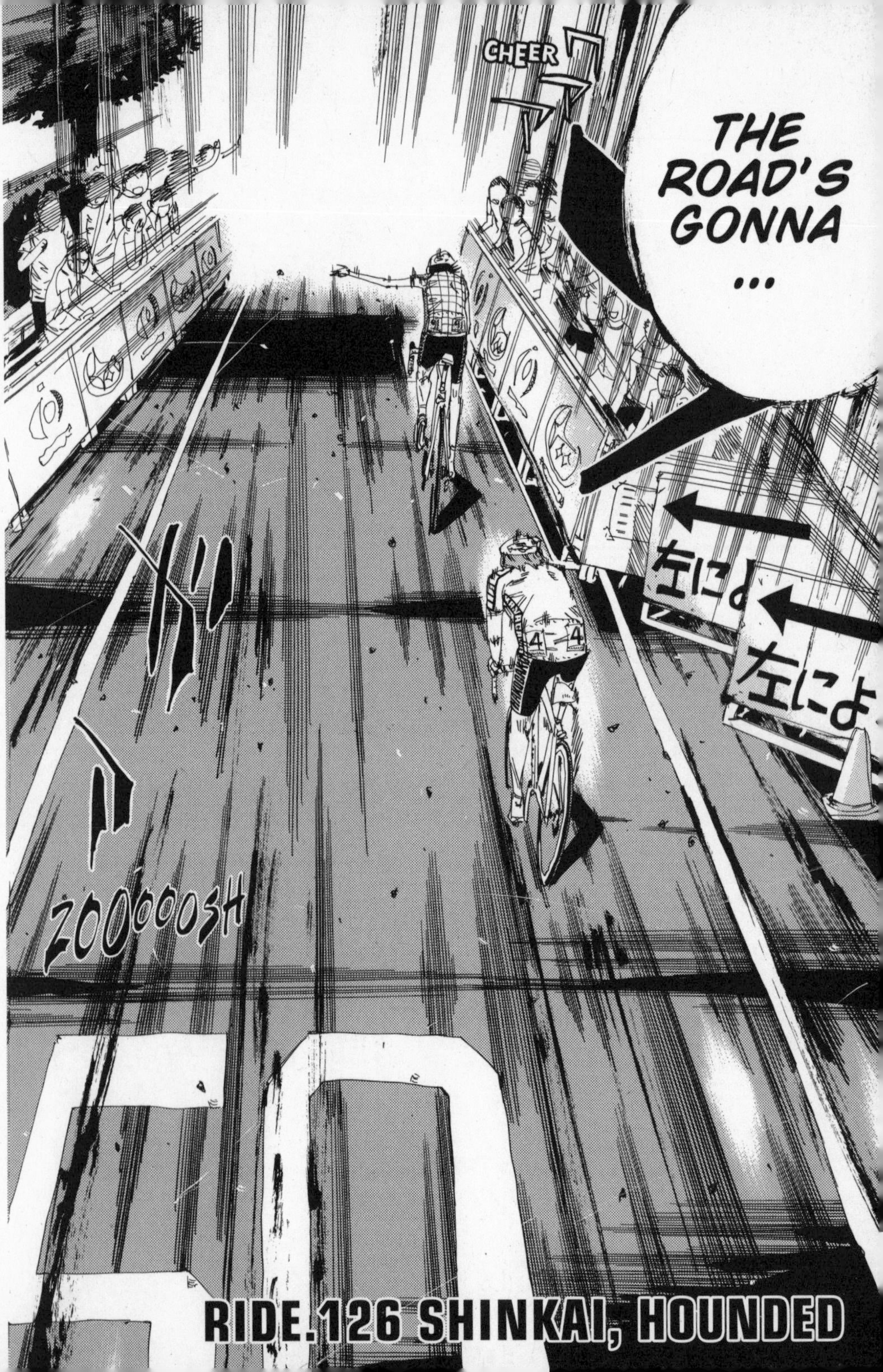
THE ROAD'S GONNA ...
CHEER
左によ
左によ
ZOOOOOOSH

RIDE.126 SHINKAI, HOUNDED

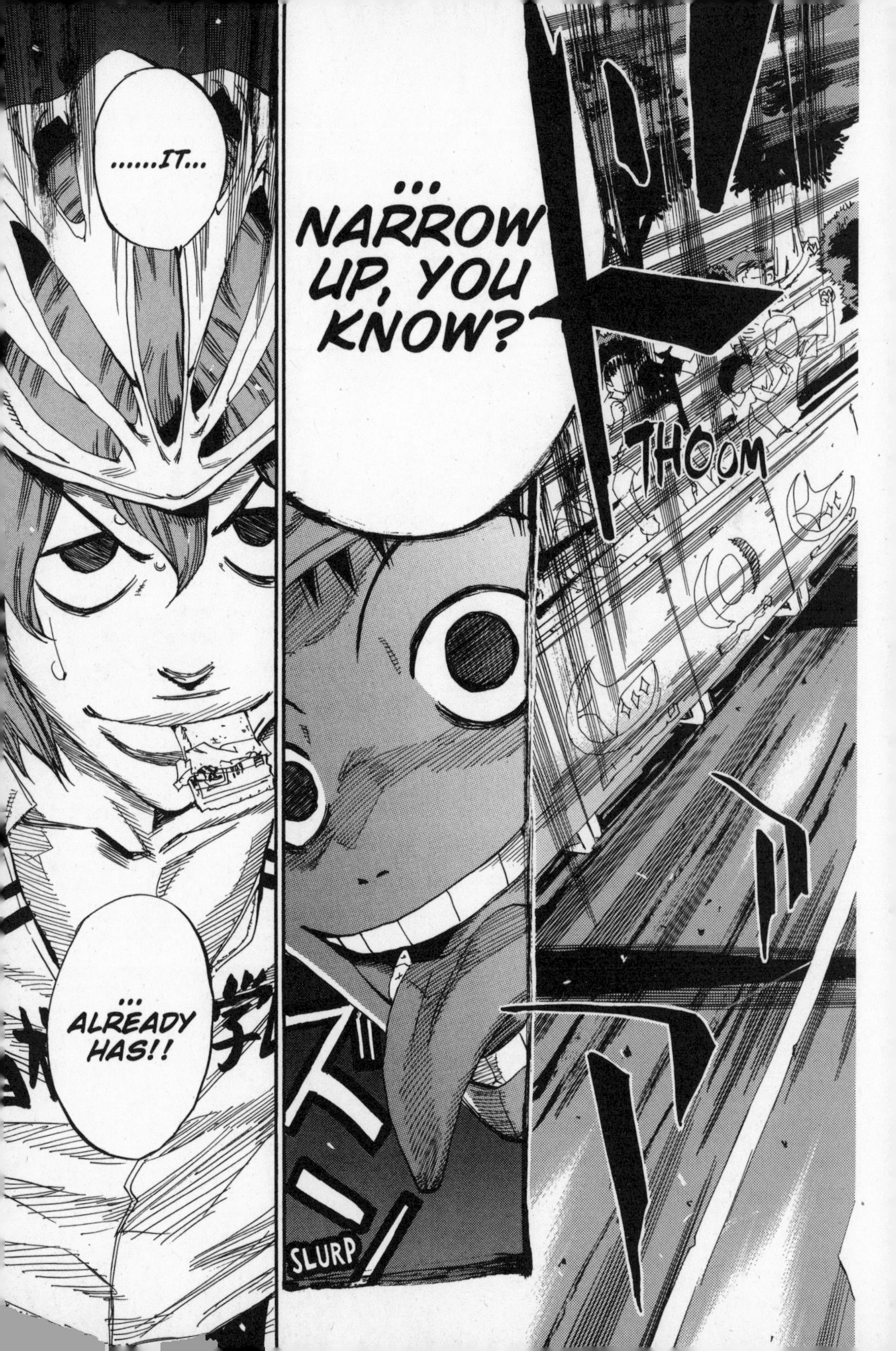
THOOM
... NARROW UP, YOU KNOW?
SLURP
......IT...
... ALREADY HAS!!

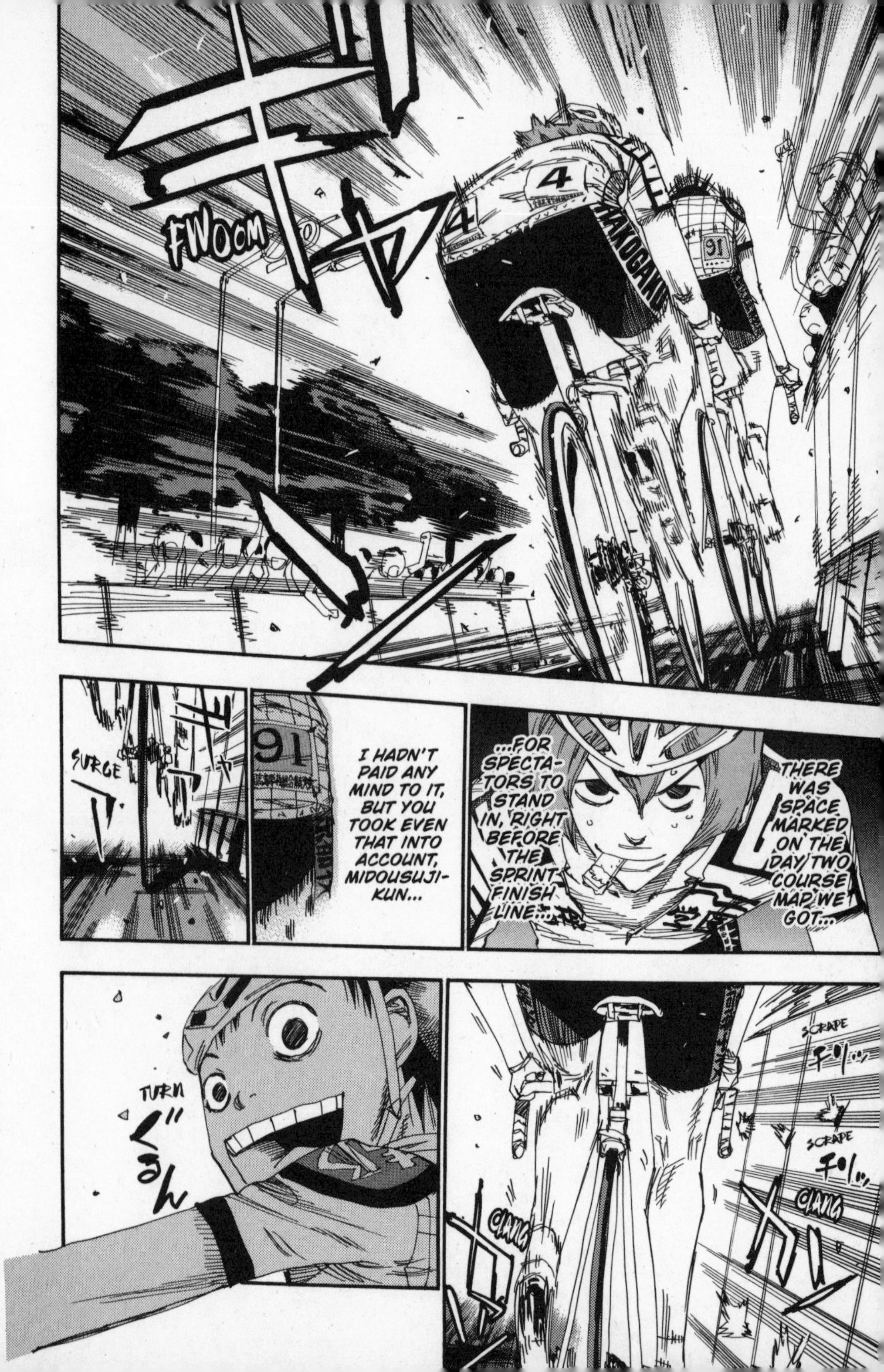
FWOOM
THERE WAS SPACE MARKED ON THE DAY TWO COURSE MAP WE GOT...
...FOR SPECTATORS TO STAND IN, RIGHT BEFORE THE SPRINT FINISH LINE...
I HADN'T PAID ANY MIND TO IT, BUT YOU TOOK EVEN THAT INTO ACCOUNT, MIDOUSUJI-KUN...
SURGE
SCRAPE
SCRAPE
CLANG
CLANG
TURN

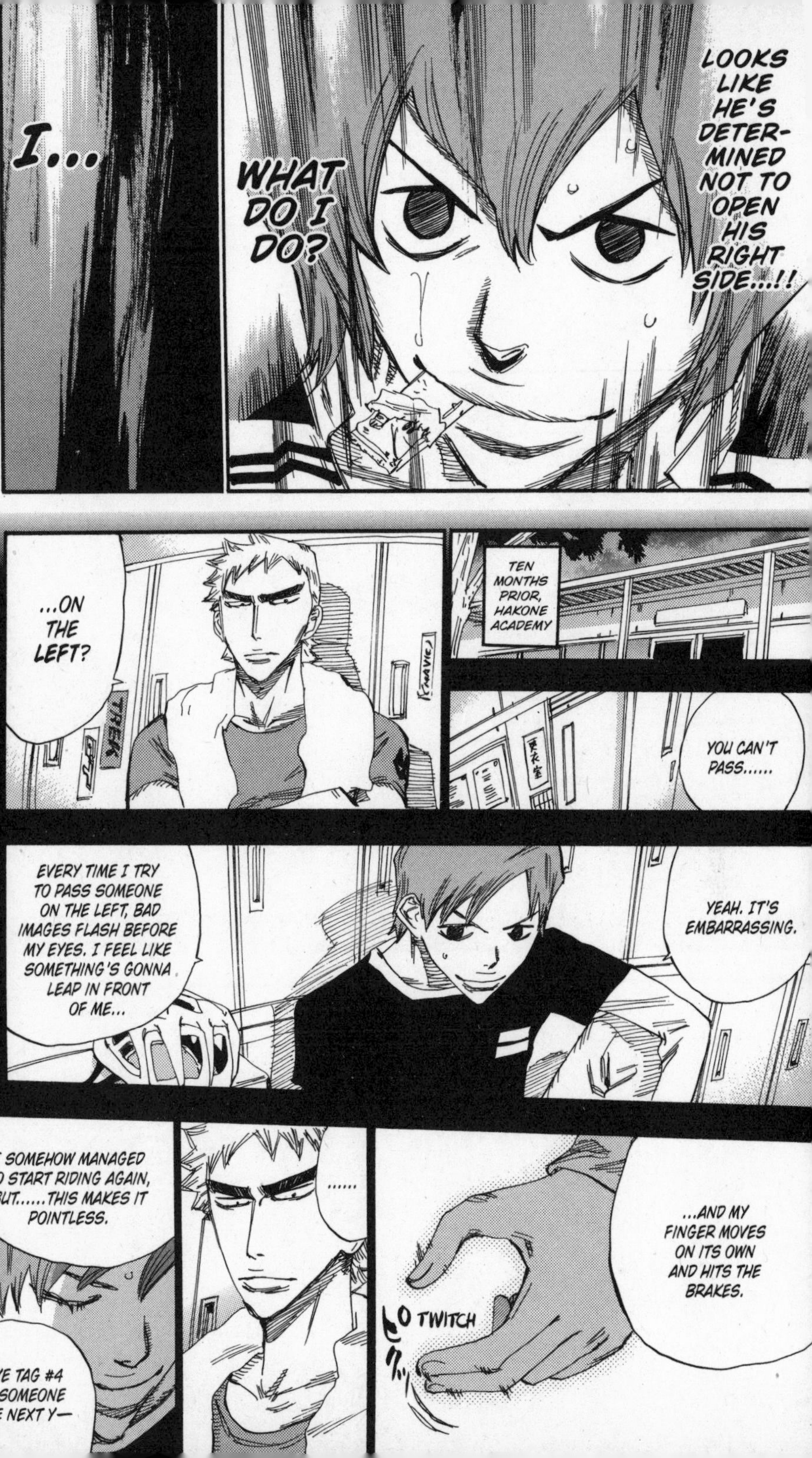
LOOKS LIKE HE'S DETERMINED NOT TO OPEN HIS RIGHT SIDE...!!
WHAT DO I DO?
I...
TEN MONTHS PRIOR, HAKONE ACADEMY
YOU CAN'T PASS......
...ON THE LEFT?
YEAH. IT'S EMBARRASSING.
EVERY TIME I TRY TO PASS SOMEONE ON THE LEFT, BAD IMAGES FLASH BEFORE MY EYES. I FEEL LIKE SOMETHING'S GONNA LEAP IN FRONT OF ME...
...AND MY FINGER MOVES ON ITS OWN AND HITS THE BRAKES.
TWITCH
......
I SOMEHOW MANAGED TO START RIDING AGAIN, BUT......THIS MAKES IT POINTLESS.
GIVE TAG #4 TO SOMEONE ELSE NEXT Y—

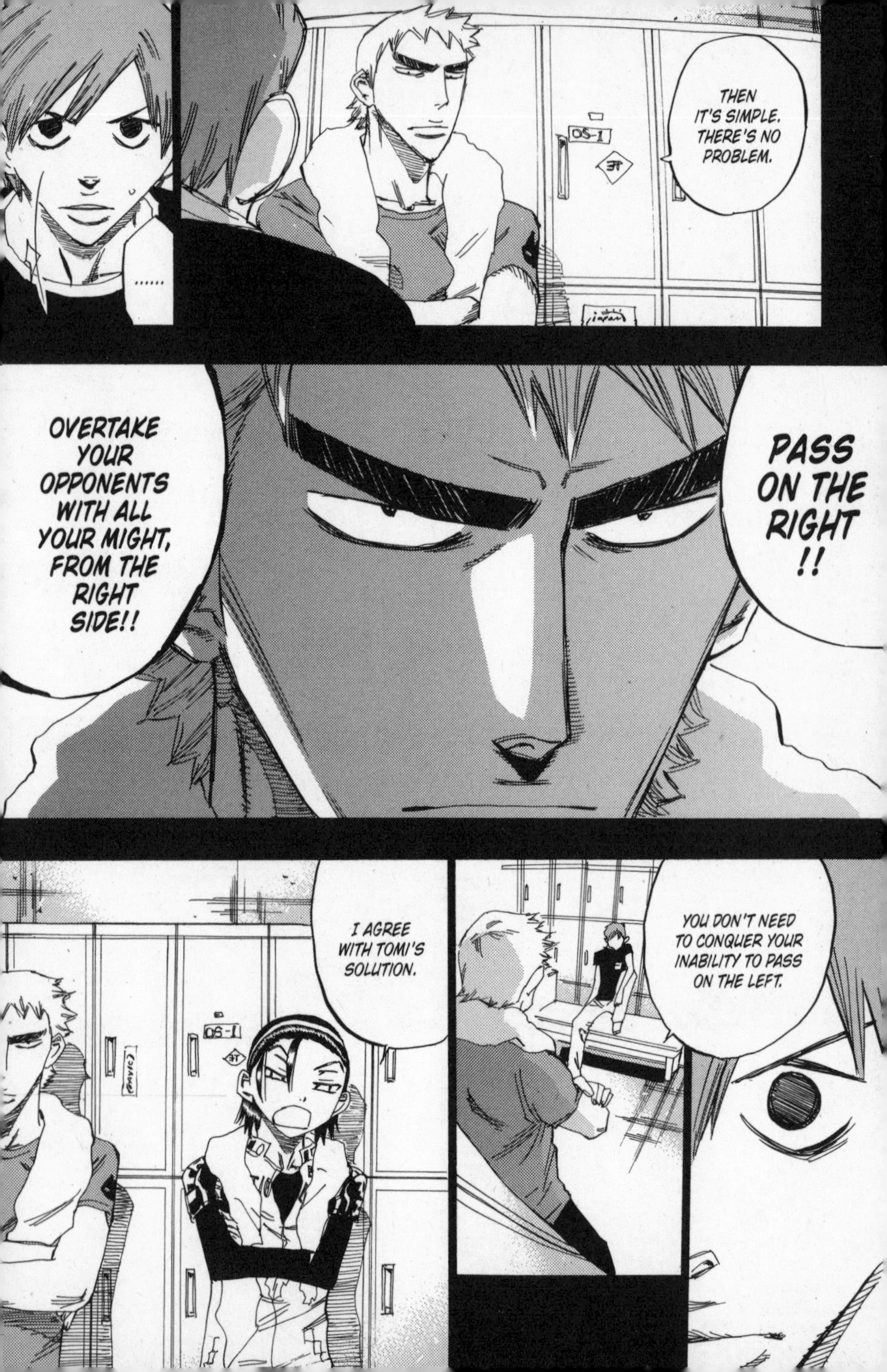
THEN IT'S SIMPLE. THERE'S NO PROBLEM.
......
PASS ON THE RIGHT!!
OVERTAKE YOUR OPPONENTS WITH ALL YOUR MIGHT, FROM THE RIGHT SIDE!!
YOU DON'T NEED TO CONQUER YOUR INABILITY TO PASS ON THE LEFT.
I AGREE WITH TOMI'S SOLUTION.

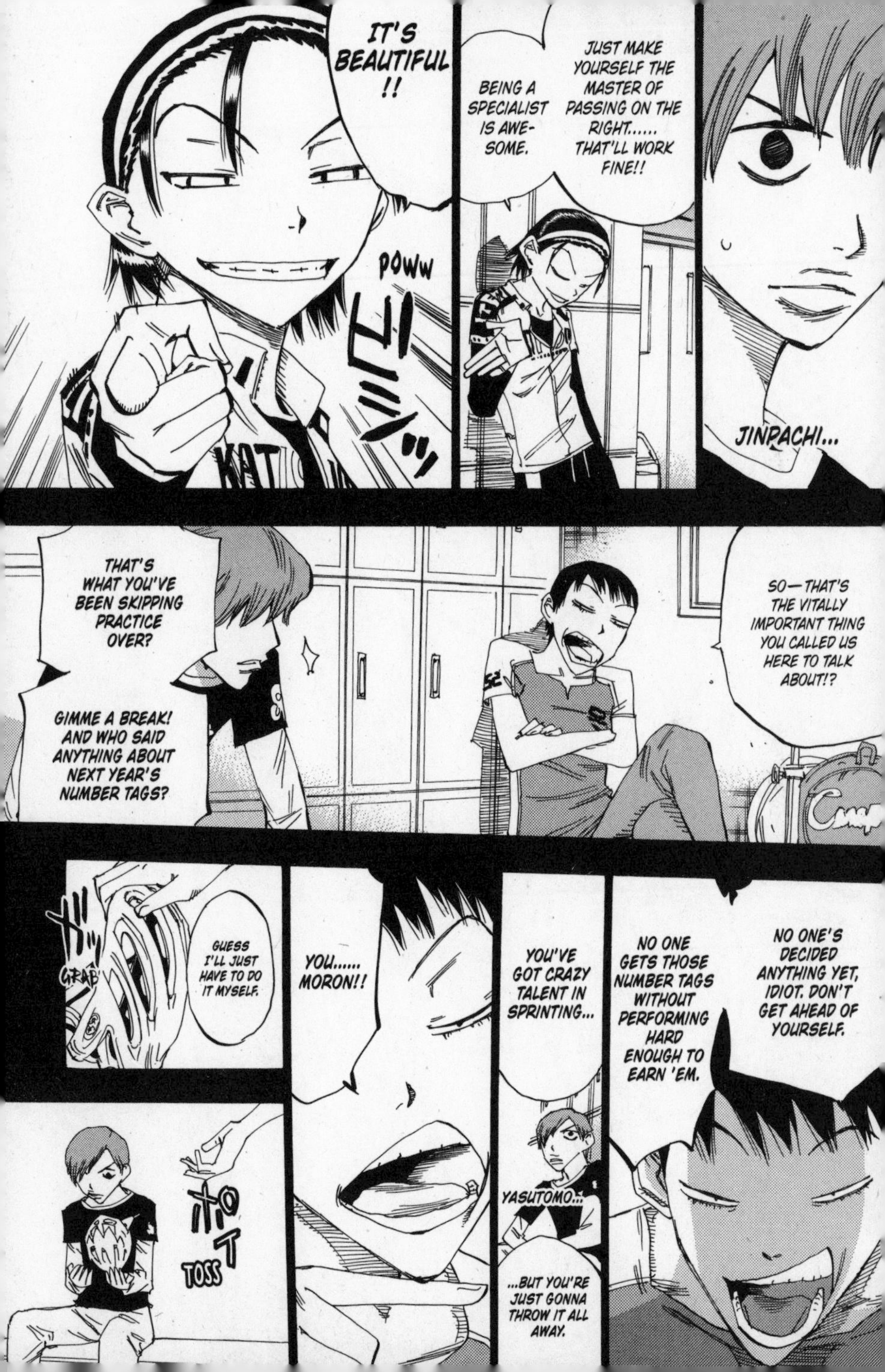
JINPACHI...
JUST MAKE YOURSELF THE MASTER OF PASSING ON THE RIGHT...... THAT'LL WORK FINE!!
BEING A SPECIALIST IS AWE-SOME.
IT'S BEAUTIFUL !!
POWW
SO—THAT'S THE VITALLY IMPORTANT THING YOU CALLED US HERE TO TALK ABOUT!?
THAT'S WHAT YOU'VE BEEN SKIPPING PRACTICE OVER?
GIMME A BREAK! AND WHO SAID ANYTHING ABOUT NEXT YEAR'S NUMBER TAGS?
NO ONE'S DECIDED ANYTHING YET, IDIOT. DON'T GET AHEAD OF YOURSELF.
NO ONE GETS THOSE NUMBER TAGS WITHOUT PERFORMING HARD ENOUGH TO EARN 'EM.
YOU'VE GOT CRAZY TALENT IN SPRINTING...
YASUTOMO...
...BUT YOU'RE JUST GONNA THROW IT ALL AWAY.
YOU...... MORON!!
GUESS I'LL JUST HAVE TO DO IT MYSELF.
GRAB
TOSS

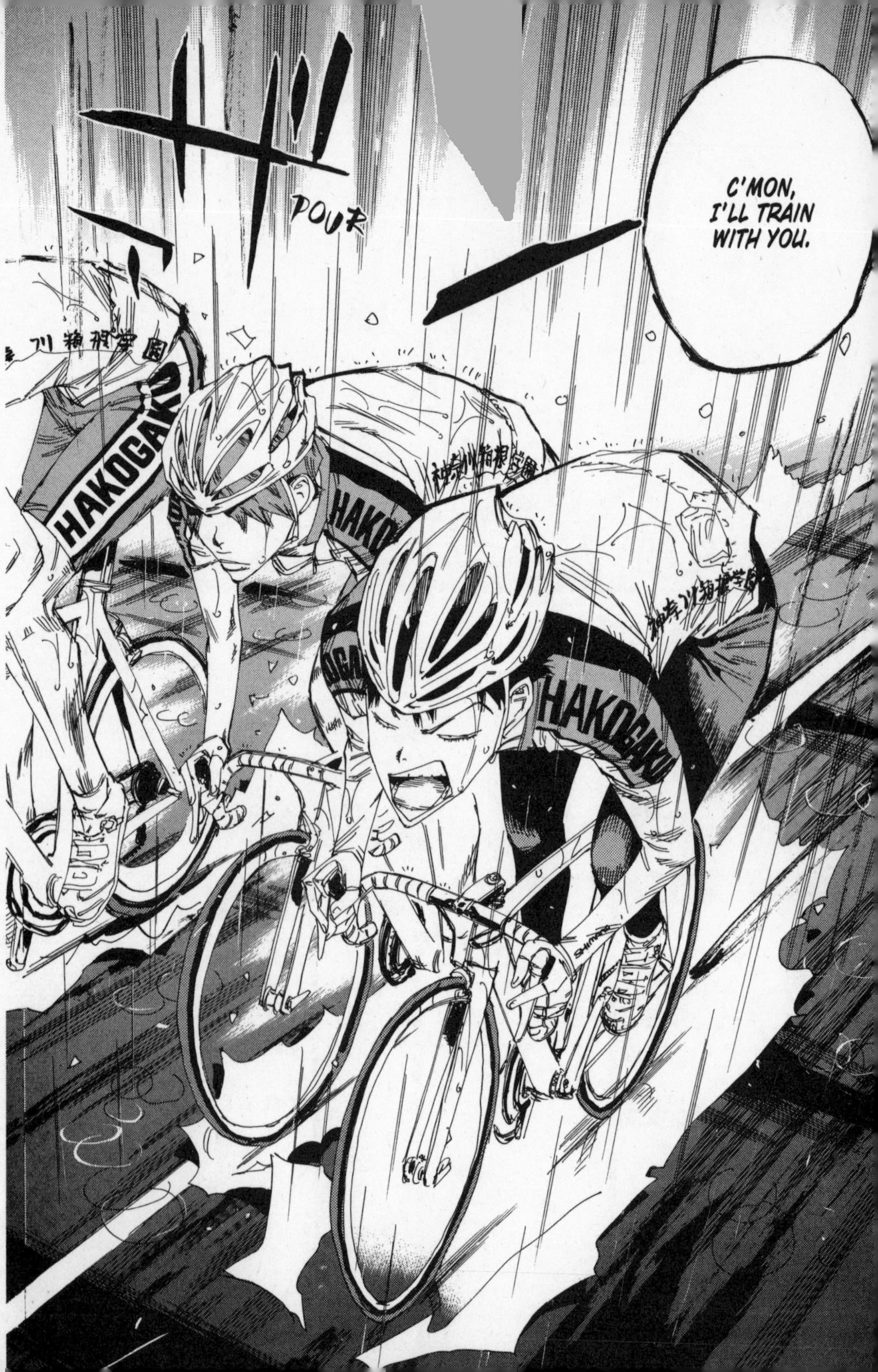
C'MON, I'LL TRAIN WITH YOU.
POUR
HAKOGAKU
HAKOGAKU
HAKOGAKU

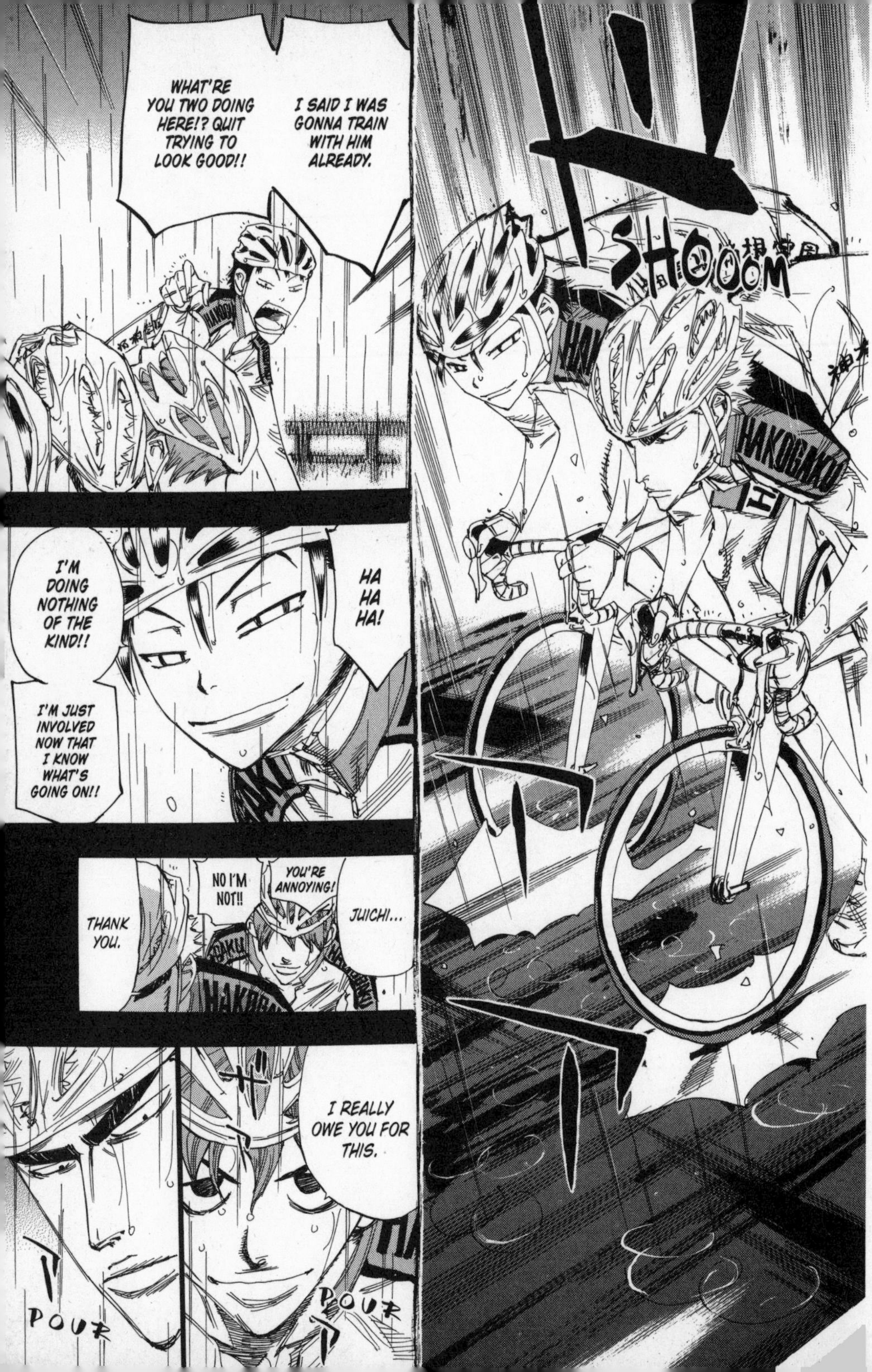
SHOOOM
I SAID I WAS GONNA TRAIN WITH HIM ALREADY.
WHAT'RE YOU TWO DOING HERE!? QUIT TRYING TO LOOK GOOD!!
HA HA HA!
I'M DOING NOTHING OF THE KIND!!
I'M JUST INVOLVED NOW THAT I KNOW WHAT'S GOING ON!!
JUICHI...
YOU'RE ANNOYING!
NO I'M NOT!!
THANK YOU.
I REALLY OWE YOU FOR THIS.
POUR
POUR

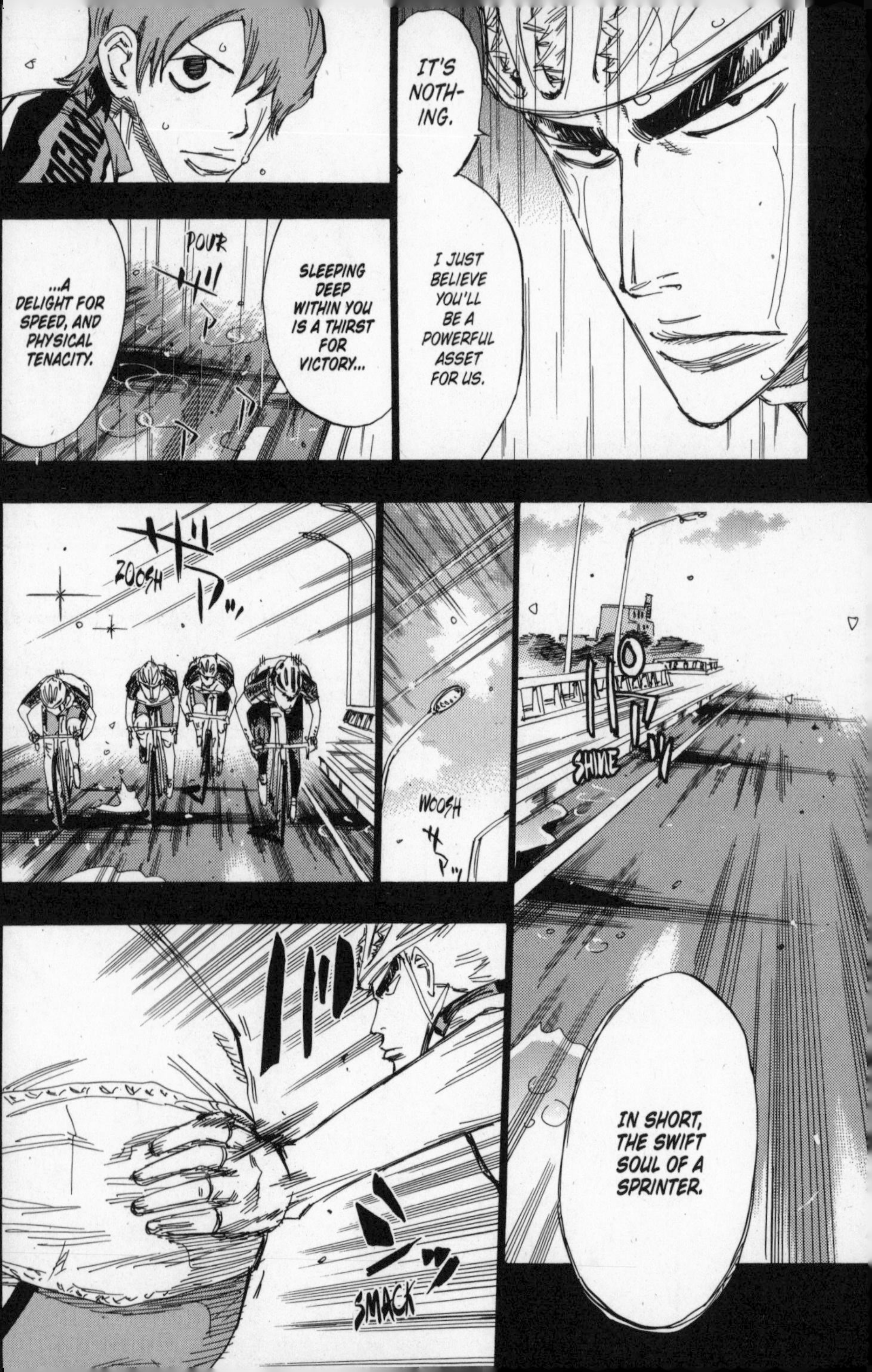
IT'S NOTH-ING.
I JUST BELIEVE YOU'LL BE A POWERFUL ASSET FOR US.
SLEEPING DEEP WITHIN YOU IS A THIRST FOR VICTORY...
POUR
...A DELIGHT FOR SPEED, AND PHYSICAL TENACITY.
SHINE
IN SHORT, THE SWIFT SOUL OF A SPRINTER.
WOOSH
ZOOSH
SMACK

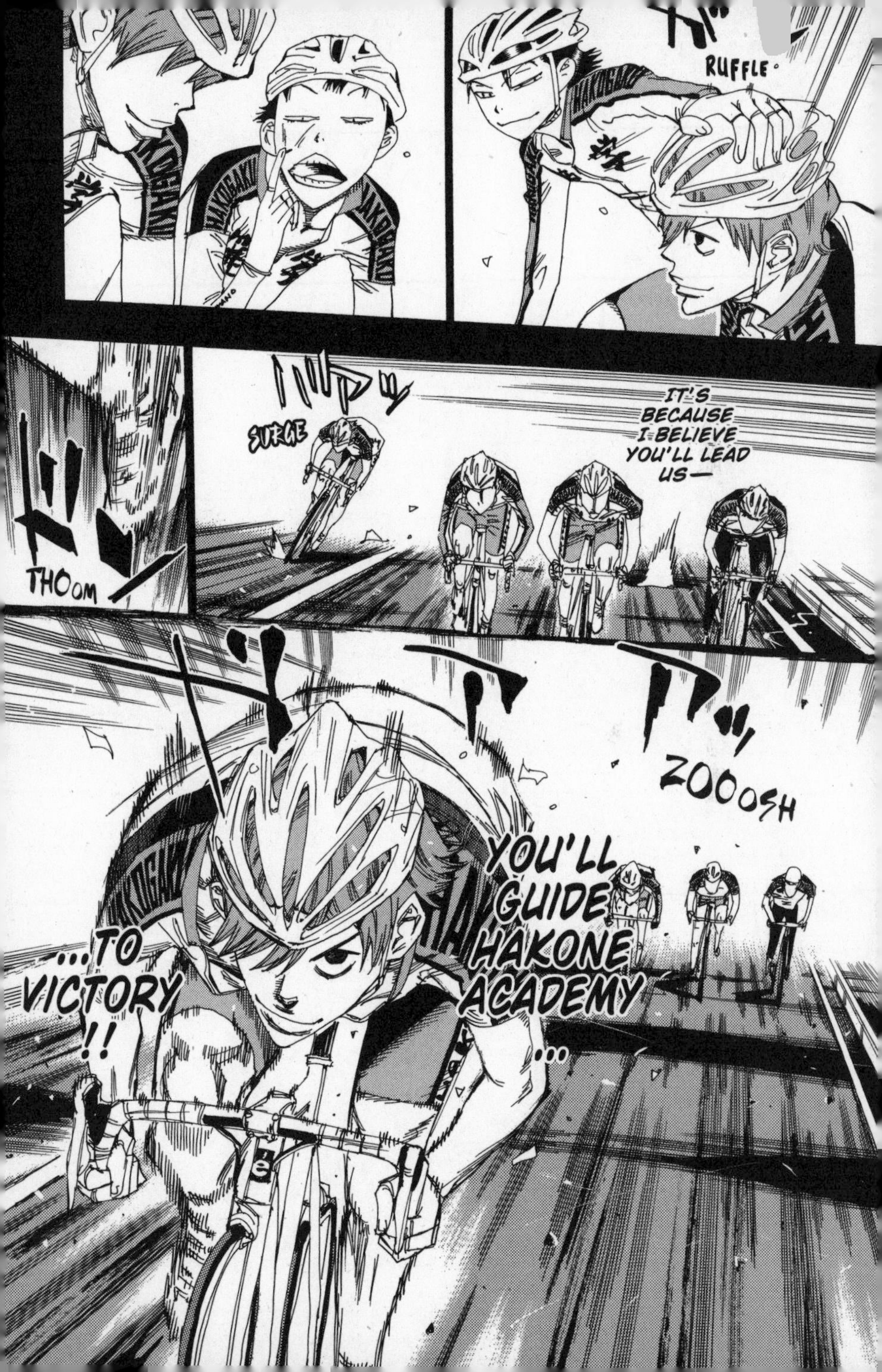
RUFFLE
SURGE
IT'S BECAUSE I BELIEVE YOU'LL LEAD US—
THOom
ZOOOSH
YOU'LL GUIDE HAKONE ACADEMY...
...TO VICTORY!!

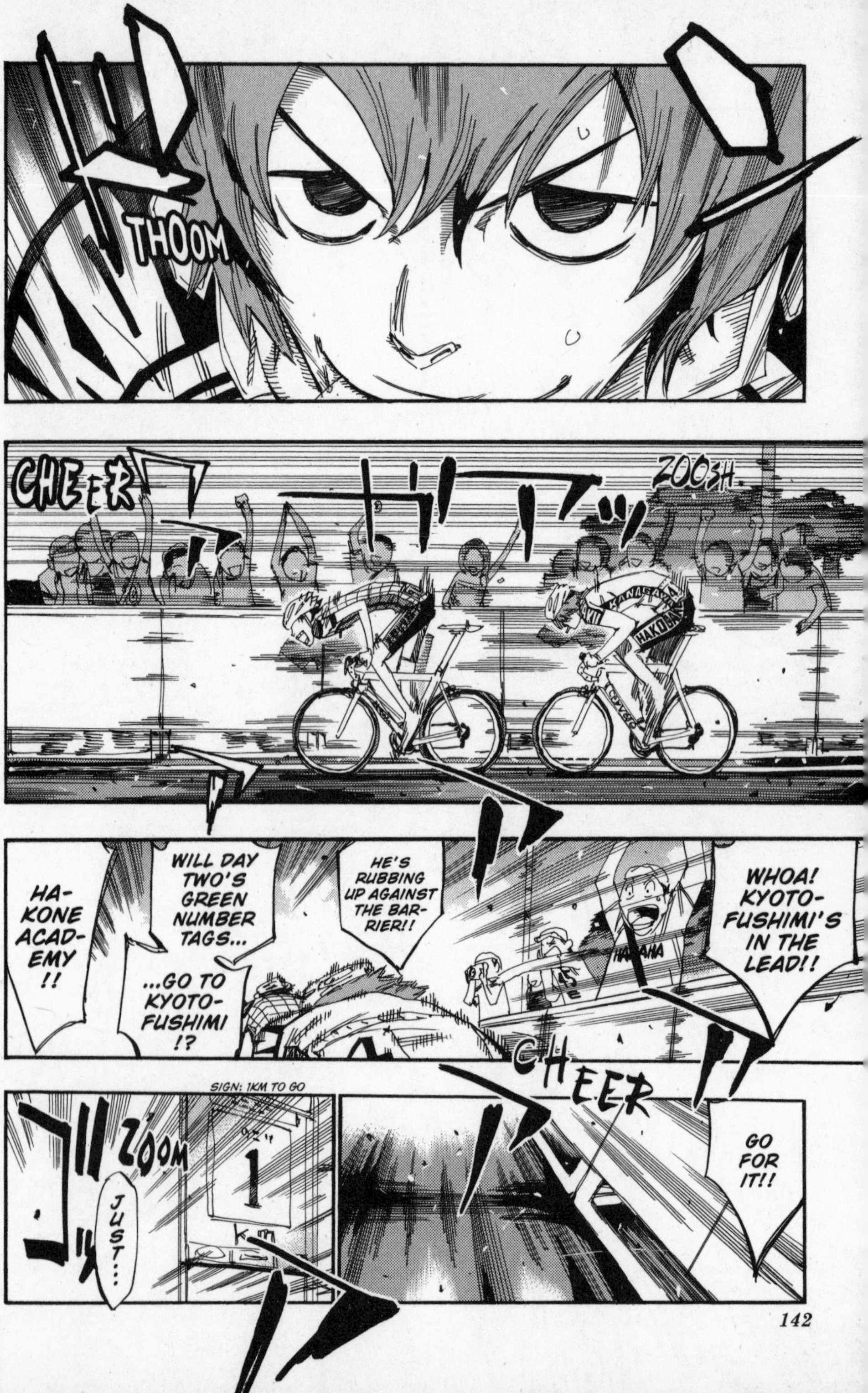
THOOM
ZOOSH
CHEER
WHOA! KYOTO-FUSHIMI'S IN THE LEAD!!
HE'S RUBBING UP AGAINST THE BARRIER!!
WILL DAY TWO'S GREEN NUMBER TAGS...
...GO TO KYOTO-FUSHIMI!?
HAKONE ACADEMY!!
CHEER
GO FOR IT!!
SIGN: 1KM TO GO
ZOOM
JUST...

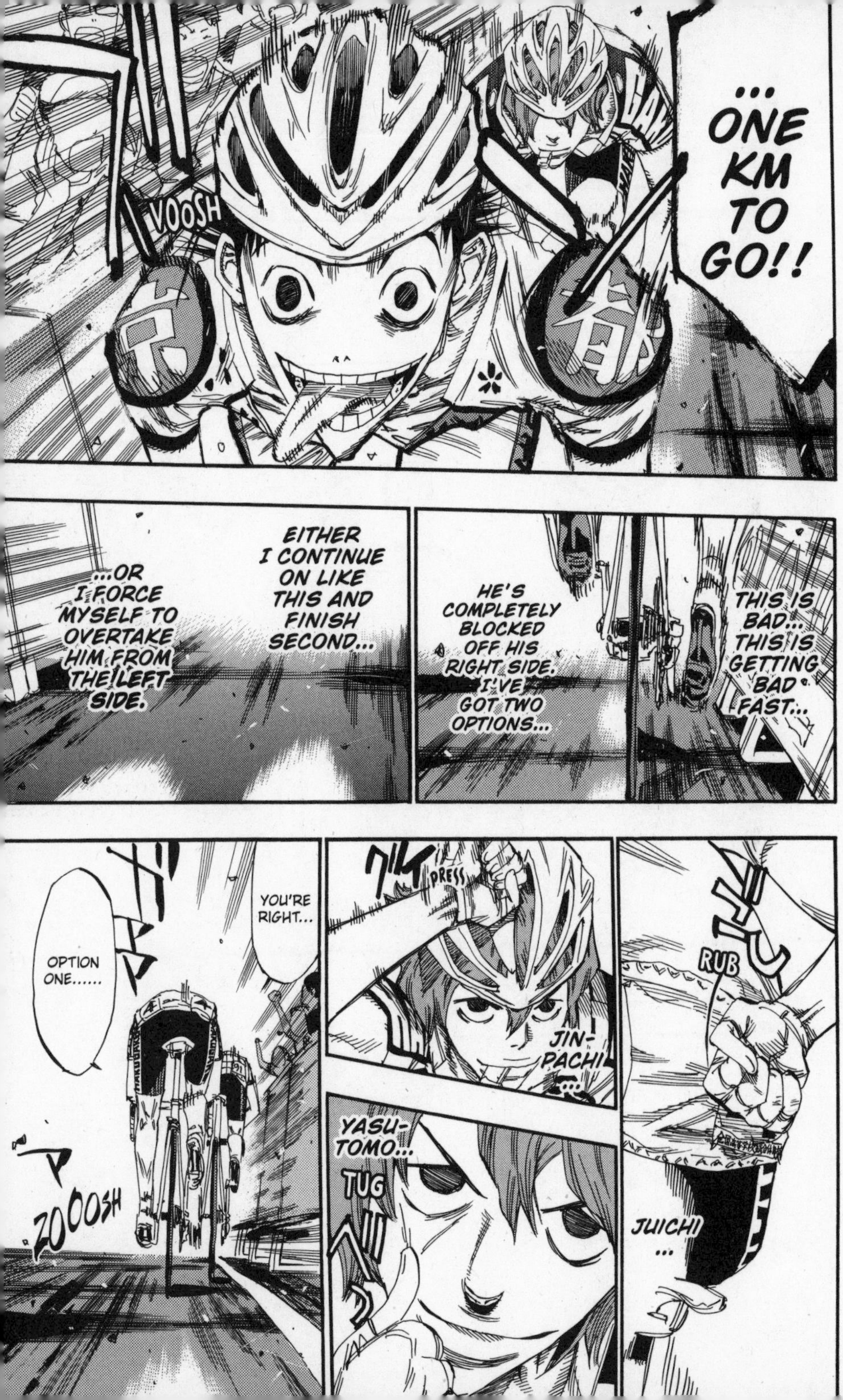
... ONE KM TO GO!!
VOOSH
THIS IS BAD... THIS IS GETTING BAD FAST...
HE'S COMPLETELY BLOCKED OFF HIS RIGHT SIDE. I'VE GOT TWO OPTIONS...
EITHER I CONTINUE ON LIKE THIS AND FINISH SECOND...
...OR I FORCE MYSELF TO OVERTAKE HIM FROM THE LEFT SIDE.
RUB
JUICHI ...
PRESS
JIN-PACHI ...
YASU-TOMO...
TUG
YOU'RE RIGHT...
OPTION ONE......
ZOOOSH

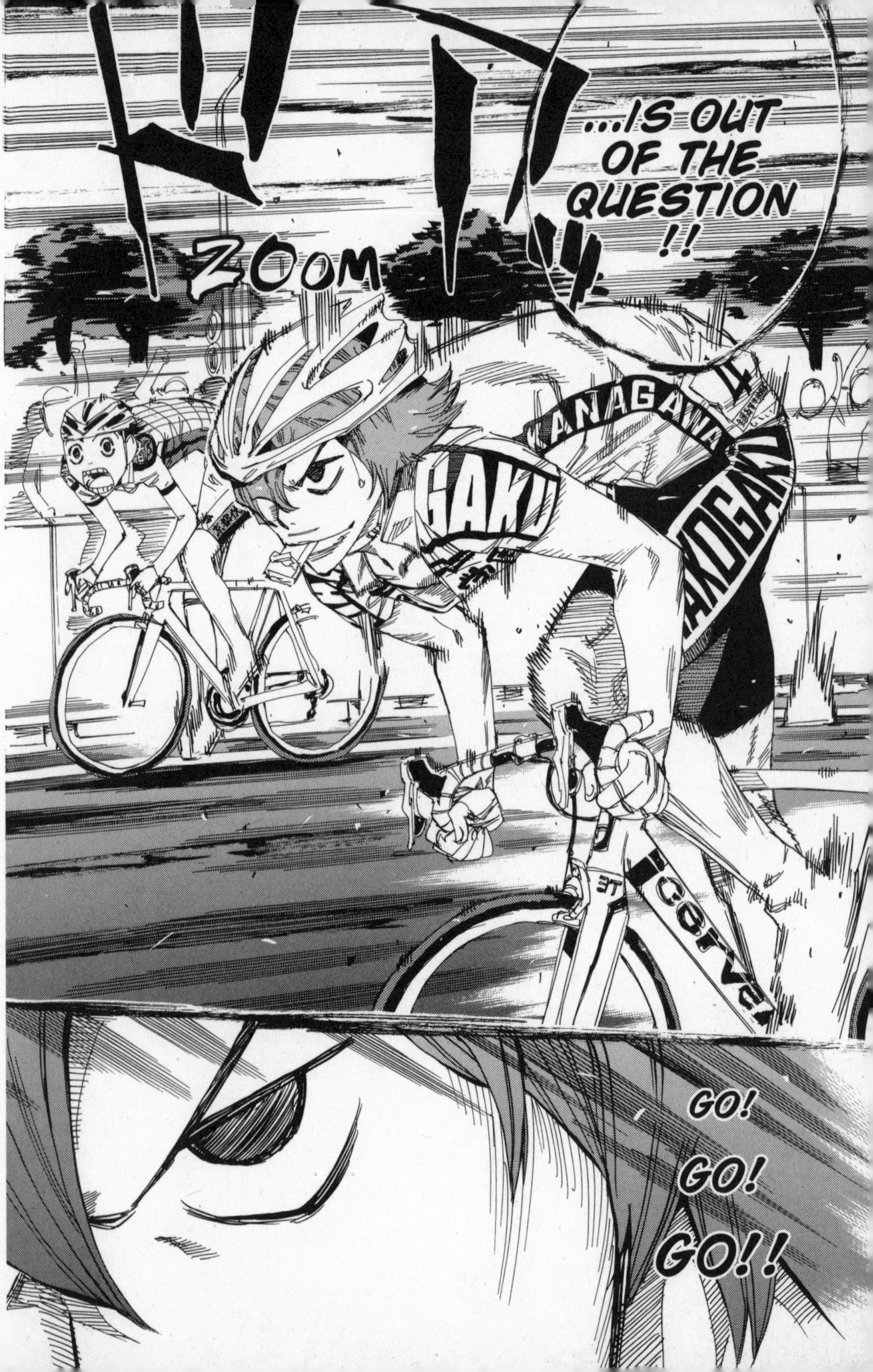
...IS OUT OF THE QUESTION!!
ZOOM
GO! GO! GO!!

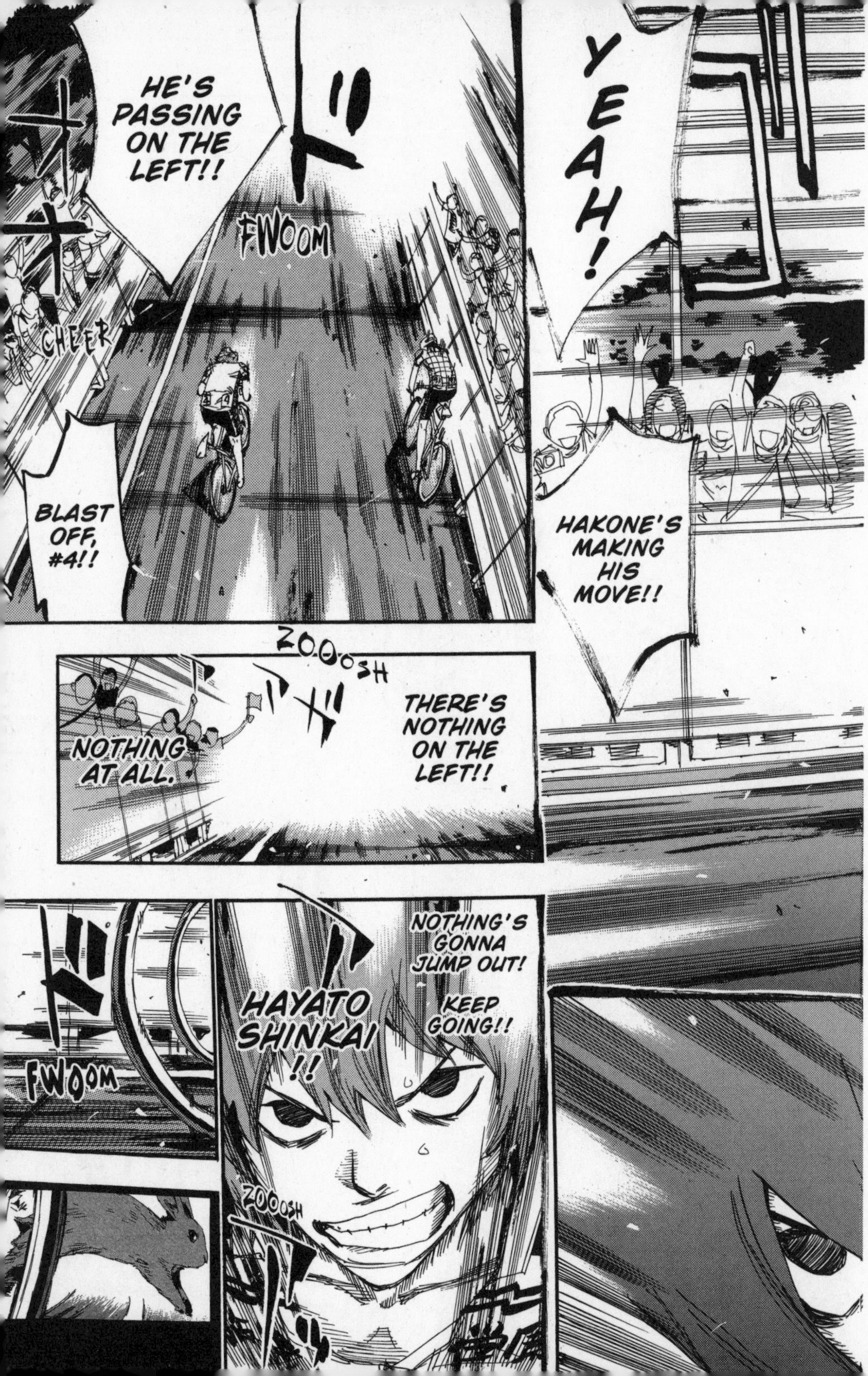
YEAH!
HAKONE'S MAKING HIS MOVE!!
HE'S PASSING ON THE LEFT!!
FWOOM
CHEER
BLAST OFF, #4!!
ZOOOSH
THERE'S NOTHING ON THE LEFT!!
NOTHING AT ALL.
NOTHING'S GONNA JUMP OUT!
KEEP GOING!!
HAYATO SHINKAI!!
ZOOOSH
FWOOM

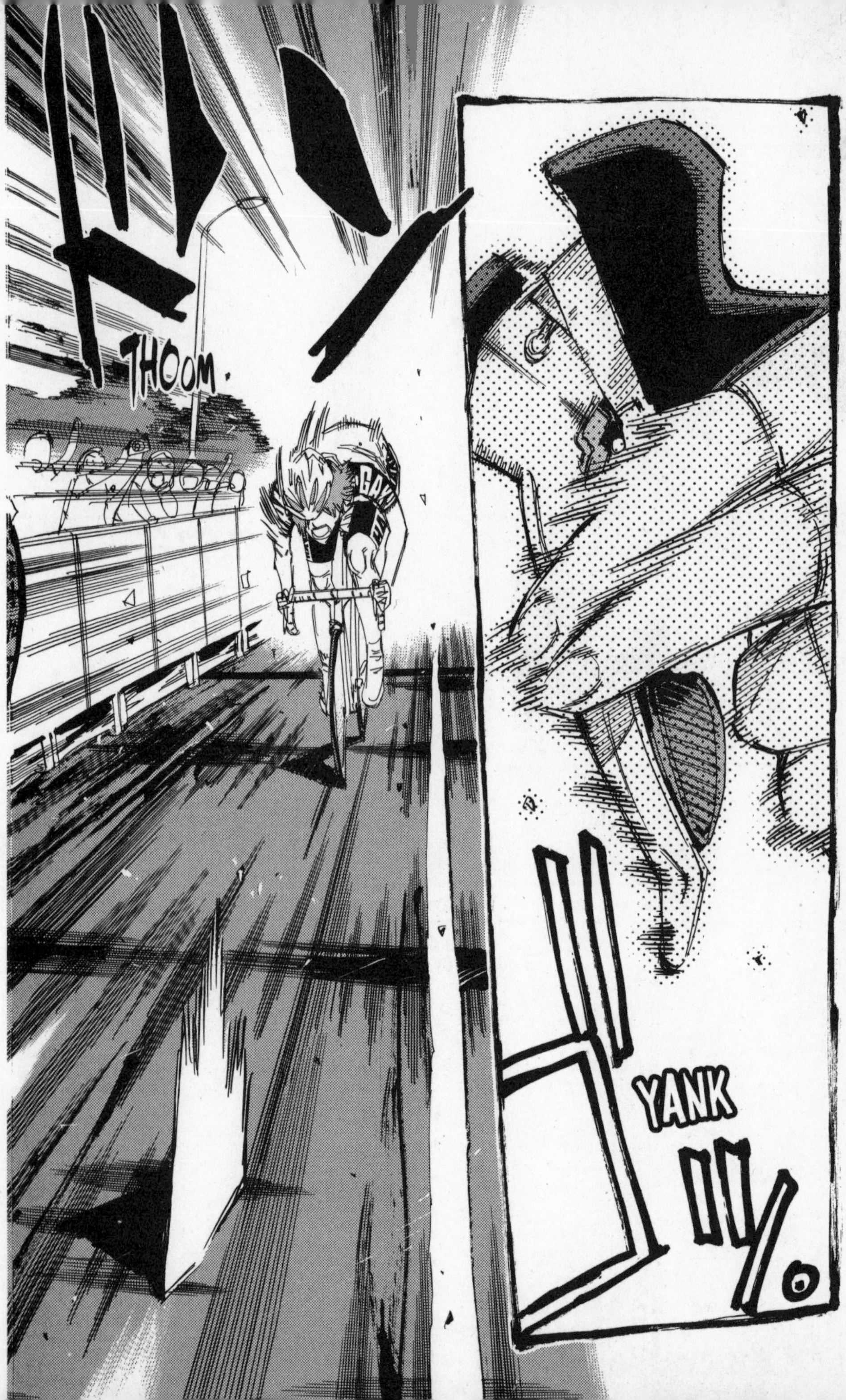
YANK
THOOM

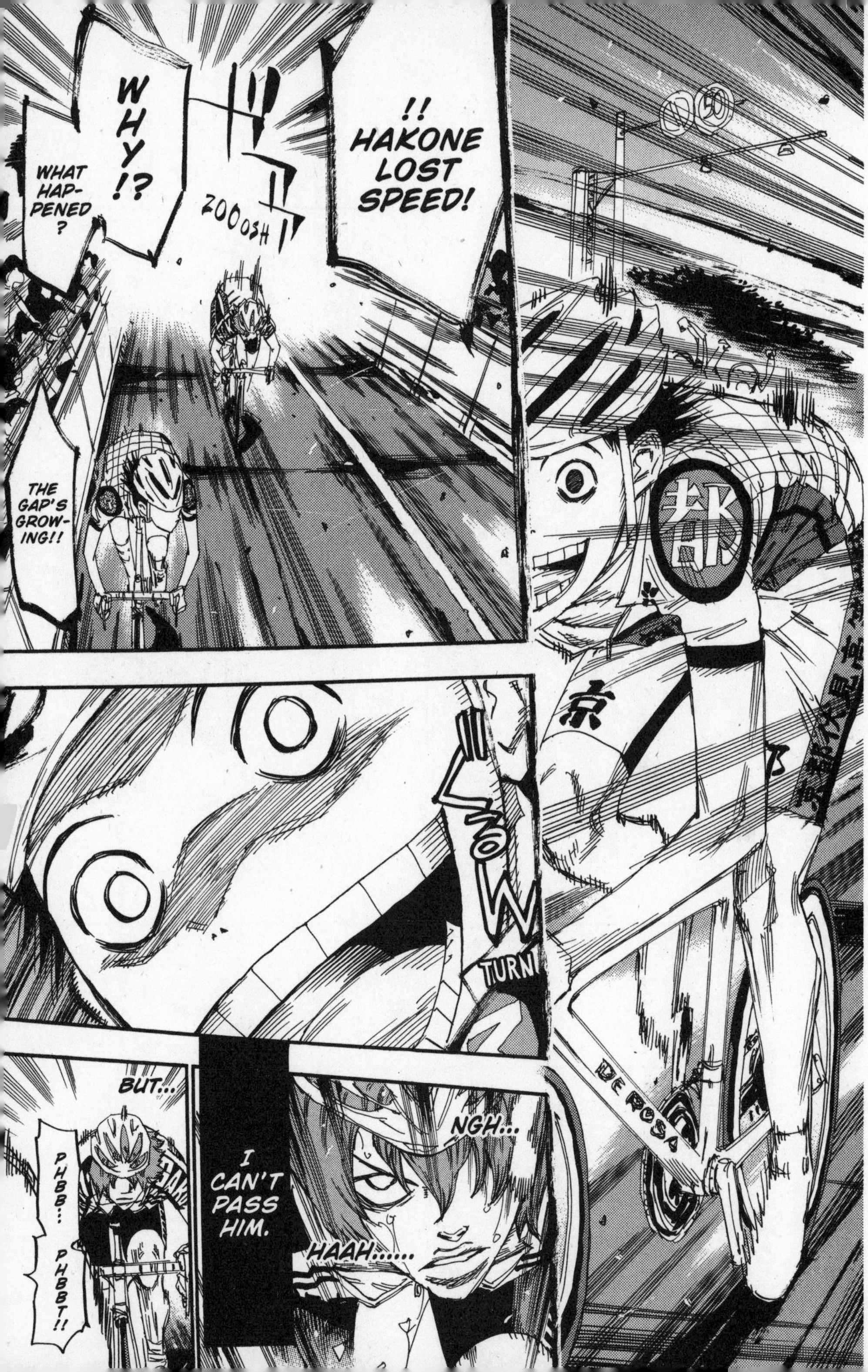
DE ROSA
!! HAKONE LOST SPEED!
ZOOOSH
WHY!?
WHAT HAP-PENED?
THE GAP'S GROW-ING!!
TURN
NGH...
HAAH......
I CAN'T PASS HIM.
BUT...
PHBB... PHBBT!!

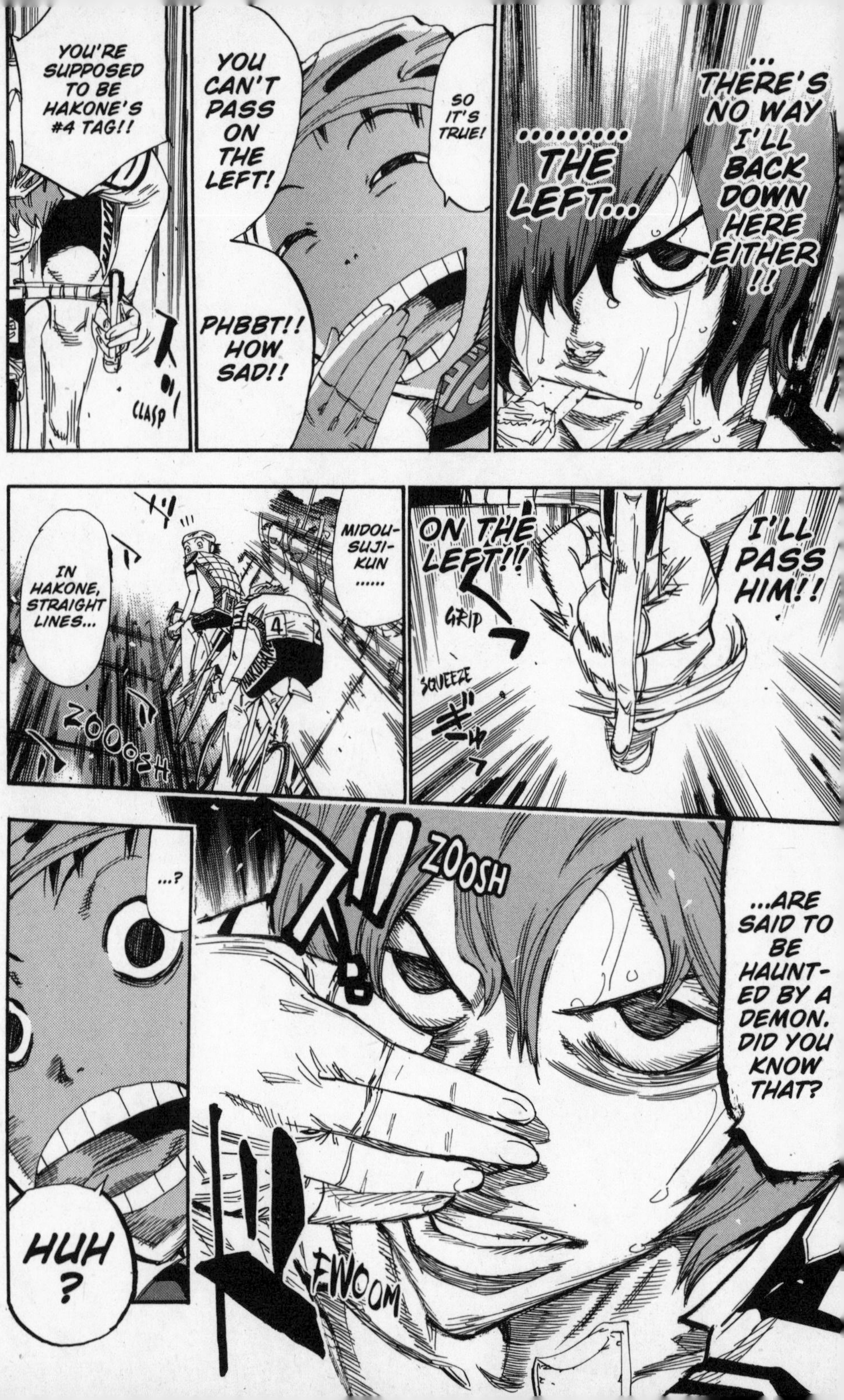

...THERE'S NO WAY I'LL BACK DOWN HERE EITHER!!
..........THE LEFT...
SO IT'S TRUE!
YOU CAN'T PASS ON THE LEFT!
PHBBT!! HOW SAD!!
YOU'RE SUPPOSED TO BE HAKONE'S #4 TAG!!
CLASP
I'LL PASS HIM!!
ON THE LEFT!!
GRIP
SQUEEZE
MIDOU-SUJI-KUN ......
IN HAKONE, STRAIGHT LINES...
ZOOOSH
...ARE SAID TO BE HAUNT-ED BY A DEMON. DID YOU KNOW THAT?
ZOOSH
...?
FWOOM
HUH?

RIDE.127 DEMON

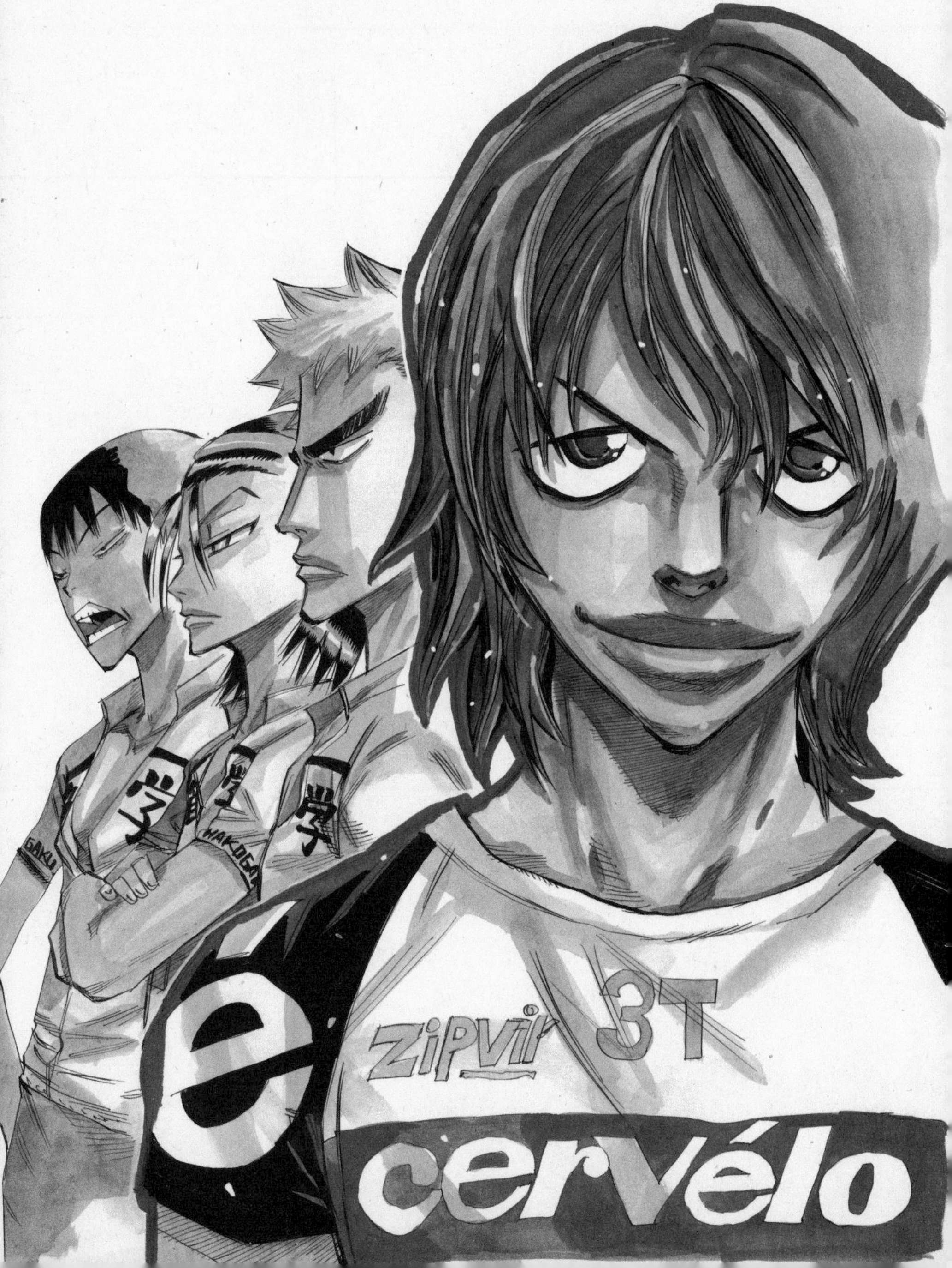
ZiPVit
3T
cervélo

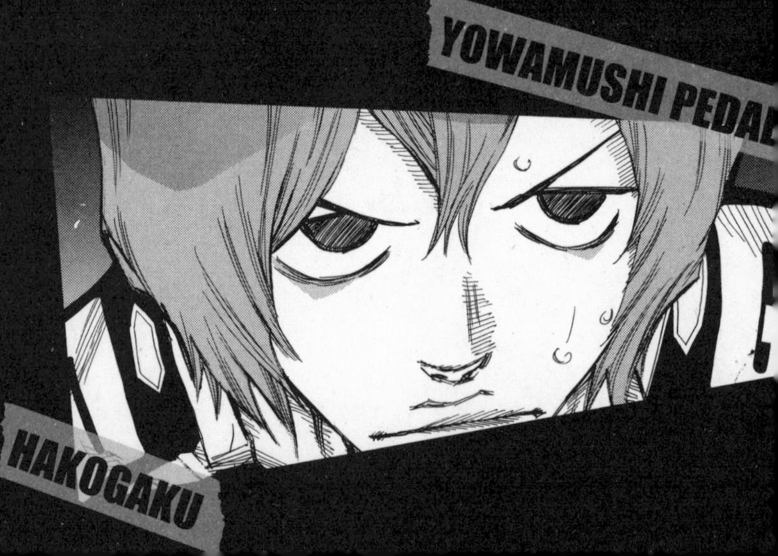
YOWAMUSHI PEDA
HAKOGAKU

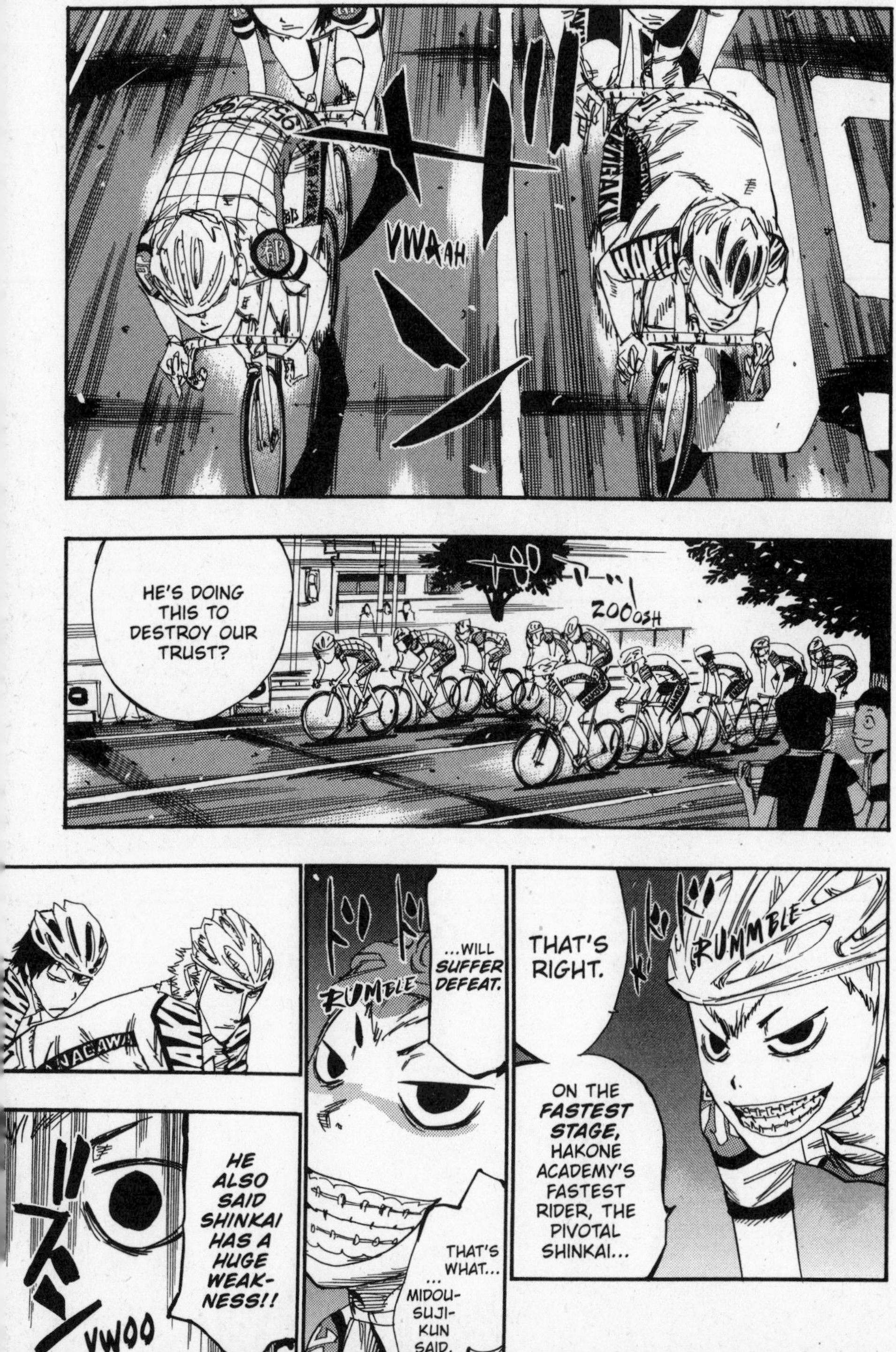
VWAAAH
HE'S DOING THIS TO DESTROY OUR TRUST?
ZOOOSH
THAT'S RIGHT.
RUMMBLE
ON THE FASTEST STAGE, HAKONE ACADEMY'S FASTEST RIDER, THE PIVOTAL SHINKAI...
...WILL SUFFER DEFEAT.
RUMBLE
THAT'S WHAT... ...MIDOU-SUJI-KUN SAID.
HE ALSO SAID SHINKAI HAS A HUGE WEAK-NESS!!
VWOO

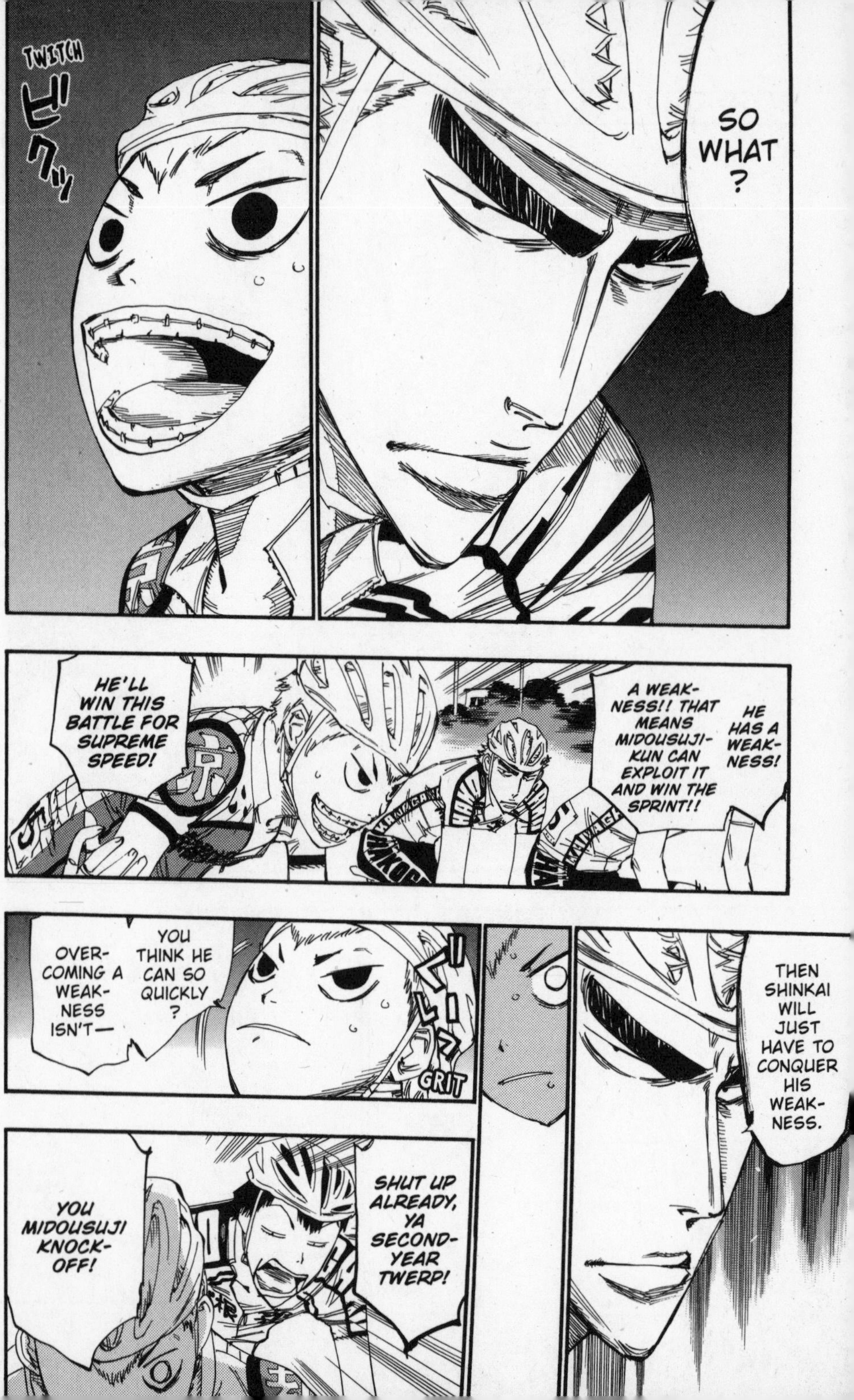
SO WHAT?
TWITCH
ビクッ
HE HAS A WEAKNESS!
A WEAKNESS!! THAT MEANS MIDOUSUJI-KUN CAN EXPLOIT IT AND WIN THE SPRINT!!
HE'LL WIN THIS BATTLE FOR SUPREME SPEED!
THEN SHINKAI WILL JUST HAVE TO CONQUER HIS WEAKNESS.
GRIT
YOU THINK HE CAN SO QUICKLY?
OVERCOMING A WEAKNESS ISN'T—
SHUT UP ALREADY, YA SECOND-YEAR TWERP!
YOU MIDOUSUJI KNOCK-OFF!

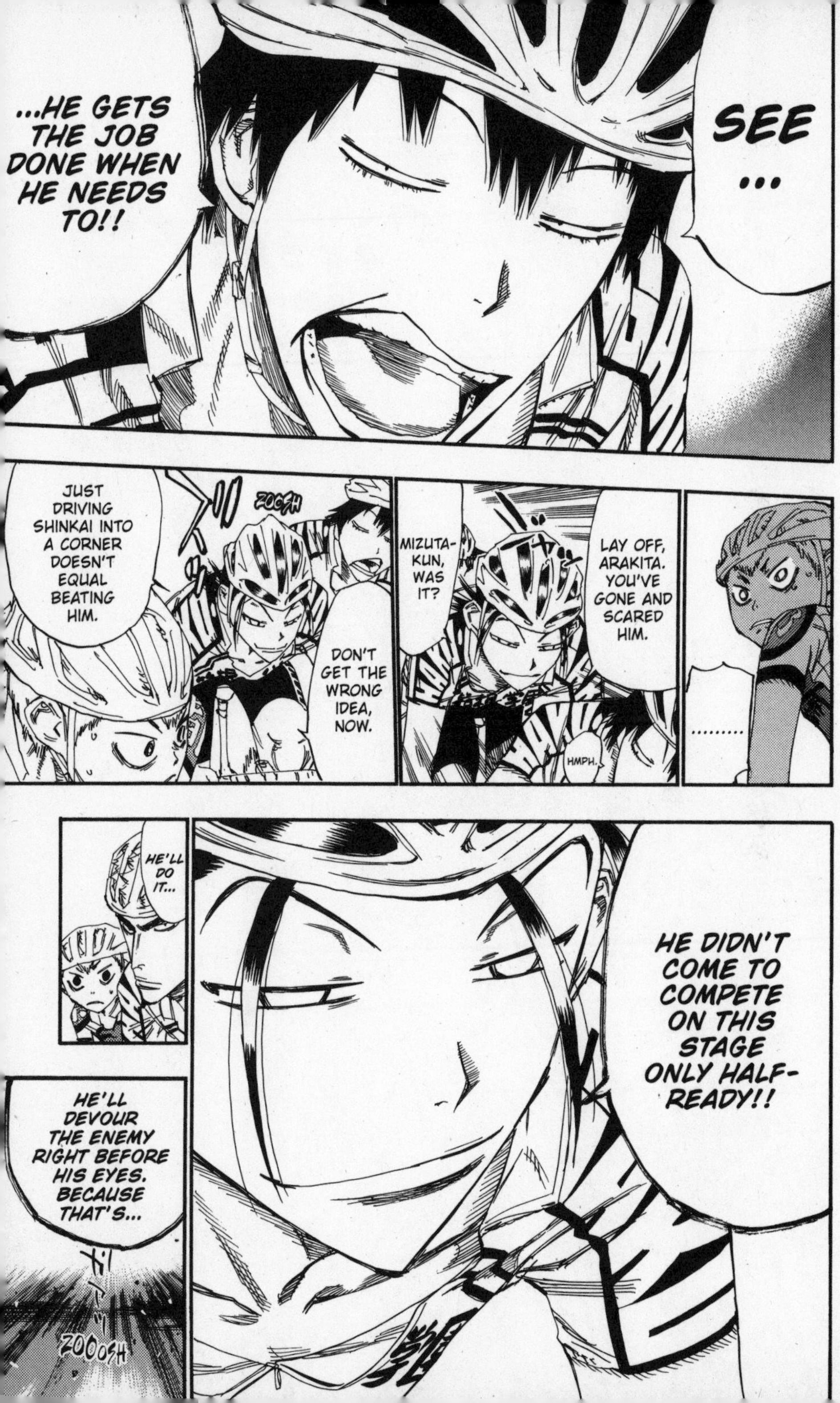
SEE...
...HE GETS THE JOB DONE WHEN HE NEEDS TO!!
....
LAY OFF, ARAKITA. YOU'VE GONE AND SCARED HIM.
MIZUTA-KUN, WAS IT?
HMPH.
ZOOSH
DON'T GET THE WRONG IDEA, NOW.
JUST DRIVING SHINKAI INTO A CORNER DOESN'T EQUAL BEATING HIM.
HE DIDN'T COME TO COMPETE ON THIS STAGE ONLY HALF-READY!!
HE'LL DO IT...
HE'LL DEVOUR THE ENEMY RIGHT BEFORE HIS EYES. BECAUSE THAT'S...
ZOOOSH

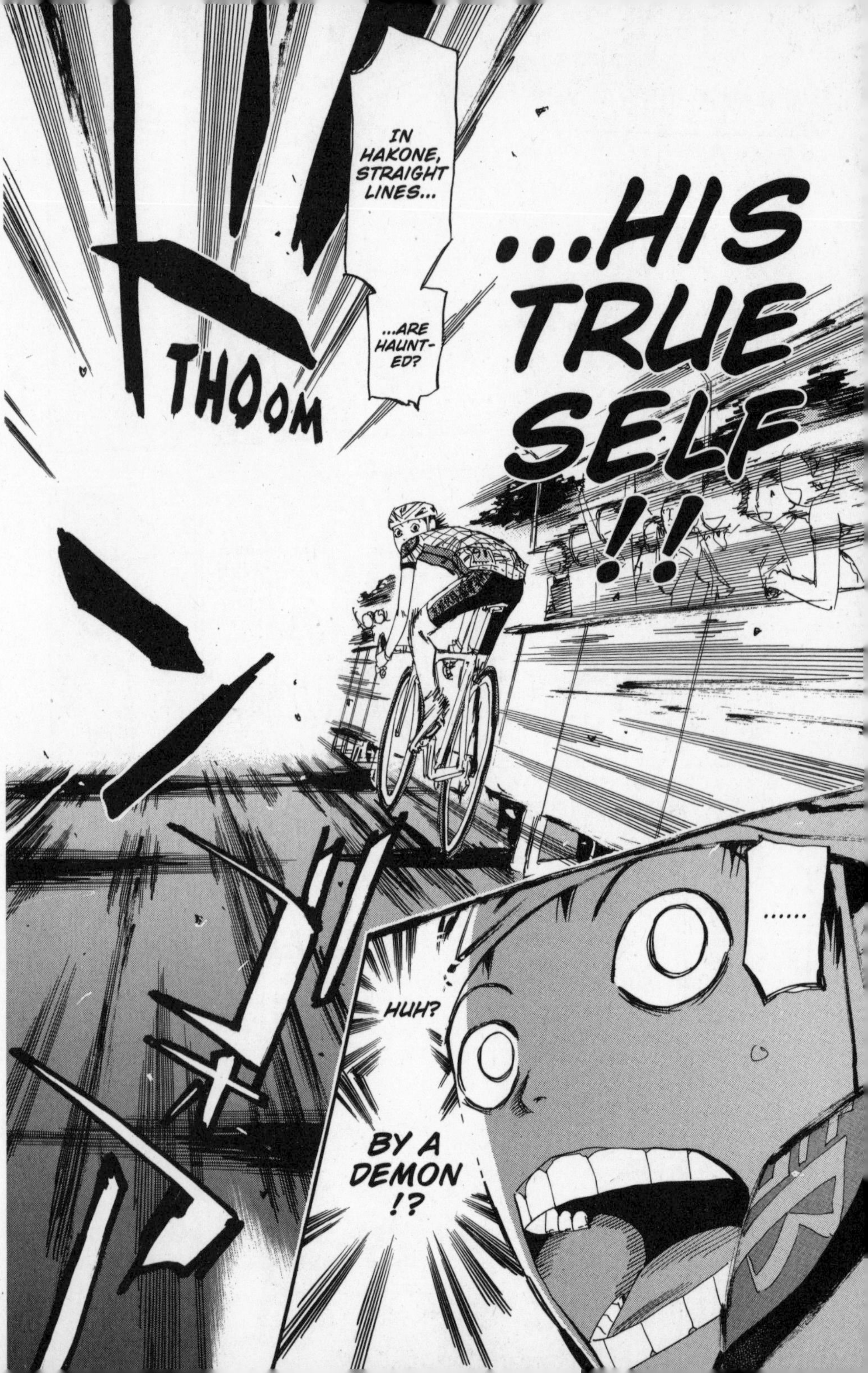
IN HAKONE, STRAIGHT LINES...
...ARE HAUNT-ED?
...HIS TRUE SELF!!
THOOM
......
HUH?
BY A DEMON!?

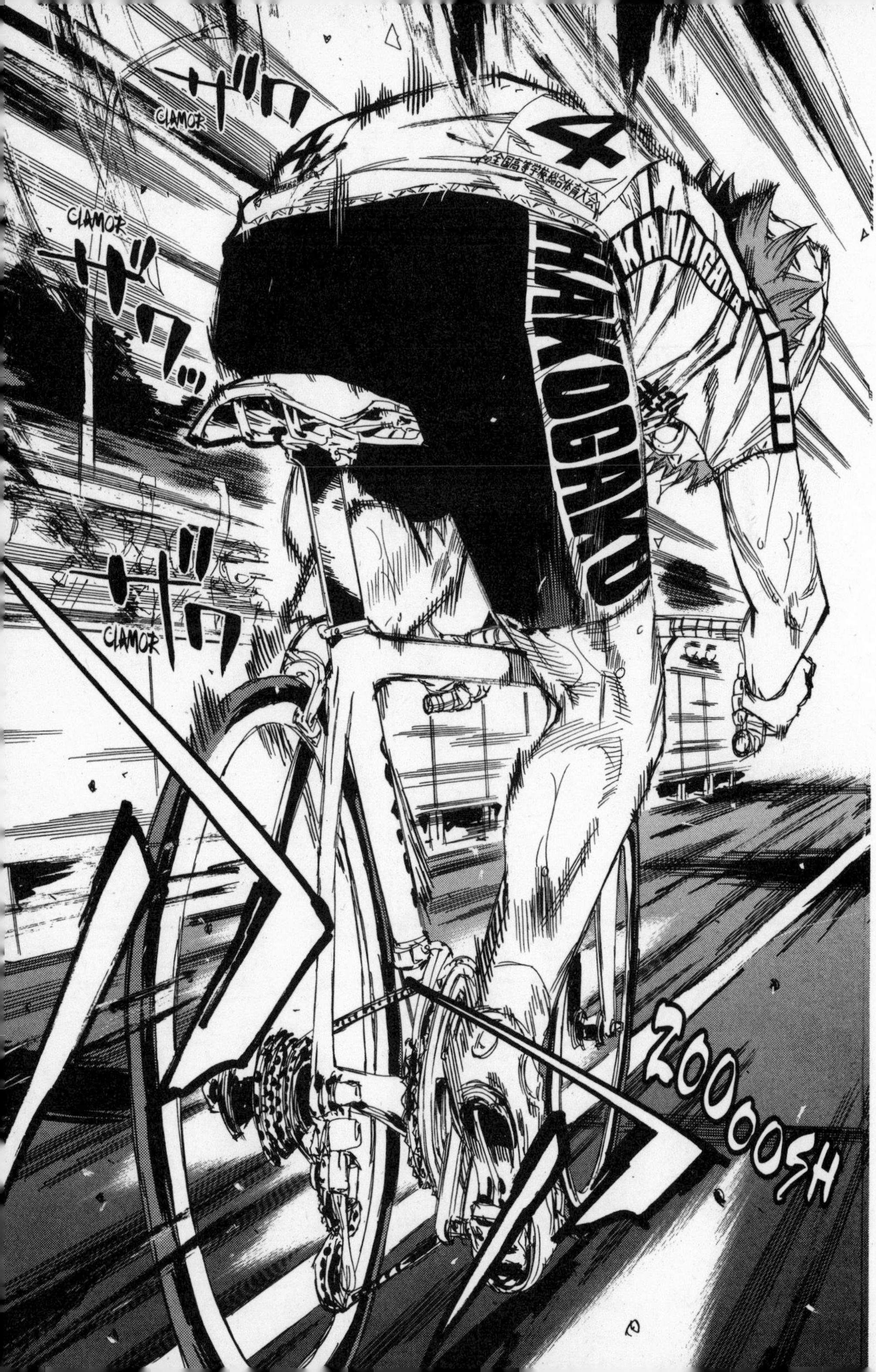

4
HAKOGAKU
ザワ
CLAMOR
ザワッ
CLAMOR
ザワ
CLAMOR
ZOOOOSH

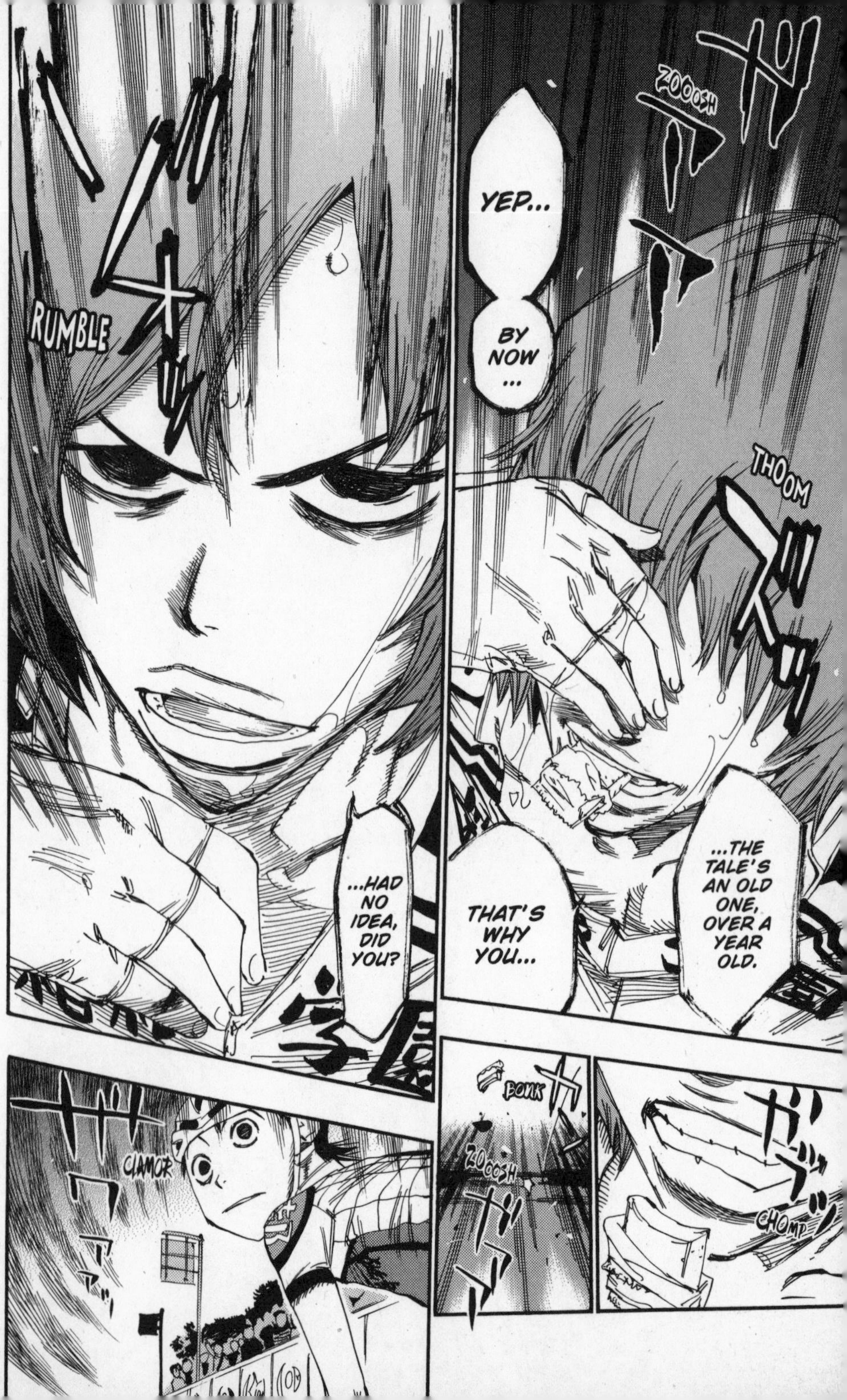
ZOOOSH
YEP...
BY NOW...
THOOM
...THE TALE'S AN OLD ONE, OVER A YEAR OLD.
THAT'S WHY YOU...
RUMBLE
...HAD NO IDEA, DID YOU?
CHOMP
BONK
ZOOOSH
CLAMOR

...CHANGED.

HIS INTEN-SITY...

JOLT

LURCH

SPASM

BULGE

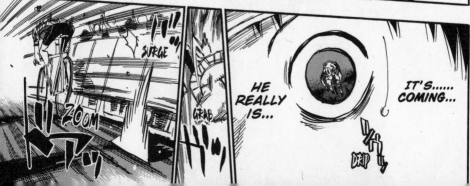

SURGE

ZOOM

GRAB

HE REALLY IS...

IT'S...... COMING...

DRIP

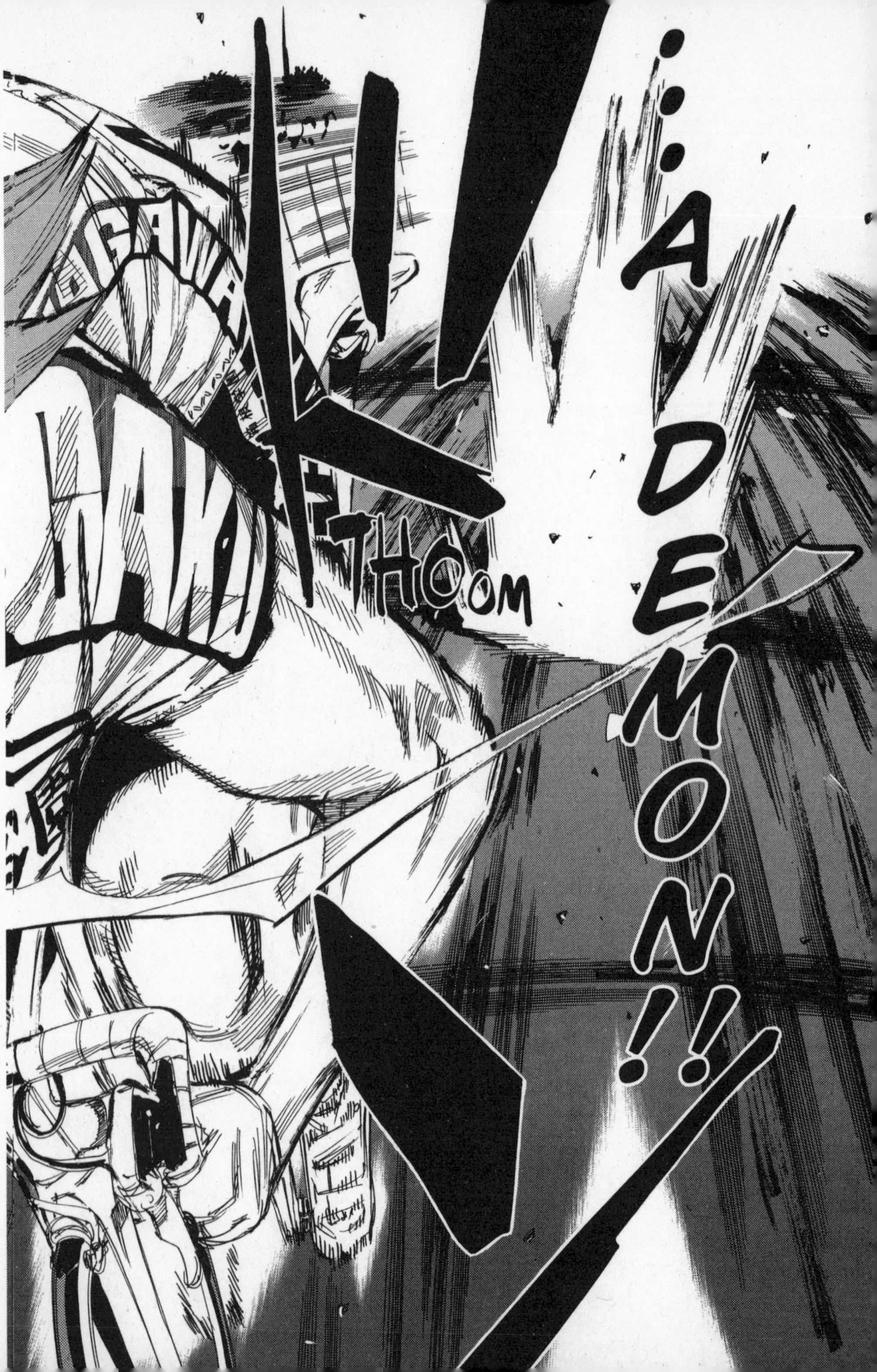

...ADEMON!!
THOOM

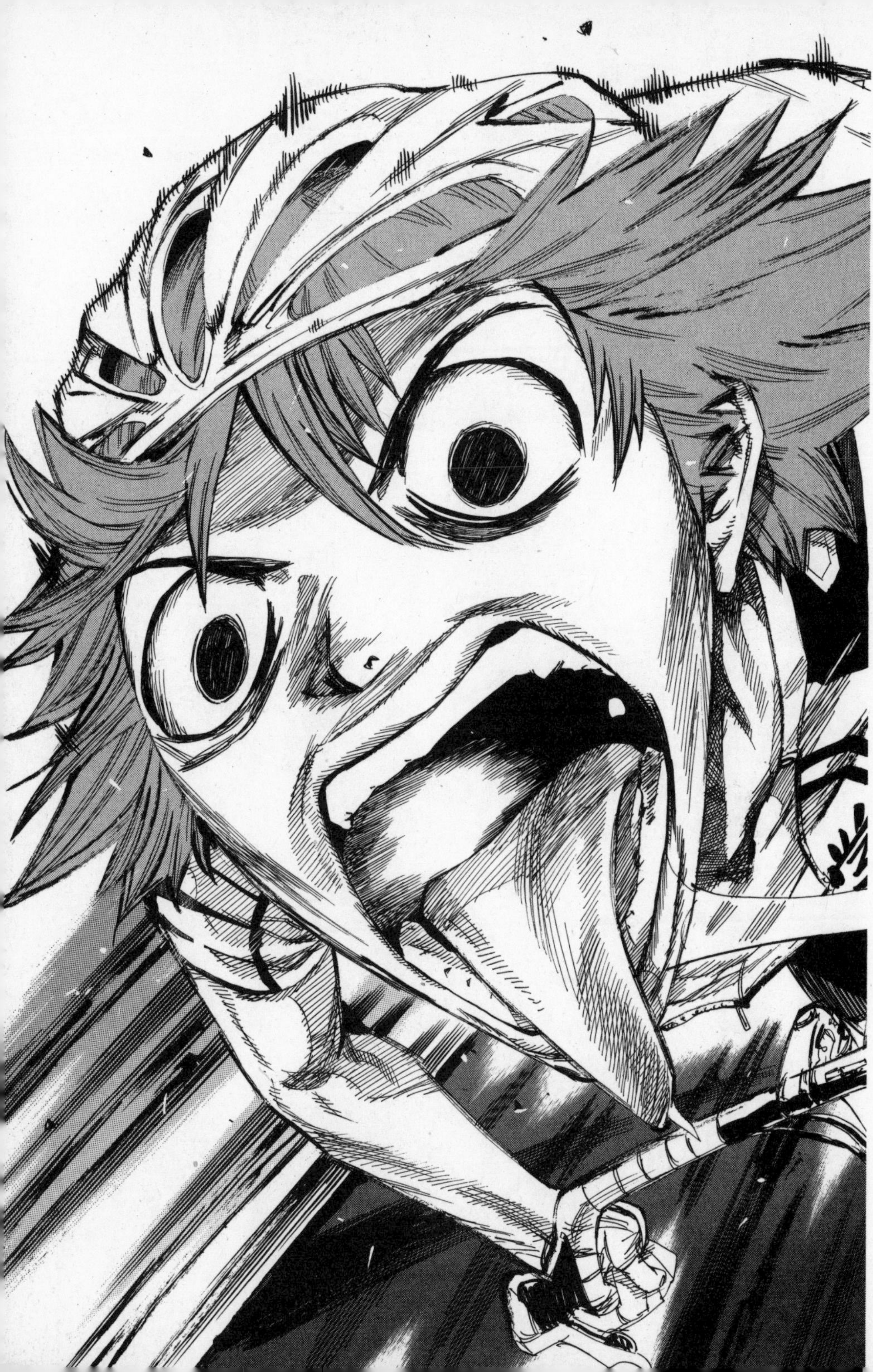

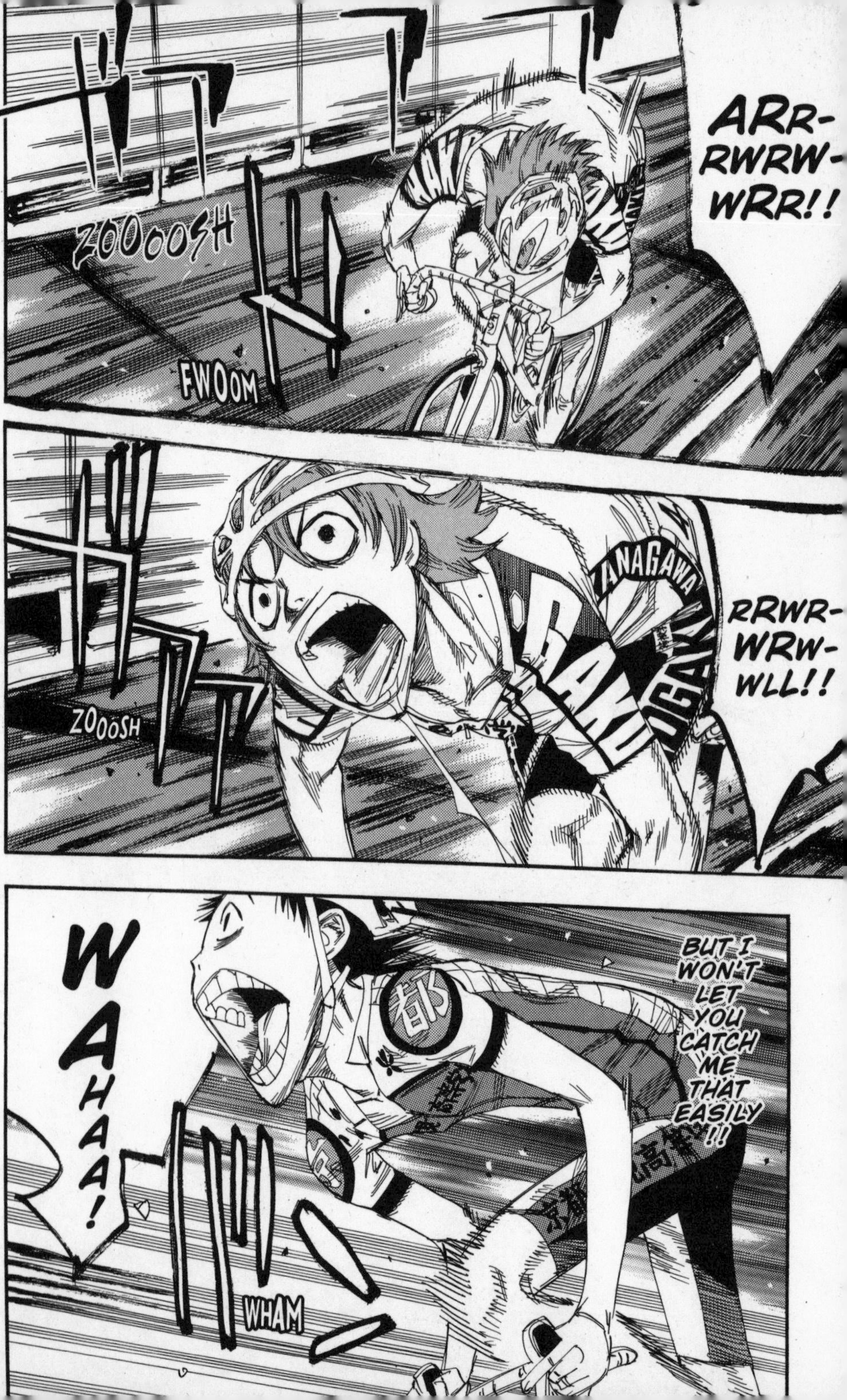
ARR-
RWRW-
WRR!!
ZOOOOSH
FWOOM
RRWR-
WRW-
WLL!!
ZOOOSH
BUT I WON'T LET YOU CATCH ME THAT EASILY!!
WAHAA!
WHAM

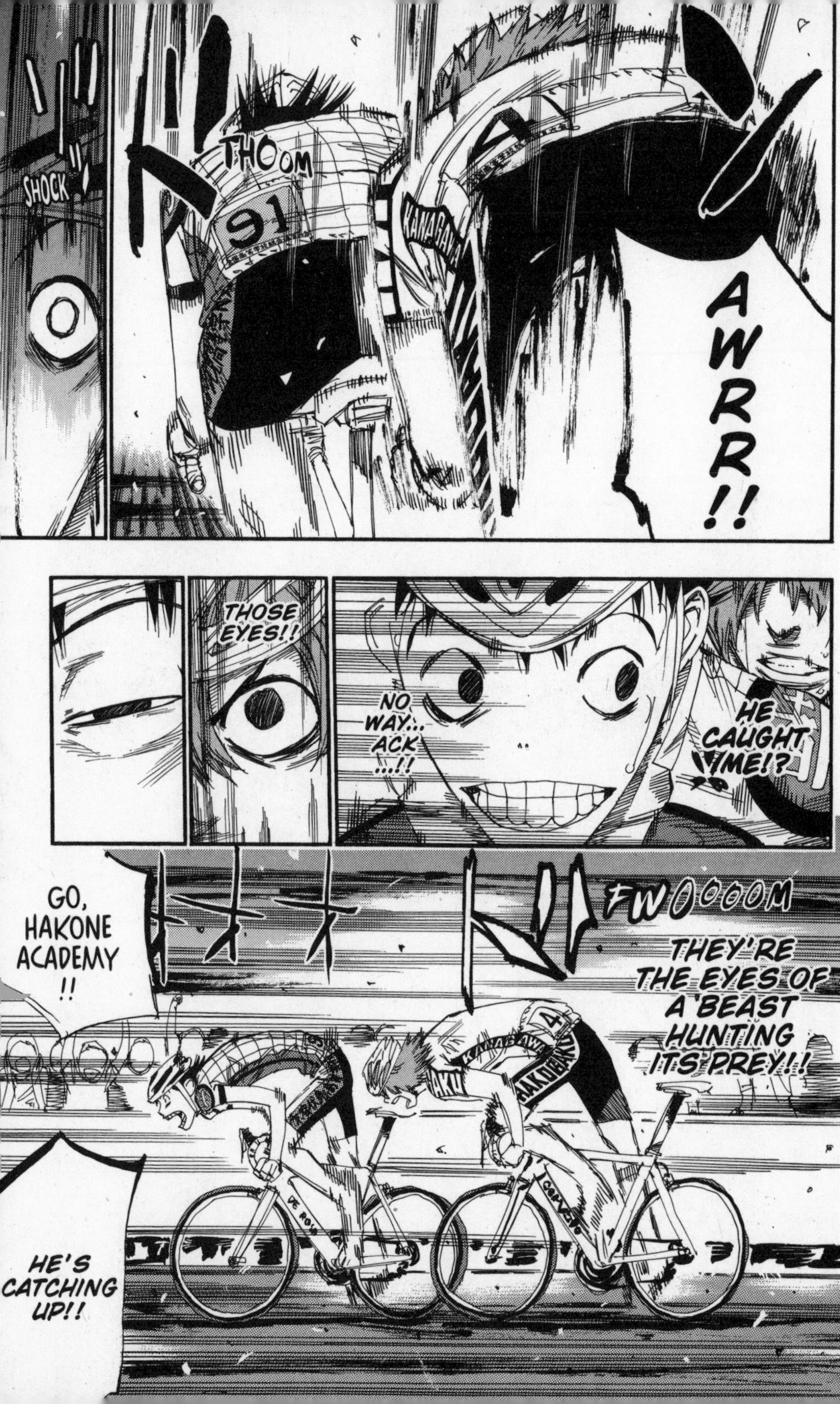
AWRR!!
THOOM
SHOCK
HE CAUGHT ME!?
NO WAY... ACK...!!
THOSE EYES!!
FWOOOOM
THEY'RE THE EYES OF A BEAST HUNTING ITS PREY!!
GO, HAKONE ACADEMY!!
HE'S CATCHING UP!!

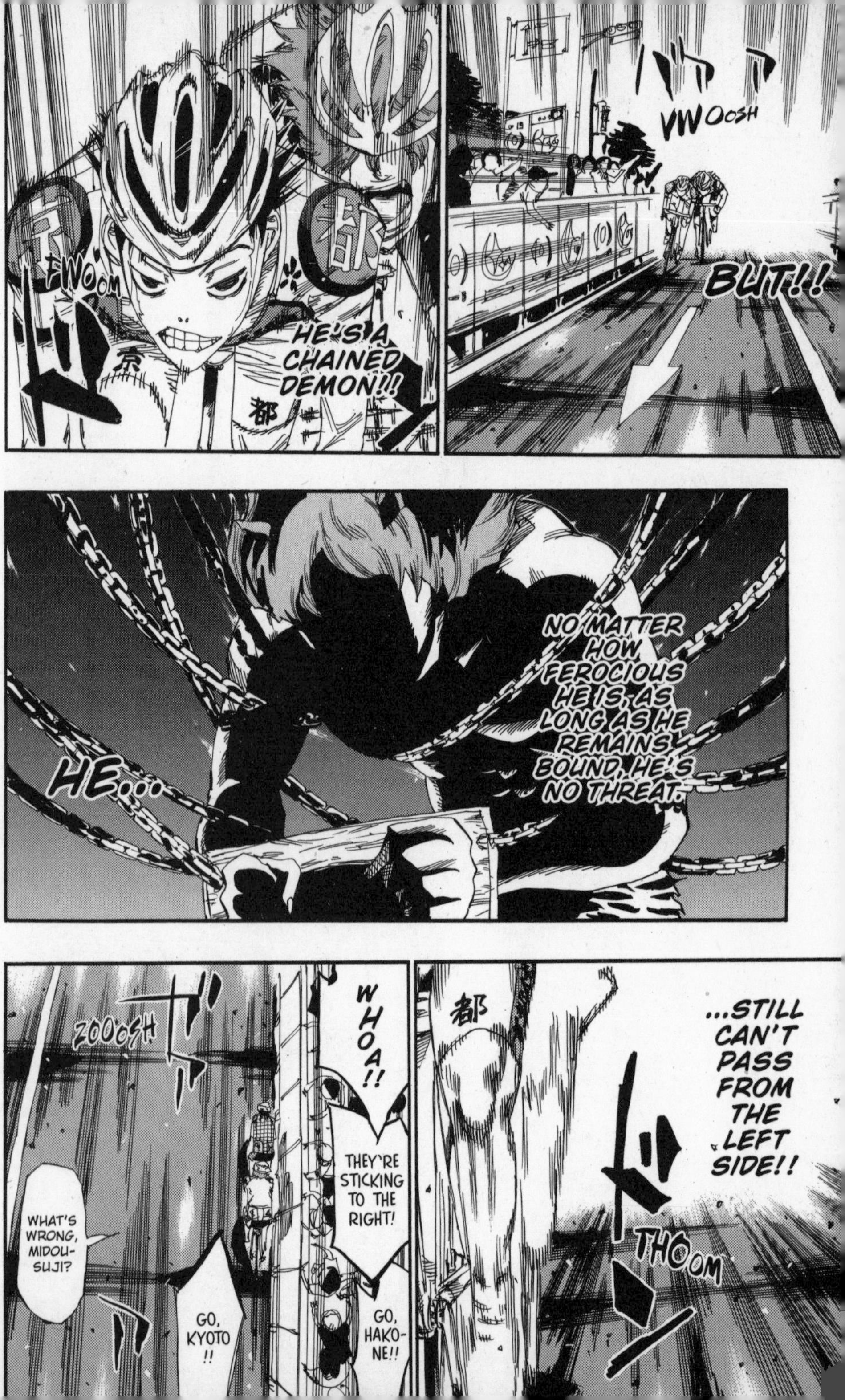
VWOOSH
BUT!!
FWOOM
HE'S A CHAINED DEMON!!
NO MATTER HOW FEROCIOUS HE IS, AS LONG AS HE REMAINS BOUND, HE'S NO THREAT.
HE...
...STILL CAN'T PASS FROM THE LEFT SIDE!!
THOOM
WHOA!!
ZOOOSH
THEY'RE STICKING TO THE RIGHT!
WHAT'S WRONG, MIDOU-SUJI?
GO, HAKO-NE!!
GO, KYOTO!!

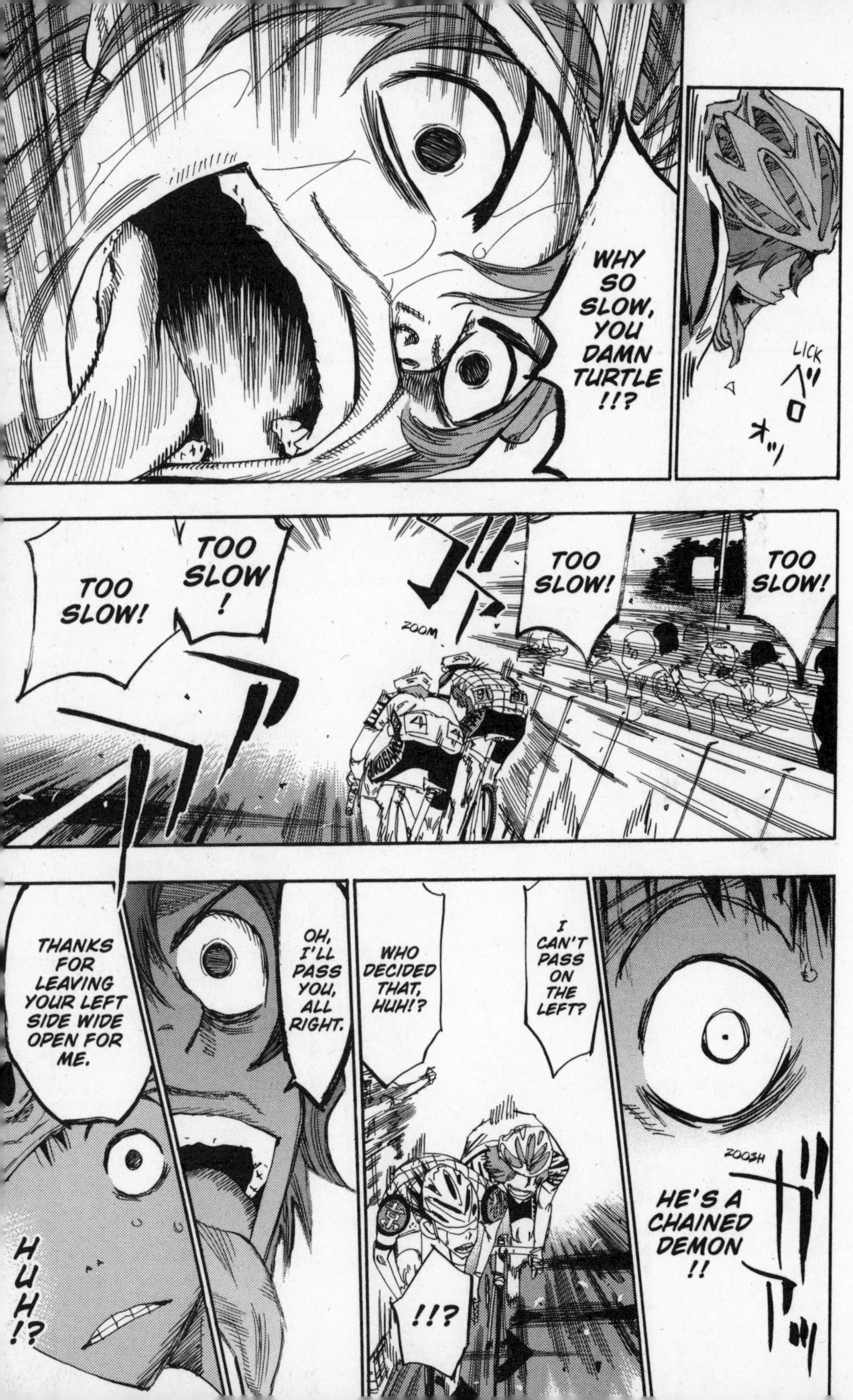
LICK
WHY SO SLOW, YOU DAMN TURTLE!!?
TOO SLOW!
TOO SLOW!
ZOOM
TOO SLOW!
TOO SLOW!
ZOOSH
HE'S A CHAINED DEMON!!
I CAN'T PASS ON THE LEFT?
WHO DECIDED THAT, HUH!?
!!?
OH, I'LL PASS YOU, ALL RIGHT.
THANKS FOR LEAVING YOUR LEFT SIDE WIDE OPEN FOR ME.
HUH!?

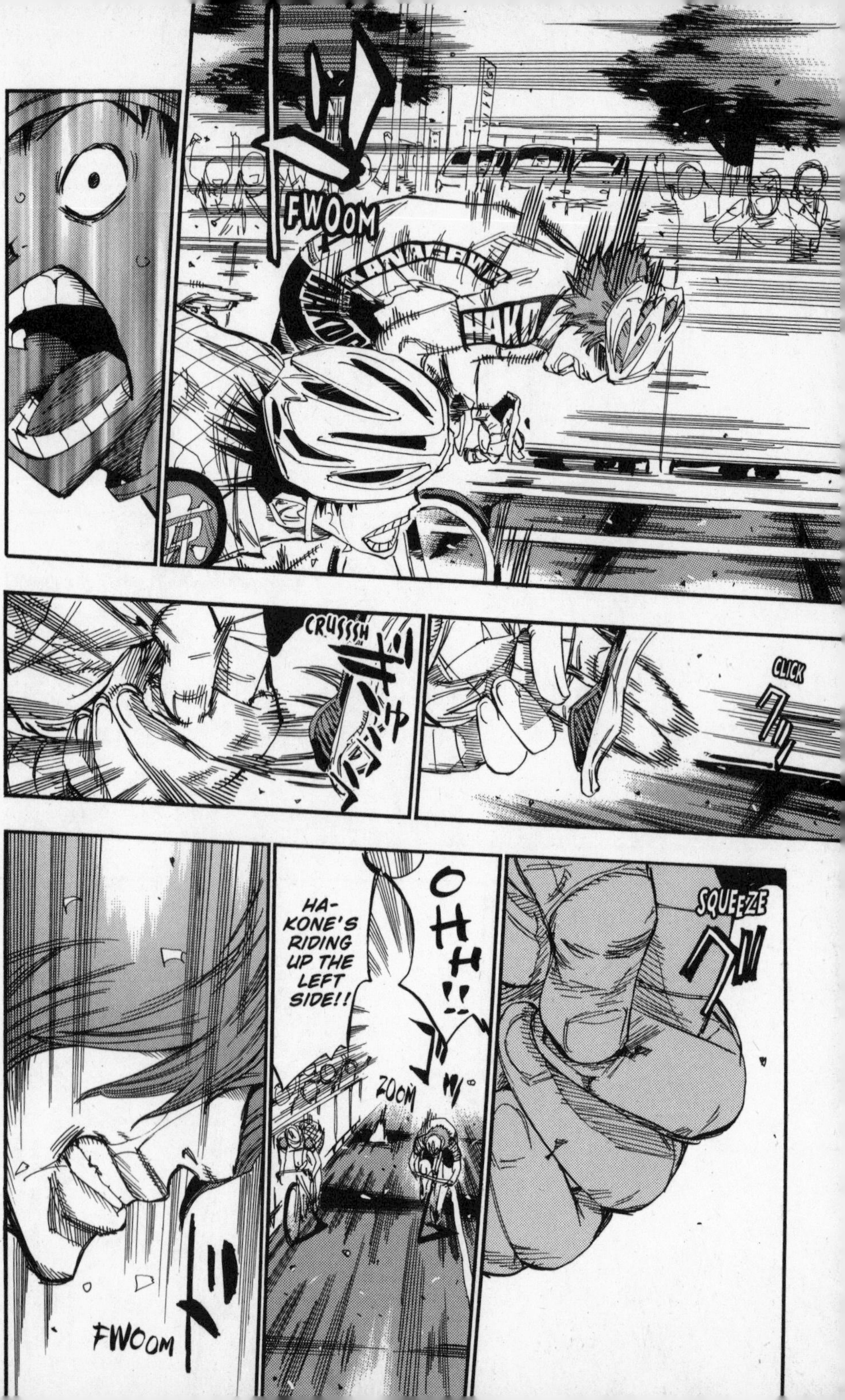
FWOOM
CLICK
CRUSSSH
SQUEEZE
OHH!!
HA-KONE'S RIDING UP THE LEFT SIDE!!
ZOOM
FWOOM

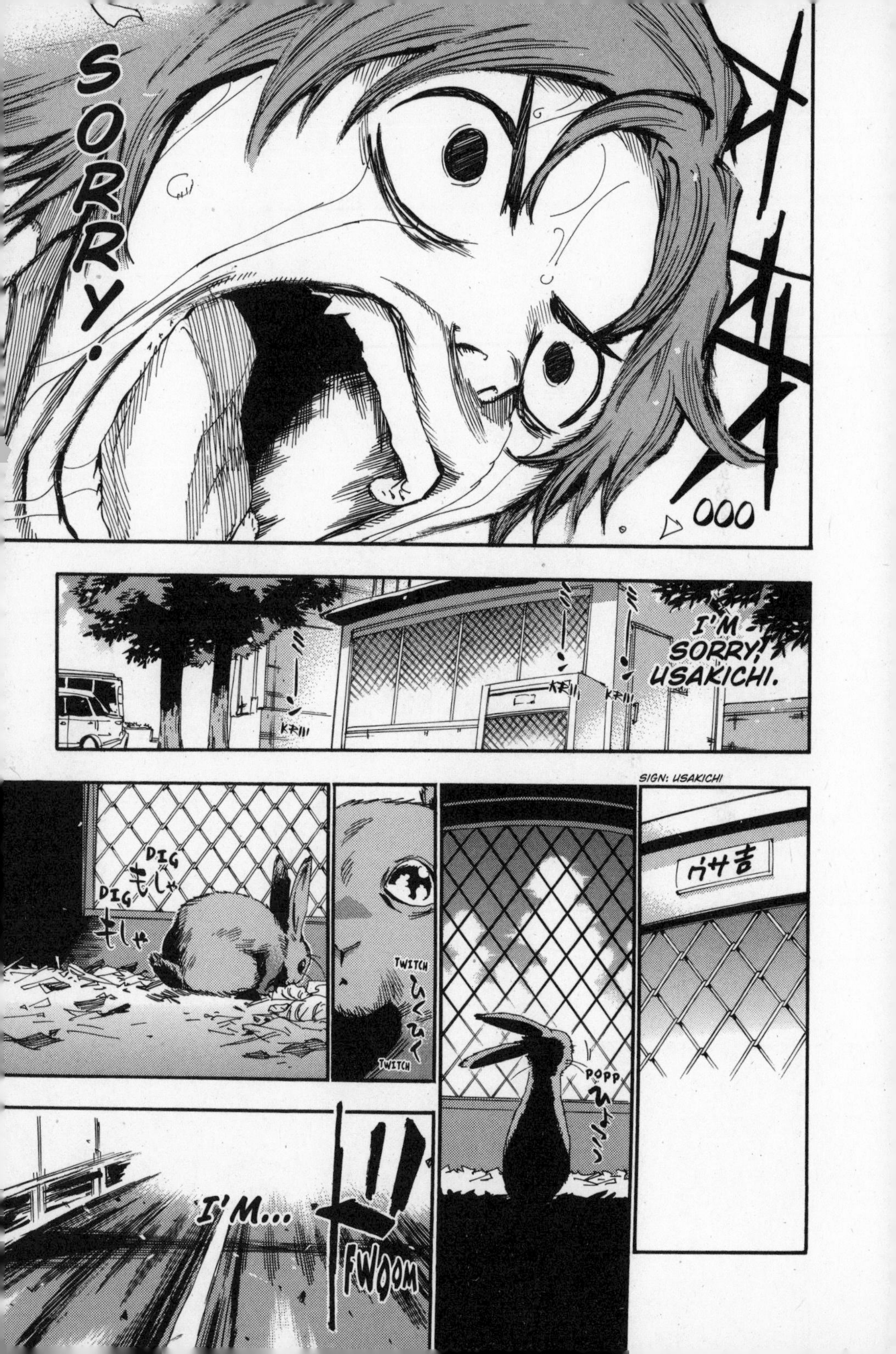
SORRY!
OOO
I'M SORRY, USAKICHI.
KRIII
KRIII
KRIII
SIGN: USAKICHI
ウサ吉
POPP
TWITCH
ひくひく
TWITCH
DIG
もしゃ
DIG
もしゃ
I'M...
FWOOM

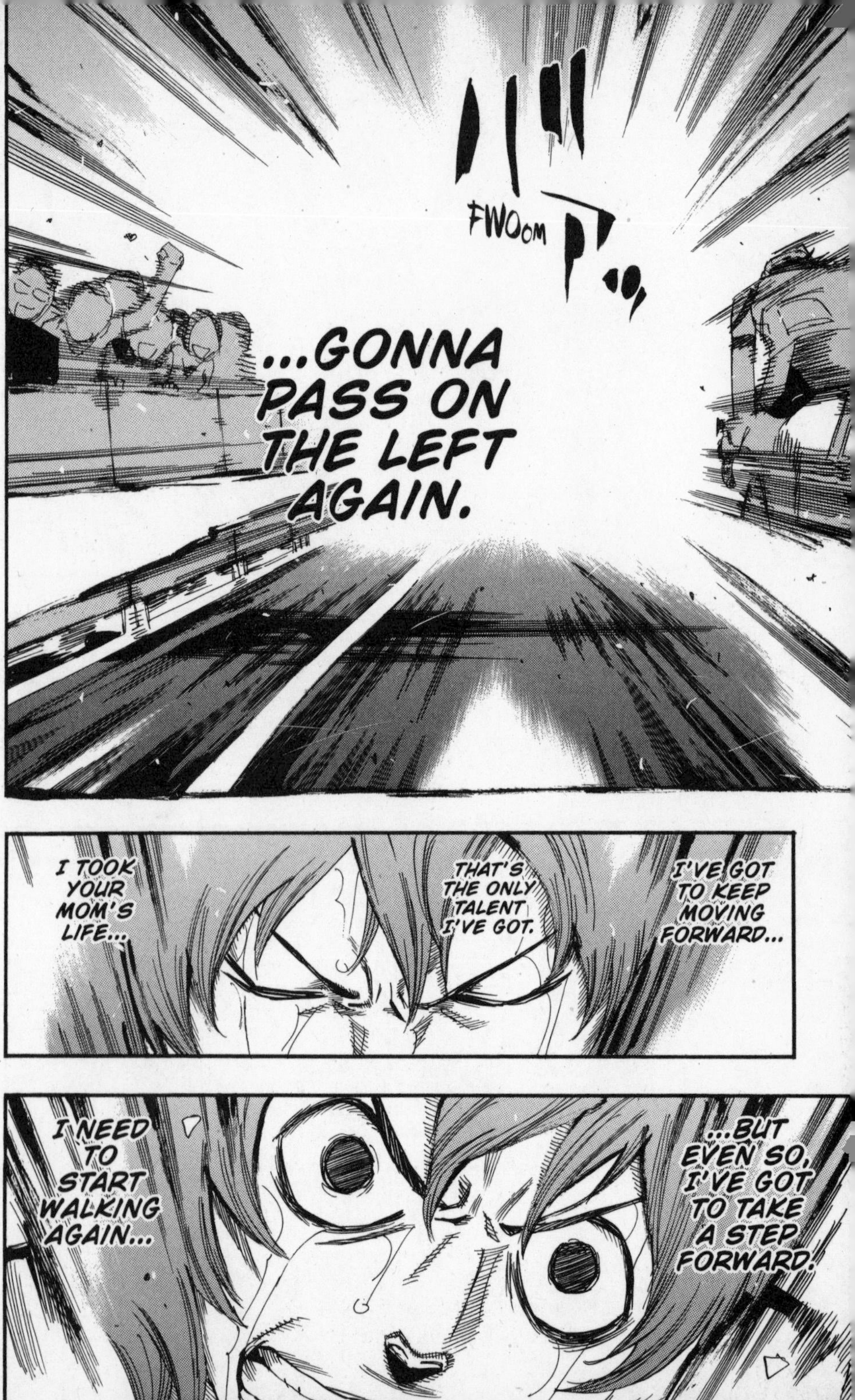
FWOOM
...GONNA PASS ON THE LEFT AGAIN.
I'VE GOT TO KEEP MOVING FORWARD...
THAT'S THE ONLY TALENT I'VE GOT.
I TOOK YOUR MOM'S LIFE...
...BUT EVEN SO, I'VE GOT TO TAKE A STEP FORWARD.
I NEED TO START WALKING AGAIN...

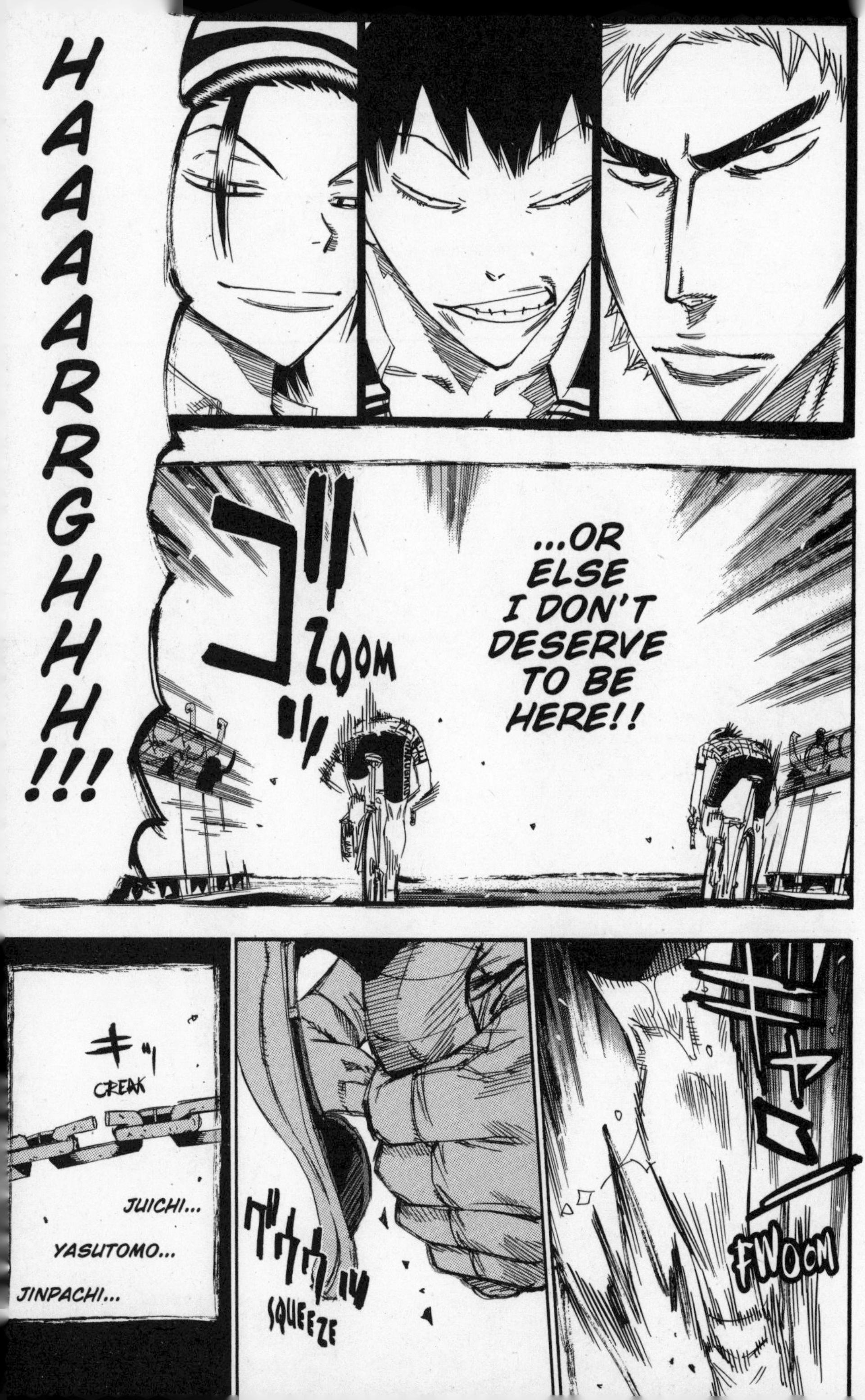
HAAAAARRRGHHHH!!!
...OR ELSE I DON'T DESERVE TO BE HERE!!
ZOOM
FWOOM
SQUEEZE
CREAK
JUICHI...
YASUTOMO...
JINPACHI...

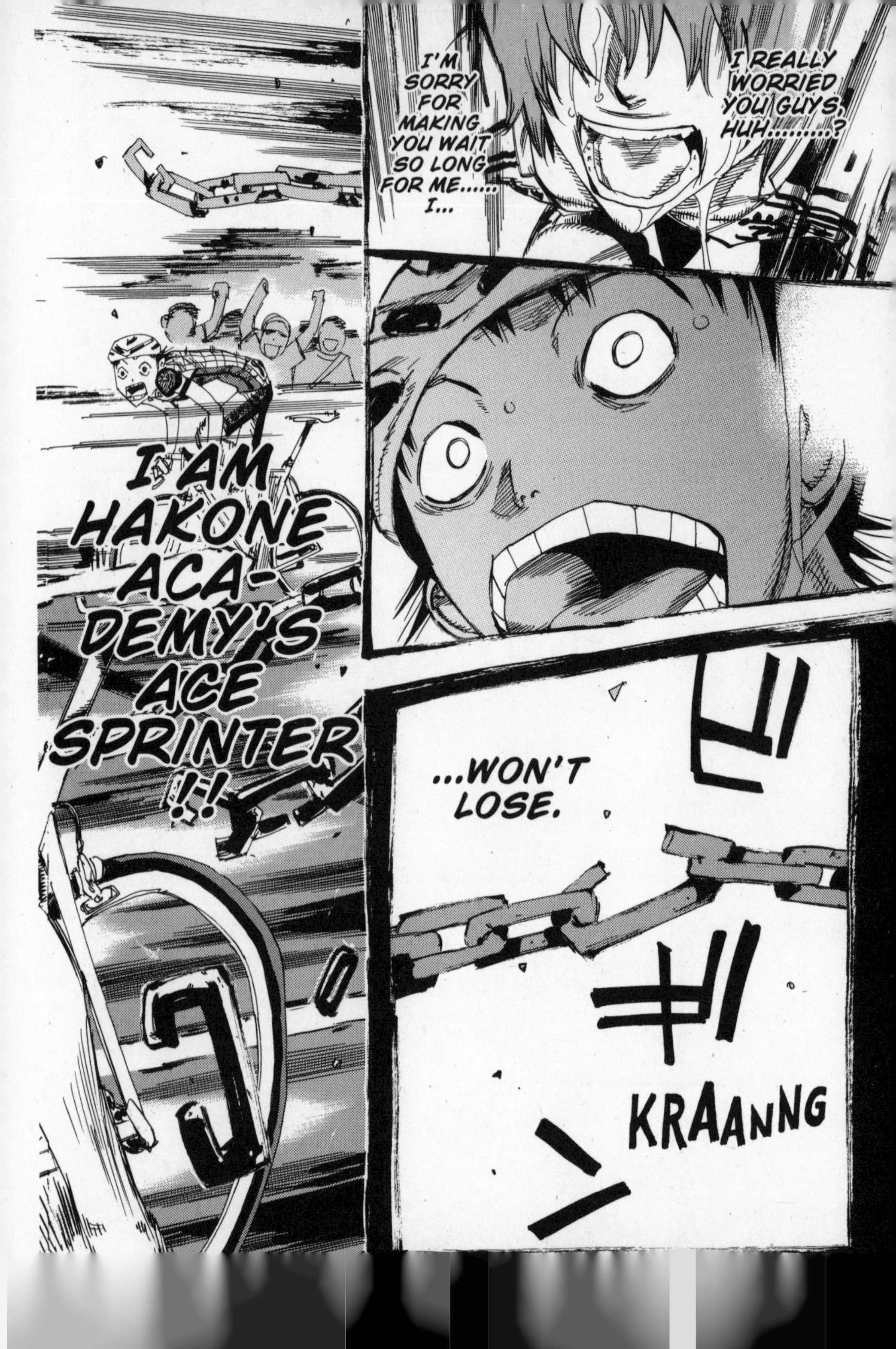
I REALLY WORRIED YOU GUYS, HUH.........?
I'M SORRY FOR MAKING YOU WAIT SO LONG FOR ME...... I...
...WON'T LOSE.
KRAANNG
I AM HAKONE ACA-DEMY'S ACE SPRINTER!!

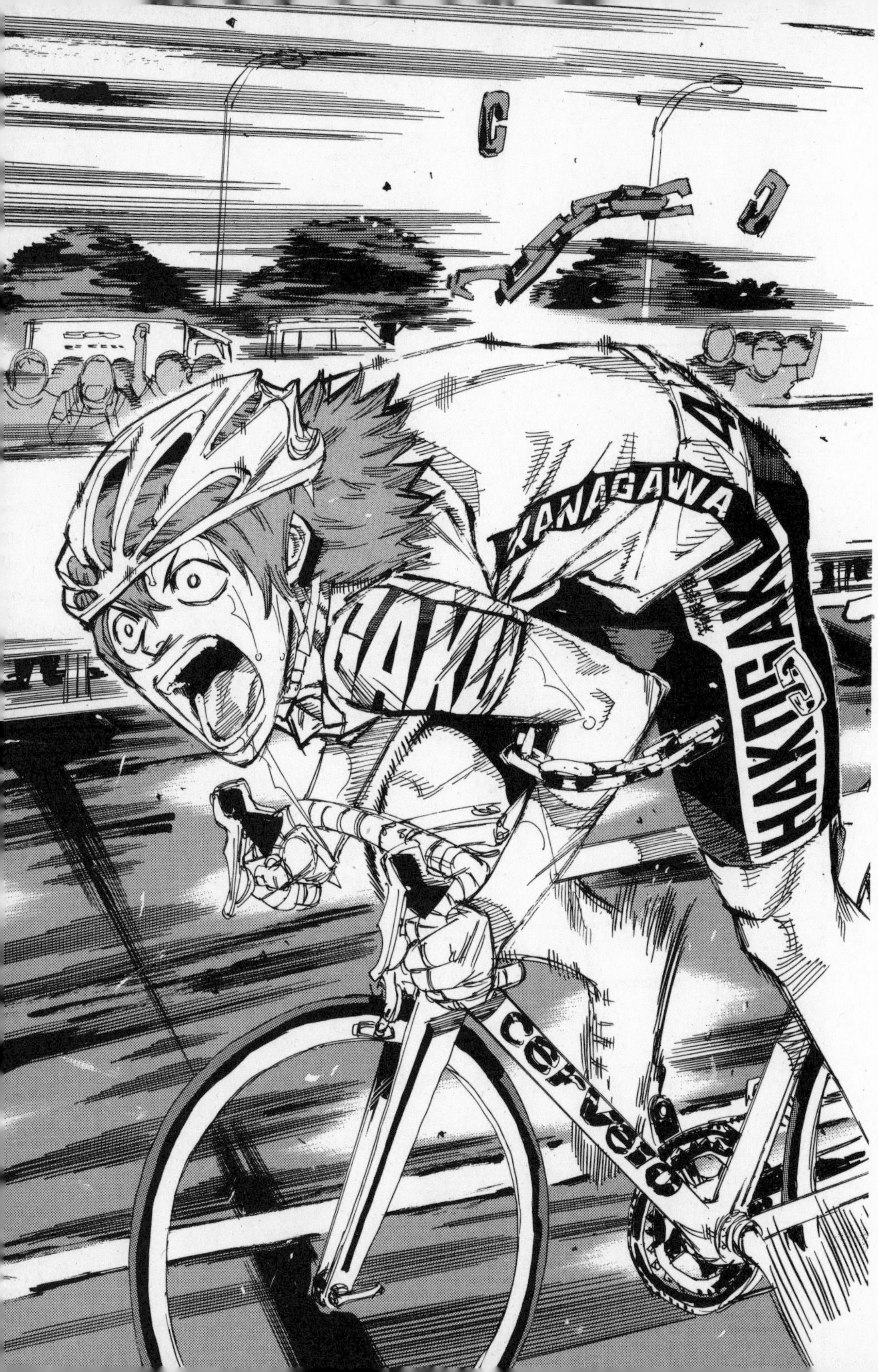
KANAGAWA
HAKOGAKU
cervelo

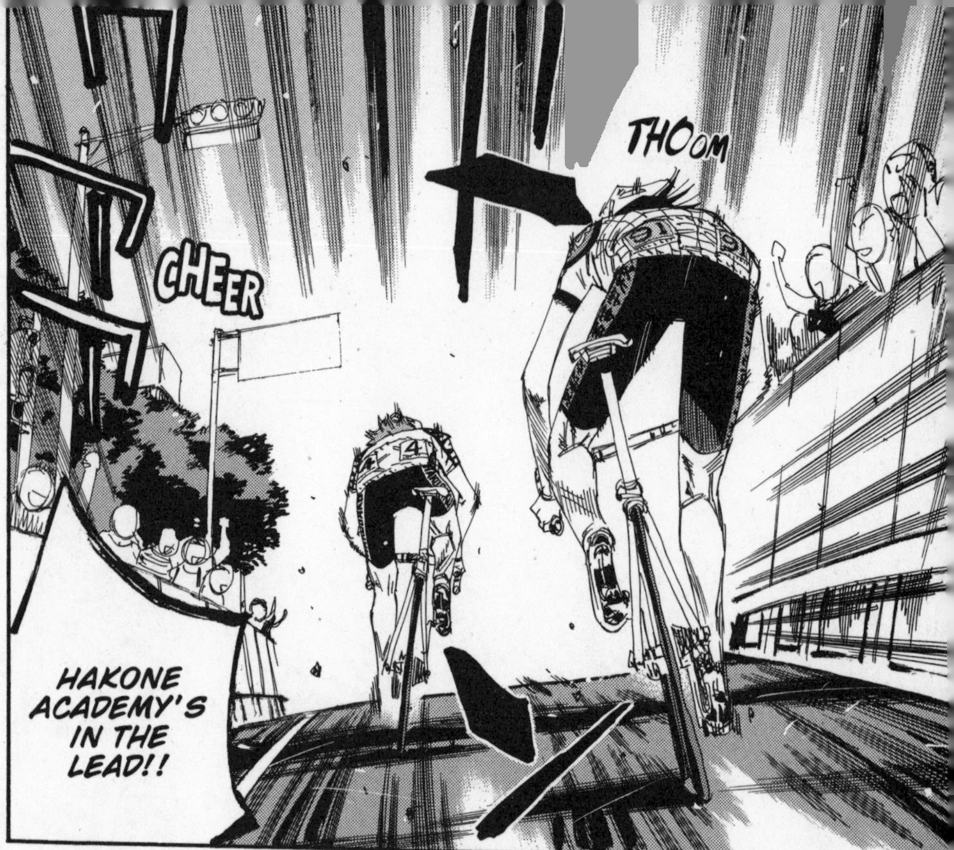
THOOM
CHEER
HAKONE ACADEMY'S IN THE LEAD!!

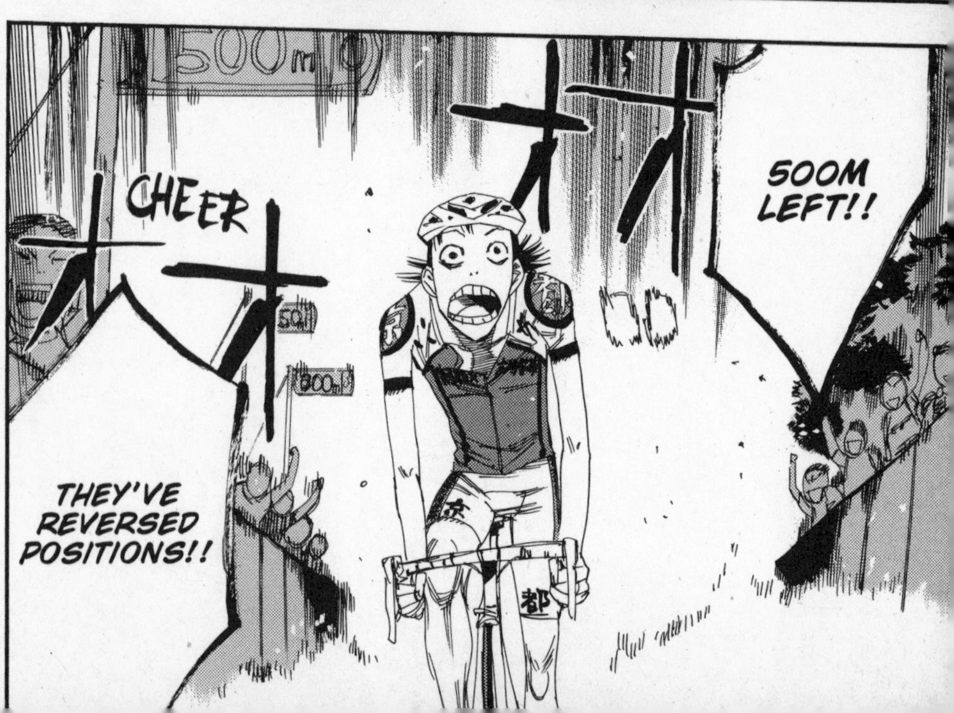
500M LEFT!!
500m
CHEER
THEY'VE REVERSED POSITIONS!!

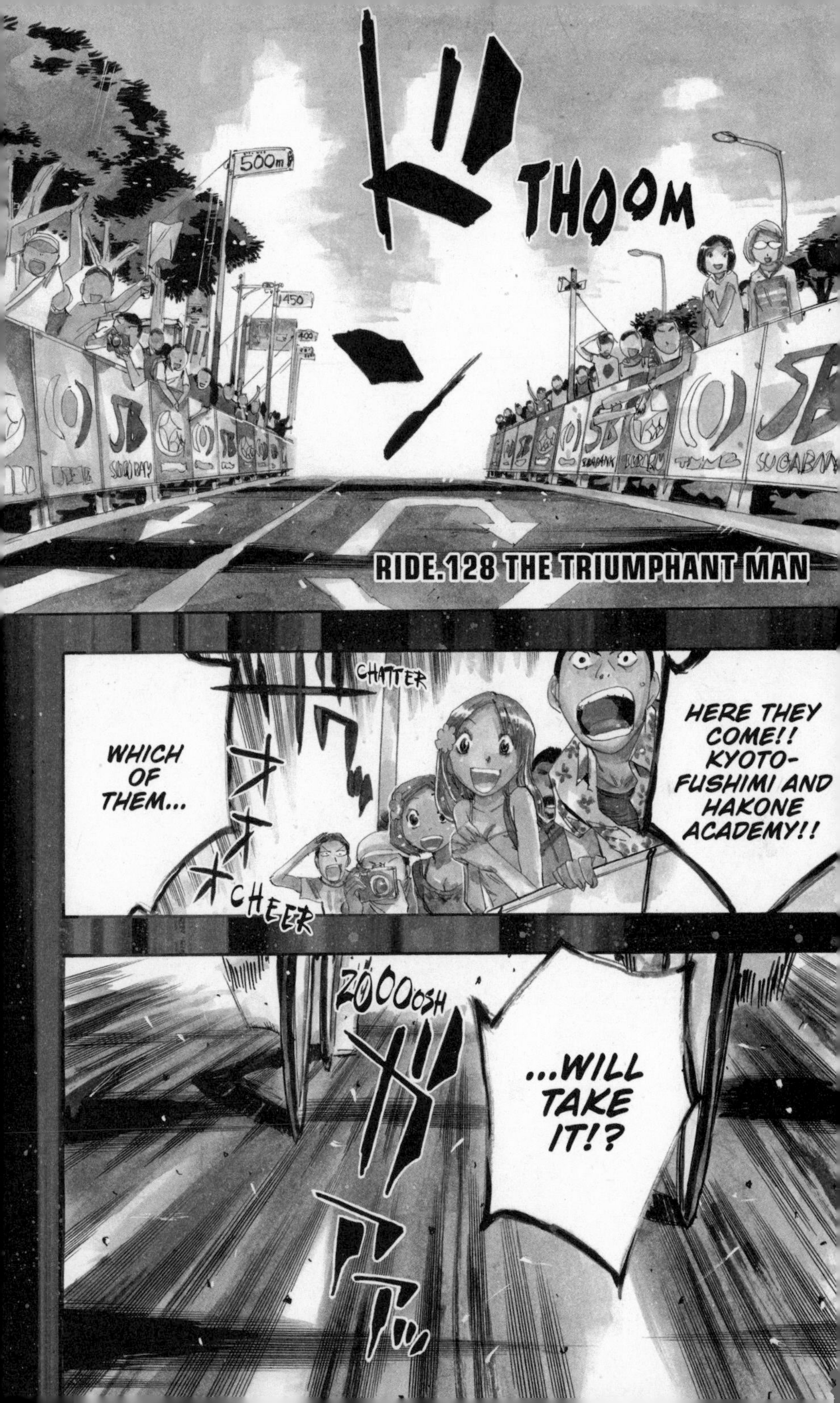
500m
450
THOOM
RIDE.128 THE TRIUMPHANT MAN
HERE THEY COME!! KYOTO-FUSHIMI AND HAKONE ACADEMY!!
CHATTER
WHICH OF THEM...
CHEER
ZOOOOSH
...WILL TAKE IT!?

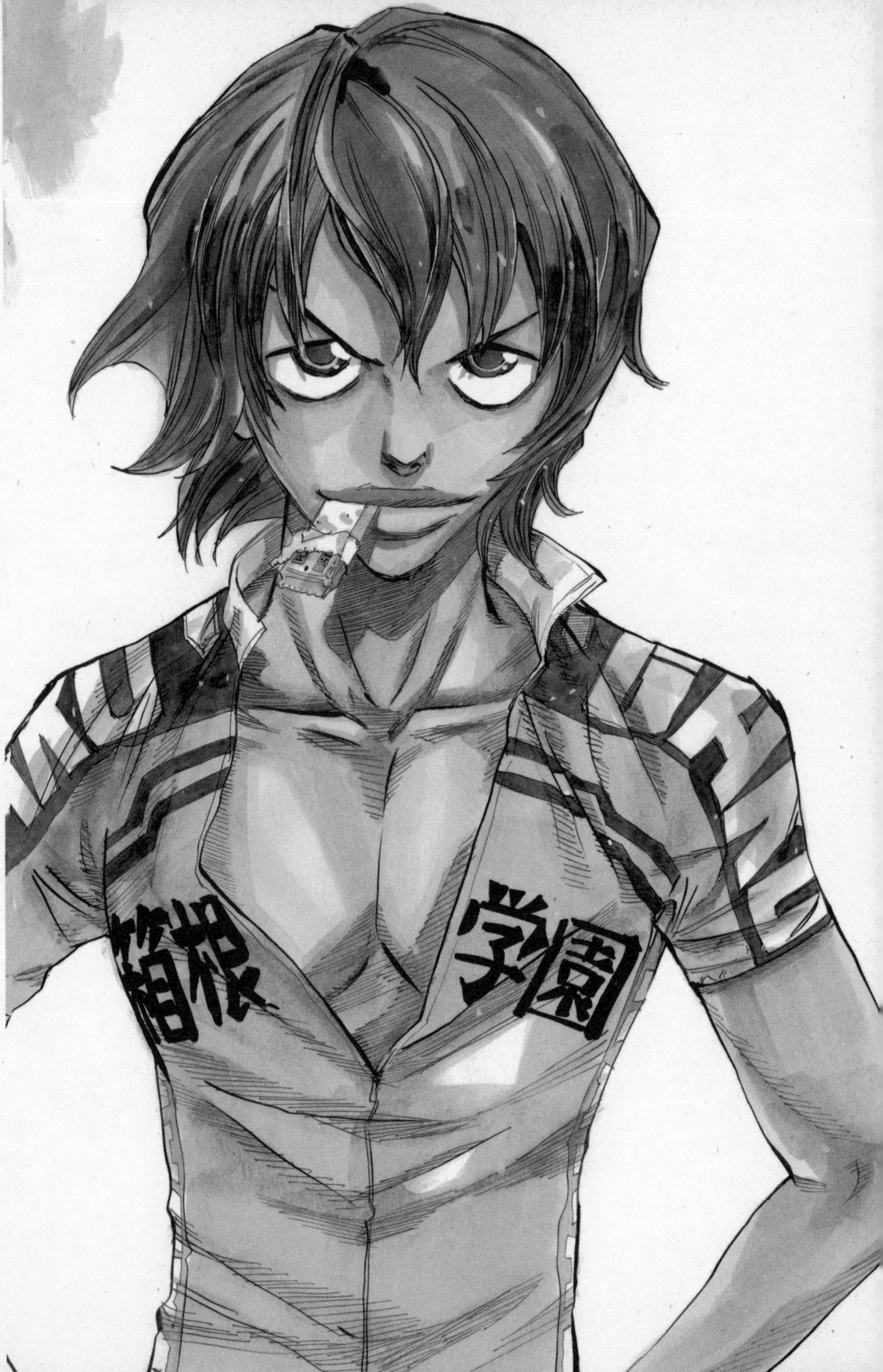
箱根
学園

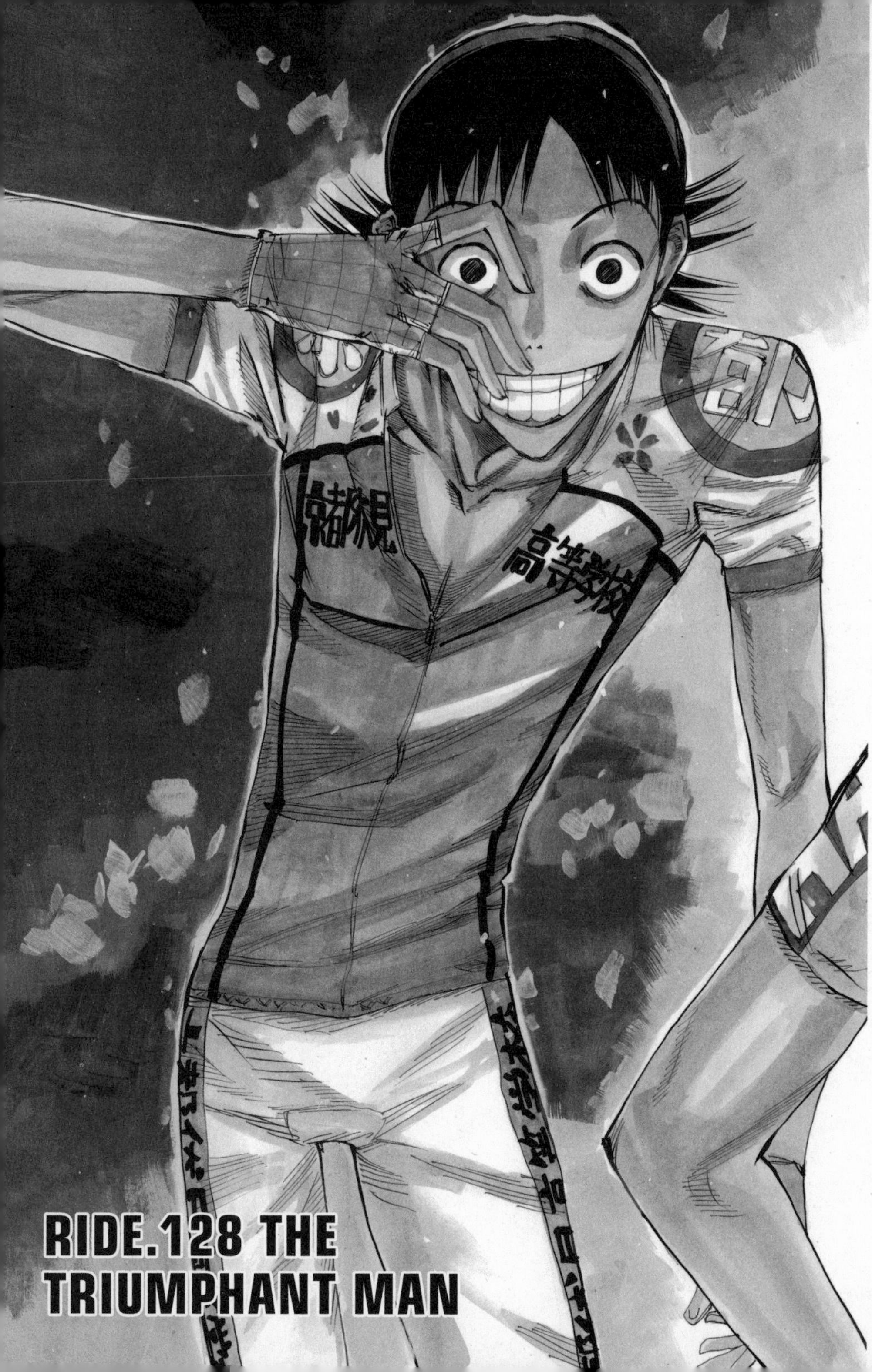

RIDE.128 THE TRIUMPHANT MAN

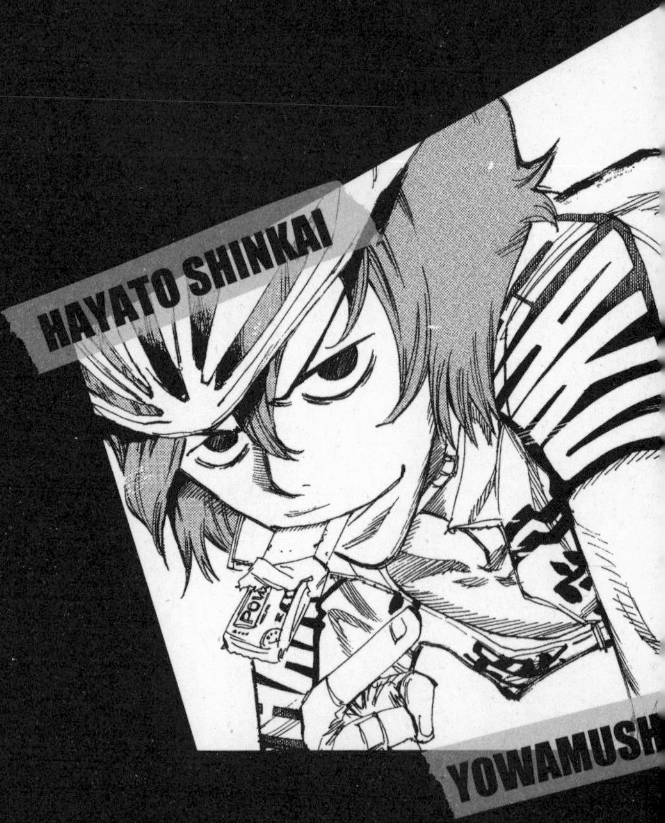
HAYATO SHINKAI

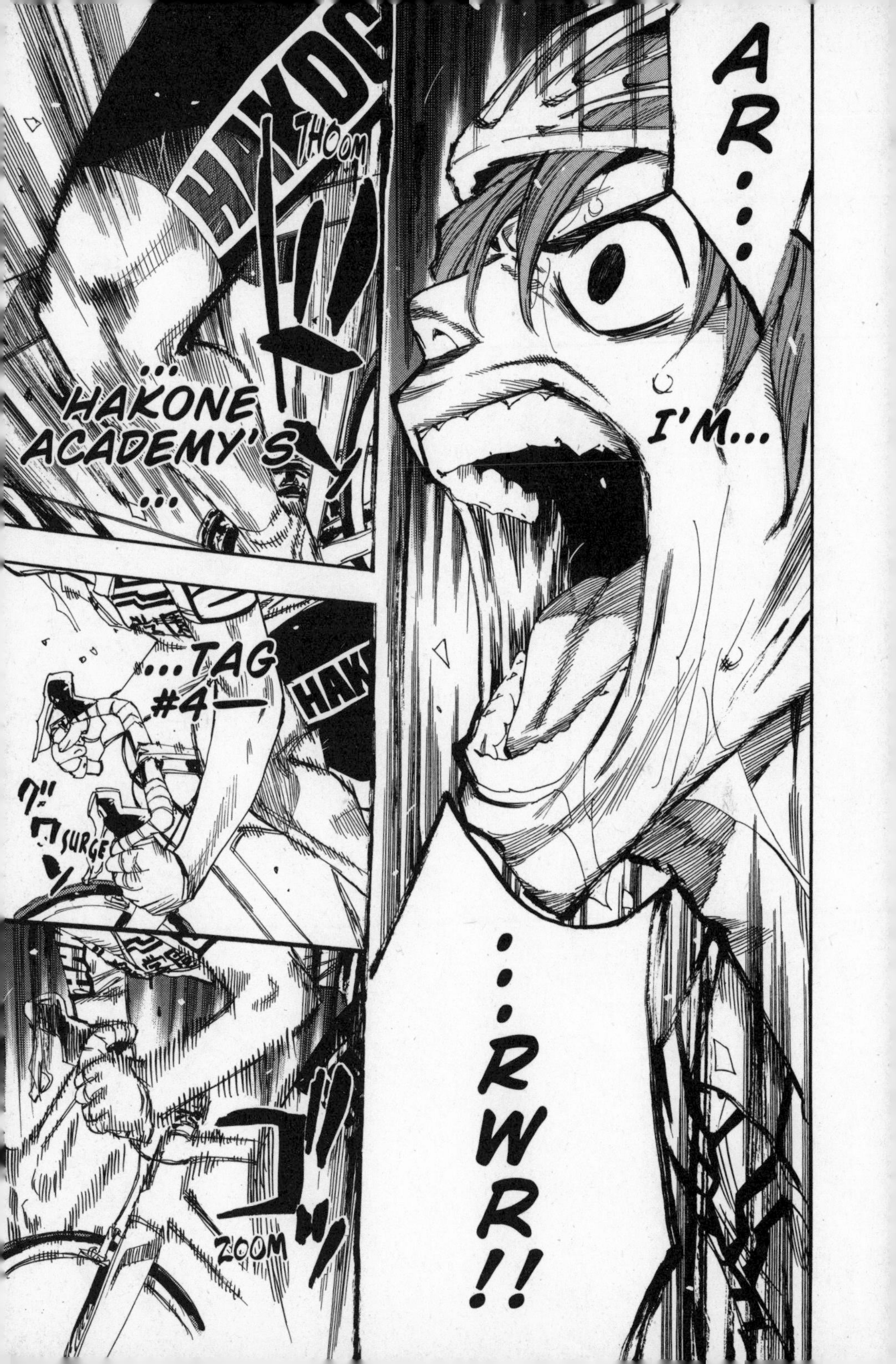
AR...
I'M...
...RWR!!
...HAKONE ACADEMY'S ...
THOOM
...TAG #4—
SURGE
ZOOM

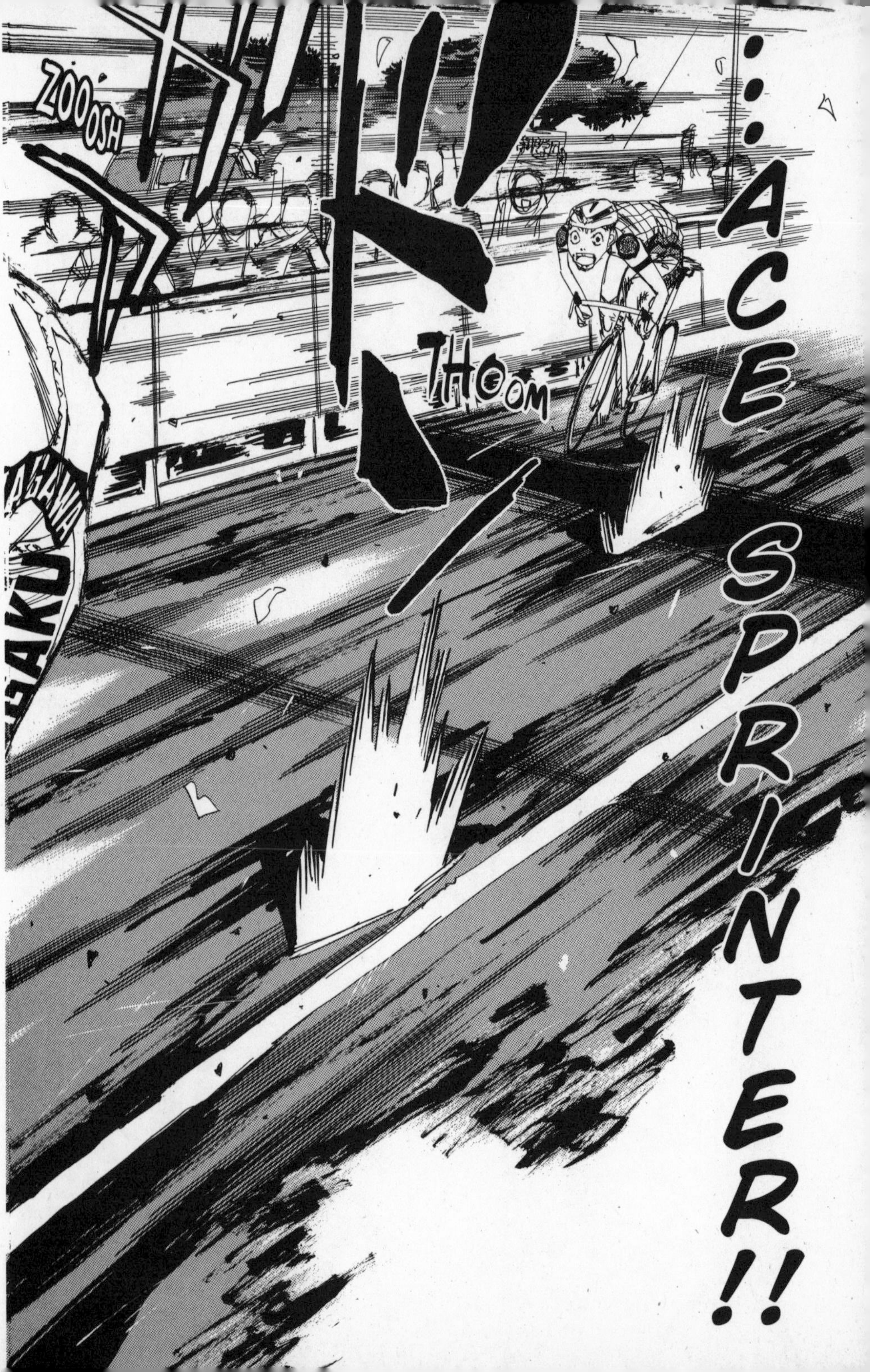
...ACE SPRINTER!!
THOOM
ZOOOSH

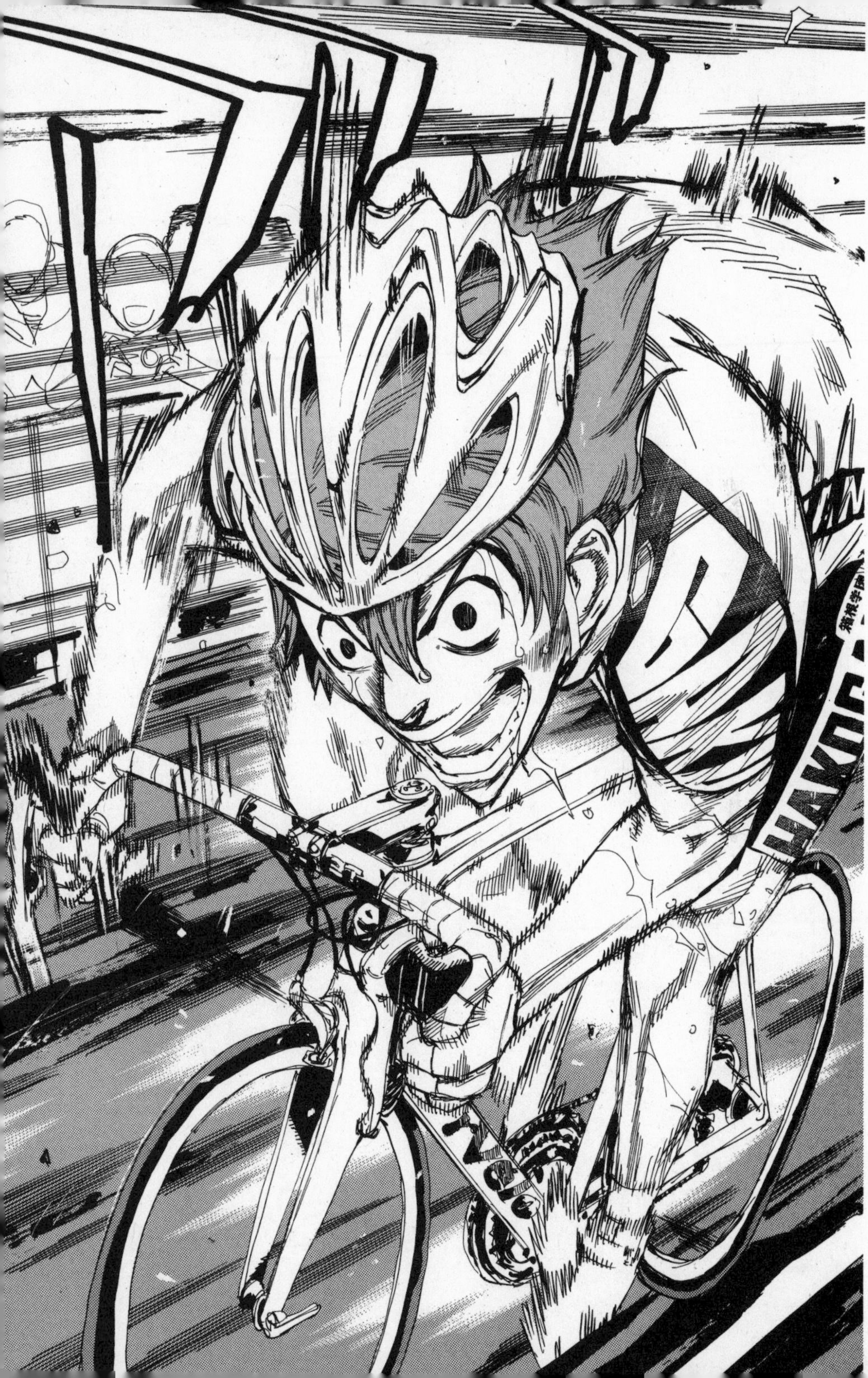

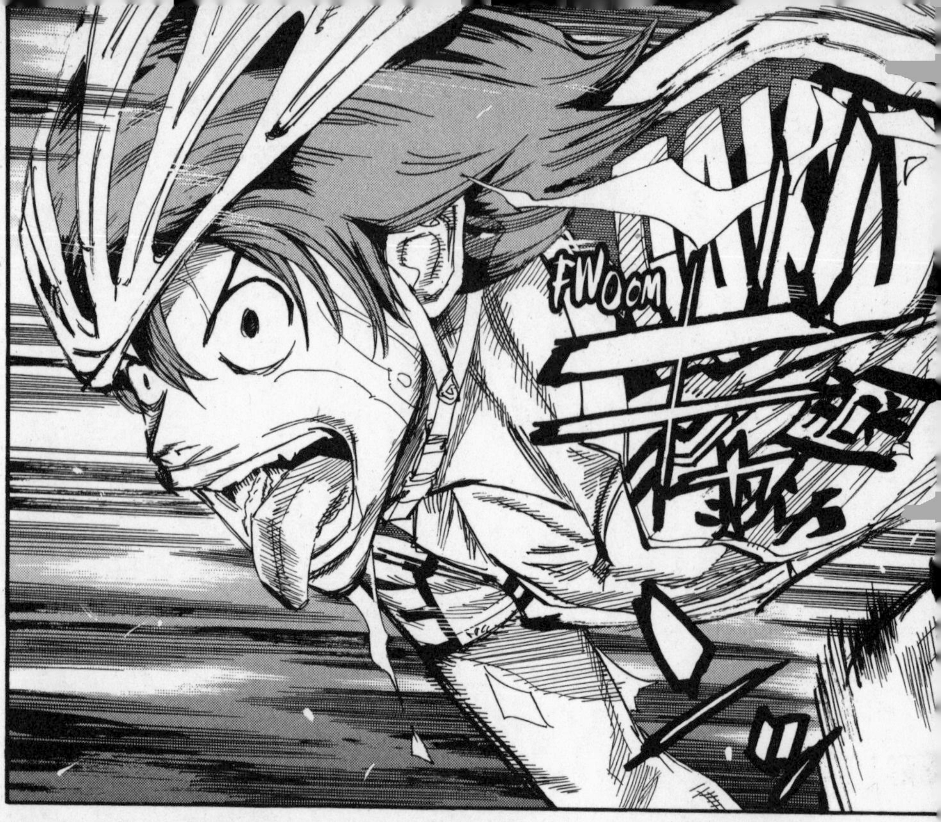
FWOOM

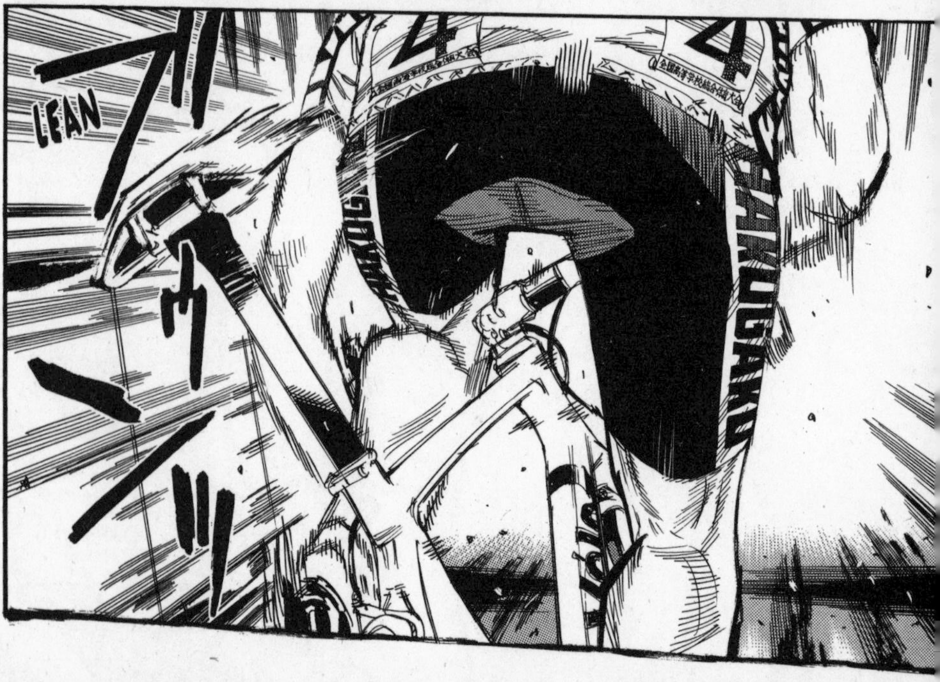
LEAN

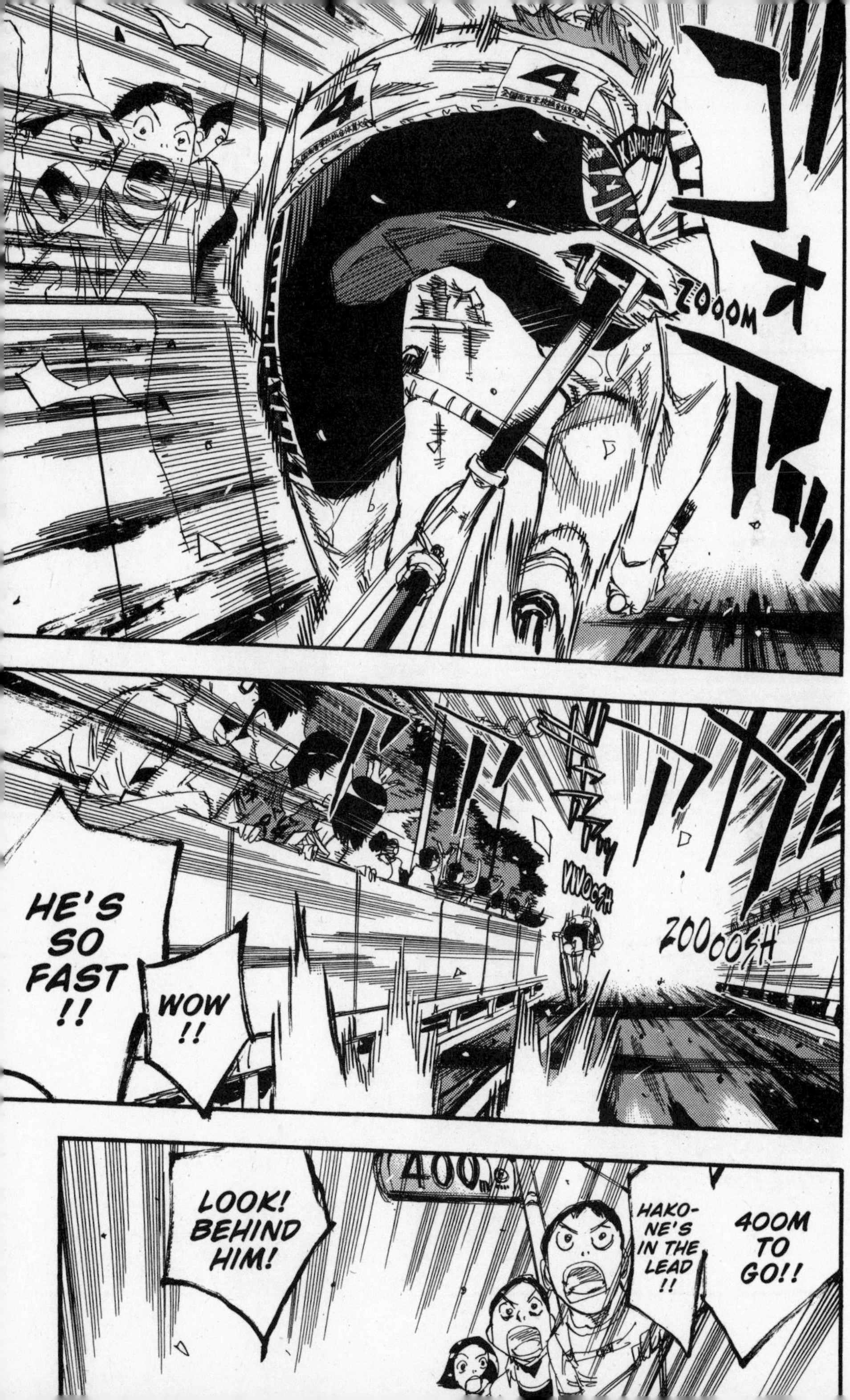
ZOOOM
ZOOOOSH
VWOOSH
WOW!!
HE'S SO FAST!!
400m
400M TO GO!!
HAKONE'S IN THE LEAD!!
LOOK! BEHIND HIM!

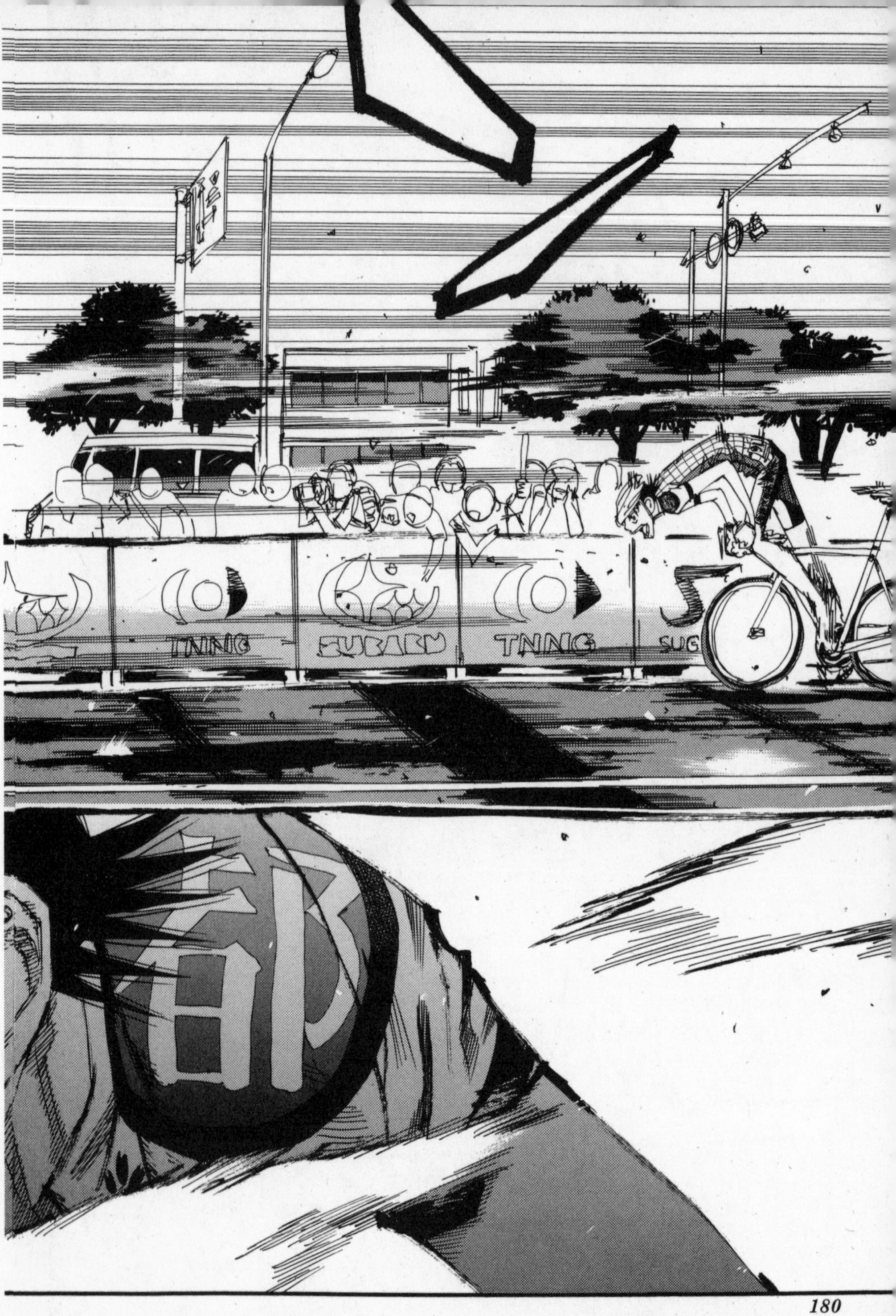
TNNG
SUBARU
TNNG

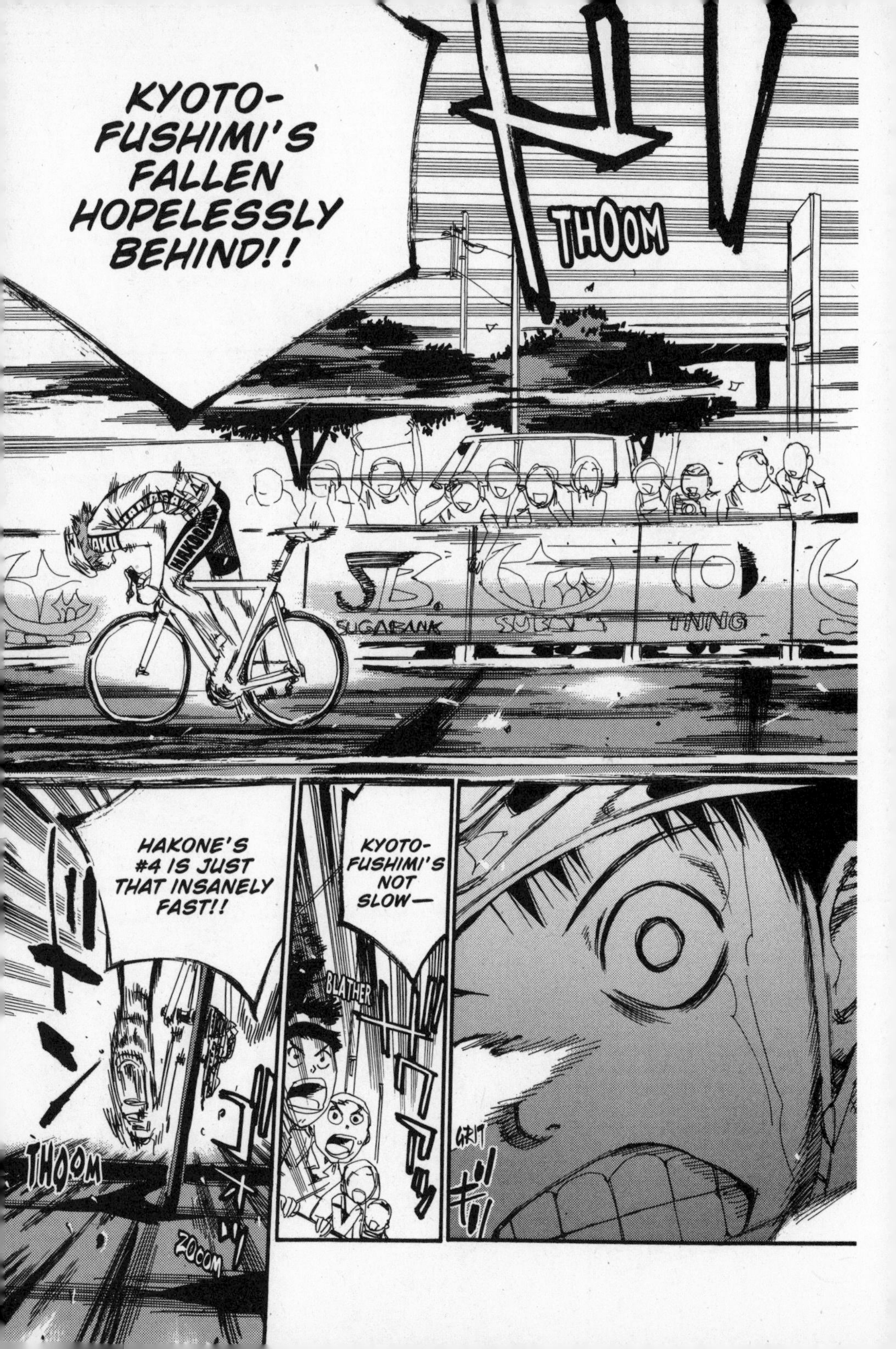
KYOTO-FUSHIMI'S FALLEN HOPELESSLY BEHIND!!
THOOM
SUGABANK
TNNG
GRIT
KYOTO-FUSHIMI'S NOT SLOW—
BLATHER
HAKONE'S #4 IS JUST THAT INSANELY FAST!!
THOOM
ZOOM

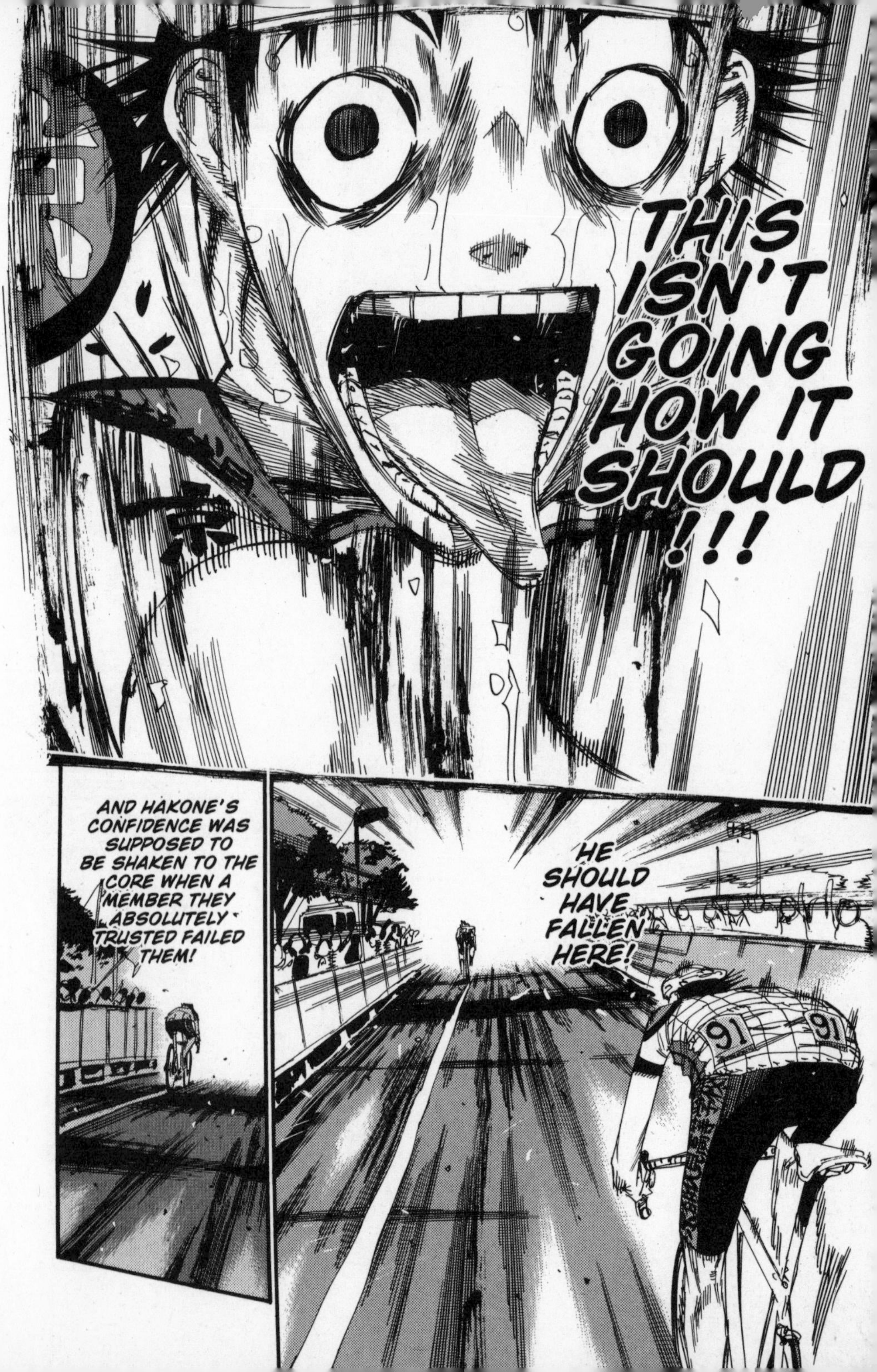
THIS ISN'T GOING HOW IT SHOULD !!!
HE SHOULD HAVE FALLEN HERE!
AND HAKONE'S CONFIDENCE WAS SUPPOSED TO BE SHAKEN TO THE CORE WHEN A MEMBER THEY ABSOLUTELY TRUSTED FAILED THEM!

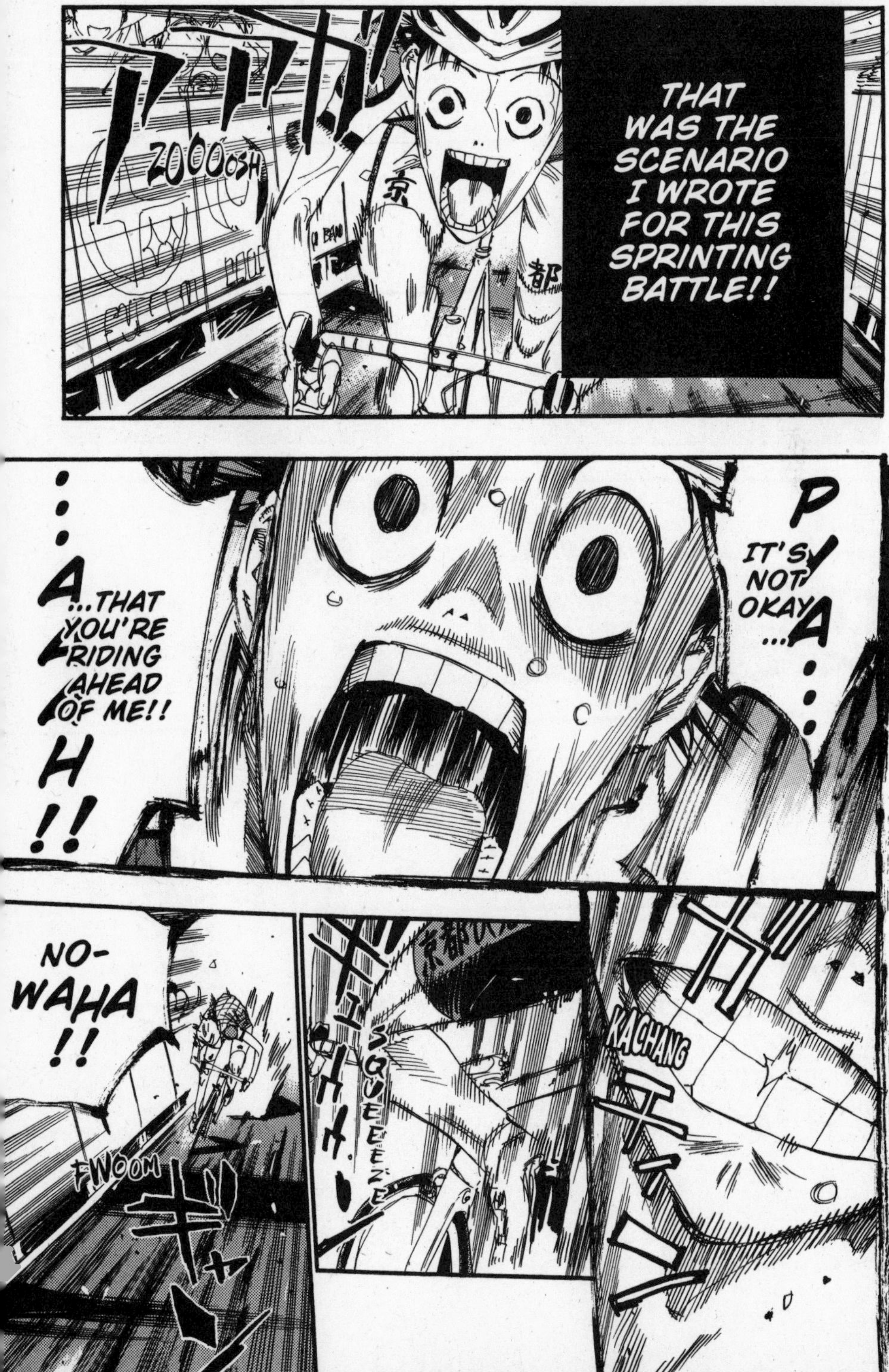
THAT WAS THE SCENARIO I WROTE FOR THIS SPRINTING BATTLE!!
ZOOOOSH
P...A...
IT'S NOT OKAY...
...A...H!!
...THAT YOU'RE RIDING AHEAD OF ME!!
KACHANG
SQUEEEZE
NO-WAHA!!
FWOOM

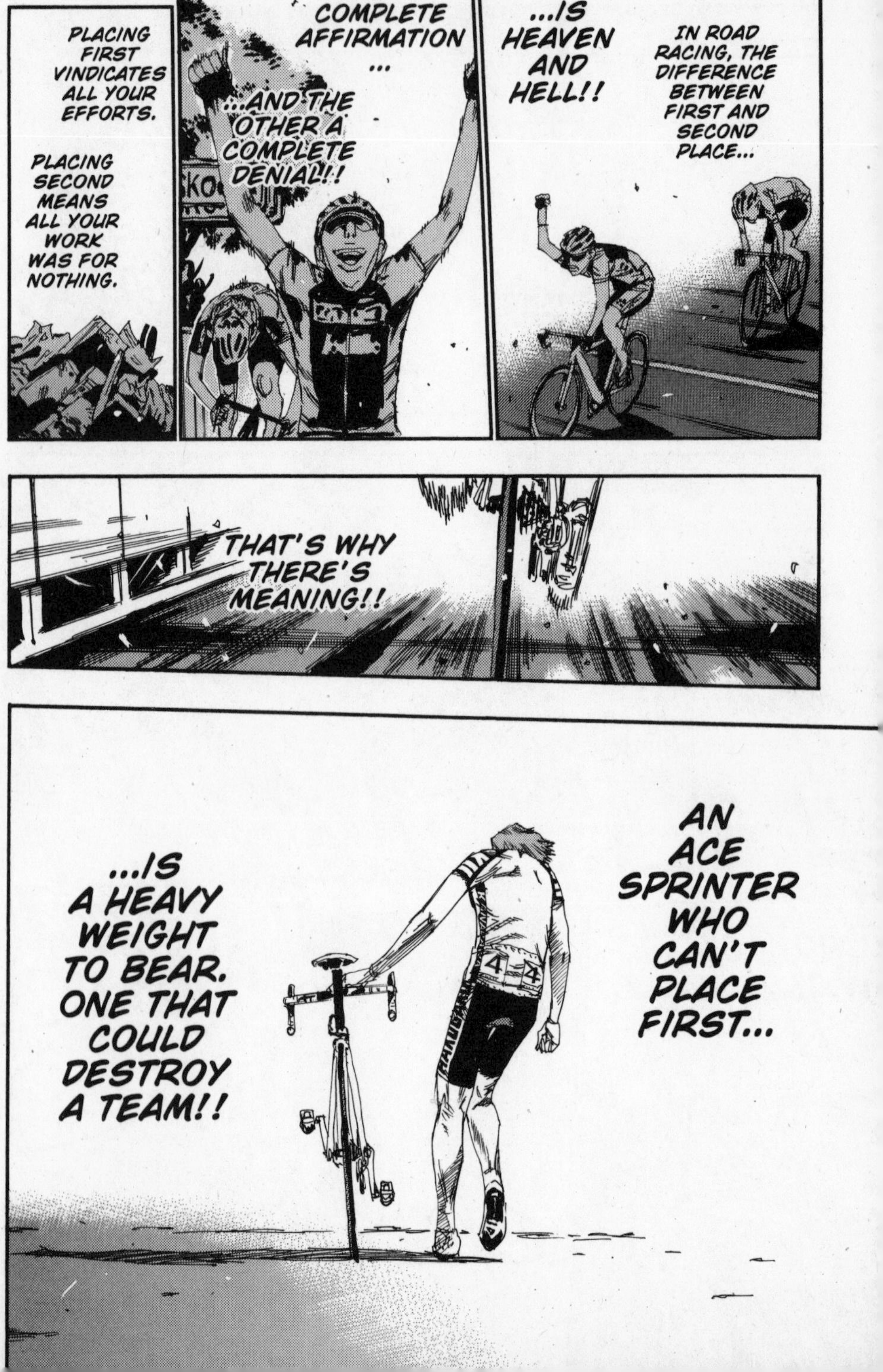
IN ROAD RACING, THE DIFFERENCE BETWEEN FIRST AND SECOND PLACE...
...IS HEAVEN AND HELL!!
ONE IS COMPLETE AFFIRMATION ...
...AND THE OTHER A COMPLETE DENIAL!!
PLACING FIRST VINDICATES ALL YOUR EFFORTS.
PLACING SECOND MEANS ALL YOUR WORK WAS FOR NOTHING.
THAT'S WHY THERE'S MEANING!!
AN ACE SPRINTER WHO CAN'T PLACE FIRST...
...IS A HEAVY WEIGHT TO BEAR. ONE THAT COULD DESTROY A TEAM!!

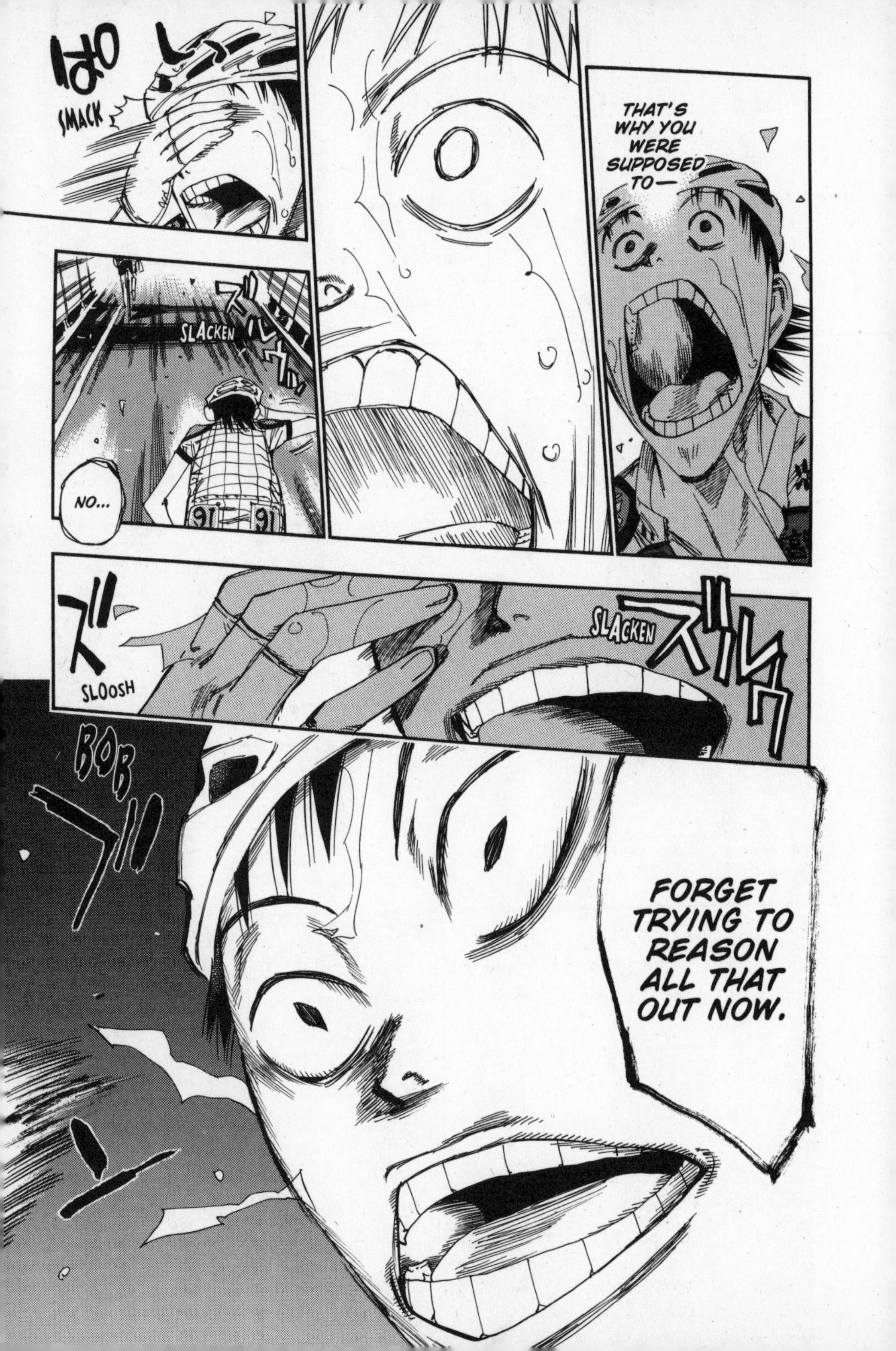
THAT'S WHY YOU WERE SUPPOSED TO—
SMACK
SLACKEN
NO...
SLACKEN
SLOOSH
FORGET TRYING TO REASON ALL THAT OUT NOW.
BOB

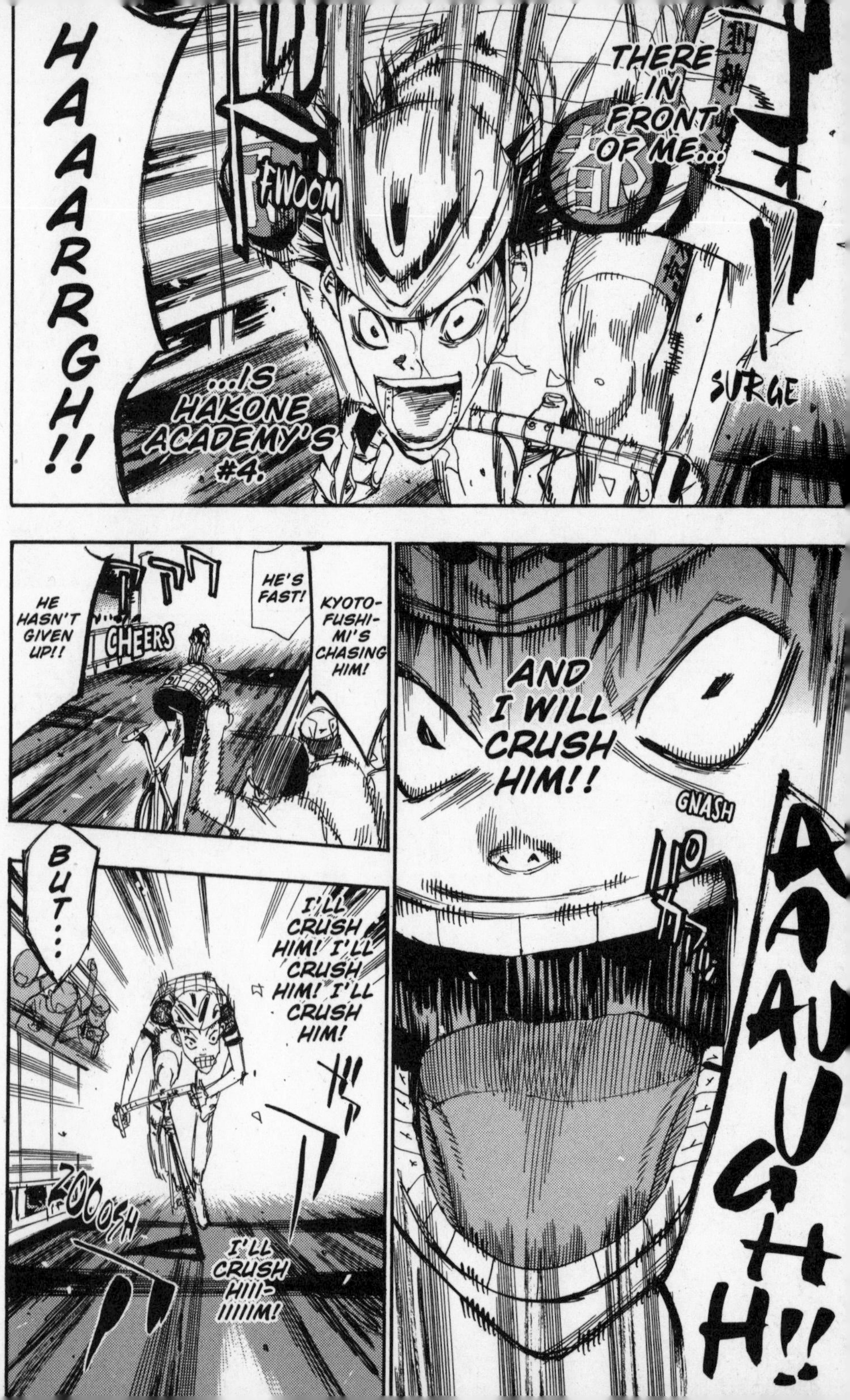
THERE IN FRONT OF ME...
FWOOM
SURGE
...IS HAKONE ACADEMY'S #4.
HAAAARRRGH!!
AND I WILL CRUSH HIM!!
GNASH
AAAUUGHH!!
HE'S FAST!
KYOTO-FUSHIMI'S CHASING HIM!
HE HASN'T GIVEN UP!!
CHEERS
BUT...
I'LL CRUSH HIM! I'LL CRUSH HIM! I'LL CRUSH HIM!
I'LL CRUSH HIII-IIIIM!
ZOOOSH

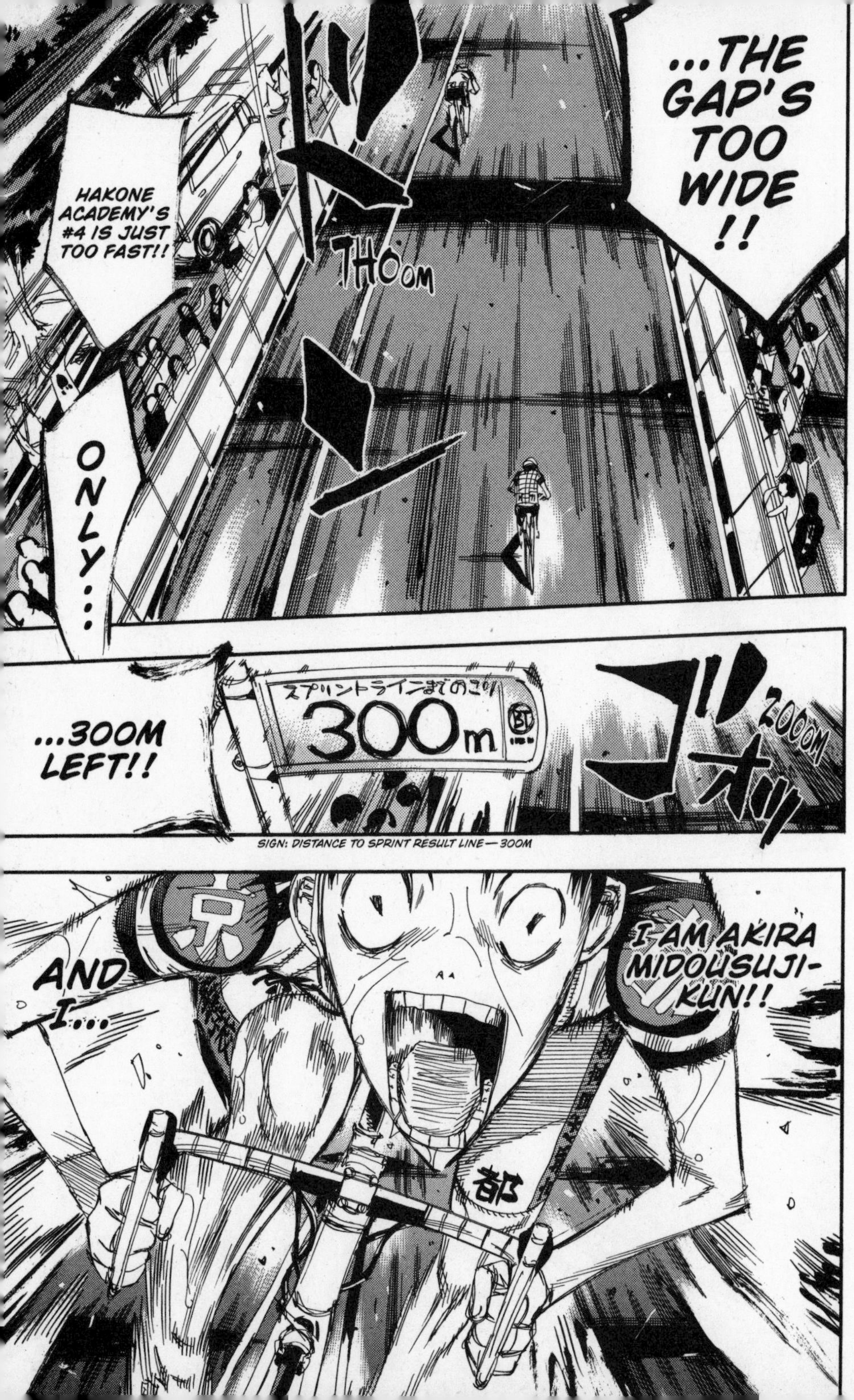
...THE GAP'S TOO WIDE!!
THOOM
HAKONE ACADEMY'S #4 IS JUST TOO FAST!!
ONLY...
ZOOOM
スプリントラインまでのこり
300m
...300M LEFT!!
SIGN: DISTANCE TO SPRINT RESULT LINE—300M
I AM AKIRA MIDOUSUJI-KUN!!
AND I...

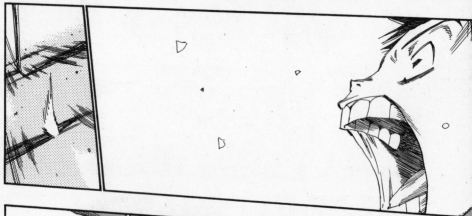

200 METERS LEFT!!

I SEE THE FINISH LINE AHEAD !!

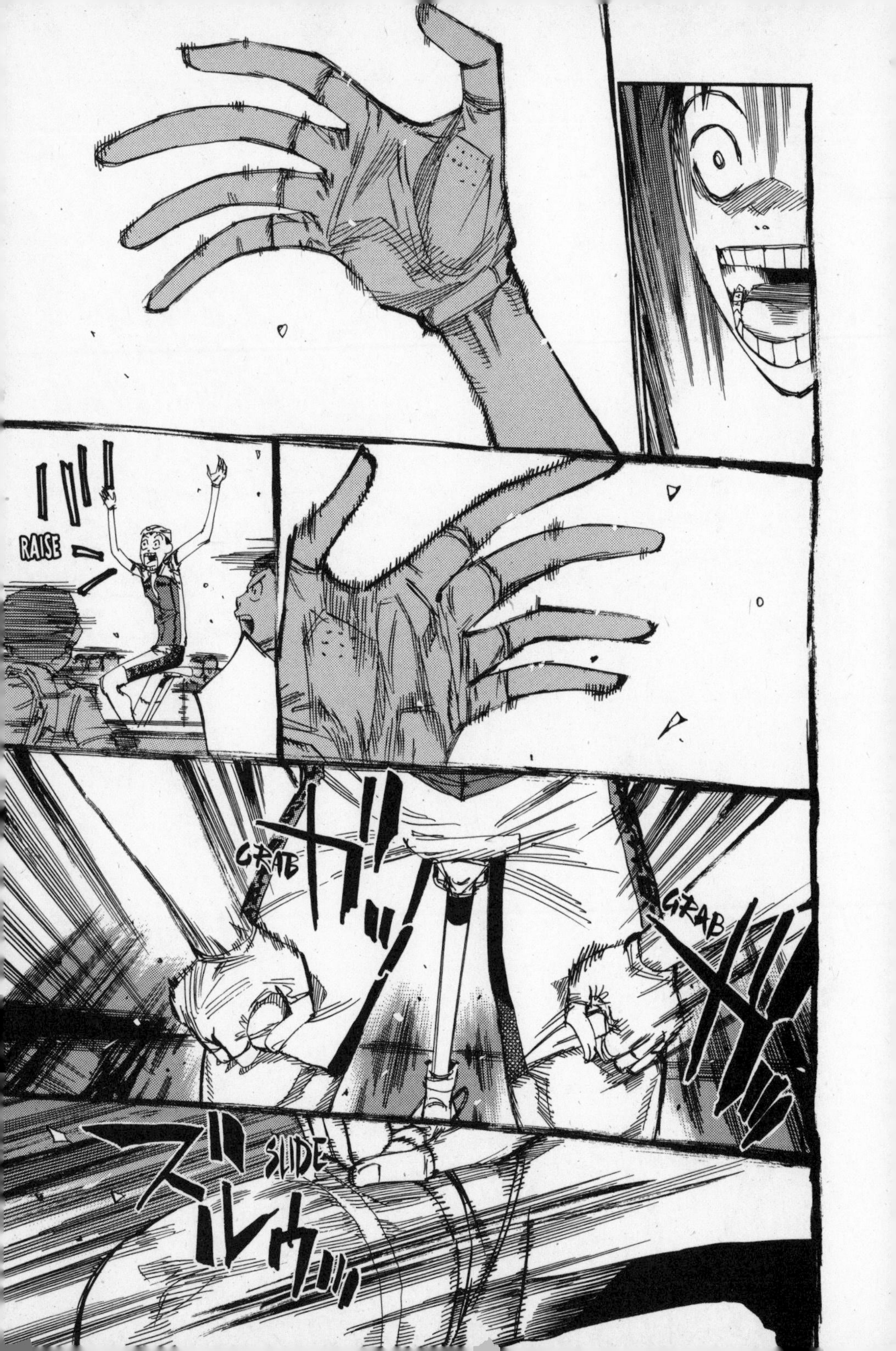
RAISE
GRAB
GRAB
SLIDE

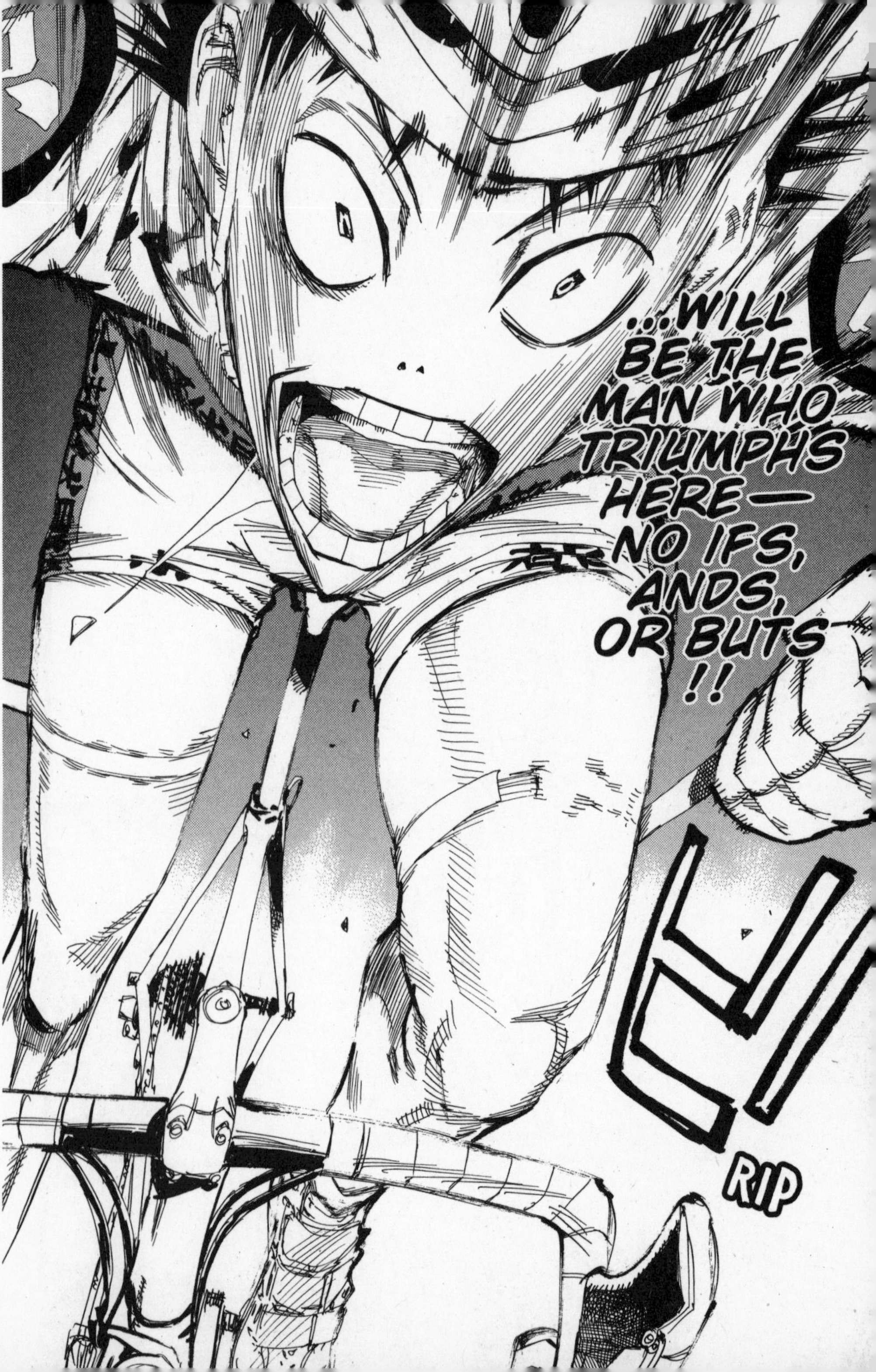
...WILL BE THE MAN WHO TRIUMPHS HERE— NO IFS, ANDS, OR BUTS!!
RIP

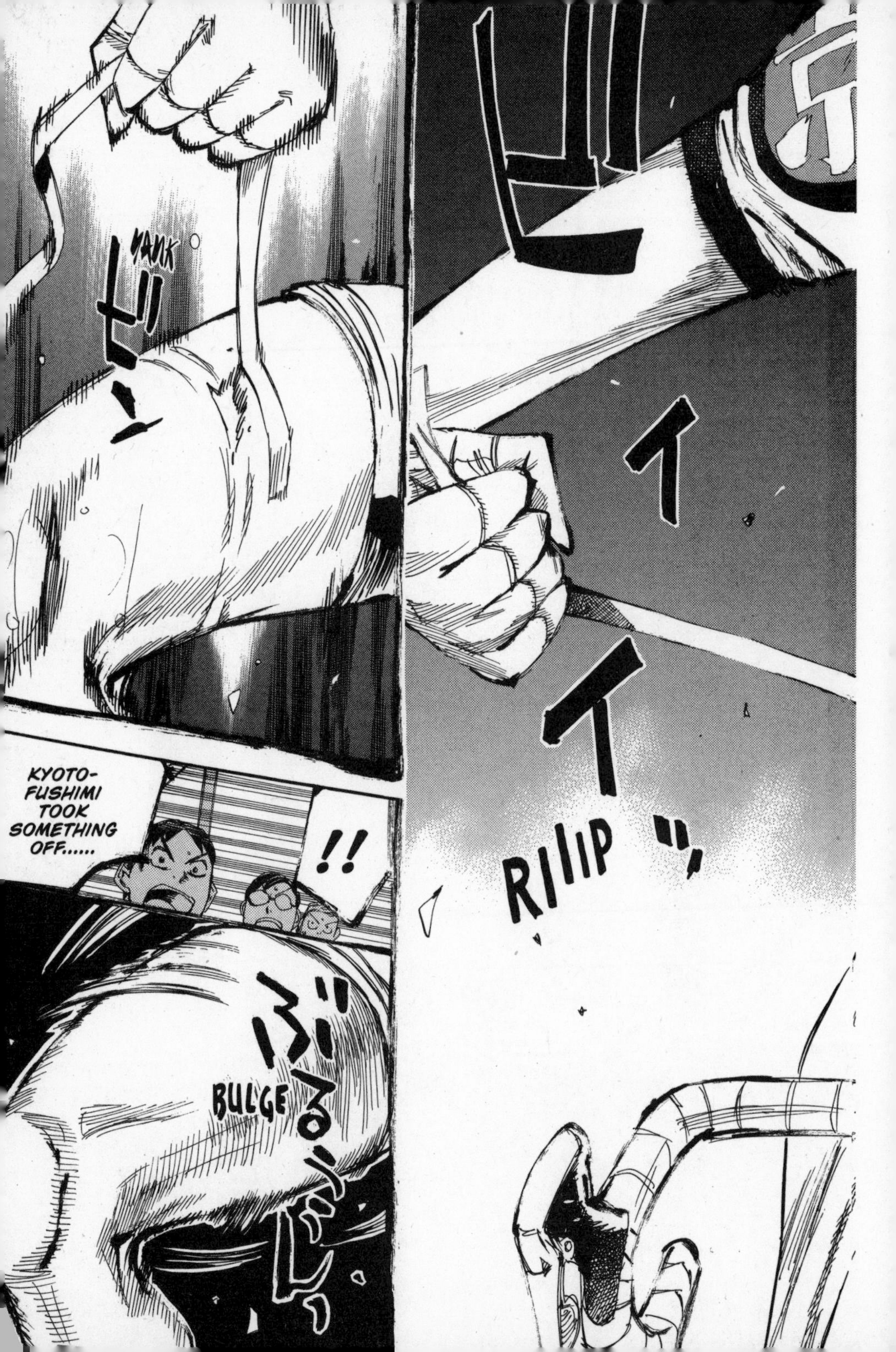
RIIIP
YANK
KYOTO-FUSHIMI TOOK SOMETHING OFF......
!!
BULGE

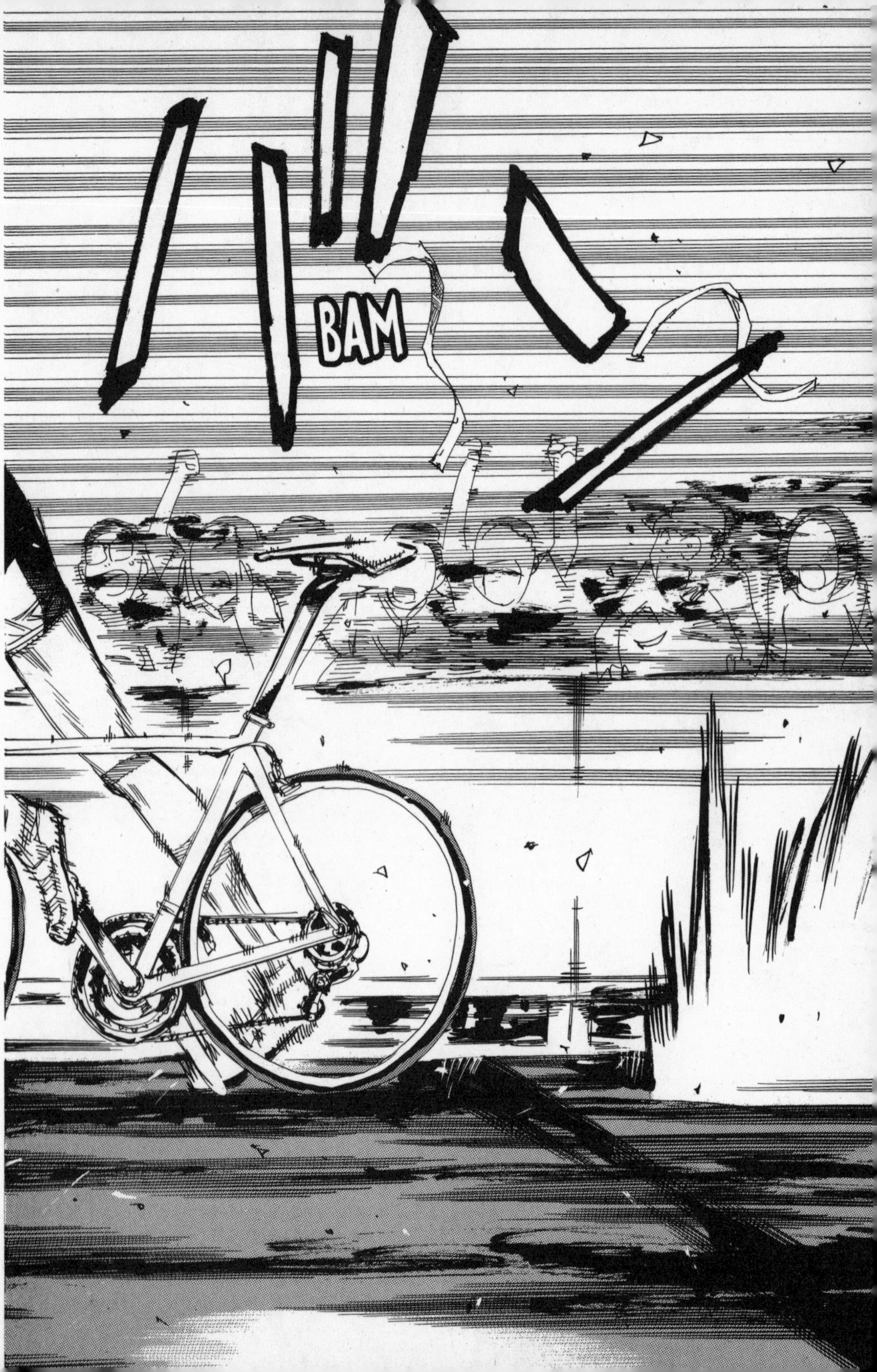
BAM

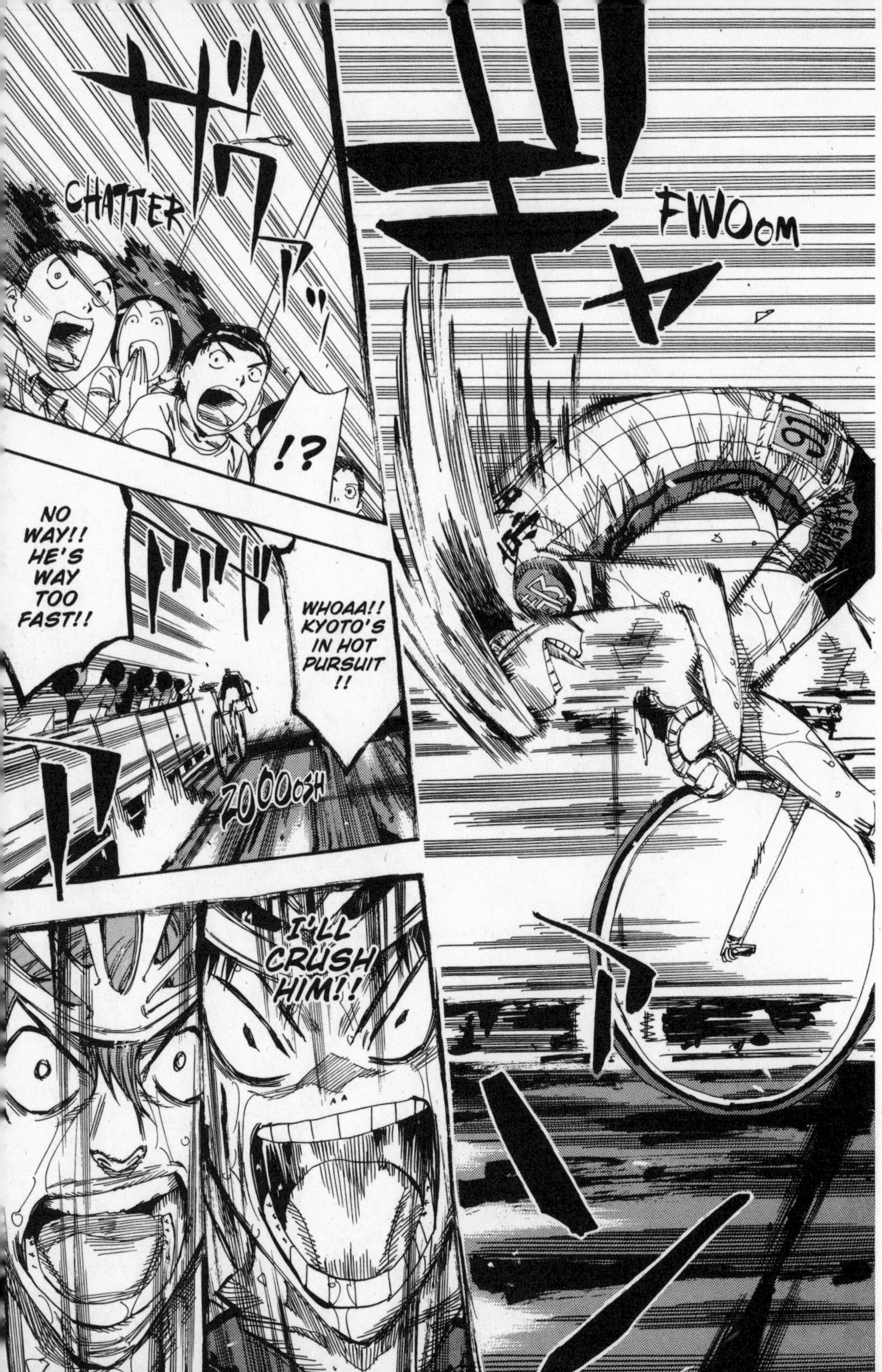
FWOOM
CHATTER
!?
WHOAA!! KYOTO'S IN HOT PURSUIT!!
NO WAY!! HE'S WAY TOO FAST!!
ZOOOOSH
I'LL CRUSH HIM!!

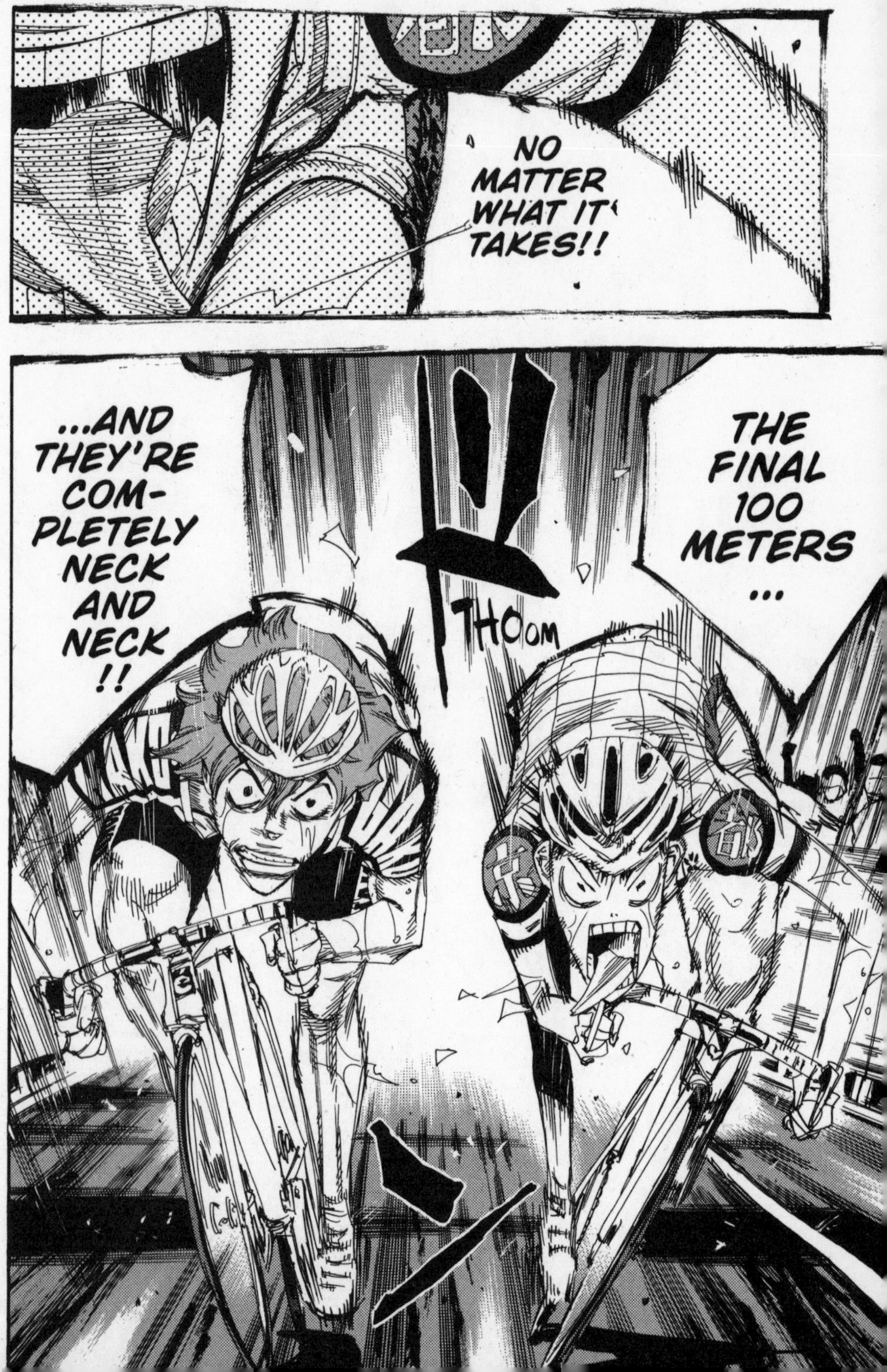
NO MATTER WHAT IT TAKES!!
THE FINAL 100 METERS...
THOOM
...AND THEY'RE COM-PLETELY NECK AND NECK!!

LET'S EXPLAIN SOME STUFF.

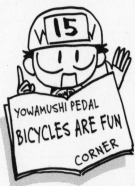

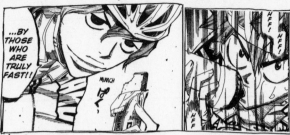

15
YOWAMUSHI PEDAL
BICYCLES ARE FUN
CORNER

HFF! HFF!
HFF
...BY THOSE WHO ARE TRULY FAST!!
MUNCH

THIS TIME, LET'S DISCUSS THESE ENERGY SNACKS THAT SHINKAI-SAN IS MUNCHING ON THROUGHOUT THE STORY.

ROAD RACES TEND TO TAKE FOUR TO FIVE HOURS FOR A SINGLE RACE, AND IN ANY CASE, BICYCLE-RIDING IN GENERAL BURNS A LOT OF CALORIES. THAT'S WHY RACERS **NEED TO EAT AND DRINK** DURING A RACE. THOSE WHO DON'T EAT WILL VERY SUDDENLY FIND THEMSELVES UNABLE TO CONTINUE PEDALING. THE SAME GOES FOR NOT KEEPING HYDRATED. WHILE YOU RIDE, YOUR BODY LOSES SEVERAL LITERS OF WATER THROUGH SWEAT, SO IT'S IMPORTANT TO KEEP REPLENISHING IT. THAT SAID, THIS DOESN'T APPLY ONLY TO RACERS. WHETHER YOU'RE RIDING CASUALLY AROUND TOWN OR JUST RIDING SLOWLY, YOU'LL STILL BURN THROUGH A SURPRISING AMOUNT OF CALORIES. YOUR BODY WILL SEND ITS USUAL WARNING SIGNALS LIKE "I'M HUNGRY" OR "I'M THIRSTY" TO YOU, OF COURSE. BUT ACTUALLY, IF YOU WAIT TO EAT OR DRINK UNTIL YOU SENSE THOSE THINGS, IT WILL ALREADY BE TOO LATE. (MEANING YOUR BODY WILL SOON CEASE TO FUNCTION AT PEAK PERFORMANCE.) BEFORE YOU GET TO THAT POINT, IT'S IMPORTANT THAT YOU CONTINUALLY REPLENISH YOUR ENERGY A LITTLE AT A TIME.

SPORTS NUTRITION FOODS FOR CYCLING ARE SOLD IN STORES!

TALK WITH THE STORE WORKERS ABOUT THE VARIETIES THEY OFFER!

THERE ARE MANY KINDS, INCLUDING BOTH BARS AND GELS, AND RIDERS EAT A MIX OF THEM BASED ON THEIR CONDITION.

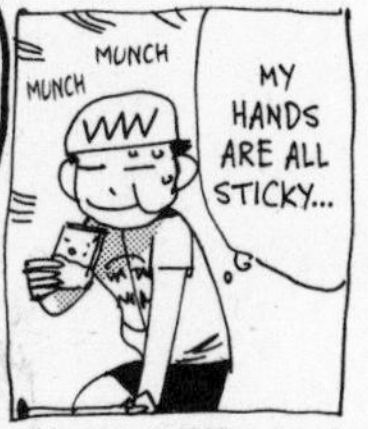

MUNCH
MUNCH
MY HANDS ARE ALL STICKY...

BECAUSE IT'S A HIGH-CALORIE FOOD.

THAT CAN HAPPEN. (LOL!)

BARS

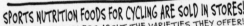

COMES IN FLAVORS LIKE CHOCOLATE AND PEANUT

GELS

BAR
on
POWER
GEL
PRO
SENSYU

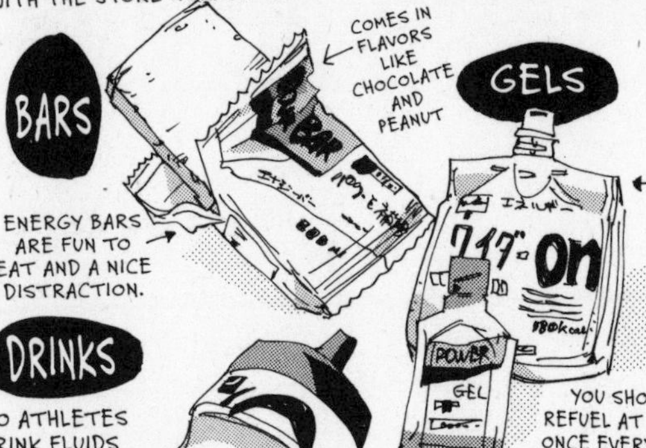

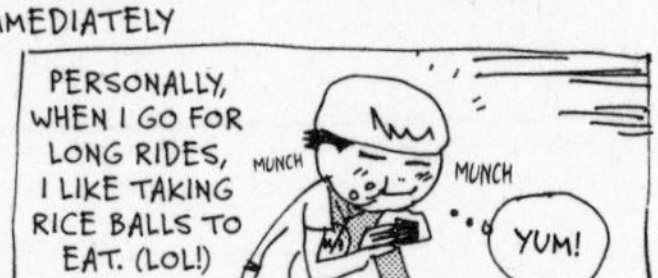

REPLENISHES ENERGY IMMEDIATELY

ENERGY BARS ARE FUN TO EAT AND A NICE DISTRACTION.

PERSONALLY, WHEN I GO FOR LONG RIDES, I LIKE TAKING RICE BALLS TO EAT. (LOL!)
MUNCH
MUNCH
YUM!

DRINKS

PRO ATHLETES DRINK FLUIDS SPECIALLY FORMULATED BY THEIR TEAM.

YOU SHOULD REFUEL AT LEAST ONCE EVERY 30-60 MINUTES!

AN ADULT MALE TYPICALLY USES ABOUT 2,500 CALORIES PER DAY. A CYCLIST WILL BURN 7,500 CALORIES IN A SINGLE RACE.

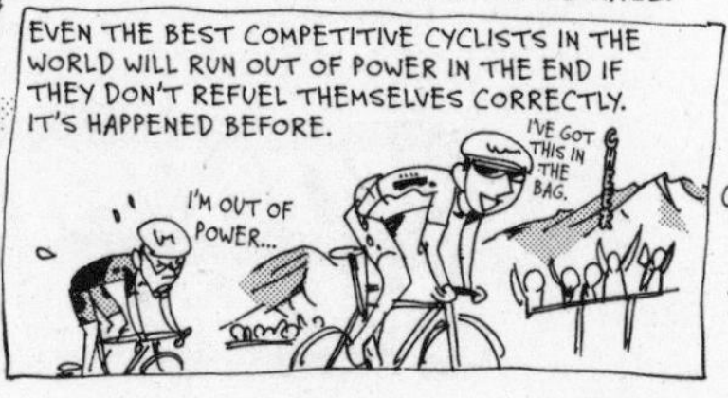

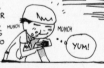

EVEN THE BEST COMPETITIVE CYCLISTS IN THE WORLD WILL RUN OUT OF POWER IN THE END IF THEY DON'T REFUEL THEMSELVES CORRECTLY. IT'S HAPPENED BEFORE.

I'VE GOT THIS IN THE BAG.
I'M OUT OF POWER...

WHEN YOU GO RIDING, BE SURE TO BRING PLENTY OF FOOD AND DRINK!!

EVEN A CHOCOLATE BAR IS GOOD.
CHOCO
CALORIE BAR
TABE
SPORTS

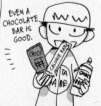

- REFUELING AFTER RIDING TO AID IN RECOVERY IS SUPER-IMPORTANT TOO!

YOWAMUSHI PEDAL

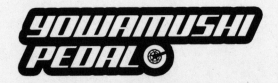

RIDE.129 THE FASTEST AND THE STRONGEST

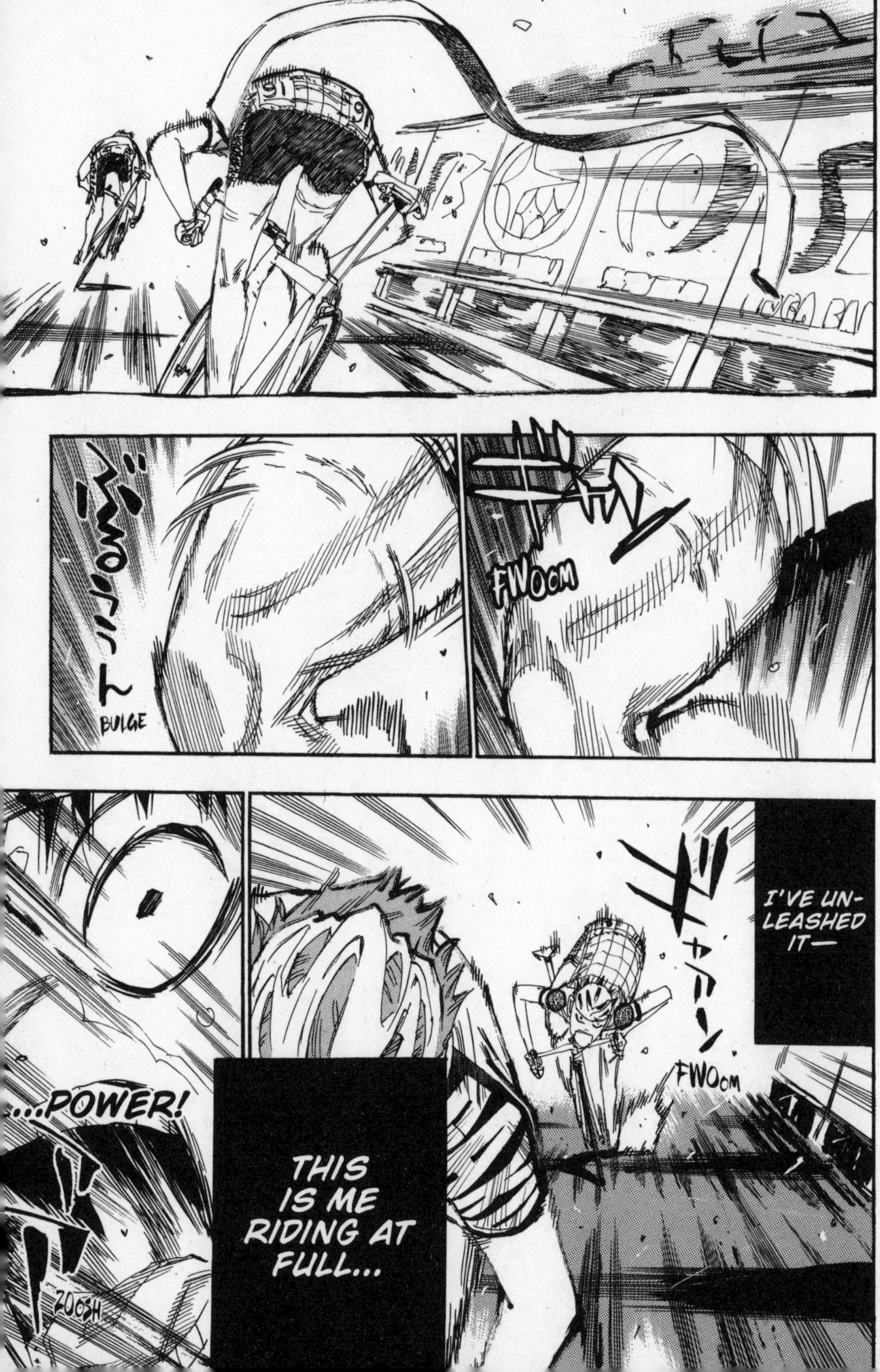
FWOOM
BULGE
I'VE UN-LEASHED IT—
FWOOM
THIS IS ME RIDING AT FULL...
...POWER!
ZOOSH

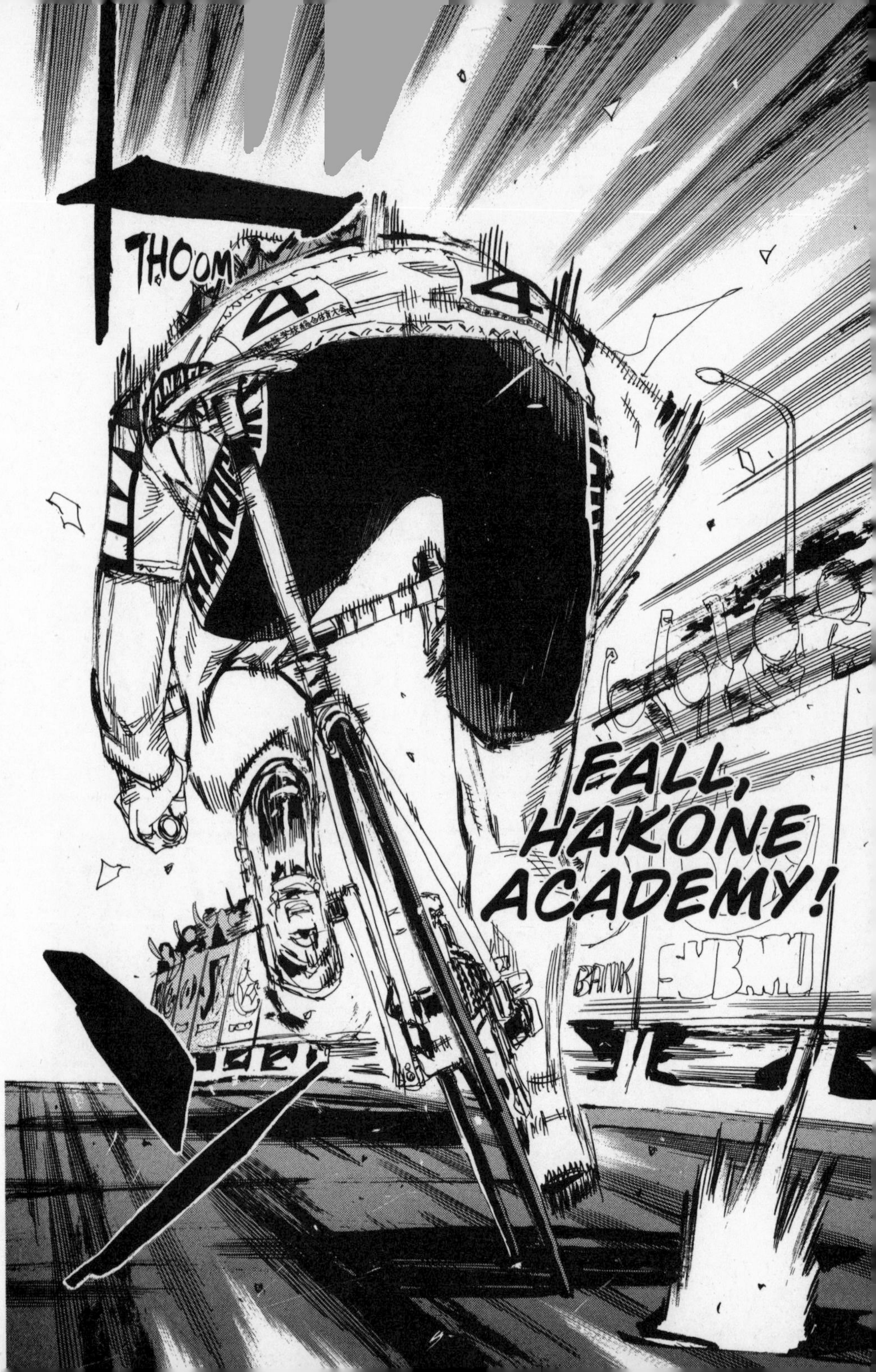
THOOM
FALL, HAKONE ACADEMY!

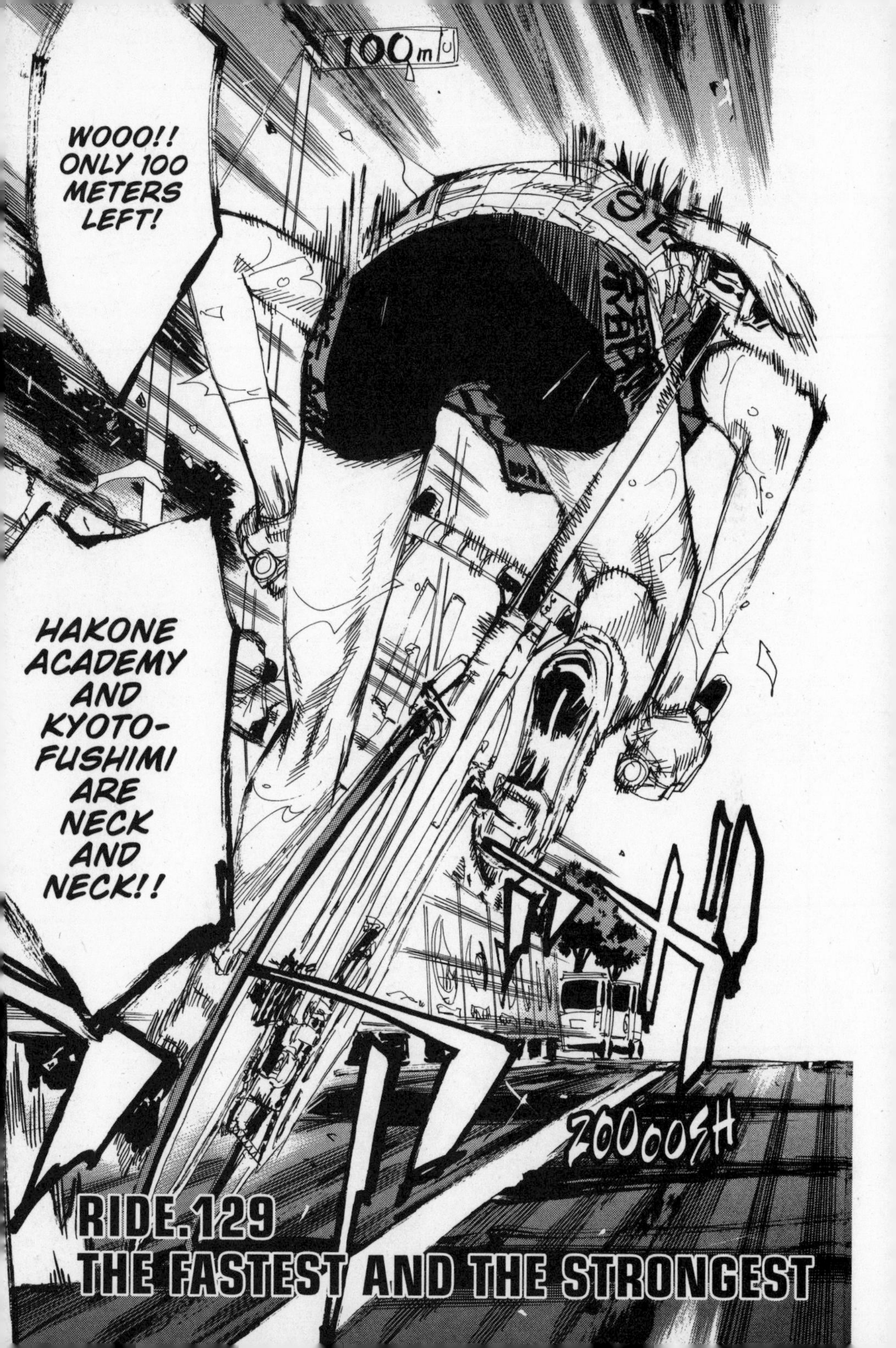
100m
WOOO!! ONLY 100 METERS LEFT!
HAKONE ACADEMY AND KYOTO-FUSHIMI ARE NECK AND NECK!!
ZOOOOSH

RIDE.129 THE FASTEST AND THE STRONGEST

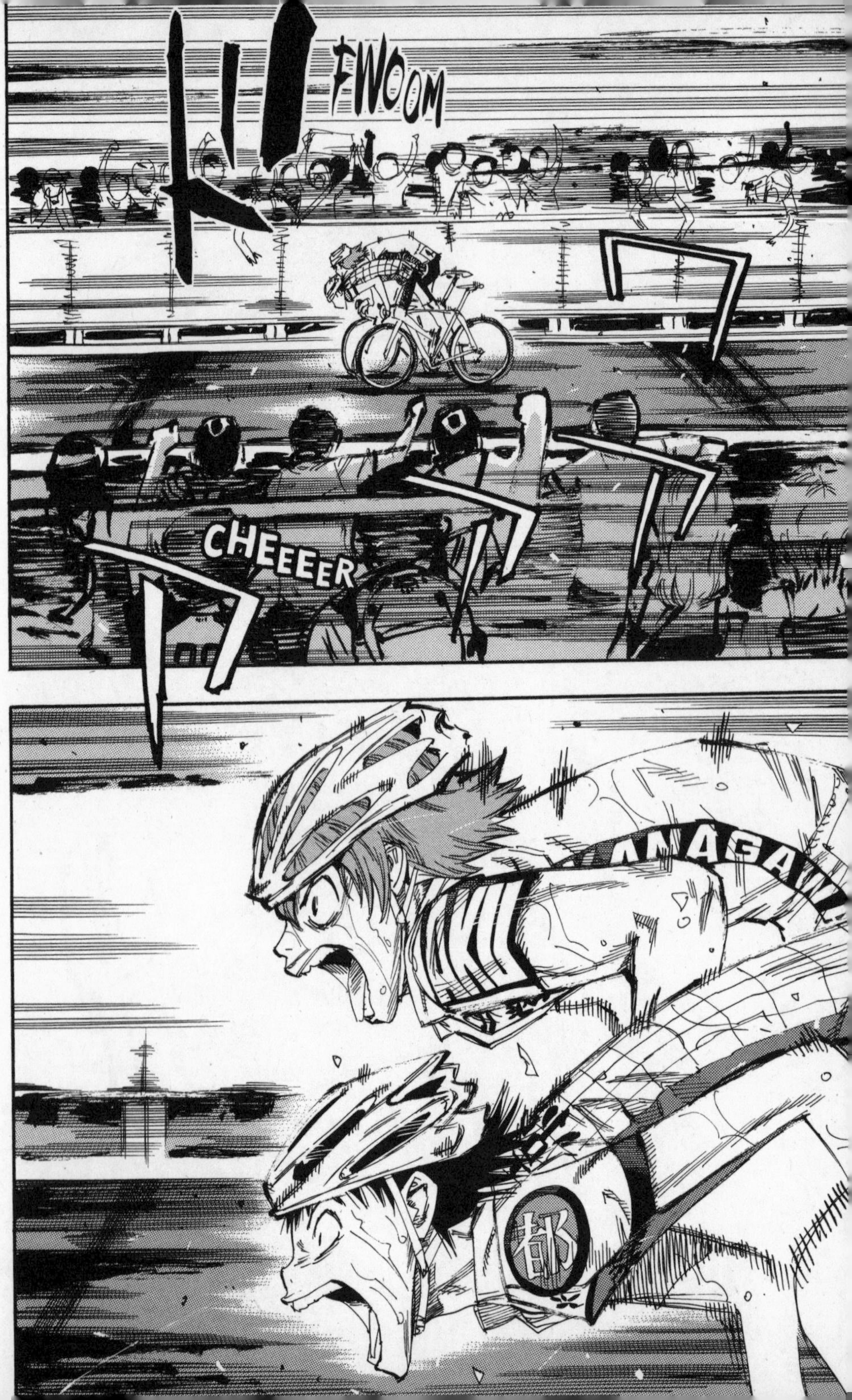
FWOOM
CHEEEER

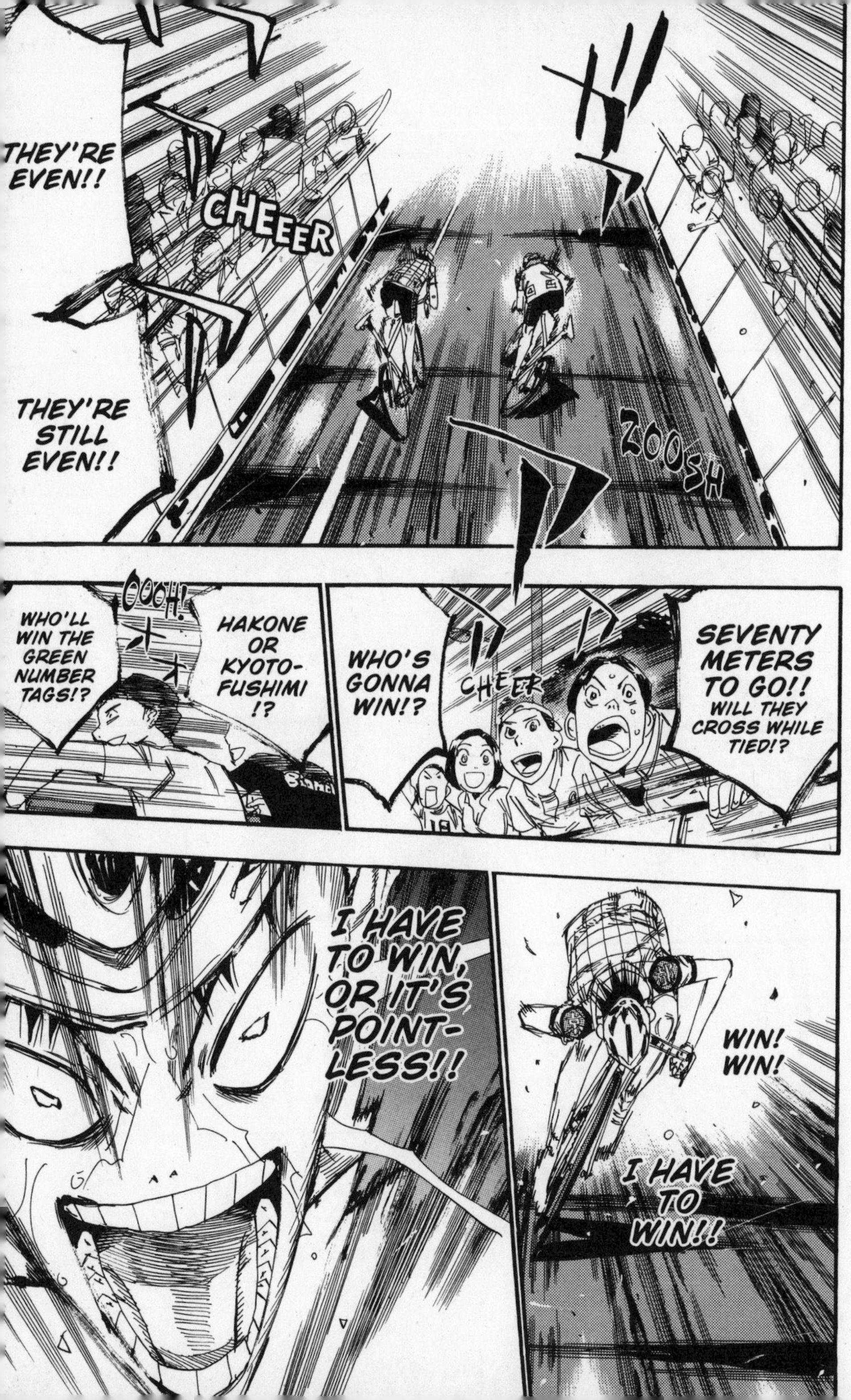
THEY'RE EVEN!!
CHEEER
ZOOSH
THEY'RE STILL EVEN!!
SEVENTY METERS TO GO!!
WILL THEY CROSS WHILE TIED!?
CHEER
WHO'S GONNA WIN!?
HAKONE OR KYOTO-FUSHIMI!?
OOOH!
WHO'LL WIN THE GREEN NUMBER TAGS!?
WIN! WIN!
I HAVE TO WIN!!
I HAVE TO WIN, OR IT'S POINTLESS!!

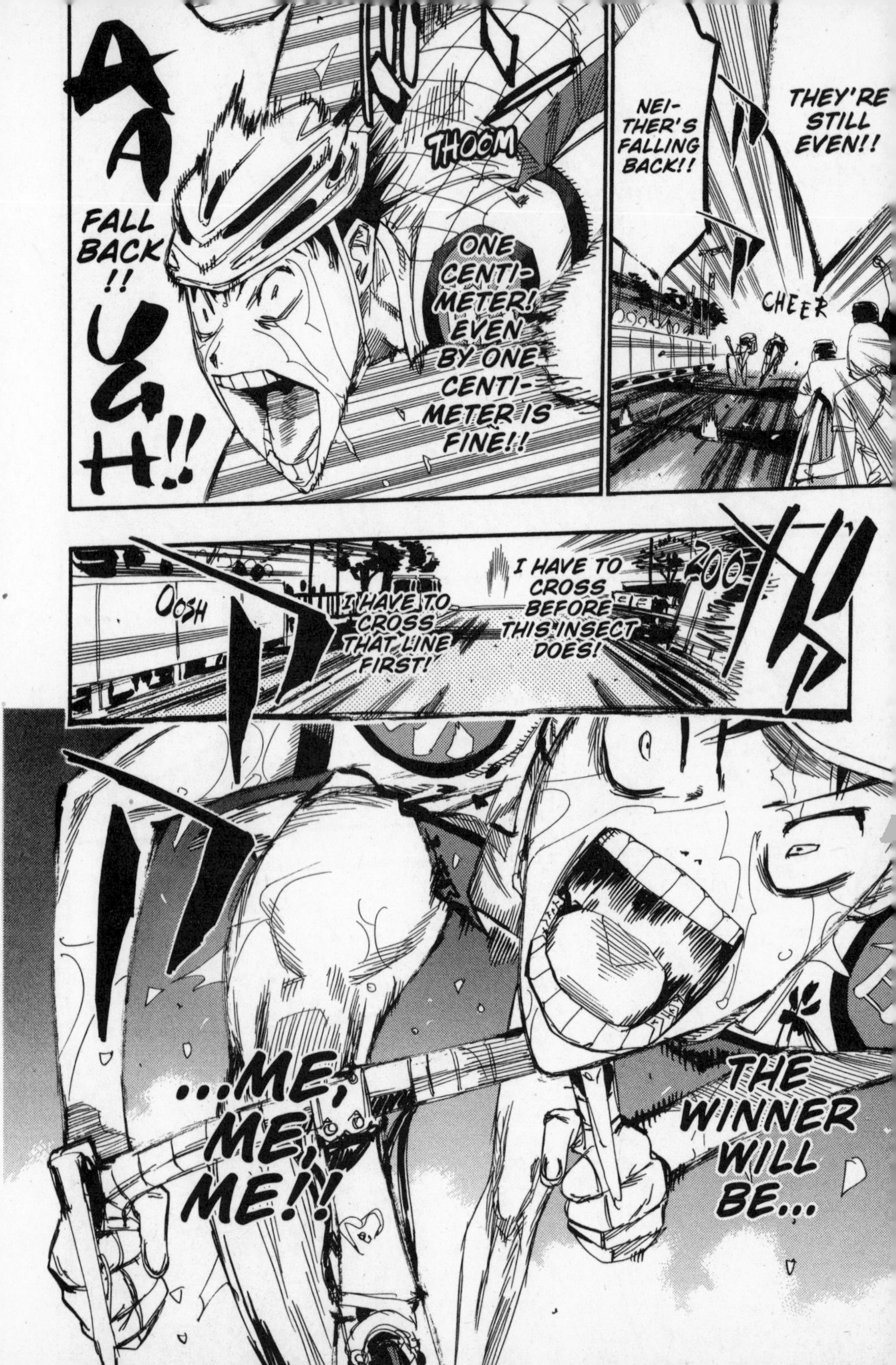
THEY'RE STILL EVEN!!
NEI-THER'S FALLING BACK!!
CHEER
THOOM
ONE CENTI-METER! EVEN BY ONE CENTI-METER IS FINE!!
FALL BACK!!
AAUGH!!
200
I HAVE TO CROSS BEFORE THIS INSECT DOES!
I HAVE TO CROSS THAT LINE FIRST!
OOSH
THE WINNER WILL BE...
...ME, ME, ME!!

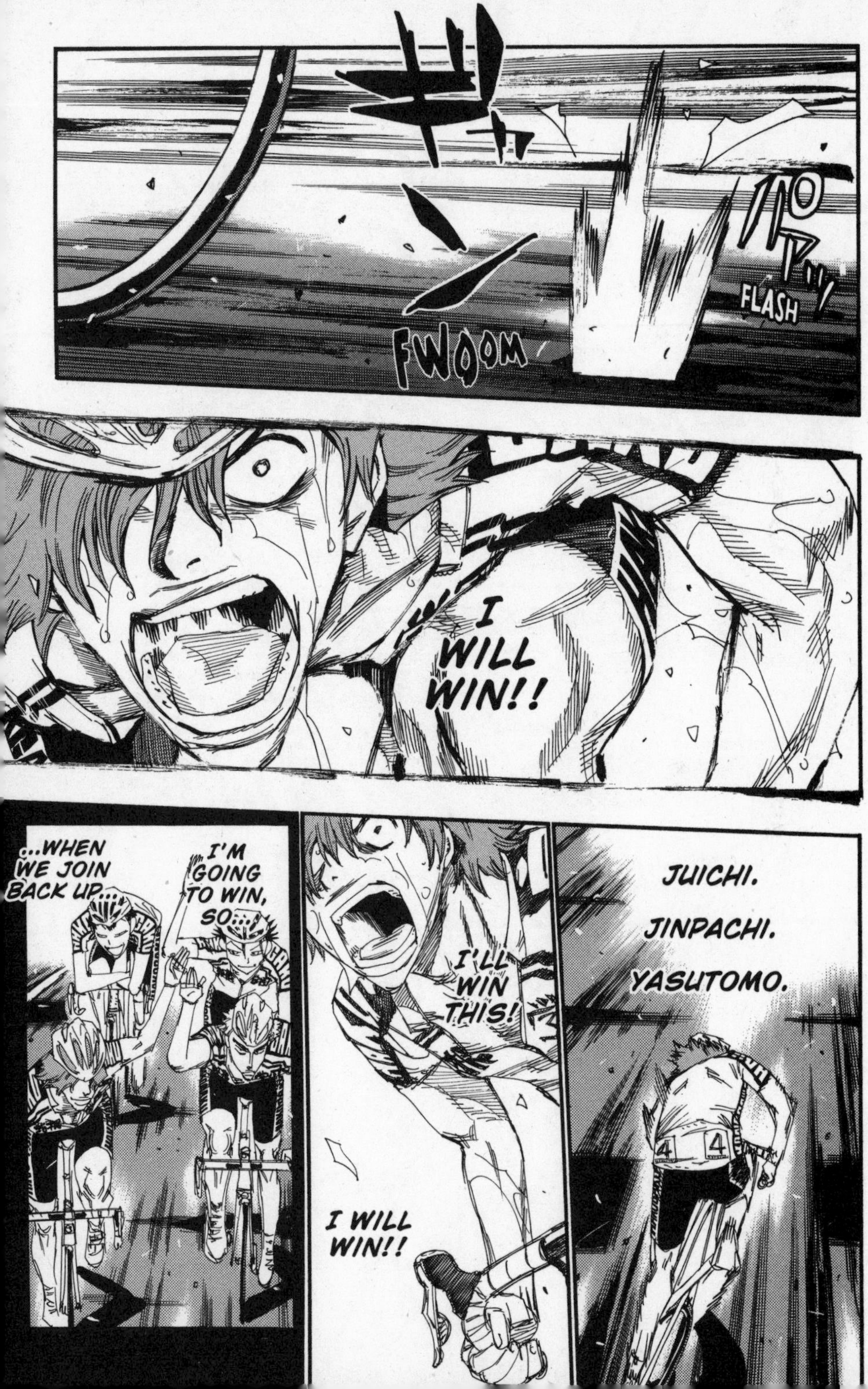
FLASH
FWOOM
I WILL WIN!!
JUICHI.
JINPACHI.
YASUTOMO.
I'LL WIN THIS!
I WILL WIN!!
I'M GOING TO WIN, SO...
...WHEN WE JOIN BACK UP...

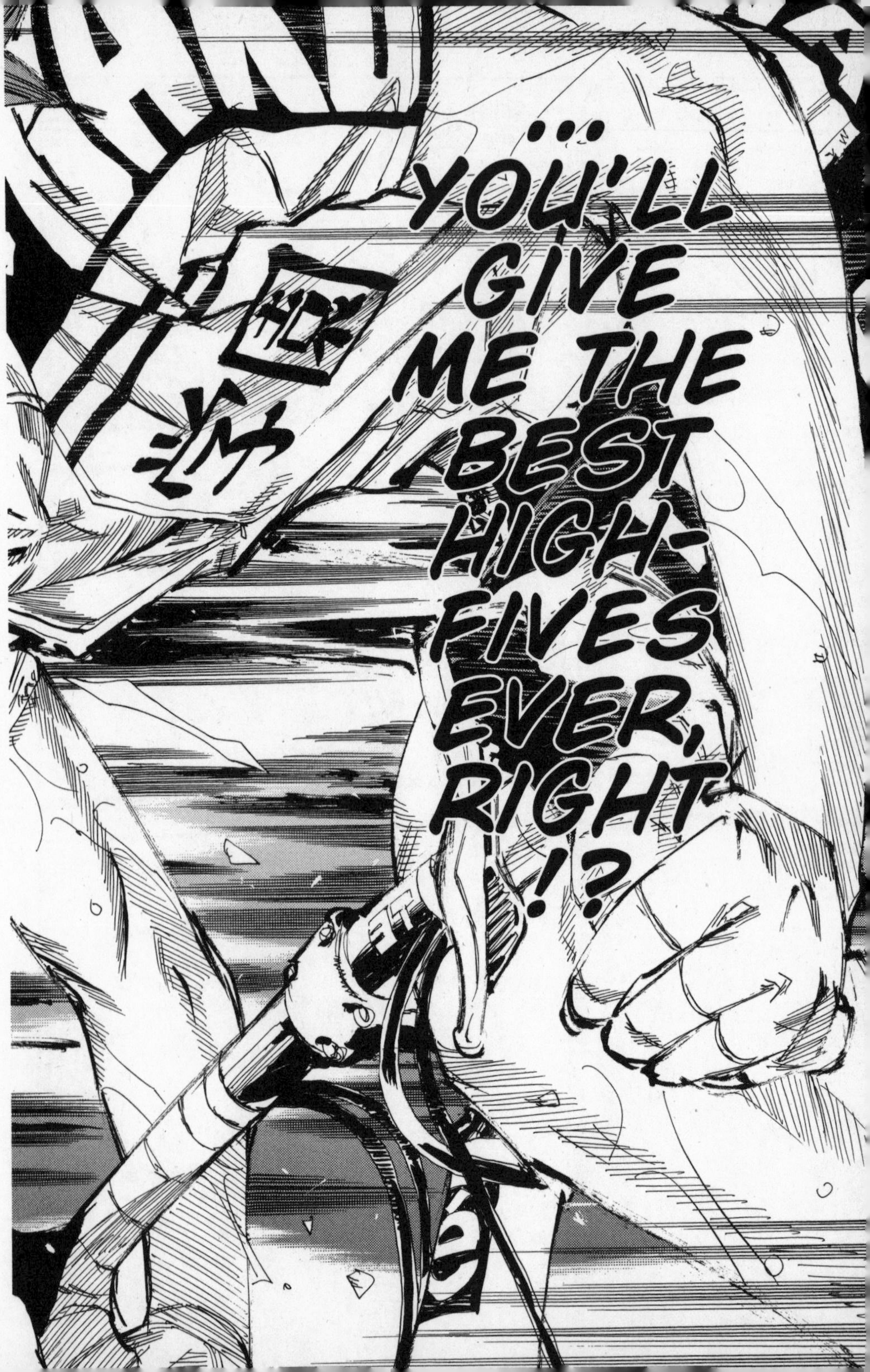
...YOU'LL GIVE ME THE BEST HIGH-FIVES EVER, RIGHT!?

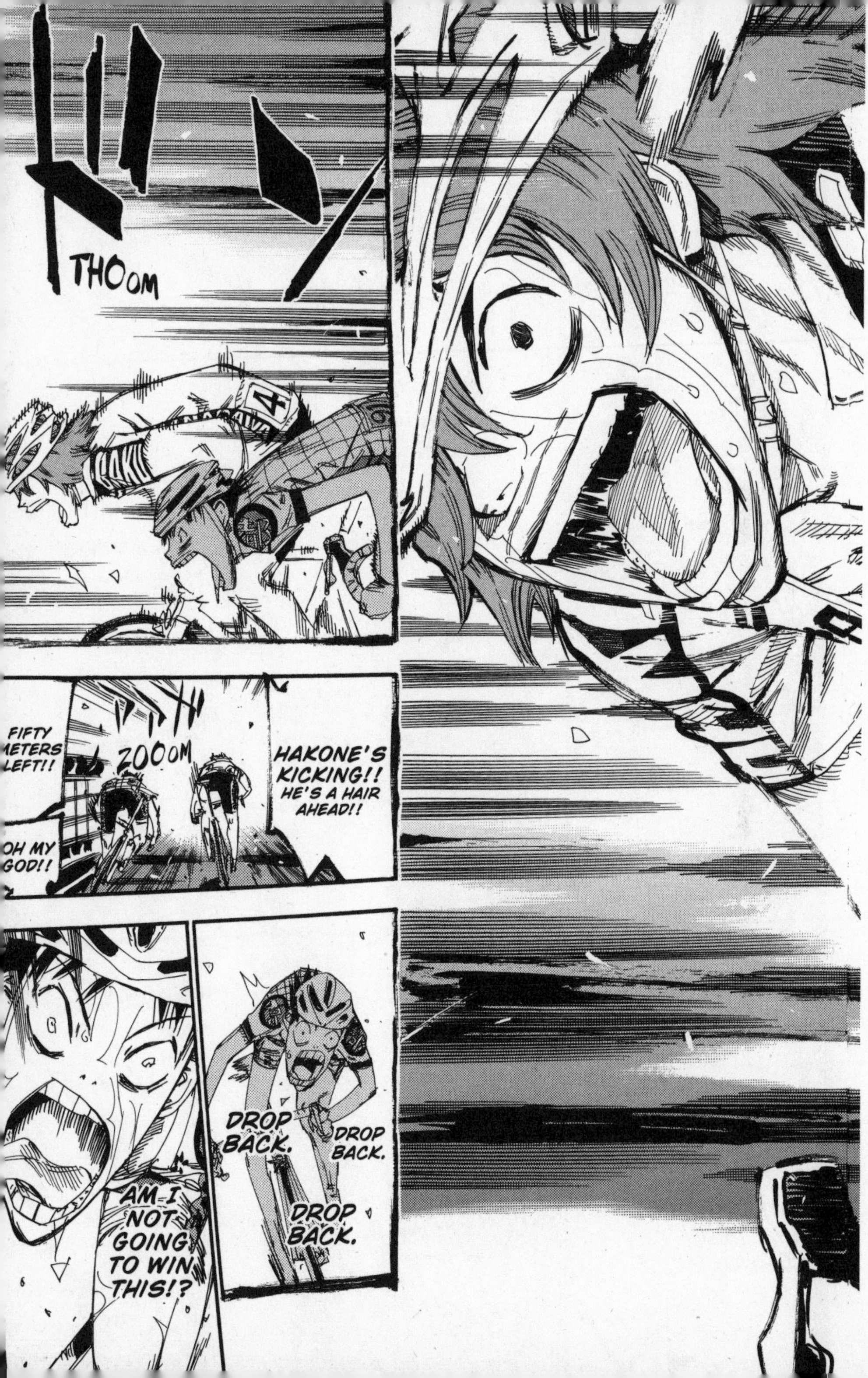
THOOM
HAKONE'S KICKING!! HE'S A HAIR AHEAD!!
ZOOOM
FIFTY METERS LEFT!!
OH MY GOD!!
DROP BACK.
DROP BACK.
DROP BACK.
AM I NOT GOING TO WIN THIS!?

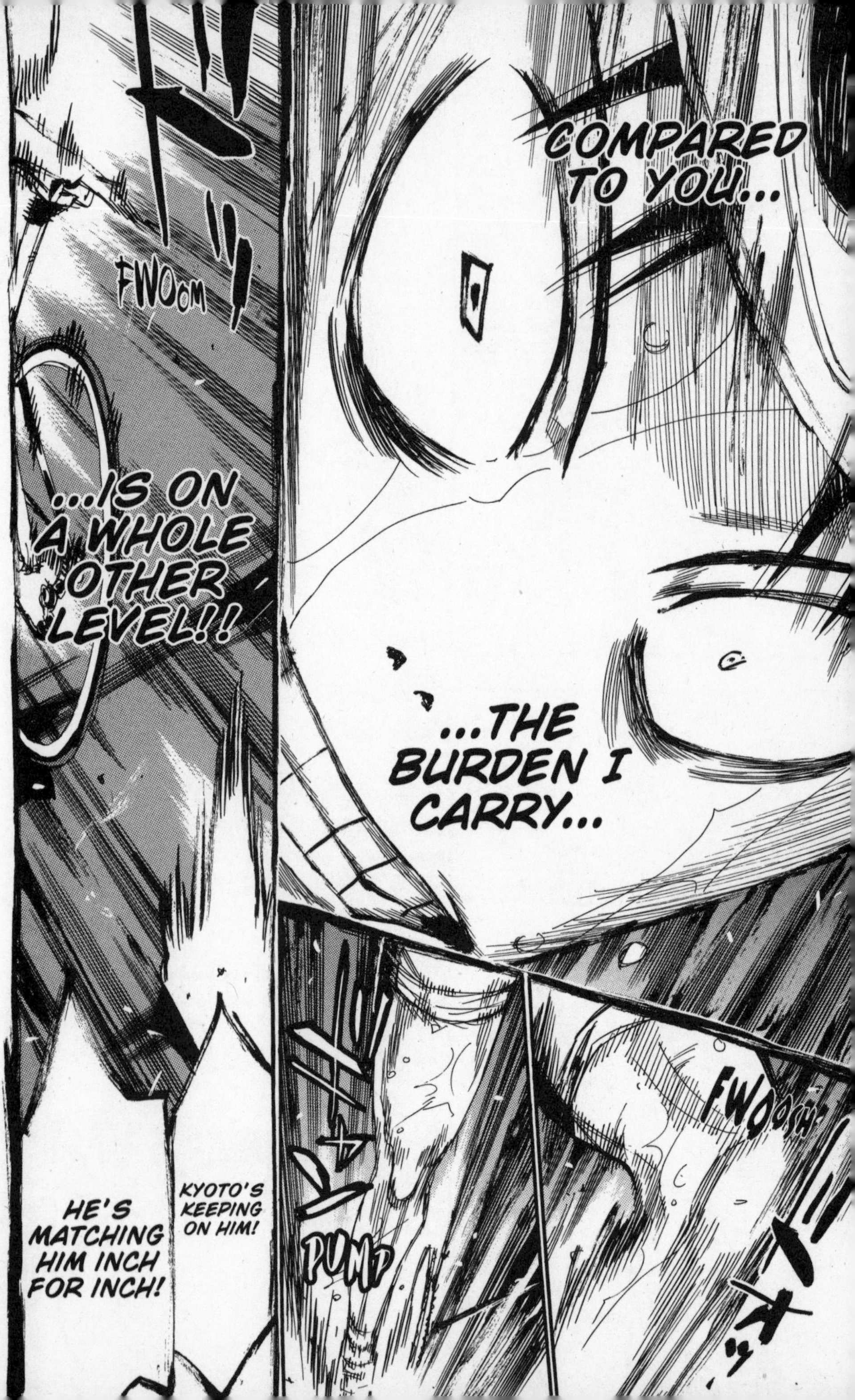
COMPARED TO YOU...
...THE BURDEN I CARRY...
FWOOSH
PUMP
FWOOM
...IS ON A WHOLE OTHER LEVEL!!
KYOTO'S KEEPING ON HIM!
HE'S MATCHING HIM INCH FOR INCH!

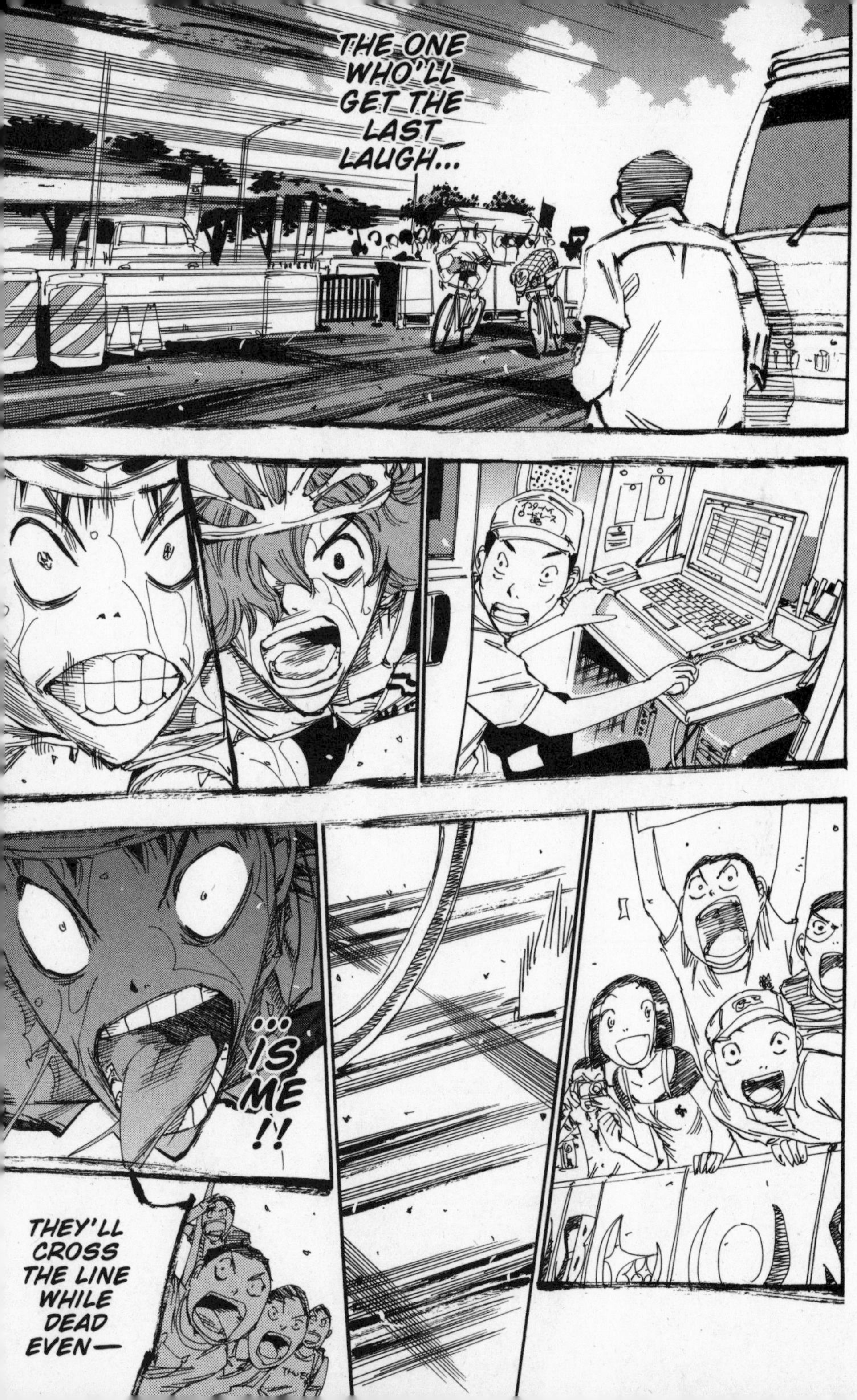
THE ONE WHO'LL GET THE LAST LAUGH...
...IS ME!!
THEY'LL CROSS THE LINE WHILE DEAD EVEN—

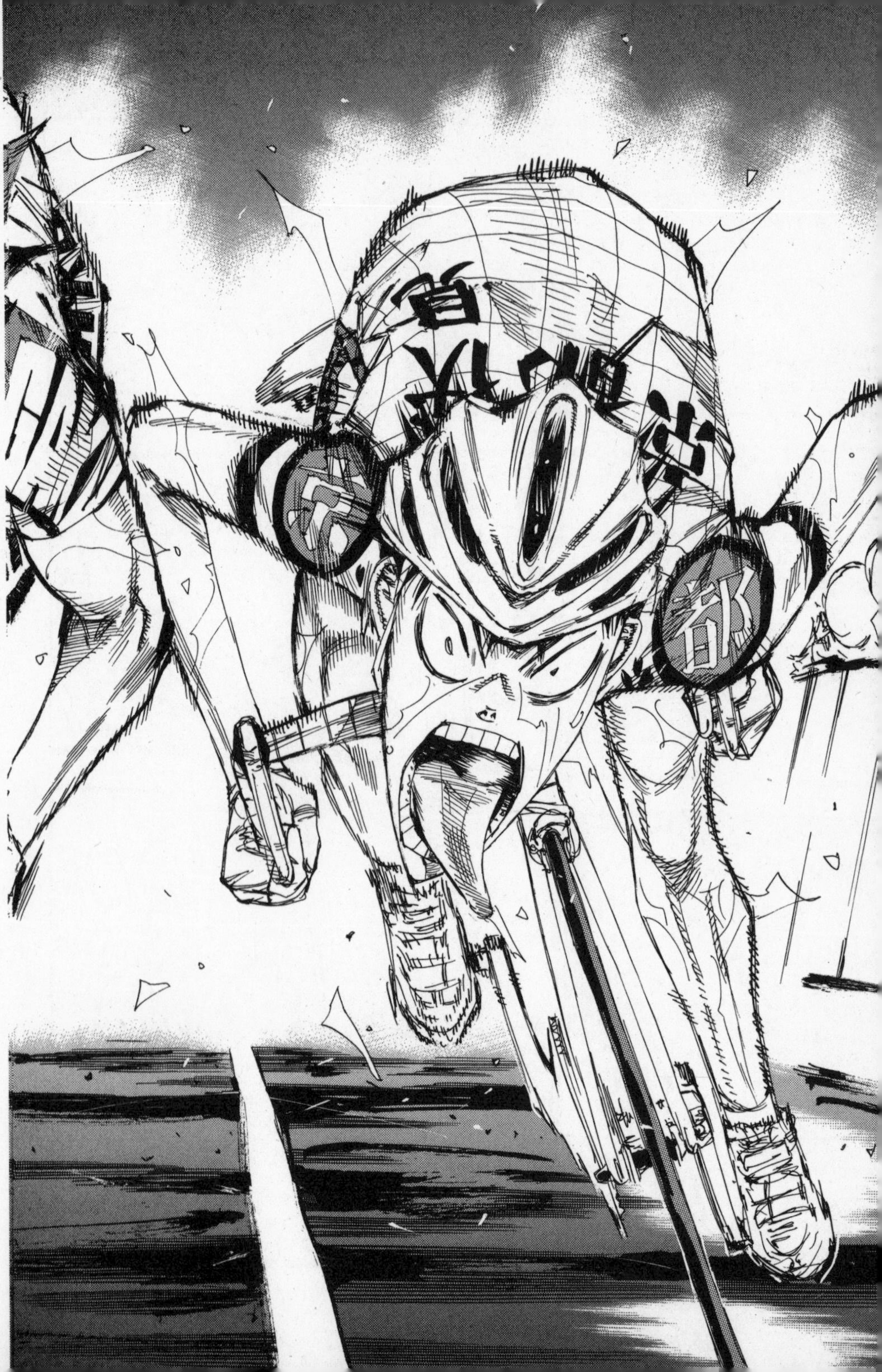
部

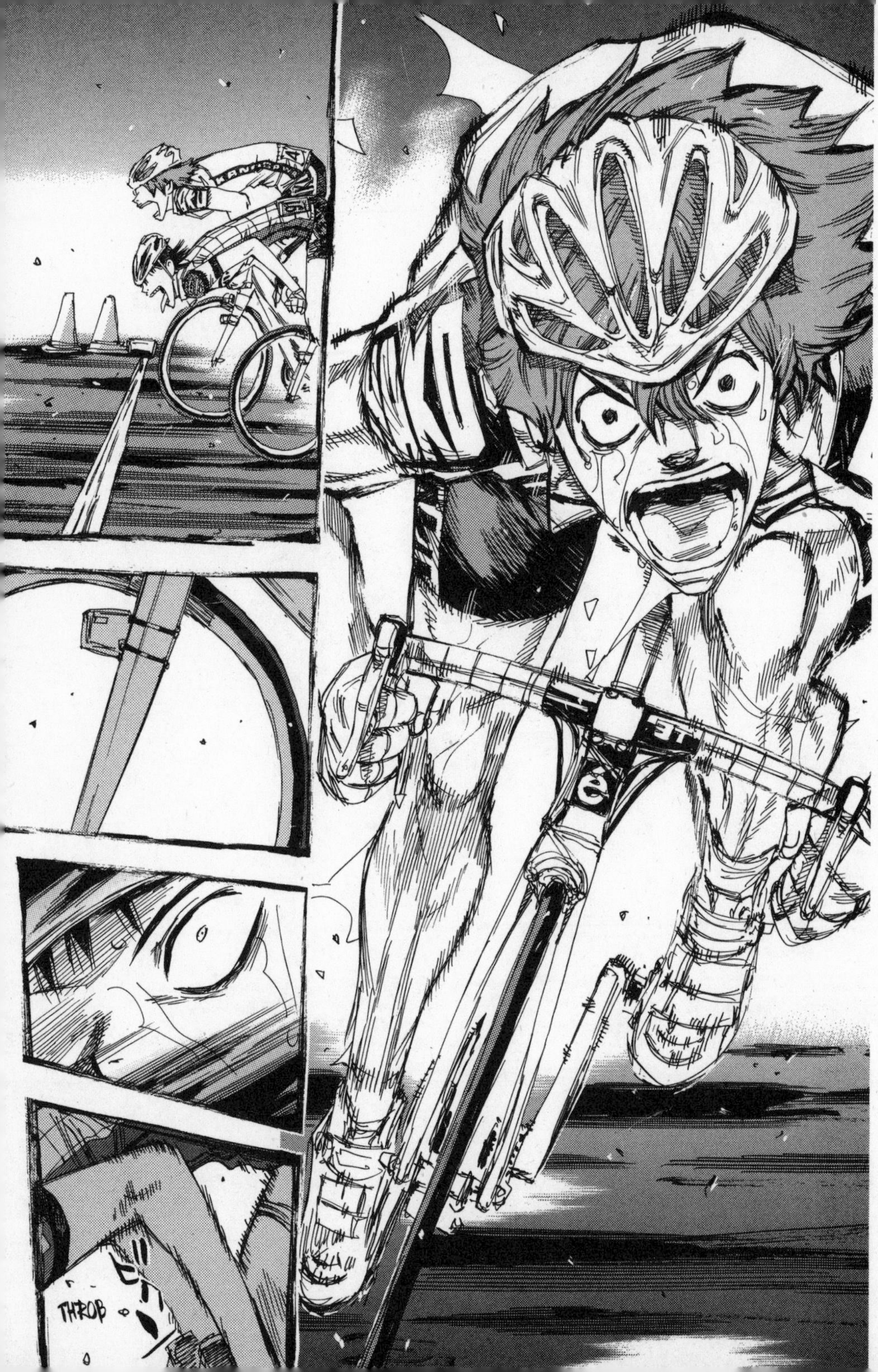
THROB

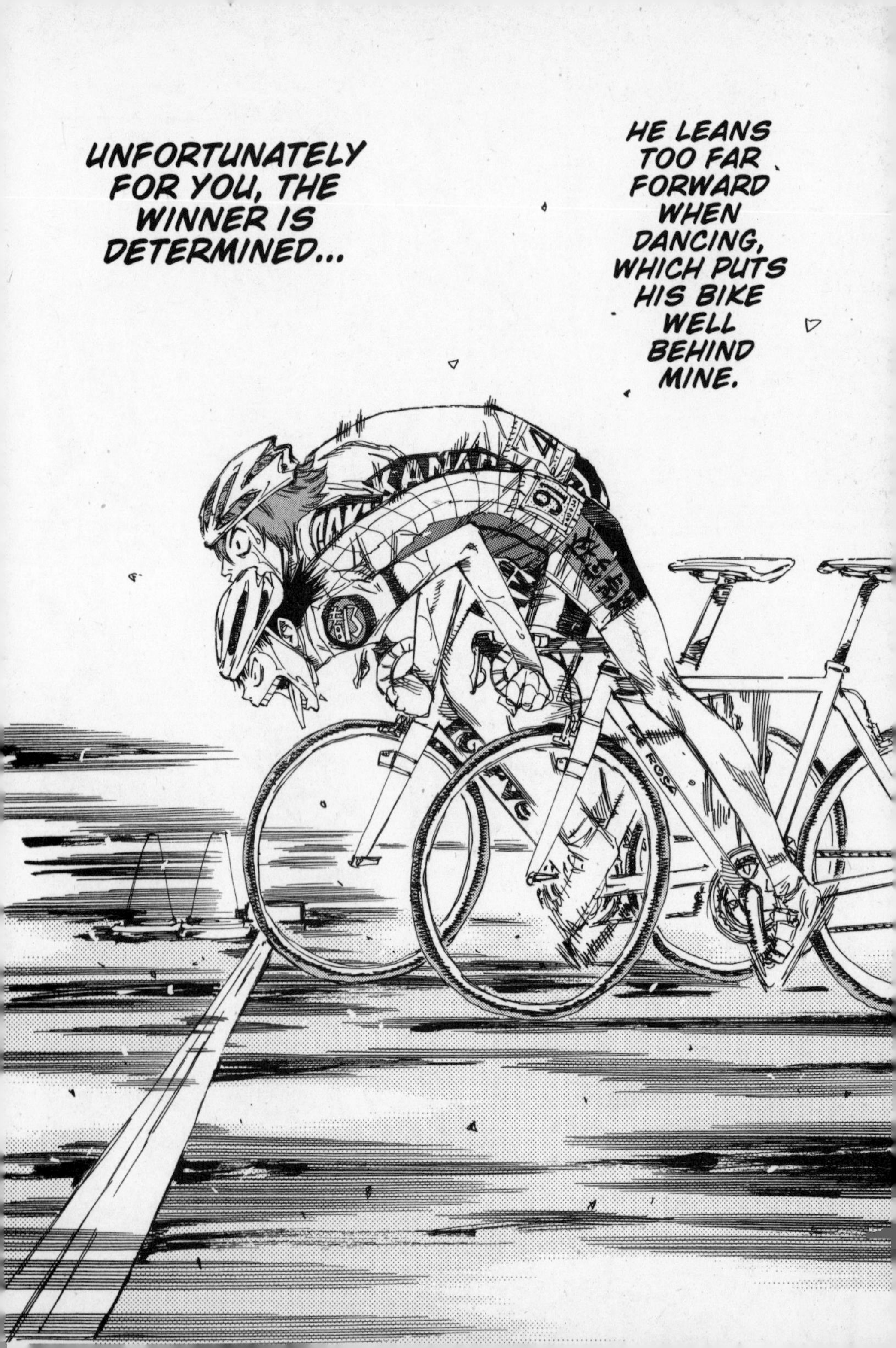
HE LEANS TOO FAR FORWARD WHEN DANCING, WHICH PUTS HIS BIKE WELL BEHIND MINE.
UNFORTUNATELY FOR YOU, THE WINNER IS DETERMINED...

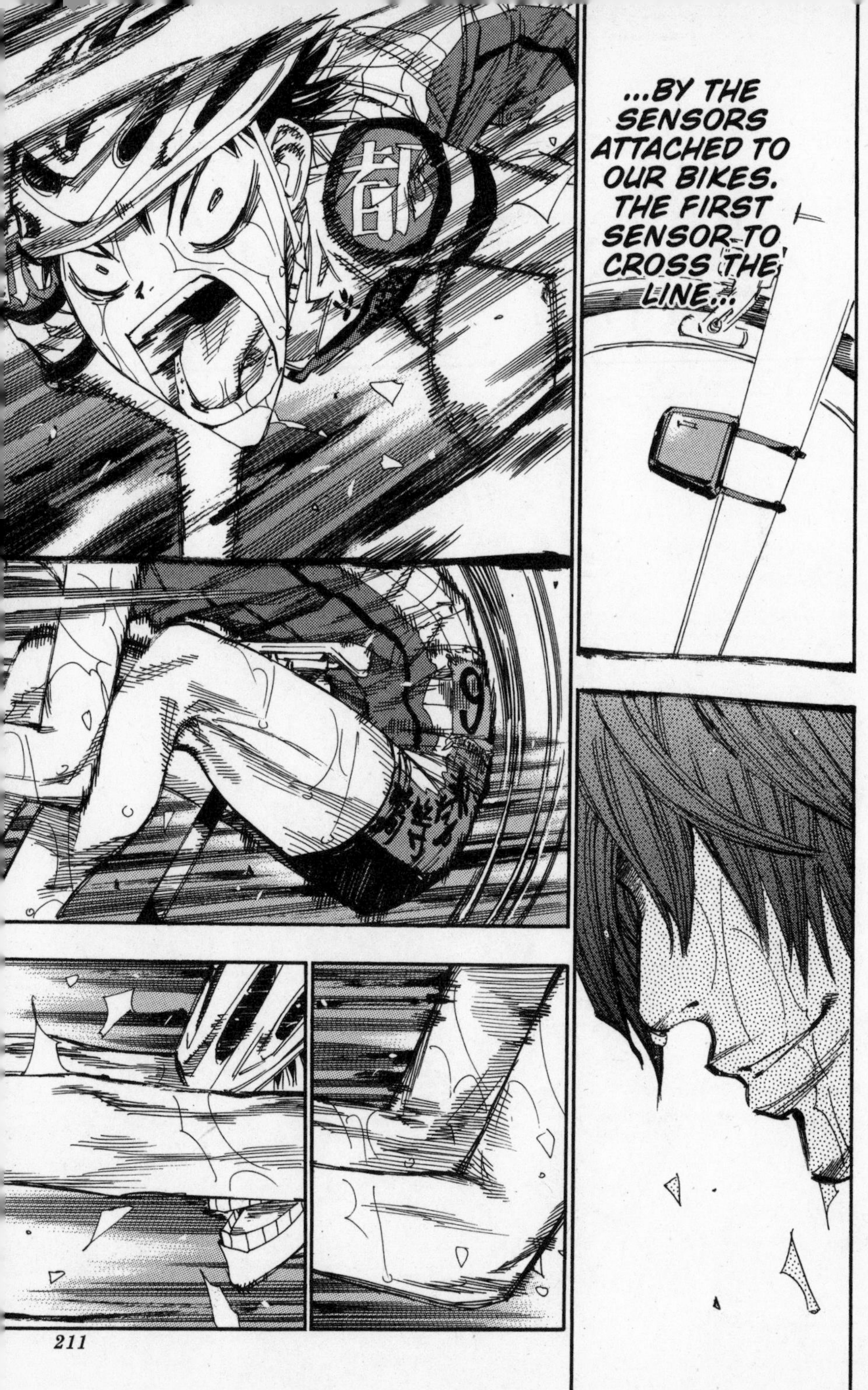
...BY THE SENSORS ATTACHED TO OUR BIKES. THE FIRST SENSOR TO CROSS THE LINE...

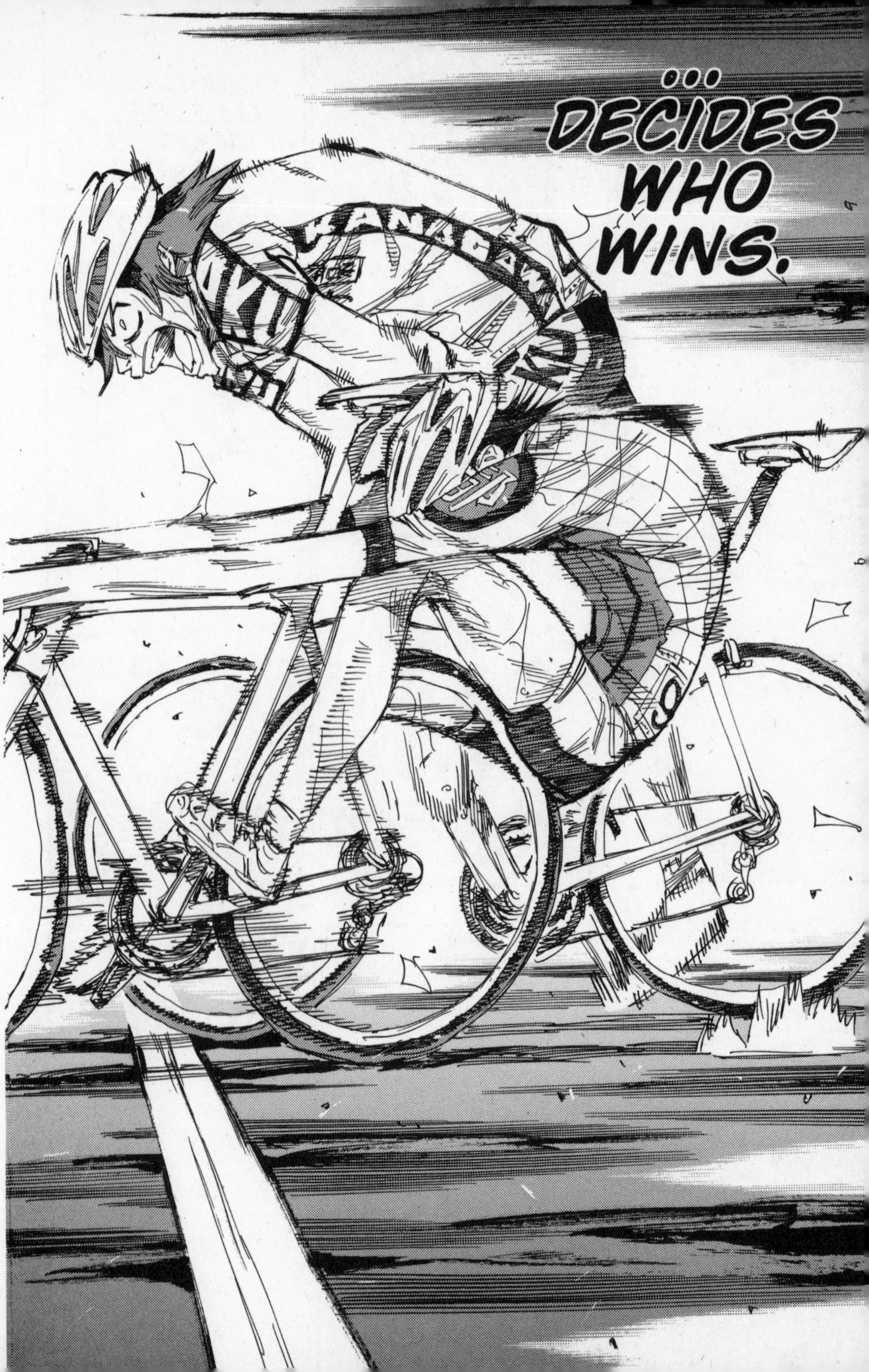
...DECIDES WHO WINS.

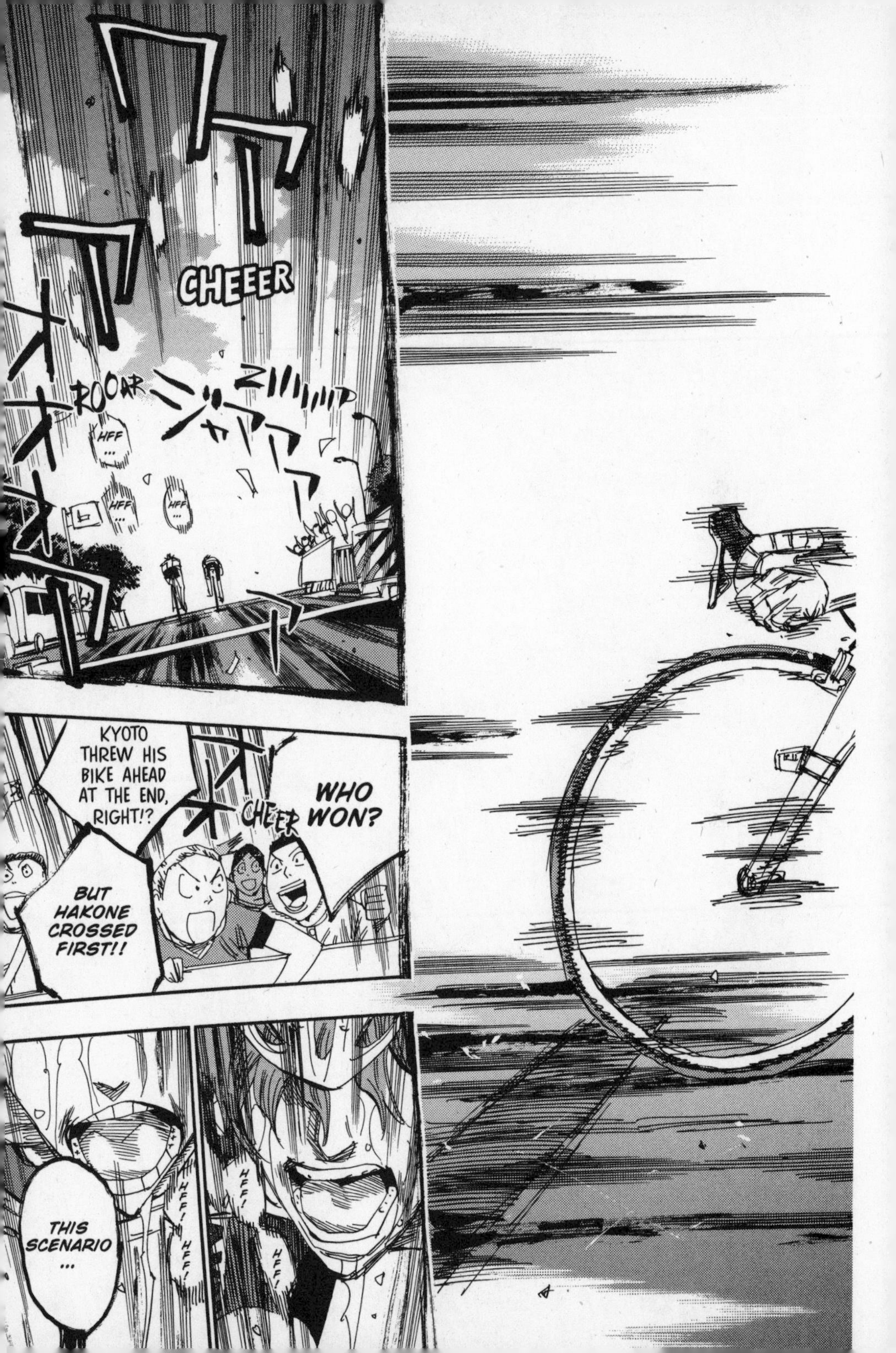
CHEEER
ZIIIIIIIP
ROOAR
HFF...
HFF...
HFF...
WHO WON?
CHEER
KYOTO THREW HIS BIKE AHEAD AT THE END, RIGHT!?
BUT HAKONE CROSSED FIRST!!
HFF! HFF!
HFF! HFF!
THIS SCENARIO...

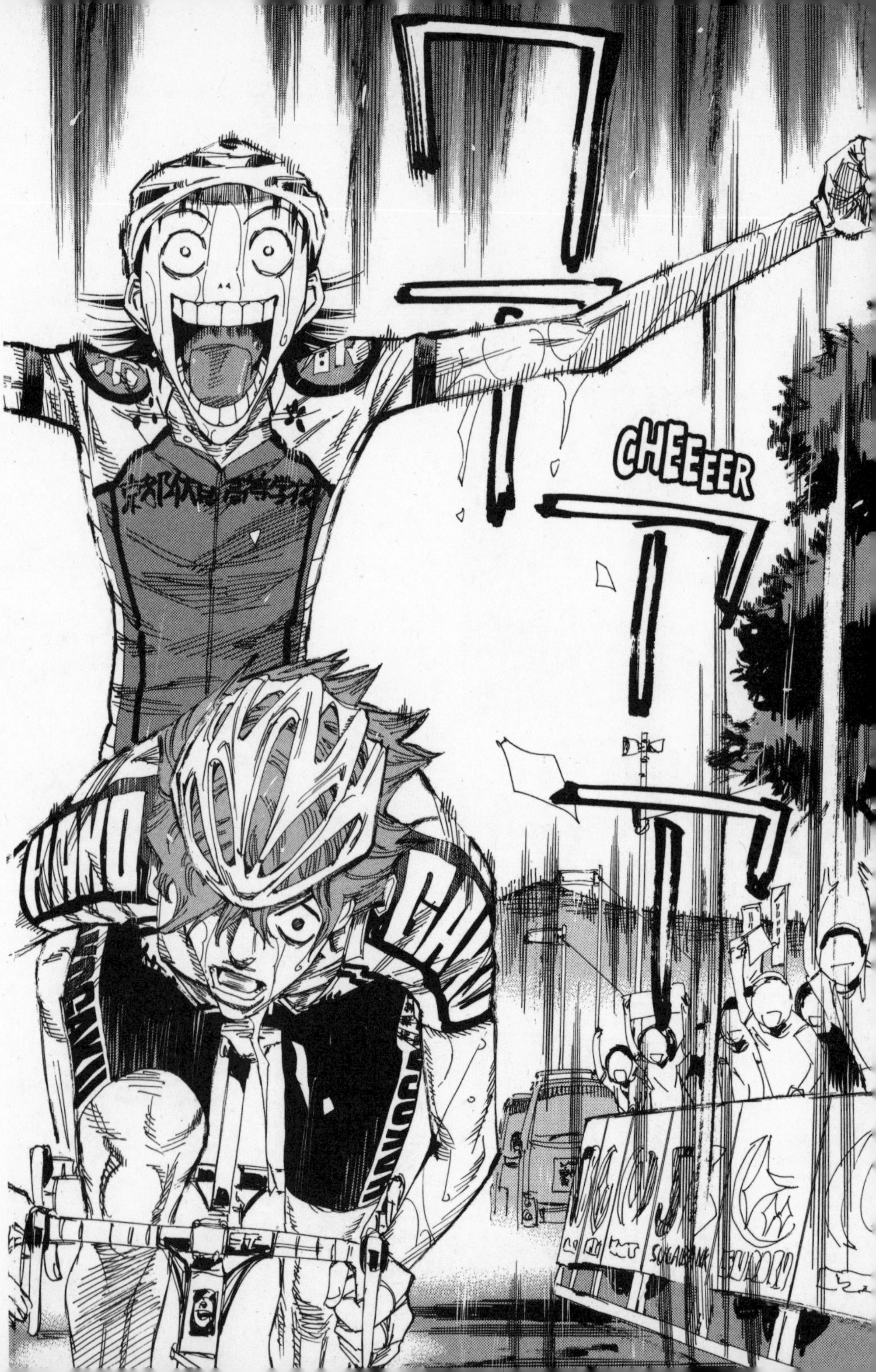
CHEEEER

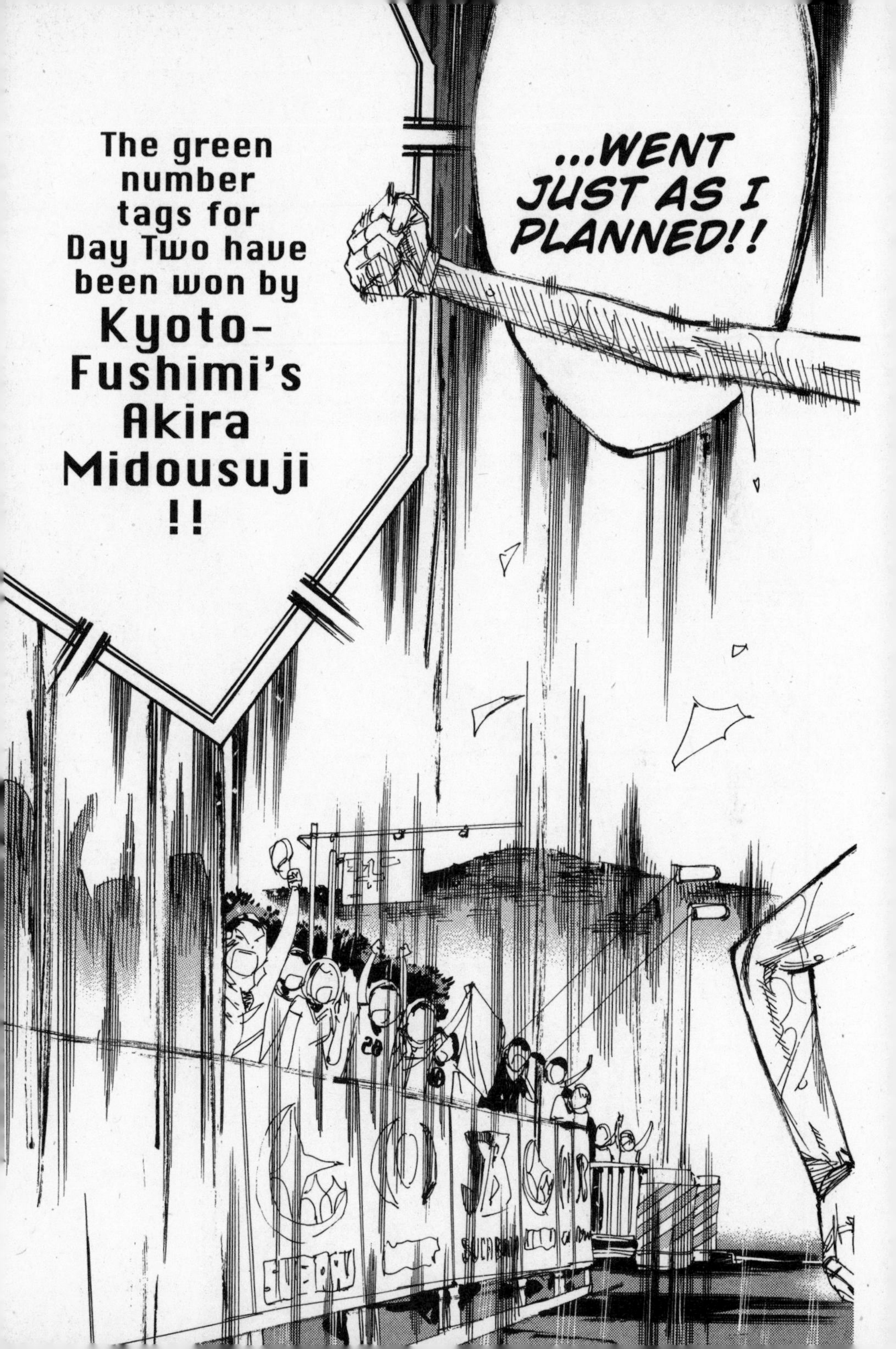
...WENT JUST AS I PLANNED!!
The green number tags for Day Two have been won by Kyoto-Fushimi's Akira Midousuji!!

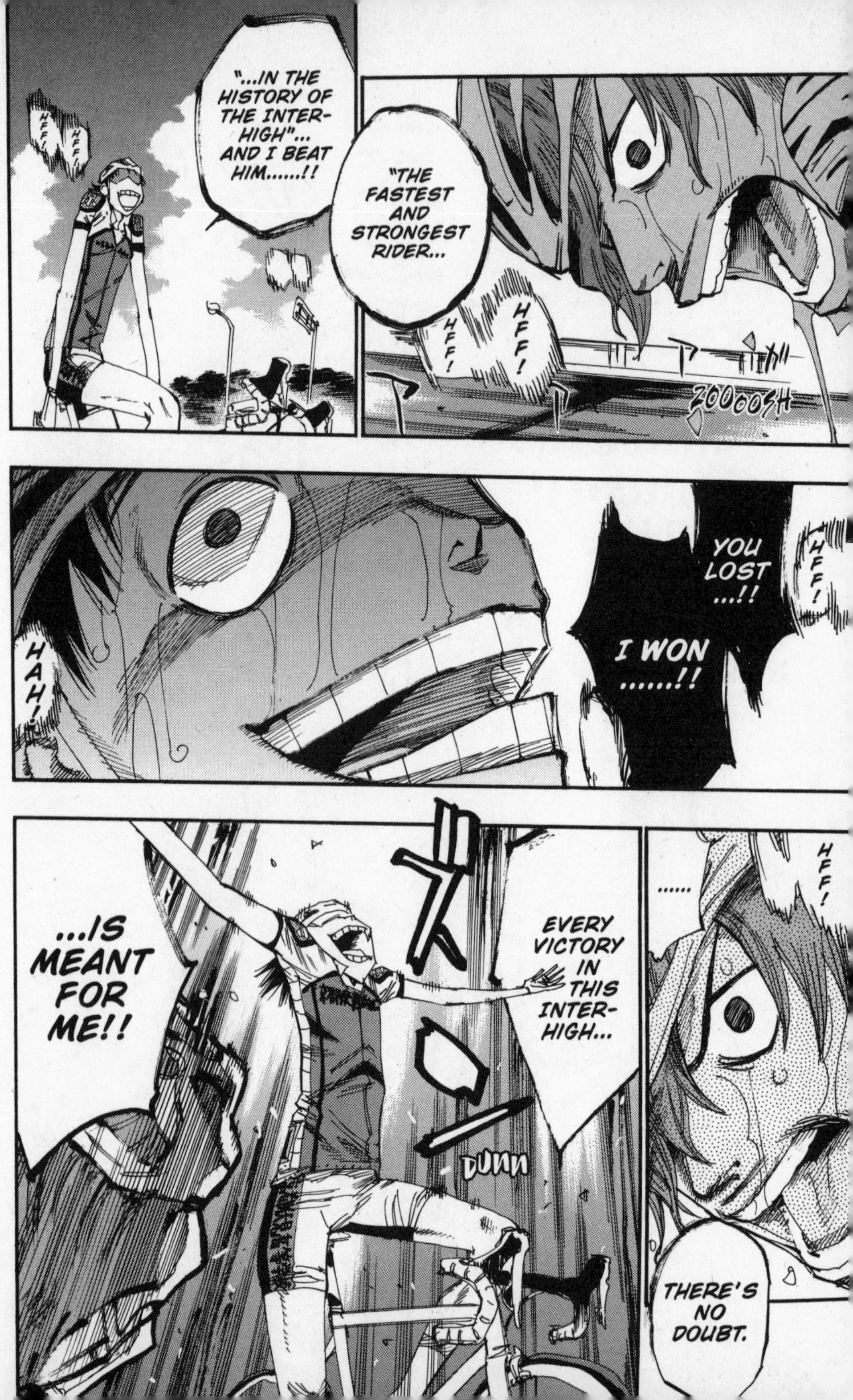
"THE FASTEST AND STRONGEST RIDER...
HFF! HFF!
ZOOOOSH
"...IN THE HISTORY OF THE INTER-HIGH"... AND I BEAT HIM......!!
HFF! HFF!
HFF!
YOU LOST ...!!
I WON ......!!
HAH!
HFF!
......
THERE'S NO DOUBT.
EVERY VICTORY IN THIS INTER-HIGH...
...IS MEANT FOR ME!!
DUNN

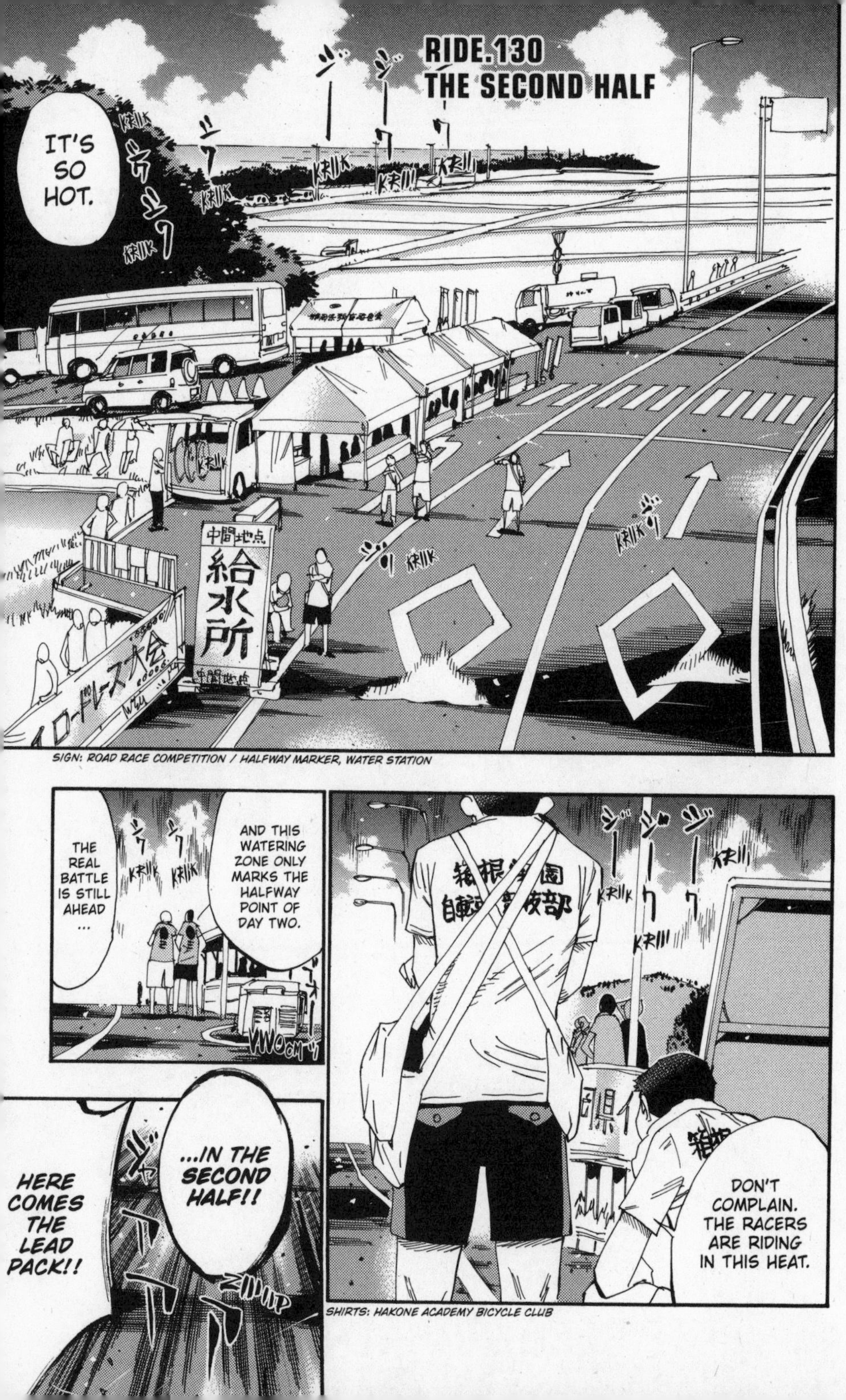
RIDE.130
THE SECOND HALF
IT'S SO HOT.
KRIIK
DON'T COMPLAIN. THE RACERS ARE RIDING IN THIS HEAT.
AND THIS WATERING ZONE ONLY MARKS THE HALFWAY POINT OF DAY TWO.
THE REAL BATTLE IS STILL AHEAD...
...IN THE SECOND HALF!!
HERE COMES THE LEAD PACK!!
SIGN: ROAD RACE COMPETITION / HALFWAY MARKER, WATER STATION
SHIRTS: HAKONE ACADEMY BICYCLE CLUB

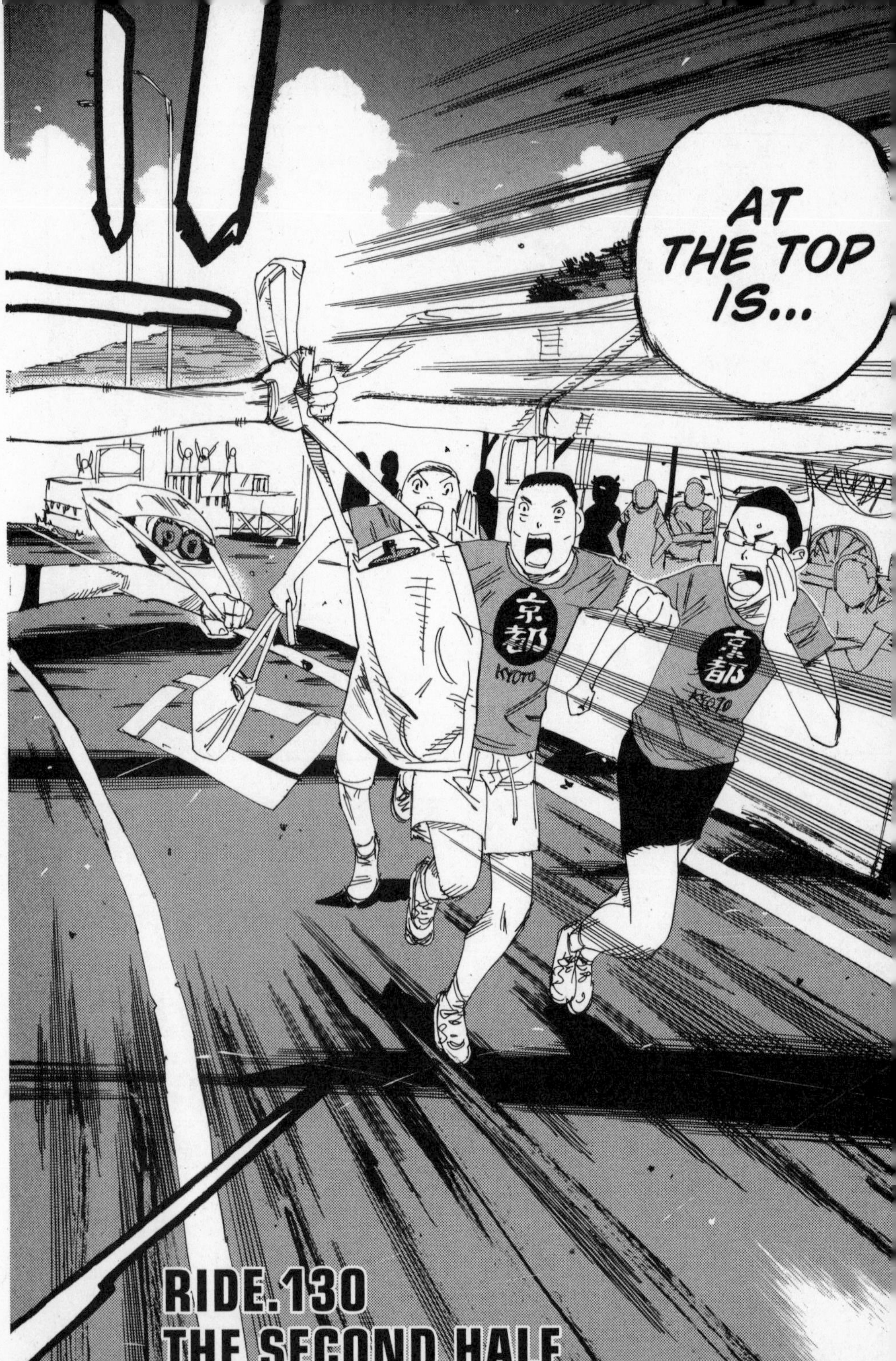
AT THE TOP IS...
京都
KYOTO
京都
KYOTO
RIDE.130
THE SECOND HALF

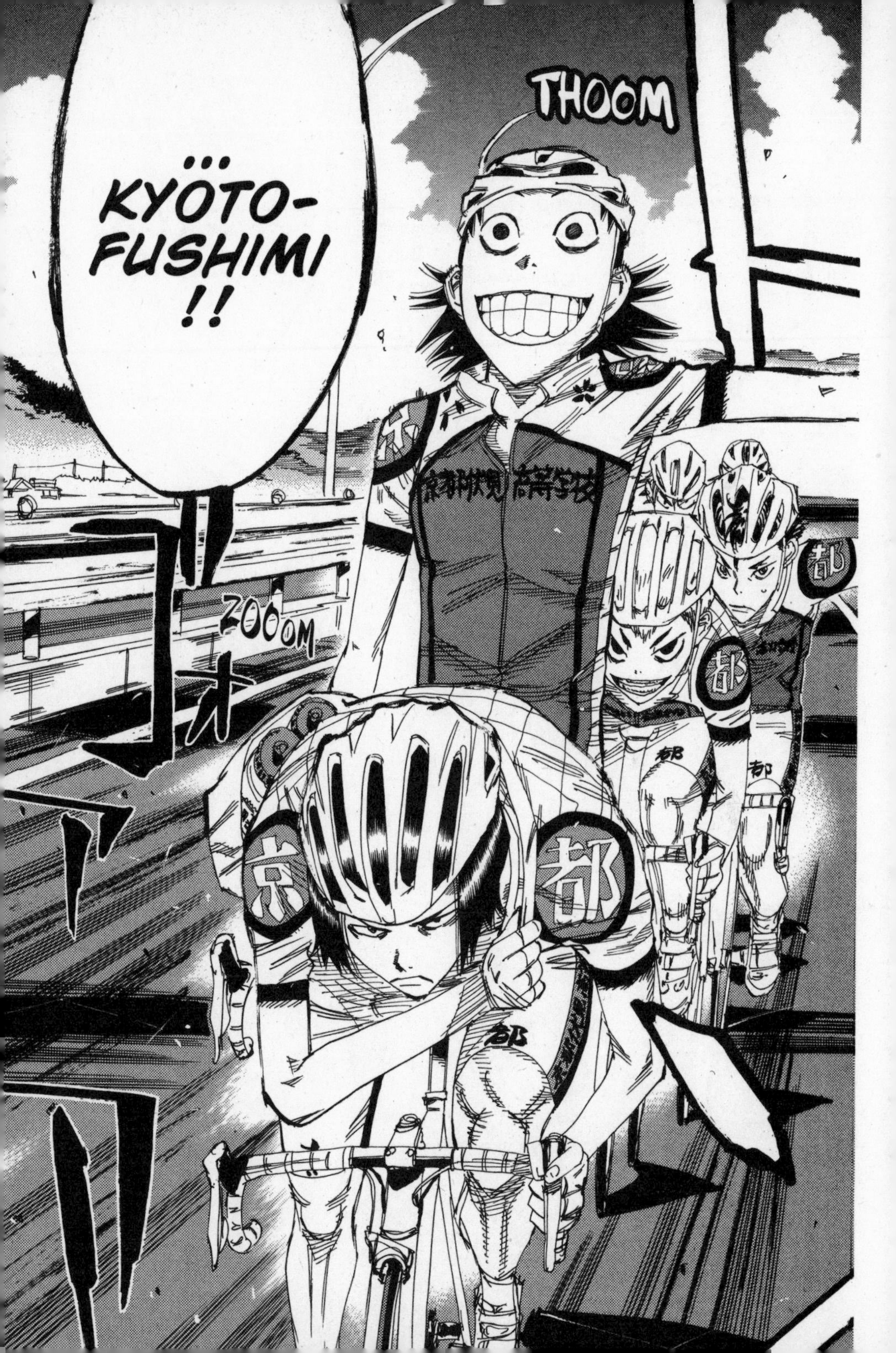
THOOM
...KYÖTO-FUSHIMI!!
ZOOOM

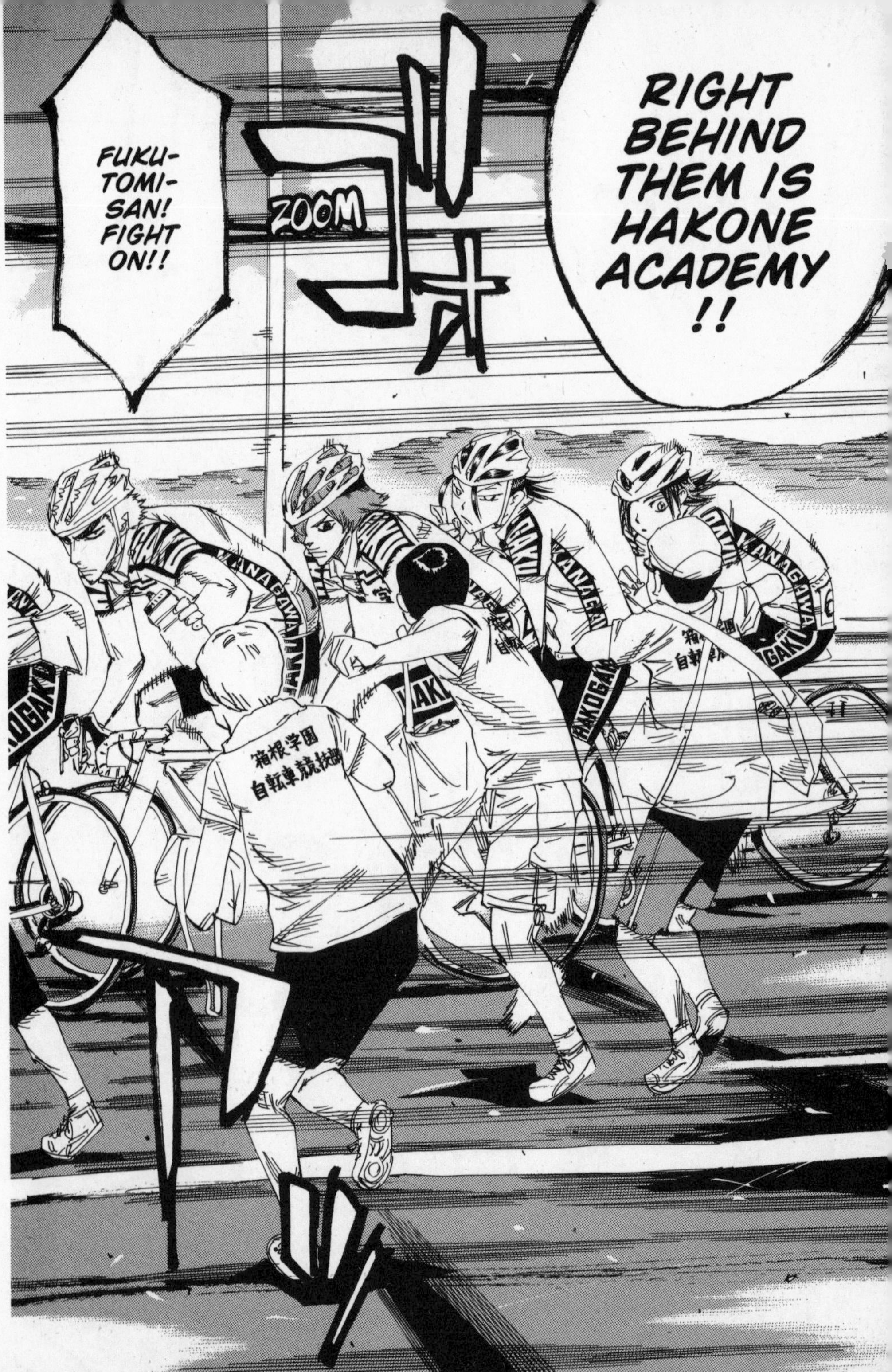
RIGHT BEHIND THEM IS HAKONE ACADEMY!!
ZOOM
FUKU-TOMI-SAN! FIGHT ON!!

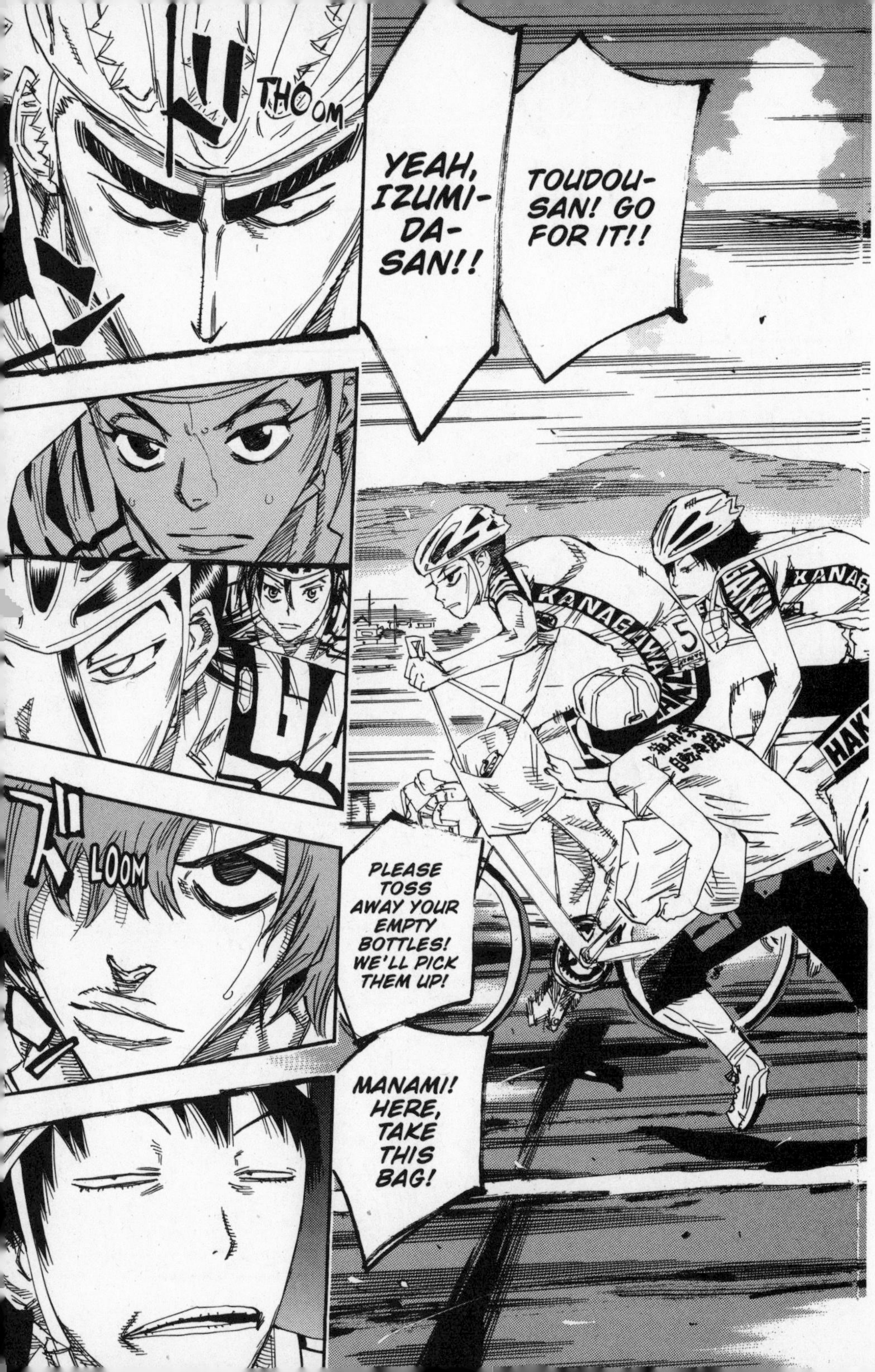
TOUDOU-SAN! GO FOR IT!!
YEAH, IZUMI-DA-SAN!!
PLEASE TOSS AWAY YOUR EMPTY BOTTLES! WE'LL PICK THEM UP!
MANAMI! HERE, TAKE THIS BAG!
THOOM
LOOM

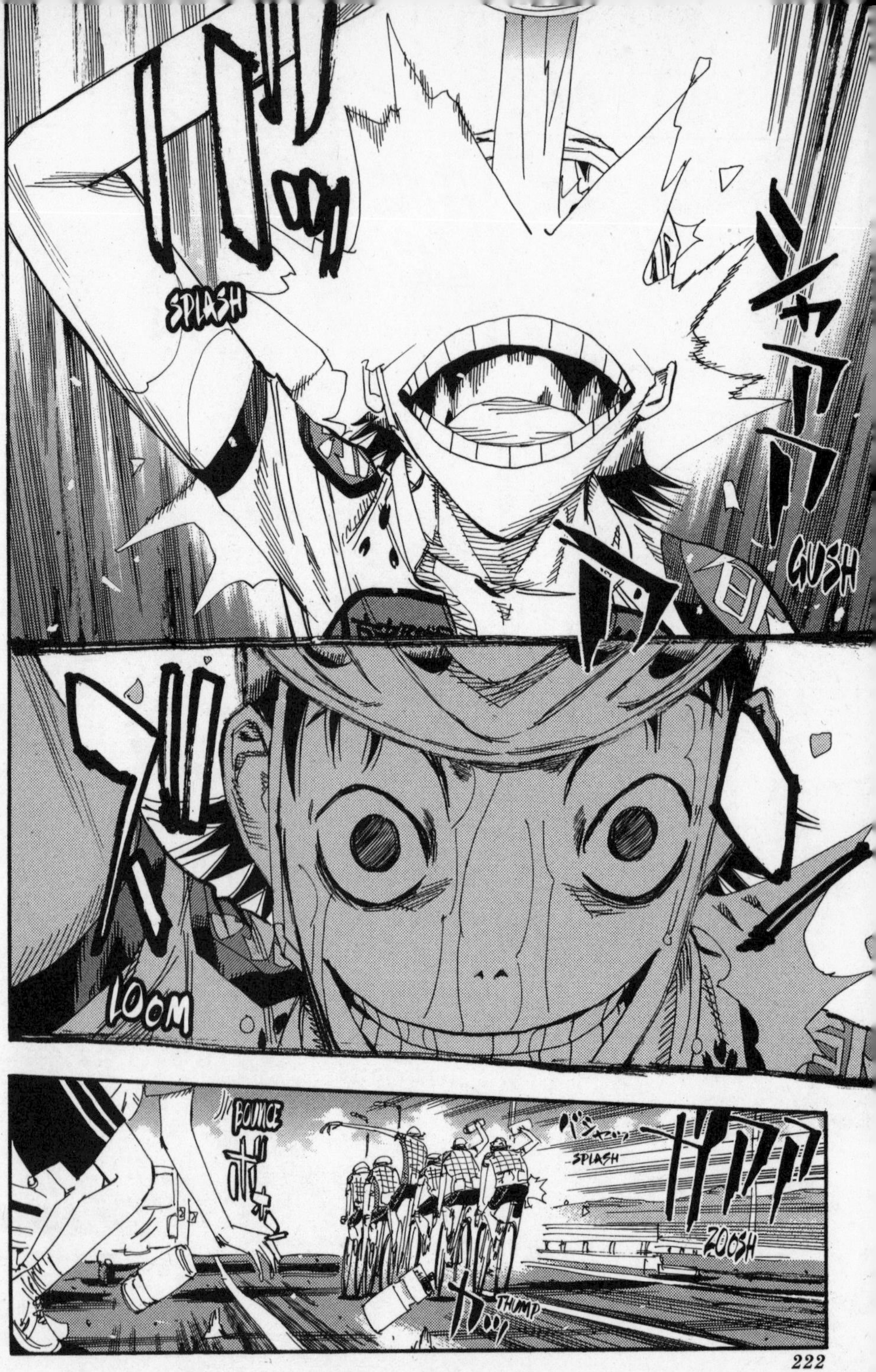

シャアアア!
GUSH
SPLASH
LOOM
ZOOSH
バシャッ
SPLASH
THUMP
BOUNCE

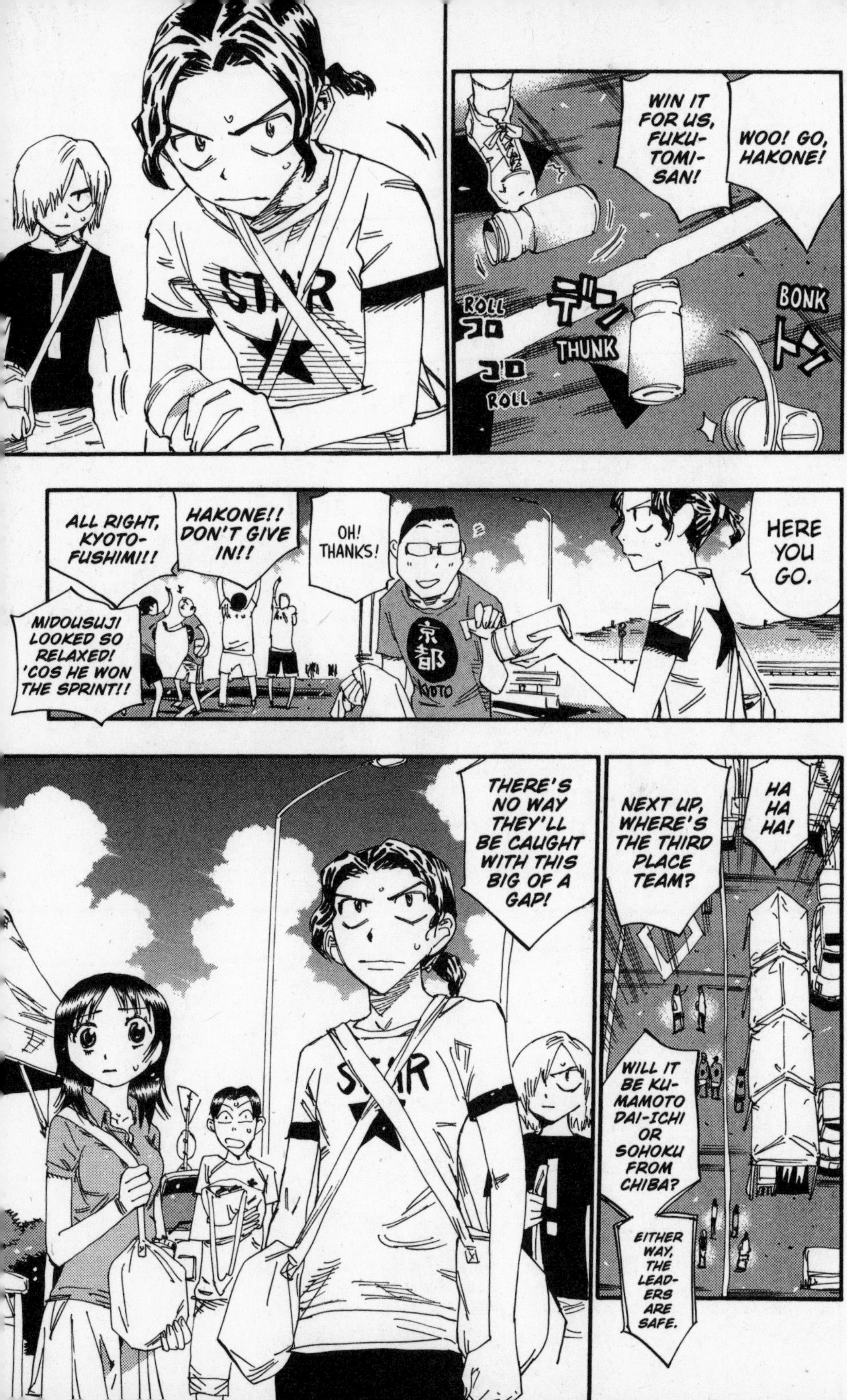
WOO! GO, HAKONE!
WIN IT FOR US, FUKUTOMI-SAN!
BONK
THUNK
ROLL
ROLL
HERE YOU GO.
OH! THANKS!
HAKONE!! DON'T GIVE IN!!
ALL RIGHT, KYOTO-FUSHIMI!!
MIDOUSUJI LOOKED SO RELAXED! 'COS HE WON THE SPRINT!!
HA HA HA!
NEXT UP, WHERE'S THE THIRD PLACE TEAM?
WILL IT BE KUMAMOTO DAI-ICHI OR SOHOKU FROM CHIBA?
EITHER WAY, THE LEADERS ARE SAFE.
THERE'S NO WAY THEY'LL BE CAUGHT WITH THIS BIG OF A GAP!

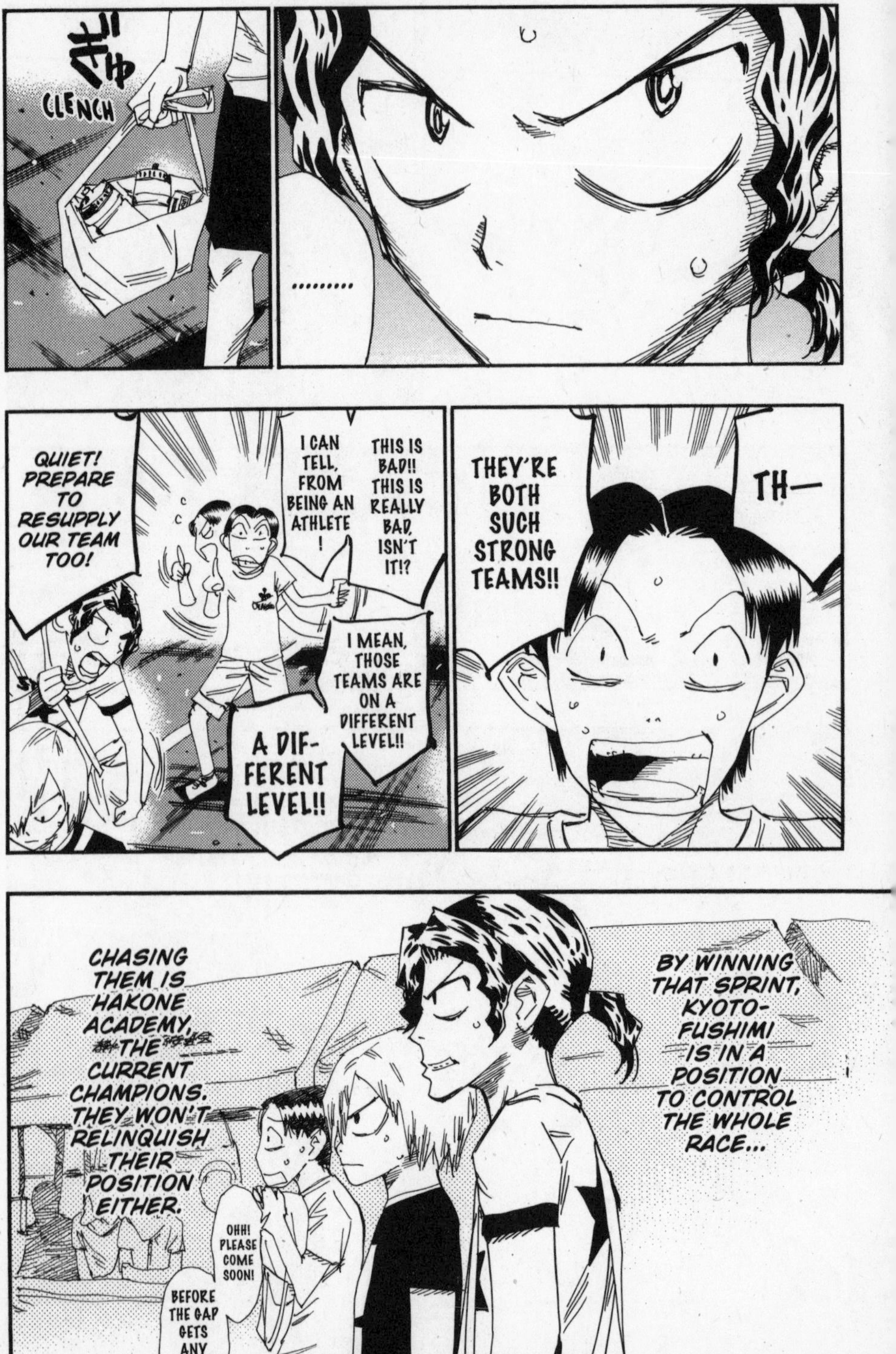

....
ぎゅ
CLENCH
TH—
THEY'RE BOTH SUCH STRONG TEAMS!!
THIS IS BAD!! THIS IS REALLY BAD, ISN'T IT!?
I CAN TELL, FROM BEING AN ATHLETE!
I MEAN, THOSE TEAMS ARE ON A DIFFERENT LEVEL!!
A DIFFERENT LEVEL!!
QUIET! PREPARE TO RESUPPLY OUR TEAM TOO!
BY WINNING THAT SPRINT, KYOTO-FUSHIMI IS IN A POSITION TO CONTROL THE WHOLE RACE...
CHASING THEM IS HAKONE ACADEMY, THE CURRENT CHAMPIONS. THEY WON'T RELINQUISH THEIR POSITION EITHER.
OHH! PLEASE COME SOON!
BEFORE THE GAP GETS ANY WIDER!

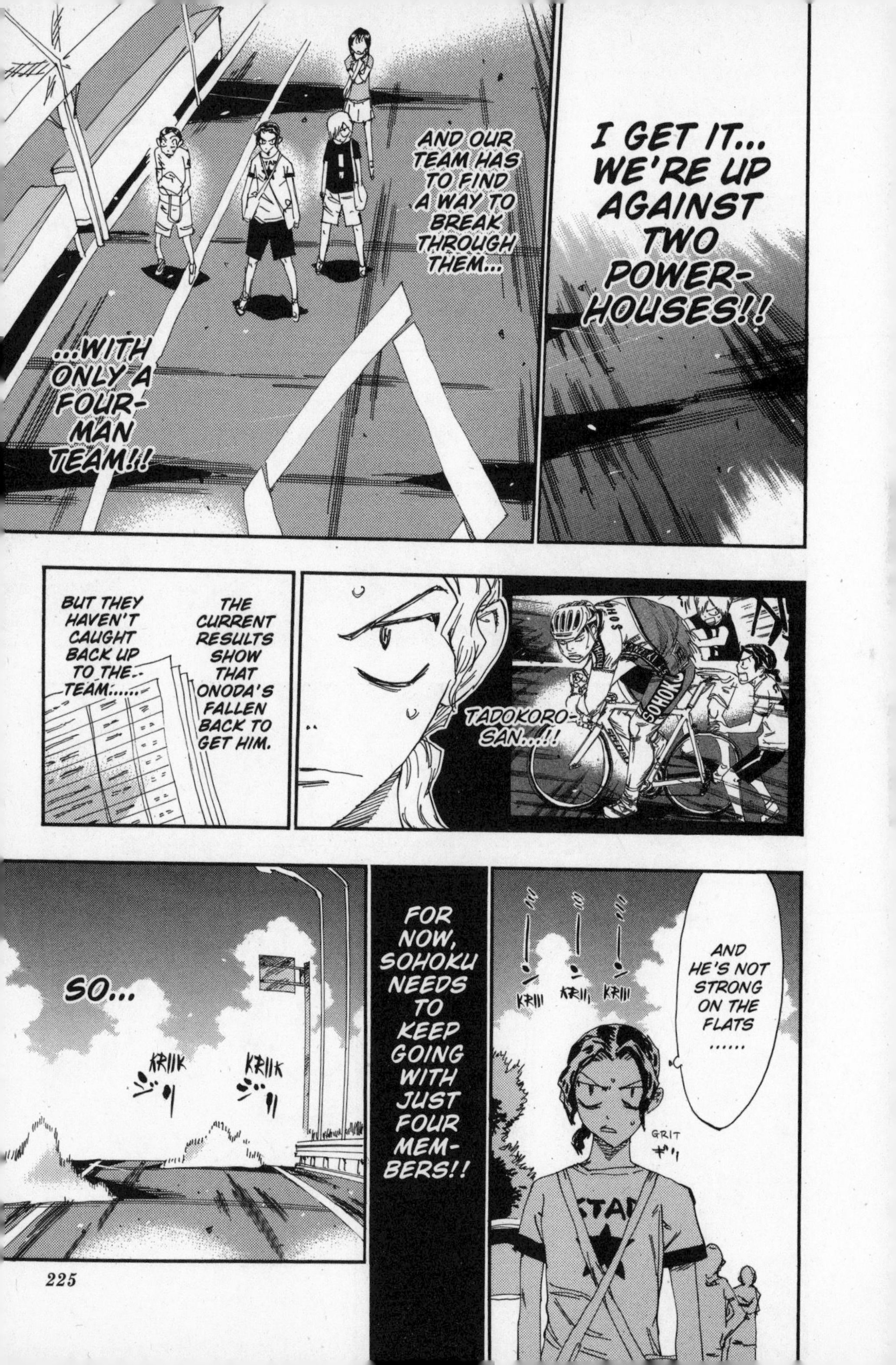
I GET IT... WE'RE UP AGAINST TWO POWER-HOUSES!!
AND OUR TEAM HAS TO FIND A WAY TO BREAK THROUGH THEM...
...WITH ONLY A FOUR-MAN TEAM!!
TADOKORO-SAN...!!
..
THE CURRENT RESULTS SHOW THAT ONODA'S FALLEN BACK TO GET HIM.
BUT THEY HAVEN'T CAUGHT BACK UP TO THE TEAM......
KRIII
KRIII
KRIII
AND HE'S NOT STRONG ON THE FLATS ......
GRIT
FOR NOW, SOHOKU NEEDS TO KEEP GOING WITH JUST FOUR MEM-BERS!!
SO...
KRIIK
KRIIK

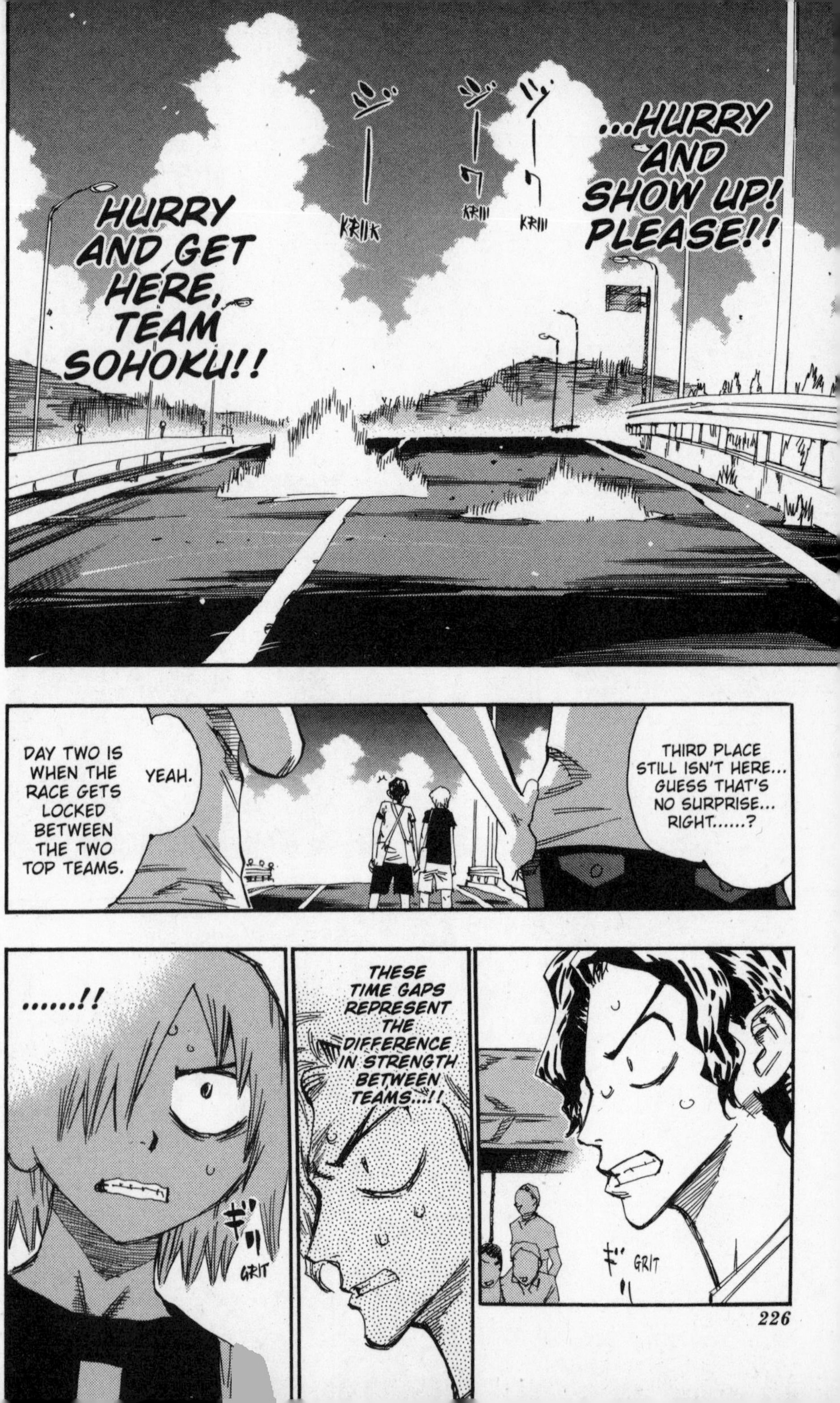

...HURRY AND SHOW UP! PLEASE!!
KRIII
KRIII
KRIIK
HURRY AND GET HERE, TEAM SOHOKU!!
THIRD PLACE STILL ISN'T HERE... GUESS THAT'S NO SURPRISE... RIGHT......?
YEAH.
DAY TWO IS WHEN THE RACE GETS LOCKED BETWEEN THE TWO TOP TEAMS.
GRIT
THESE TIME GAPS REPRESENT THE DIFFERENCE IN STRENGTH BETWEEN TEAMS...!!
......!!
GRIT

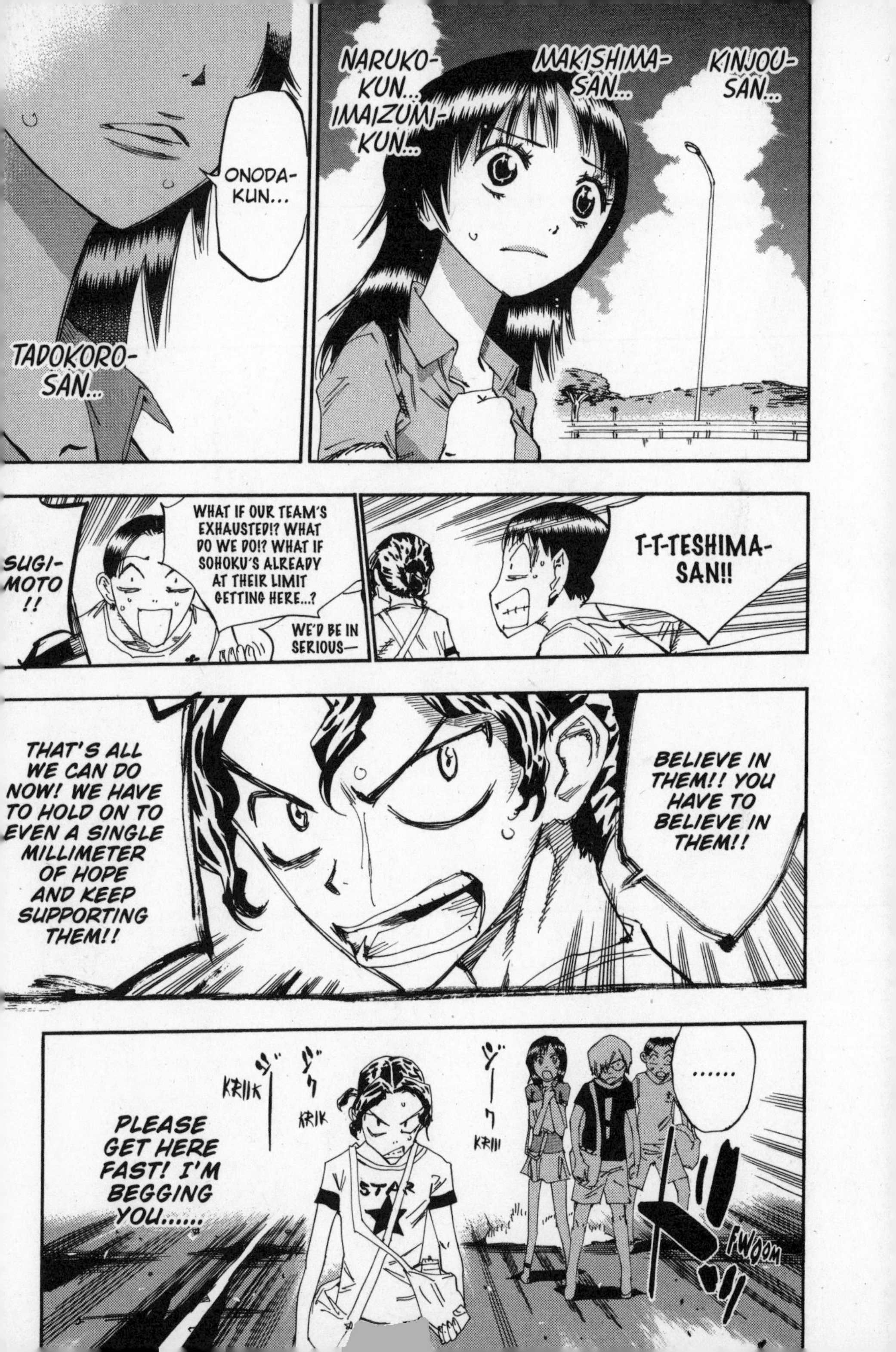
KINJOU-SAN...
MAKISHIMA-SAN...
NARUKO-KUN... IMAIZUMI-KUN...
ONODA-KUN...
TADOKORO-SAN...
T-T-TESHIMA-SAN!!
WHAT IF OUR TEAM'S EXHAUSTED!? WHAT DO WE DO!? WHAT IF SOHOKU'S ALREADY AT THEIR LIMIT GETTING HERE...?
WE'D BE IN SERIOUS—
SUGI-MOTO!!
BELIEVE IN THEM!! YOU HAVE TO BELIEVE IN THEM!!
THAT'S ALL WE CAN DO NOW! WE HAVE TO HOLD ON TO EVEN A SINGLE MILLIMETER OF HOPE AND KEEP SUPPORTING THEM!!
......
FWOOM
KRIII
KRIK
KRIIK
PLEASE GET HERE FAST! I'M BEGGING YOU......

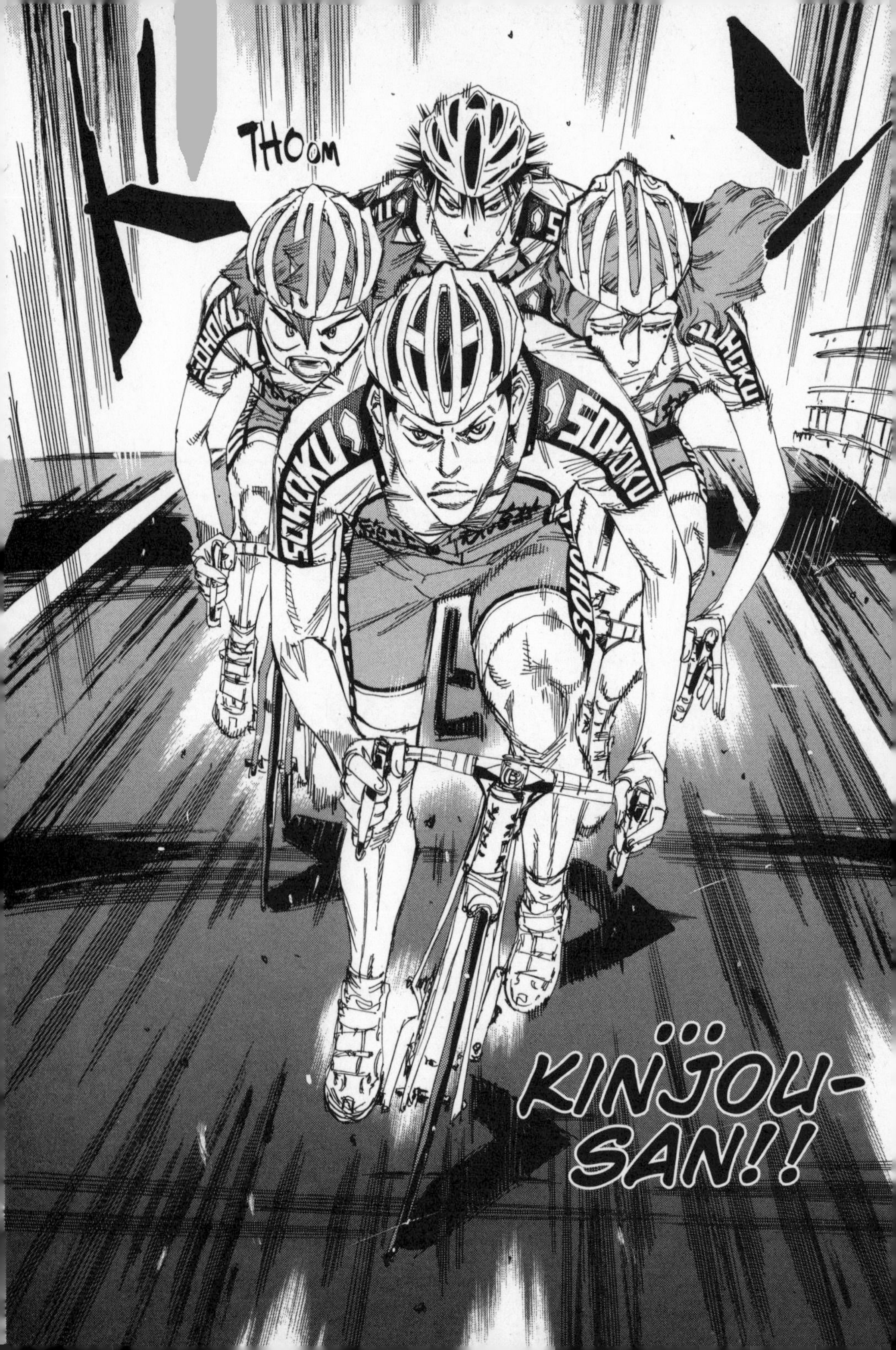
THOOM
KINJOU-SAN!!

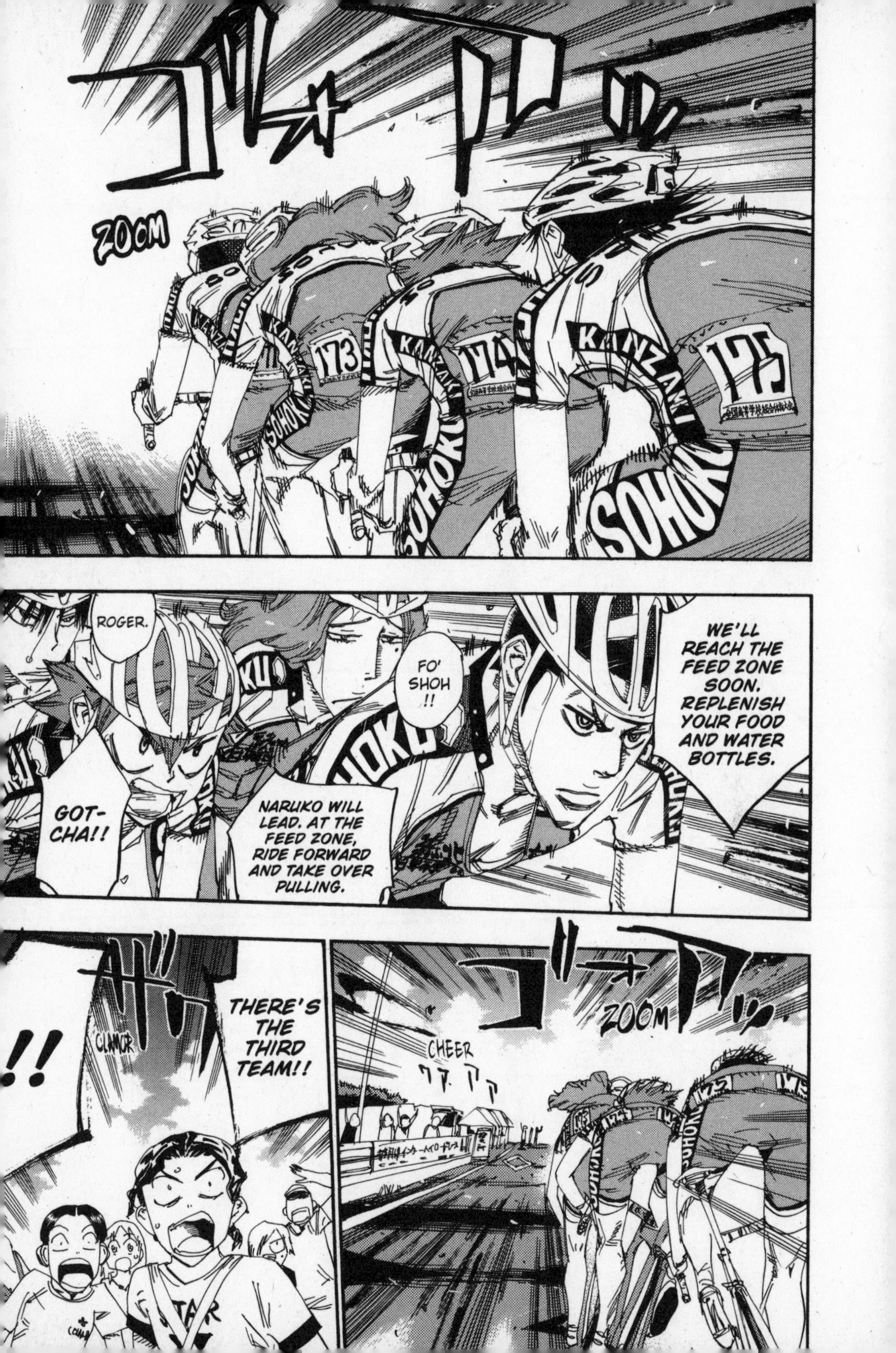
ZOOM
WE'LL REACH THE FEED ZONE SOON. REPLENISH YOUR FOOD AND WATER BOTTLES.
FO' SHOH!!
NARUKO WILL LEAD. AT THE FEED ZONE, RIDE FORWARD AND TAKE OVER PULLING.
ROGER.
GOT-CHA!!
ZOOM
CHEER
THERE'S THE THIRD TEAM!!
CLAMOR
!!

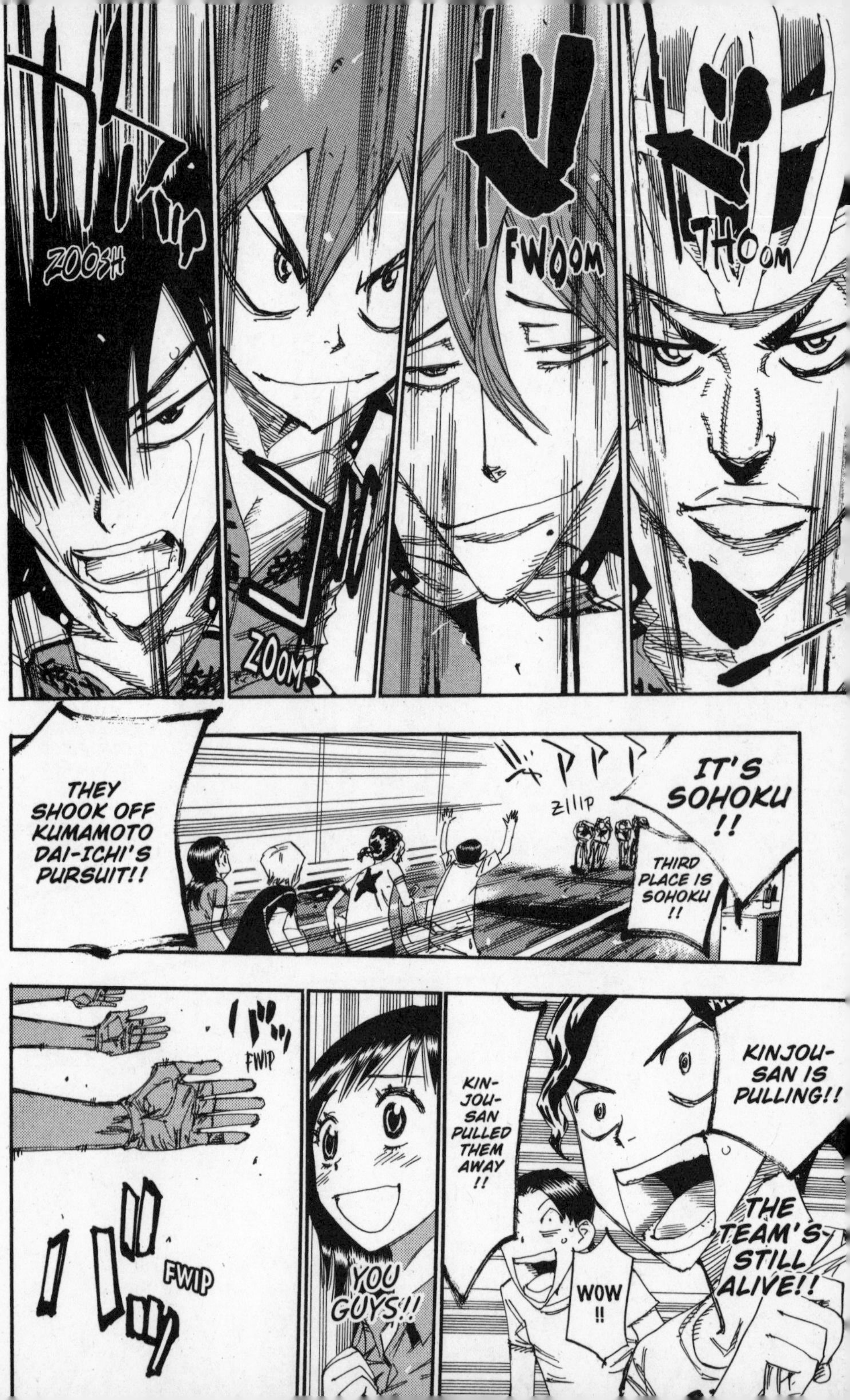
THOOM
FWOOM
ZOOM!
ZIP
ZOOSH
IT'S SOHOKU!!
THIRD PLACE IS SOHOKU!!
ZIIIP
THEY SHOOK OFF KUMAMOTO DAI-ICHI'S PURSUIT!!
KINJOU-SAN IS PULLING!!
THE TEAM'S STILL ALIVE!!
WOW!!
KIN-JOU-SAN PULLED THEM AWAY!!
YOU GUYS!!
FWIP
FWIP

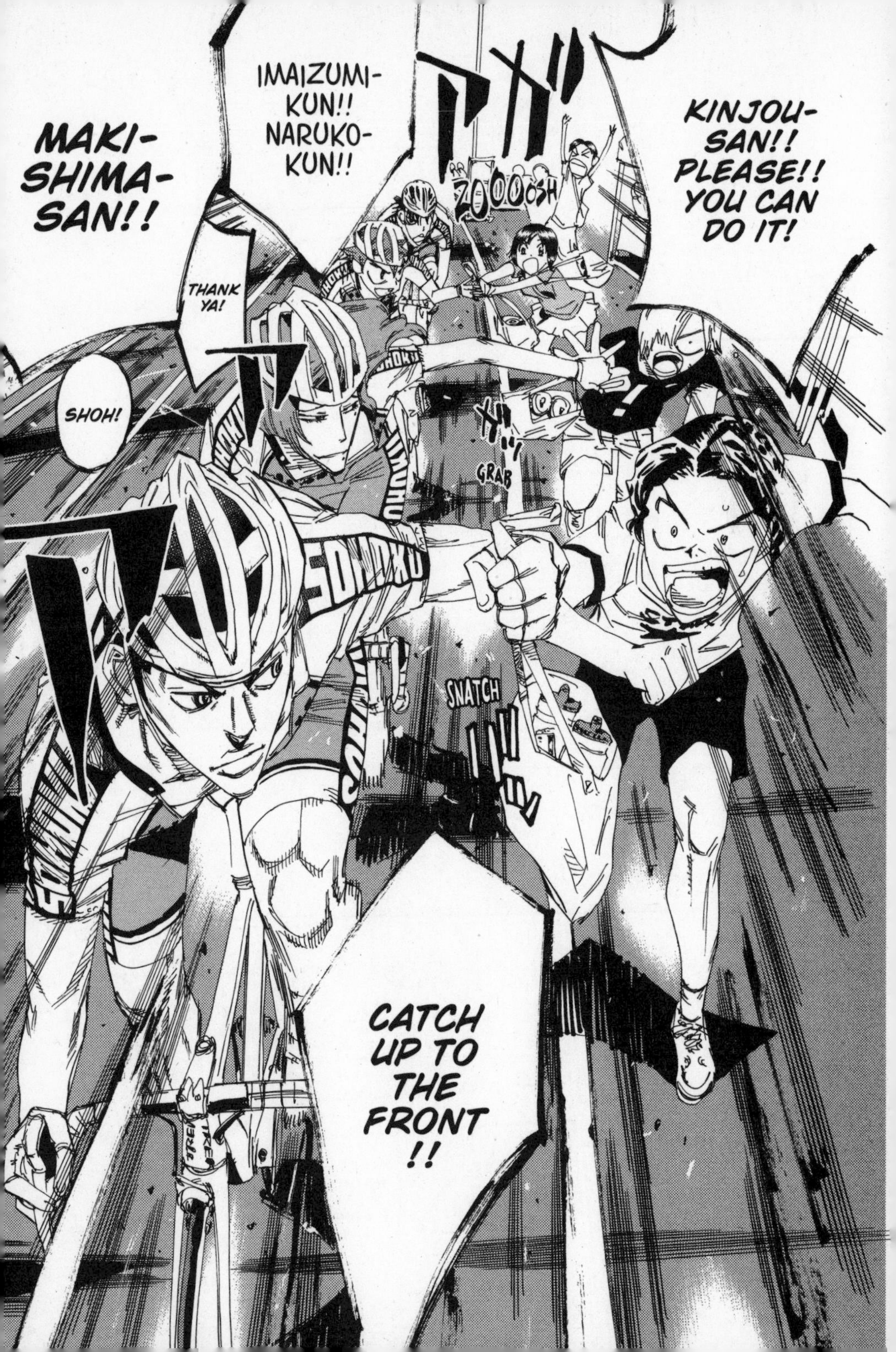
KINJOU-SAN!! PLEASE!! YOU CAN DO IT!
IMAIZUMI-KUN!! NARUKO-KUN!!
MAKI-SHIMA-SAN!!
ZOOOOSH
THANK YA!
GRAB
SHOH!
SNATCH
CATCH UP TO THE FRONT!!

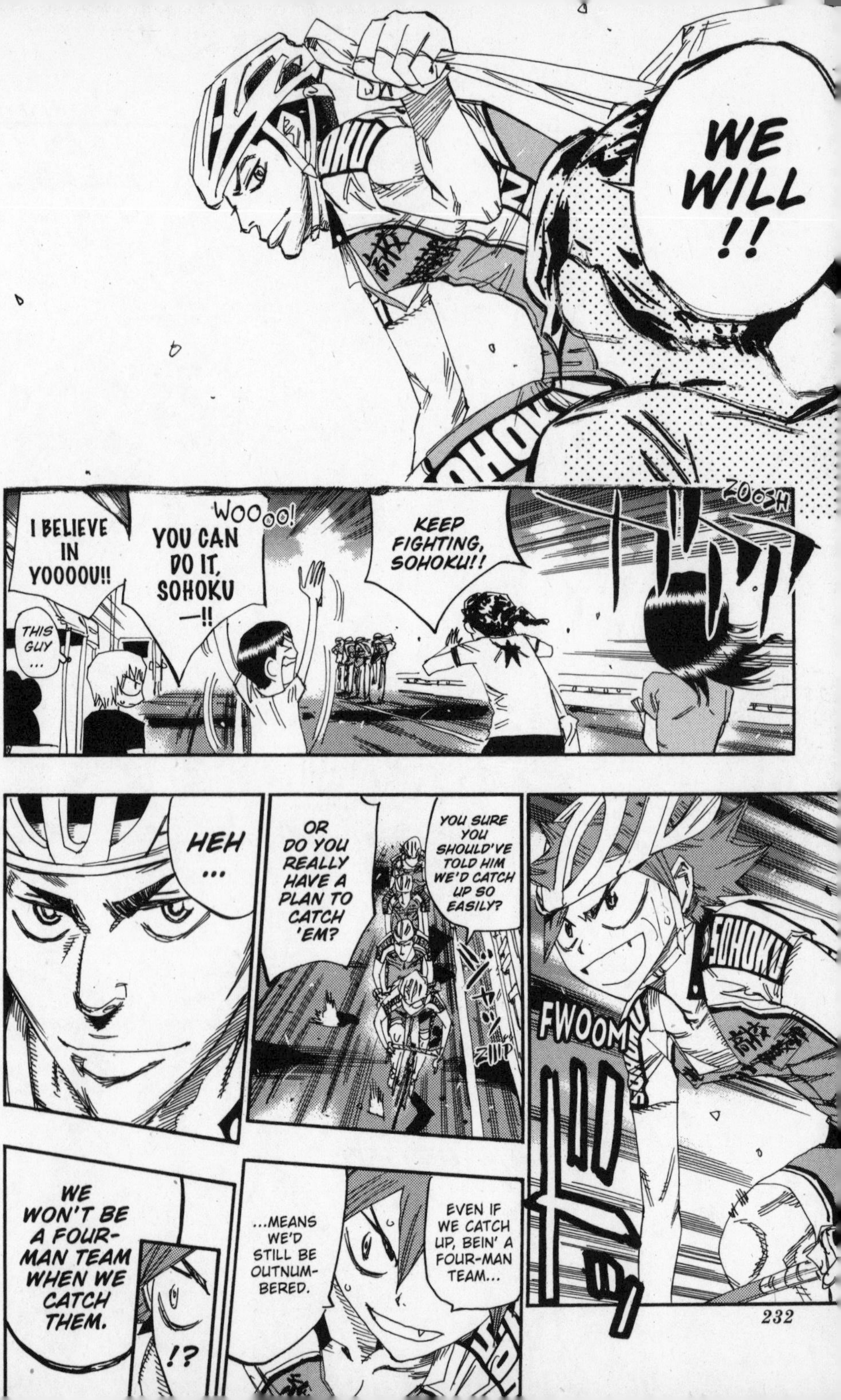
WE WILL!!
ZOOSH
KEEP FIGHTING, SOHOKU!!
WOOooo!
YOU CAN DO IT, SOHOKU—!!
I BELIEVE IN YOOOOU!!
THIS GUY...
FWOOM
YOU SURE YOU SHOULD'VE TOLD HIM WE'D CATCH UP SO EASILY?
OR DO YOU REALLY HAVE A PLAN TO CATCH 'EM?
ZIIP
HEH...
EVEN IF WE CATCH UP, BEIN' A FOUR-MAN TEAM...
...MEANS WE'D STILL BE OUTNUMBERED.
WE WON'T BE A FOUR-MAN TEAM WHEN WE CATCH THEM.
!?

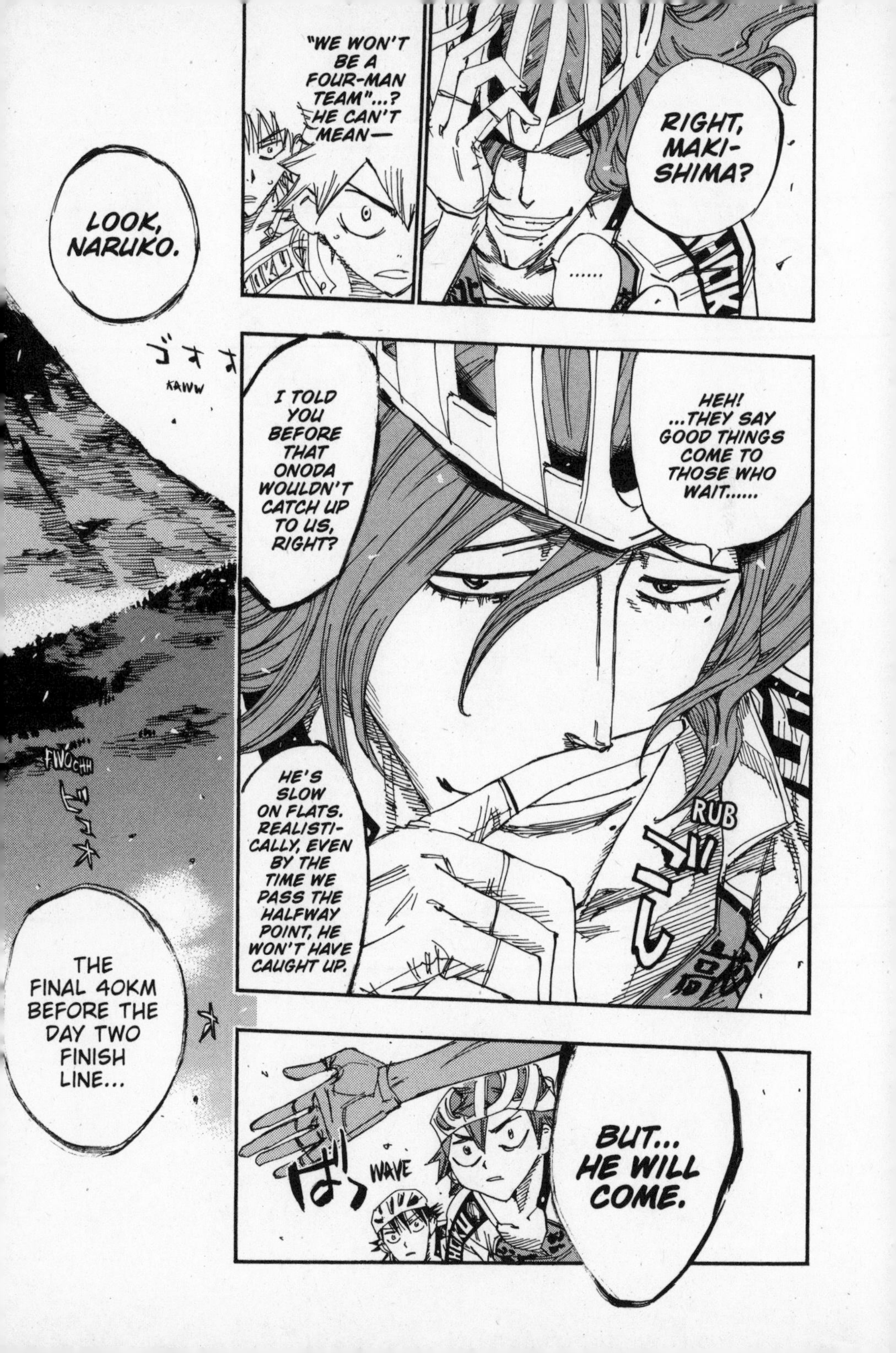
RIGHT, MAKI-SHIMA?
......
"WE WON'T BE A FOUR-MAN TEAM"...? HE CAN'T MEAN—
LOOK, NARUKO.
HEH! ...THEY SAY GOOD THINGS COME TO THOSE WHO WAIT......
I TOLD YOU BEFORE THAT ONODA WOULDN'T CATCH UP TO US, RIGHT?
RUB
HE'S SLOW ON FLATS. REALISTI-CALLY, EVEN BY THE TIME WE PASS THE HALFWAY POINT, HE WON'T HAVE CAUGHT UP.
ゴオオ
KAWW
FWOCHH
THE FINAL 40KM BEFORE THE DAY TWO FINISH LINE...
BUT... HE WILL COME.
WAVE

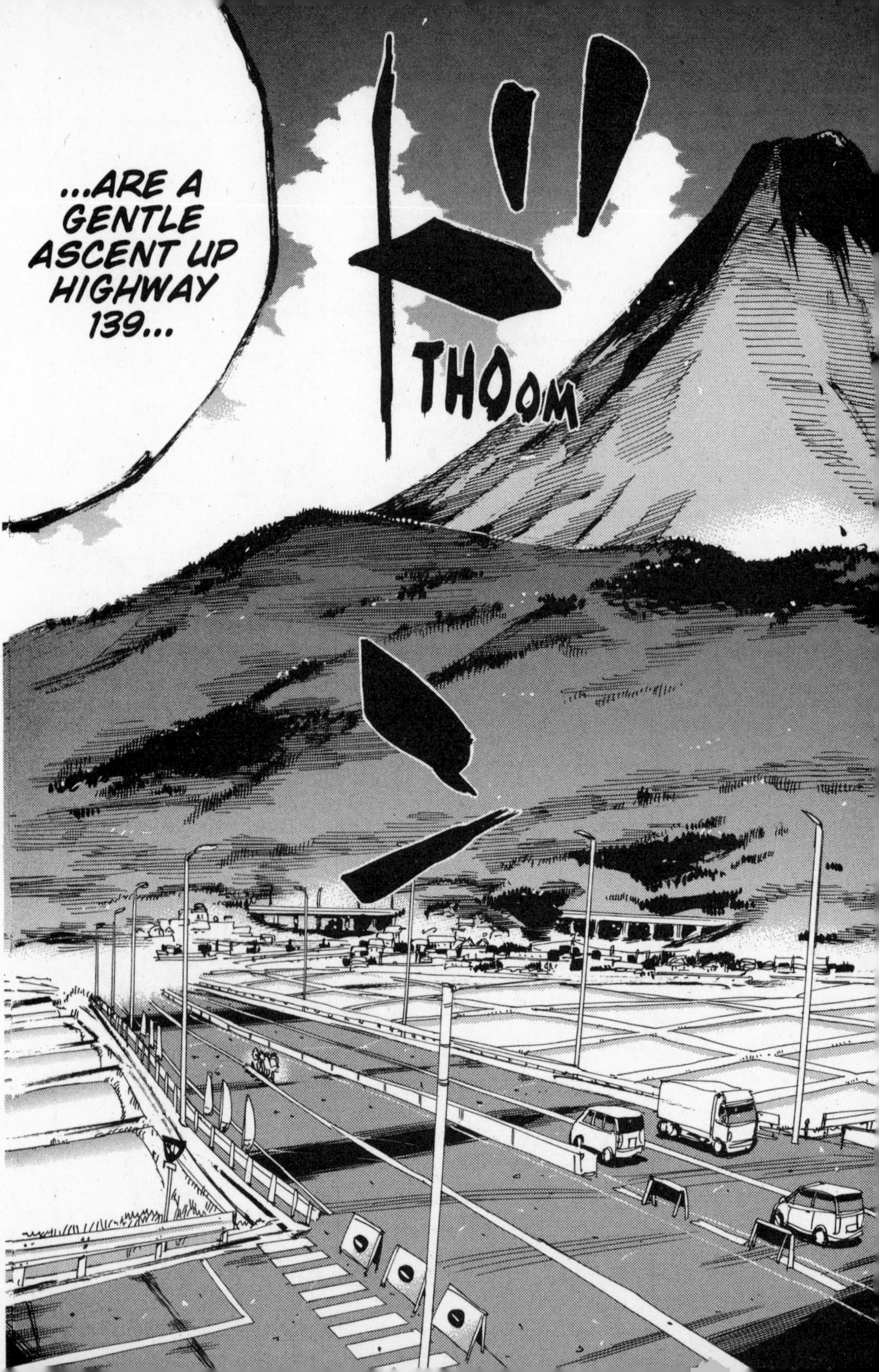
...ARE A GENTLE ASCENT UP HIGHWAY 139...
THOOM

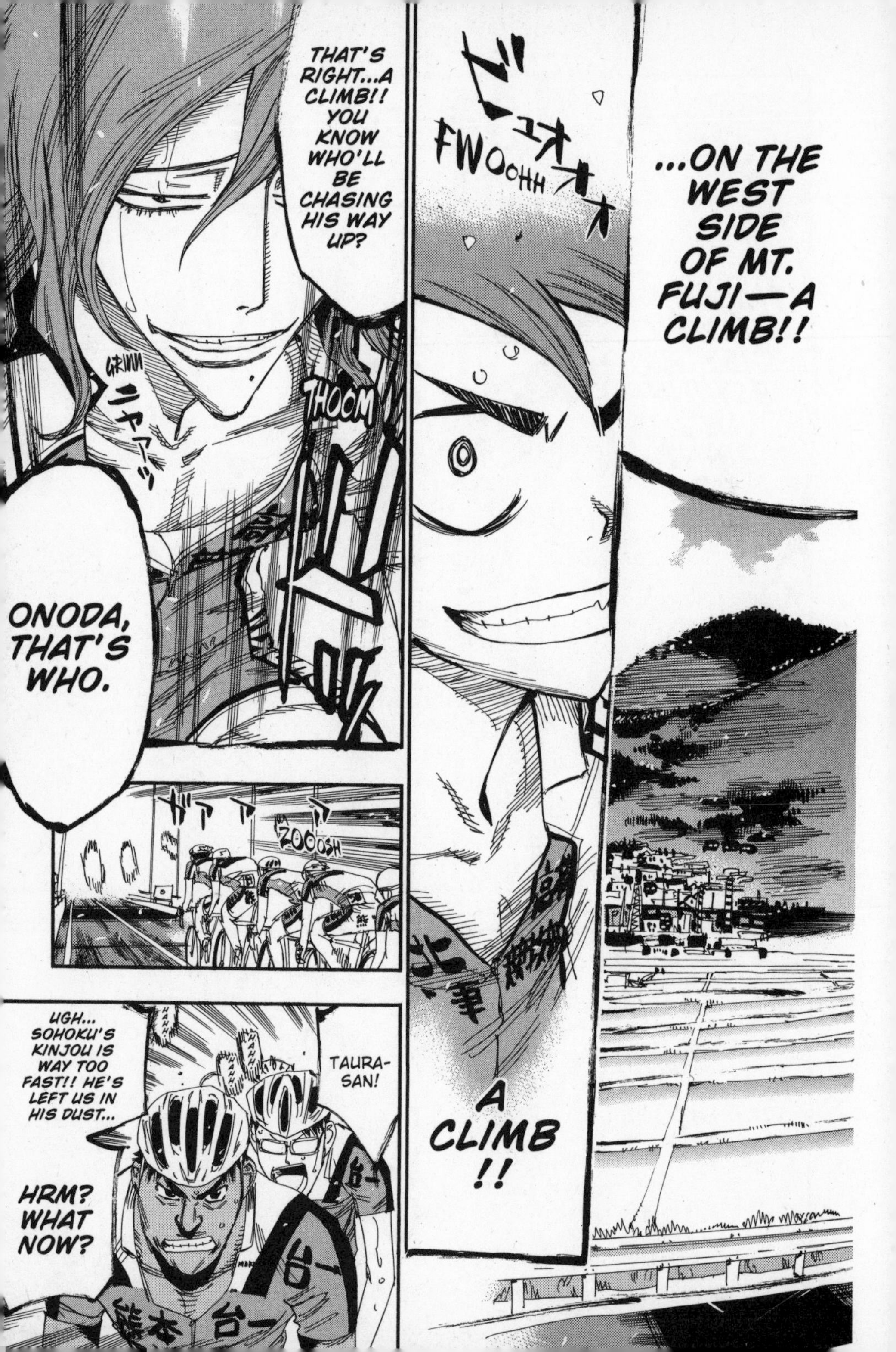
...ON THE WEST SIDE OF MT. FUJI—A CLIMB!!
FWOOHHH
A CLIMB!!
THAT'S RIGHT...A CLIMB!! YOU KNOW WHO'LL BE CHASING HIS WAY UP?
GRINN
ニヤァーッ
THOOM
ONODA, THAT'S WHO.
ZOOOSH
TAURA-SAN!
UGH... SOHOKU'S KINJOU IS WAY TOO FAST!! HE'S LEFT US IN HIS DUST...
HRM? WHAT NOW?

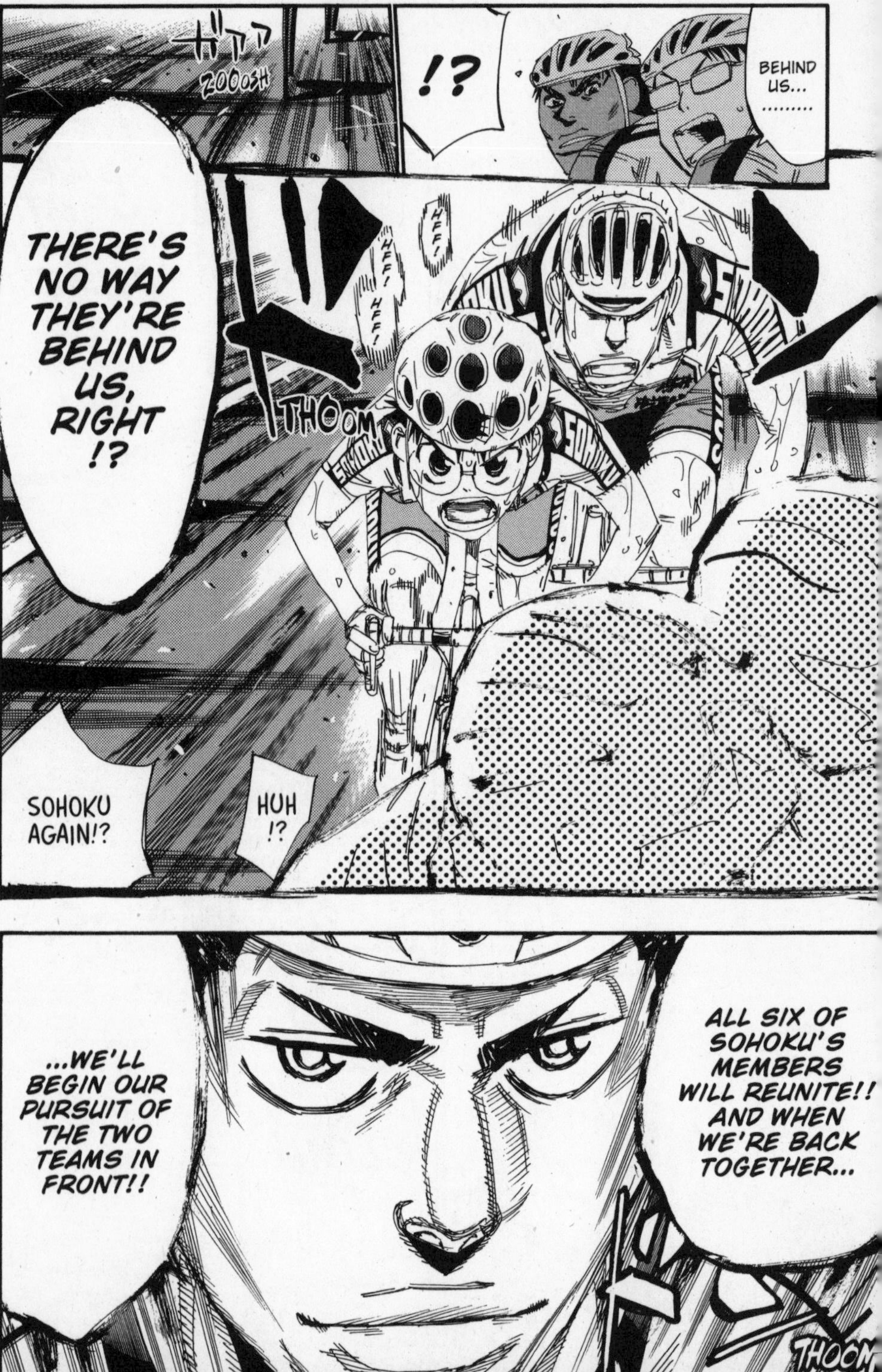
BEHIND US... ....
!?
ZOOOSH
THERE'S NO WAY THEY'RE BEHIND US, RIGHT!?
HFF! HFF! HFF! HFF!
THOOM
HUH!?
SOHOKU AGAIN!?
ALL SIX OF SOHOKU'S MEMBERS WILL REUNITE!! AND WHEN WE'RE BACK TOGETHER...
...WE'LL BEGIN OUR PURSUIT OF THE TWO TEAMS IN FRONT!!
THOOM

RIDE.131 ONODA'S RIDE

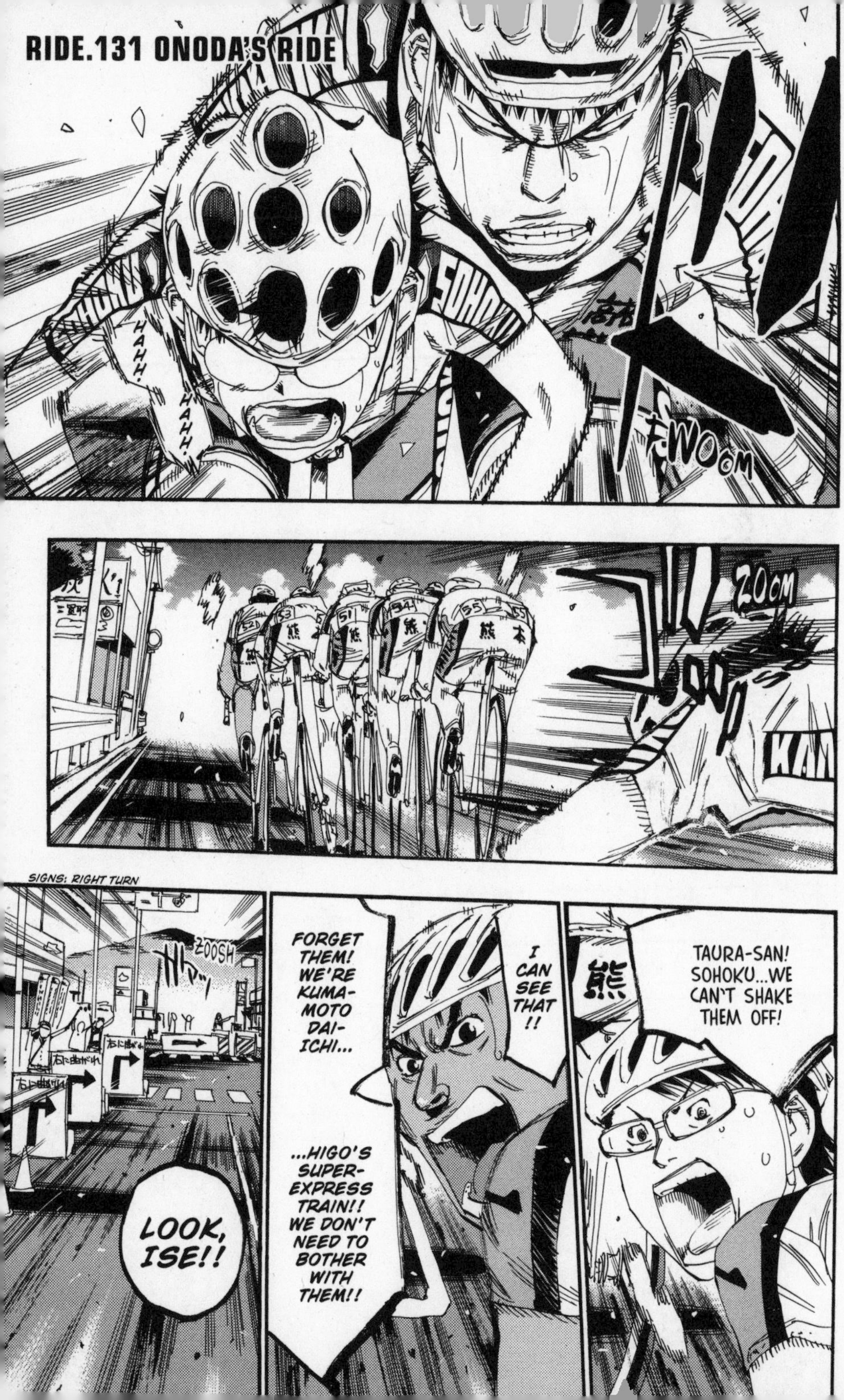

HAHH
HAHH
FWOOM
ZOOM
KAN
SIGNS: RIGHT TURN
ZOOSH
TAURA-SAN! SOHOKU...WE CAN'T SHAKE THEM OFF!
I CAN SEE THAT!!
FORGET THEM! WE'RE KUMAMOTO DAIICHI...
...HIGO'S SUPER-EXPRESS TRAIN!! WE DON'T NEED TO BOTHER WITH THEM!!
LOOK, ISE!!

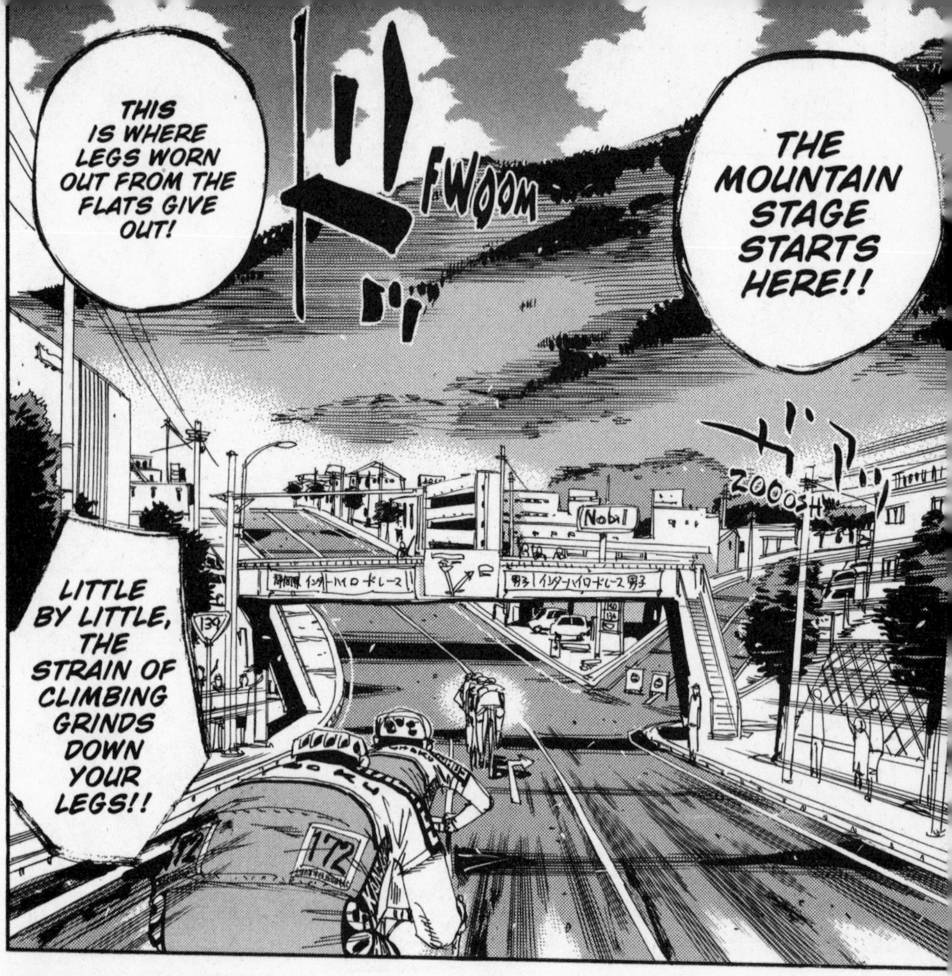
THE MOUNTAIN STAGE STARTS HERE!!
FWOOM
THIS IS WHERE LEGS WORN OUT FROM THE FLATS GIVE OUT!
ZOOOSH
LITTLE BY LITTLE, THE STRAIN OF CLIMBING GRINDS DOWN YOUR LEGS!!
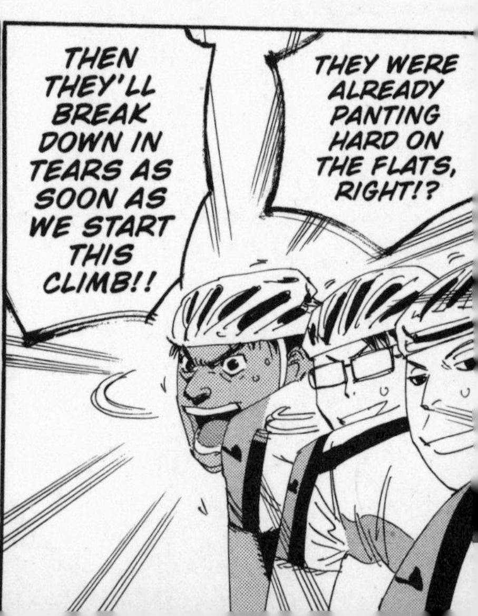
THEY WERE ALREADY PANTING HARD ON THE FLATS, RIGHT!?
THEN THEY'LL BREAK DOWN IN TEARS AS SOON AS WE START THIS CLIMB!!
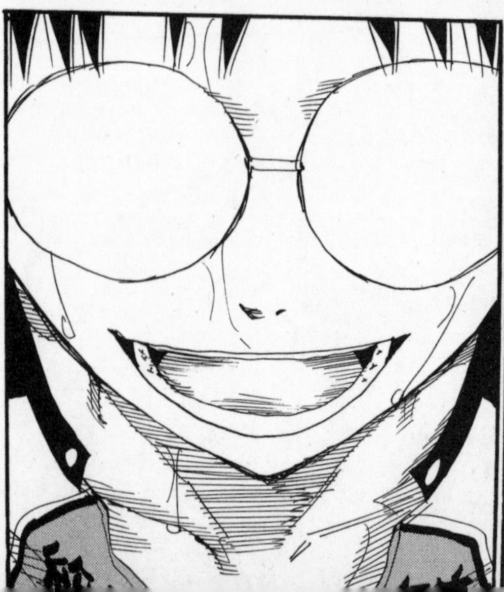

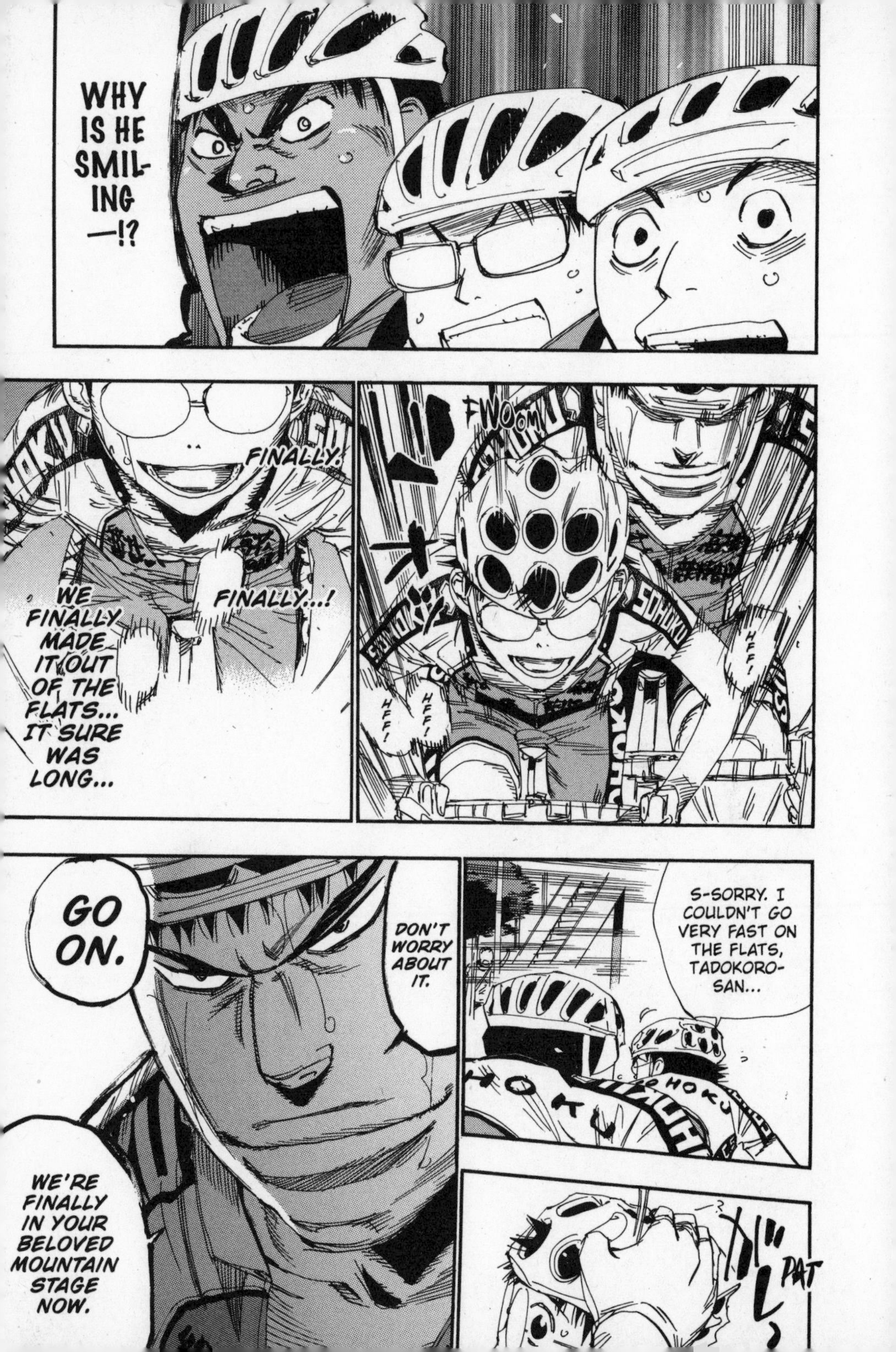
WHY IS HE SMILING—!?
FWOOM
HFF!
HFF!
HFF!
FINALLY.
FINALLY...!
WE FINALLY MADE IT OUT OF THE FLATS... IT SURE WAS LONG...
S-SORRY. I COULDN'T GO VERY FAST ON THE FLATS, TADOKORO-SAN...
PAT
DON'T WORRY ABOUT IT.
GO ON.
WE'RE FINALLY IN YOUR BELOVED MOUNTAIN STAGE NOW.

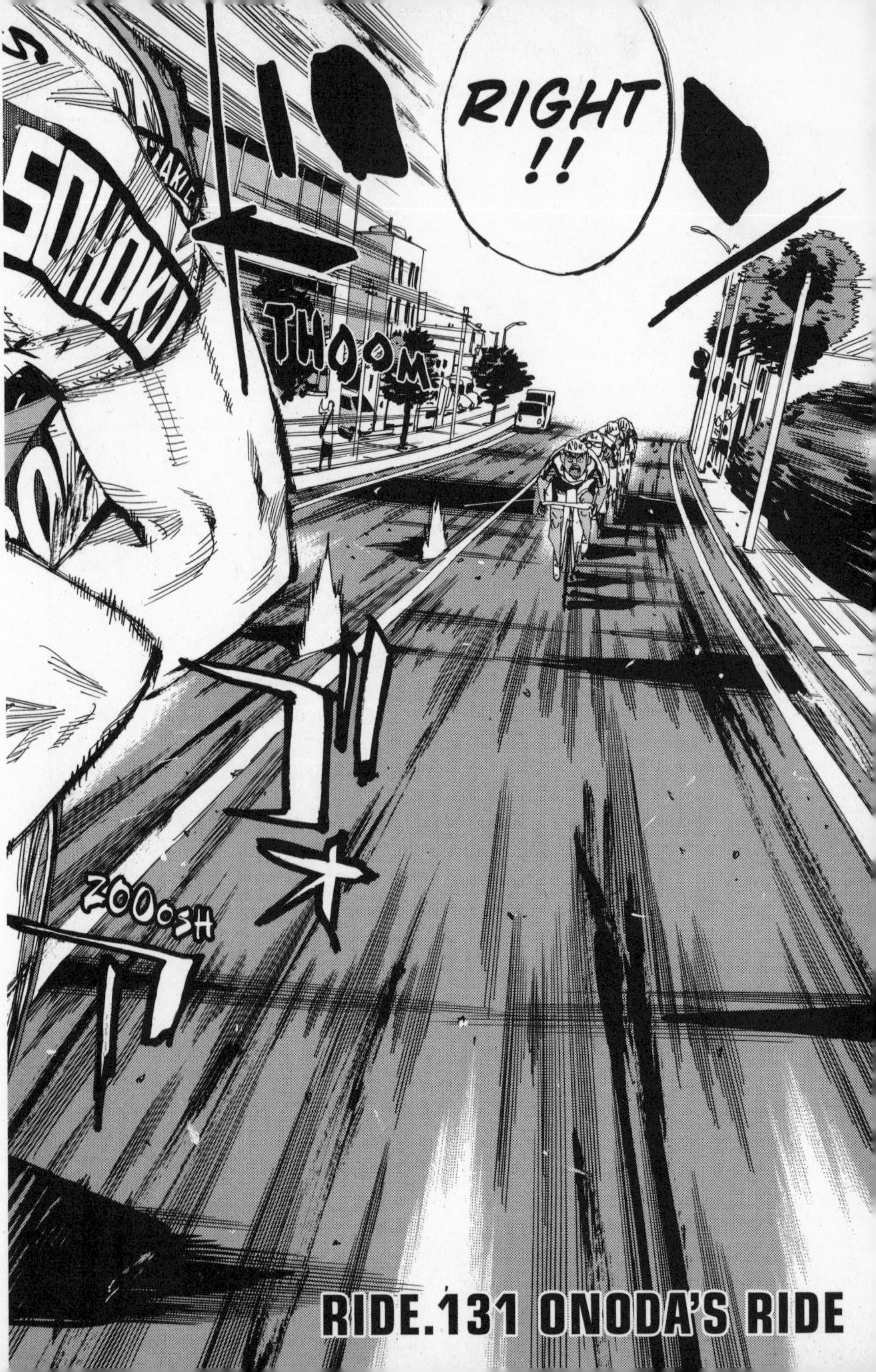
RIGHT !!
THOOM
SOHOKU
ZOOOOSH

RIDE.131 ONODA'S RIDE

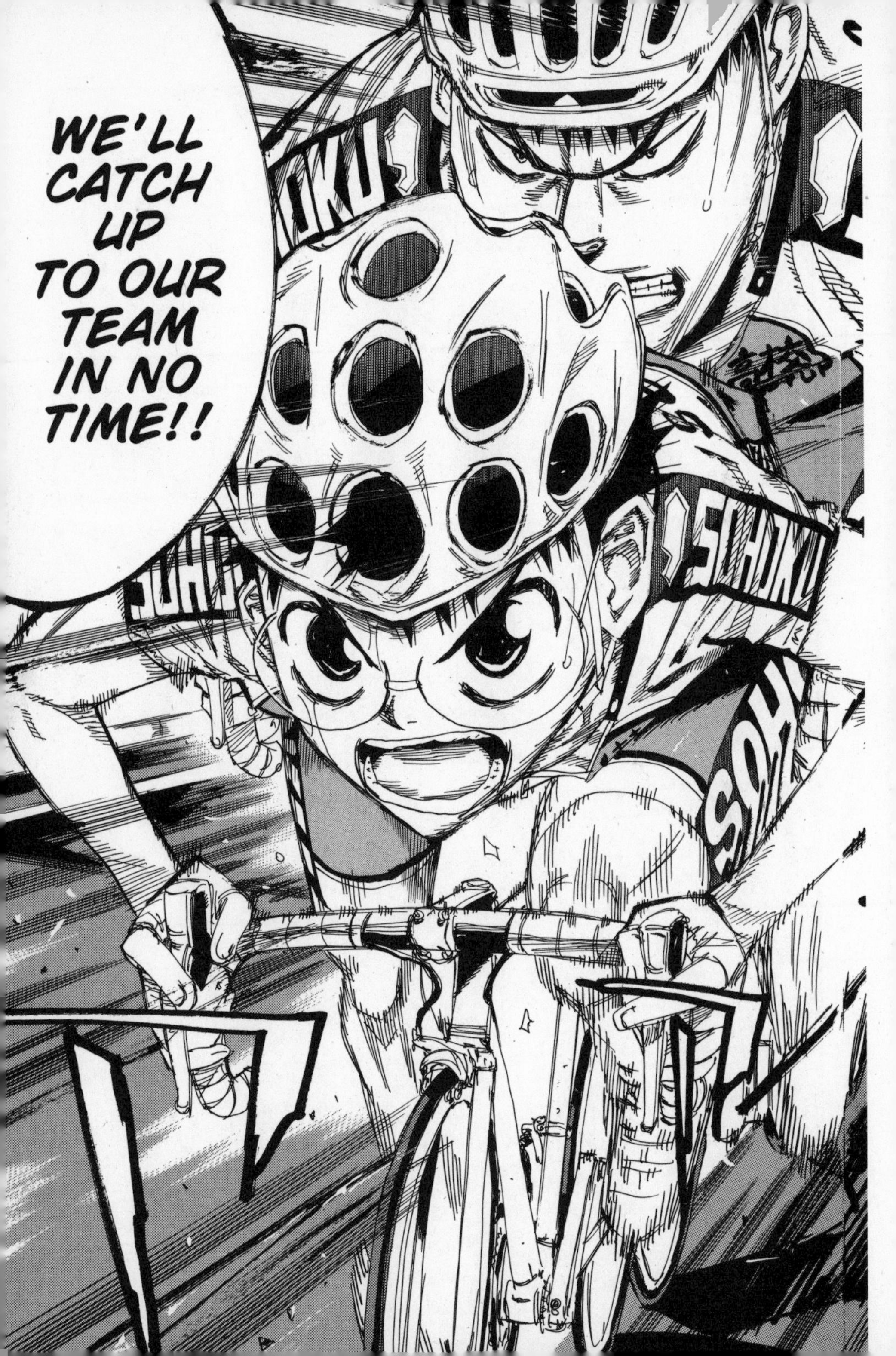
WE'LL CATCH UP TO OUR TEAM IN NO TIME!!

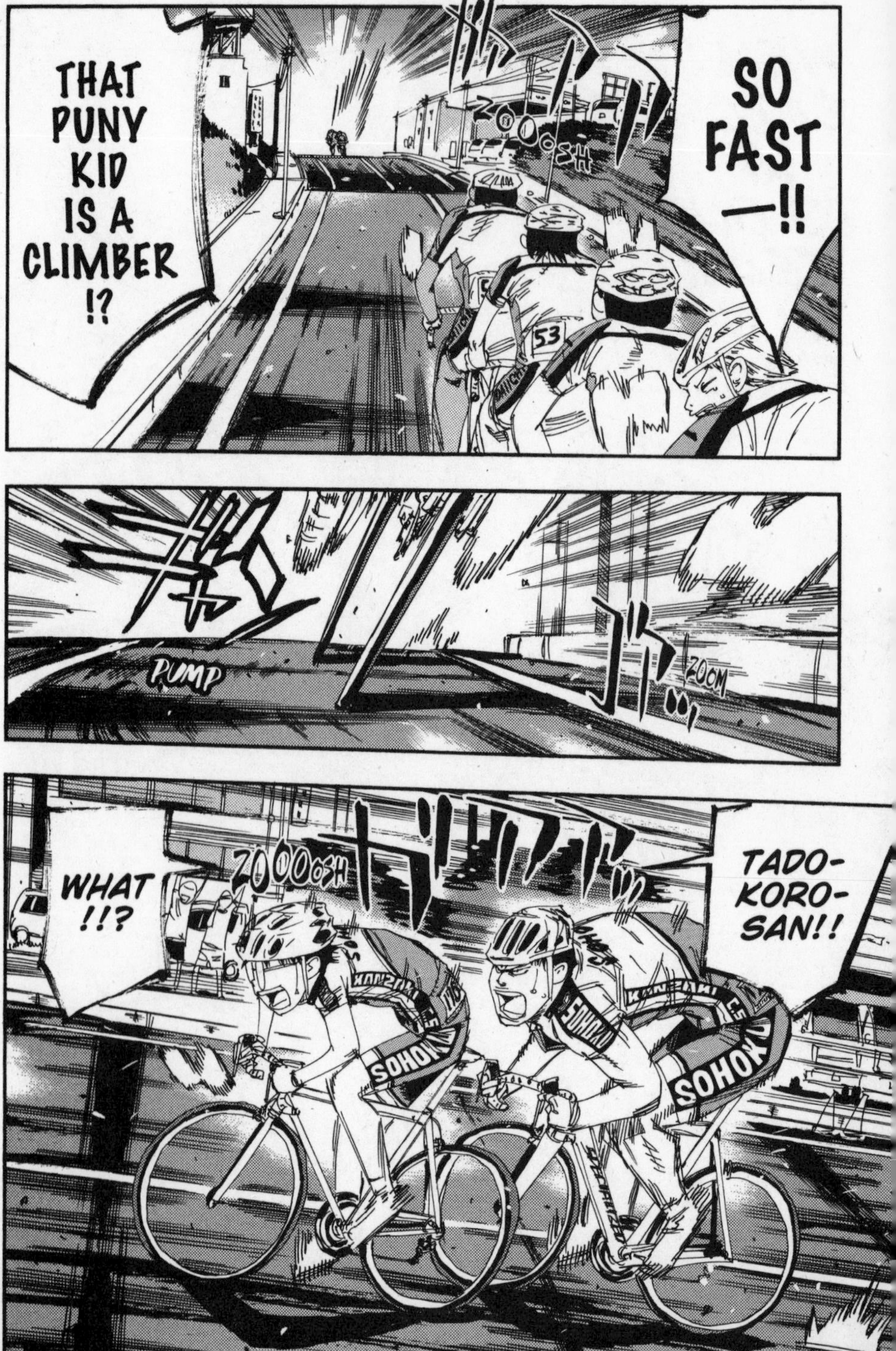
SO FAST—!!
ZOOOOSH
THAT PUNY KID IS A CLIMBER!?
ZOOM
PUMP
TADO-KORO-SAN!!
ZOOOOSH
WHAT!!?

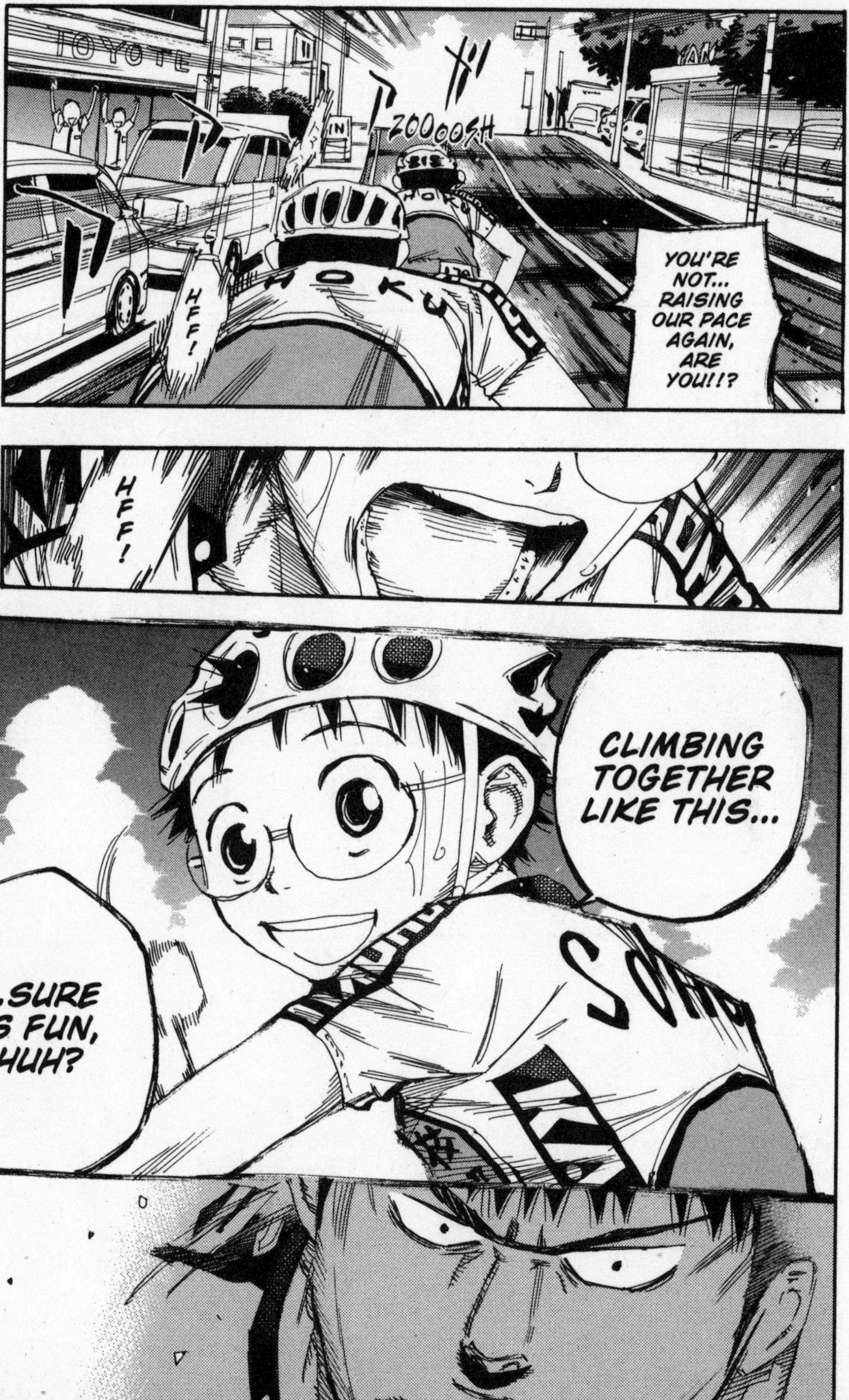
TOYOTE
ZOOOOSH
YOU'RE NOT... RAISING OUR PACE AGAIN, ARE YOU!!?
HFF!
HFF!
CLIMBING TOGETHER LIKE THIS...
...SURE IS FUN, HUH?

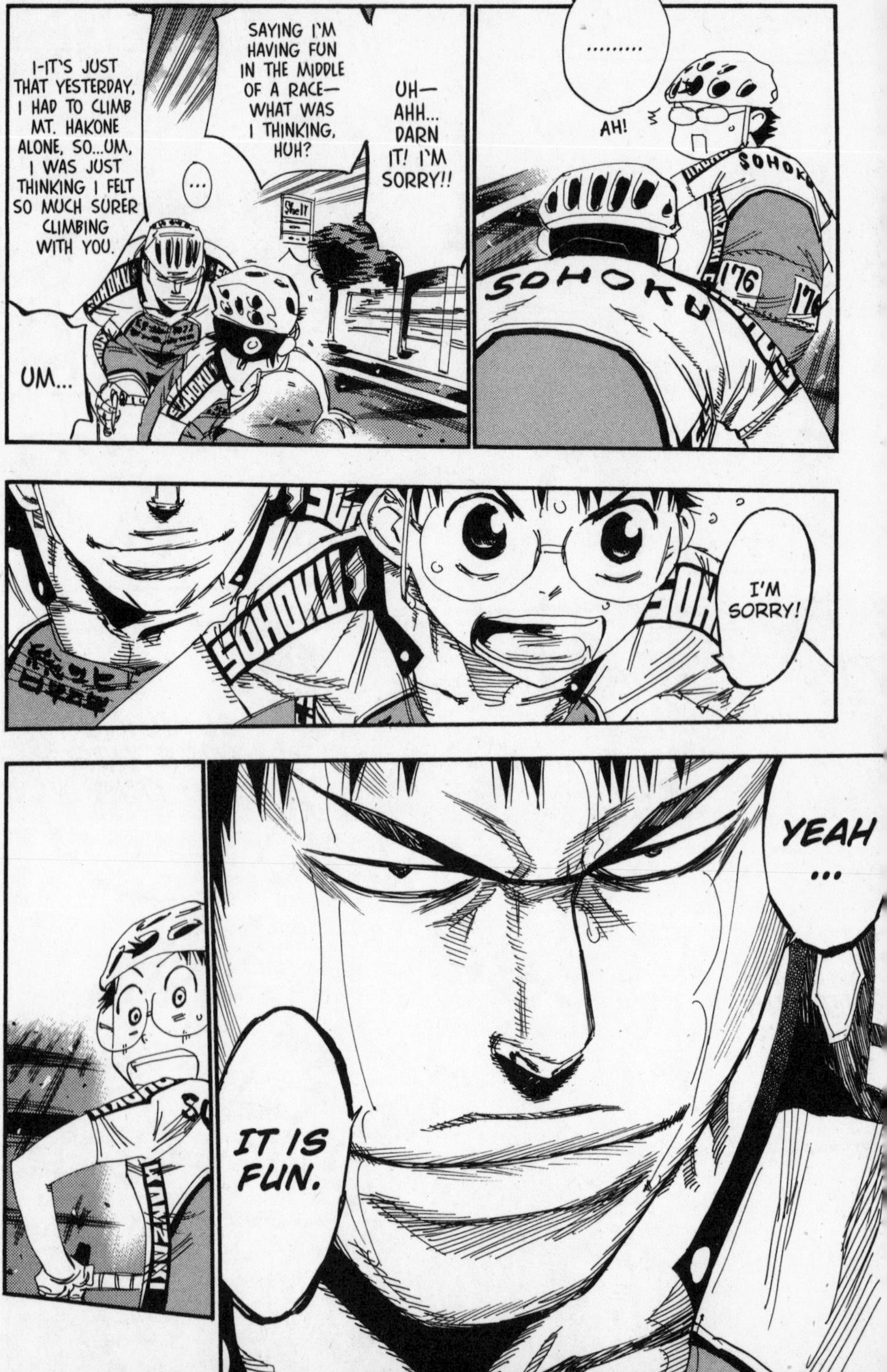
....
AH!
UH— AHH... DARN IT! I'M SORRY!!
SAYING I'M HAVING FUN IN THE MIDDLE OF A RACE— WHAT WAS I THINKING, HUH?
...
UM...
I-IT'S JUST THAT YESTERDAY, I HAD TO CLIMB MT. HAKONE ALONE, SO...UM, I WAS JUST THINKING I FELT SO MUCH SURER CLIMBING WITH YOU.
I'M SORRY!
YEAH ...
IT IS FUN.

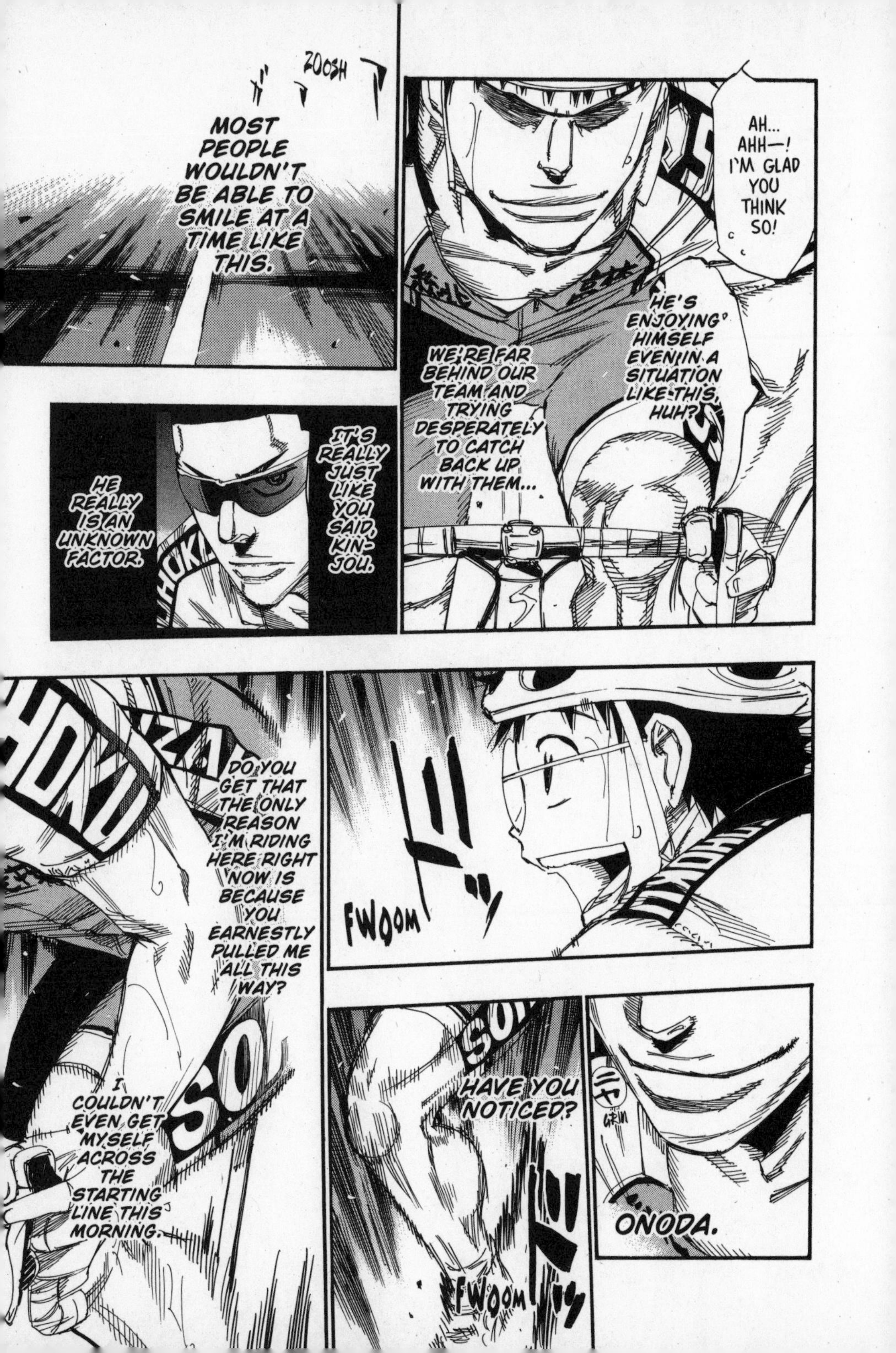

AH... AHH—! I'M GLAD YOU THINK SO!
HE'S ENJOYING HIMSELF EVEN IN A SITUATION LIKE THIS, HUH?
WE'RE FAR BEHIND OUR TEAM AND TRYING DESPERATELY TO CATCH BACK UP WITH THEM...
ZOOSH
MOST PEOPLE WOULDN'T BE ABLE TO SMILE AT A TIME LIKE THIS.
IT'S REALLY JUST LIKE YOU SAID, KINJOU.
HE REALLY IS AN UNKNOWN FACTOR.
FWOOM
HAVE YOU NOTICED?
GRIN
ONODA.
FWOOM
DO YOU GET THAT THE ONLY REASON I'M RIDING HERE RIGHT NOW IS BECAUSE YOU EARNESTLY PULLED ME ALL THIS WAY?
I COULDN'T EVEN GET MYSELF ACROSS THE STARTING LINE THIS MORNING.

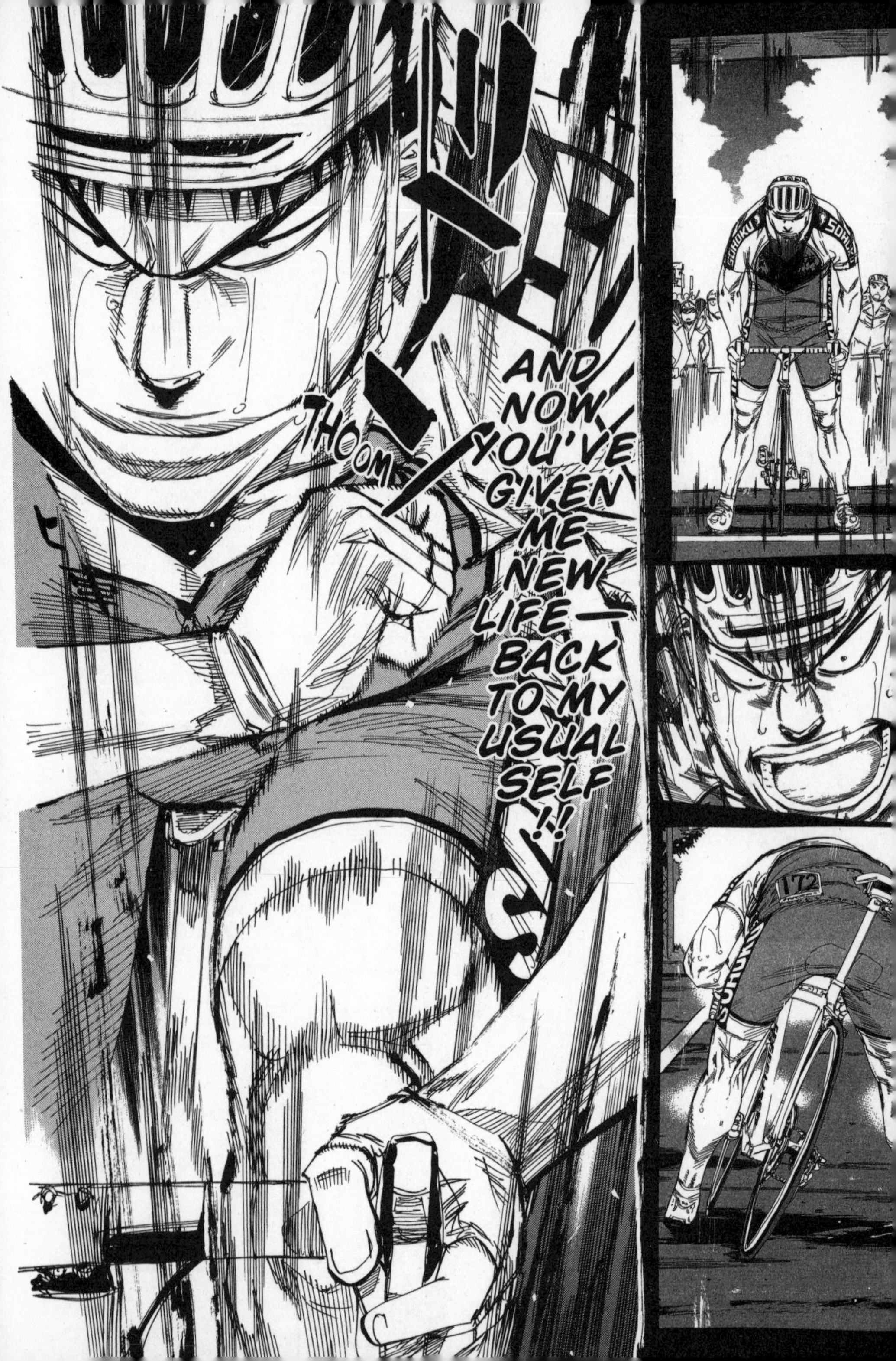
THOOM
AND NOW YOU'VE GIVEN ME NEW LIFE— BACK TO MY USUAL SELF!!

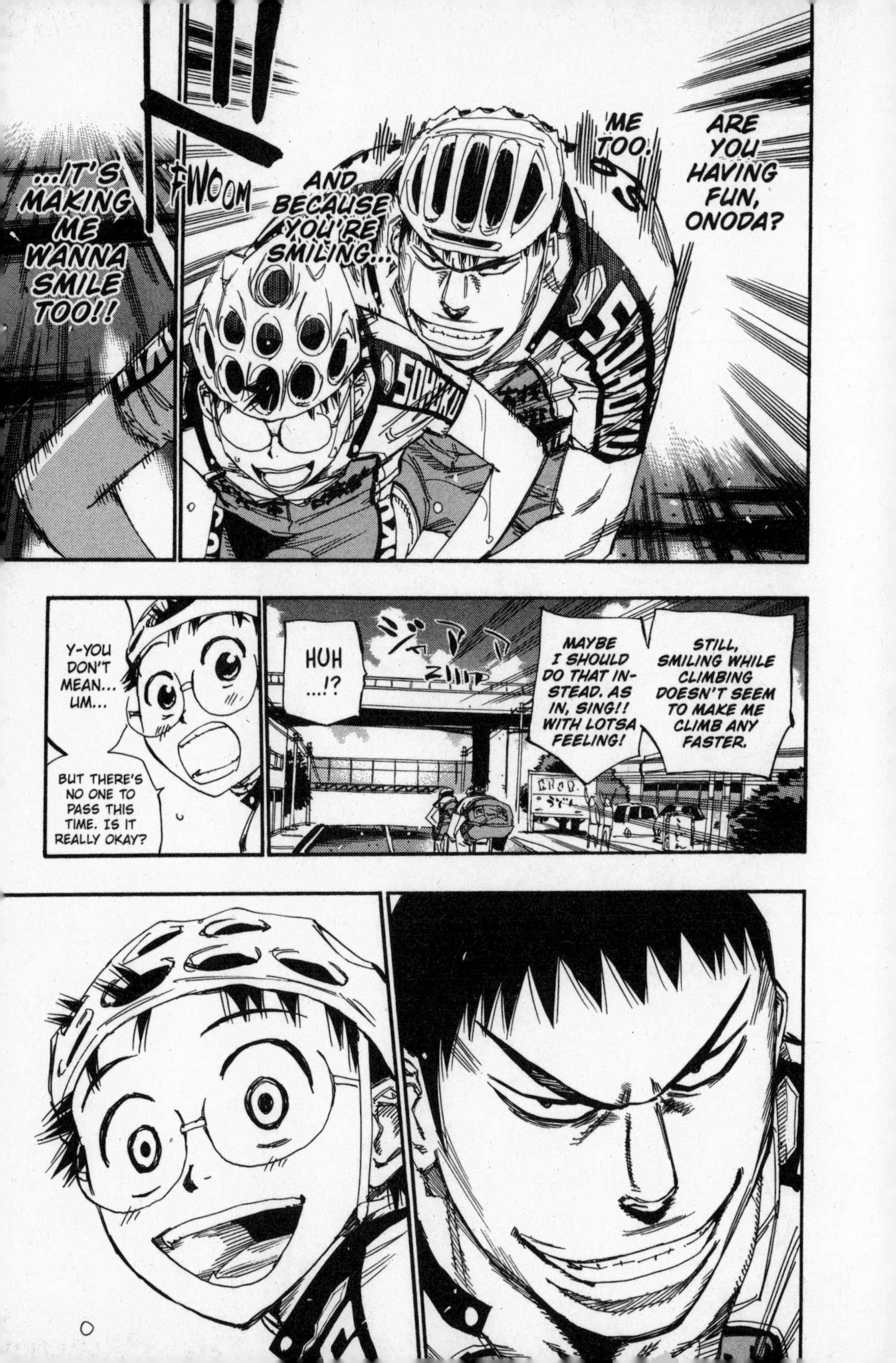
ARE YOU HAVING FUN, ONODA?
ME TOO.
AND BECAUSE YOU'RE SMILING...
FWOOM
...IT'S MAKING ME WANNA SMILE TOO!!
STILL, SMILING WHILE CLIMBING DOESN'T SEEM TO MAKE ME CLIMB ANY FASTER.
MAYBE I SHOULD DO THAT IN-STEAD. AS IN, SING!! WITH LOTSA FEELING!
HUH ...!?
Y-YOU DON'T MEAN... UM...
BUT THERE'S NO ONE TO PASS THIS TIME. IS IT REALLY OKAY?

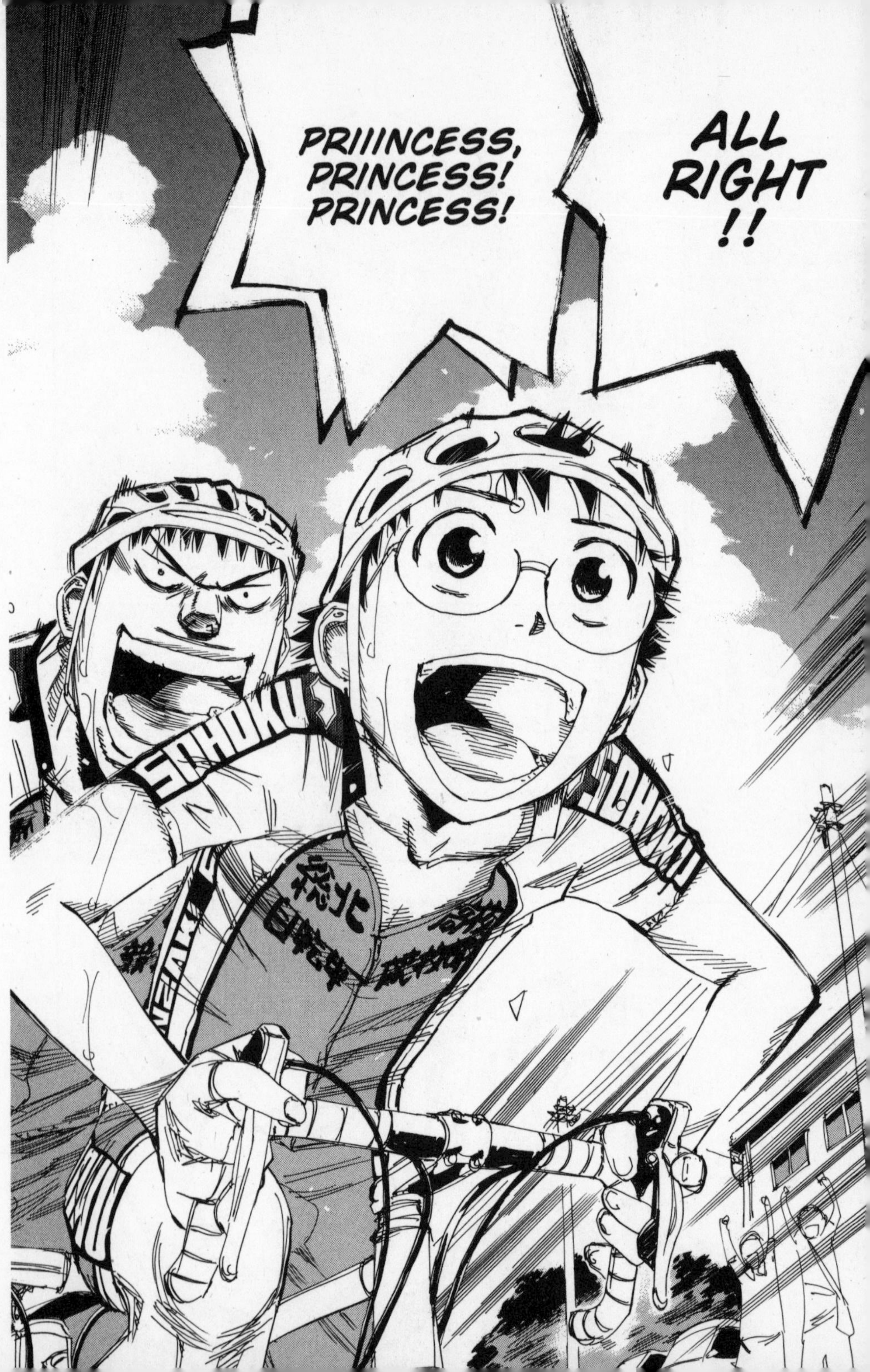
ALL RIGHT !!
PRIIINCESS, PRINCESS! PRINCESS!

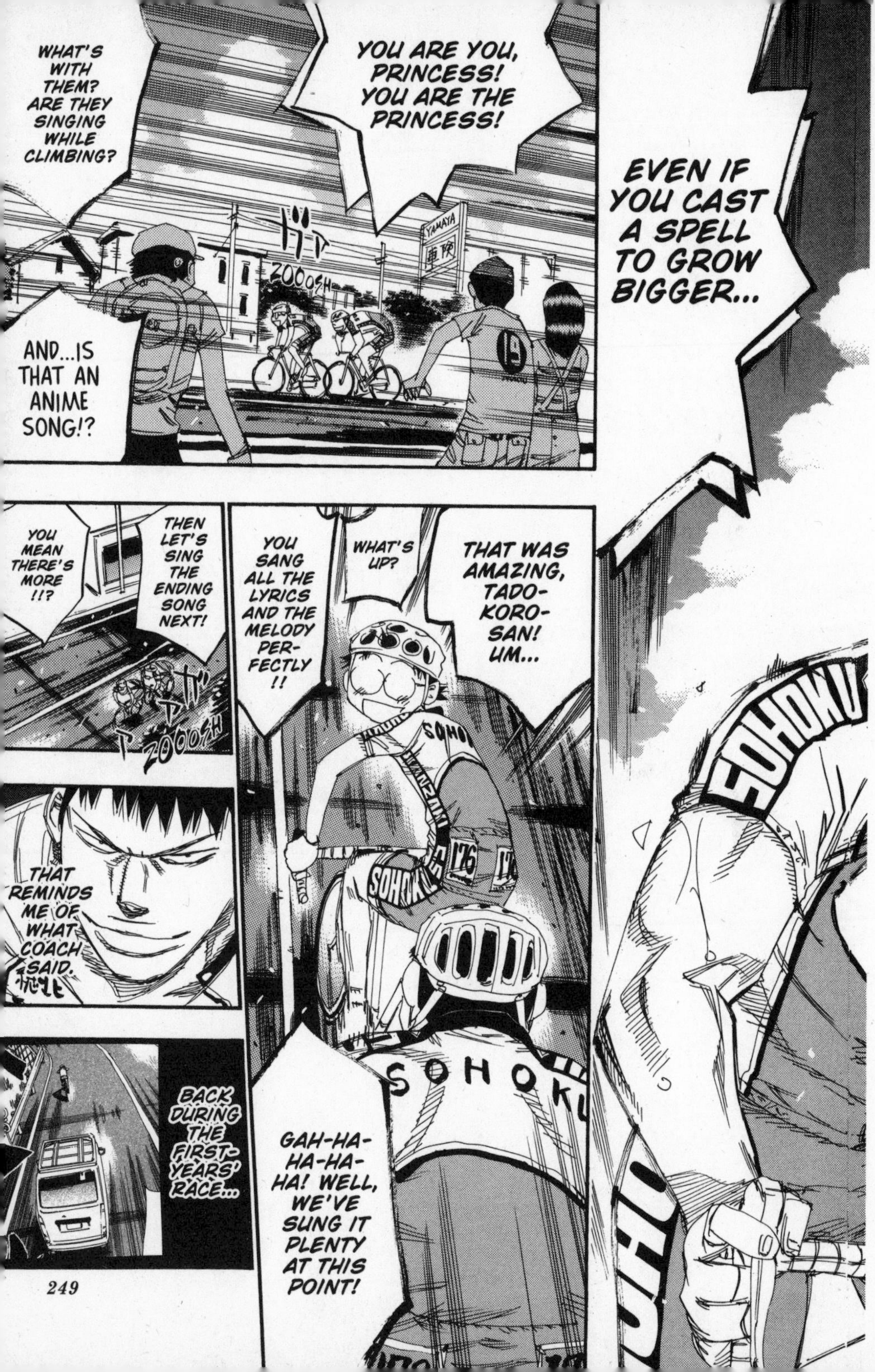
EVEN IF YOU CAST A SPELL TO GROW BIGGER...
YOU ARE YOU, PRINCESS! YOU ARE THE PRINCESS!
ZOOOSH
WHAT'S WITH THEM? ARE THEY SINGING WHILE CLIMBING?
AND...IS THAT AN ANIME SONG!?
THAT WAS AMAZING, TADOKORO-SAN! UM...
WHAT'S UP?
YOU SANG ALL THE LYRICS AND THE MELODY PERFECTLY!!
SOHOKU
GAH-HA-HA-HA! WELL, WE'VE SUNG IT PLENTY AT THIS POINT!
THEN LET'S SING THE ENDING SONG NEXT!
YOU MEAN THERE'S MORE!!?
ZOOOSH
THAT REMINDS ME OF WHAT COACH SAID.
BACK DURING THE FIRST-YEARS' RACE...

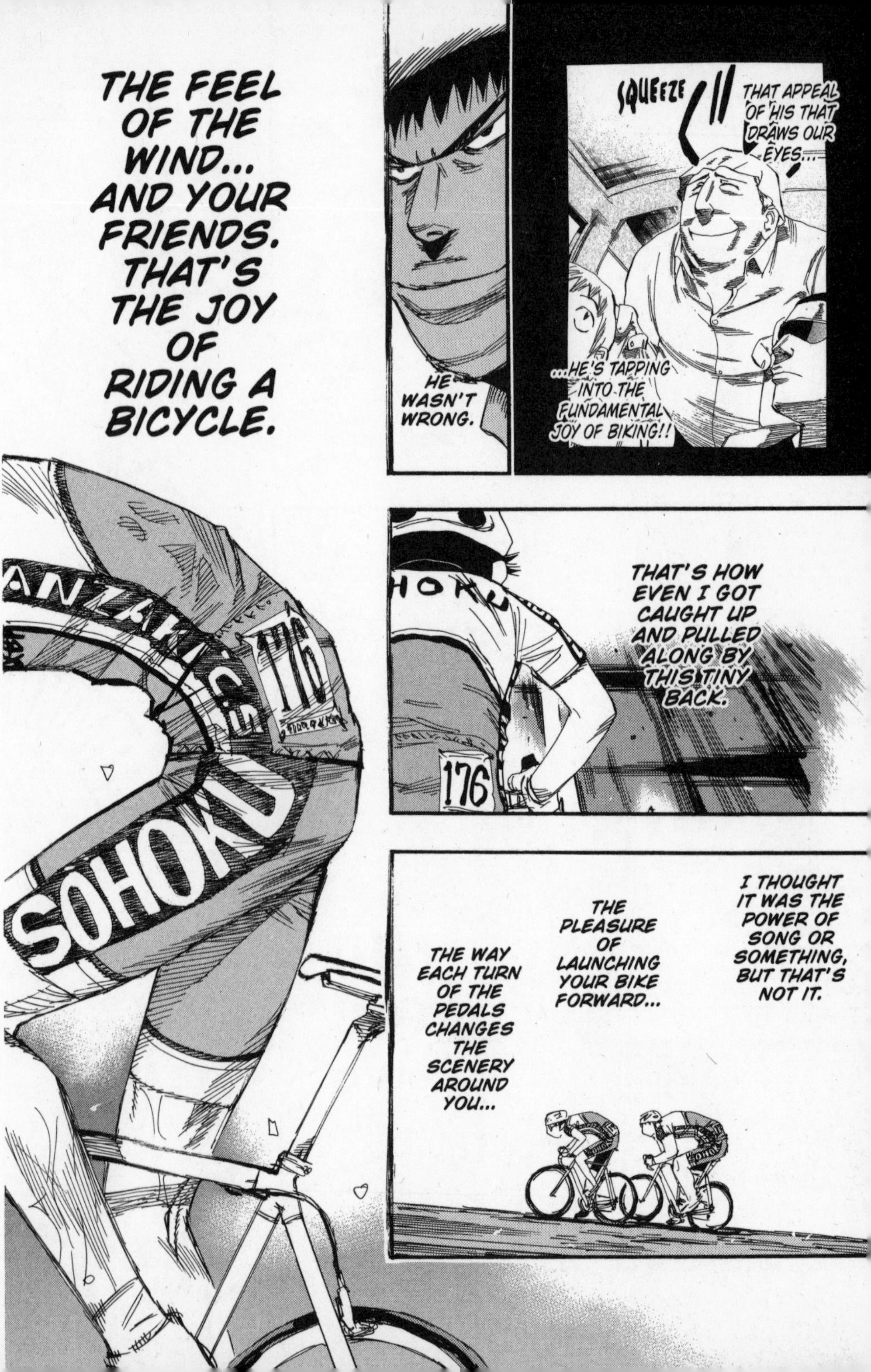
SQUEEZE
THAT APPEAL OF HIS THAT DRAWS OUR EYES...
...HE'S TAPPING INTO THE FUNDAMENTAL JOY OF BIKING!!
HE WASN'T WRONG.
THAT'S HOW EVEN I GOT CAUGHT UP AND PULLED ALONG BY THIS TINY BACK.
176
I THOUGHT IT WAS THE POWER OF SONG OR SOMETHING, BUT THAT'S NOT IT.
THE PLEASURE OF LAUNCHING YOUR BIKE FORWARD...
THE WAY EACH TURN OF THE PEDALS CHANGES THE SCENERY AROUND YOU...
THE FEEL OF THE WIND... AND YOUR FRIENDS. THAT'S THE JOY OF RIDING A BICYCLE.
SOHOKU
176

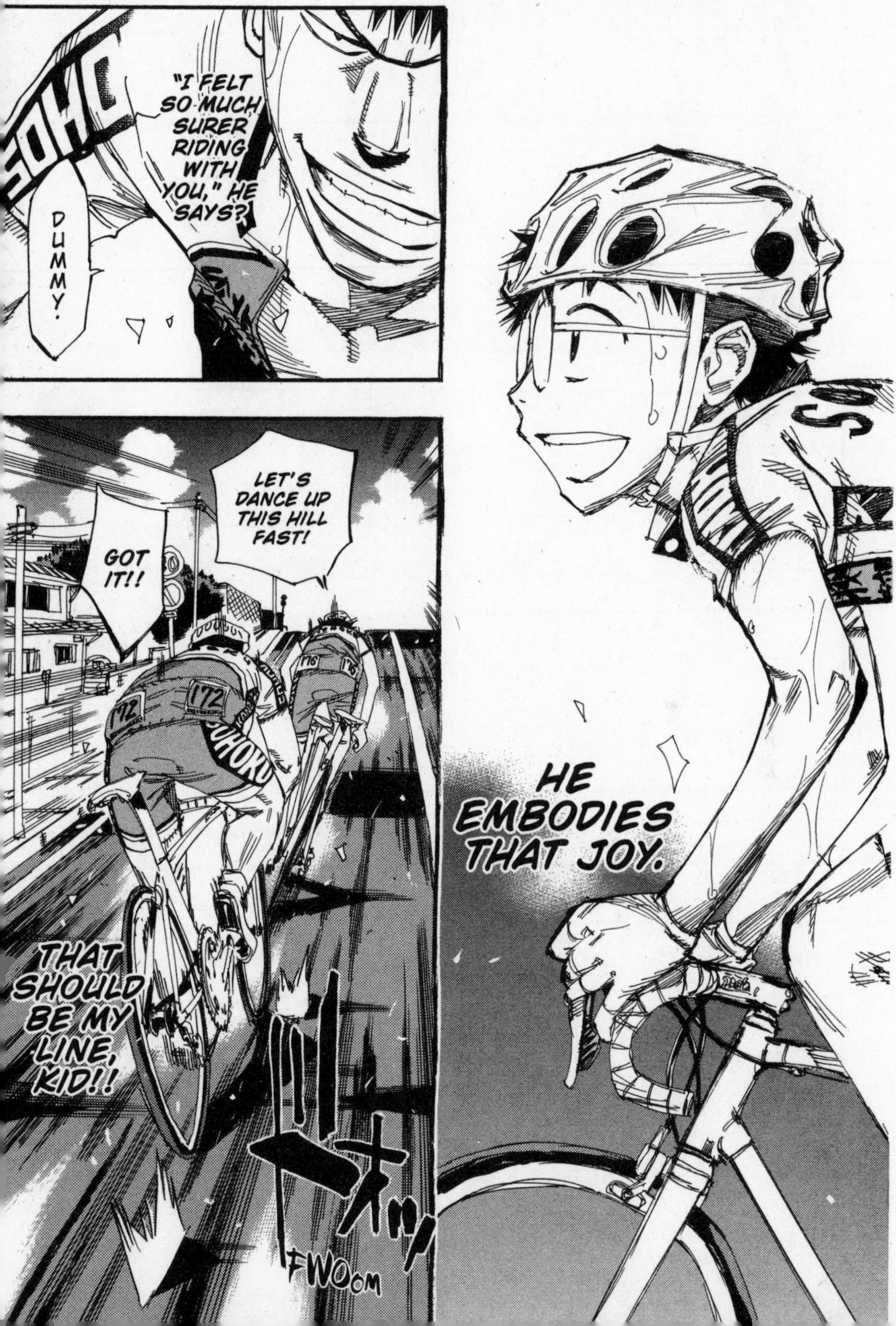
HE EMBODIES THAT JOY.
"I FELT SO MUCH SURER RIDING WITH YOU," HE SAYS?
DUMMY.
LET'S DANCE UP THIS HILL FAST!
GOT IT!!
THAT SHOULD BE MY LINE, KID!!
FWOOM

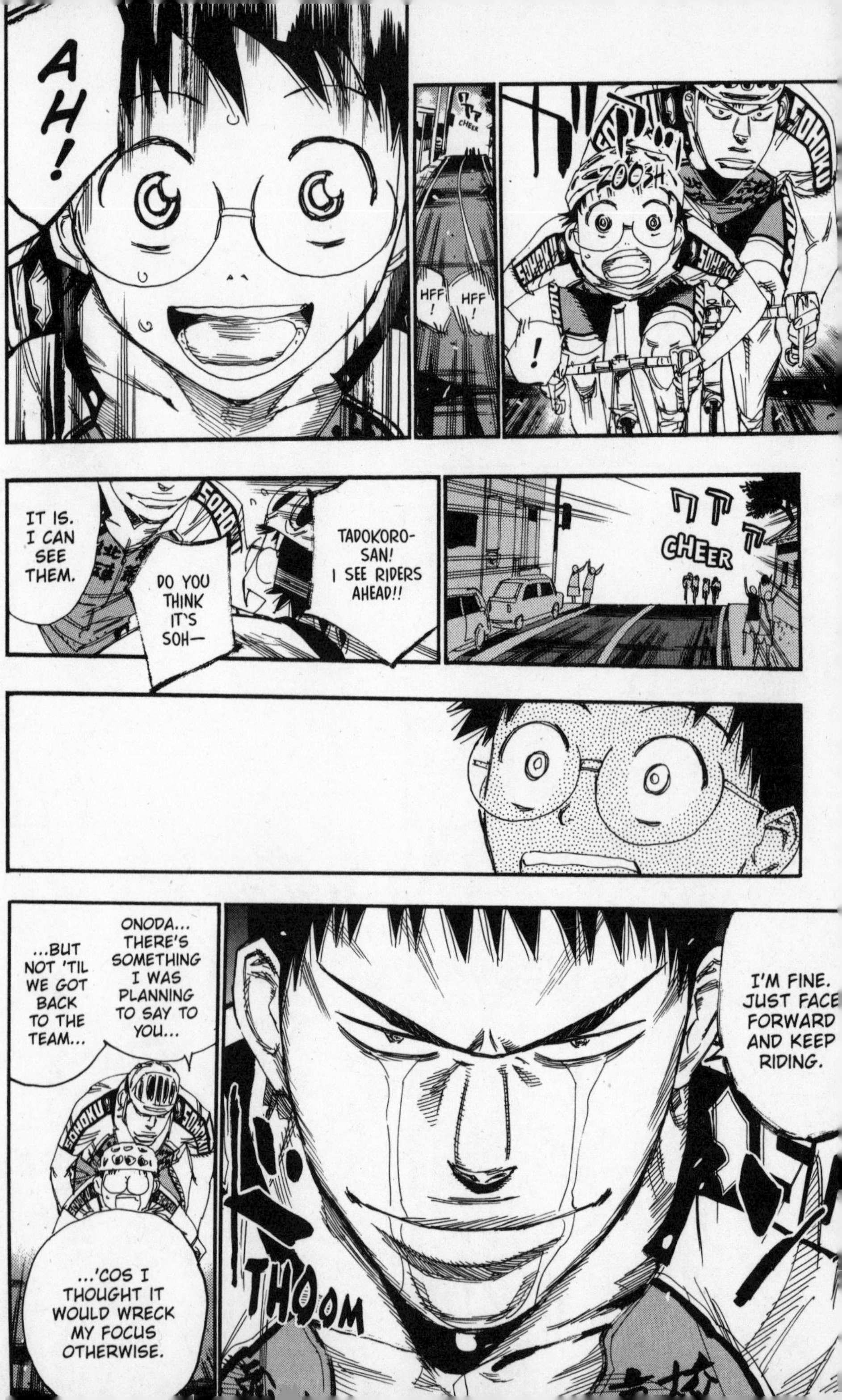
ZOOSH
!
CHEER
HFF!
HFF!
AH!
CHEER
TADOKORO-SAN! I SEE RIDERS AHEAD!!
DO YOU THINK IT'S SOH—
IT IS. I CAN SEE THEM.
I'M FINE. JUST FACE FORWARD AND KEEP RIDING.
THOOM
ONODA... THERE'S SOMETHING I WAS PLANNING TO SAY TO YOU...
...BUT NOT 'TIL WE GOT BACK TO THE TEAM...
...'COS I THOUGHT IT WOULD WRECK MY FOCUS OTHERWISE.

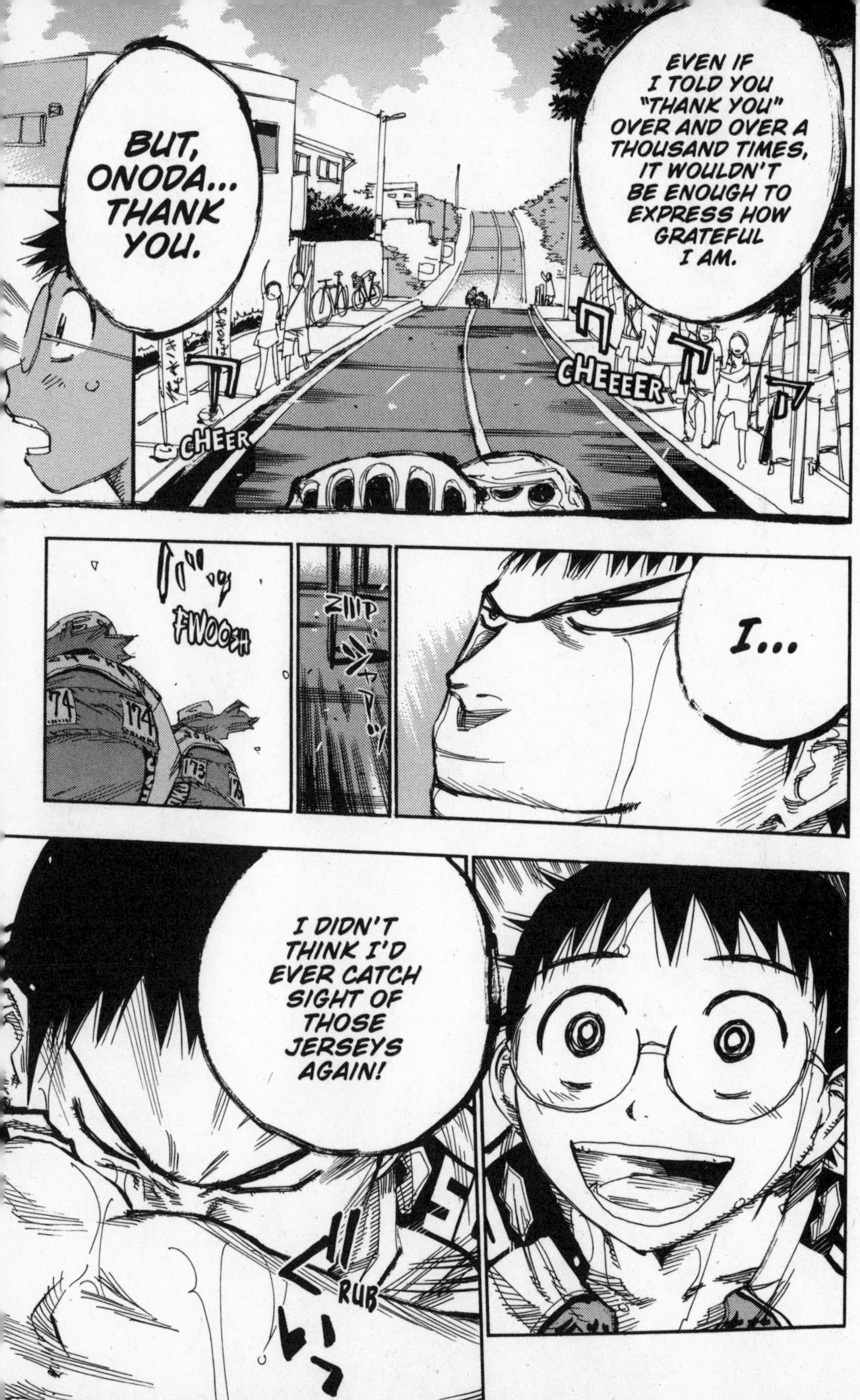
EVEN IF I TOLD YOU "THANK YOU" OVER AND OVER A THOUSAND TIMES, IT WOULDN'T BE ENOUGH TO EXPRESS HOW GRATEFUL I AM.
BUT, ONODA... THANK YOU.
CHEEEER
CHEER
I...
ZIIIP
FWOOSH
I DIDN'T THINK I'D EVER CATCH SIGHT OF THOSE JERSEYS AGAIN!
RUB

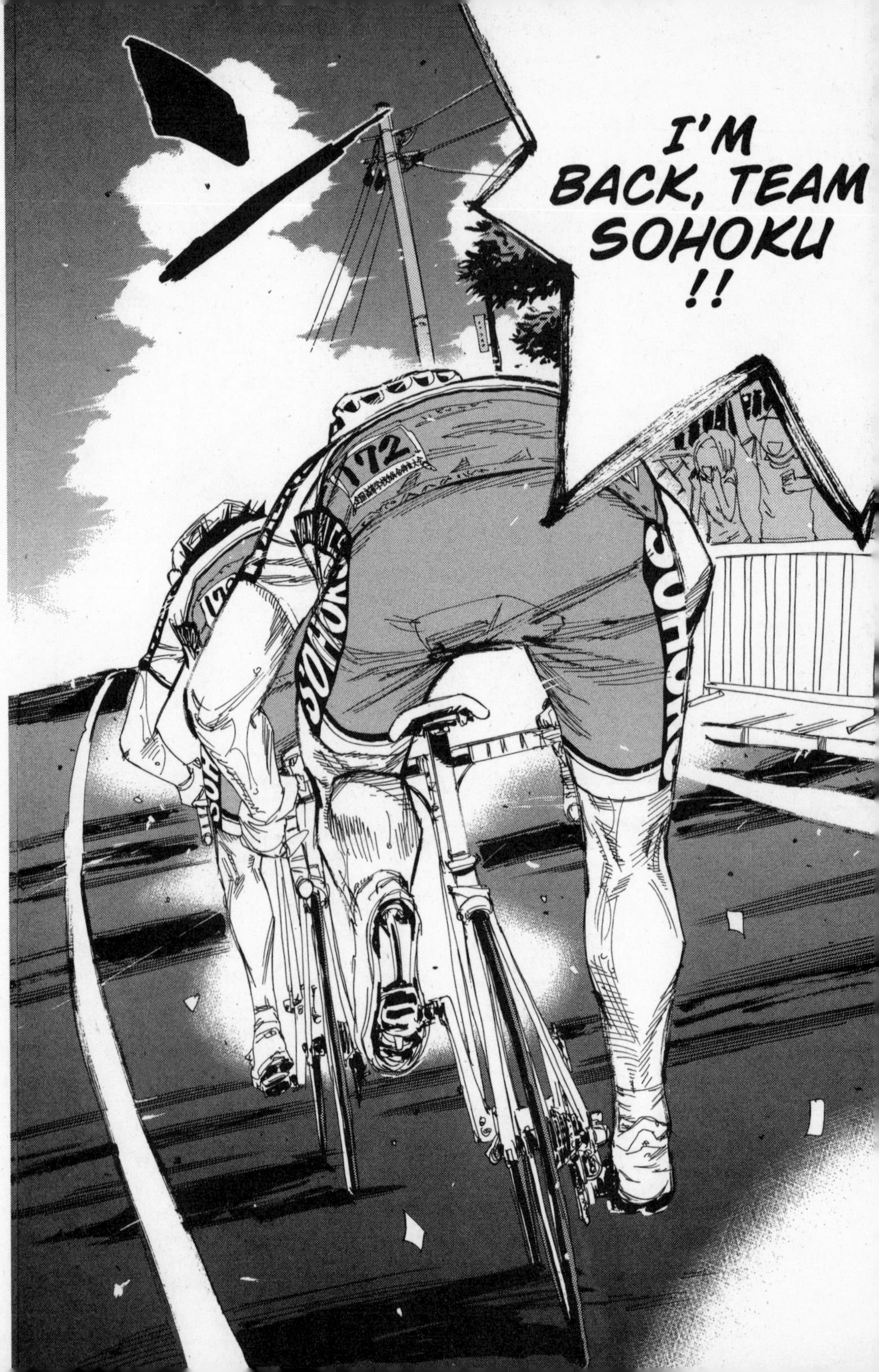
I'M BACK, TEAM SOHOKU !!

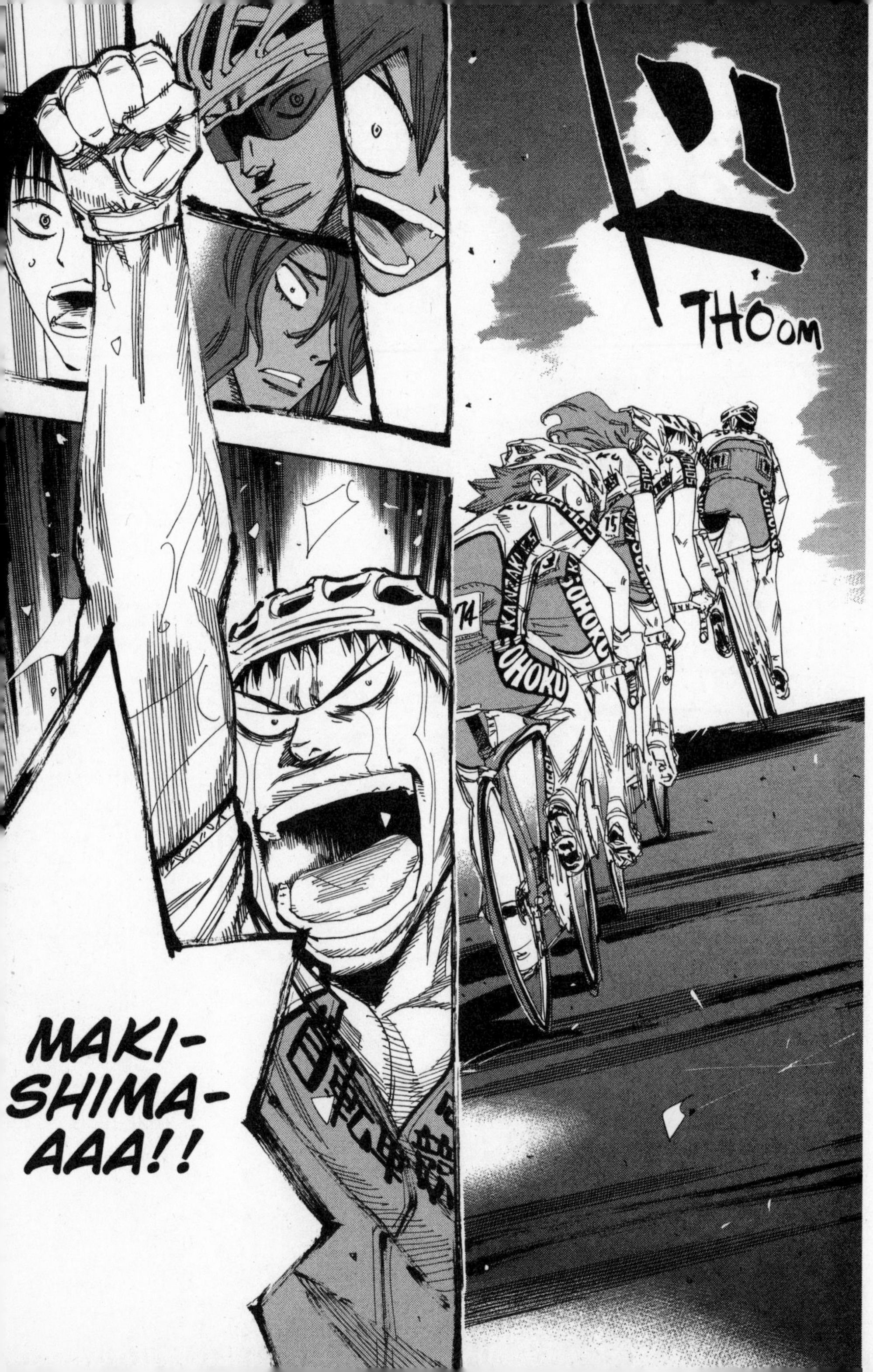
THOom
MAKI-SHIMA-AAA!!

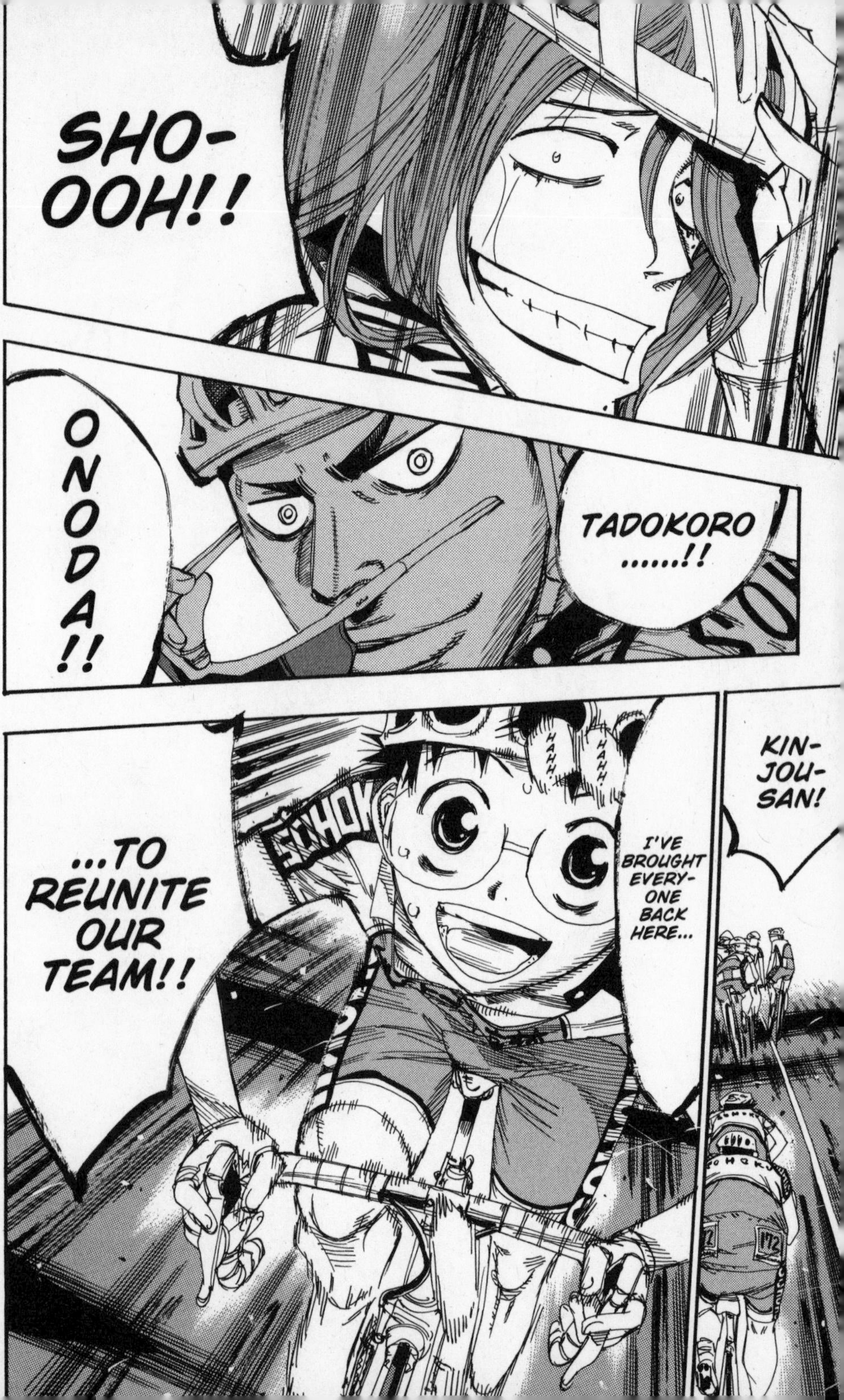
SHO-OOH!!
TADOKORO ......!!
ONODA!!
KIN-JOU-SAN!
HAHH HAHH
I'VE BROUGHT EVERY-ONE BACK HERE...
...TO REUNITE OUR TEAM!!

RIDE.132 SOHOKU UNITE!!

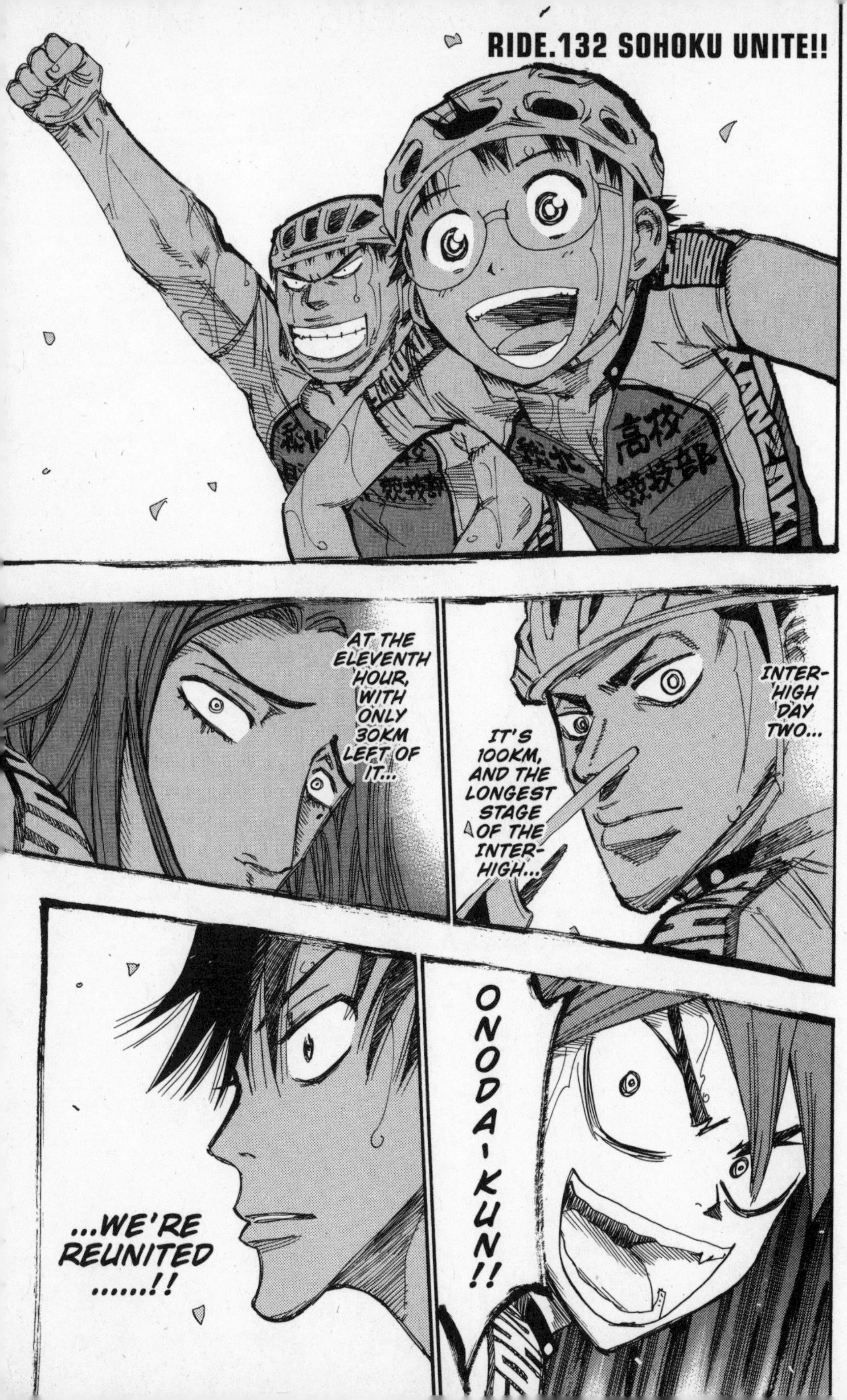
INTER-HIGH DAY TWO...
IT'S 100KM, AND THE LONGEST STAGE OF THE INTER-HIGH...
AT THE ELEVENTH HOUR, WITH ONLY 30KM LEFT OF IT...
ONODA-KUN!!
...WE'RE REUNITED ......!!

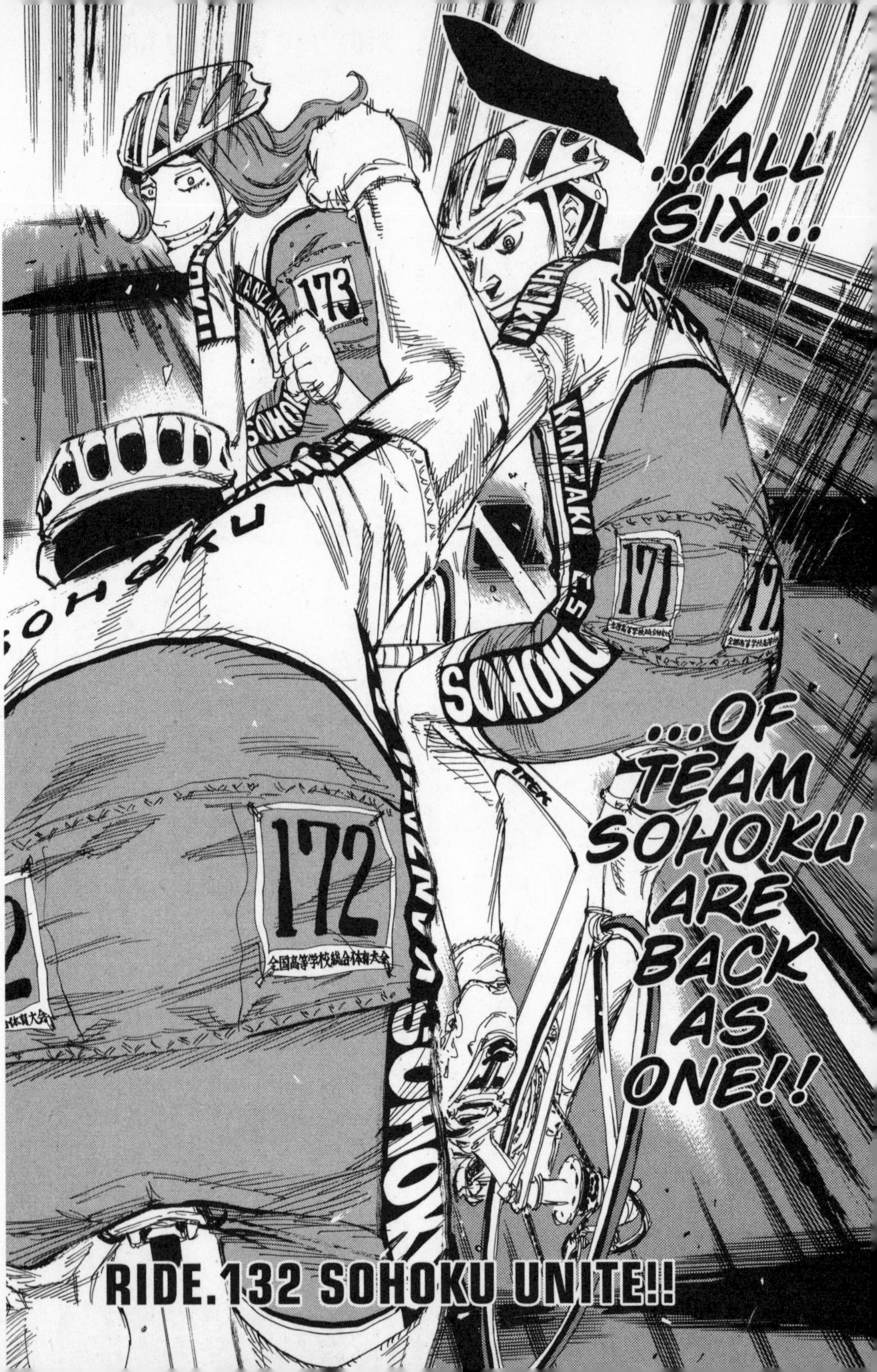
...ALL SIX...
...OF TEAM SOHOKU ARE BACK AS ONE!!

RIDE.132 SOHOKU UNITE!!

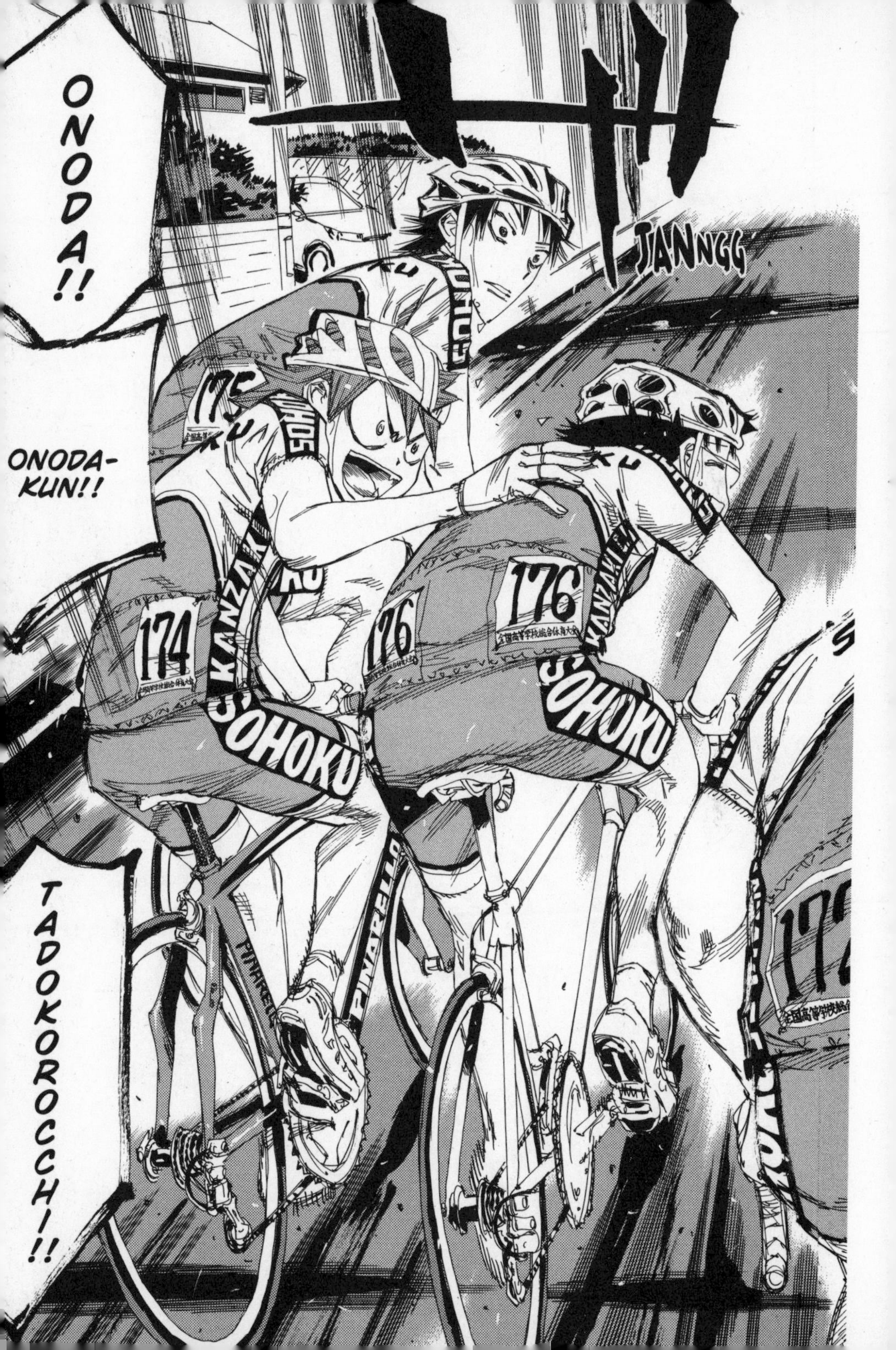
JANNGG
ONODA!!
ONODA-KUN!!
TADOKOROCCHI!!

KIN-JOU-SAN!

HAAH! HAAH!

HAAH!

ZIIP!

I'M SORRY FOR THE WAIT.

ORDERS... ONODA.

I BROUGHT EVERY-ONE BACK...

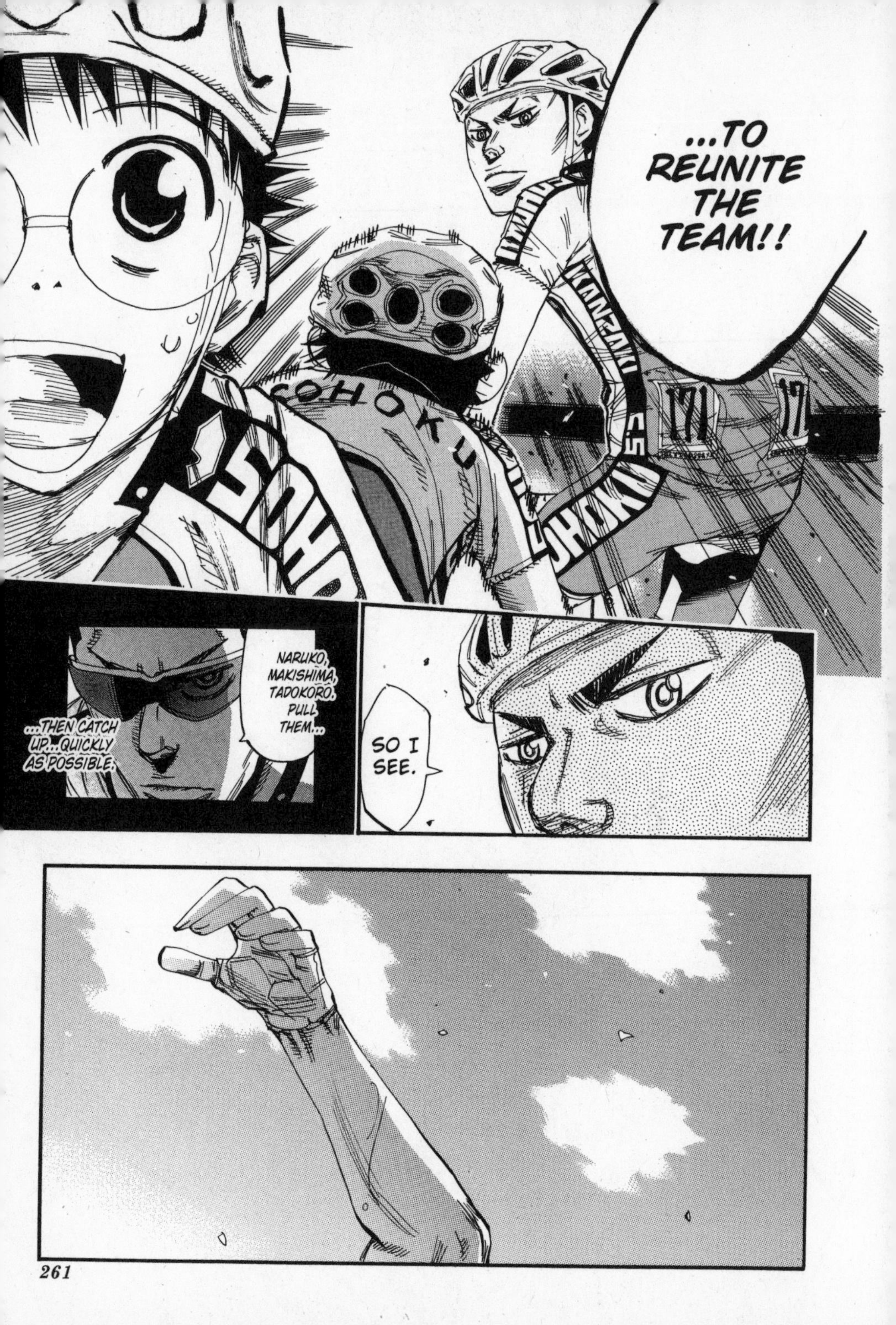
...TO REUNITE THE TEAM!!
SO I SEE.
NARUKO, MAKISHIMA, TADOKORO. PULL THEM...
...THEN CATCH UP...QUICKLY AS POSSIBLE.

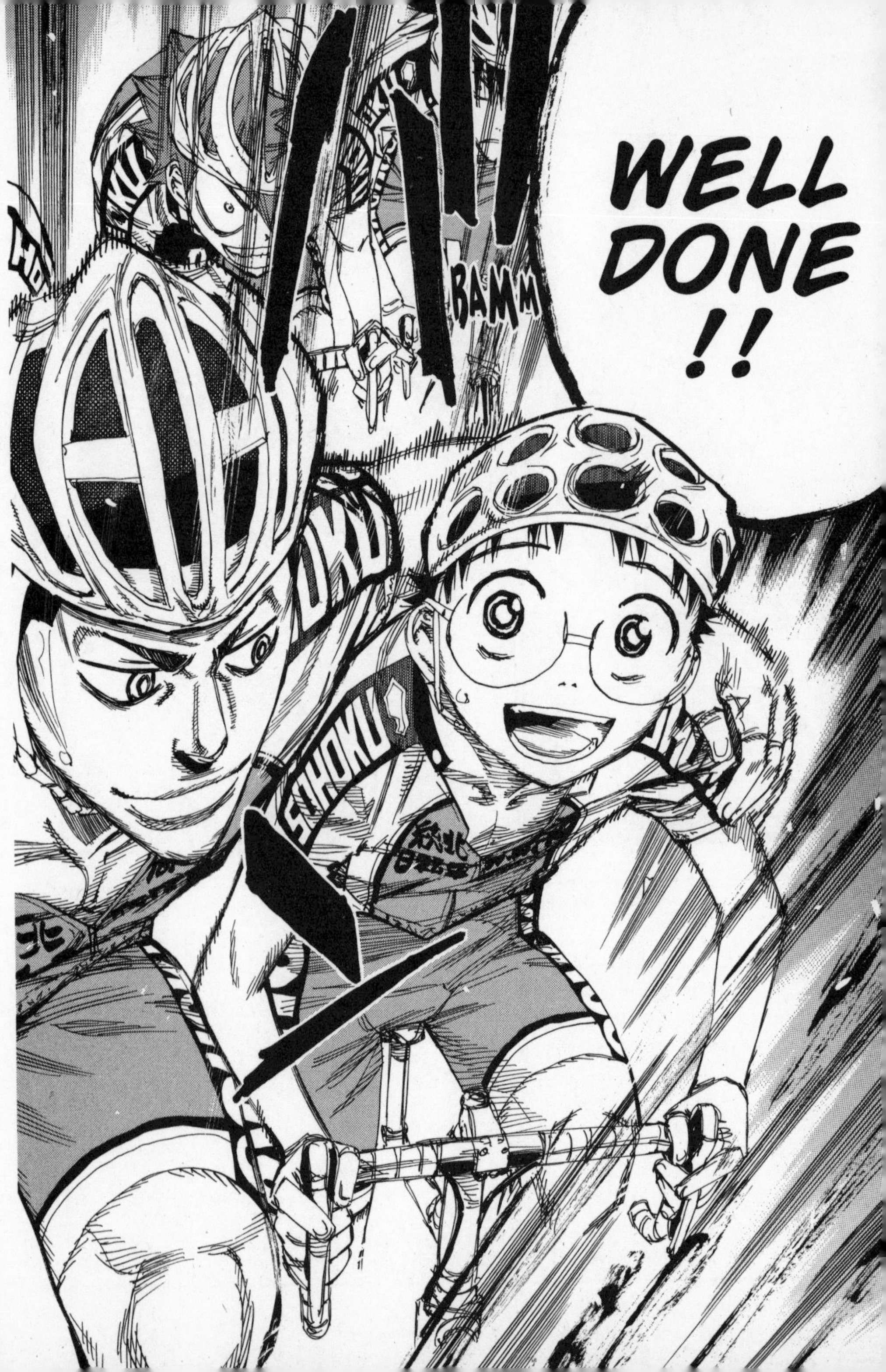
WELL DONE !!
BAMM

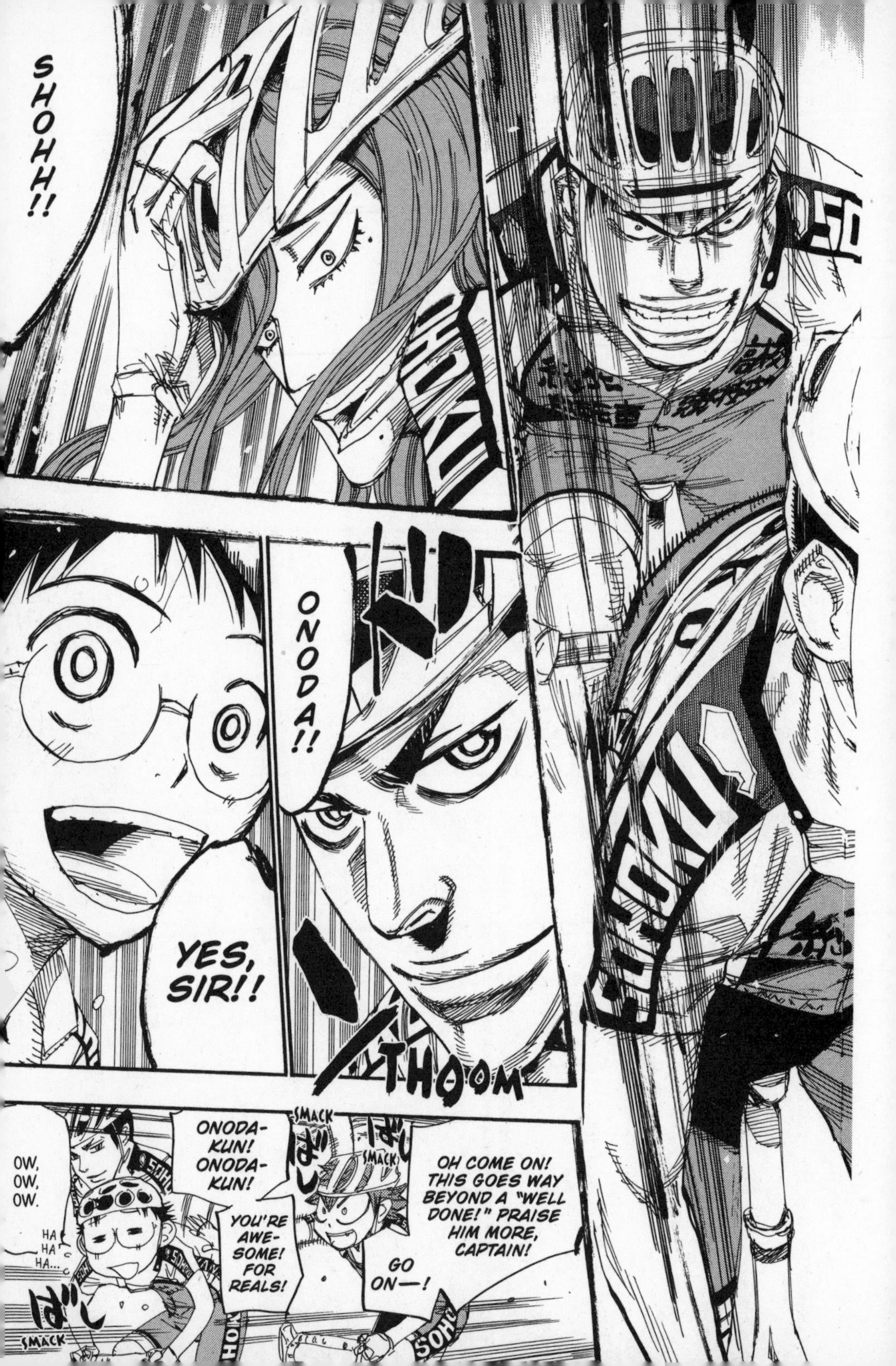
SHOHHH!!
ONODA!!
THOOM
YES, SIR!!
OH COME ON! THIS GOES WAY BEYOND A "WELL DONE!" PRAISE HIM MORE, CAPTAIN!
GO ON—!
SMACK
SMACK
ONODA-KUN! ONODA-KUN!
YOU'RE AWE-SOME! FOR REALS!
HA HA HA...
OW, OW, OW.
SMACK

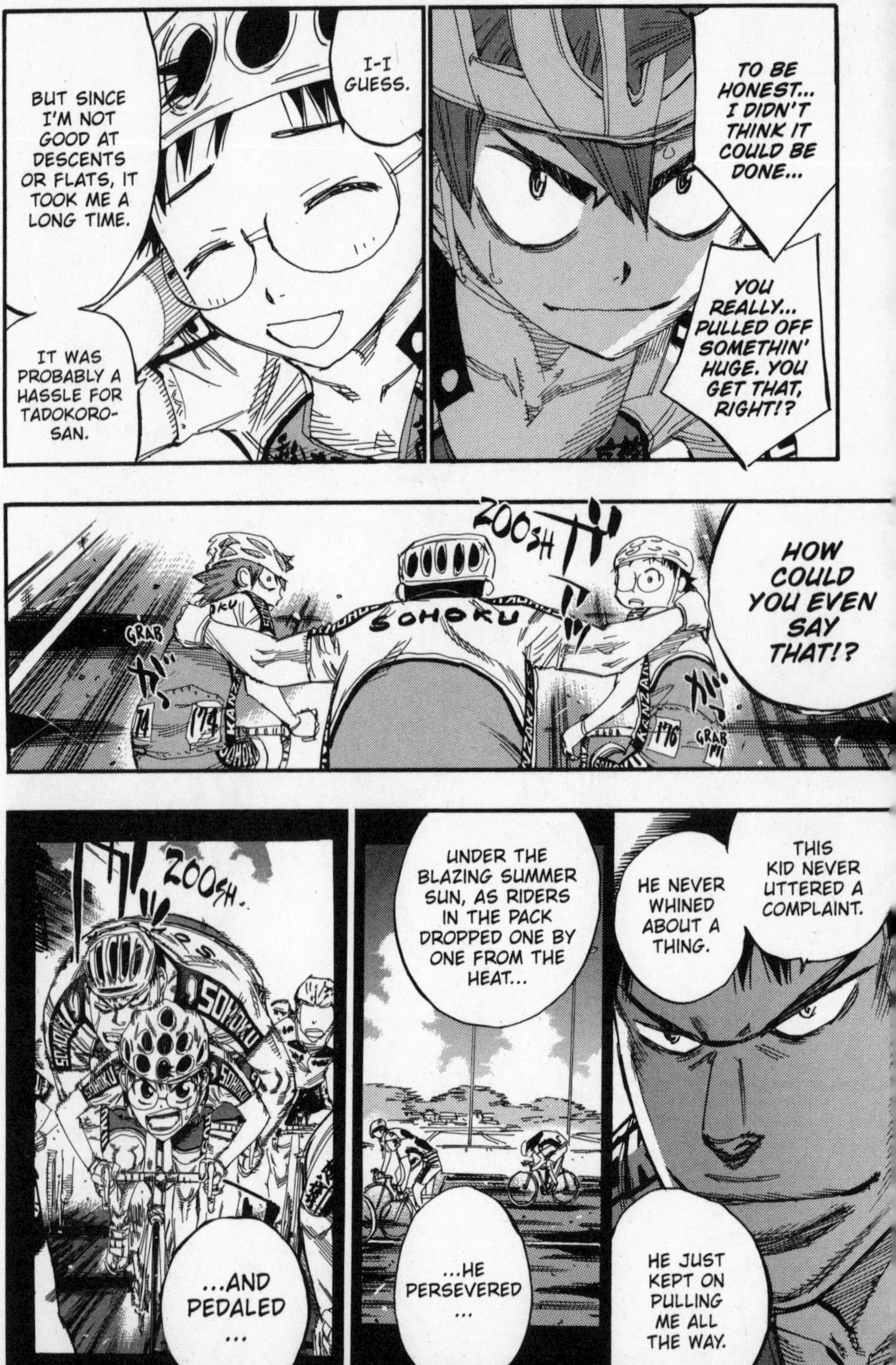
TO BE HONEST... I DIDN'T THINK IT COULD BE DONE...
YOU REALLY... PULLED OFF SOMETHIN' HUGE. YOU GET THAT, RIGHT!?
I-I GUESS.
BUT SINCE I'M NOT GOOD AT DESCENTS OR FLATS, IT TOOK ME A LONG TIME.
IT WAS PROBABLY A HASSLE FOR TADOKORO-SAN.
HOW COULD YOU EVEN SAY THAT!?
ZOOSH
SOHOKU
GRAB
GRAB
THIS KID NEVER UTTERED A COMPLAINT.
HE NEVER WHINED ABOUT A THING.
HE JUST KEPT ON PULLING ME ALL THE WAY.
UNDER THE BLAZING SUMMER SUN, AS RIDERS IN THE PACK DROPPED ONE BY ONE FROM THE HEAT...
...HE PERSEVERED...
ZOOSH..
...AND PEDALED...

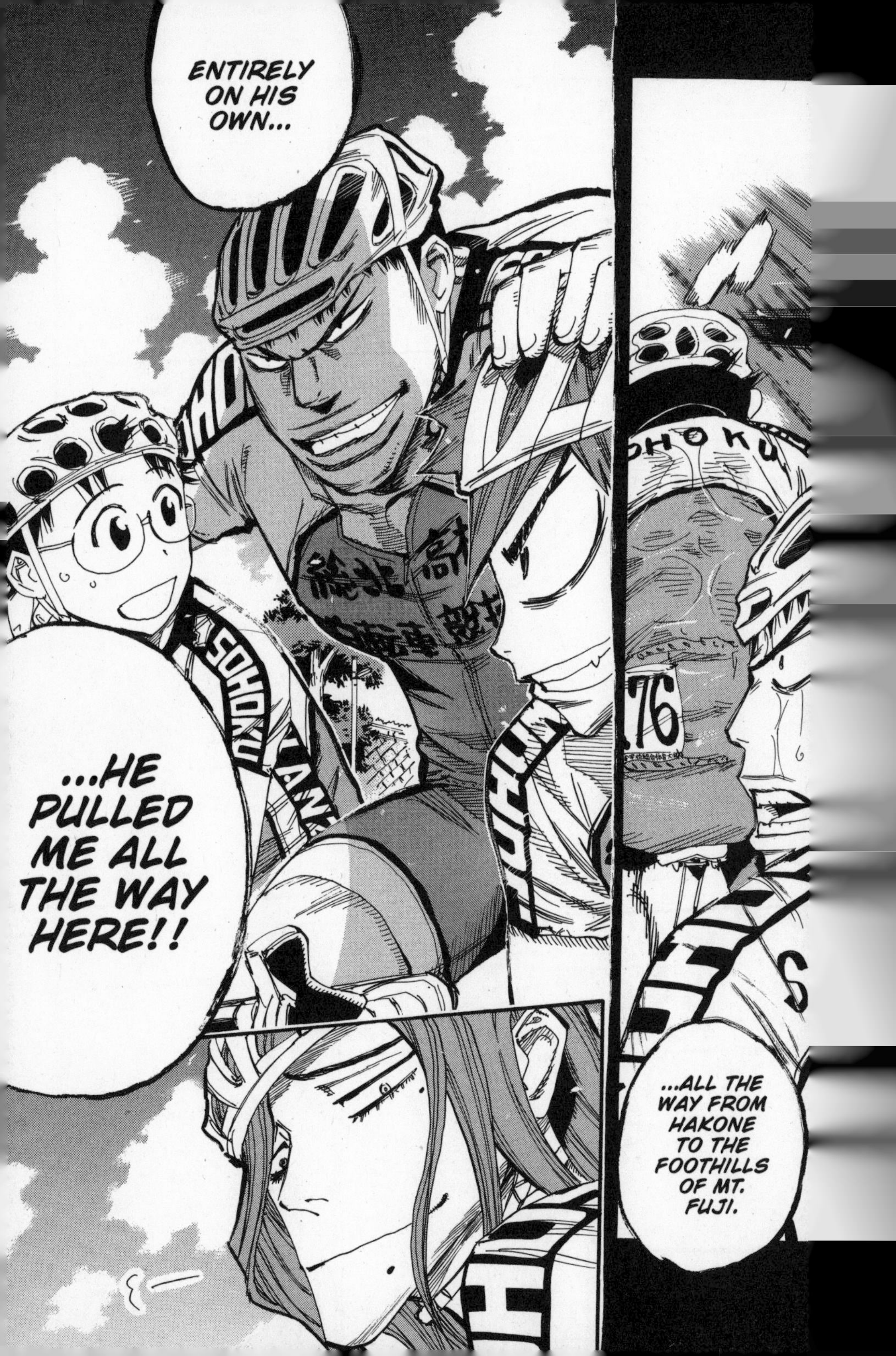
...ALL THE WAY FROM HAKONE TO THE FOOTHILLS OF MT. FUJI.
ENTIRELY ON HIS OWN...
...HE PULLED ME ALL THE WAY HERE!!

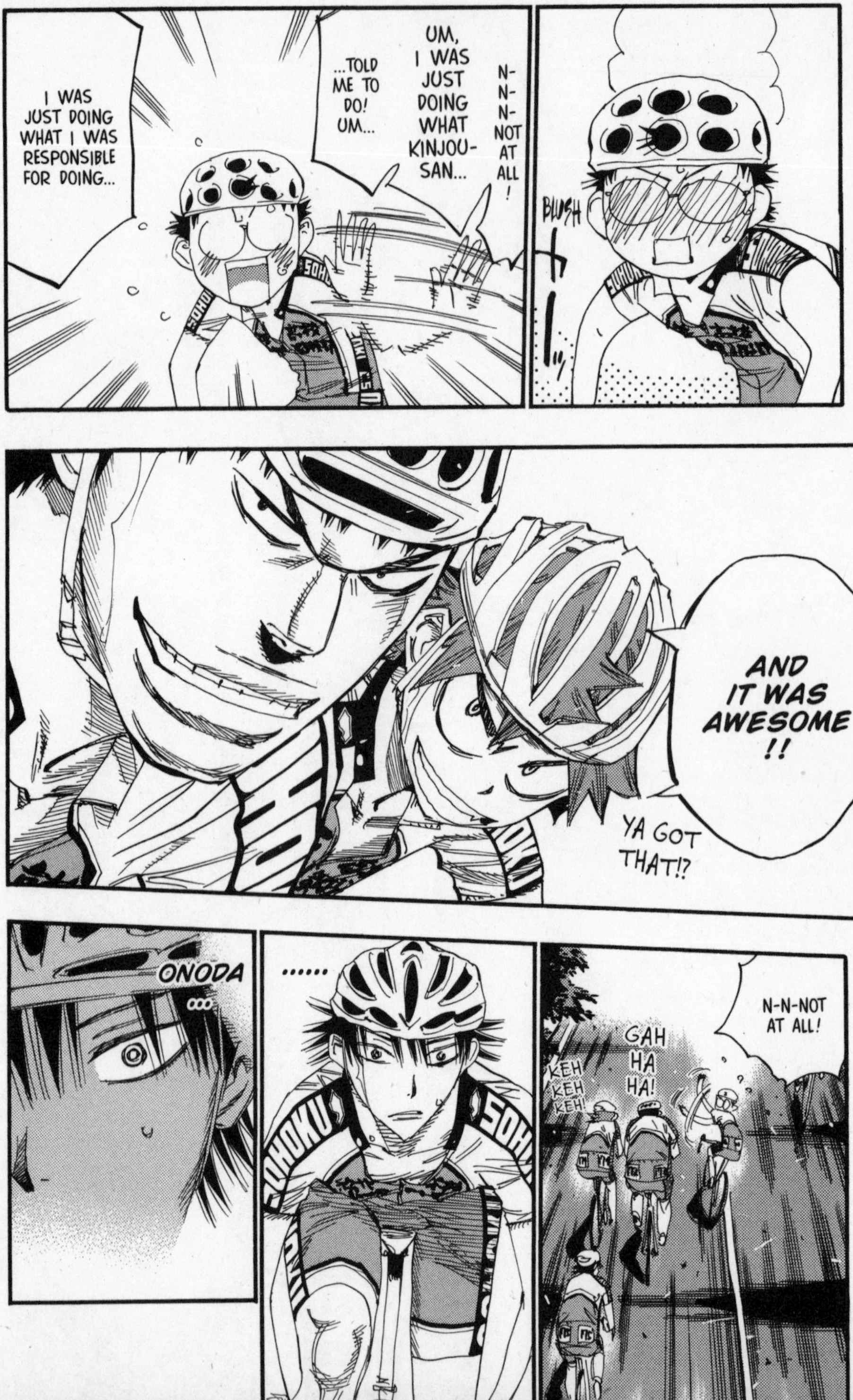
BLUSH
N-N-N-NOT AT ALL!
UM, I WAS JUST DOING WHAT KINJOU-SAN...
...TOLD ME TO DO! UM...
I WAS JUST DOING WHAT I WAS RESPONSIBLE FOR DOING...
AND IT WAS AWESOME!!
YA GOT THAT!?
N-N-NOT AT ALL!
GAH HA HA!
KEH KEH KEH
......
ONODA...

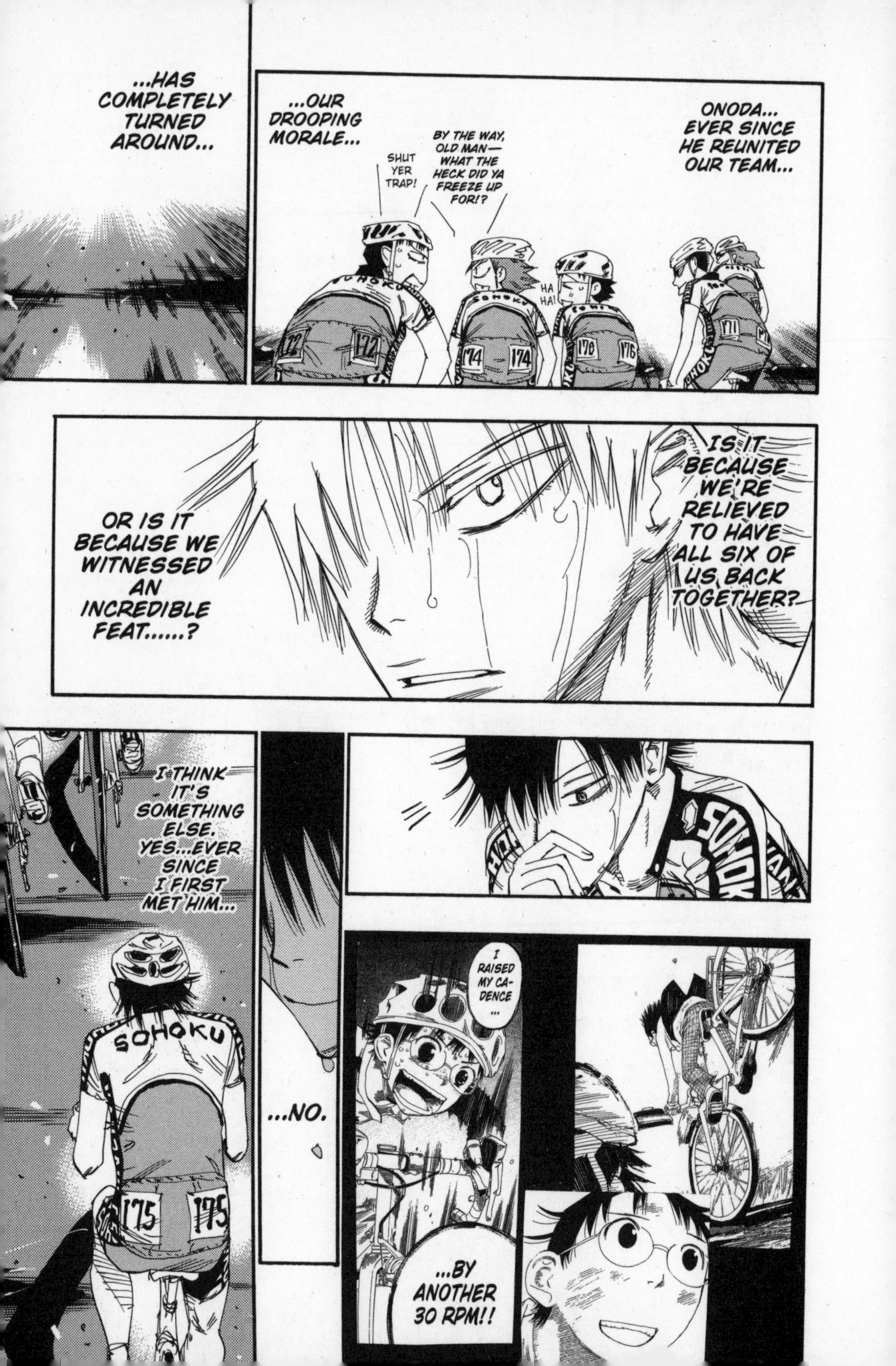
ONODA... EVER SINCE HE REUNITED OUR TEAM...
...OUR DROOPING MORALE...
BY THE WAY, OLD MAN—WHAT THE HECK DID YA FREEZE UP FOR!?
SHUT YER TRAP!
HA HA!
...HAS COMPLETELY TURNED AROUND...
IS IT BECAUSE WE'RE RELIEVED TO HAVE ALL SIX OF US BACK TOGETHER?
OR IS IT BECAUSE WE WITNESSED AN INCREDIBLE FEAT......?
I RAISED MY CA-DENCE...
...BY ANOTHER 30 RPM!!
...NO.
I THINK IT'S SOMETHING ELSE. YES...EVER SINCE I FIRST MET HIM...

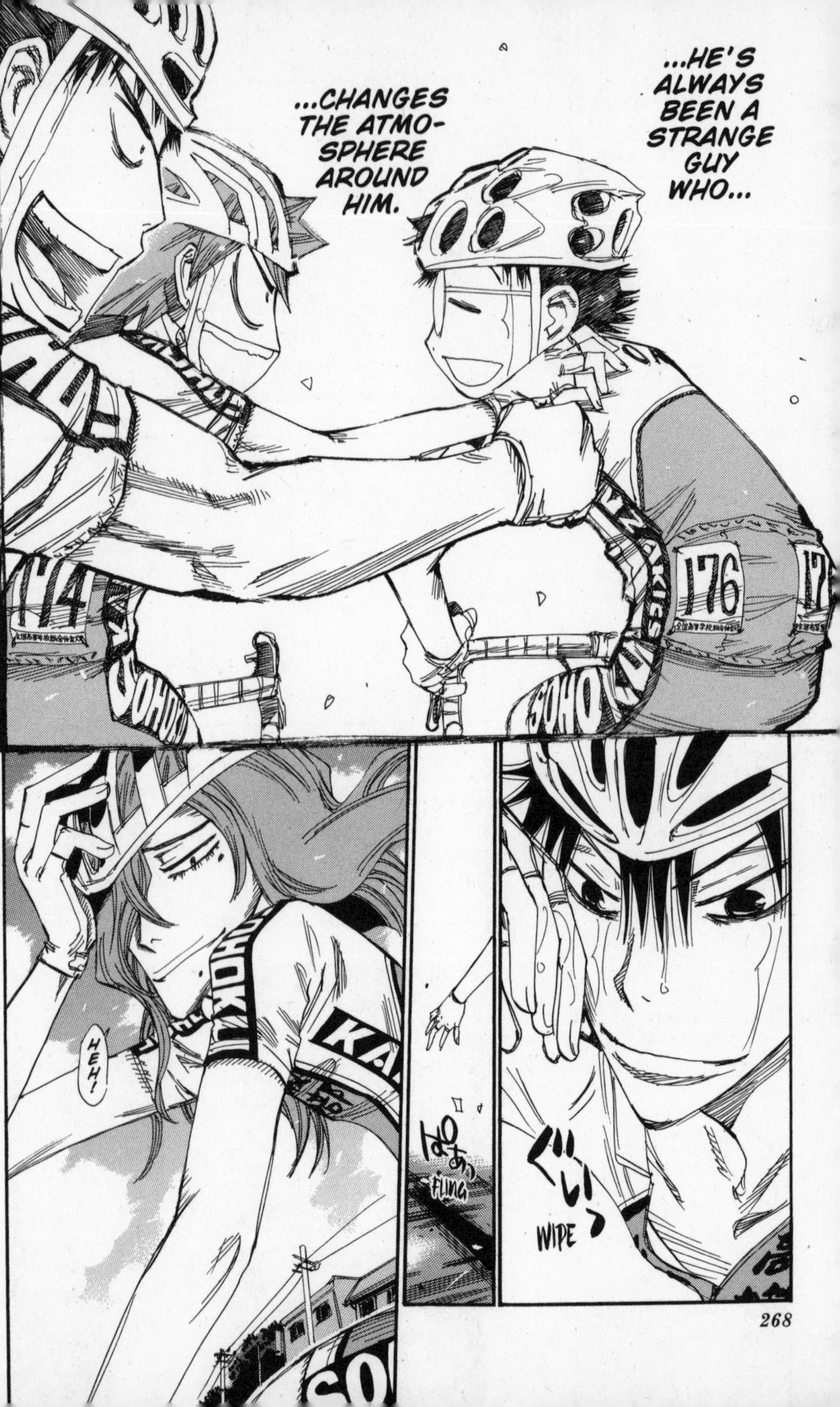
...HE'S ALWAYS BEEN A STRANGE GUY WHO...
...CHANGES THE ATMO-SPHERE AROUND HIM.
WIPE
FLING
HEH!

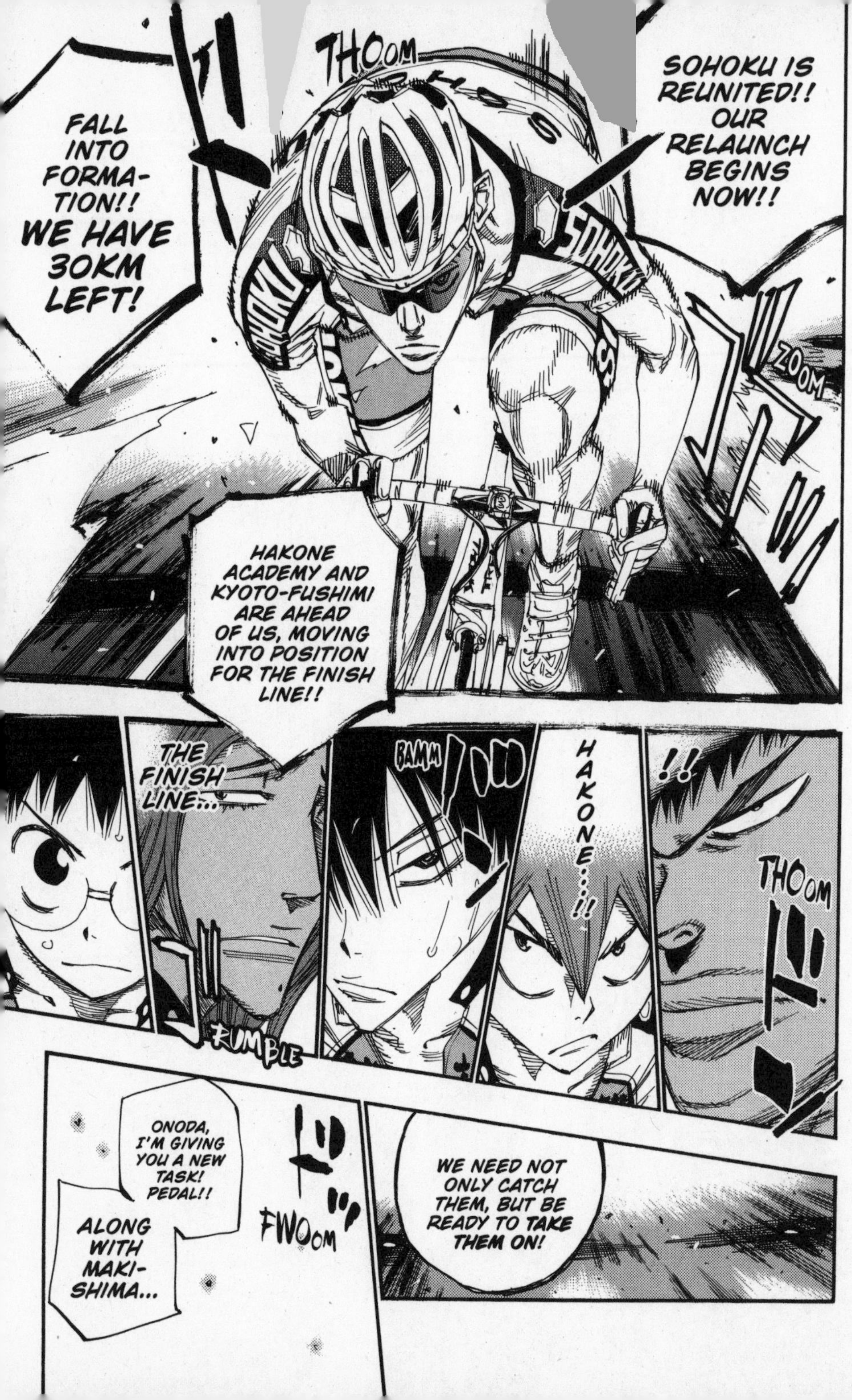
SOHOKU IS REUNITED!! OUR RELAUNCH BEGINS NOW!!
THOOM
FALL INTO FORMATION!! WE HAVE 30KM LEFT!
ZOOM
HAKONE ACADEMY AND KYOTO-FUSHIMI ARE AHEAD OF US, MOVING INTO POSITION FOR THE FINISH LINE!!
!!
THOOM
HAKONE...!!
BAMM
THE FINISH LINE...
RUMBLE
WE NEED NOT ONLY CATCH THEM, BUT BE READY TO TAKE THEM ON!
FWOOM
ONODA, I'M GIVING YOU A NEW TASK! PEDAL!!
ALONG WITH MAKISHIMA...

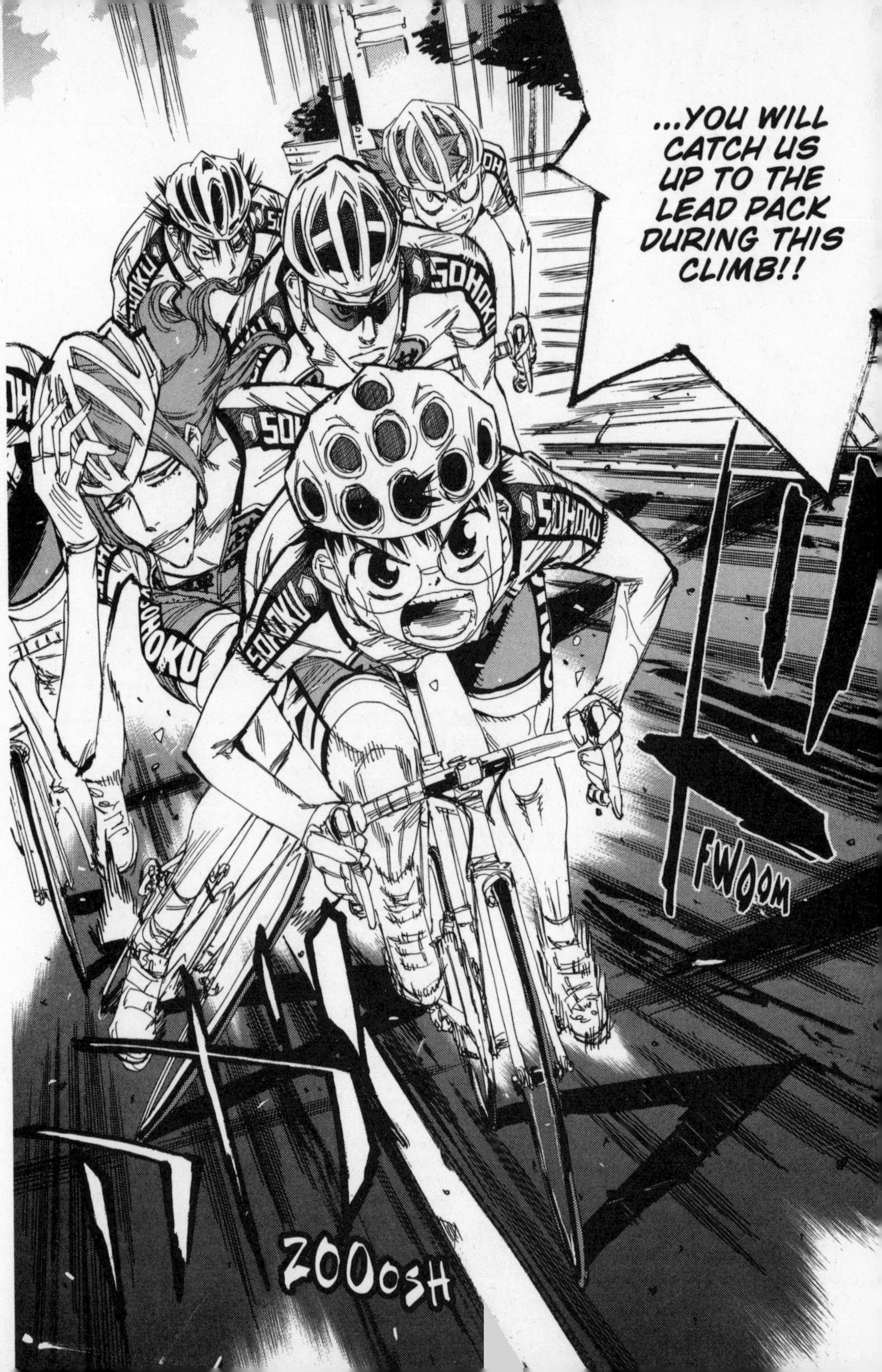
...YOU WILL CATCH US UP TO THE LEAD PACK DURING THIS CLIMB!!
FWOOM
ZOOOOSH

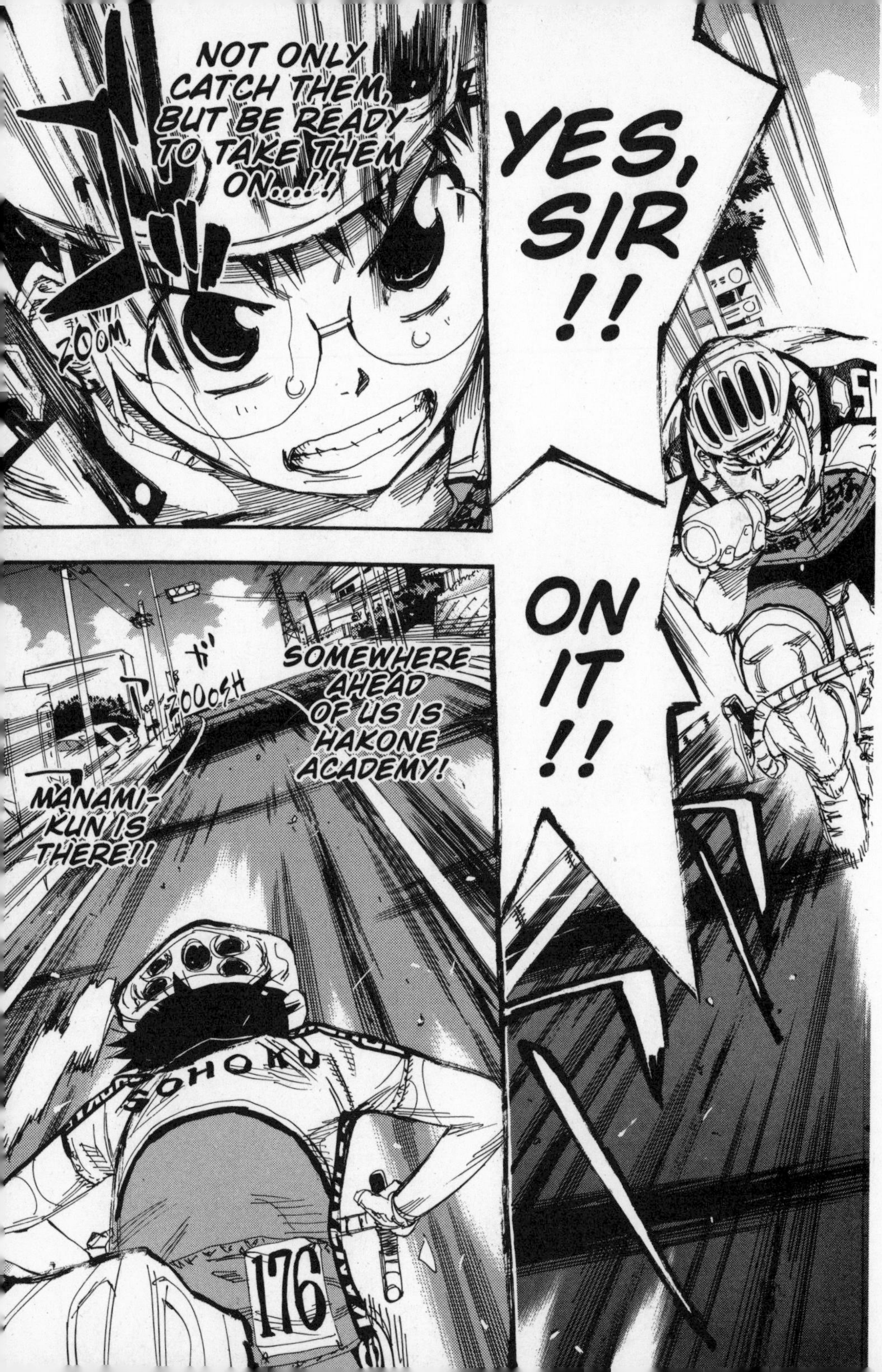

YES, SIR!!
ON IT!!
NOT ONLY CATCH THEM, BUT BE READY TO TAKE THEM ON...!!
ZOOM
SOMEWHERE AHEAD OF US IS HAKONE ACADEMY!
MANAMI-KUN IS THERE!!
ZOOOSH
SOHOKU
176

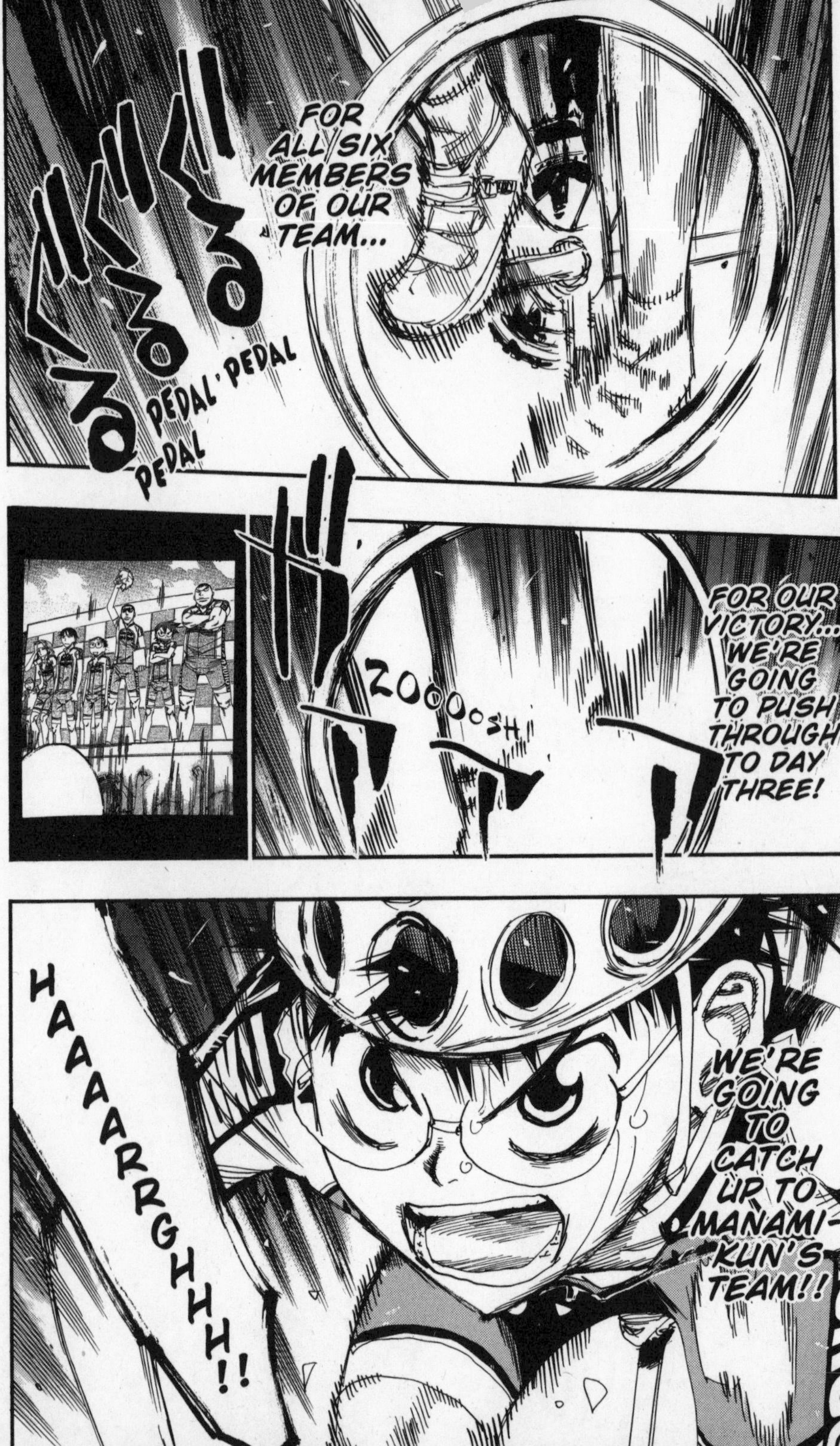
FOR ALL SIX MEMBERS OF OUR TEAM...
PEDAL PEDAL PEDAL
FOR OUR VICTORY... WE'RE GOING TO PUSH THROUGH TO DAY THREE!
ZOOOOOSH
WE'RE GOING TO CATCH UP TO MANAMI-KUN'S TEAM!!
HAAAARRGHHH!!

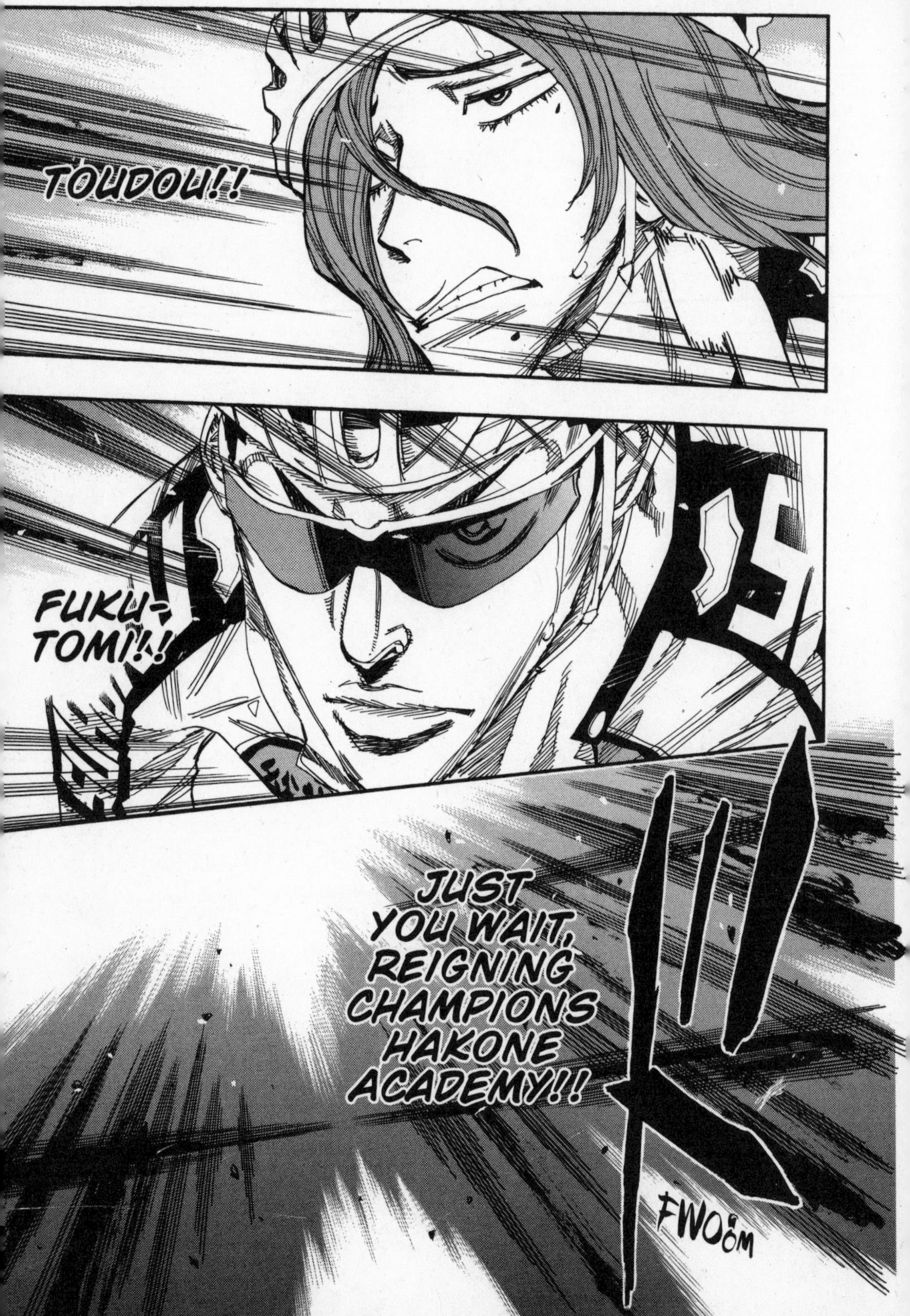
TOUDOU!!
FUKU-TOMI!!
JUST YOU WAIT, REIGNING CHAMPIONS HAKONE ACADEMY!!
FWOOM

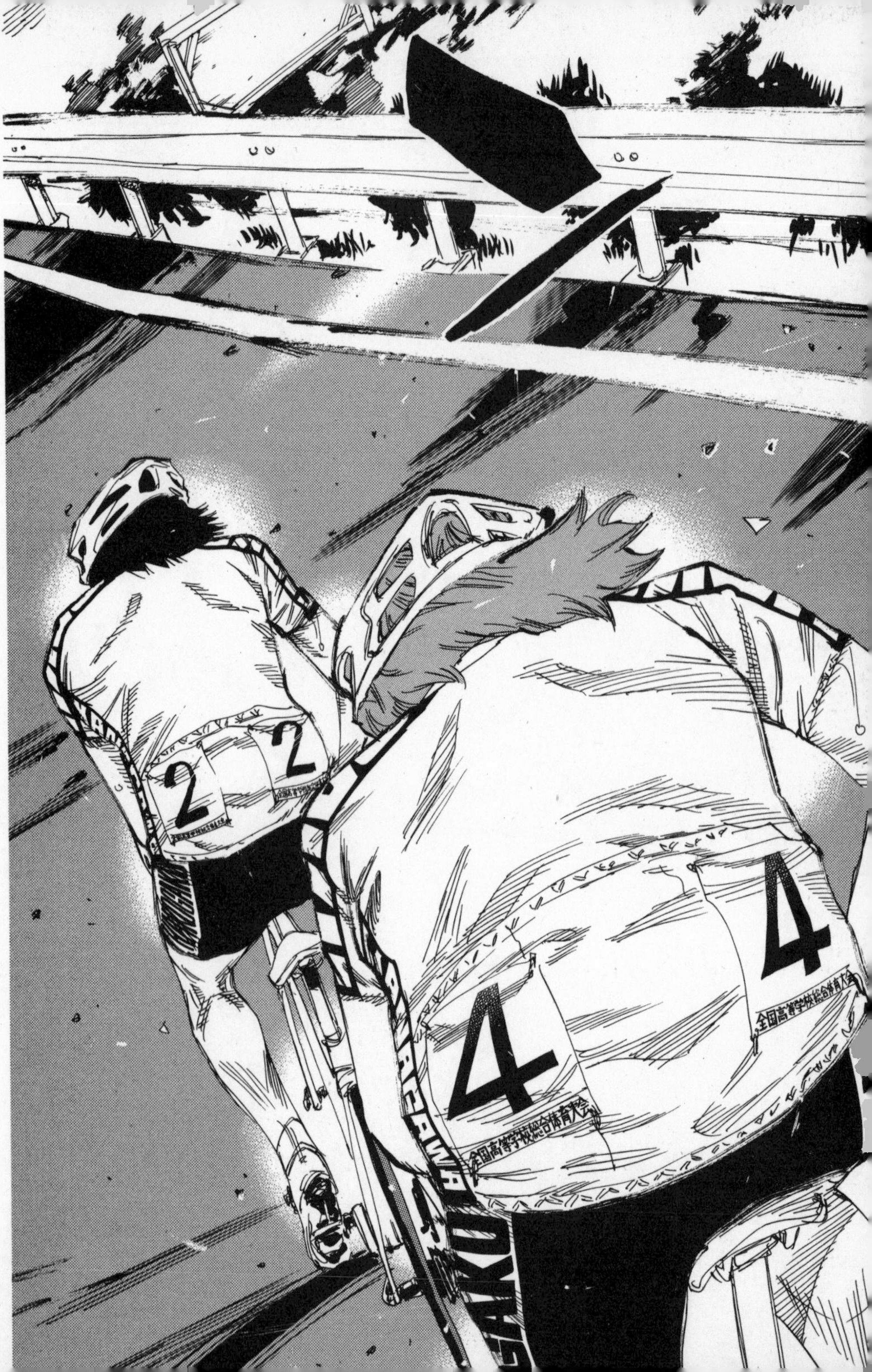
4
全国高等学校総合体育大会

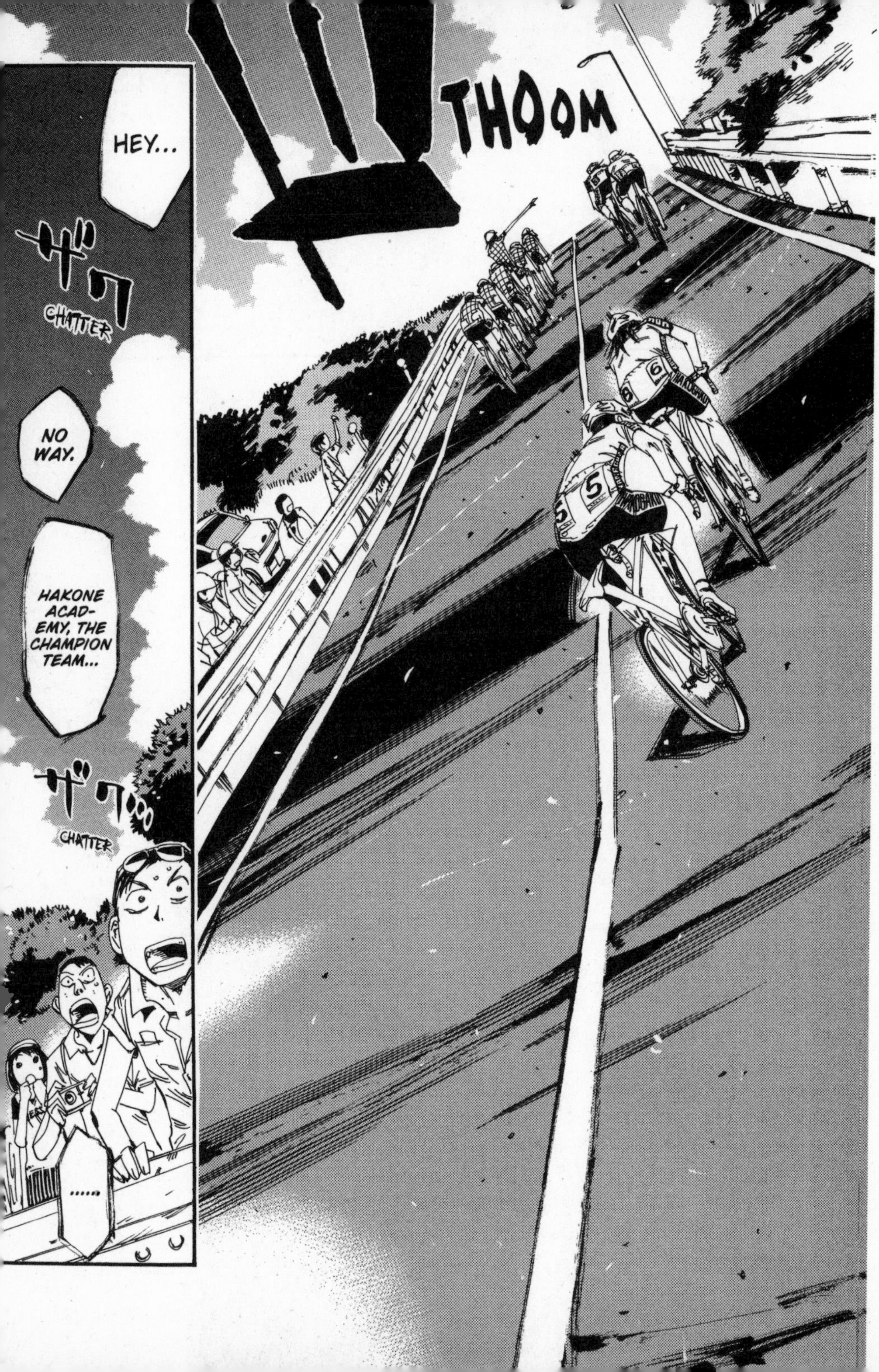
THOOM
HEY...
ザワ
CHATTER
NO WAY.
HAKONE ACADEMY, THE CHAMPION TEAM...
ザワ
CHATTER
......

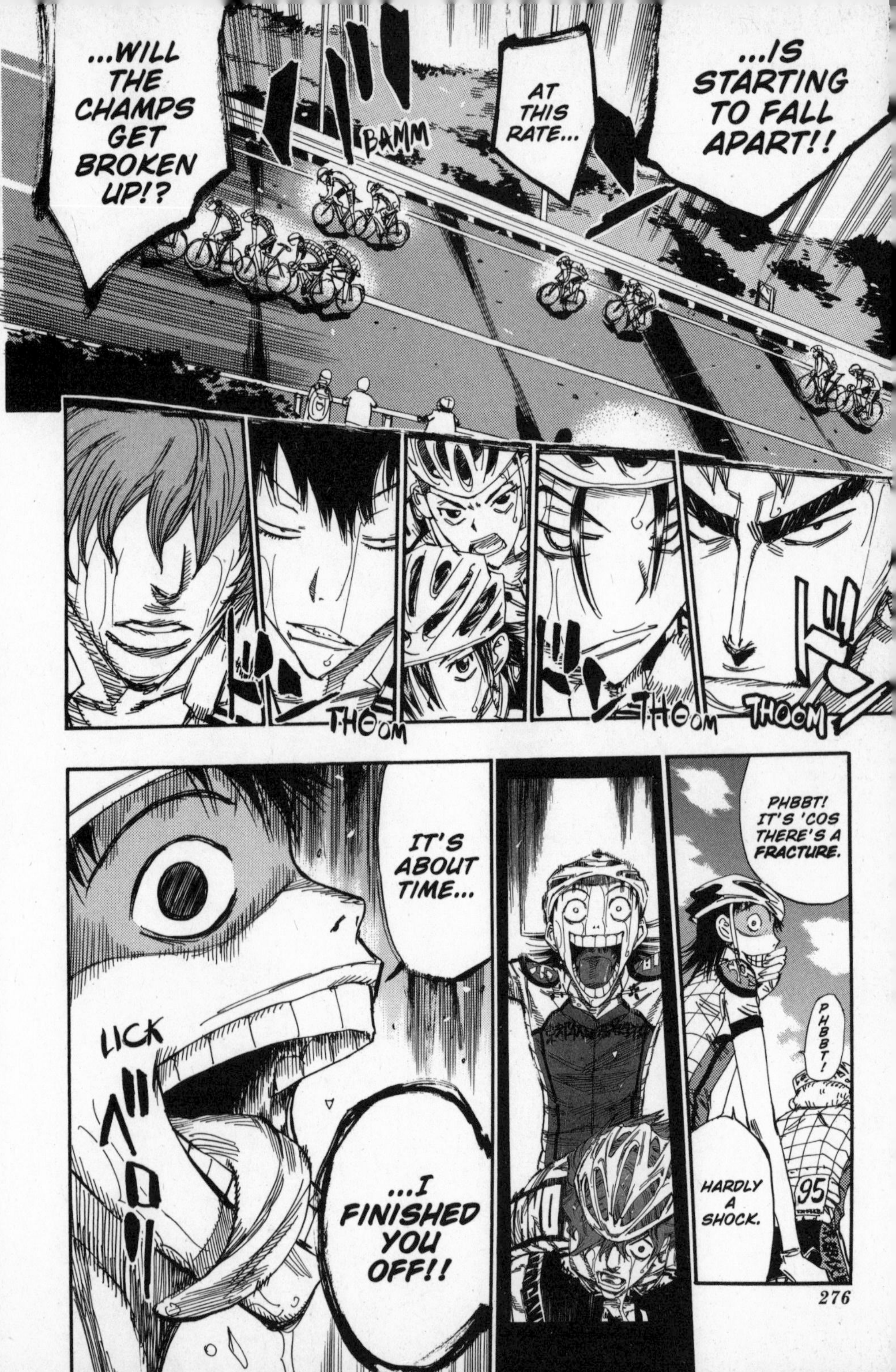

...IS STARTING TO FALL APART!!
AT THIS RATE...
BAMM
...WILL THE CHAMPS GET BROKEN UP!?
THOOM
THOOM
THOOM
PHBBT! IT'S 'COS THERE'S A FRACTURE.
PHBBT!
HARDLY A SHOCK.
95
IT'S ABOUT TIME...
LICK
...I FINISHED YOU OFF!!

RIDE.133 THE SPRINTERS' END

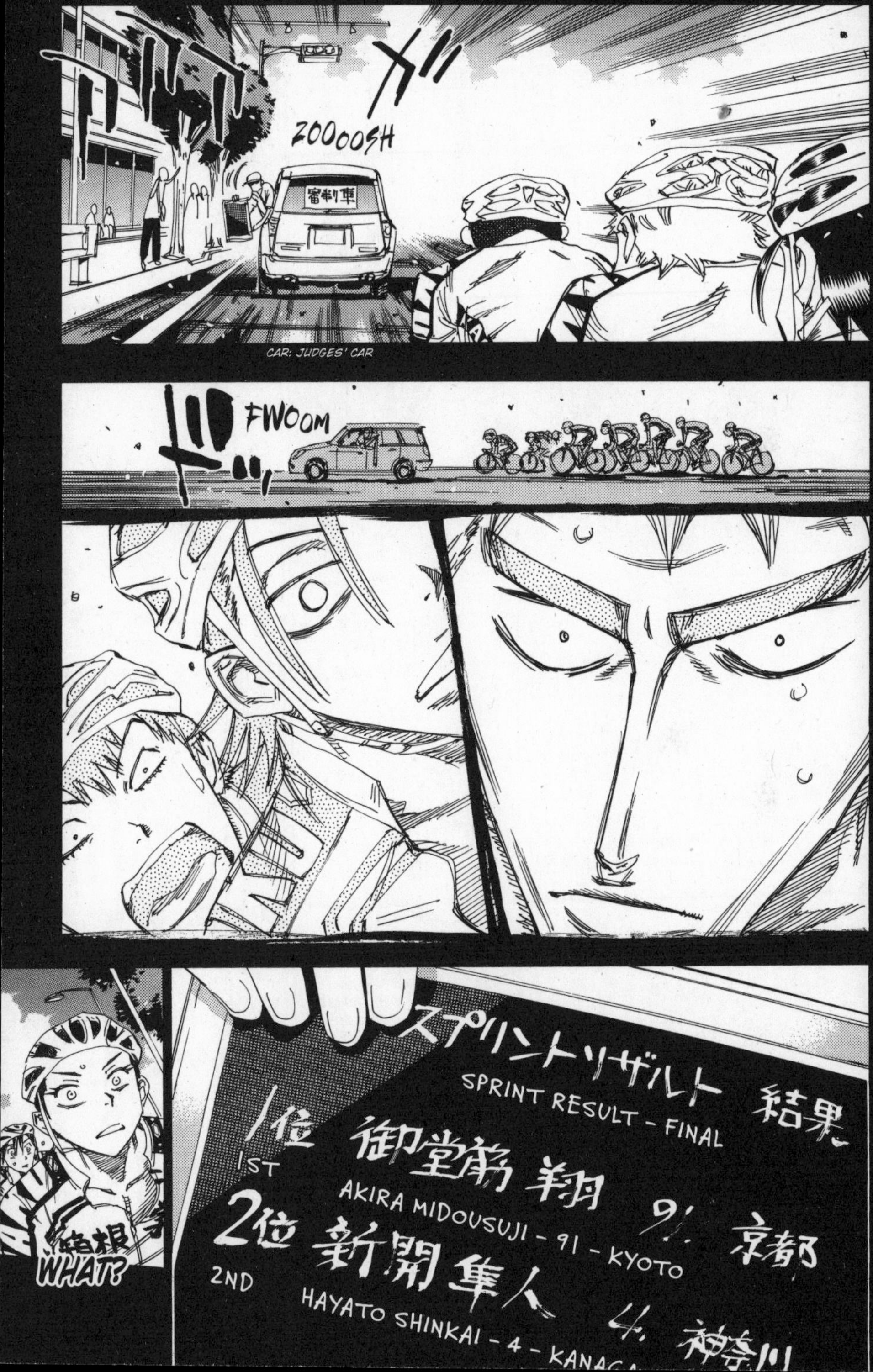
ZOOOOSH
審判車
CAR: JUDGES' CAR
FWOOM
スプリントリザルト 結果
SPRINT RESULT - FINAL
1位 御堂筋 翔 91 京都
1ST
AKIRA MIDOUSUJI - 91 - KYOTO
2位 新開 隼人 4 神奈川
2ND
HAYATO SHINKAI - 4 - KANAGA
WHAT?

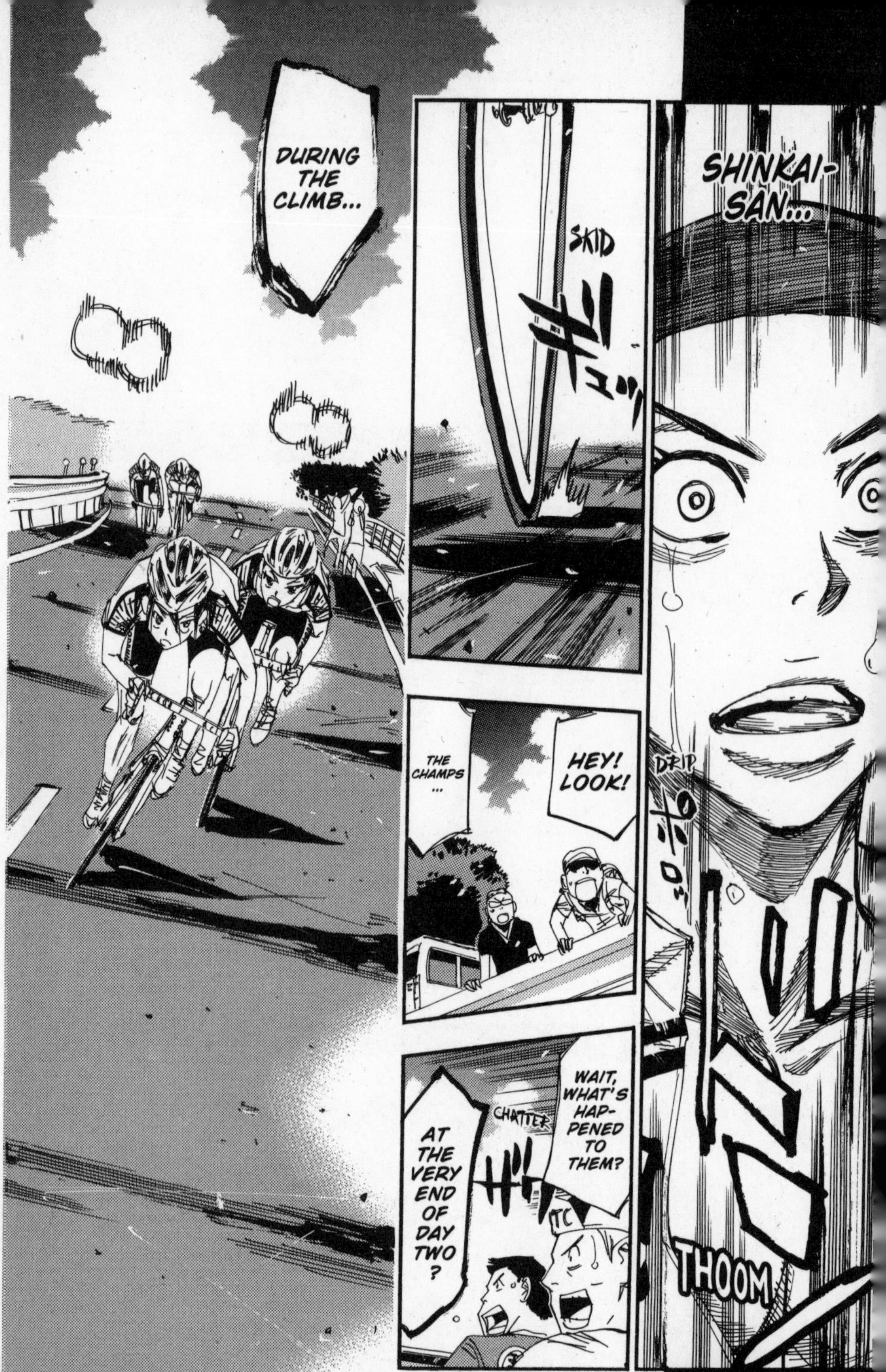
SHINKAI-SAN...
DRIP
THOOM
SKID
HEY! LOOK!
THE CHAMPS...
WAIT, WHAT'S HAP-PENED TO THEM?
CHATTER
AT THE VERY END OF DAY TWO?
DURING THE CLIMB...

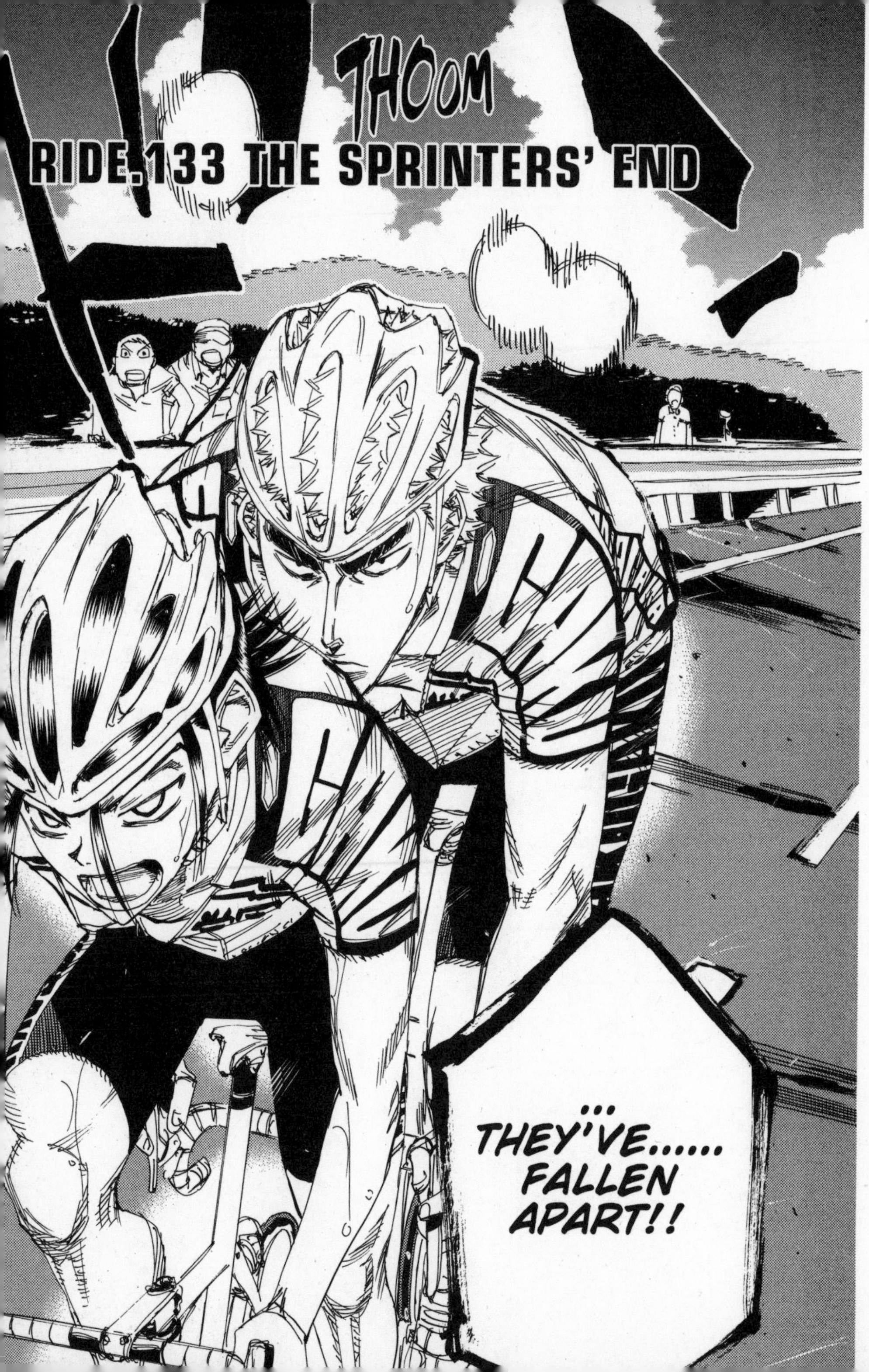
THOOM
RIDE.133 THE SPRINTERS' END
...THEY'VE...... FALLEN APART!!

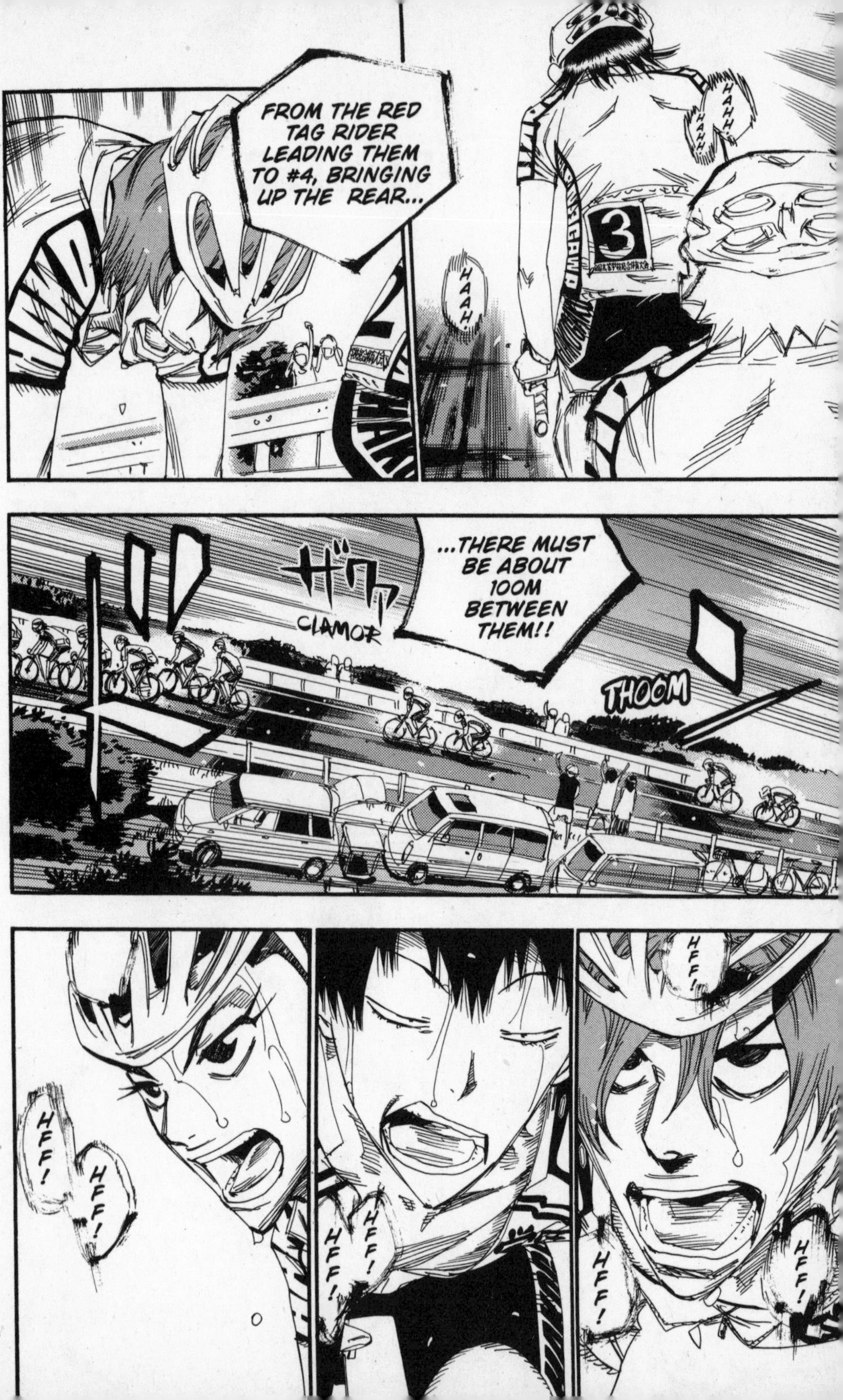
FROM THE RED TAG RIDER LEADING THEM TO #4, BRINGING UP THE REAR...
HAHH
HAHH
HAAH
THOOM
...THERE MUST BE ABOUT 100M BETWEEN THEM!!
ザワ
CLAMOR
HFF!
HFF!
HFF!
HFF!
HFF!
HFF!

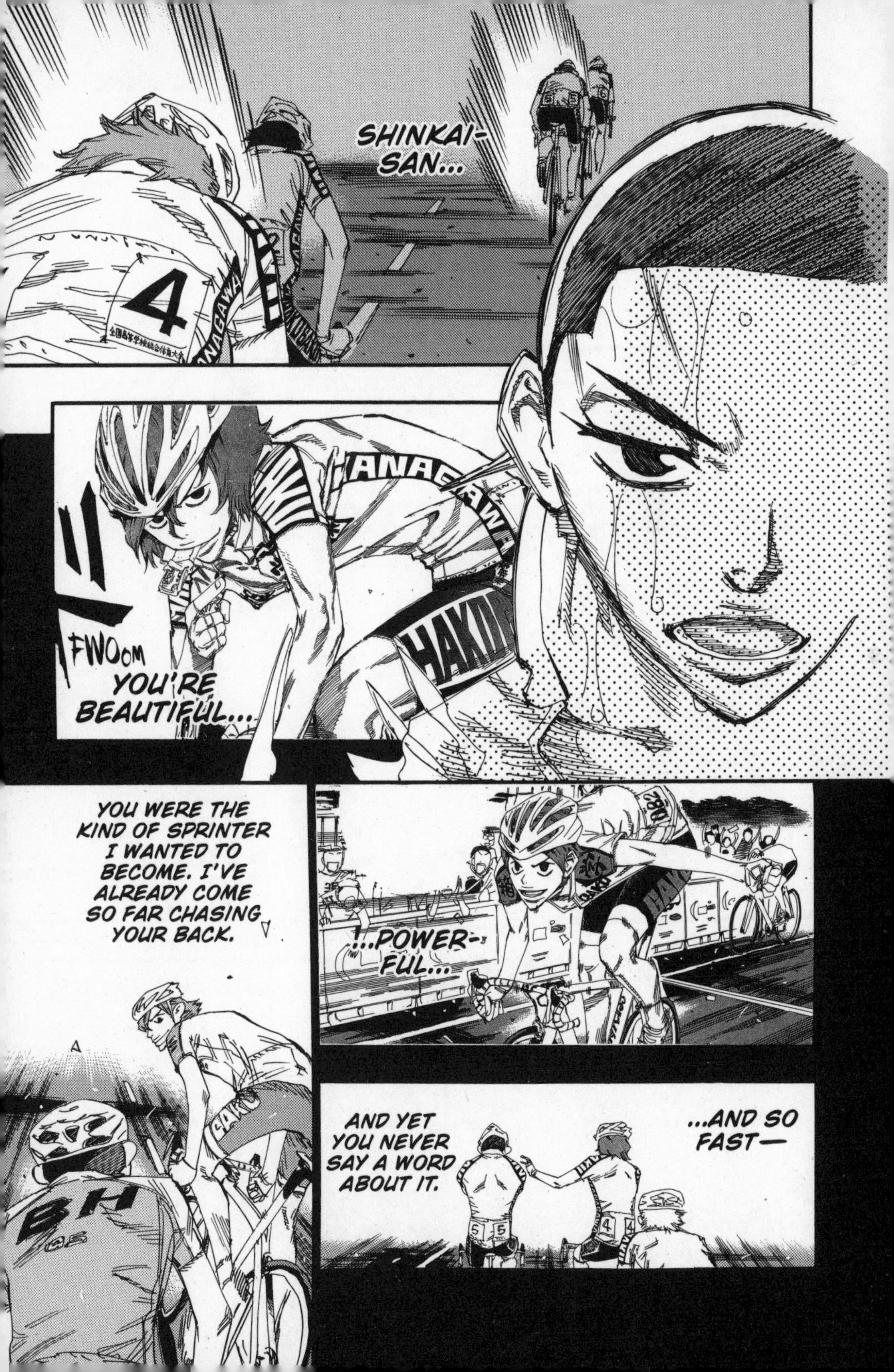
SHINKAI-SAN...
FWOOM
YOU'RE BEAUTIFUL...
!..POWER-FUL...
...AND SO FAST—
AND YET YOU NEVER SAY A WORD ABOUT IT.
YOU WERE THE KIND OF SPRINTER I WANTED TO BECOME. I'VE ALREADY COME SO FAR CHASING YOUR BACK.

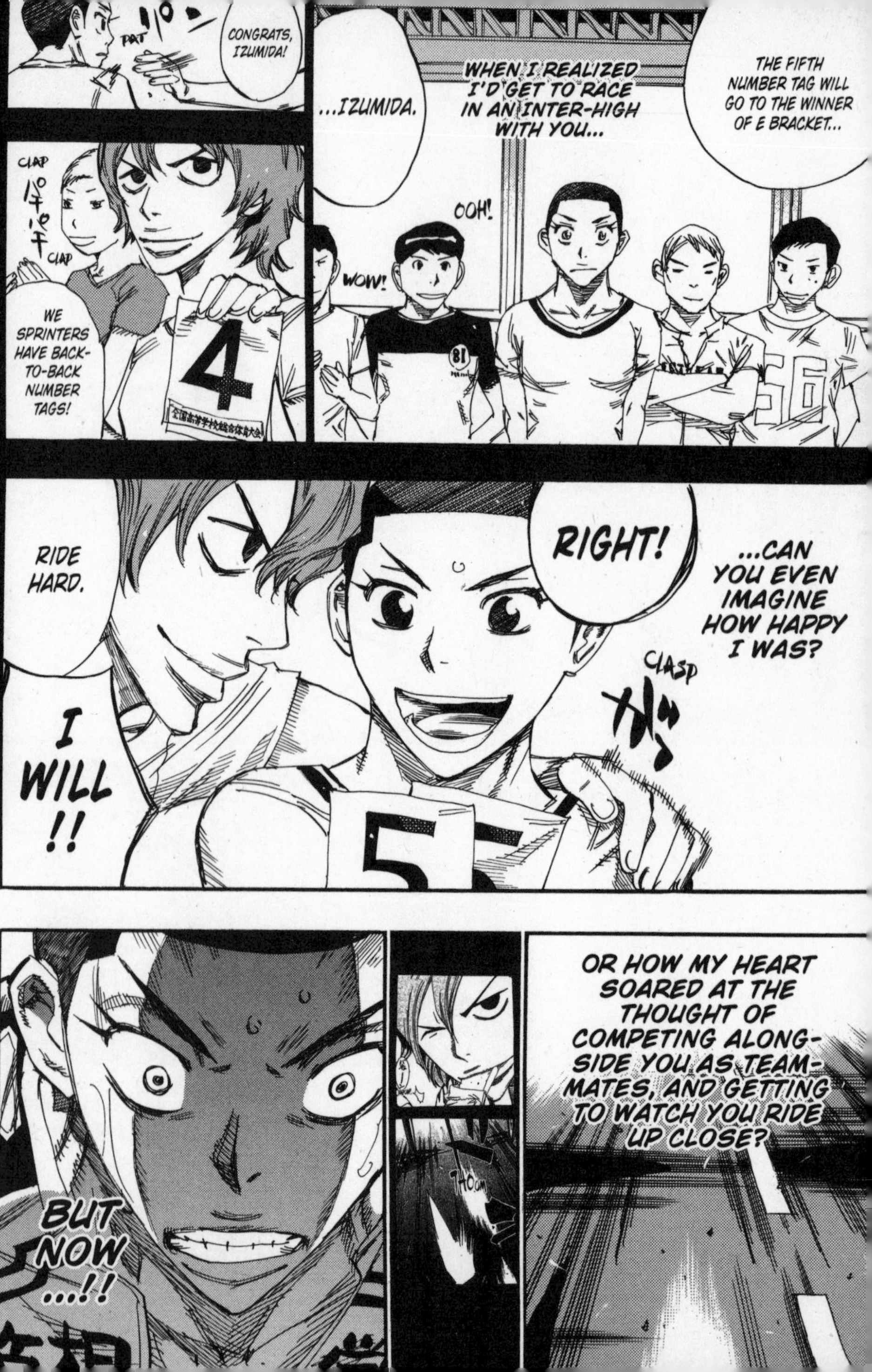
THE FIFTH NUMBER TAG WILL GO TO THE WINNER OF E BRACKET...
WHEN I REALIZED I'D GET TO RACE IN AN INTER-HIGH WITH YOU...
...IZUMIDA.
OOH!
WOW!
CONGRATS, IZUMIDA!
PAT
CLAP
CLAP
WE SPRINTERS HAVE BACK-TO-BACK NUMBER TAGS!
RIGHT!
...CAN YOU EVEN IMAGINE HOW HAPPY I WAS?
CLASP
RIDE HARD.
I WILL!!
OR HOW MY HEART SOARED AT THE THOUGHT OF COMPETING ALONG-SIDE YOU AS TEAM-MATES, AND GETTING TO WATCH YOU RIDE UP CLOSE?
BUT NOW...!!

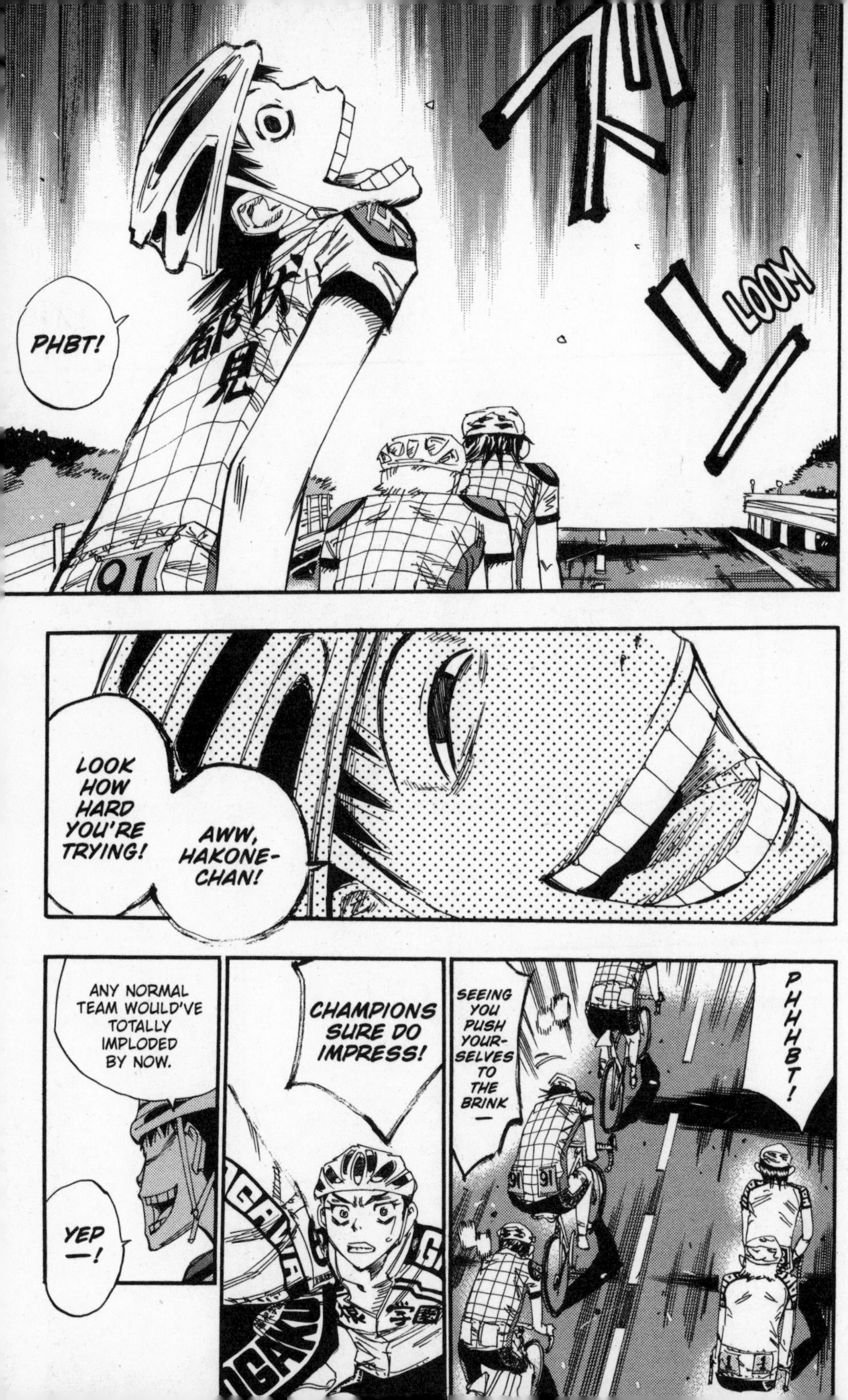
LOOM
PHBT!
AWW, HAKONE-CHAN!
LOOK HOW HARD YOU'RE TRYING!
PHHHBT!
SEEING YOU PUSH YOUR-SELVES TO THE BRINK—
CHAMPIONS SURE DO IMPRESS!
ANY NORMAL TEAM WOULD'VE TOTALLY IMPLODED BY NOW.
YEP—!

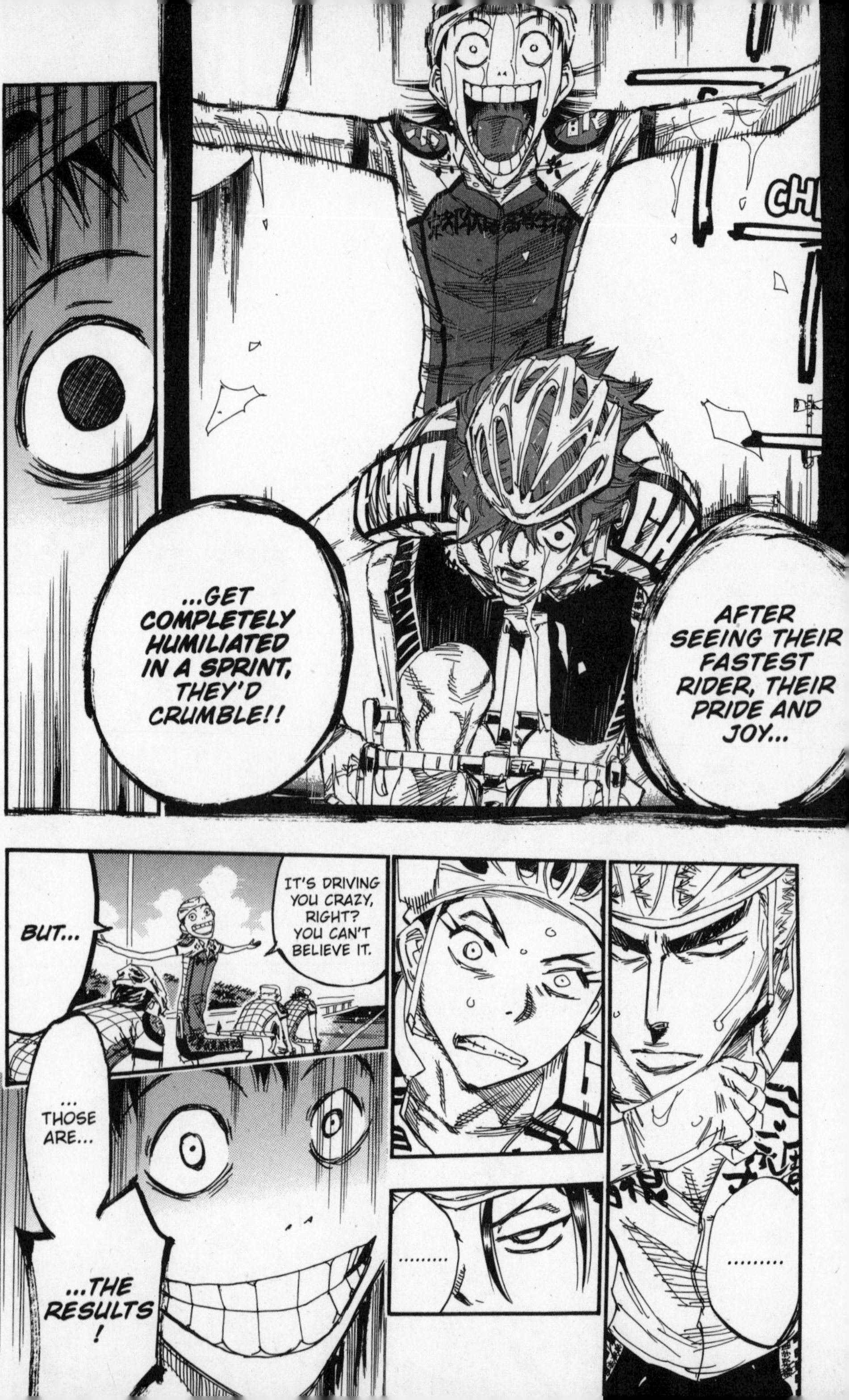
AFTER SEEING THEIR FASTEST RIDER, THEIR PRIDE AND JOY...
...GET COMPLETELY HUMILIATED IN A SPRINT, THEY'D CRUMBLE!!
....
....
IT'S DRIVING YOU CRAZY, RIGHT? YOU CAN'T BELIEVE IT.
BUT...
...THOSE ARE...
...THE RESULTS!

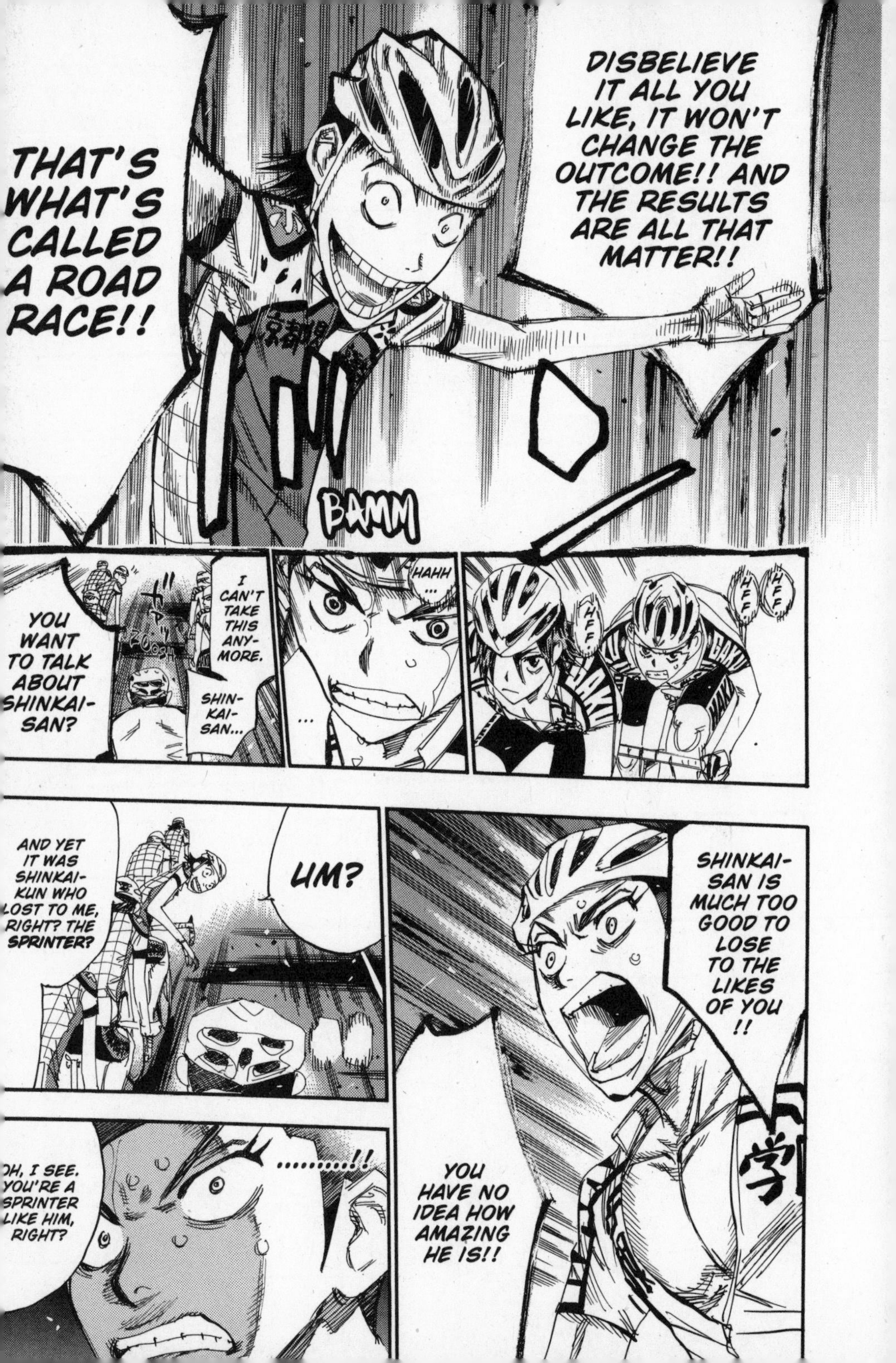

DISBELIEVE IT ALL YOU LIKE, IT WON'T CHANGE THE OUTCOME!! AND THE RESULTS ARE ALL THAT MATTER!!
THAT'S WHAT'S CALLED A ROAD RACE!!
BAMM
HFF
HFF
HFF
HAHH...
...
I CAN'T TAKE THIS ANYMORE.
SHIN-KAI-SAN...
ZOOSH
YOU WANT TO TALK ABOUT SHINKAI-SAN?
SHINKAI-SAN IS MUCH TOO GOOD TO LOSE TO THE LIKES OF YOU!!
YOU HAVE NO IDEA HOW AMAZING HE IS!!
UM?
AND YET IT WAS SHINKAI-KUN WHO LOST TO ME, RIGHT? THE SPRINTER?
..........!!
OH, I SEE. YOU'RE A SPRINTER LIKE HIM, RIGHT?

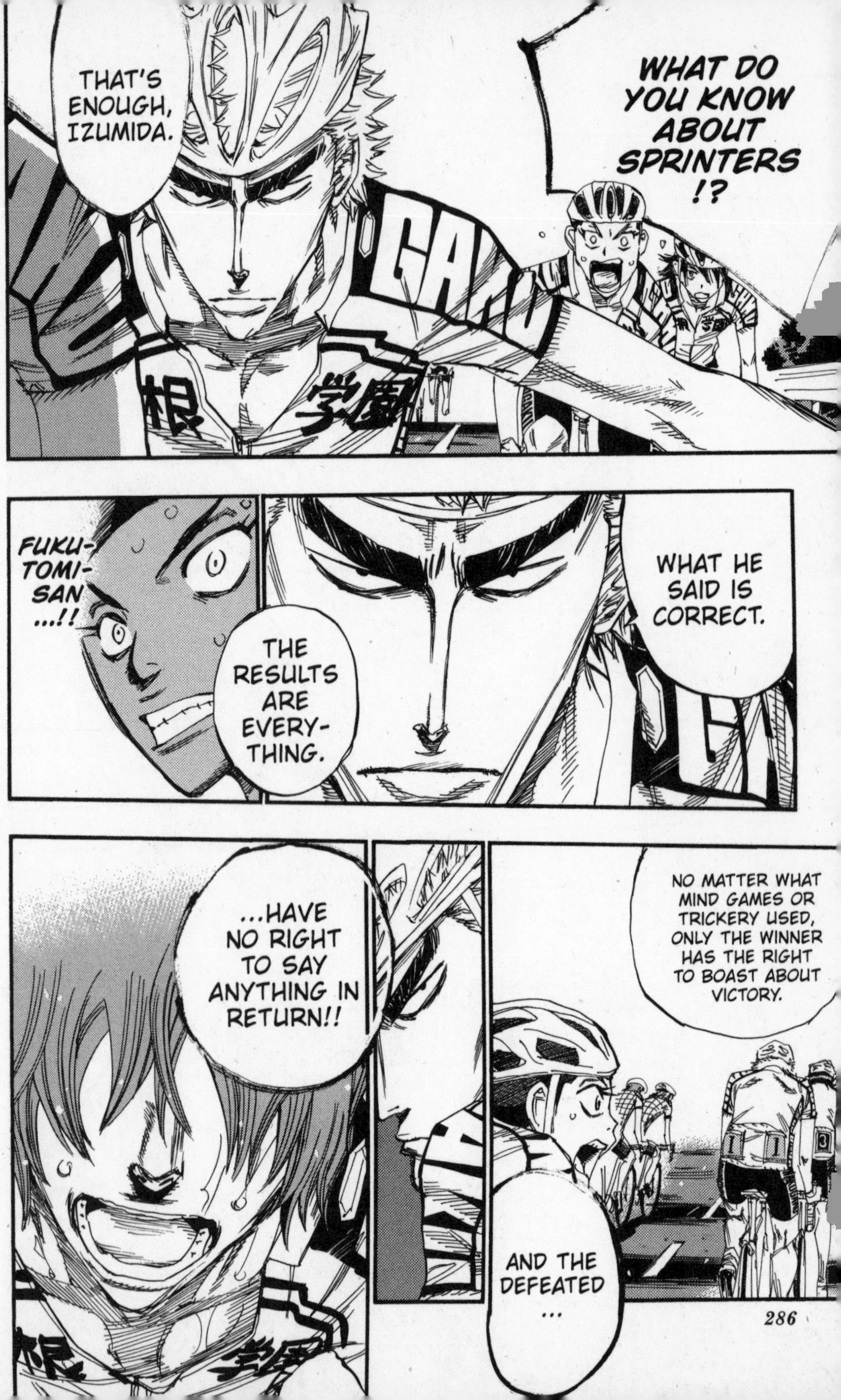
WHAT DO YOU KNOW ABOUT SPRINTERS !?
THAT'S ENOUGH, IZUMIDA.
WHAT HE SAID IS CORRECT.
THE RESULTS ARE EVERY-THING.
FUKU-TOMI-SAN ...!!
NO MATTER WHAT MIND GAMES OR TRICKERY USED, ONLY THE WINNER HAS THE RIGHT TO BOAST ABOUT VICTORY.
AND THE DEFEATED ...
...HAVE NO RIGHT TO SAY ANYTHING IN RETURN!!

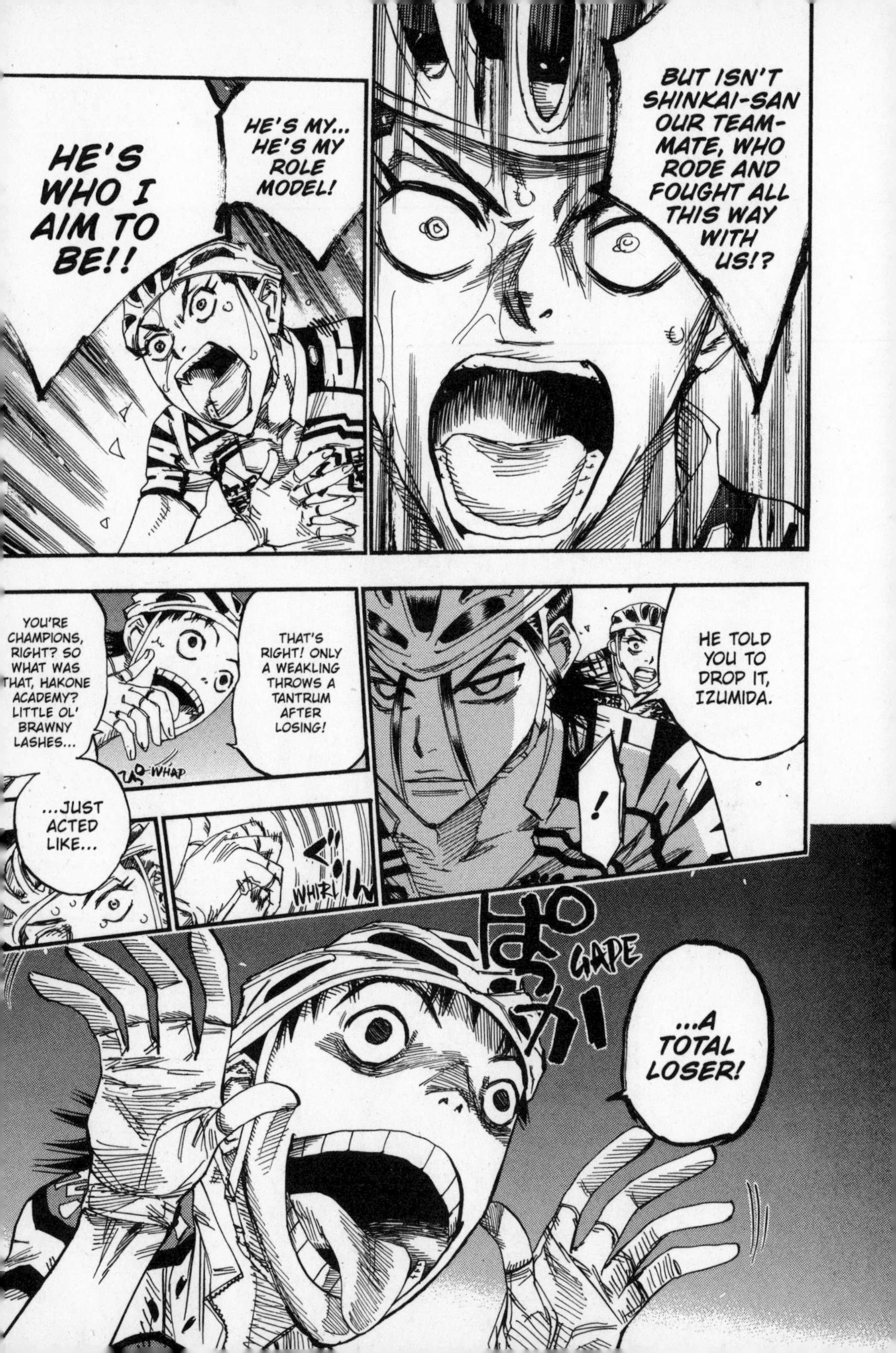
BUT ISN'T SHINKAI-SAN OUR TEAM-MATE, WHO RODE AND FOUGHT ALL THIS WAY WITH US!?
HE'S MY... HE'S MY ROLE MODEL!
HE'S WHO I AIM TO BE!!
HE TOLD YOU TO DROP IT, IZUMIDA.
!
THAT'S RIGHT! ONLY A WEAKLING THROWS A TANTRUM AFTER LOSING!
YOU'RE CHAMPIONS, RIGHT? SO WHAT WAS THAT, HAKONE ACADEMY? LITTLE OL' BRAWNY LASHES...
WHAP
WHIRL
...JUST ACTED LIKE...
GAPE
...A TOTAL LOSER!

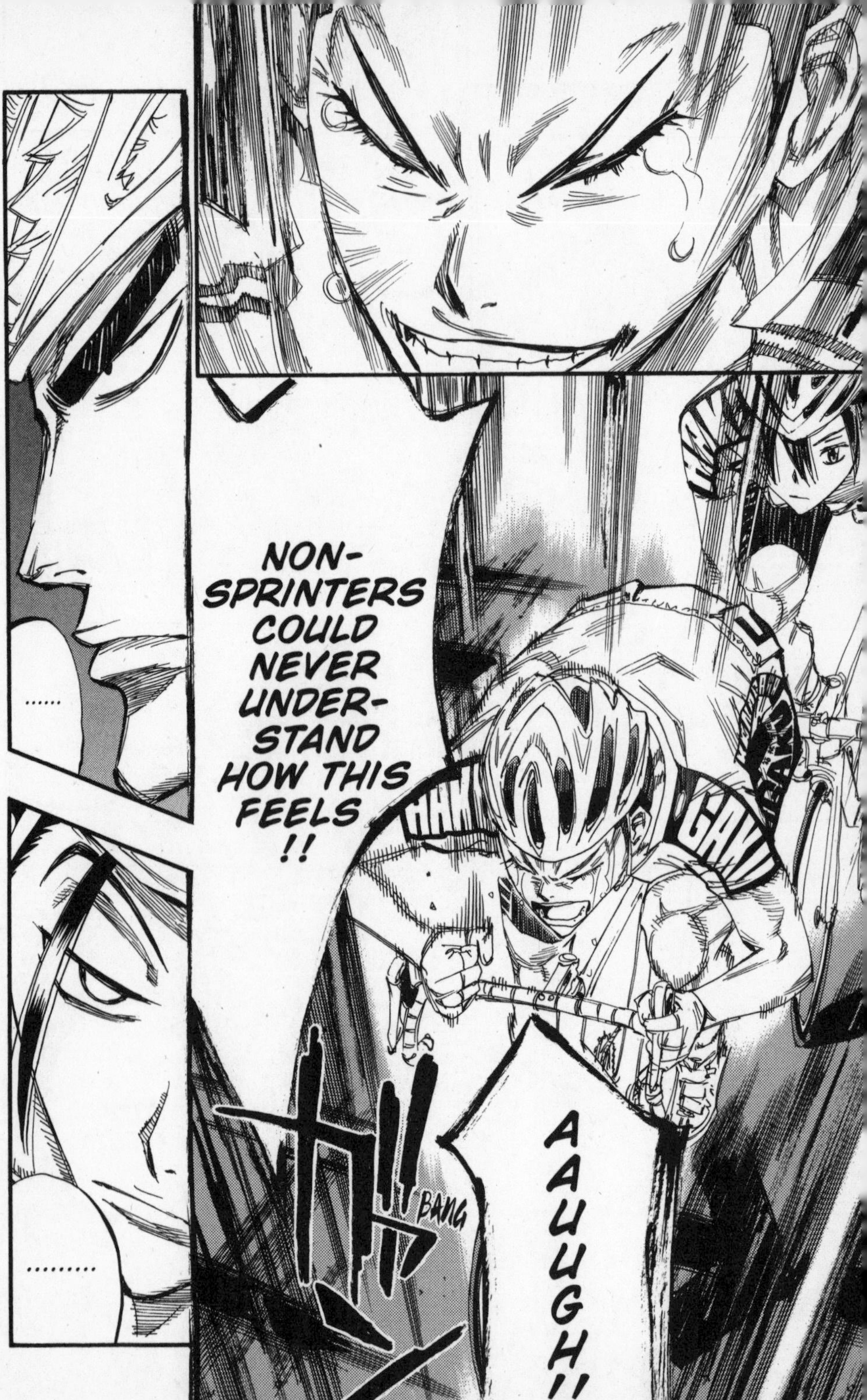
NON-SPRINTERS COULD NEVER UNDERSTAND HOW THIS FEELS!!
AAUUGH!!
BANG
......
....

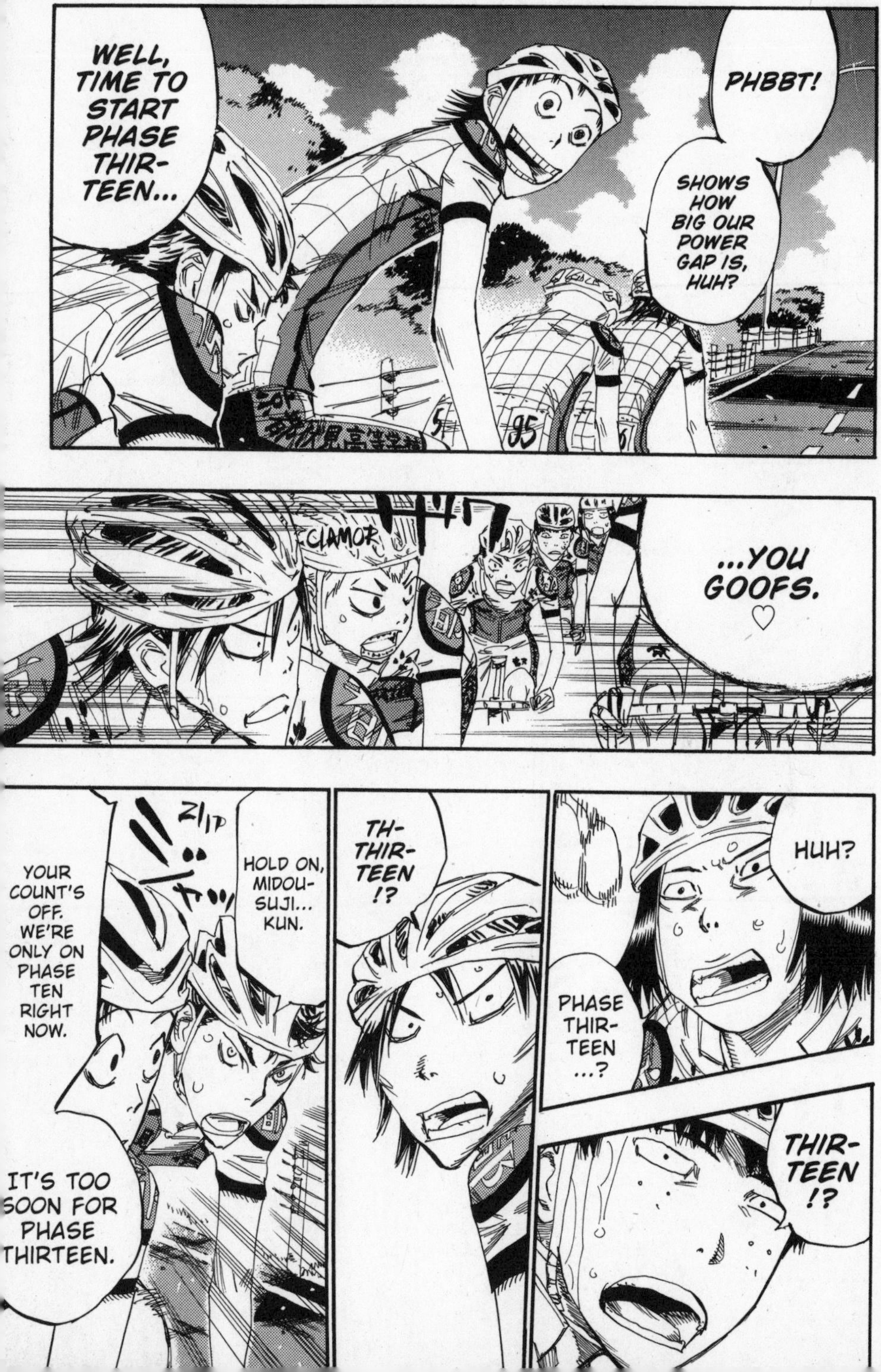
PHBBT!
SHOWS HOW BIG OUR POWER GAP IS, HUH?
WELL, TIME TO START PHASE THIRTEEN...
...YOU GOOFS. ♡
CLAMOR
HUH?
PHASE THIRTEEN...?
THIRTEEN!?
TH-THIRTEEN!?
HOLD ON, MIDOUSUJI... KUN.
ZIIP
YOUR COUNT'S OFF. WE'RE ONLY ON PHASE TEN RIGHT NOW.
IT'S TOO SOON FOR PHASE THIRTEEN.

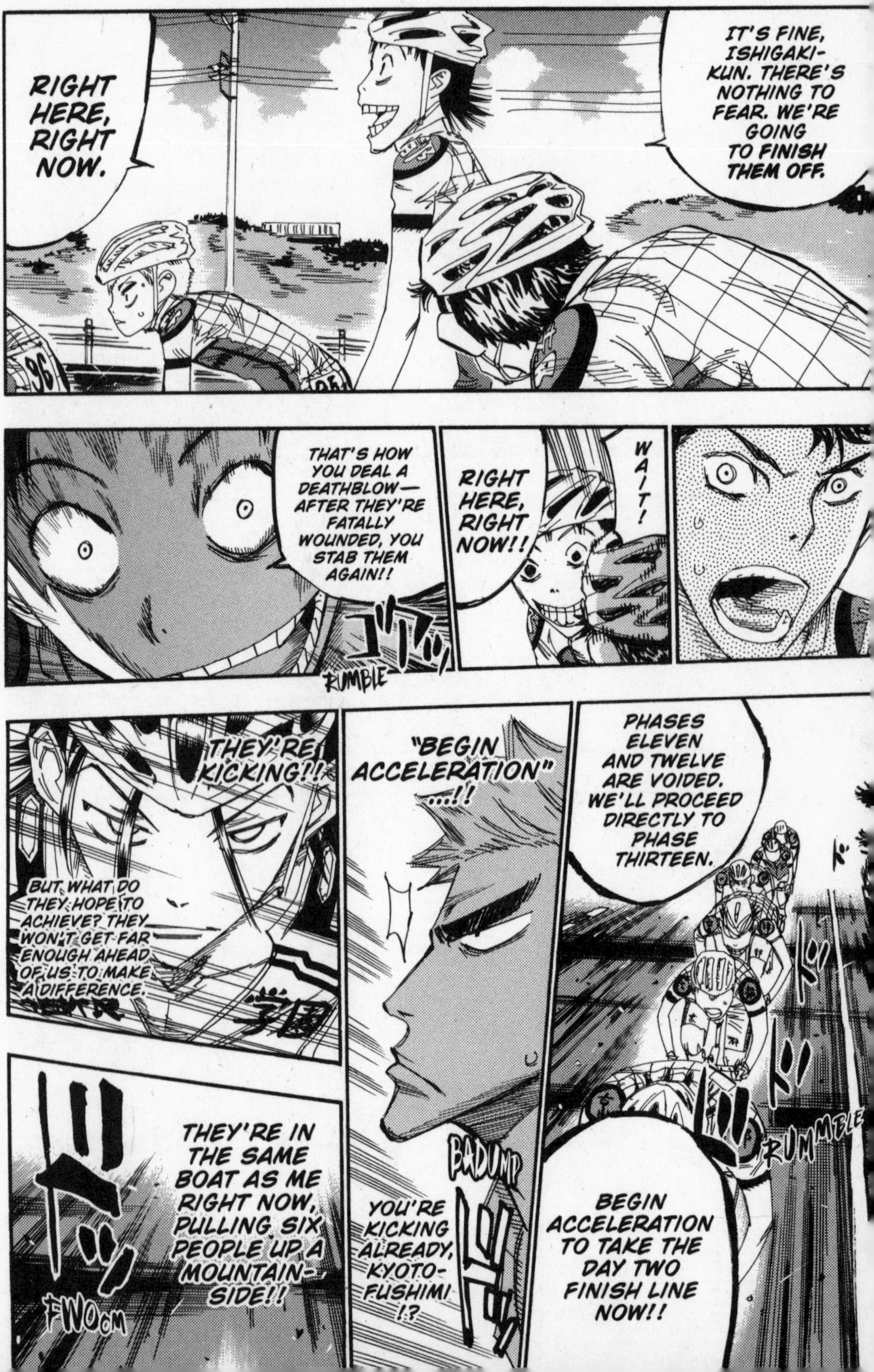
IT'S FINE, ISHIGAKI-KUN. THERE'S NOTHING TO FEAR. WE'RE GOING TO FINISH THEM OFF.
RIGHT HERE, RIGHT NOW.
WAIT!
RIGHT HERE, RIGHT NOW!!
THAT'S HOW YOU DEAL A DEATHBLOW—AFTER THEY'RE FATALLY WOUNDED, YOU STAB THEM AGAIN!!
RUMBLE
PHASES ELEVEN AND TWELVE ARE VOIDED. WE'LL PROCEED DIRECTLY TO PHASE THIRTEEN.
RUMMBLE
BEGIN ACCELERATION TO TAKE THE DAY TWO FINISH LINE NOW!!
"BEGIN ACCELERATION" ...!!
BADUMP
YOU'RE KICKING ALREADY, KYOTO-FUSHIMI!?
THEY'RE KICKING!!
BUT WHAT DO THEY HOPE TO ACHIEVE? THEY WON'T GET FAR ENOUGH AHEAD OF US TO MAKE A DIFFERENCE.
THEY'RE IN THE SAME BOAT AS ME RIGHT NOW, PULLING SIX PEOPLE UP A MOUNTAIN-SIDE!!
FWOOM

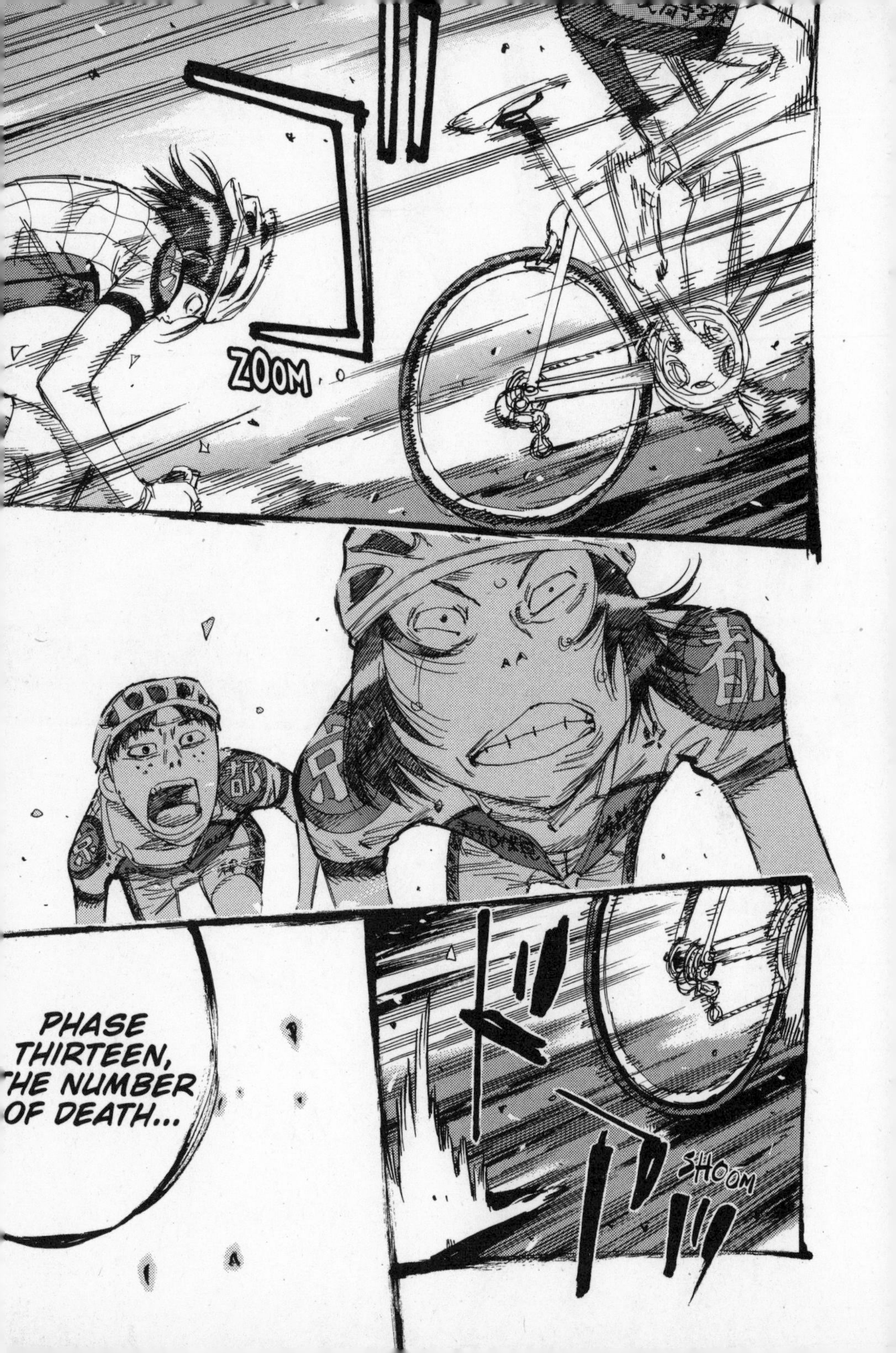
ZOOM
SHOOM
PHASE THIRTEEN, THE NUMBER OF DEATH...

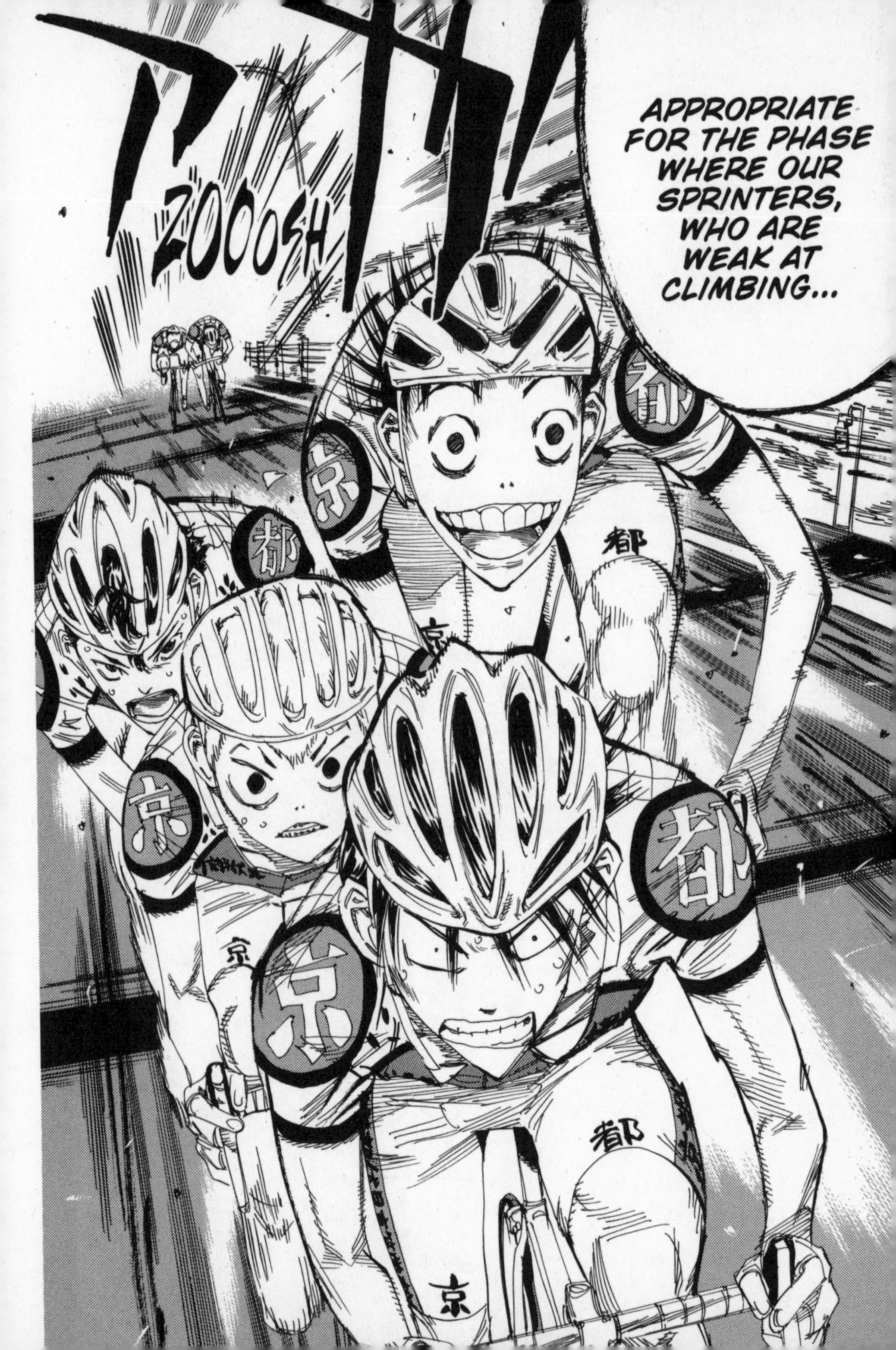
APPROPRIATE FOR THE PHASE WHERE OUR SPRINTERS, WHO ARE WEAK AT CLIMBING...
ZOOOSH

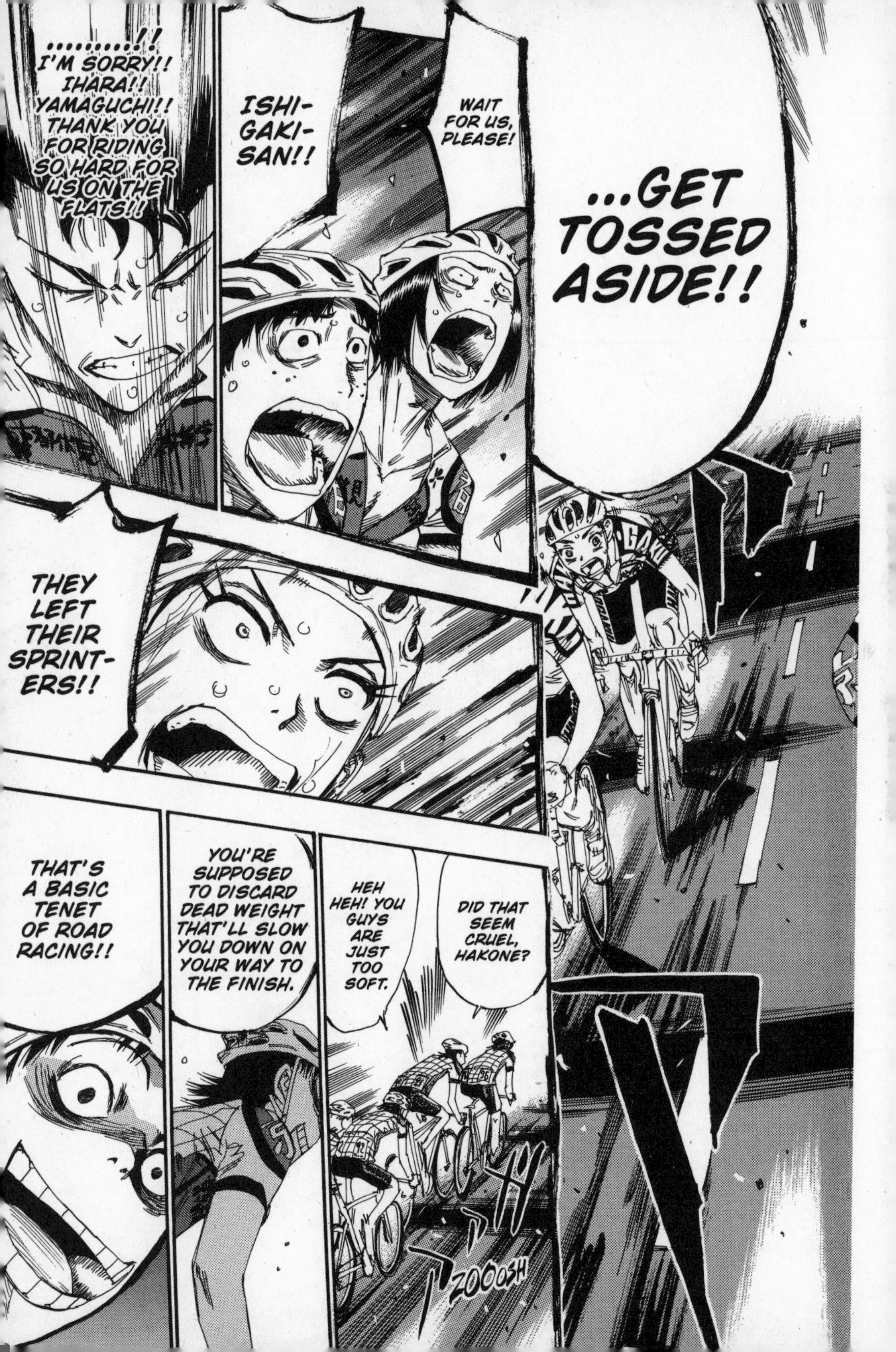
...GET TOSSED ASIDE!!
WAIT FOR US, PLEASE!
ISHI-GAKI-SAN!!
..........!! I'M SORRY!! IHARA!! YAMAGUCHI!! THANK YOU FOR RIDING SO HARD FOR US ON THE FLATS!!
THEY LEFT THEIR SPRINT-ERS!!
DID THAT SEEM CRUEL, HAKONE?
HEH HEH! YOU GUYS ARE JUST TOO SOFT.
ZOOOSH
YOU'RE SUPPOSED TO DISCARD DEAD WEIGHT THAT'LL SLOW YOU DOWN ON YOUR WAY TO THE FINISH.
THAT'S A BASIC TENET OF ROAD RACING!!

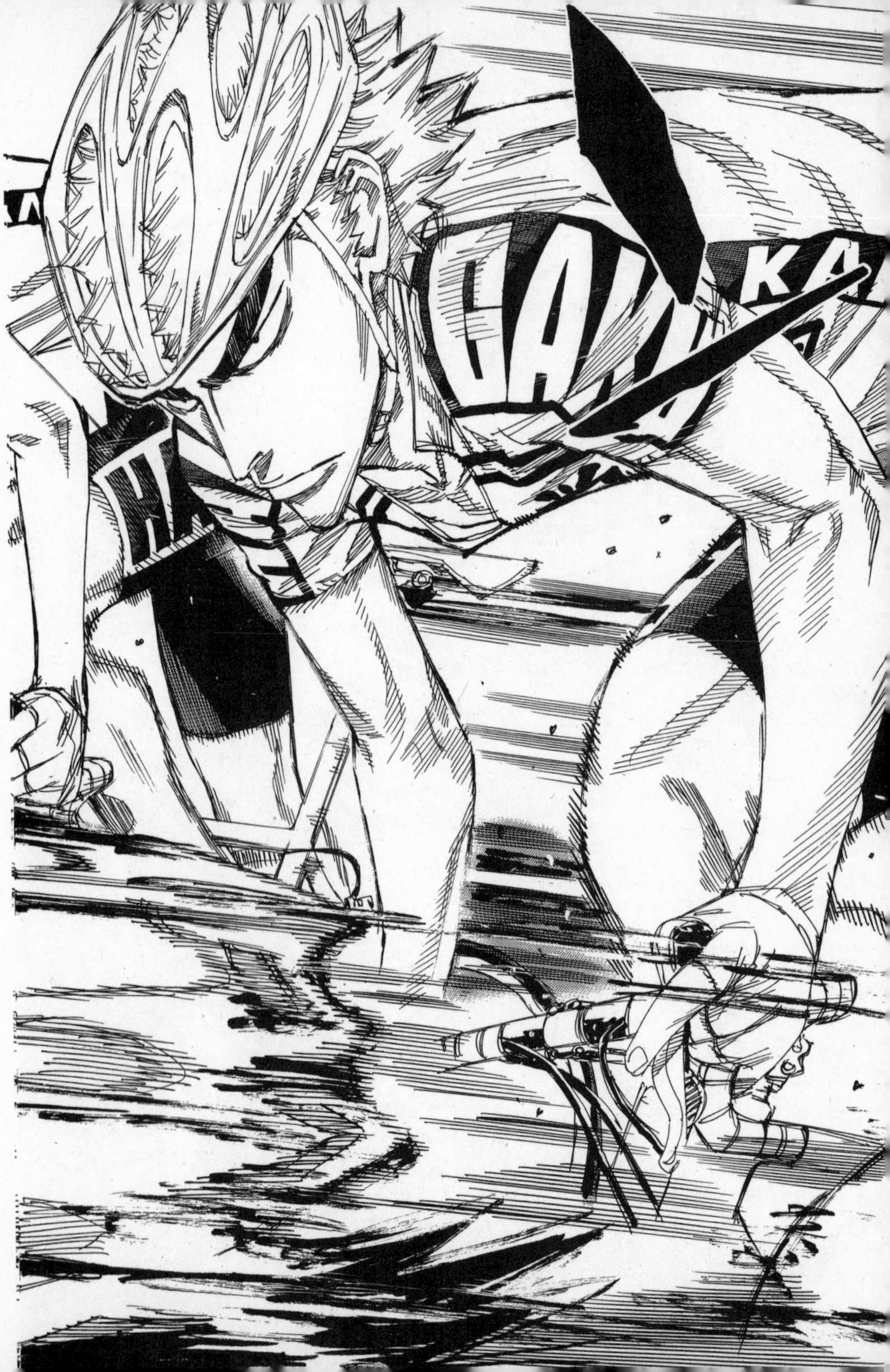
KA

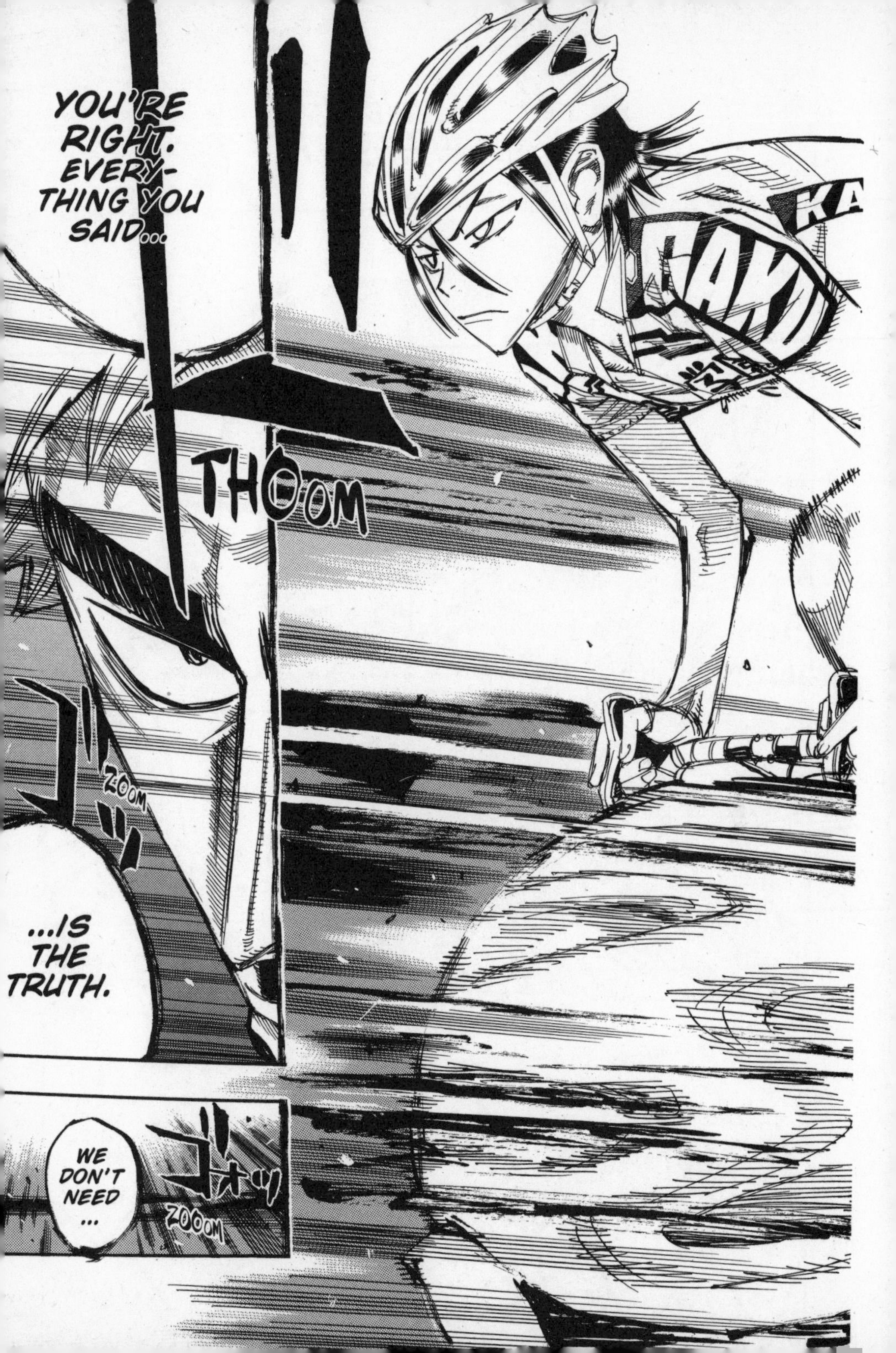
YOU'RE RIGHT. EVERYTHING YOU SAID...
THOOM
ZOOM
...IS THE TRUTH.
WE DON'T NEED ...
ZOOM

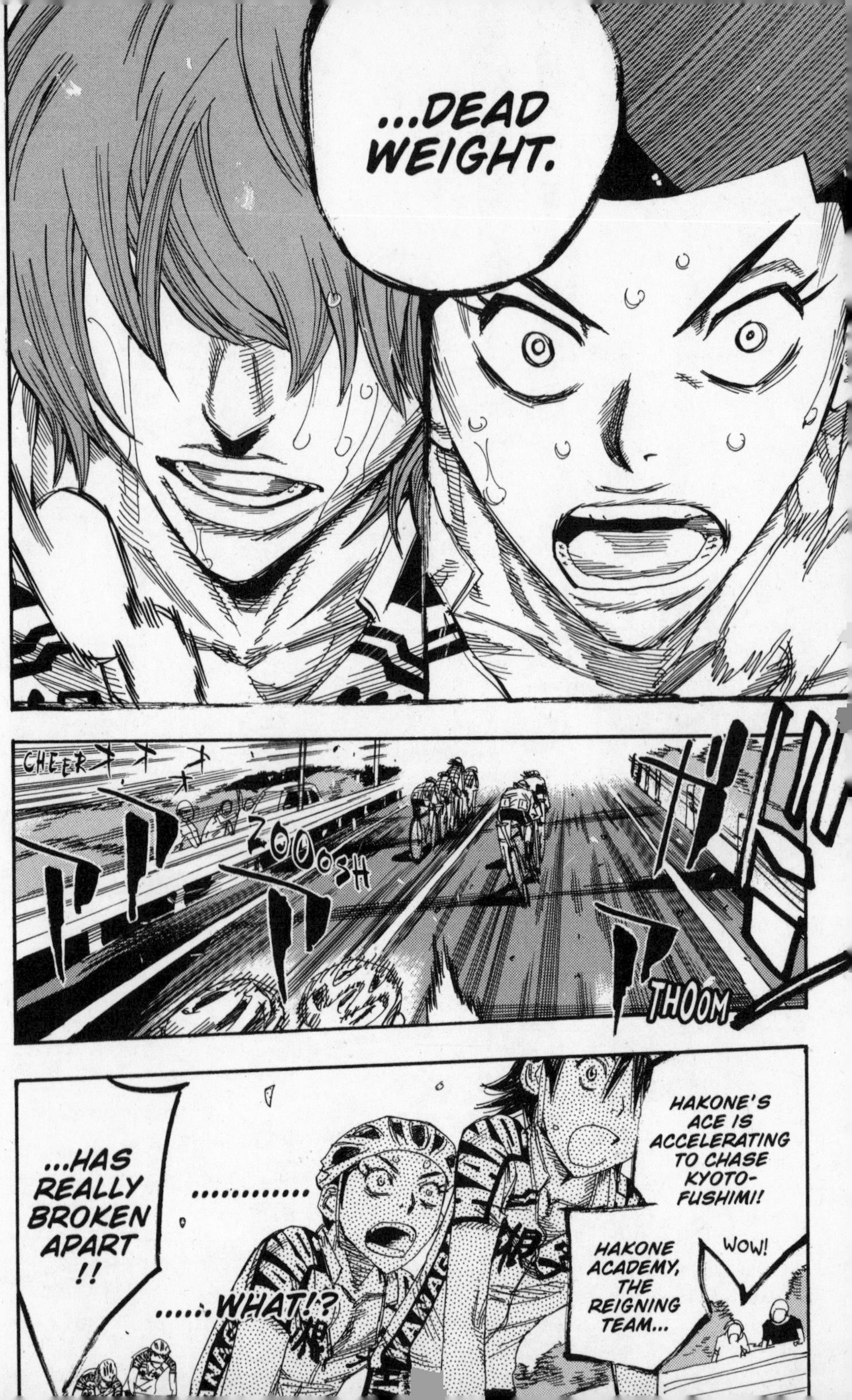
...DEAD WEIGHT.
THOOM
ZOOOSH
CHEER
HAKONE'S ACE IS ACCELERATING TO CHASE KYOTO-FUSHIMI!
WOW!
HAKONE ACADEMY, THE REIGNING TEAM...
...HAS REALLY BROKEN APART!!
....
.....WHAT!?

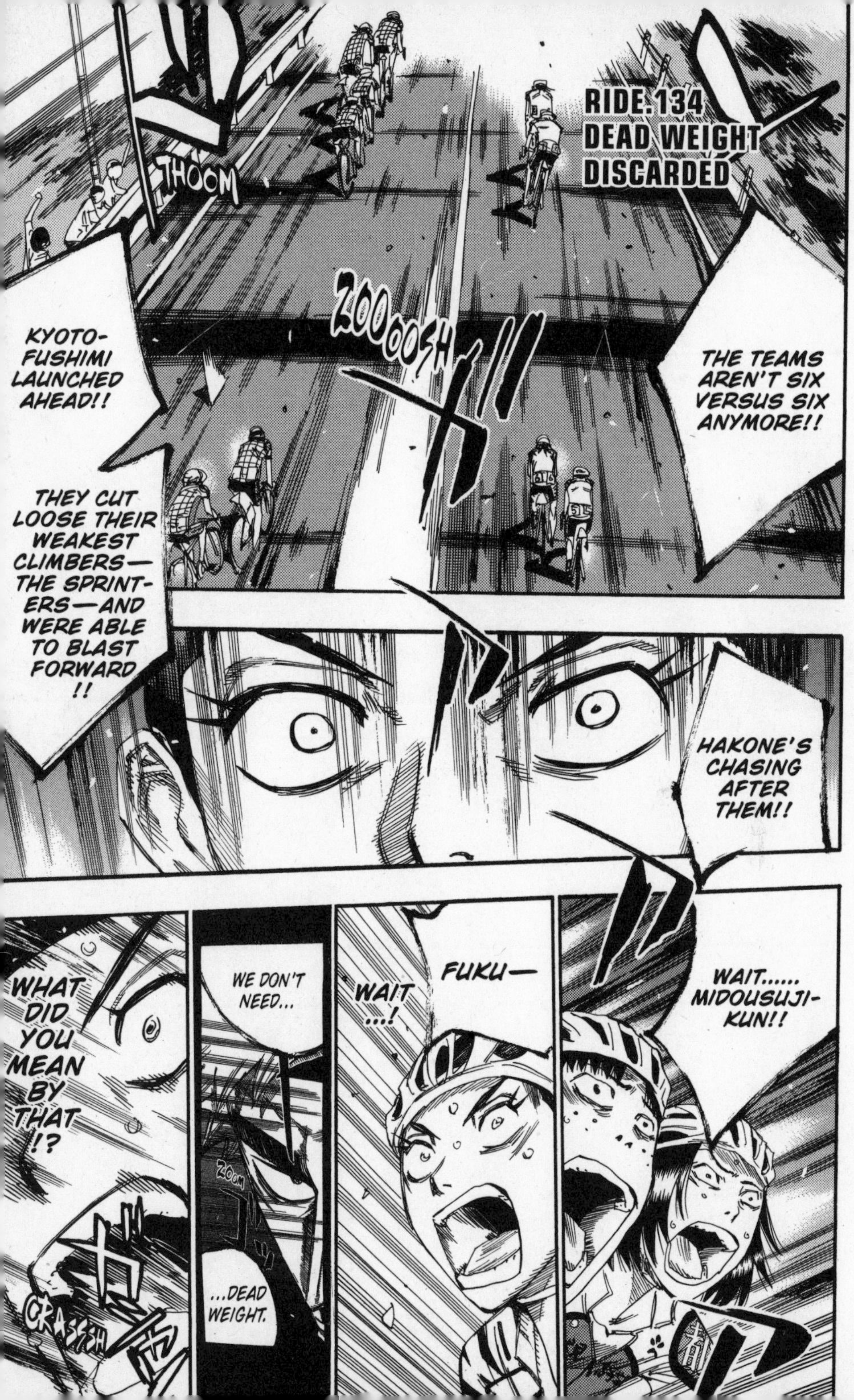
RIDE. 134
DEAD WEIGHT DISCARDED
THOOM
ZOOOOSH
THE TEAMS AREN'T SIX VERSUS SIX ANYMORE!!
KYOTO-FUSHIMI LAUNCHED AHEAD!!
THEY CUT LOOSE THEIR WEAKEST CLIMBERS—THE SPRINT-ERS—AND WERE ABLE TO BLAST FORWARD!!
HAKONE'S CHASING AFTER THEM!!
WAIT...... MIDOUSUJI-KUN!!
FUKU—
WAIT ...!
WE DON'T NEED...
...DEAD WEIGHT.
ZOOM
WHAT DID YOU MEAN BY THAT!?
CRASSH

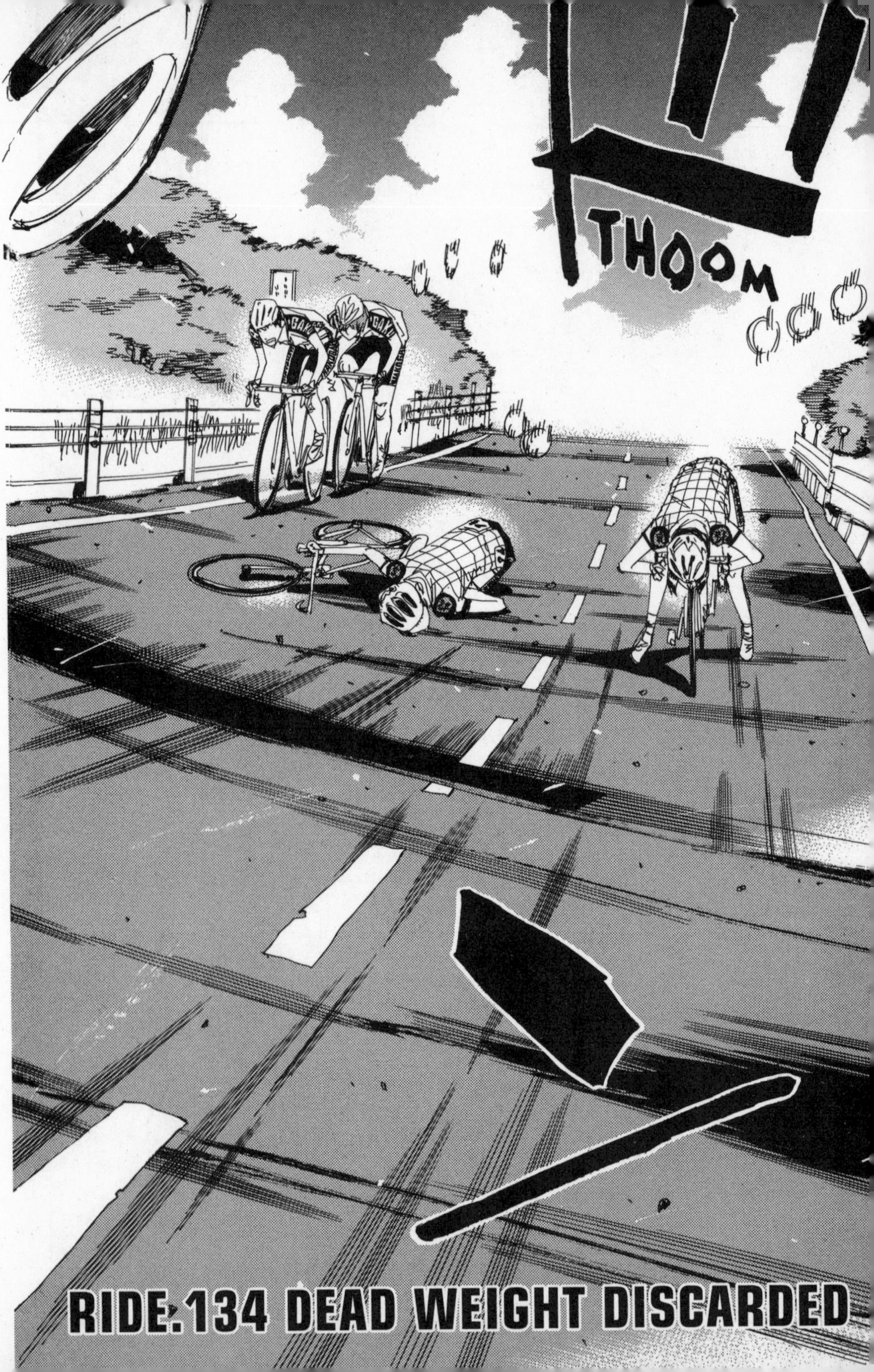
THOOM
RIDE.134 DEAD WEIGHT DISCARDED

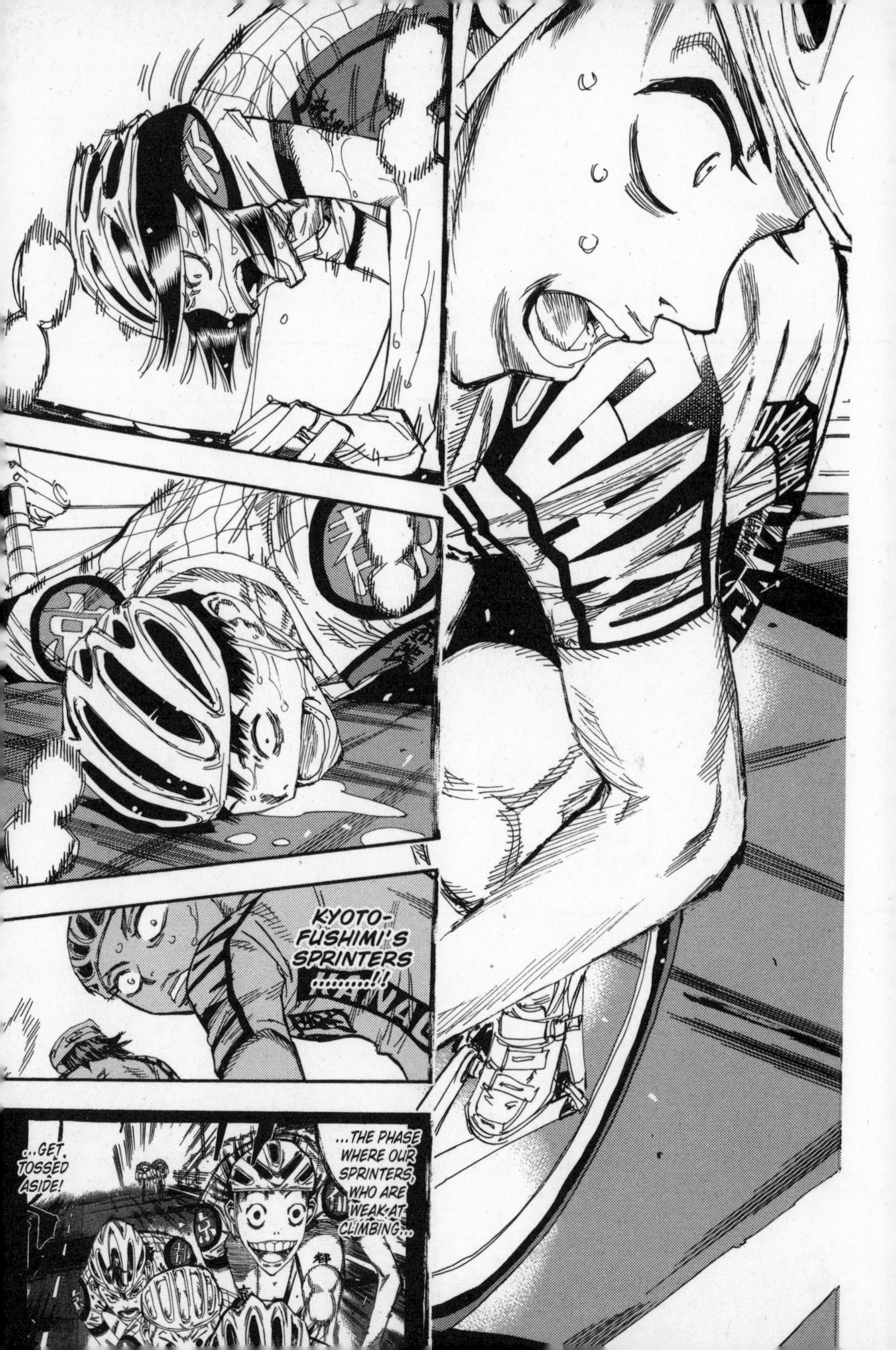
KYOTO-FUSHIMI'S SPRINTERS ....!!
...THE PHASE WHERE OUR SPRINTERS, WHO ARE WEAK AT CLIMBING...
...GET TOSSED ASIDE!

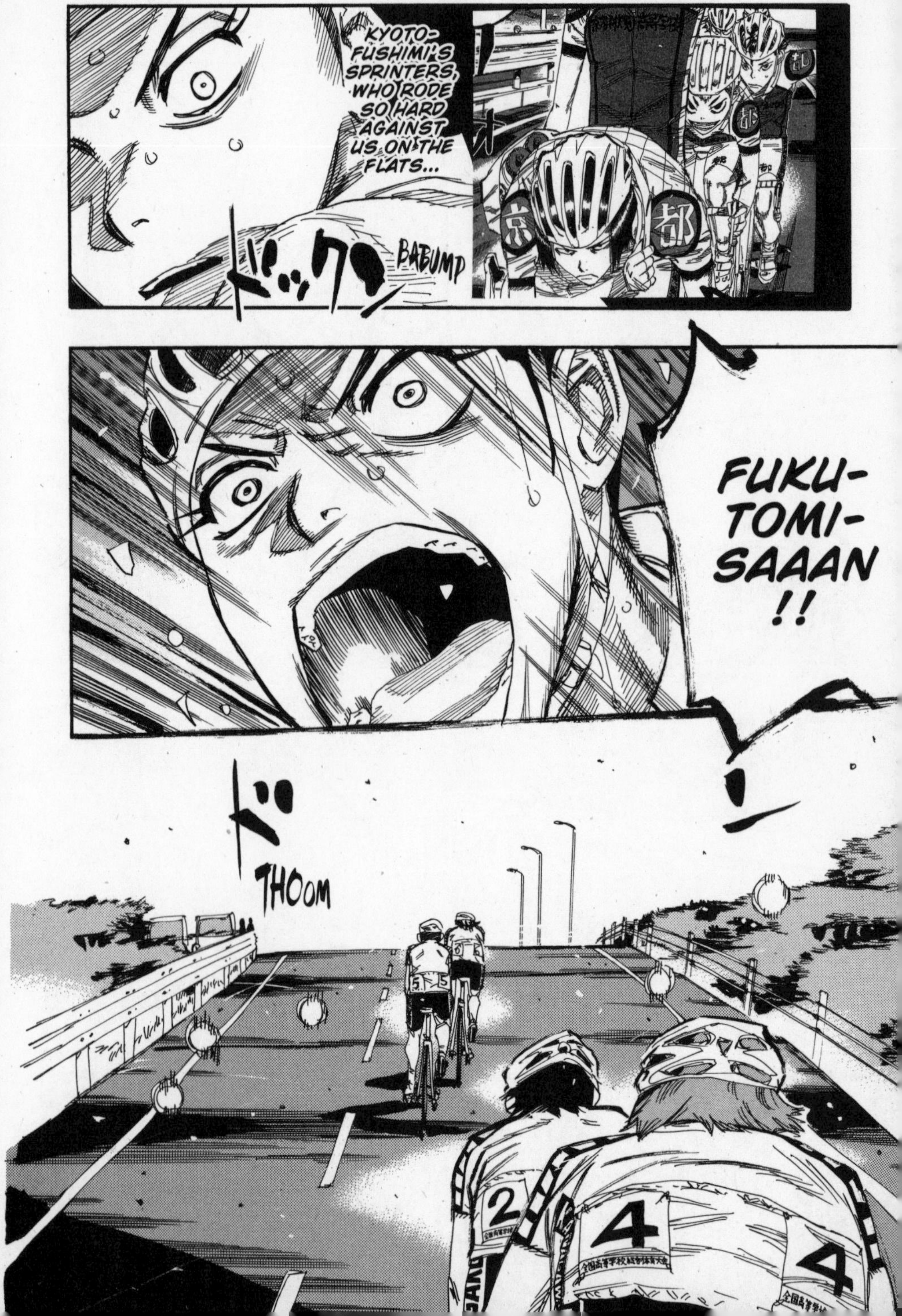
KYOTO-FUSHIMI'S SPRINTERS, WHO RODE SO HARD AGAINST US ON THE FLATS...
ドックン
BABUMP
FUKUTOMI-SAAAN!!
ド
THOOM

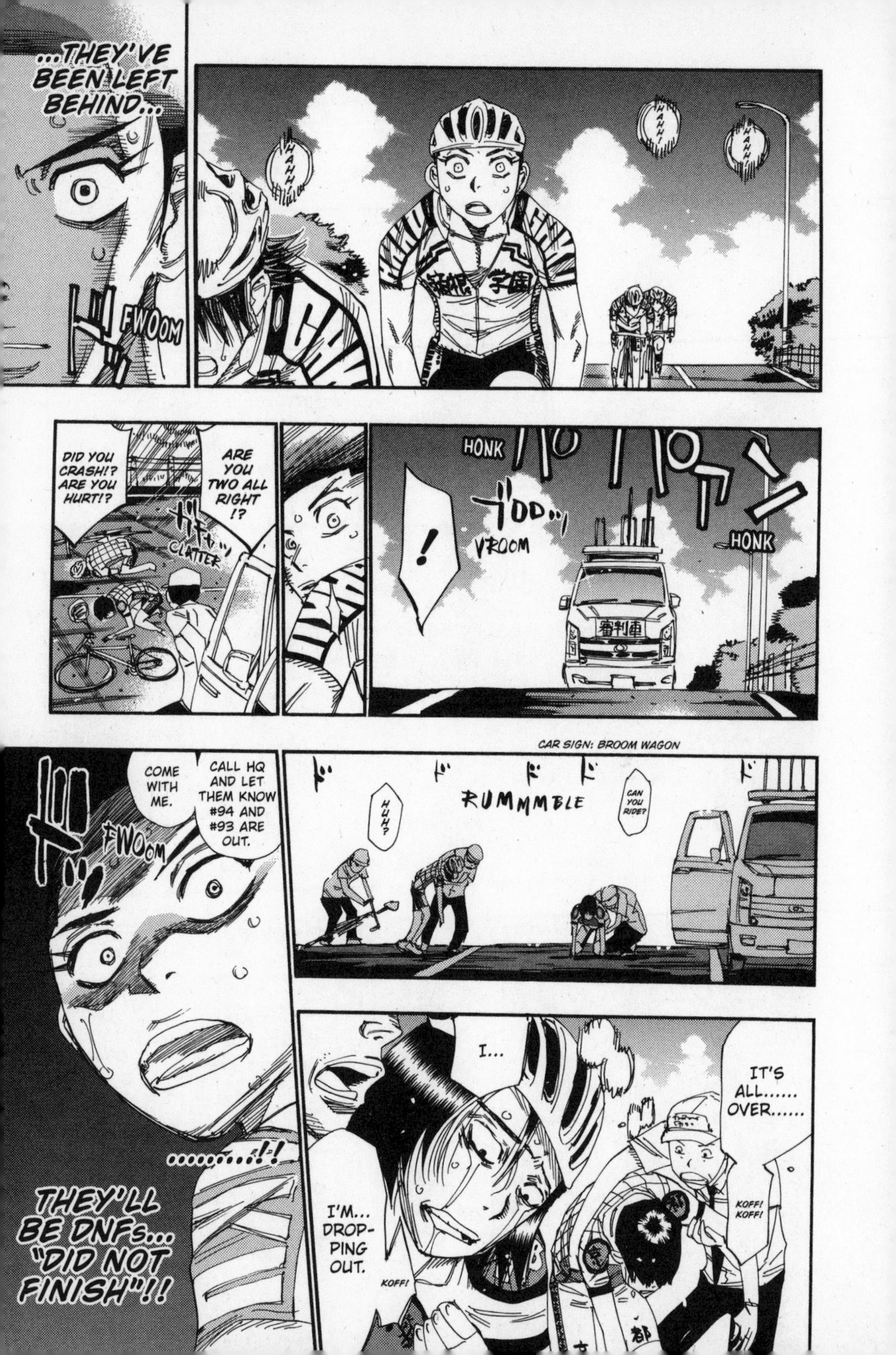
HAHH!
HAHH!
HAHH!
...THEY'VE BEEN LEFT BEHIND...
FWOOM
HONK
!
VROOM
HONK
CAR SIGN: BROOM WAGON
ARE YOU TWO ALL RIGHT!?
DID YOU CRASH!? ARE YOU HURT!?
CLATTER
RUMMMBLE
CAN YOU RIDE?
HUH?
IT'S ALL...... OVER......
I...
I'M... DROPPING OUT.
KOFF! KOFF!
KOFF!
CALL HQ AND LET THEM KNOW #94 AND #93 ARE OUT.
COME WITH ME.
FWOOM
.........!!
THEY'LL BE DNFs... "DID NOT FINISH"!!

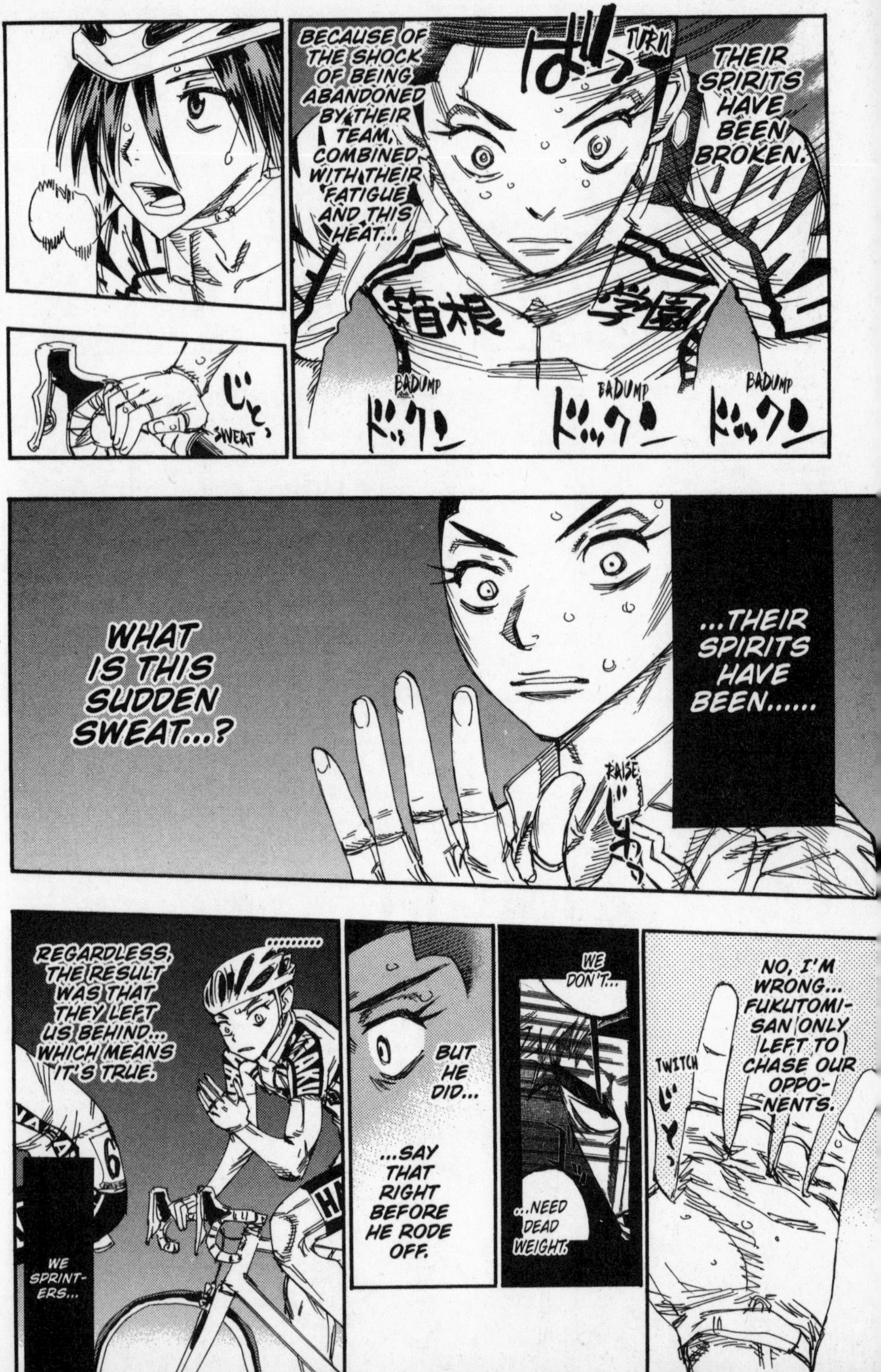

THEIR SPIRITS HAVE BEEN BROKEN.
TURN
BECAUSE OF THE SHOCK OF BEING ABANDONED BY THEIR TEAM, COMBINED WITH THEIR FATIGUE AND THIS HEAT...
箱根学園
BADUMP
BADUMP
BADUMP
SWEAT
...THEIR SPIRITS HAVE BEEN......
RAISE
WHAT IS THIS SUDDEN SWEAT...?
NO, I'M WRONG... FUKUTOMI-SAN ONLY LEFT TO CHASE OUR OPPONENTS.
TWITCH
WE DON'T...
...NEED DEAD WEIGHT.
BUT HE DID...
...SAY THAT RIGHT BEFORE HE RODE OFF.
....
REGARDLESS, THE RESULT WAS THAT THEY LEFT US BEHIND... WHICH MEANS IT'S TRUE.
WE SPRINTERS...

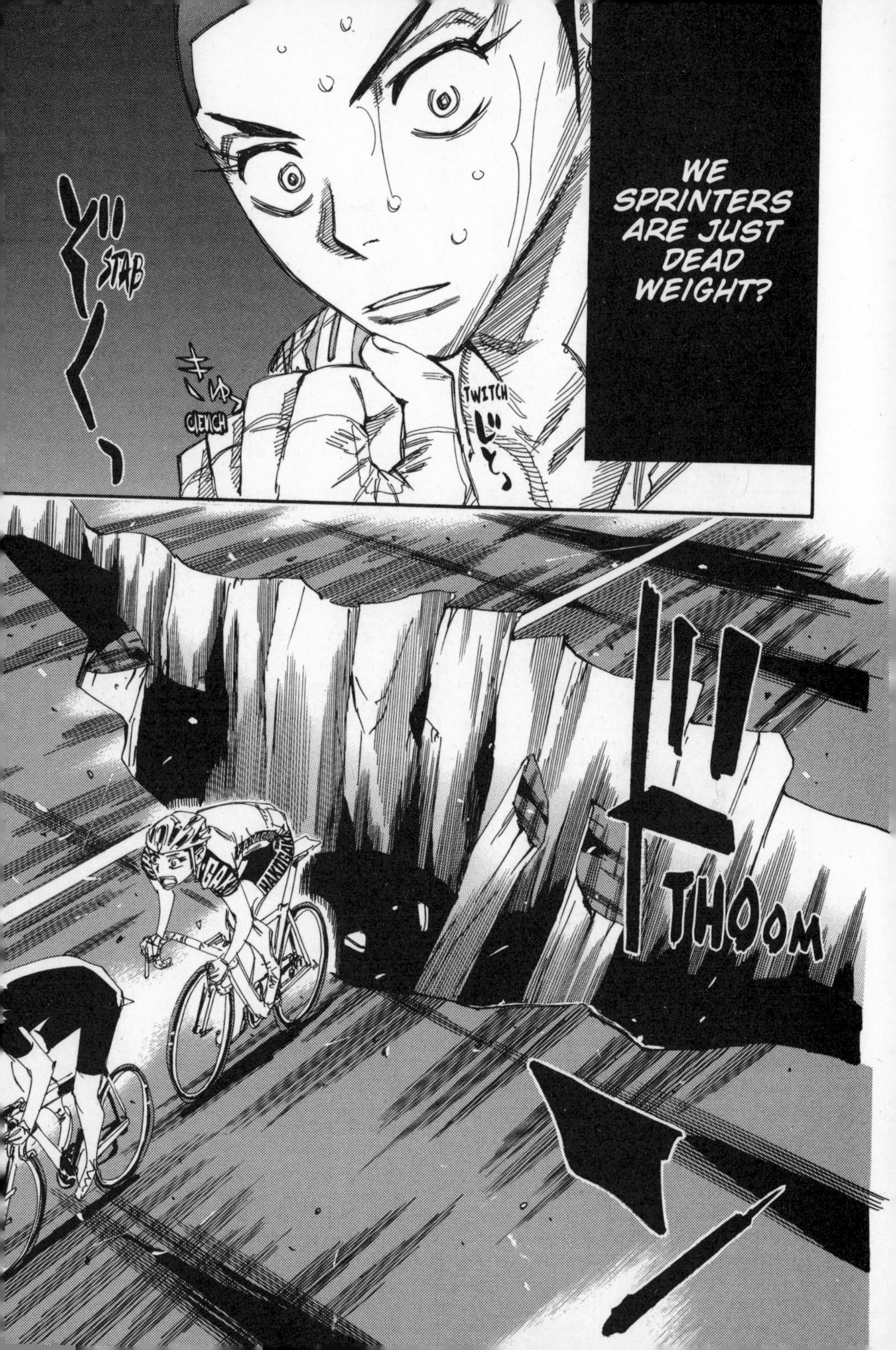
WE SPRINTERS ARE JUST DEAD WEIGHT?
TWITCH
CLENCH
STAB
THOOM

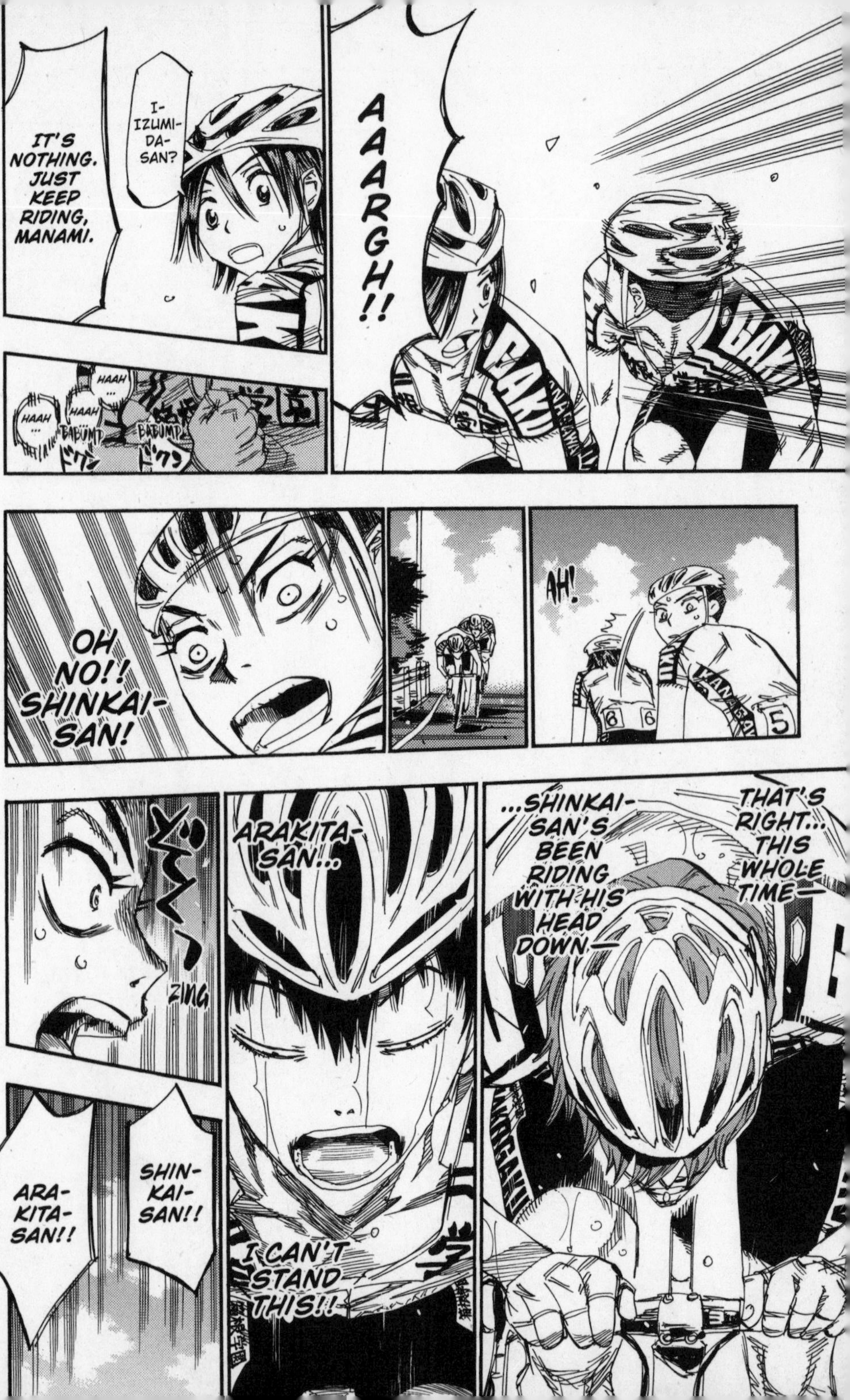
AAAARGH!!
I-IZUMI-DA-SAN?
IT'S NOTHING. JUST KEEP RIDING, MANAMI.
HAAH...
HAAH
HAAH...
BABUMP
BABUMP
AH!
OH NO!! SHINKAI-SAN!
THAT'S RIGHT... THIS WHOLE TIME—
...SHINKAI-SAN'S BEEN RIDING WITH HIS HEAD DOWN—
ARAKITA-SAN...
I CAN'T STAND THIS!!
ZING
SHIN-KAI-SAN!!
ARA-KITA-SAN!!

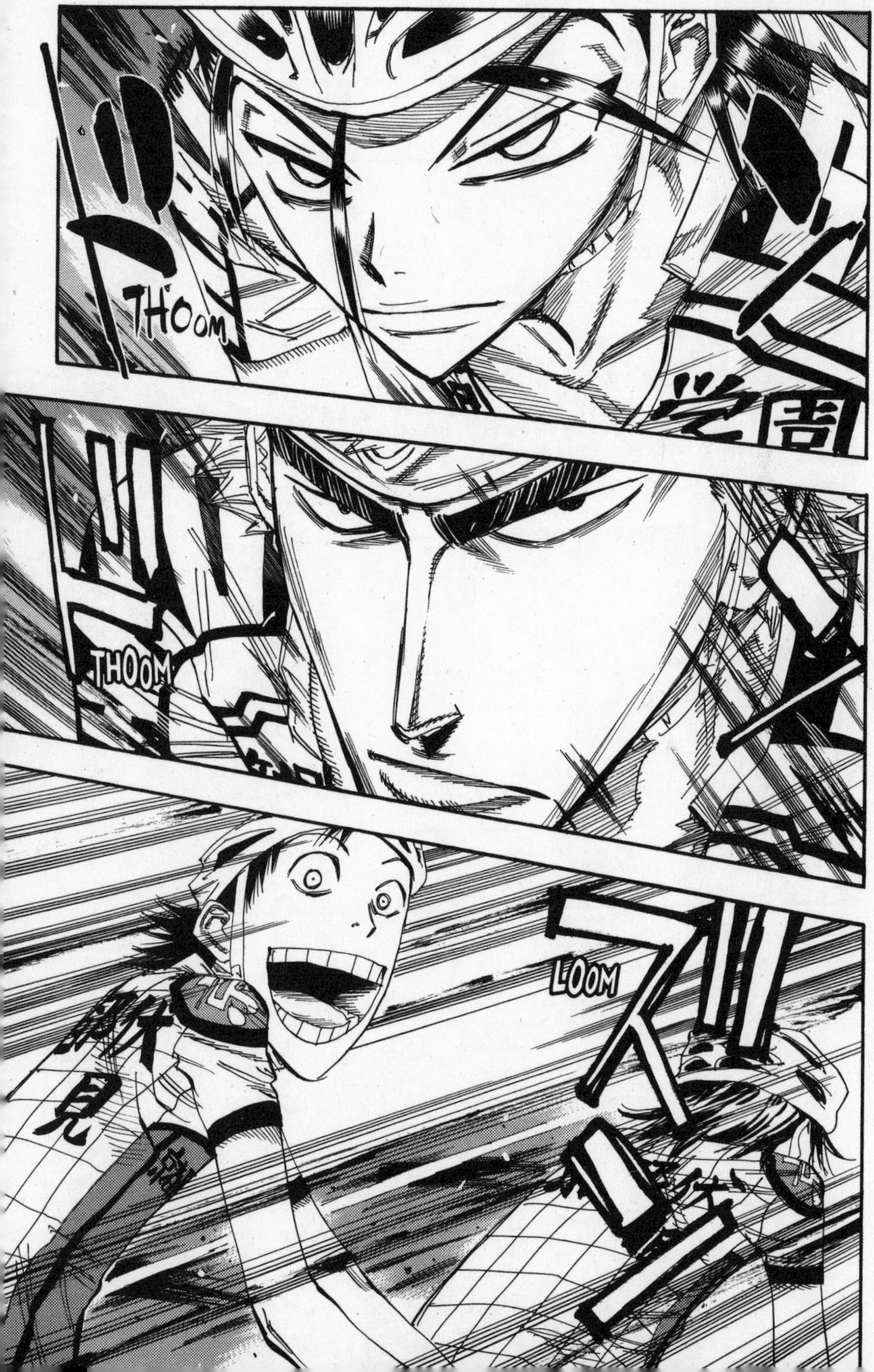
THOOM
THOOM
LOOM

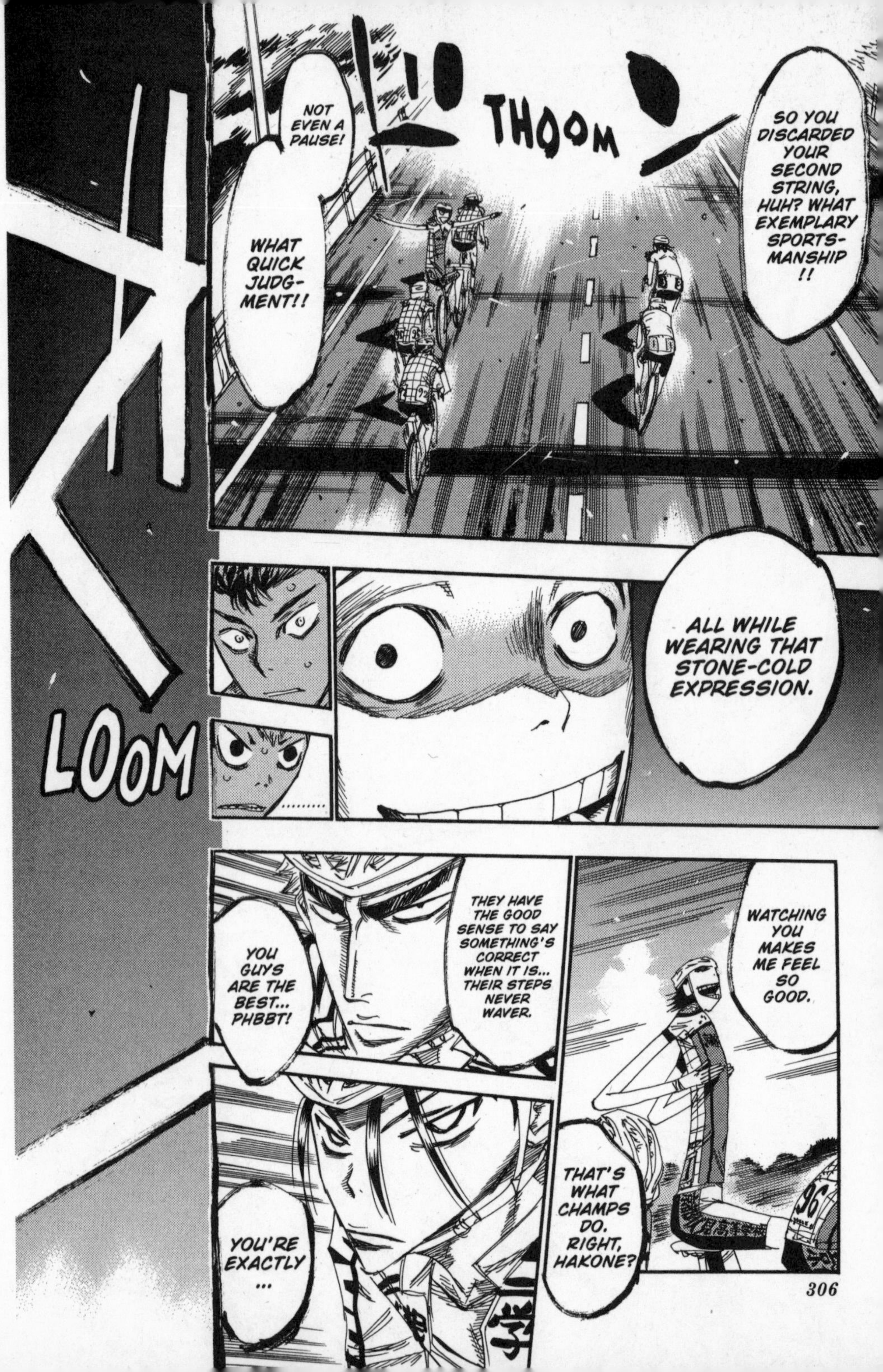
SO YOU DISCARDED YOUR SECOND STRING, HUH? WHAT EXEMPLARY SPORTS-MANSHIP!!
THOOM
NOT EVEN A PAUSE!
WHAT QUICK JUDG-MENT!!
ALL WHILE WEARING THAT STONE-COLD EXPRESSION.
....
LOOM
WATCHING YOU MAKES ME FEEL SO GOOD.
THAT'S WHAT CHAMPS DO. RIGHT, HAKONE?
THEY HAVE THE GOOD SENSE TO SAY SOMETHING'S CORRECT WHEN IT IS... THEIR STEPS NEVER WAVER.
YOU GUYS ARE THE BEST... PHBBT!
YOU'RE EXACTLY ...

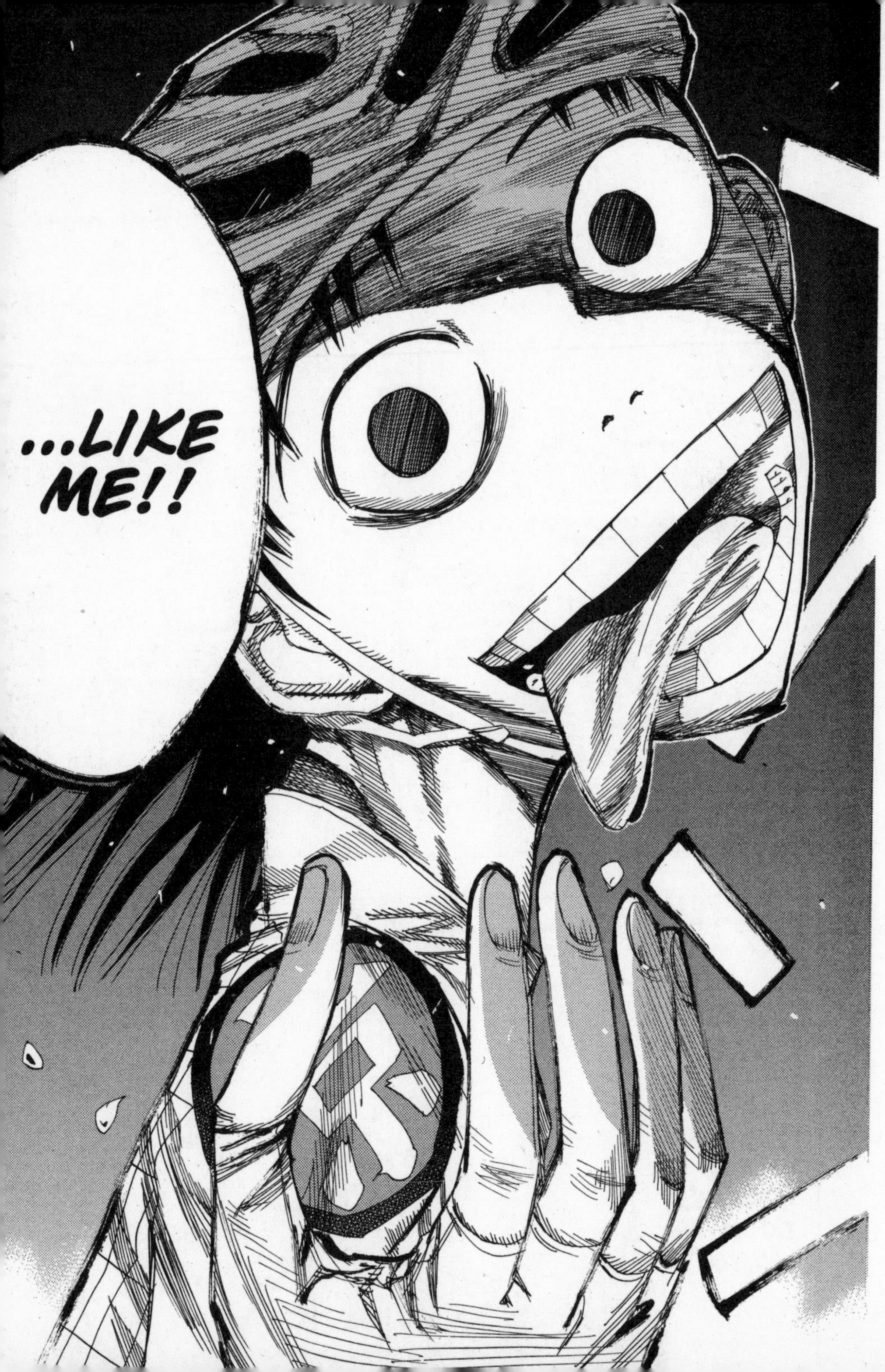
...LIKE ME!!

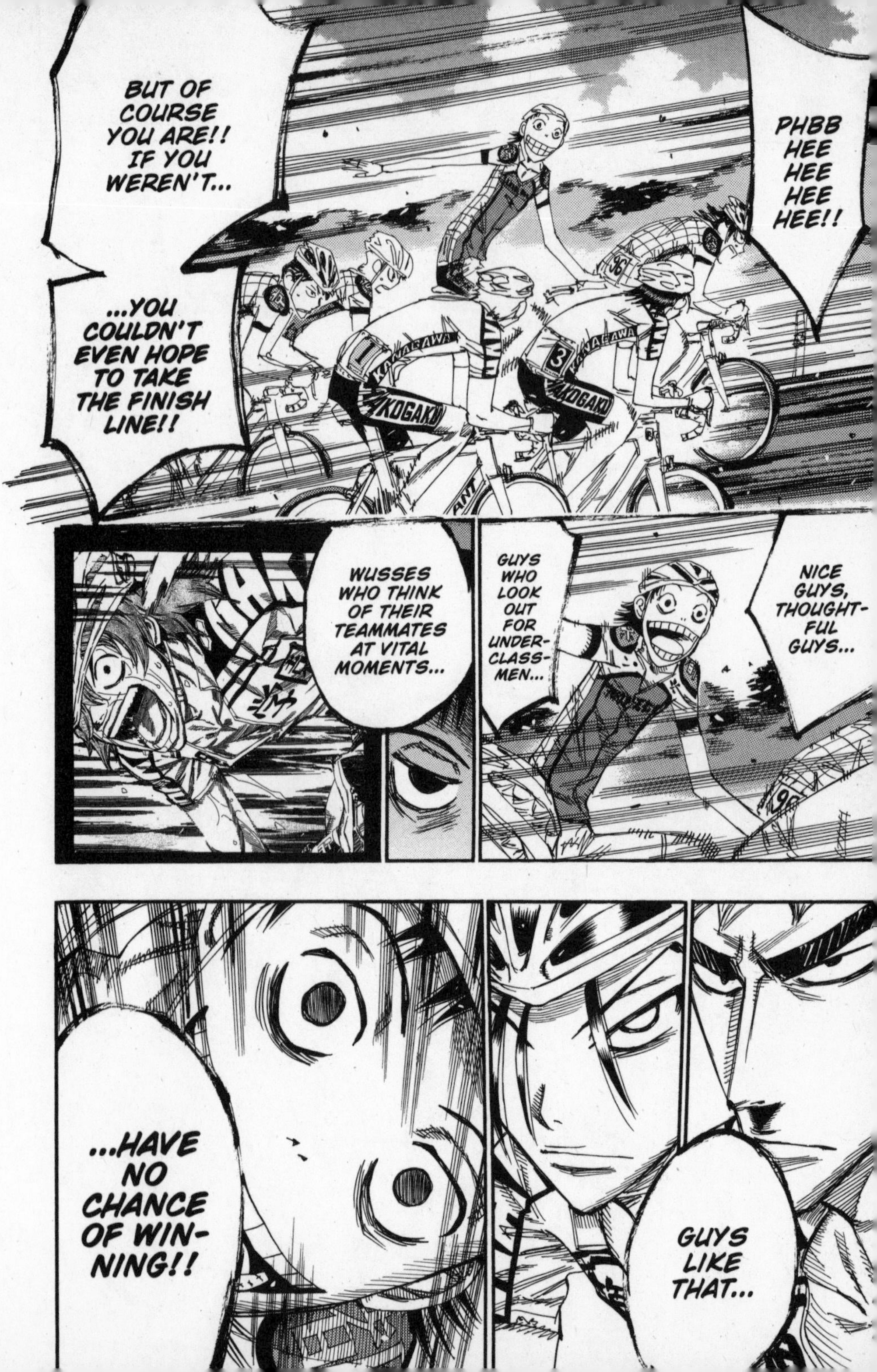
PHBB HEE HEE HEE HEE!!
BUT OF COURSE YOU ARE!! IF YOU WEREN'T...
...YOU COULDN'T EVEN HOPE TO TAKE THE FINISH LINE!!
NICE GUYS, THOUGHT-FUL GUYS...
GUYS WHO LOOK OUT FOR UNDER-CLASS-MEN...
WUSSES WHO THINK OF THEIR TEAMMATES AT VITAL MOMENTS...
GUYS LIKE THAT...
...HAVE NO CHANCE OF WIN-NING!!

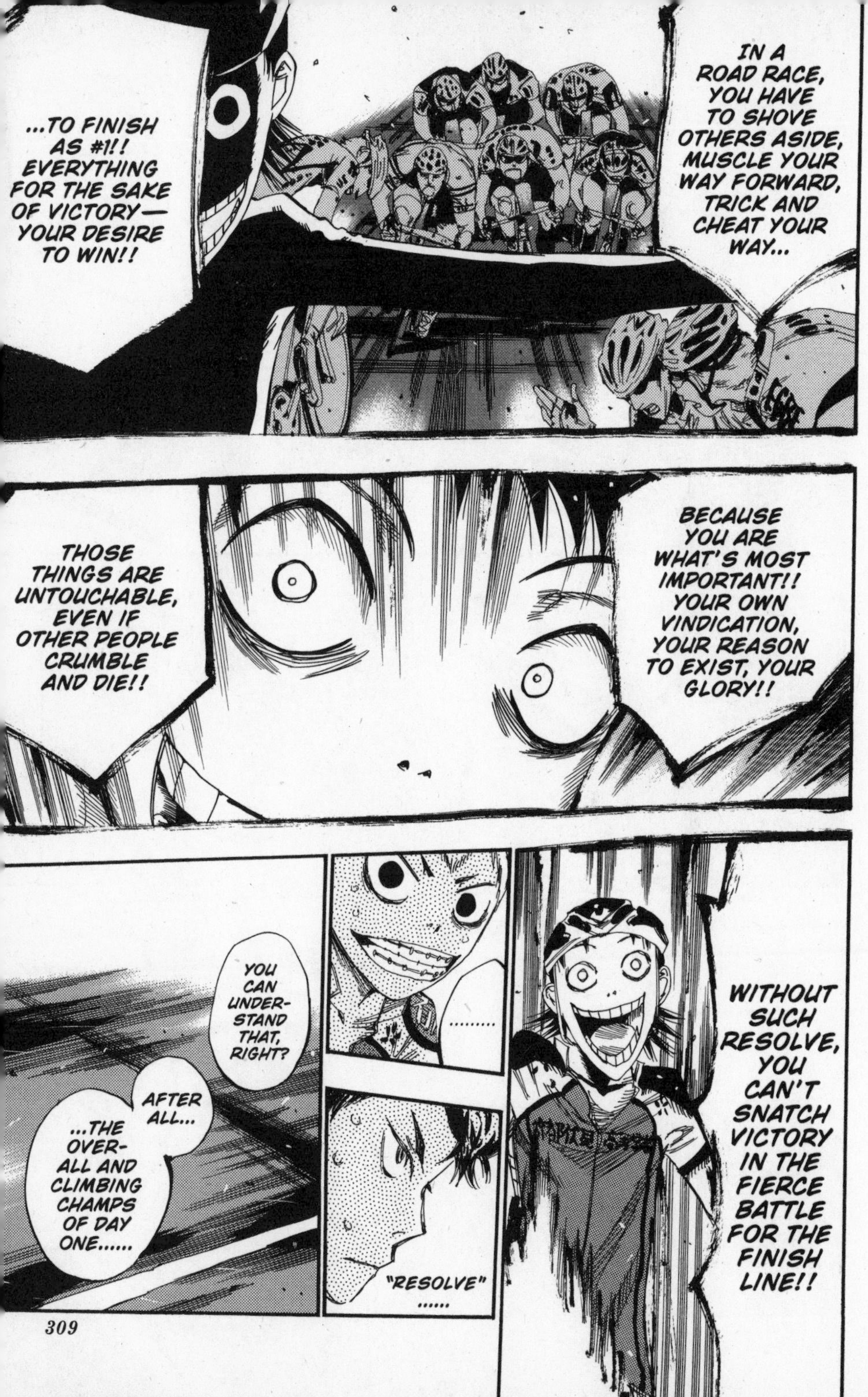
IN A ROAD RACE, YOU HAVE TO SHOVE OTHERS ASIDE, MUSCLE YOUR WAY FORWARD, TRICK AND CHEAT YOUR WAY...
...TO FINISH AS #1!! EVERYTHING FOR THE SAKE OF VICTORY—YOUR DESIRE TO WIN!!
BECAUSE YOU ARE WHAT'S MOST IMPORTANT!! YOUR OWN VINDICATION, YOUR REASON TO EXIST, YOUR GLORY!!
THOSE THINGS ARE UNTOUCHABLE, EVEN IF OTHER PEOPLE CRUMBLE AND DIE!!
WITHOUT SUCH RESOLVE, YOU CAN'T SNATCH VICTORY IN THE FIERCE BATTLE FOR THE FINISH LINE!!
YOU CAN UNDER-STAND THAT, RIGHT?
....
"RESOLVE"......
AFTER ALL...
...THE OVER-ALL AND CLIMBING CHAMPS OF DAY ONE......

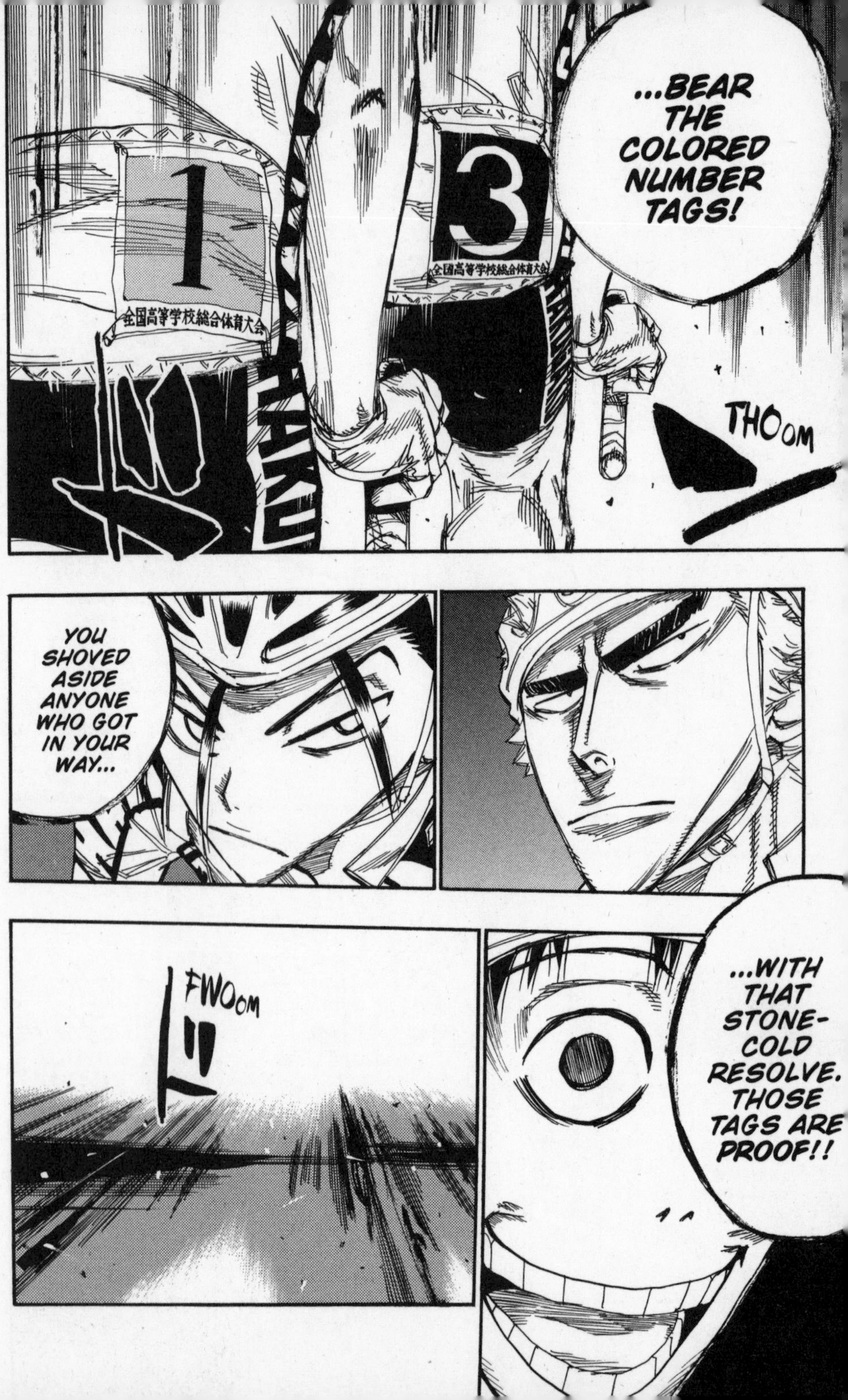
...BEAR THE COLORED NUMBER TAGS!
1
3
全国高等学校総合体育大会
THOom
YOU SHOVED ASIDE ANYONE WHO GOT IN YOUR WAY...
...WITH THAT STONE-COLD RESOLVE. THOSE TAGS ARE PROOF!!
FWOom

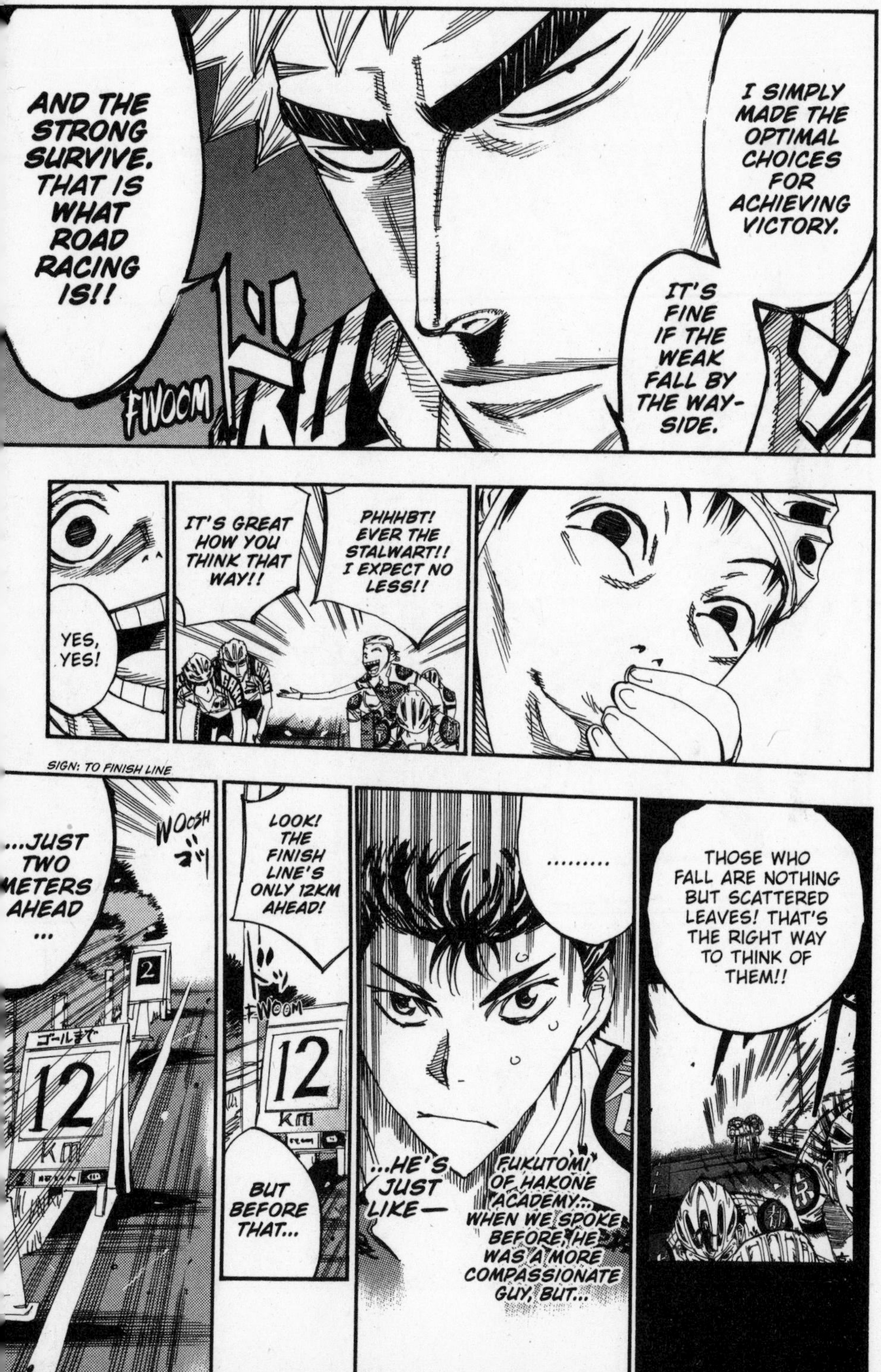
I SIMPLY MADE THE OPTIMAL CHOICES FOR ACHIEVING VICTORY.
IT'S FINE IF THE WEAK FALL BY THE WAY-SIDE.
AND THE STRONG SURVIVE. THAT IS WHAT ROAD RACING IS!!
FWOOM
PHHHBT! EVER THE STALWART!! I EXPECT NO LESS!!
IT'S GREAT HOW YOU THINK THAT WAY!!
YES, YES!
SIGN: TO FINISH LINE
THOSE WHO FALL ARE NOTHING BUT SCATTERED LEAVES! THAT'S THE RIGHT WAY TO THINK OF THEM!!
....
FUKUTOMI OF HAKONE ACADEMY... WHEN WE SPOKE BEFORE, HE WAS A MORE COMPASSIONATE GUY, BUT...
...HE'S JUST LIKE—
LOOK! THE FINISH LINE'S ONLY 12KM AHEAD!
FWOOM
12 km
BUT BEFORE THAT...
WOOSH
...JUST TWO METERS AHEAD ...
ゴールまで
12 km

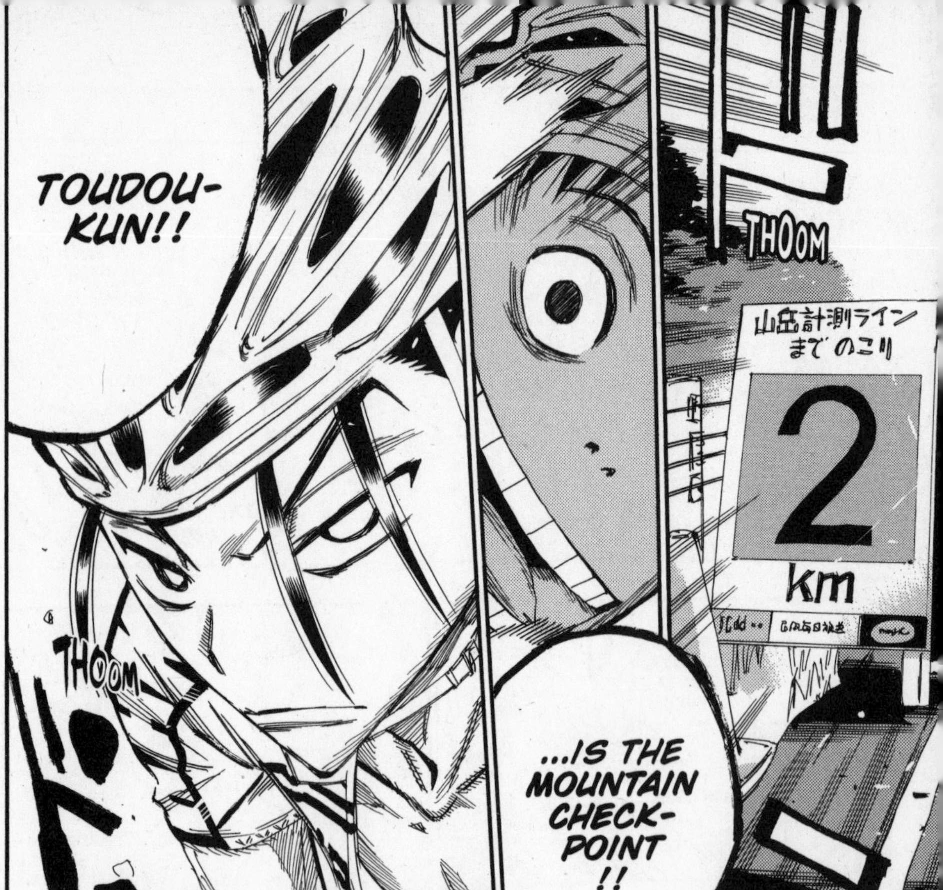
THOOM
山岳計測ライン
までのこり
2
km
...IS THE MOUNTAIN CHECKPOINT!!
TOUDOU-KUN!!
THOOM

SIGN: DISTANCE TO MOUNTAIN CHECKPOINT

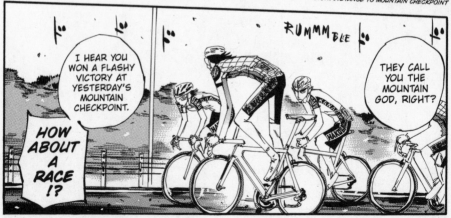

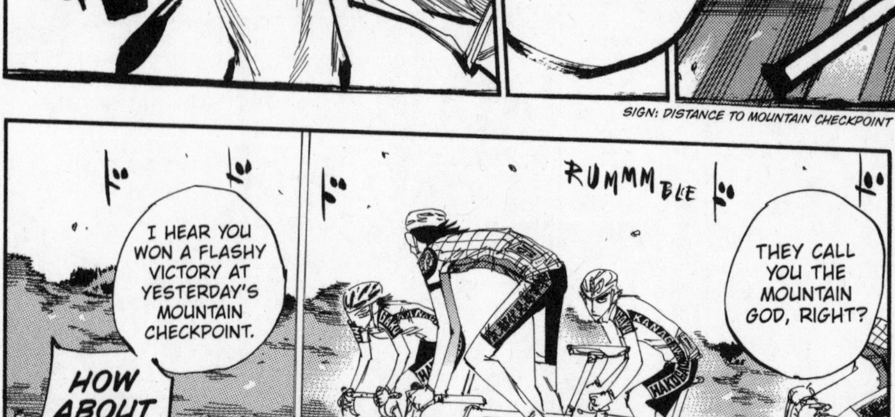
RUMMMBLE
THEY CALL YOU THE MOUNTAIN GOD, RIGHT?
I HEAR YOU WON A FLASHY VICTORY AT YESTERDAY'S MOUNTAIN CHECKPOINT.
HOW ABOUT A RACE!?

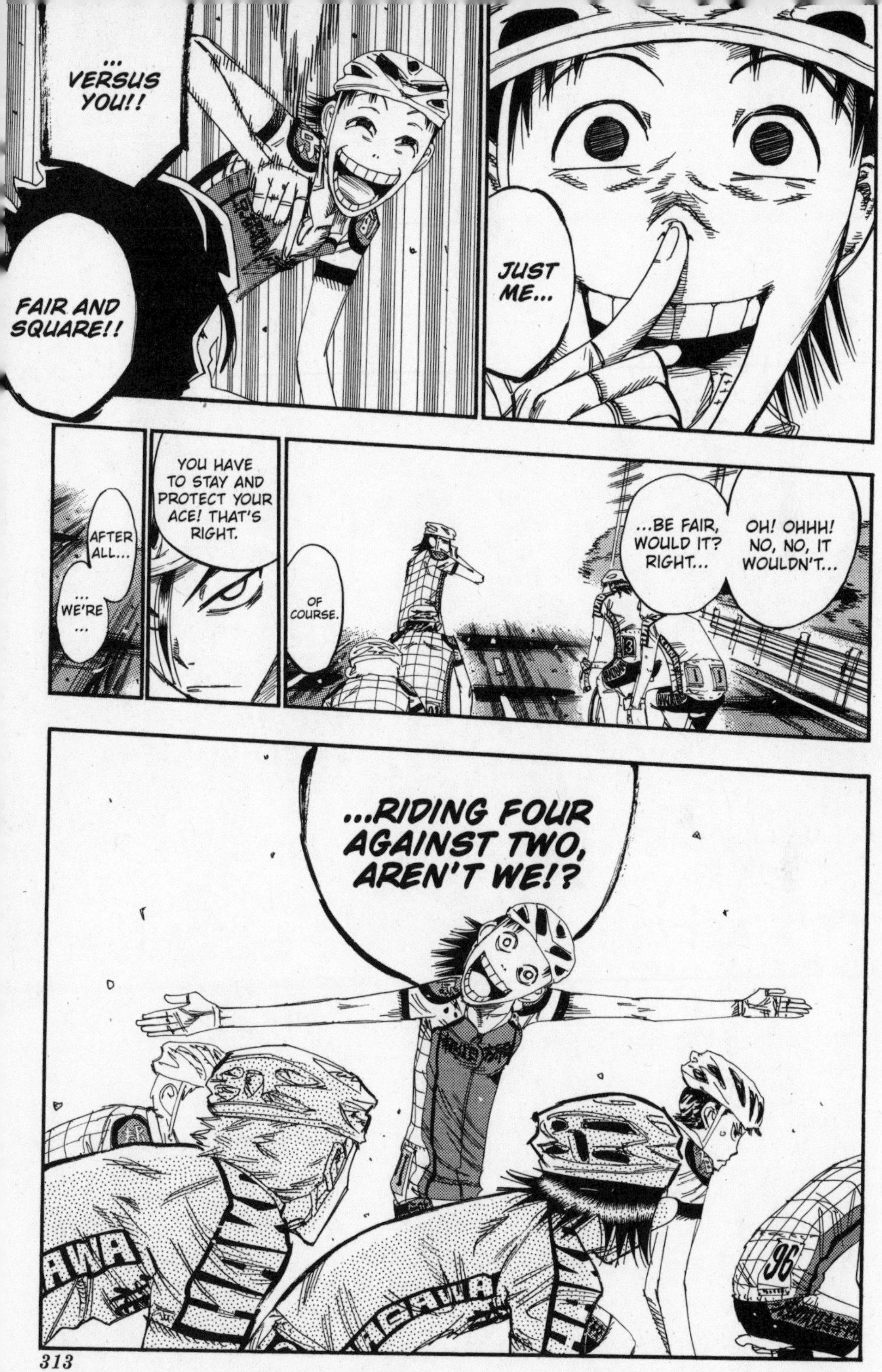
JUST ME...
...VERSUS YOU!!
FAIR AND SQUARE!!
OH! OHHH! NO, NO, IT WOULDN'T...
...BE FAIR, WOULD IT? RIGHT...
OF COURSE.
YOU HAVE TO STAY AND PROTECT YOUR ACE! THAT'S RIGHT.
AFTER ALL...
...WE'RE...
...RIDING FOUR AGAINST TWO, AREN'T WE!?

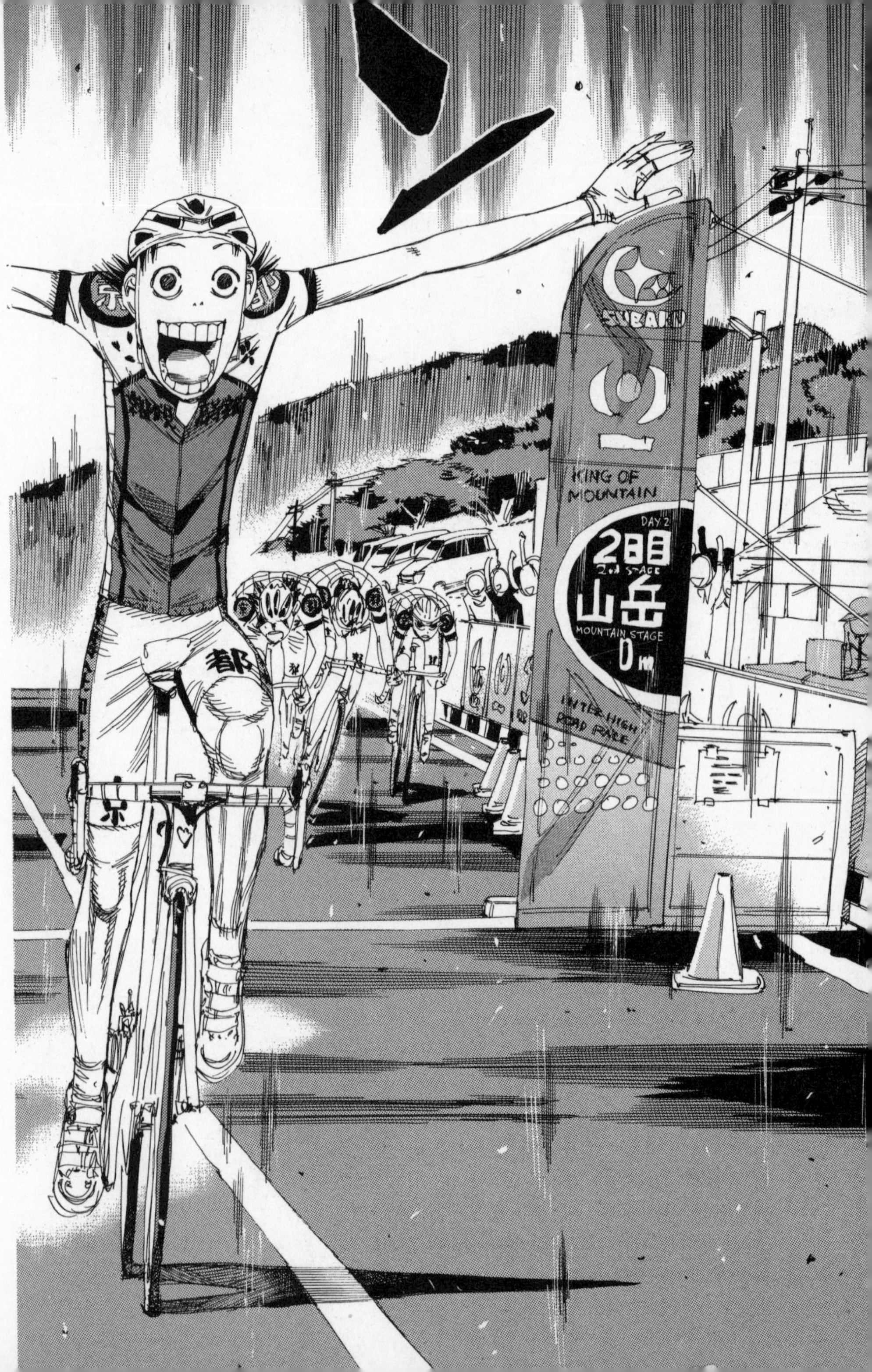
KING OF MOUNTAIN
DAY 2
2日目
2nd STAGE
山岳
MOUNTAIN STAGE
0m
INTER HIGH ROAD RACE

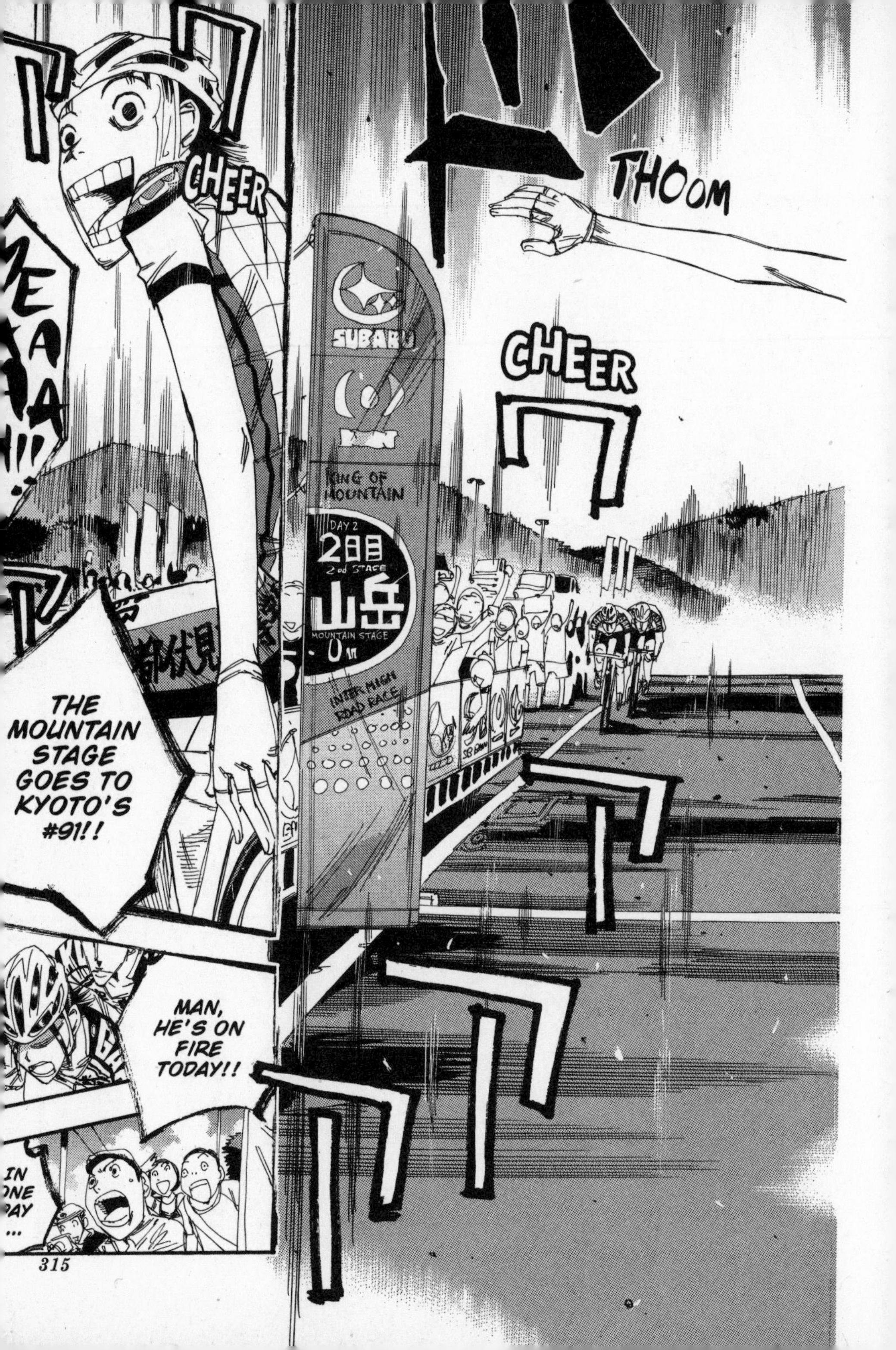
THOOM
CHEER
SUBARU
KING OF MOUNTAIN
DAY 2
2日目
2nd STAGE
山岳
MOUNTAIN STAGE
0m
INTER HIGH ROAD RACE
CHEER
THE MOUNTAIN STAGE GOES TO KYOTO'S #91!!
MAN, HE'S ON FIRE TODAY!!
IN ONE AY ...

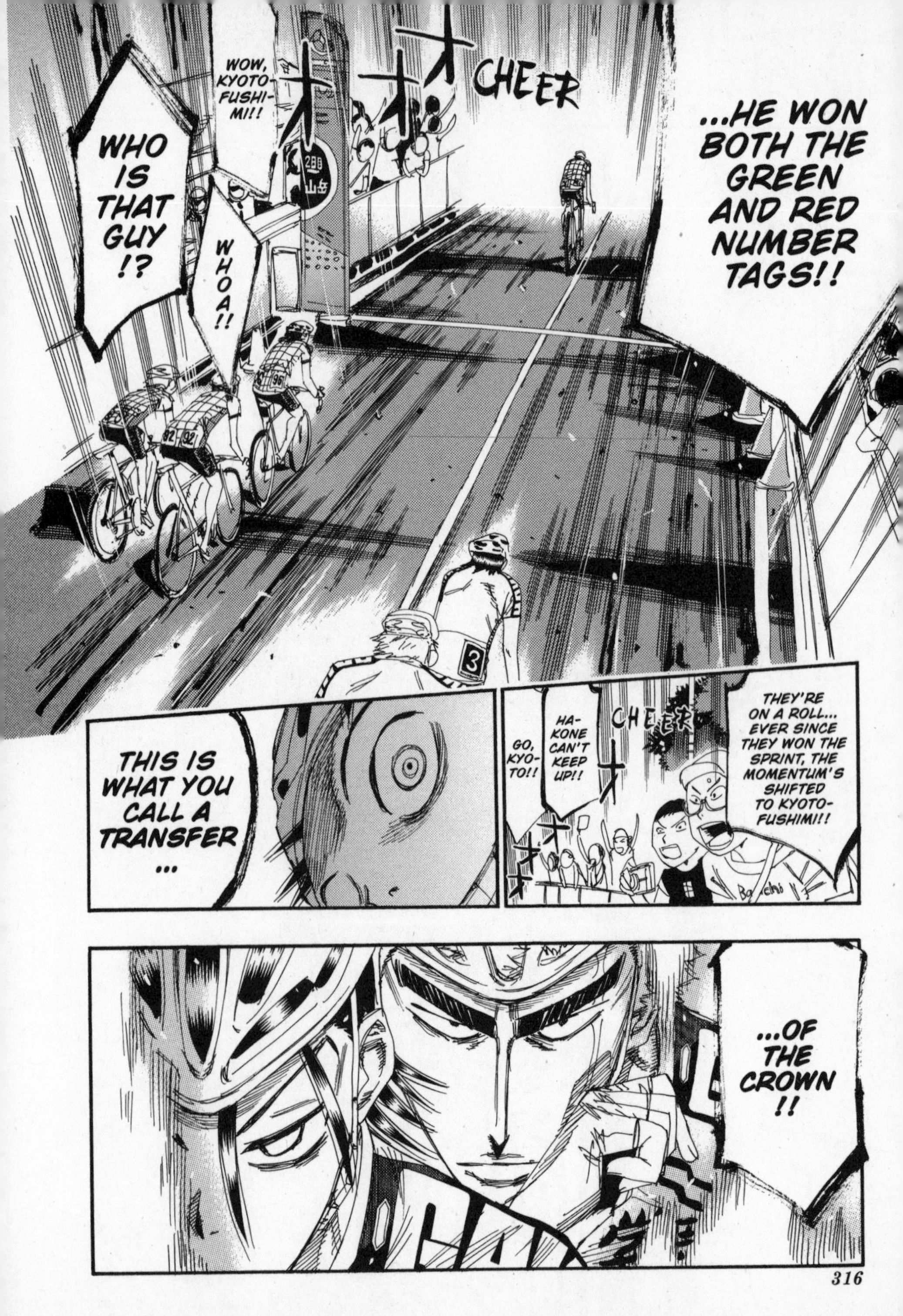
...HE WON BOTH THE GREEN AND RED NUMBER TAGS!!
CHEER
WOW, KYOTO-FUSHIMI!!
WHOA!!
WHO IS THAT GUY!?
THEY'RE ON A ROLL... EVER SINCE THEY WON THE SPRINT, THE MOMENTUM'S SHIFTED TO KYOTO-FUSHIMI!!
CHEER
HA-KONE CAN'T KEEP UP!!
GO, KYOTO!!
THIS IS WHAT YOU CALL A TRANSFER...
...OF THE CROWN!!

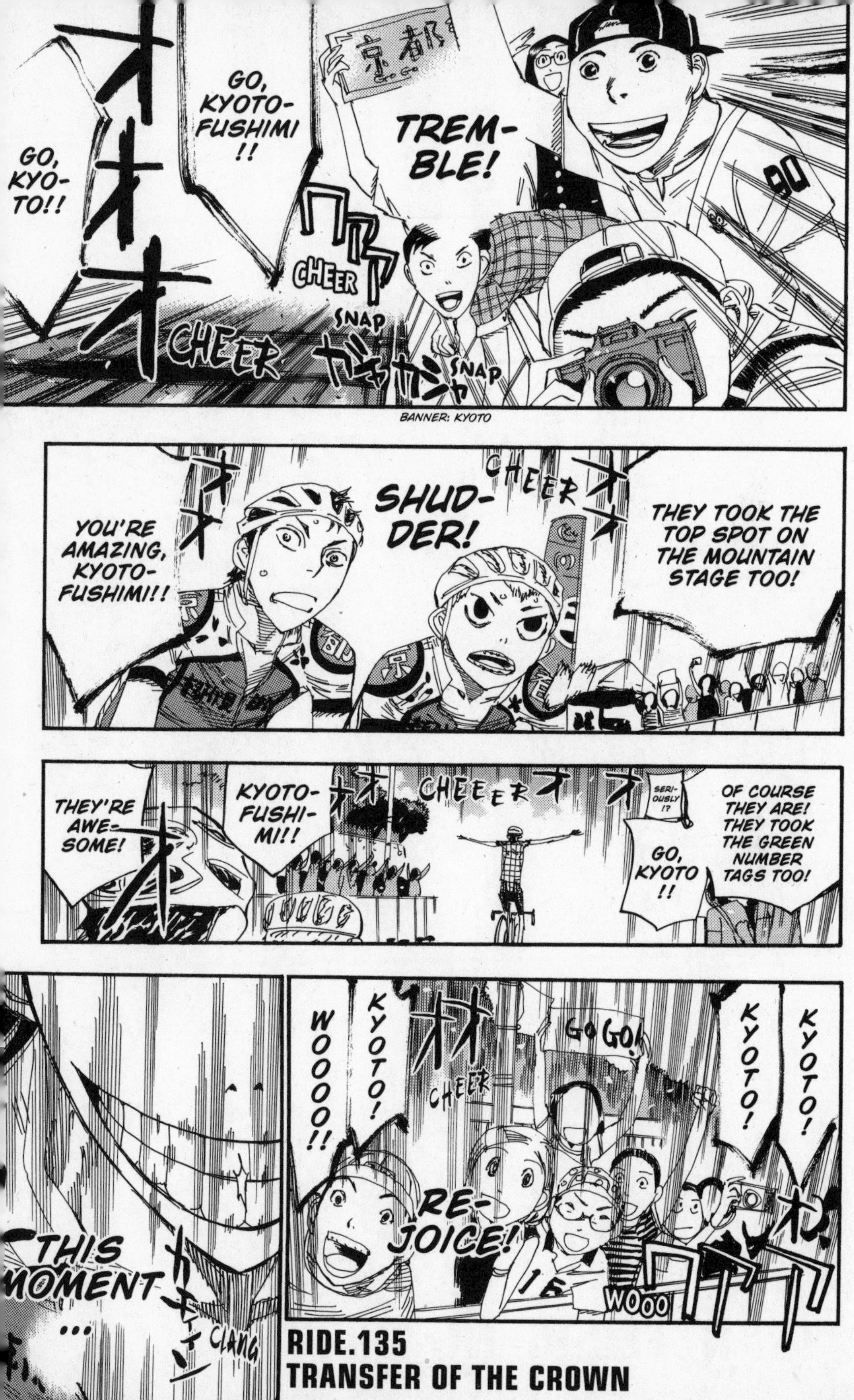
TREMBLE!
GO, KYOTO-FUSHIMI!!
GO, KYOTO!!
CHEER
SNAP
SNAP
CHEER
BANNER: KYOTO
THEY TOOK THE TOP SPOT ON THE MOUNTAIN STAGE TOO!
CHEER
SHUDDER!
YOU'RE AMAZING, KYOTO-FUSHIMI!!
OF COURSE THEY ARE! THEY TOOK THE GREEN NUMBER TAGS TOO!
SERIOUSLY!?
GO, KYOTO!!
CHEEER
KYOTO-FUSHIMI!!
THEY'RE AWESOME!
KYOTO!
KYOTO!
GO GO!
KYOTO!
WOOOOO!!
CHEER
REJOICE!
WOOO
THIS MOMENT...
CLANG

RIDE.135
TRANSFER OF THE CROWN

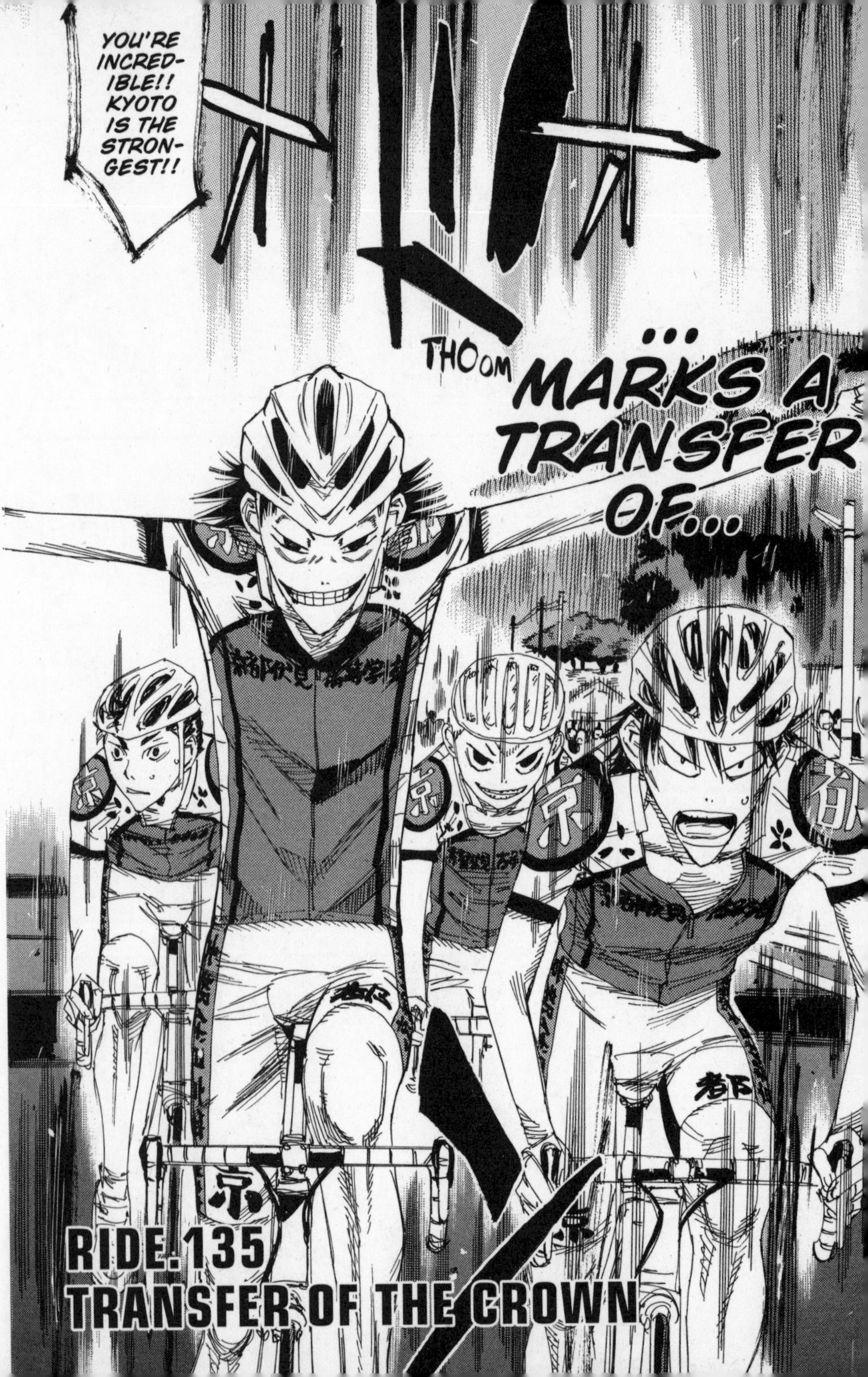
YOU'RE INCREDIBLE!! KYOTO IS THE STRONGEST!!
...MARKS A TRANSFER OF...
THOOM
RIDE. 135
TRANSFER OF THE CROWN

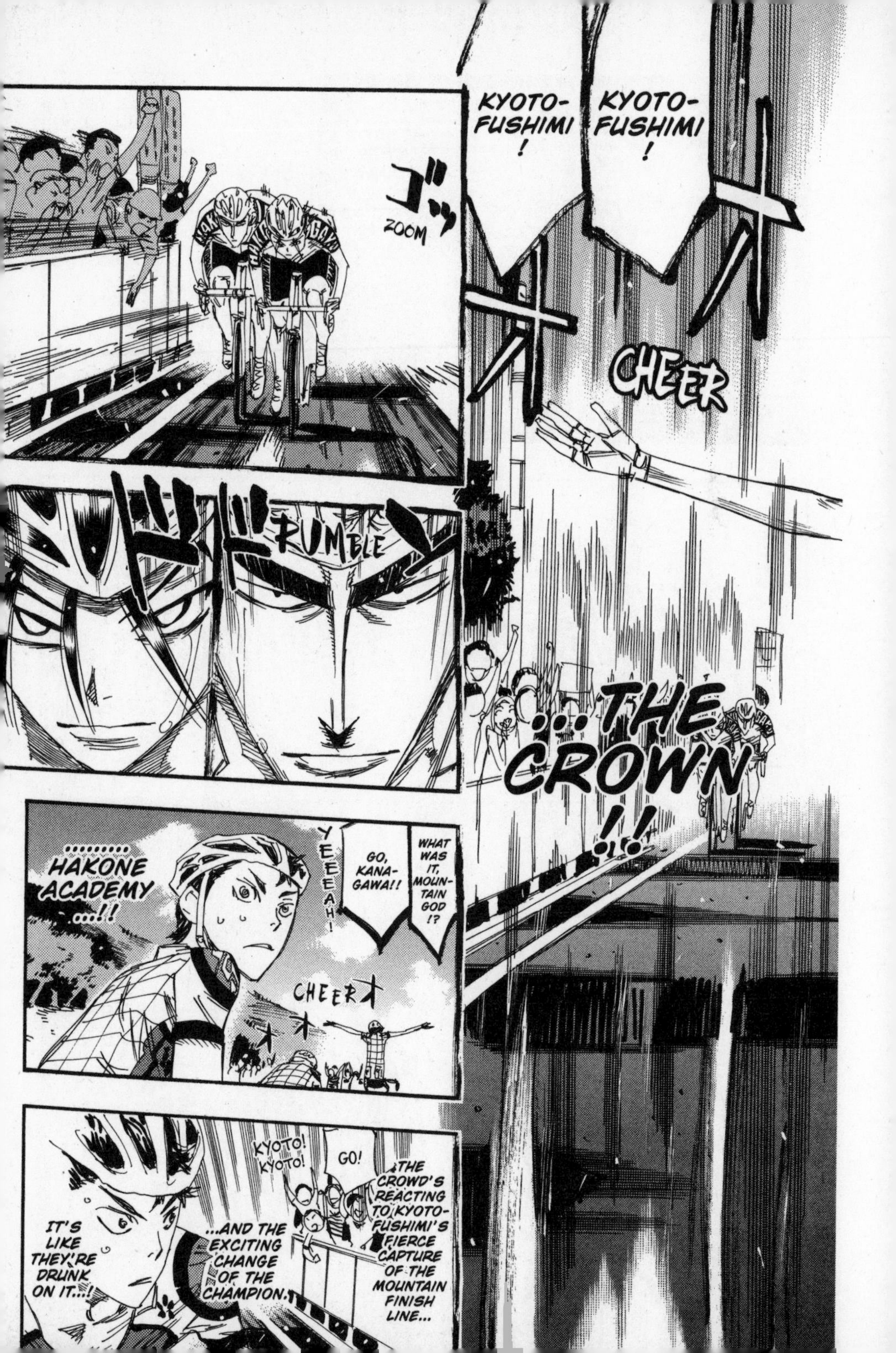
KYOTO-FUSHIMI!
KYOTO-FUSHIMI!
CHEER
...THE CROWN!!
ZOOM
RUMBLE
WHAT WAS IT, MOUNTAIN GOD!?
GO, KANAGAWA!!
YEEEAH!
..........HAKONE ACADEMY ...!!
CHEER
THE CROWD'S REACTING TO KYOTO-FUSHIMI'S FIERCE CAPTURE OF THE MOUNTAIN FINISH LINE...
GO!
KYOTO! KYOTO!
...AND THE EXCITING CHANGE OF THE CHAMPION.
IT'S LIKE THEY'RE DRUNK ON IT...!

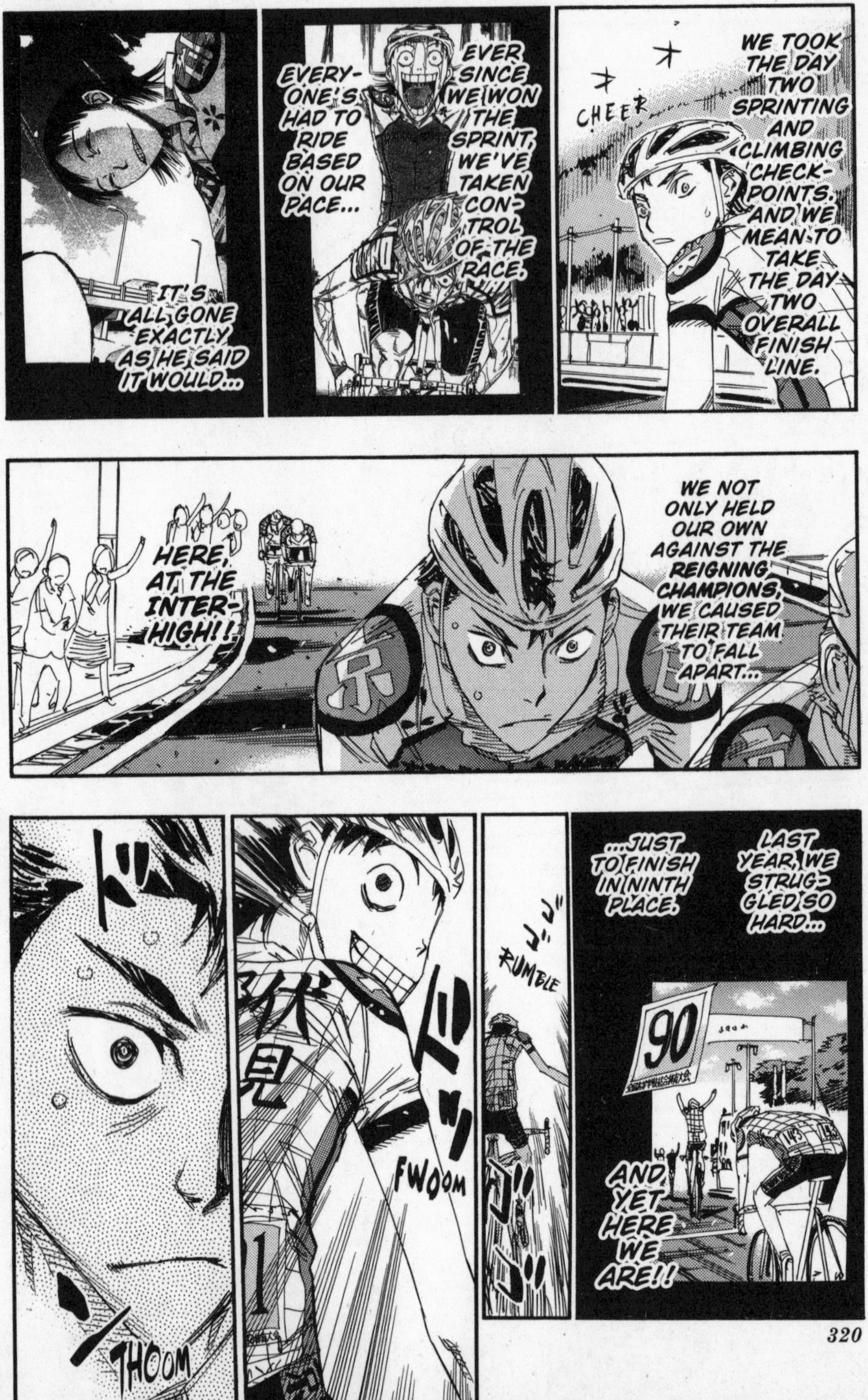
CHEER
WE TOOK THE DAY TWO SPRINTING AND CLIMBING CHECK-POINTS. AND WE MEAN TO TAKE THE DAY TWO OVERALL FINISH LINE.
EVER SINCE WE WON THE SPRINT, WE'VE TAKEN CON-TROL OF THE RACE.
EVERY-ONE'S HAD TO RIDE BASED ON OUR PACE...
IT'S ALL GONE EXACTLY AS HE SAID IT WOULD...
WE NOT ONLY HELD OUR OWN AGAINST THE REIGNING CHAMPIONS, WE CAUSED THEIR TEAM TO FALL APART...
HERE, AT THE INTER-HIGH!!
LAST YEAR, WE STRUG-GLED SO HARD...
...JUST TO FINISH IN NINTH PLACE.
90
AND YET HERE WE ARE!!
RUMBLE
FWOOM
THOOM

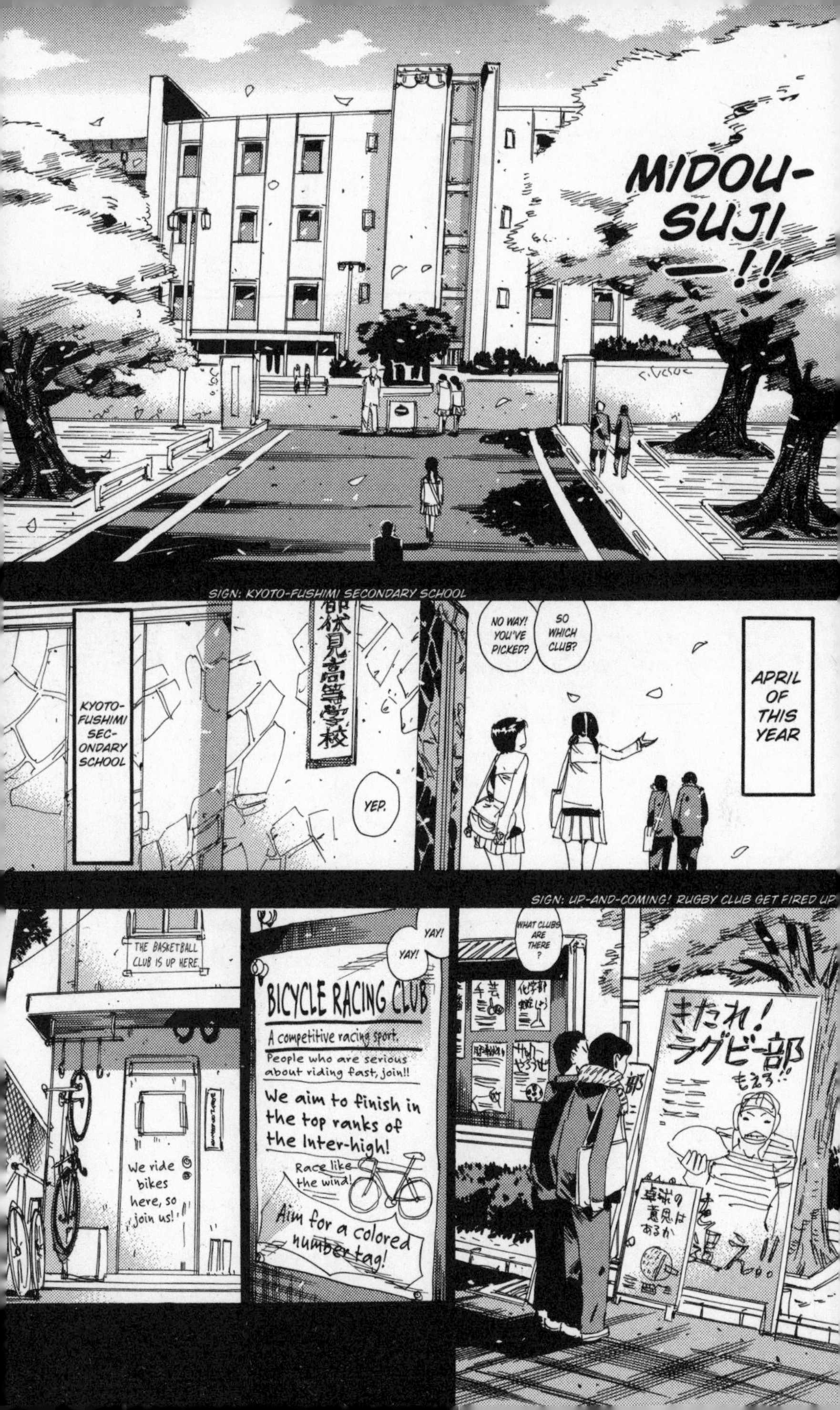
MIDOU-SUJI—!!
SIGN: KYOTO-FUSHIMI SECONDARY SCHOOL
APRIL OF THIS YEAR
SO WHICH CLUB?
NO WAY! YOU'VE PICKED?
YEP.
KYOTO-FUSHIMI SECONDARY SCHOOL
SIGN: UP-AND-COMING! RUGBY CLUB GET FIRED UP
WHAT CLUBS ARE THERE?
きたれ！ラグビー部
YAY!
YAY!
BICYCLE RACING CLUB
A competitive racing sport.
People who are serious about riding fast, join!!
We aim to finish in the top ranks of the Inter-high!
Race like the wind!
Aim for a colored number tag!
THE BASKETBALL CLUB IS UP HERE.
We ride bikes here, so join us!

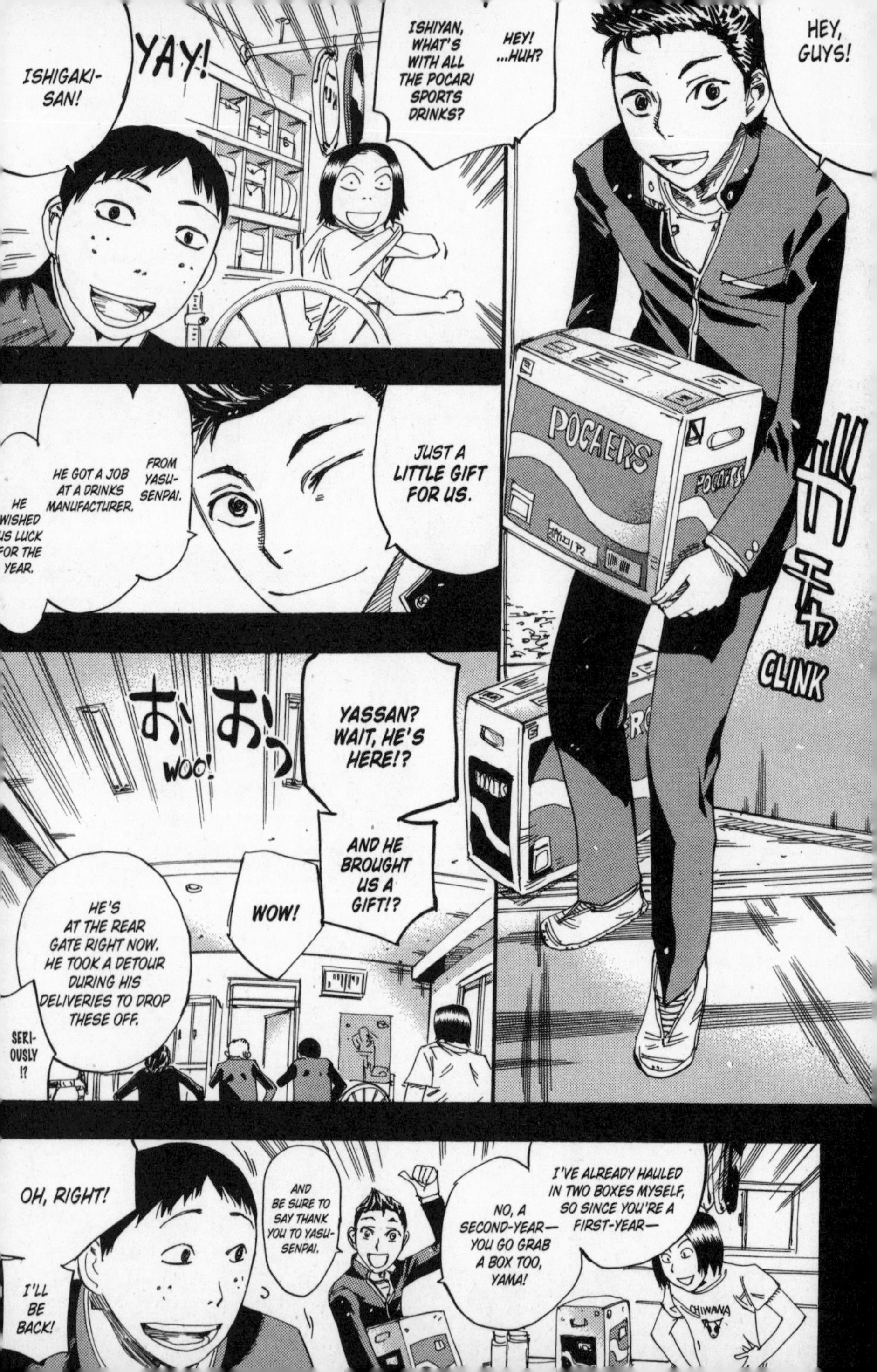
HEY, GUYS!
POCAERS
POCAERS
CLINK
HEY! ...HUH?
ISHIYAN, WHAT'S WITH ALL THE POCARI SPORTS DRINKS?
YAY!
ISHIGAKI-SAN!
JUST A LITTLE GIFT FOR US.
FROM YASU-SENPAI.
HE GOT A JOB AT A DRINKS MANUFACTURER.
HE WISHED US LUCK FOR THE YEAR.
YASSAN? WAIT, HE'S HERE!?
AND HE BROUGHT US A GIFT!?
おおっ
WOO!
WOW!
HE'S AT THE REAR GATE RIGHT NOW. HE TOOK A DETOUR DURING HIS DELIVERIES TO DROP THESE OFF.
SERIOUSLY!?
I'VE ALREADY HAULED IN TWO BOXES MYSELF, SO SINCE YOU'RE A FIRST-YEAR—
NO, A SECOND-YEAR— YOU GO GRAB A BOX TOO, YAMA!
AND BE SURE TO SAY THANK YOU TO YASU-SENPAI.
OH, RIGHT!
I'LL BE BACK!
CHIWANA

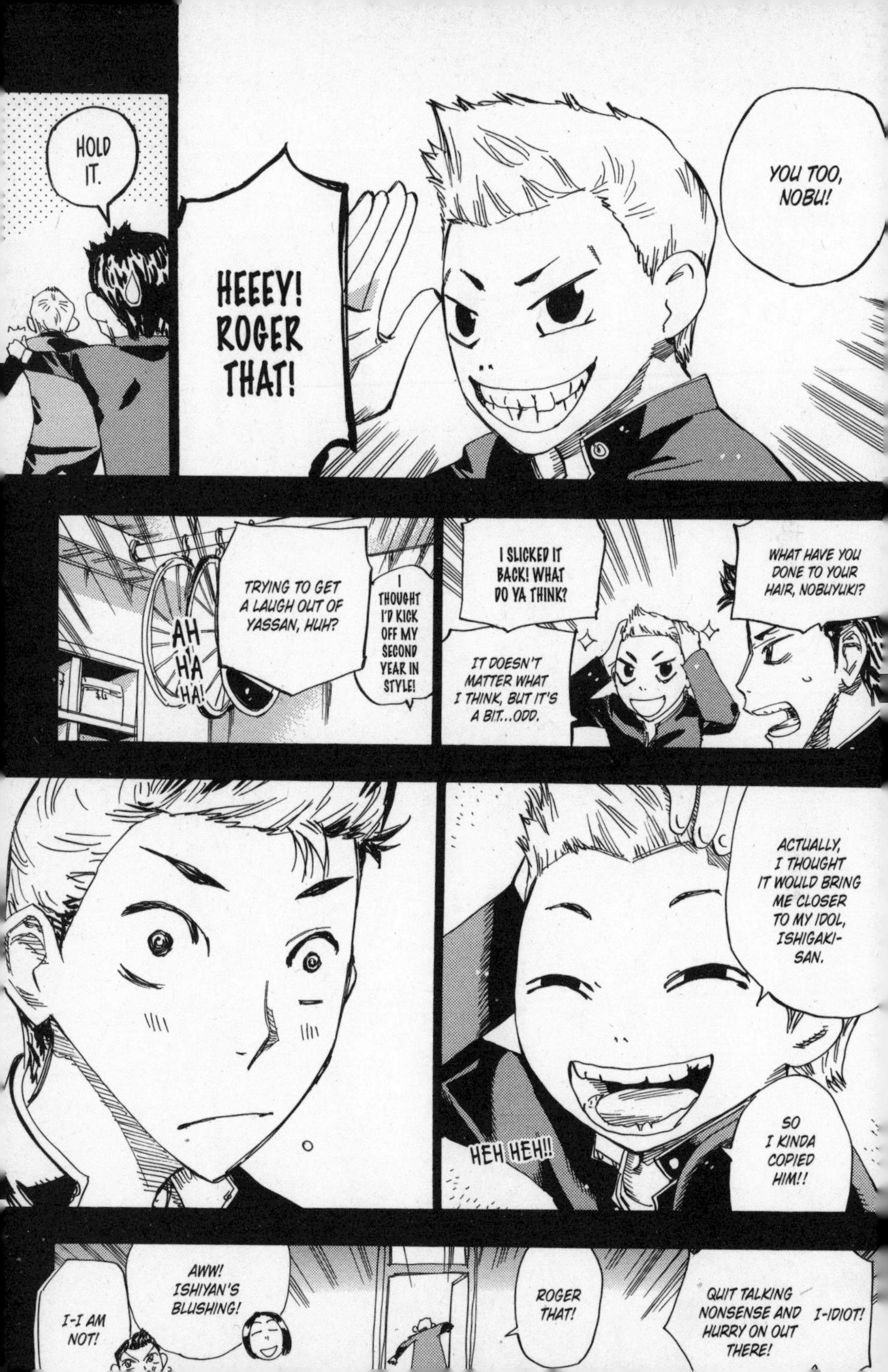
YOU TOO, NOBU!
HEEEY! ROGER THAT!
HOLD IT.
WHAT HAVE YOU DONE TO YOUR HAIR, NOBUYUKI?
I SLICKED IT BACK! WHAT DO YA THINK?
IT DOESN'T MATTER WHAT I THINK, BUT IT'S A BIT...ODD.
I THOUGHT I'D KICK OFF MY SECOND YEAR IN STYLE!
TRYING TO GET A LAUGH OUT OF YASSAN, HUH?
AH HA HA!
ACTUALLY, I THOUGHT IT WOULD BRING ME CLOSER TO MY IDOL, ISHIGAKI-SAN.
SO I KINDA COPIED HIM!!
HEH HEH!!
I-IDIOT!
QUIT TALKING NONSENSE AND HURRY ON OUT THERE!
ROGER THAT!
AWW! ISHIYAN'S BLUSHING!
I-I AM NOT!

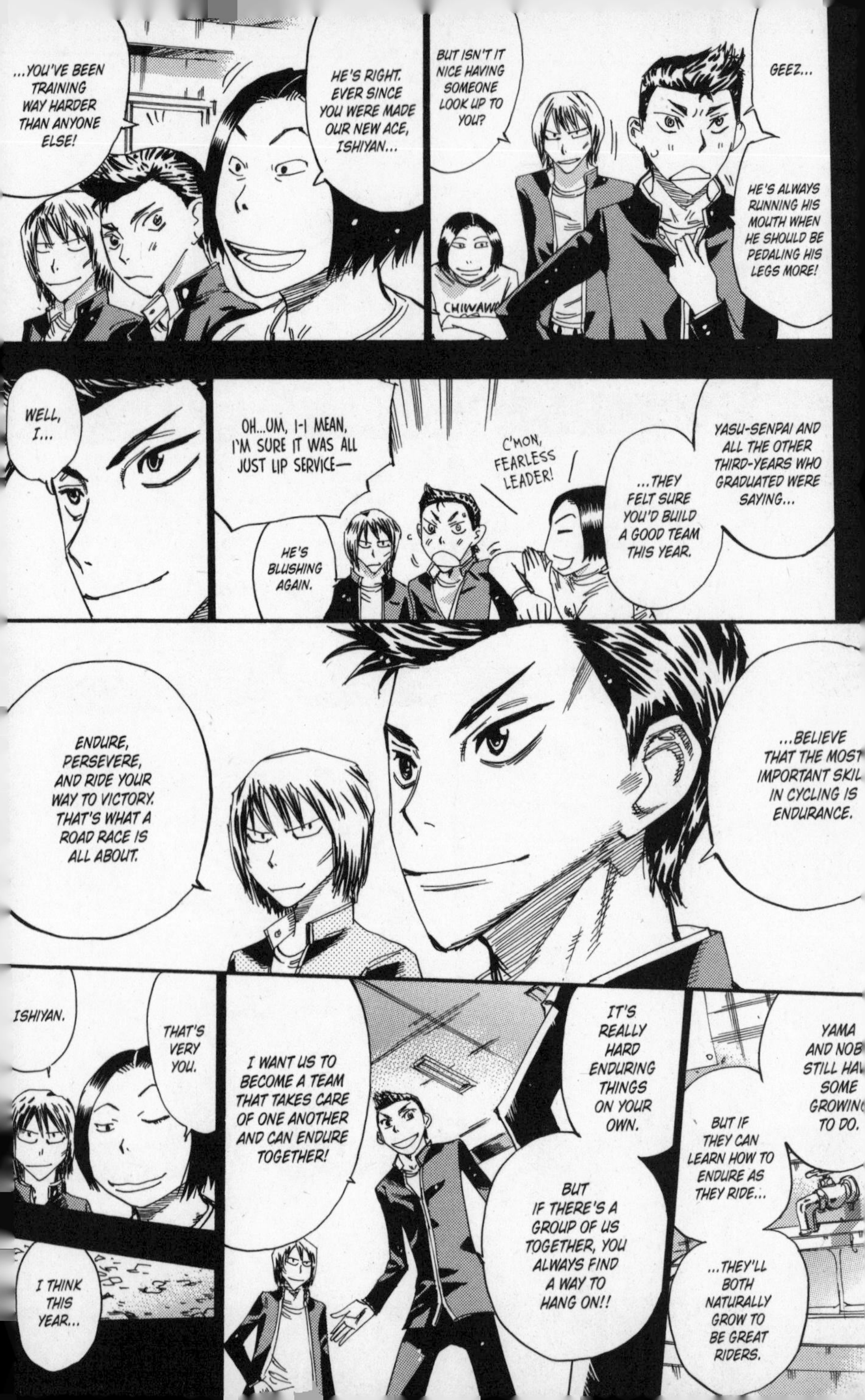
GEEZ...
HE'S ALWAYS RUNNING HIS MOUTH WHEN HE SHOULD BE PEDALING HIS LEGS MORE!
CHIWAW
BUT ISN'T IT NICE HAVING SOMEONE LOOK UP TO YOU?
HE'S RIGHT. EVER SINCE YOU WERE MADE OUR NEW ACE, ISHIYAN...
...YOU'VE BEEN TRAINING WAY HARDER THAN ANYONE ELSE!
YASU-SENPAI AND ALL THE OTHER THIRD-YEARS WHO GRADUATED WERE SAYING...
...THEY FELT SURE YOU'D BUILD A GOOD TEAM THIS YEAR.
C'MON, FEARLESS LEADER!
OH...UM, I-I MEAN, I'M SURE IT WAS ALL JUST LIP SERVICE—
HE'S BLUSHING AGAIN.
WELL, I...
...BELIEVE THAT THE MOST IMPORTANT SKIL IN CYCLING IS ENDURANCE.
ENDURE, PERSEVERE, AND RIDE YOUR WAY TO VICTORY. THAT'S WHAT A ROAD RACE IS ALL ABOUT.
YAMA AND NOB STILL HAV SOME GROWIN TO DO.
BUT IF THEY CAN LEARN HOW TO ENDURE AS THEY RIDE...
...THEY'LL BOTH NATURALLY GROW TO BE GREAT RIDERS.
IT'S REALLY HARD ENDURING THINGS ON YOUR OWN.
BUT IF THERE'S A GROUP OF US TOGETHER, YOU ALWAYS FIND A WAY TO HANG ON!!
I WANT US TO BECOME A TEAM THAT TAKES CARE OF ONE ANOTHER AND CAN ENDURE TOGETHER!
THAT'S VERY YOU.
ISHIYAN.
I THINK THIS YEAR...

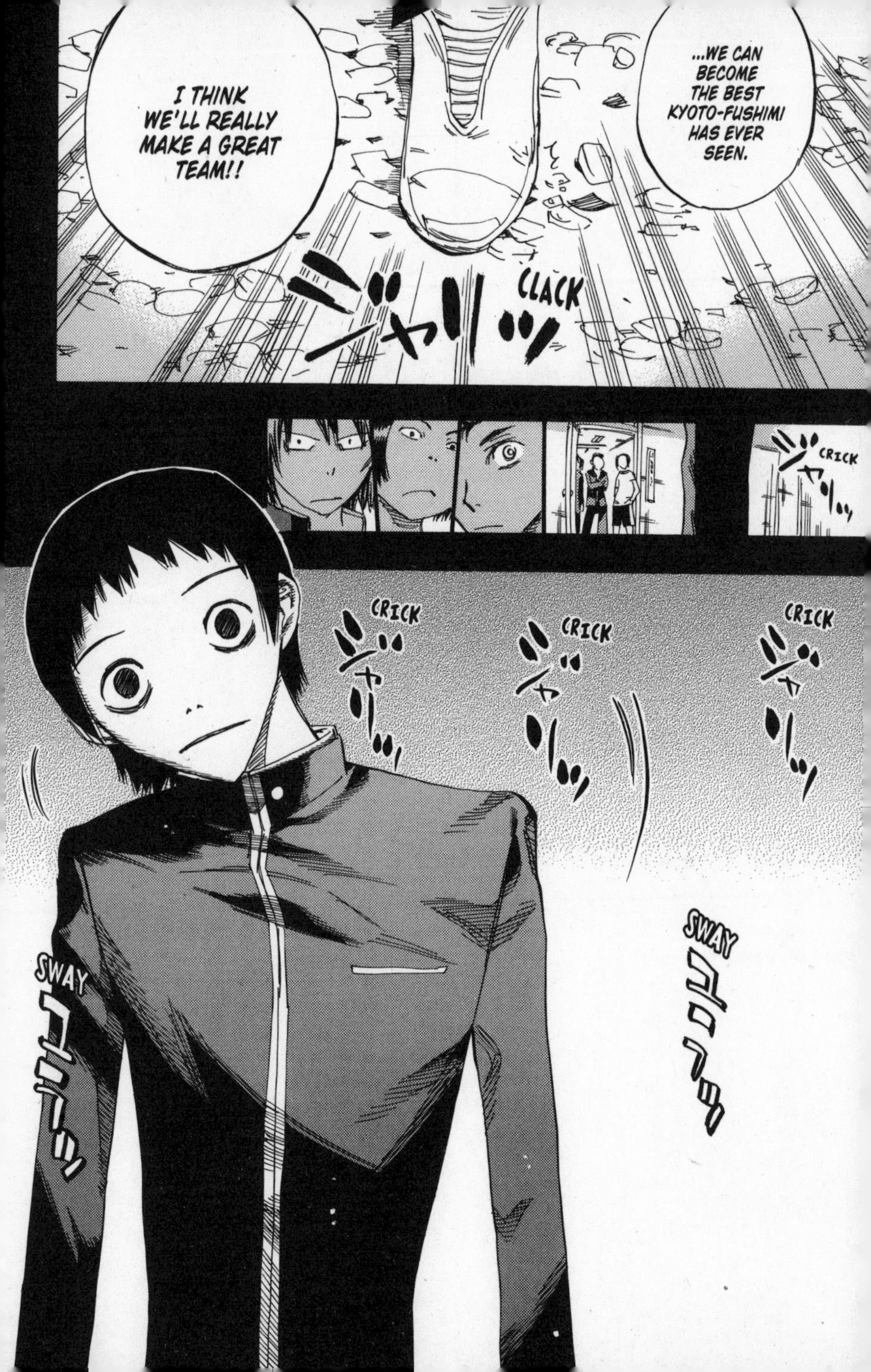
...WE CAN BECOME THE BEST KYOTO-FUSHIMI HAS EVER SEEN.
I THINK WE'LL REALLY MAKE A GREAT TEAM!!
CLACK
ジャリッ
CRICK
CRICK
CRICK
CRICK
SWAY
SWAY

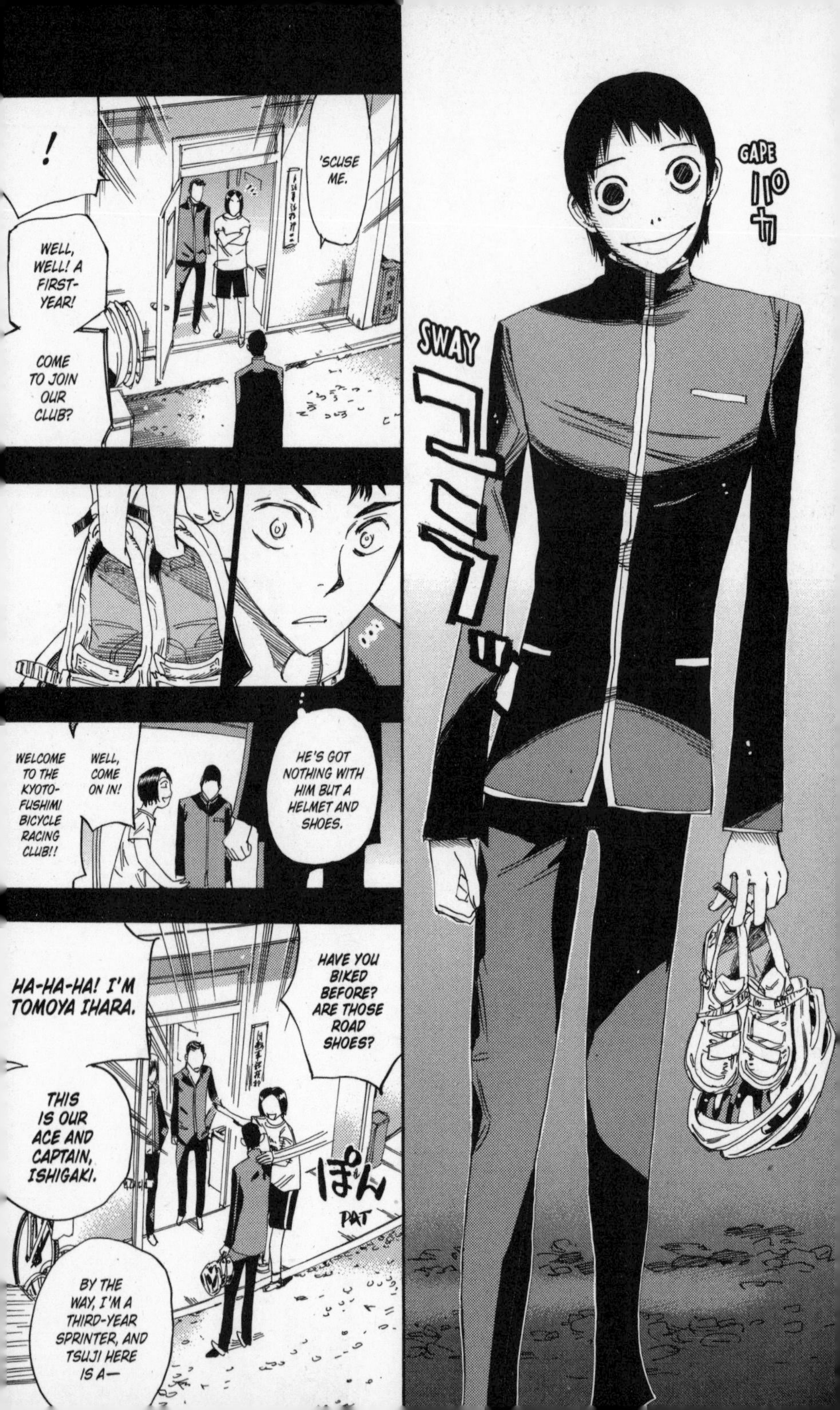
GAPE
パカ
SWAY
'SCUSE ME.
!
WELL, WELL! A FIRST-YEAR!
COME TO JOIN OUR CLUB?
HE'S GOT NOTHING WITH HIM BUT A HELMET AND SHOES.
WELL, COME ON IN!
WELCOME TO THE KYOTO-FUSHIMI BICYCLE RACING CLUB!!
HAVE YOU BIKED BEFORE? ARE THOSE ROAD SHOES?
HA-HA-HA! I'M TOMOYA IHARA.
THIS IS OUR ACE AND CAPTAIN, ISHIGAKI.
ぽん
PAT
BY THE WAY, I'M A THIRD-YEAR SPRINTER, AND TSUJI HERE IS A—

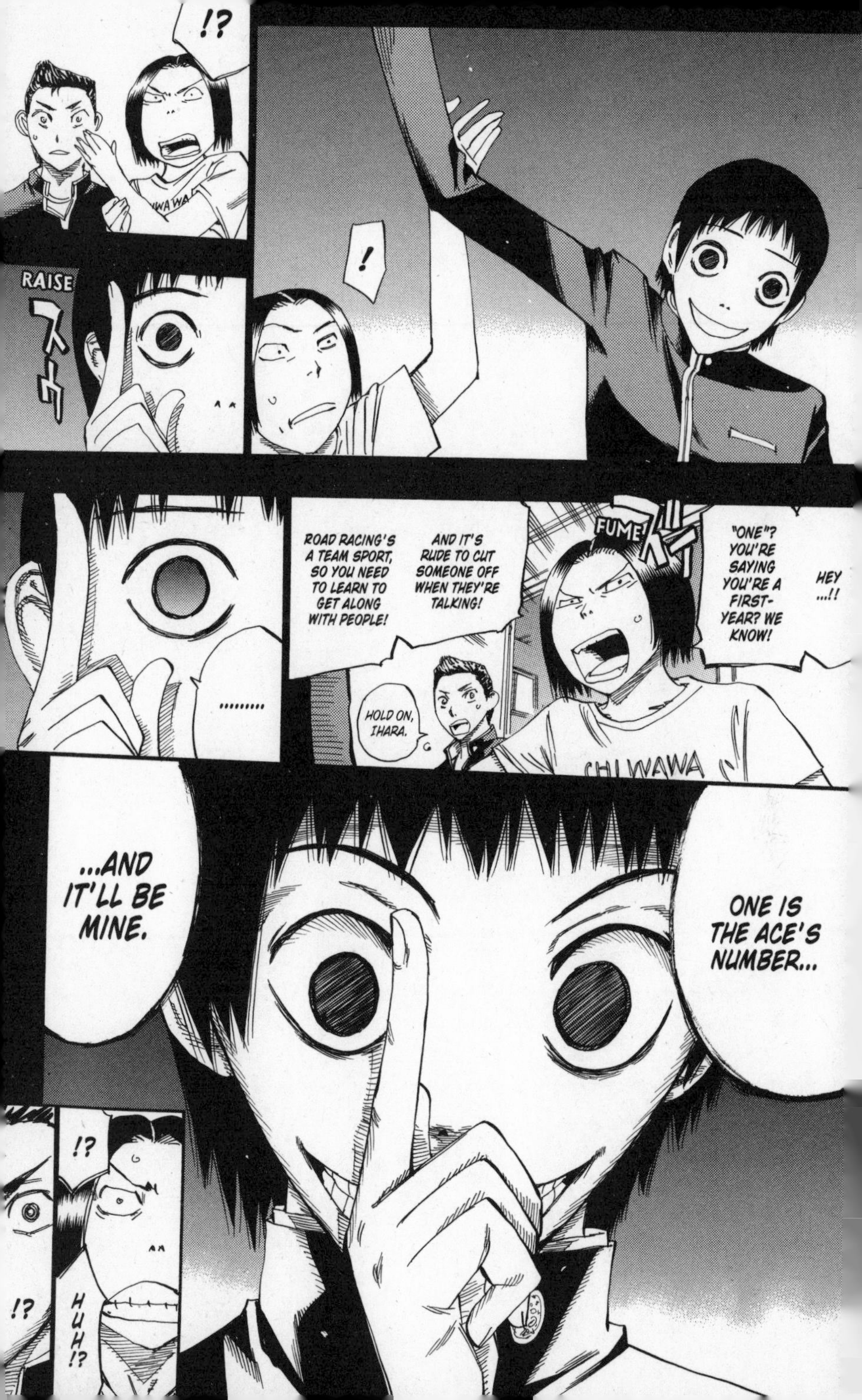
!
!?
RAISE
HEY ...!!
"ONE"? YOU'RE SAYING YOU'RE A FIRST-YEAR? WE KNOW!
FUME
AND IT'S RUDE TO CUT SOMEONE OFF WHEN THEY'RE TALKING!
ROAD RACING'S A TEAM SPORT, SO YOU NEED TO LEARN TO GET ALONG WITH PEOPLE!
HOLD ON, IHARA.
....
ONE IS THE ACE'S NUMBER...
...AND IT'LL BE MINE.
!?
HUH!?
!?

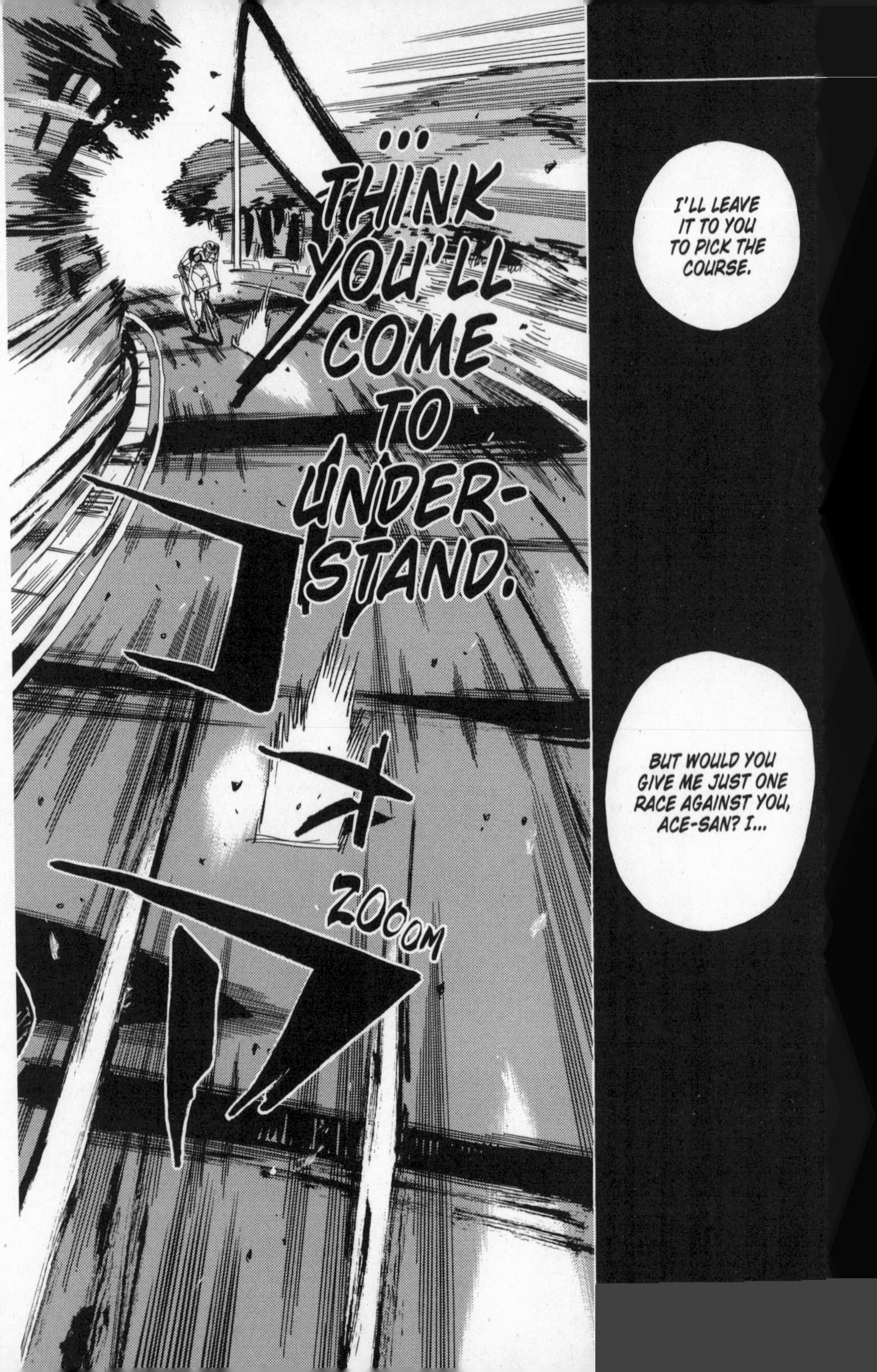
I'LL LEAVE IT TO YOU TO PICK THE COURSE.
BUT WOULD YOU GIVE ME JUST ONE RACE AGAINST YOU, ACE-SAN? I...
...THINK YOU'LL COME TO UNDER-STAND.
ZOOOM

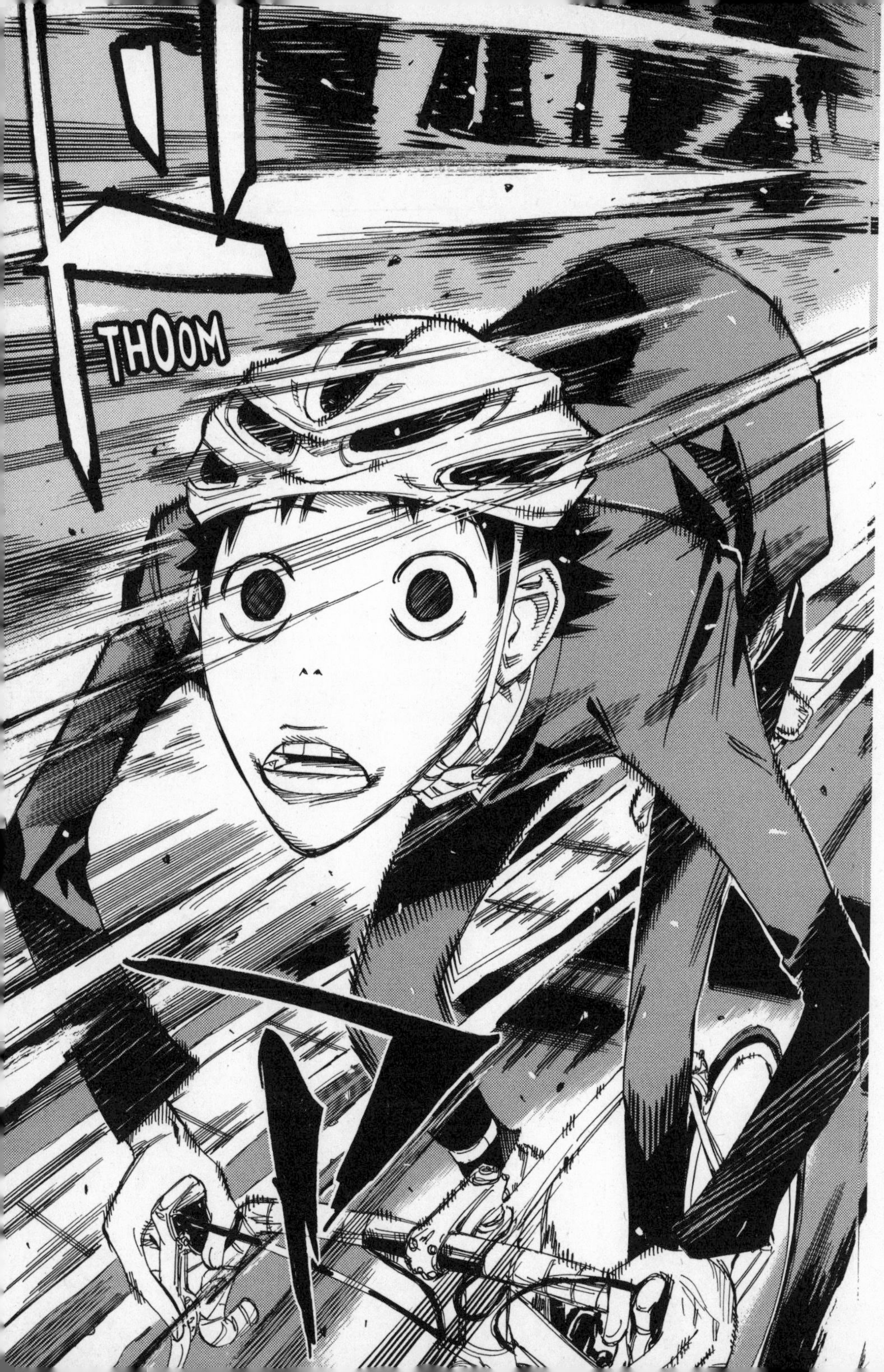
THOOM

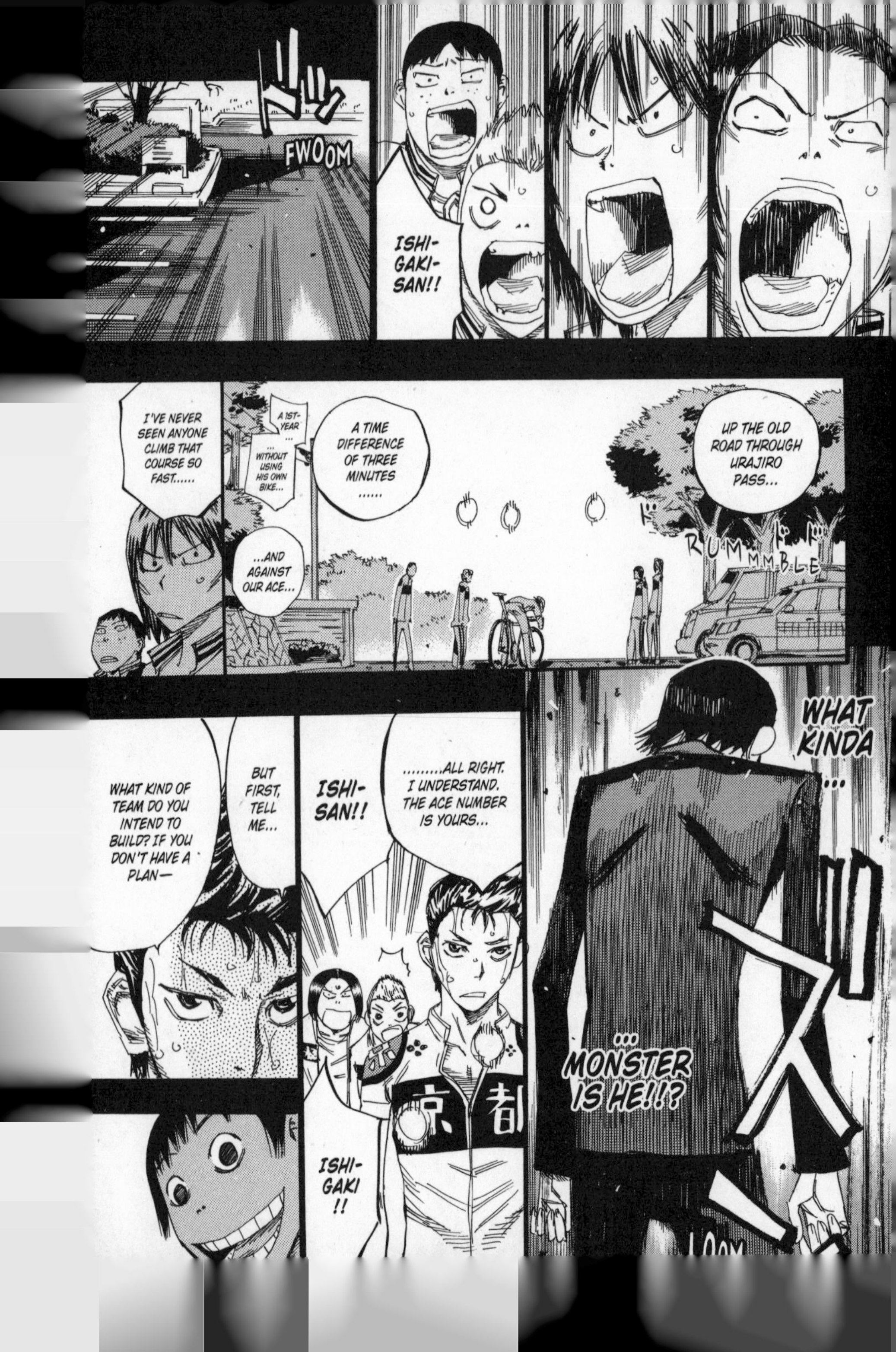

ISHI-GAKI-SAN!!
FWOOM
UP THE OLD ROAD THROUGH URAJIRO PASS...
RUMMMBLE
A TIME DIFFERENCE OF THREE MINUTES ......
A 1ST-YEAR ... WITHOUT USING HIS OWN BIKE...
...AND AGAINST OUR ACE...
I'VE NEVER SEEN ANYONE CLIMB THAT COURSE SO FAST......
WHAT KINDA ...
...MONSTER IS HE!!?
........ALL RIGHT. I UNDERSTAND. THE ACE NUMBER IS YOURS...
ISHI-SAN!!
京都
ISHI-GAKI !!
BUT FIRST, TELL ME...
WHAT KIND OF TEAM DO YOU INTEND TO BUILD? IF YOU DON'T HAVE A PLAN—

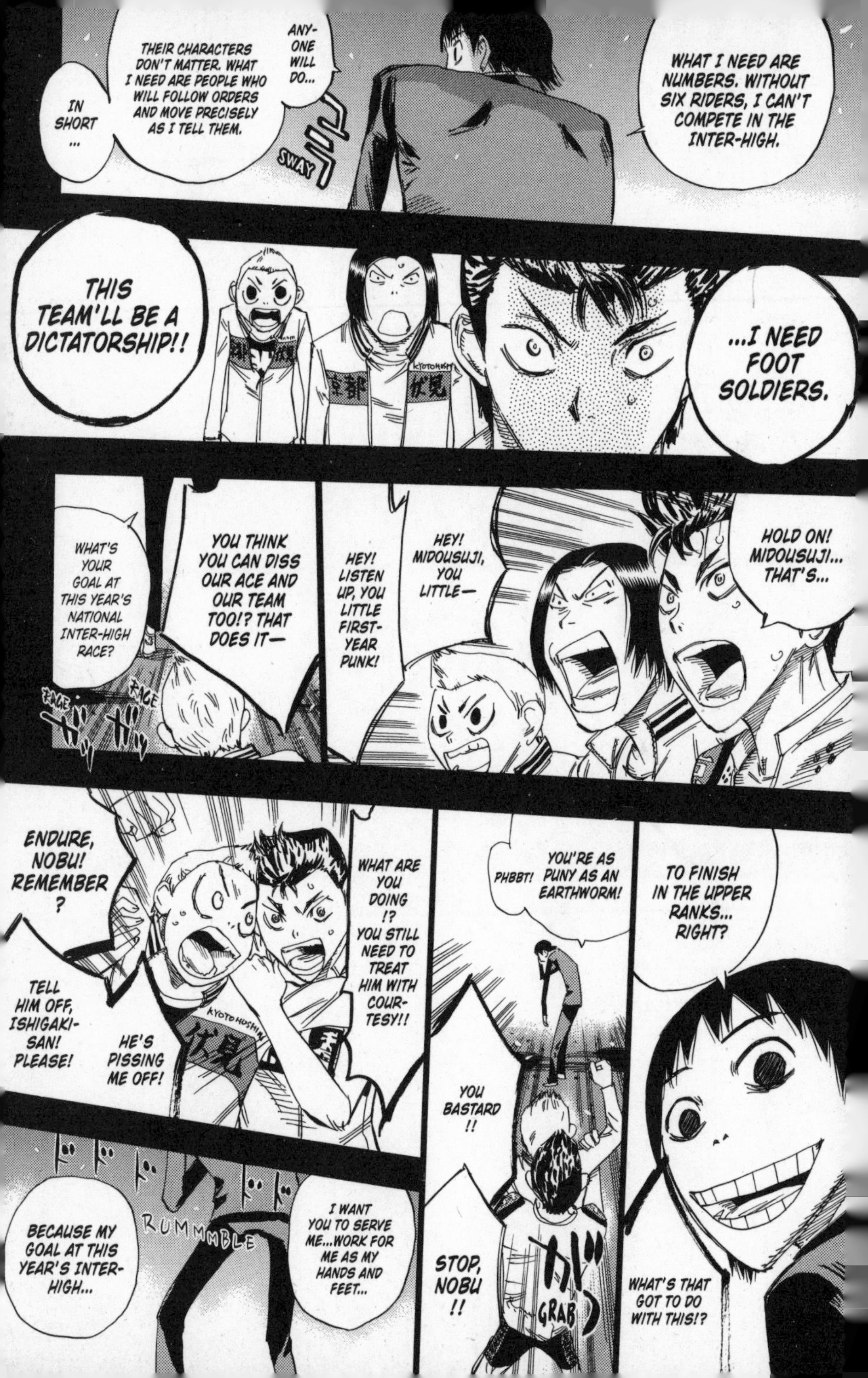
WHAT I NEED ARE NUMBERS. WITHOUT SIX RIDERS, I CAN'T COMPETE IN THE INTER-HIGH.
ANY-ONE WILL DO...
THEIR CHARACTERS DON'T MATTER. WHAT I NEED ARE PEOPLE WHO WILL FOLLOW ORDERS AND MOVE PRECISELY AS I TELL THEM.
IN SHORT...
SWAY
...I NEED FOOT SOLDIERS.
THIS TEAM'LL BE A DICTATORSHIP!!
HOLD ON! MIDOUSUJI... THAT'S...
HEY! MIDOUSUJI, YOU LITTLE—
HEY! LISTEN UP, YOU LITTLE FIRST-YEAR PUNK!
YOU THINK YOU CAN DISS OUR ACE AND OUR TEAM TOO!? THAT DOES IT—
WHAT'S YOUR GOAL AT THIS YEAR'S NATIONAL INTER-HIGH RACE?
RAGE
RAGE
TO FINISH IN THE UPPER RANKS... RIGHT?
WHAT'S THAT GOT TO DO WITH THIS!?
YOU'RE AS PUNY AS AN EARTHWORM!
PHBBT!
YOU BASTARD!!
STOP, NOBU!!
GRAB
WHAT ARE YOU DOING!? YOU STILL NEED TO TREAT HIM WITH COURTESY!!
ENDURE, NOBU! REMEMBER?
TELL HIM OFF, ISHIGAKI-SAN! PLEASE!
HE'S PISSING ME OFF!
I WANT YOU TO SERVE ME...WORK FOR ME AS MY HANDS AND FEET...
BECAUSE MY GOAL AT THIS YEAR'S INTER-HIGH...
RUMMMBLE

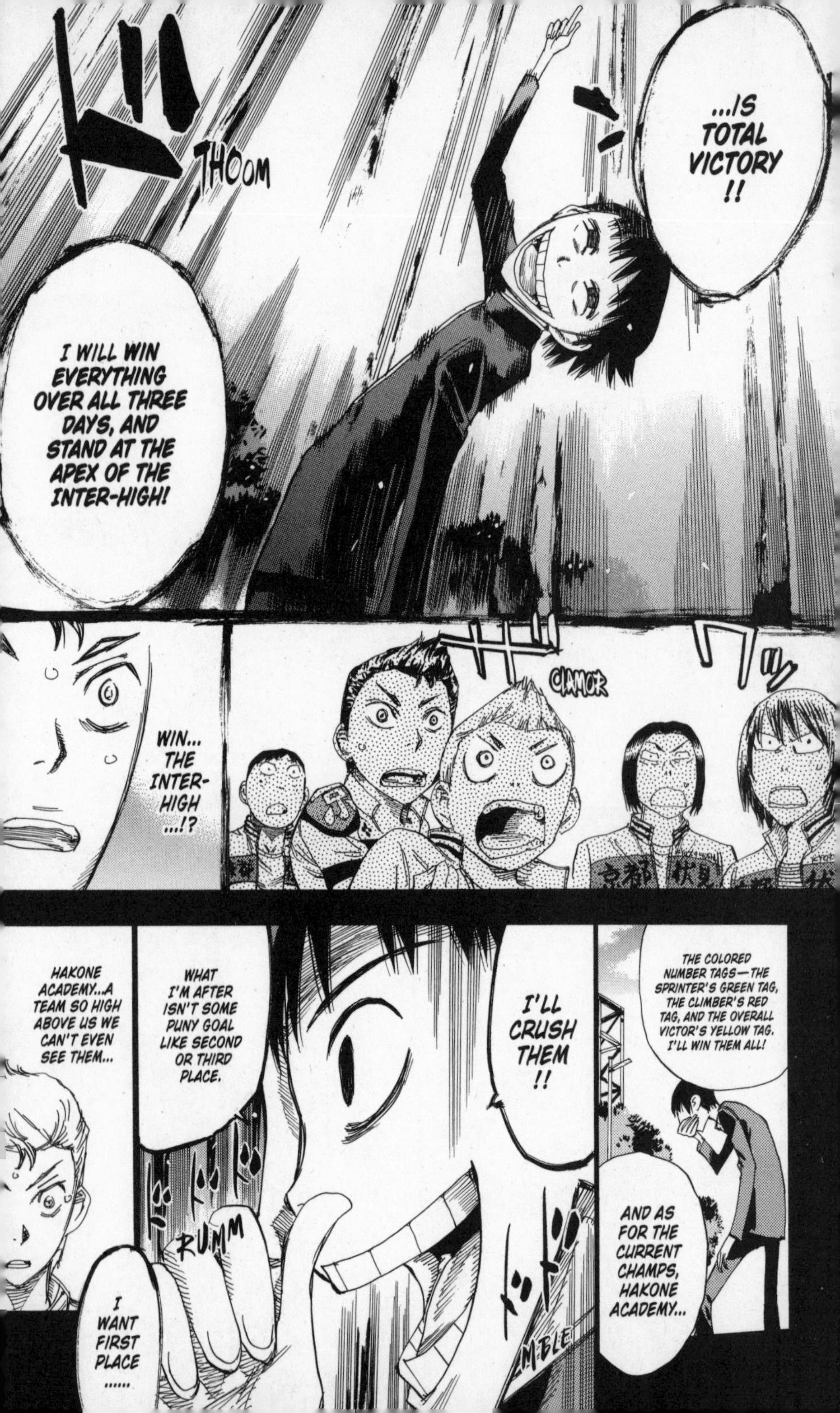

...IS TOTAL VICTORY !!
THOOM
I WILL WIN EVERYTHING OVER ALL THREE DAYS, AND STAND AT THE APEX OF THE INTER-HIGH!
CLAMOR
WIN... THE INTER-HIGH ...!?
THE COLORED NUMBER TAGS—THE SPRINTER'S GREEN TAG, THE CLIMBER'S RED TAG, AND THE OVERALL VICTOR'S YELLOW TAG. I'LL WIN THEM ALL!
AND AS FOR THE CURRENT CHAMPS, HAKONE ACADEMY...
MBLE
I'LL CRUSH THEM !!
RUMM
I WANT FIRST PLACE ......
WHAT I'M AFTER ISN'T SOME PUNY GOAL LIKE SECOND OR THIRD PLACE.
HAKONE ACADEMY...A TEAM SO HIGH ABOVE US WE CAN'T EVEN SEE THEM...

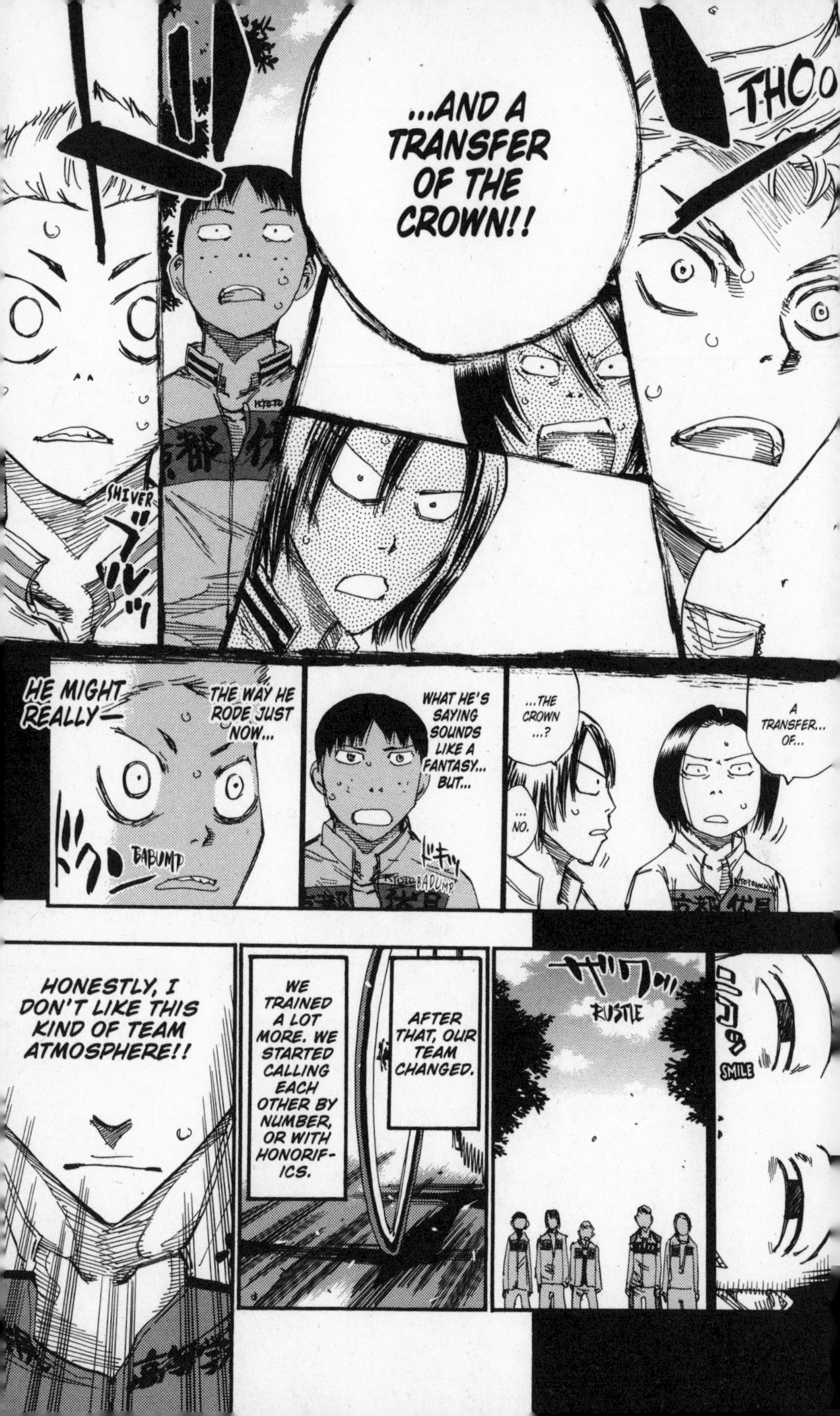
THO
...AND A TRANSFER OF THE CROWN!!
SHIVER
A TRANSFER... OF...
...THE CROWN ...?
... NO.
WHAT HE'S SAYING SOUNDS LIKE A FANTASY... BUT...
BADUMP
HE MIGHT REALLY—
THE WAY HE RODE JUST NOW...
BABUMP
SMILE
RUSTLE
AFTER THAT, OUR TEAM CHANGED.
WE TRAINED A LOT MORE. WE STARTED CALLING EACH OTHER BY NUMBER, OR WITH HONORIF- ICS.
HONESTLY, I DON'T LIKE THIS KIND OF TEAM ATMOSPHERE!!

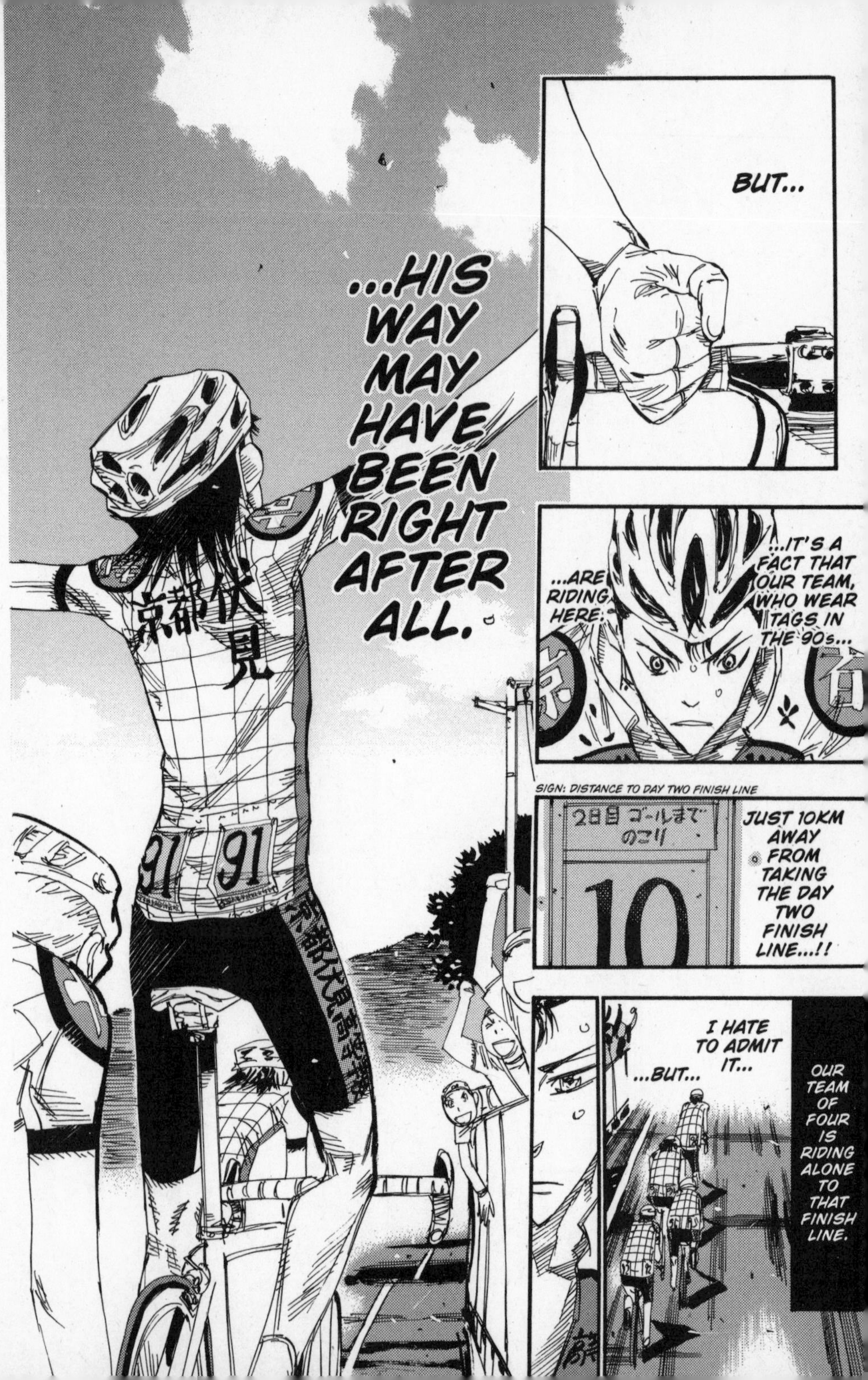
BUT...
...IT'S A FACT THAT OUR TEAM, WHO WEAR TAGS IN THE 90s...
...ARE RIDING HERE.
SIGN: DISTANCE TO DAY TWO FINISH LINE
2日目 ゴールまで のこり
10
JUST 10KM AWAY FROM TAKING THE DAY TWO FINISH LINE...!!
OUR TEAM OF FOUR IS RIDING ALONE TO THAT FINISH LINE.
I HATE TO ADMIT IT...
...BUT...
...HIS WAY MAY HAVE BEEN RIGHT AFTER ALL.

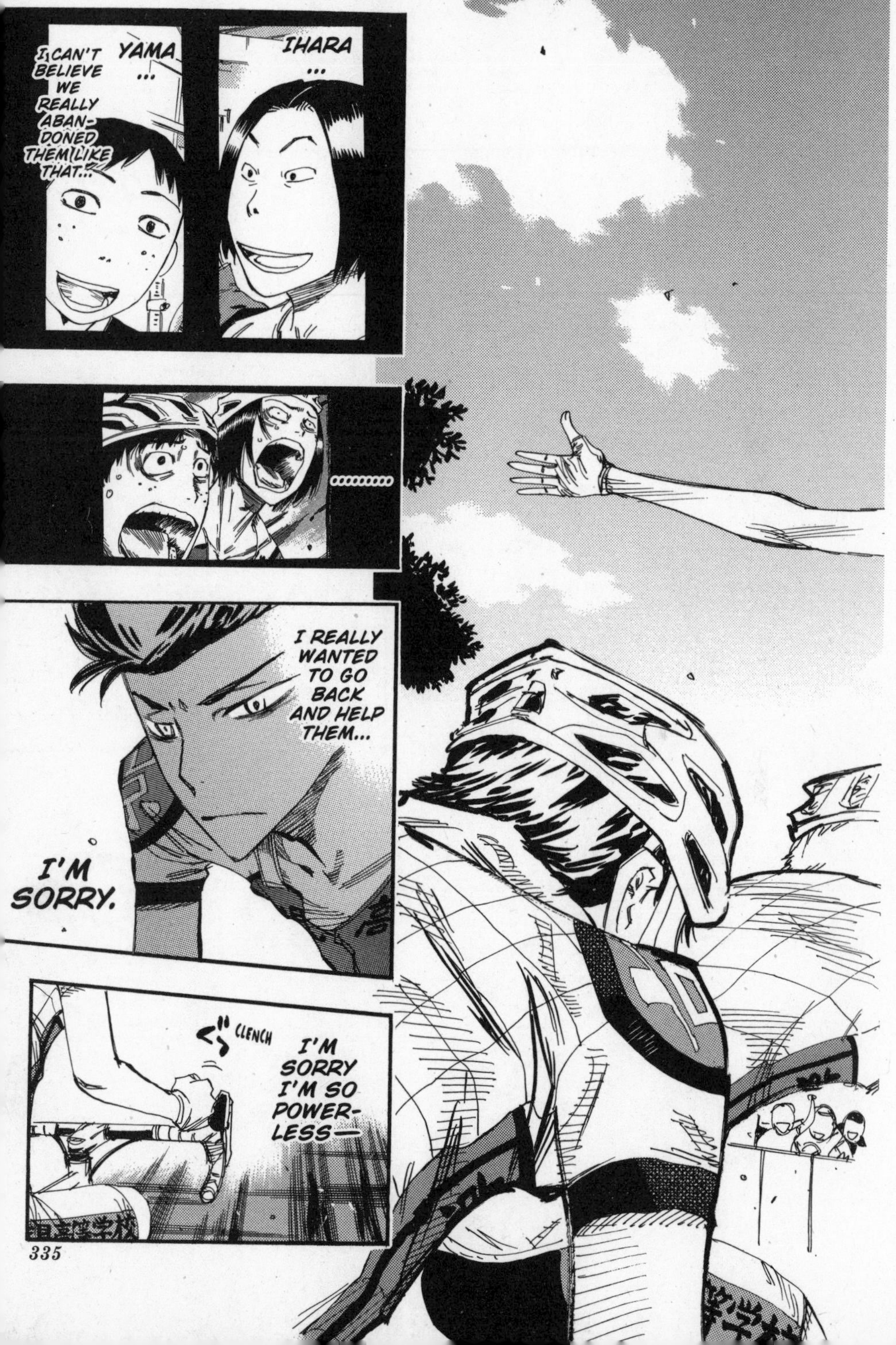
IHARA ...
YAMA ...
I CAN'T BELIEVE WE REALLY ABANDONED THEM LIKE THAT...
....
I REALLY WANTED TO GO BACK AND HELP THEM...
I'M SORRY.
CLENCH
I'M SORRY I'M SO POWERLESS—

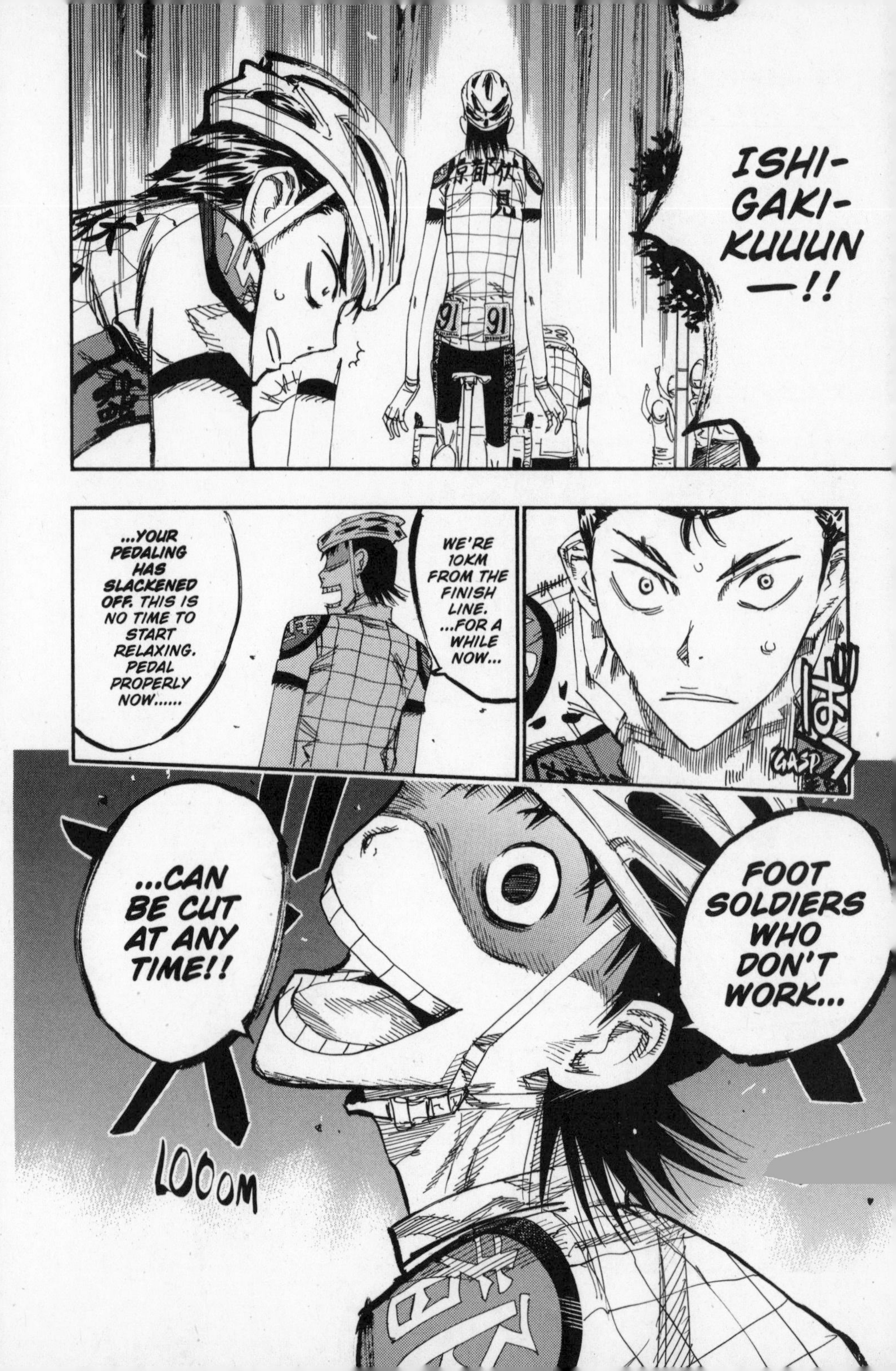
ISHI-GAKI-KUUUN—!!
GASP
WE'RE 10KM FROM THE FINISH LINE. ...FOR A WHILE NOW...
...YOUR PEDALING HAS SLACKENED OFF. THIS IS NO TIME TO START RELAXING. PEDAL PROPERLY NOW......
FOOT SOLDIERS WHO DON'T WORK...
...CAN BE CUT AT ANY TIME!!
LOOOM

RIDE.136 THE CHAMPIONS' END

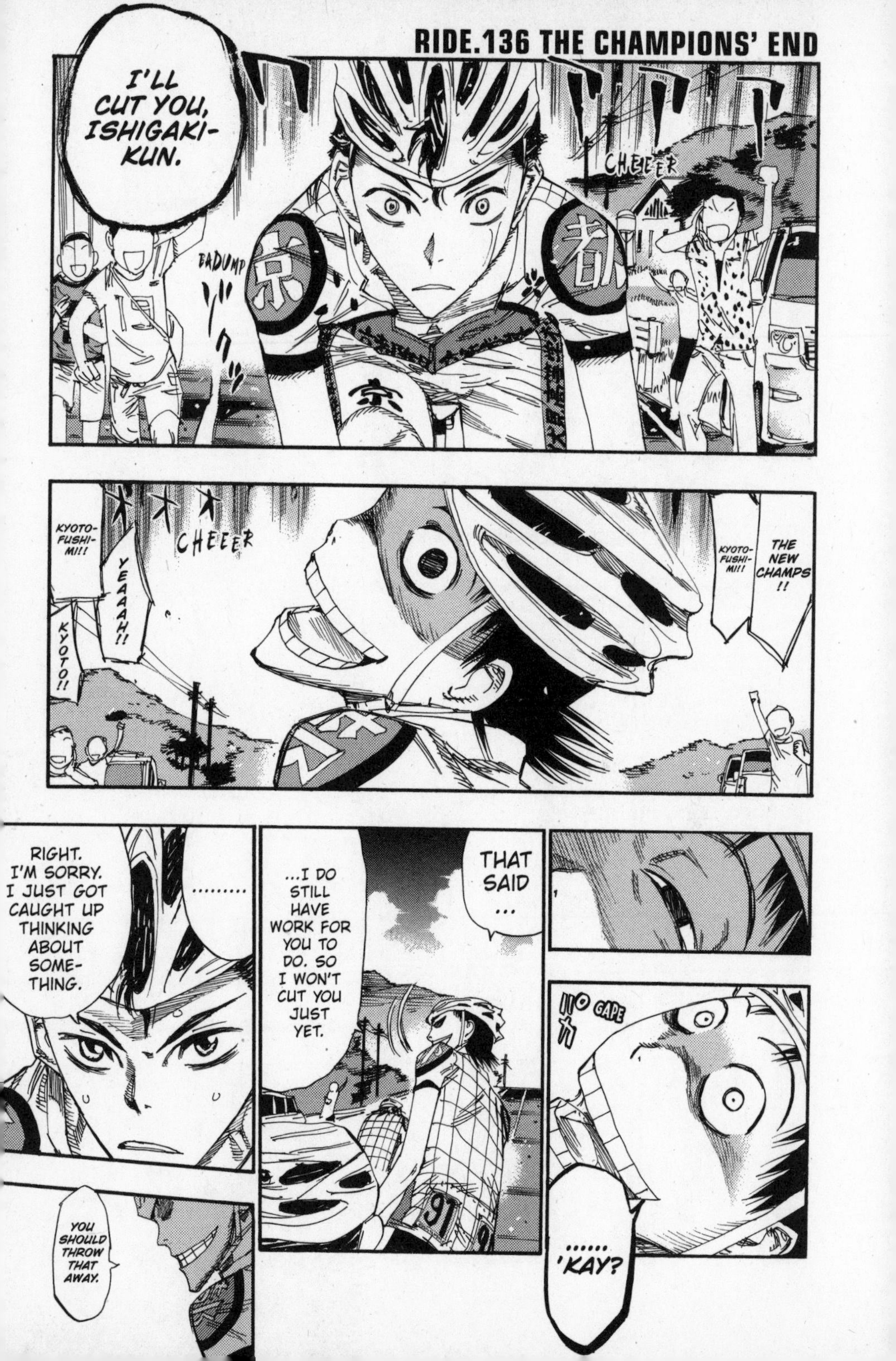
I'LL CUT YOU, ISHIGAKI-KUN.
CHEEER
BADUMP
THE NEW CHAMPS!!
KYOTO-FUSHIMI!!!
CHEEER
KYOTO-FUSHIMI!!!
YEAAAAH!!
KYOTO!!
GAPE
.......'KAY?
THAT SAID...
...I DO STILL HAVE WORK FOR YOU TO DO. SO I WON'T CUT YOU JUST YET.
....
RIGHT. I'M SORRY. I JUST GOT CAUGHT UP THINKING ABOUT SOME-THING.
YOU SHOULD THROW THAT AWAY.

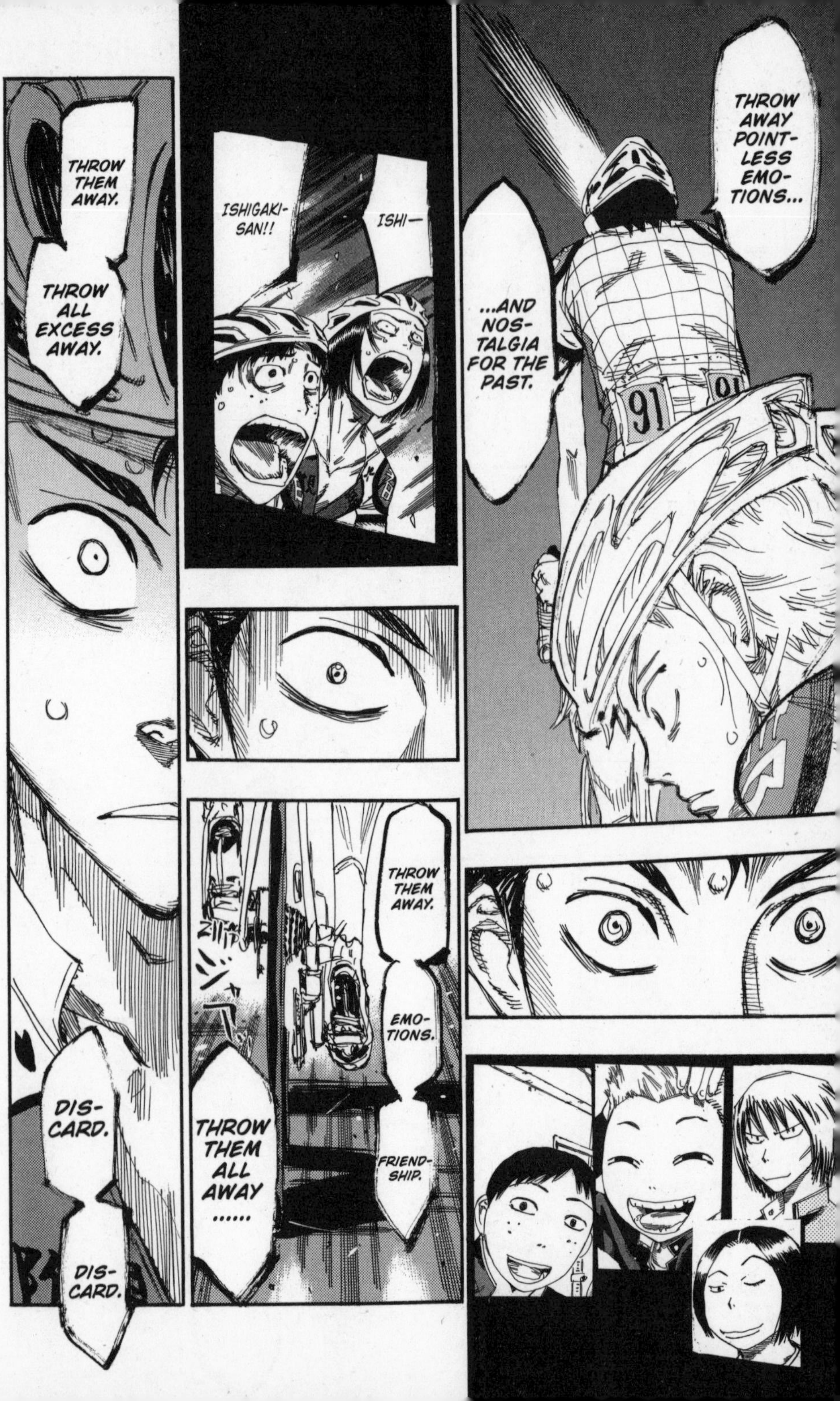
THROW AWAY POINTLESS EMOTIONS...
...AND NOSTALGIA FOR THE PAST.
ISHI—
ISHIGAKI-SAN!!
THROW THEM AWAY.
EMOTIONS.
FRIENDSHIP.
THROW THEM ALL AWAY ......
THROW THEM AWAY.
THROW ALL EXCESS AWAY.
DISCARD.
DISCARD.

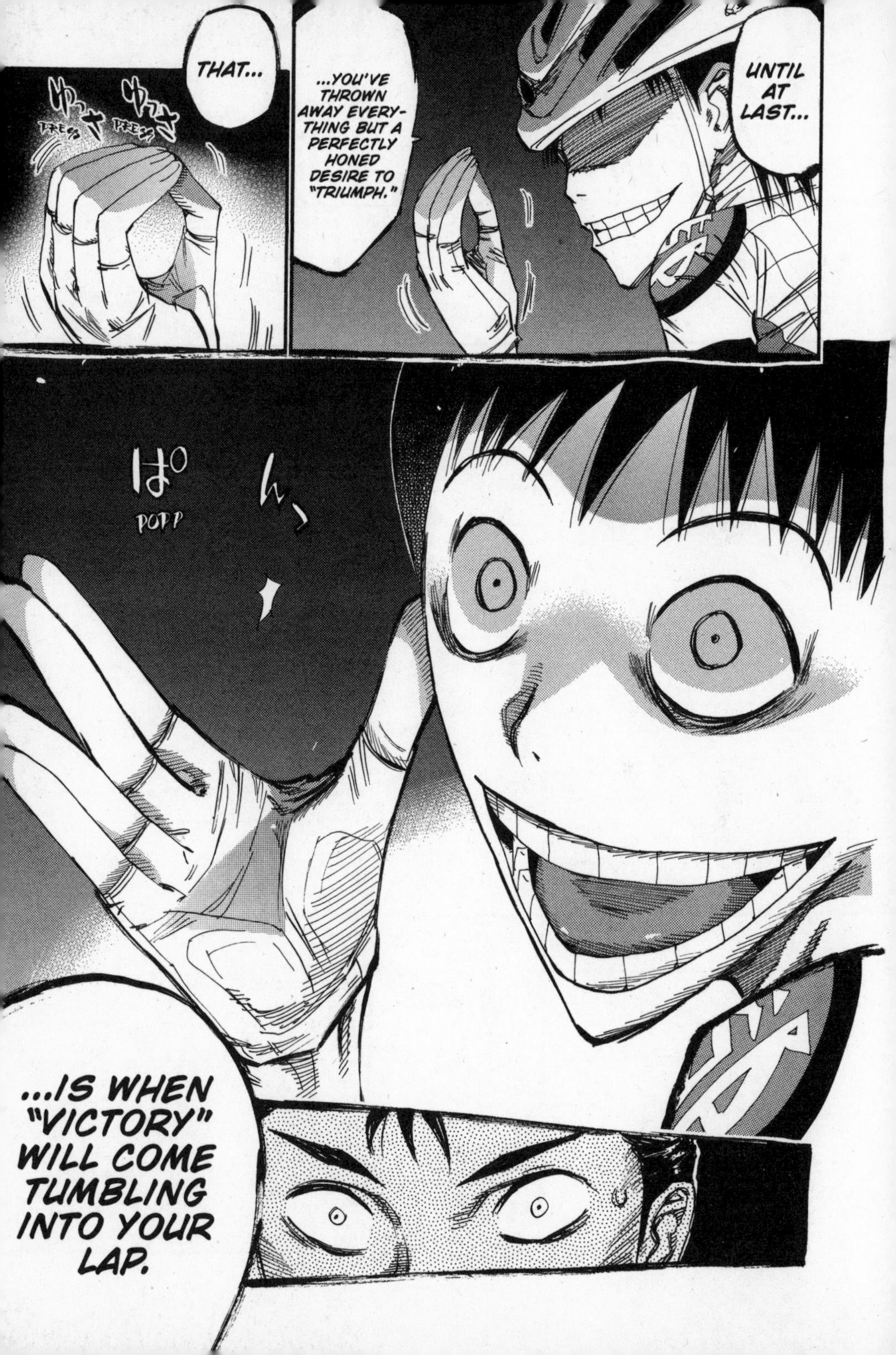
UNTIL AT LAST...
...YOU'VE THROWN AWAY EVERYTHING BUT A PERFECTLY HONED DESIRE TO "TRIUMPH."
THAT...
PRESS PRESS
ぱん
POPP
...IS WHEN "VICTORY" WILL COME TUMBLING INTO YOUR LAP.

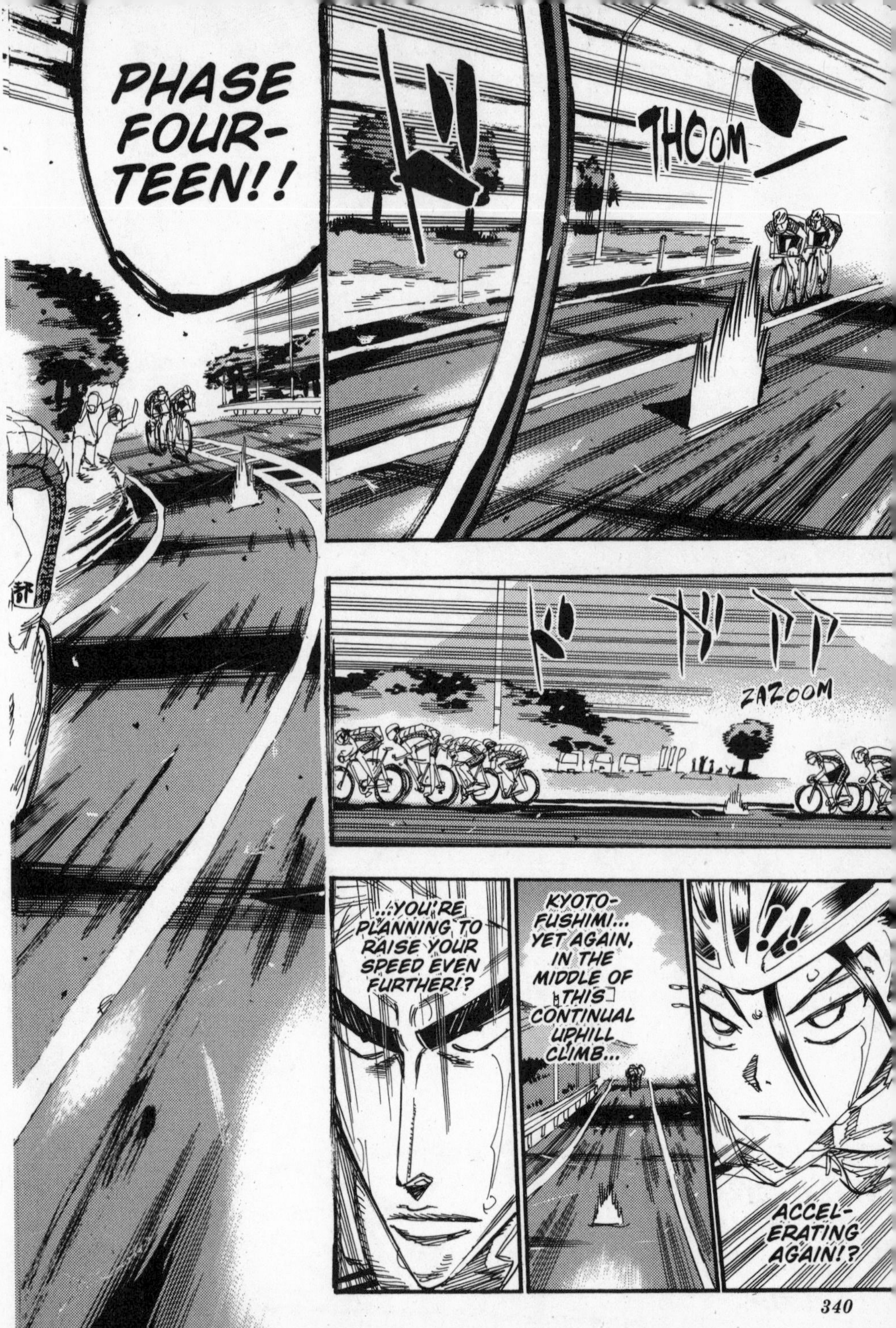
THOOM
ZAZOOM
ACCEL-ERATING AGAIN!?
KYOTO-FUSHIMI... YET AGAIN, IN THE MIDDLE OF THIS CONTINUAL UPHILL CLIMB...
...YOU'RE PLANNING TO RAISE YOUR SPEED EVEN FURTHER!?
PHASE FOUR-TEEN!!

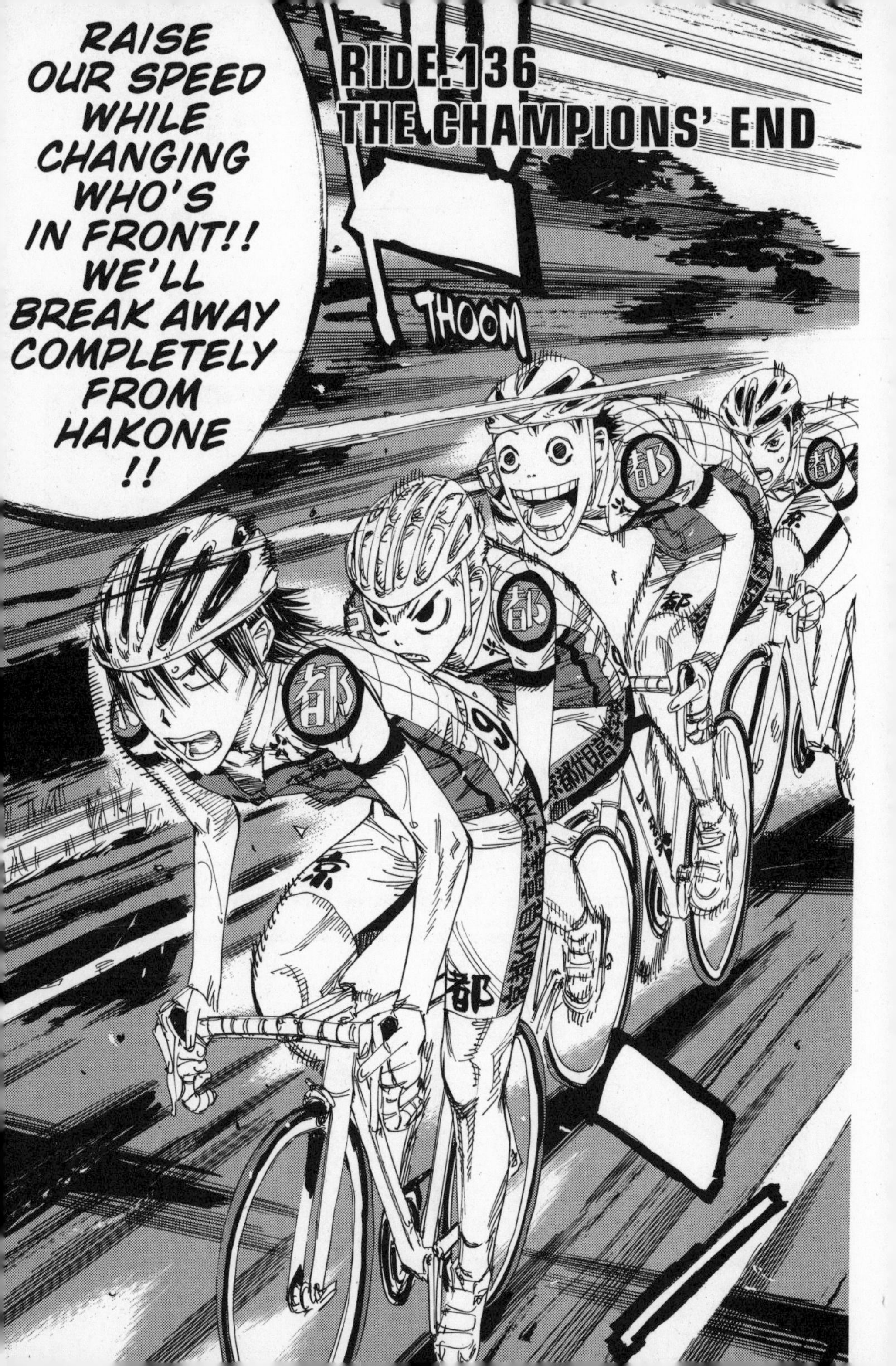
RIDE.136
THE CHAMPIONS' END
RAISE OUR SPEED WHILE CHANGING WHO'S IN FRONT!! WE'LL BREAK AWAY COMPLETELY FROM HAKONE !!
THOOM

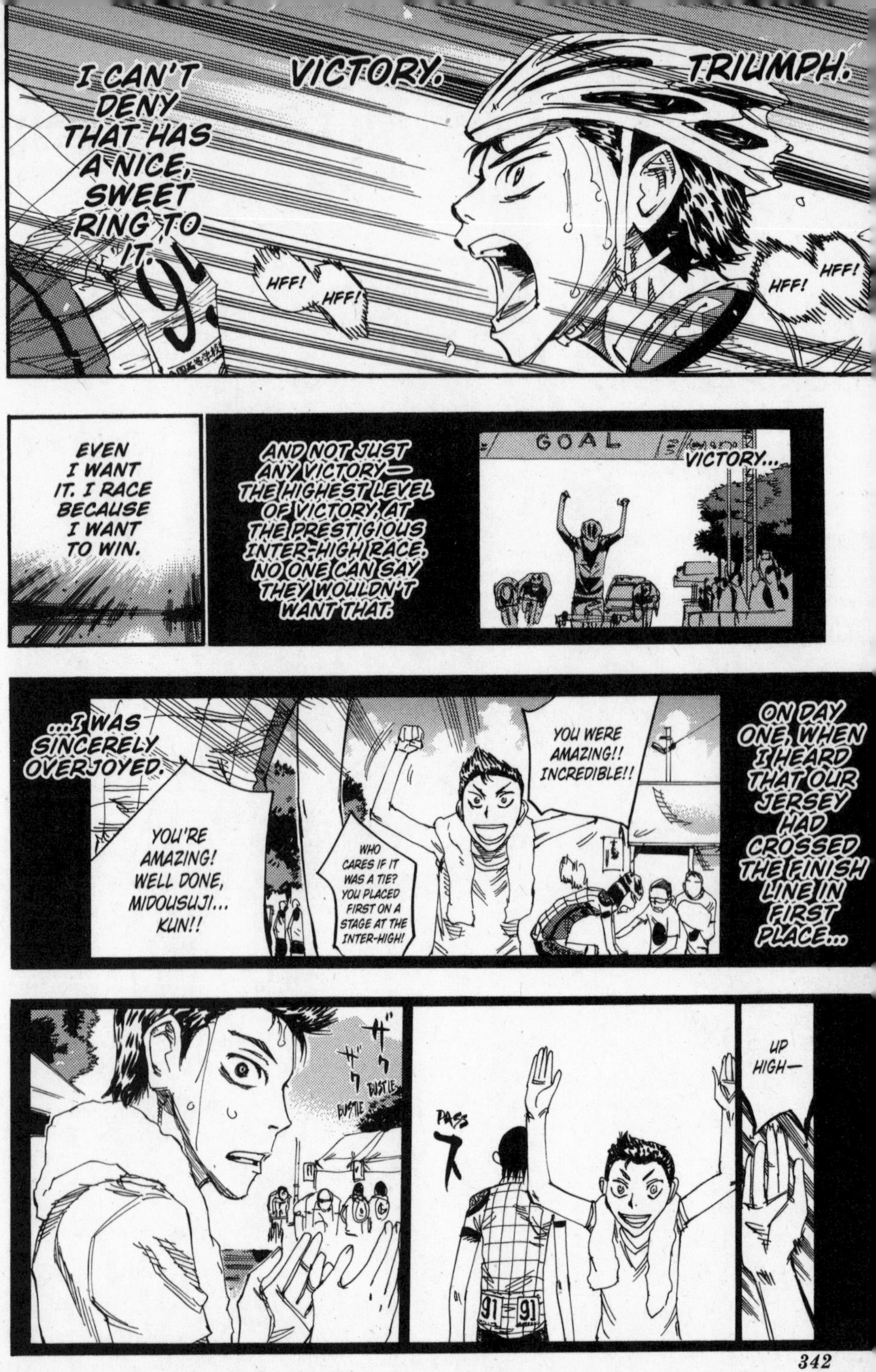
TRIUMPH.
HFF!
HFF!
VICTORY.
HFF!
HFF!
I CAN'T DENY THAT HAS A NICE, SWEET RING TO IT.
VICTORY...
AND NOT JUST ANY VICTORY— THE HIGHEST LEVEL OF VICTORY, AT THE PRESTIGIOUS INTER-HIGH RACE. NO ONE CAN SAY THEY WOULDN'T WANT THAT.
EVEN I WANT IT. I RACE BECAUSE I WANT TO WIN.
GOAL
ON DAY ONE, WHEN I HEARD THAT OUR JERSEY HAD CROSSED THE FINISH LINE IN FIRST PLACE...
YOU WERE AMAZING!! INCREDIBLE!!
...I WAS SINCERELY OVERJOYED.
WHO CARES IF IT WAS A TIE? YOU PLACED FIRST ON A STAGE AT THE INTER-HIGH!
YOU'RE AMAZING! WELL DONE, MIDOUSUJI... KUN!!
UP HIGH—
PASS
ザワ
ザワ
BUSTLE
BUSTLE

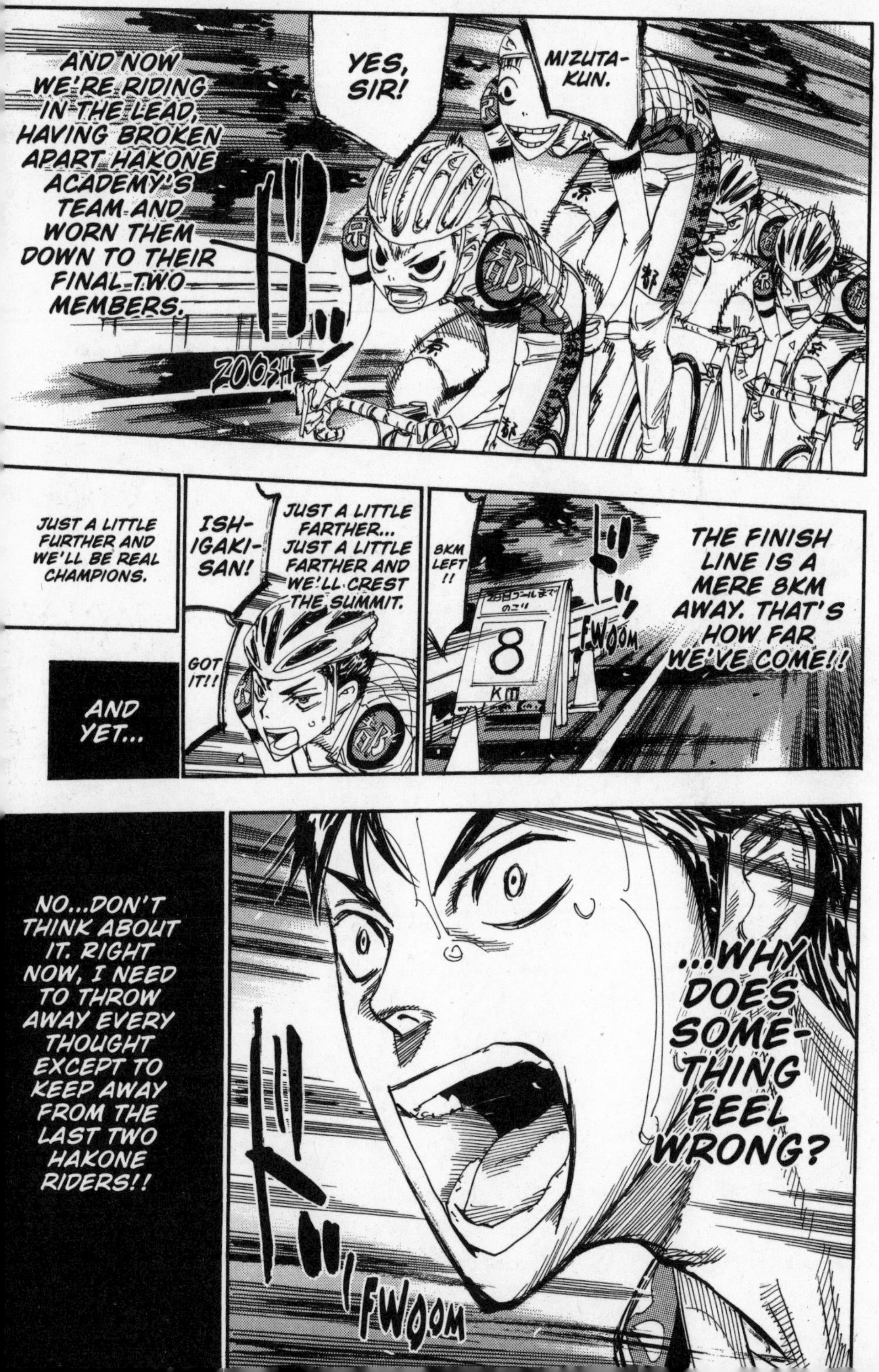
MIZUTA-KUN.
YES, SIR!
AND NOW WE'RE RIDING IN THE LEAD, HAVING BROKEN APART HAKONE ACADEMY'S TEAM AND WORN THEM DOWN TO THEIR FINAL TWO MEMBERS.
ZOOSH
THE FINISH LINE IS A MERE 8KM AWAY. THAT'S HOW FAR WE'VE COME!!
8KM LEFT!!
FWOOM
8
KM
JUST A LITTLE FARTHER... JUST A LITTLE FARTHER AND WE'LL CREST THE SUMMIT.
ISH-IGAKI-SAN!
GOT IT!!
JUST A LITTLE FURTHER AND WE'LL BE REAL CHAMPIONS.
AND YET...
...WHY DOES SOME-THING FEEL WRONG?
FWOOM
NO...DON'T THINK ABOUT IT. RIGHT NOW, I NEED TO THROW AWAY EVERY THOUGHT EXCEPT TO KEEP AWAY FROM THE LAST TWO HAKONE RIDERS!!

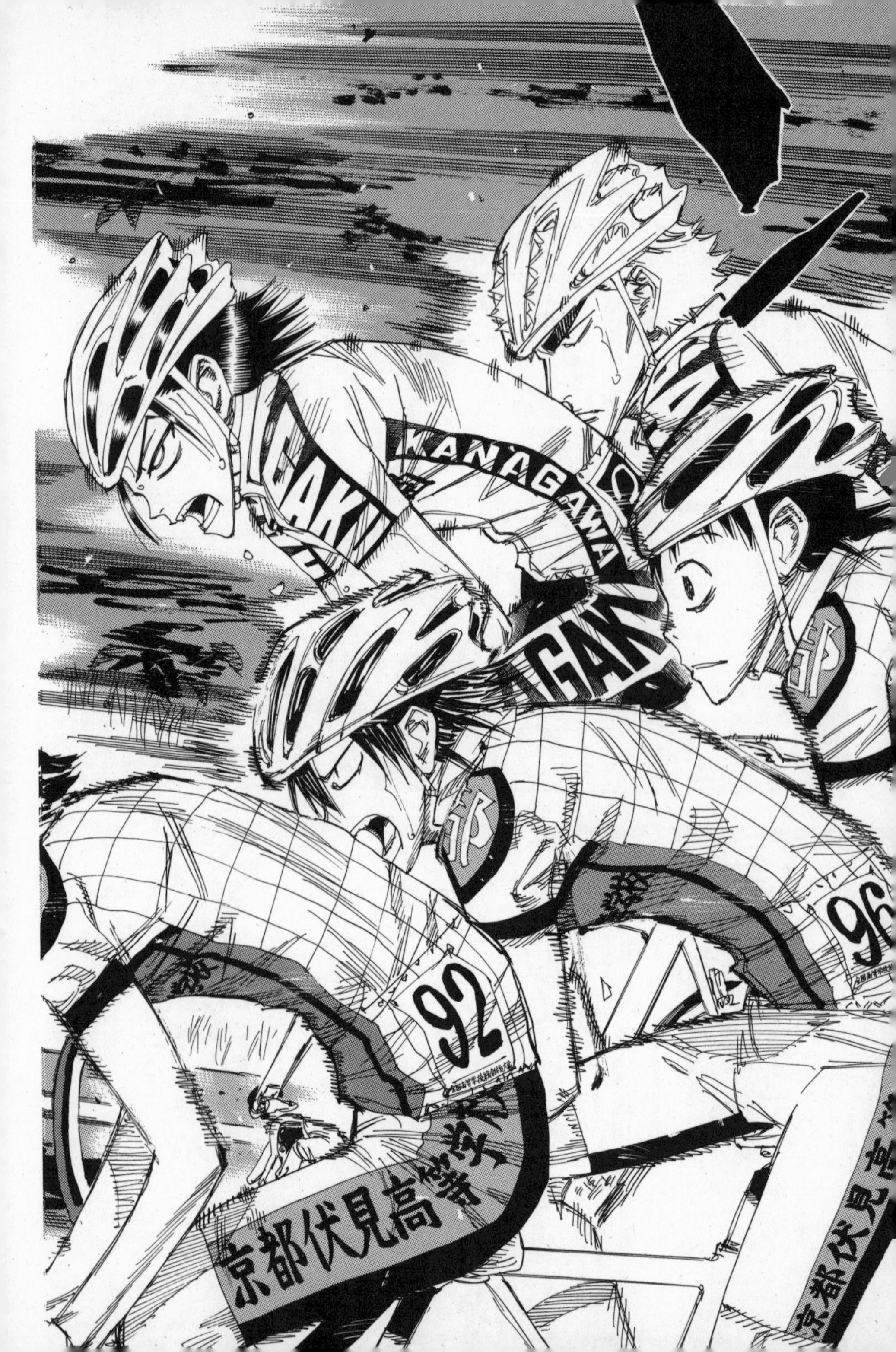
KANAGAWA
96
92
京都伏見高
京都伏見高

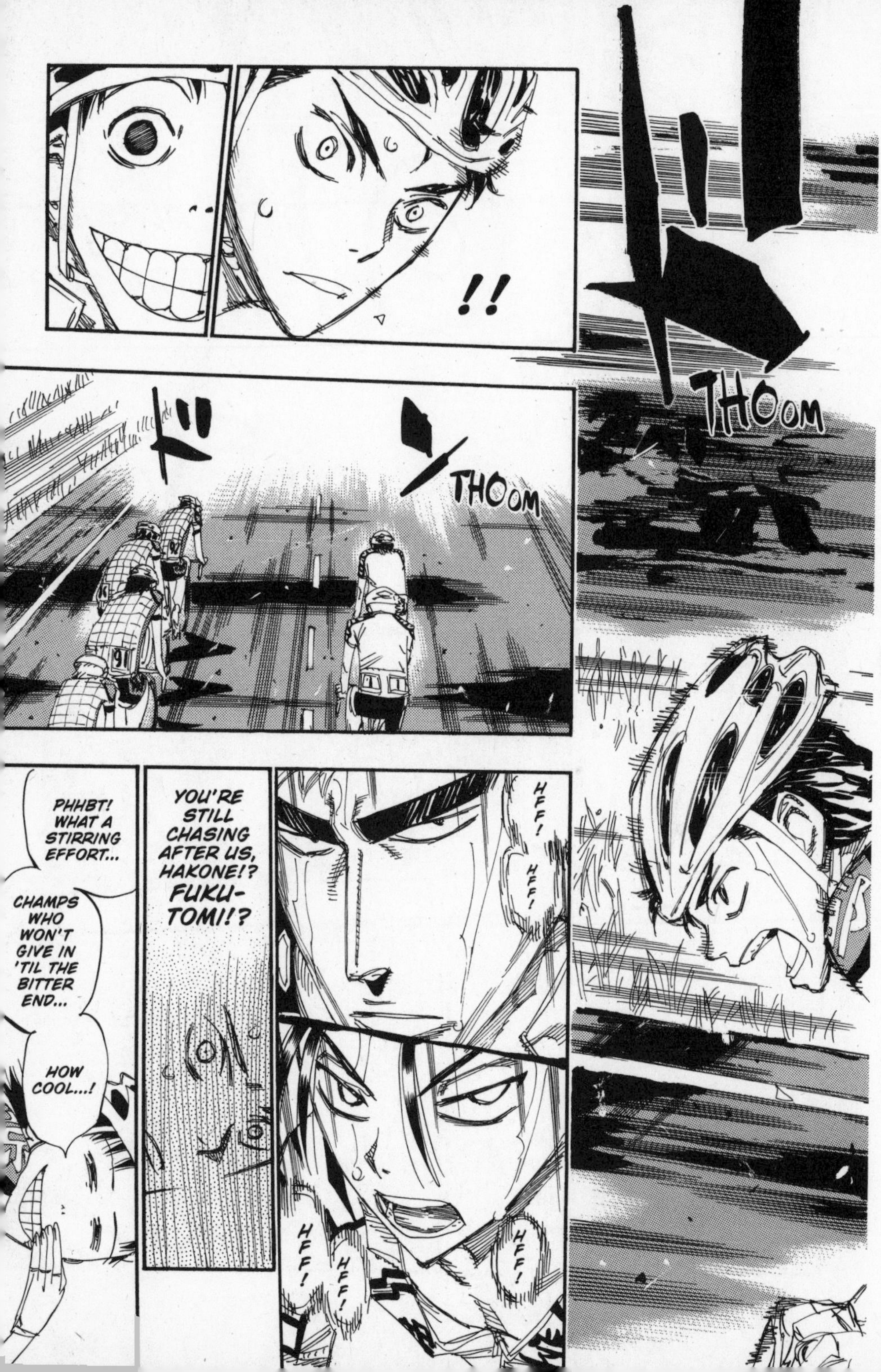
THOOM
!!
THOOM
HFF! HFF!
HFF! HFF! HFF!
YOU'RE STILL CHASING AFTER US, HAKONE!? FUKU-TOMI!?
PHHBT! WHAT A STIRRING EFFORT...
CHAMPS WHO WON'T GIVE IN 'TIL THE BITTER END...
HOW COOL...!

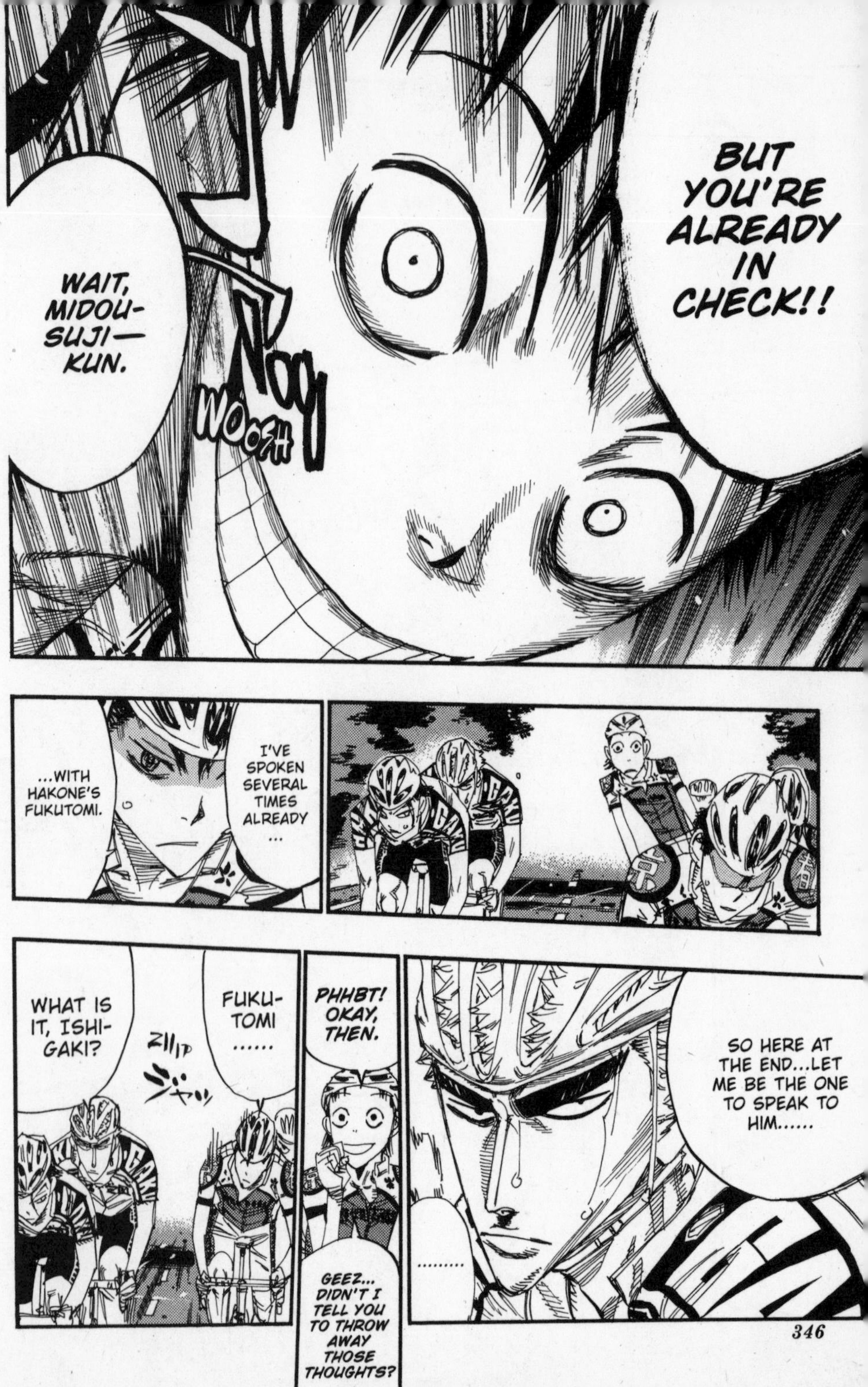
BUT YOU'RE ALREADY IN CHECK!!
WAIT, MIDOUSUJI—KUN.
WOOSH
I'VE SPOKEN SEVERAL TIMES ALREADY ...
...WITH HAKONE'S FUKUTOMI.
SO HERE AT THE END...LET ME BE THE ONE TO SPEAK TO HIM......
....
PHHBT! OKAY, THEN.
GEEZ... DIDN'T I TELL YOU TO THROW AWAY THOSE THOUGHTS?
FUKUTOMI ......
ZIIIP
WHAT IS IT, ISHIGAKI?

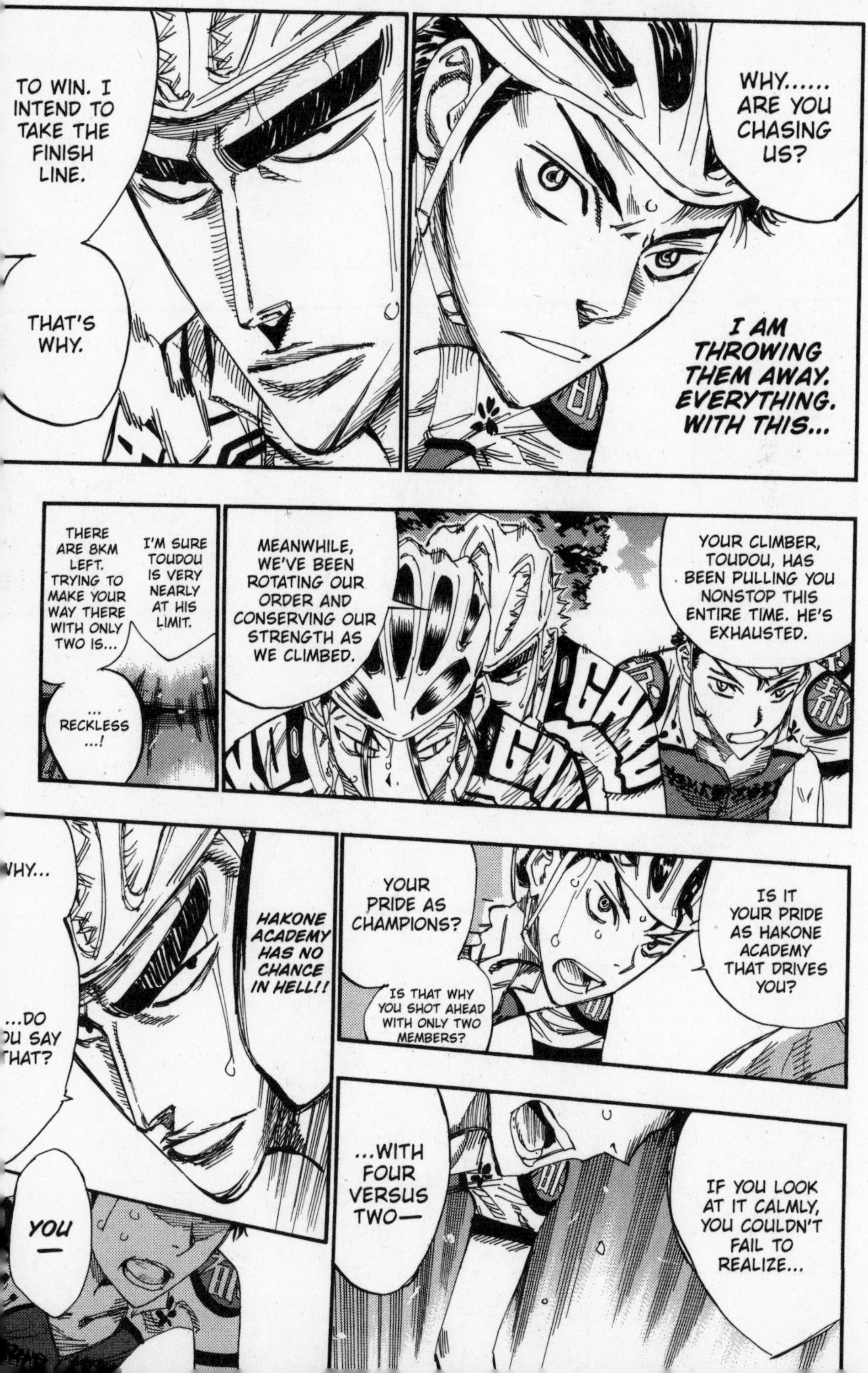
WHY...... ARE YOU CHASING US?
I AM THROWING THEM AWAY. EVERYTHING. WITH THIS...
TO WIN. I INTEND TO TAKE THE FINISH LINE.
THAT'S WHY.
YOUR CLIMBER, TOUDOU, HAS BEEN PULLING YOU NONSTOP THIS ENTIRE TIME. HE'S EXHAUSTED.
MEANWHILE, WE'VE BEEN ROTATING OUR ORDER AND CONSERVING OUR STRENGTH AS WE CLIMBED.
I'M SURE TOUDOU IS VERY NEARLY AT HIS LIMIT.
THERE ARE 8KM LEFT. TRYING TO MAKE YOUR WAY THERE WITH ONLY TWO IS...
...RECKLESS...!
IS IT YOUR PRIDE AS HAKONE ACADEMY THAT DRIVES YOU?
YOUR PRIDE AS CHAMPIONS?
IS THAT WHY YOU SHOT AHEAD WITH ONLY TWO MEMBERS?
IF YOU LOOK AT IT CALMLY, YOU COULDN'T FAIL TO REALIZE...
...WITH FOUR VERSUS TWO—
HAKONE ACADEMY HAS NO CHANCE IN HELL!!
WHY...
...DO OU SAY THAT?
YOU —

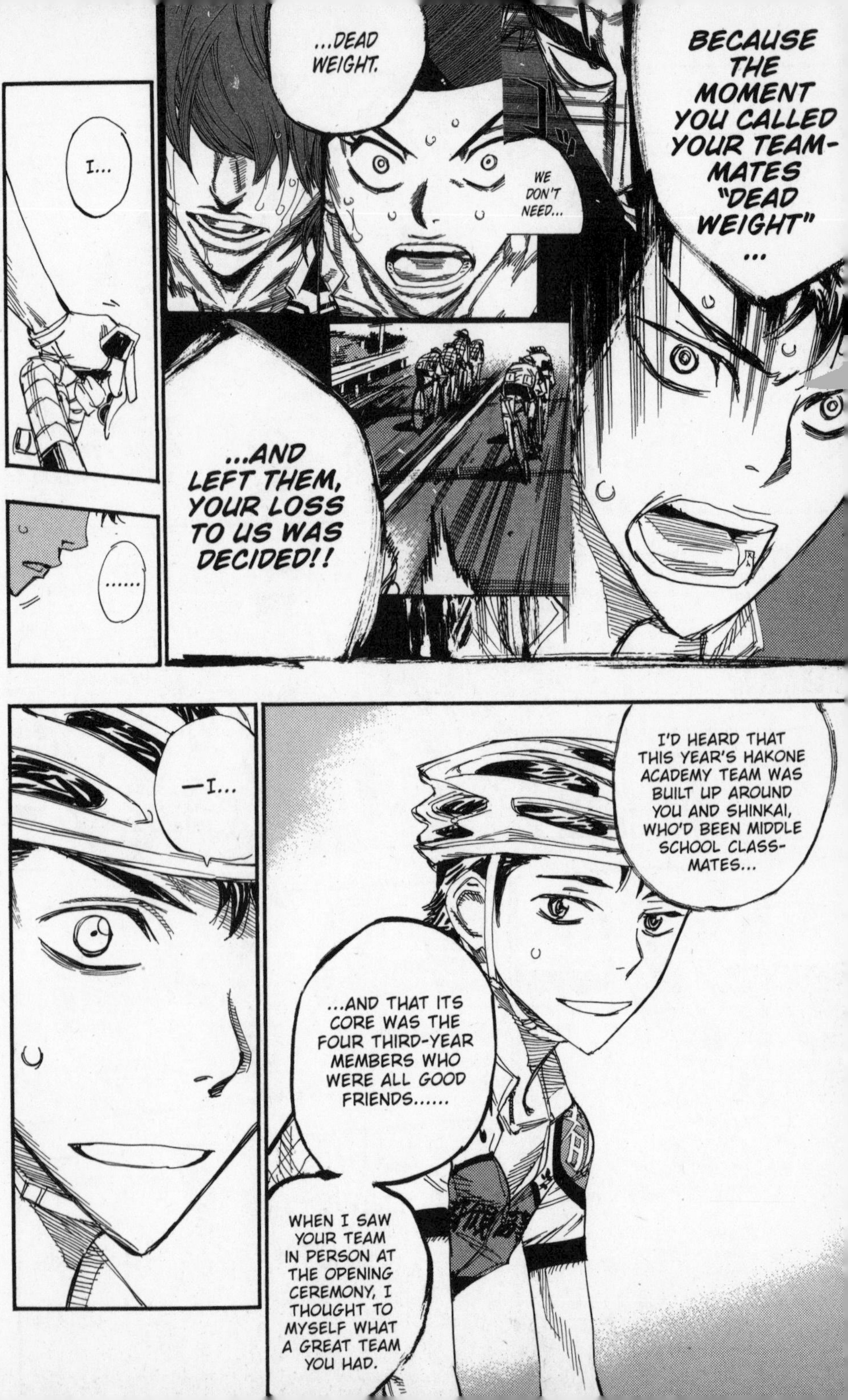
BECAUSE THE MOMENT YOU CALLED YOUR TEAM-MATES "DEAD WEIGHT"...
...DEAD WEIGHT.
WE DON'T NEED...
...AND LEFT THEM, YOUR LOSS TO US WAS DECIDED!!
I...
......
I'D HEARD THAT THIS YEAR'S HAKONE ACADEMY TEAM WAS BUILT UP AROUND YOU AND SHINKAI, WHO'D BEEN MIDDLE SCHOOL CLASS-MATES...
...AND THAT ITS CORE WAS THE FOUR THIRD-YEAR MEMBERS WHO WERE ALL GOOD FRIENDS......
WHEN I SAW YOUR TEAM IN PERSON AT THE OPENING CEREMONY, I THOUGHT TO MYSELF WHAT A GREAT TEAM YOU HAD.
—I...

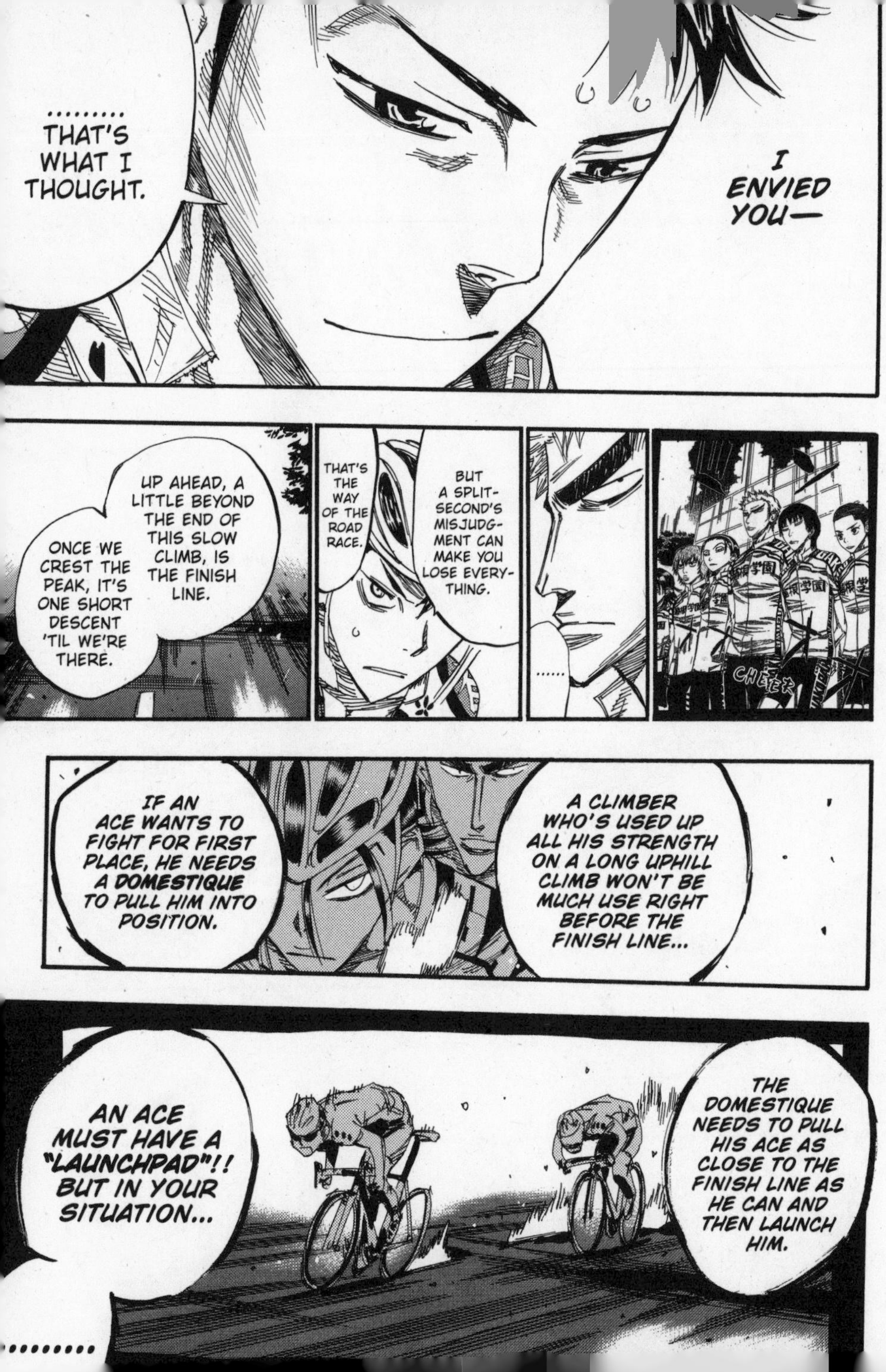
I ENVIED YOU—
....
THAT'S WHAT I THOUGHT.
CHEER
......
BUT A SPLIT-SECOND'S MISJUDG-MENT CAN MAKE YOU LOSE EVERY-THING.
THAT'S THE WAY OF THE ROAD RACE.
UP AHEAD, A LITTLE BEYOND THE END OF THIS SLOW CLIMB, IS THE FINISH LINE.
ONCE WE CREST THE PEAK, IT'S ONE SHORT DESCENT 'TIL WE'RE THERE.
A CLIMBER WHO'S USED UP ALL HIS STRENGTH ON A LONG UPHILL CLIMB WON'T BE MUCH USE RIGHT BEFORE THE FINISH LINE...
IF AN ACE WANTS TO FIGHT FOR FIRST PLACE, HE NEEDS A DOMESTIQUE TO PULL HIM INTO POSITION.
THE DOMESTIQUE NEEDS TO PULL HIS ACE AS CLOSE TO THE FINISH LINE AS HE CAN AND THEN LAUNCH HIM.
AN ACE MUST HAVE A "LAUNCHPAD"!! BUT IN YOUR SITUATION...
....

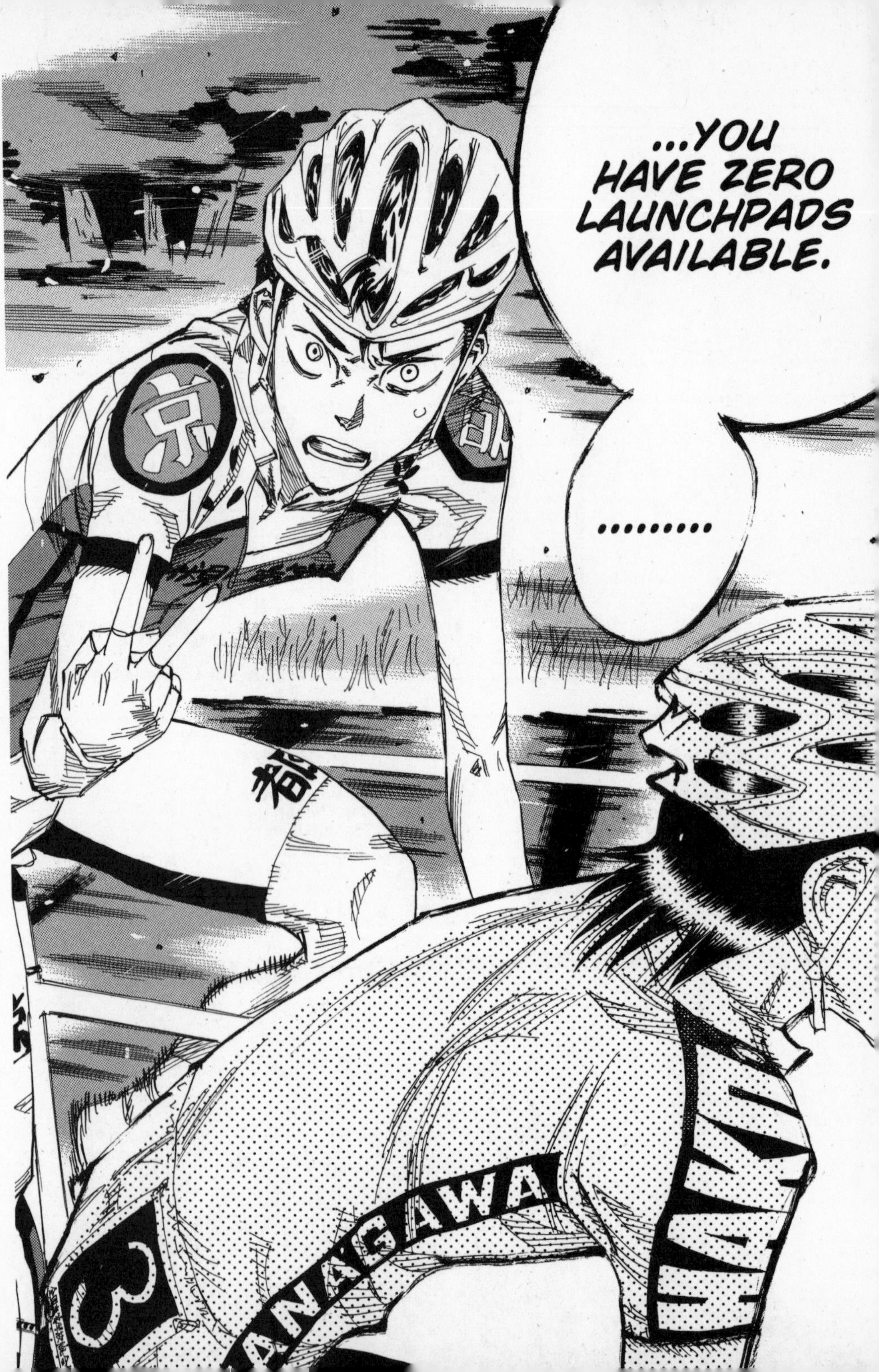
...YOU HAVE ZERO LAUNCHPADS AVAILABLE.
....

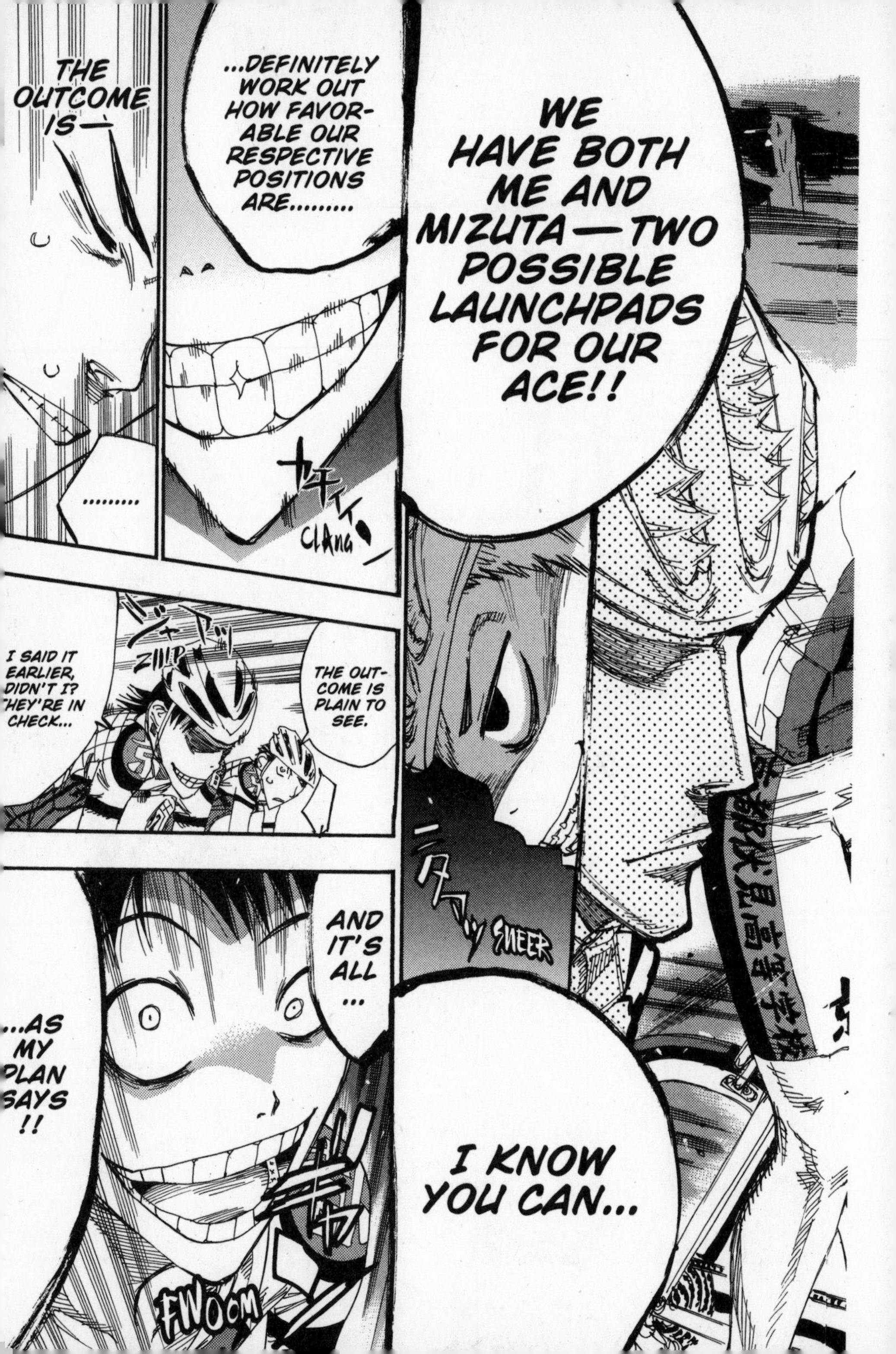
WE HAVE BOTH ME AND MIZUTA—TWO POSSIBLE LAUNCHPADS FOR OUR ACE!!
...DEFINITELY WORK OUT HOW FAVOR-ABLE OUR RESPECTIVE POSITIONS ARE.........
CLANG
THE OUTCOME IS—
....
SNEER
I KNOW YOU CAN...
THE OUT-COME IS PLAIN TO SEE.
ZIIIP
I SAID IT EARLIER, DIDN'T I? THEY'RE IN CHECK...
AND IT'S ALL ...
...AS MY PLAN SAYS!!
FWOOM

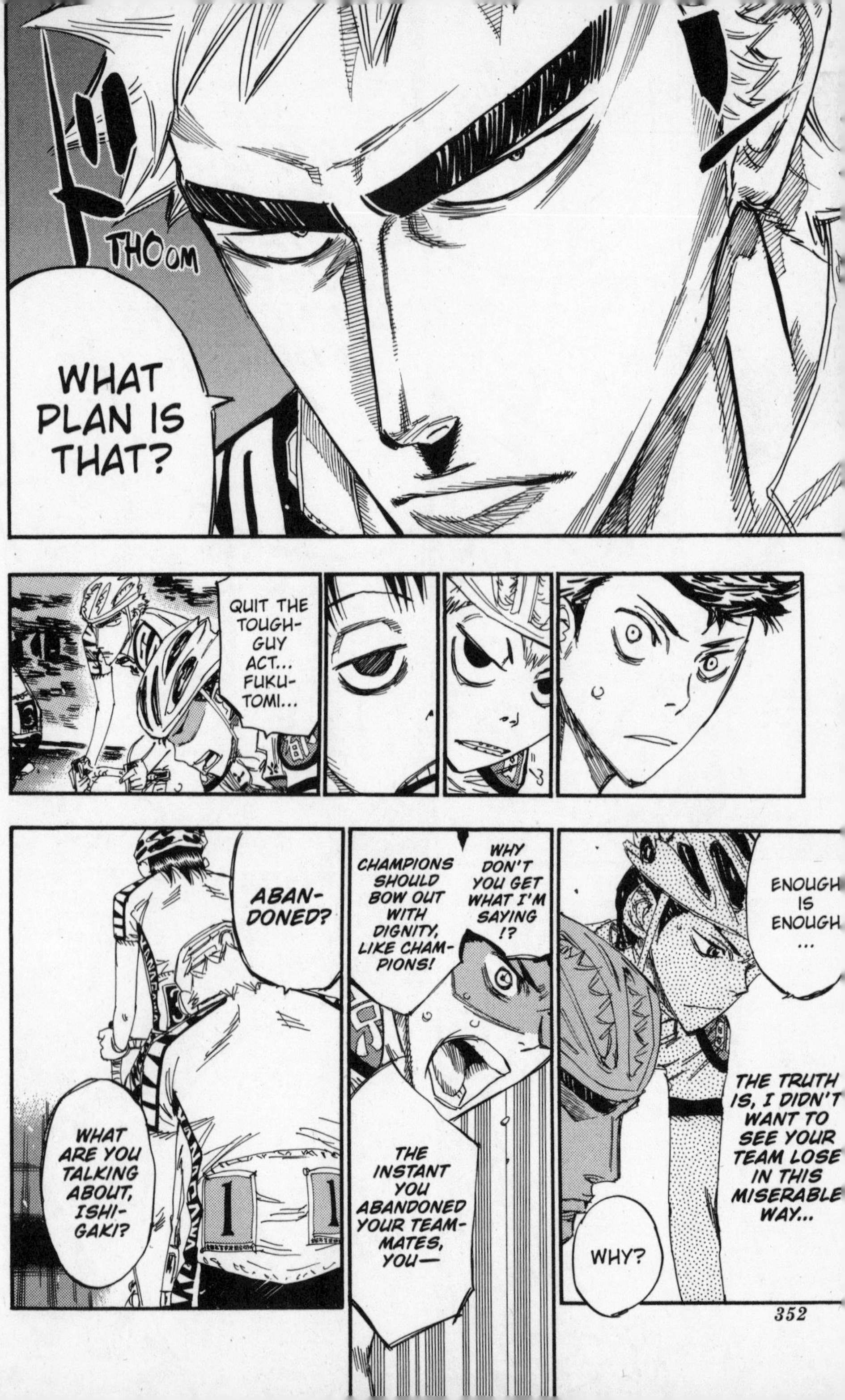
THOOM
WHAT PLAN IS THAT?
QUIT THE TOUGH-GUY ACT... FUKUTOMI...
ENOUGH IS ENOUGH...
THE TRUTH IS, I DIDN'T WANT TO SEE YOUR TEAM LOSE IN THIS MISERABLE WAY...
WHY?
WHY DON'T YOU GET WHAT I'M SAYING!?
CHAMPIONS SHOULD BOW OUT WITH DIGNITY, LIKE CHAMPIONS!
THE INSTANT YOU ABANDONED YOUR TEAMMATES, YOU—
ABANDONED?
WHAT ARE YOU TALKING ABOUT, ISHIGAKI?

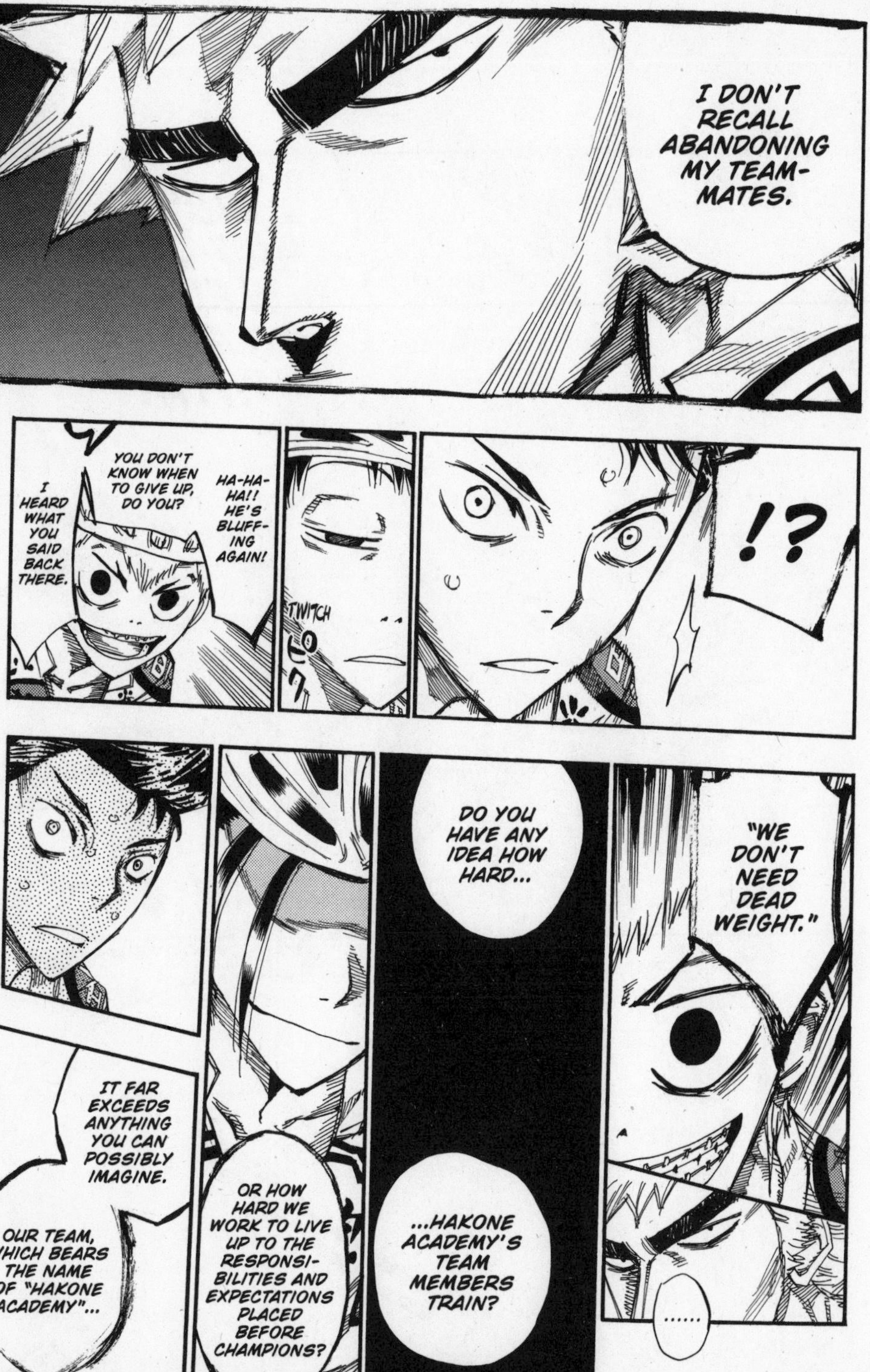
I DON'T RECALL ABANDONING MY TEAM-MATES.
!?
TWITCH
HA-HA!! HE'S BLUFF-ING AGAIN!
YOU DON'T KNOW WHEN TO GIVE UP, DO YOU?
I HEARD WHAT YOU SAID BACK THERE.
"WE DON'T NEED DEAD WEIGHT."
......
DO YOU HAVE ANY IDEA HOW HARD...
...HAKONE ACADEMY'S TEAM MEMBERS TRAIN?
OR HOW HARD WE WORK TO LIVE UP TO THE RESPONSI-BILITIES AND EXPECTATIONS PLACED BEFORE CHAMPIONS?
IT FAR EXCEEDS ANYTHING YOU CAN POSSIBLY IMAGINE.
OUR TEAM, WHICH BEARS THE NAME OF "HAKONE ACADEMY"...

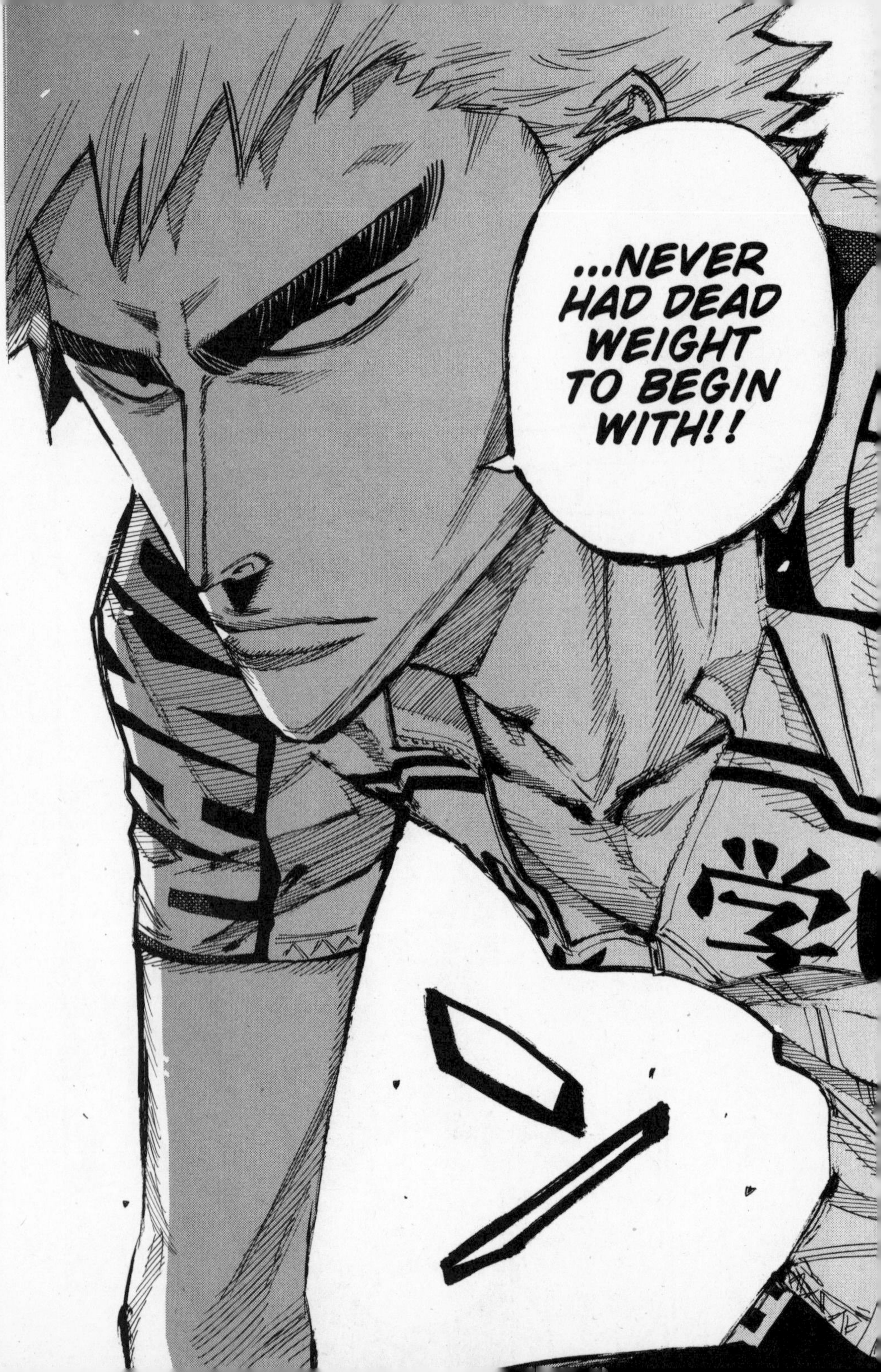
...NEVER HAD DEAD WEIGHT TO BEGIN WITH!!

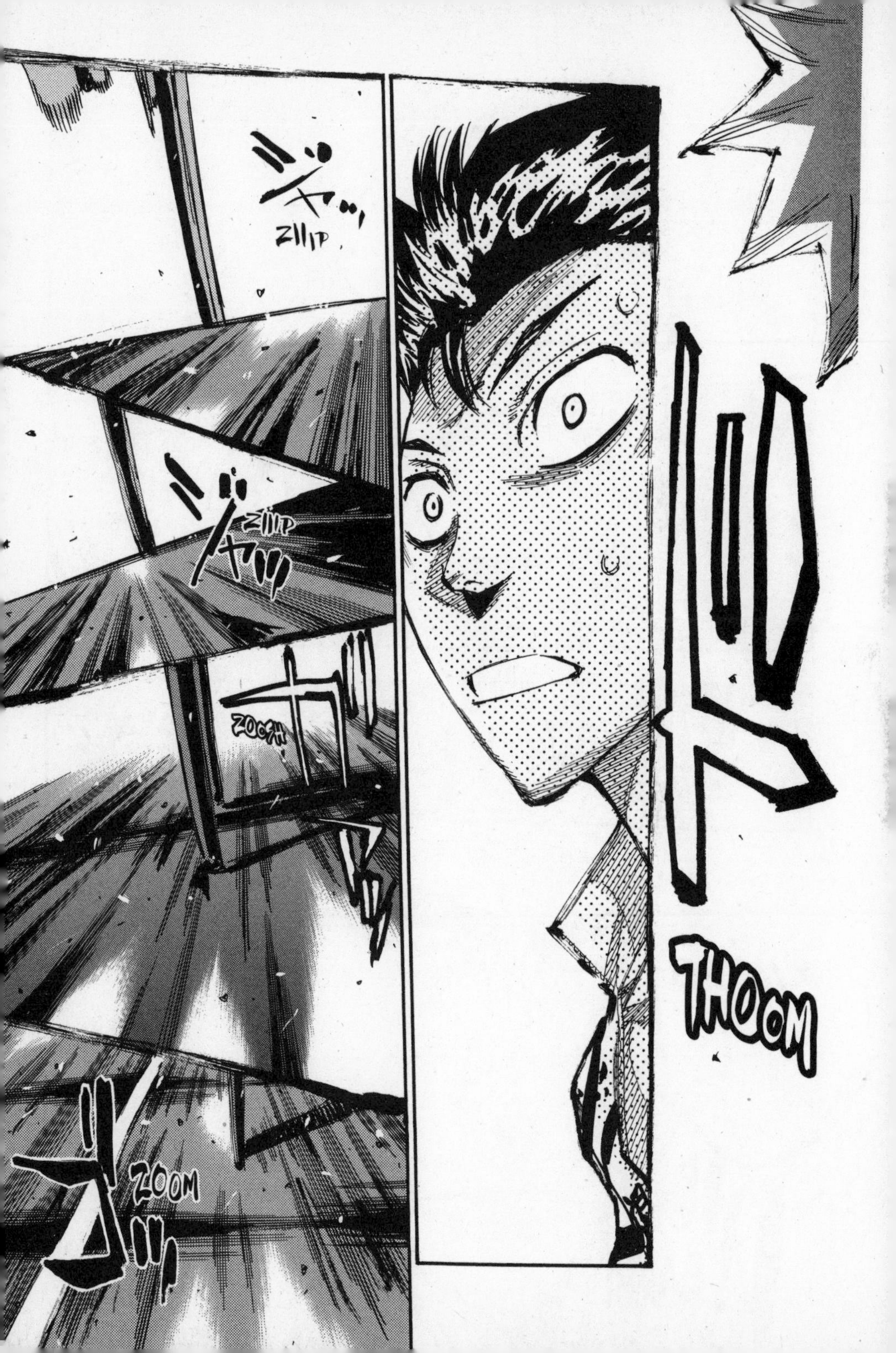
THOOM
ZIIIP
ZIIIP
ZOOSH
ZOOM

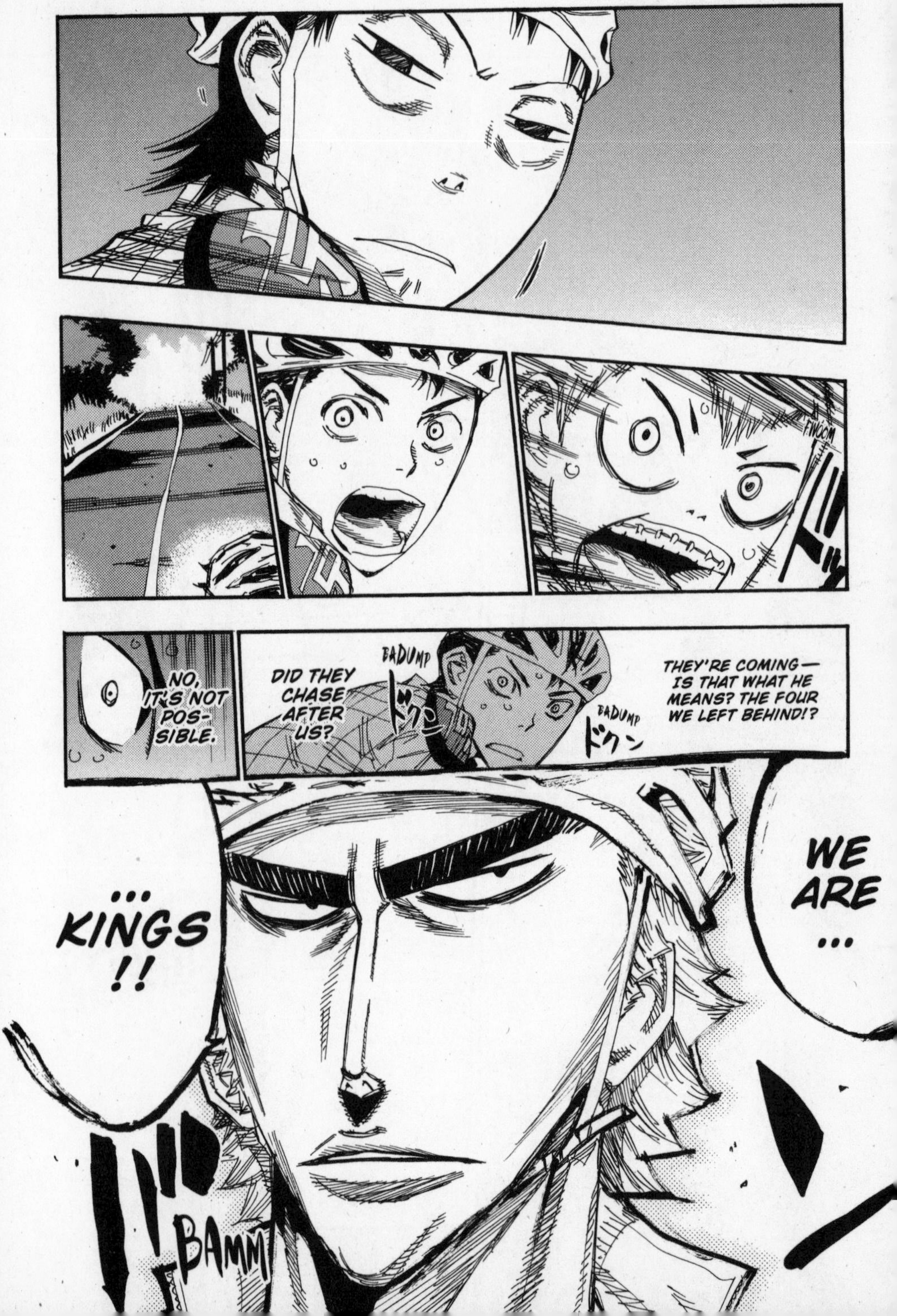
FWOOM
THEY'RE COMING— IS THAT WHAT HE MEANS? THE FOUR WE LEFT BEHIND!?
BADUMP ドクン
DID THEY CHASE AFTER US?
BADUMP ドクン
NO, IT'S NOT POS-SIBLE.
WE ARE ...
... KINGS !!
BAMM

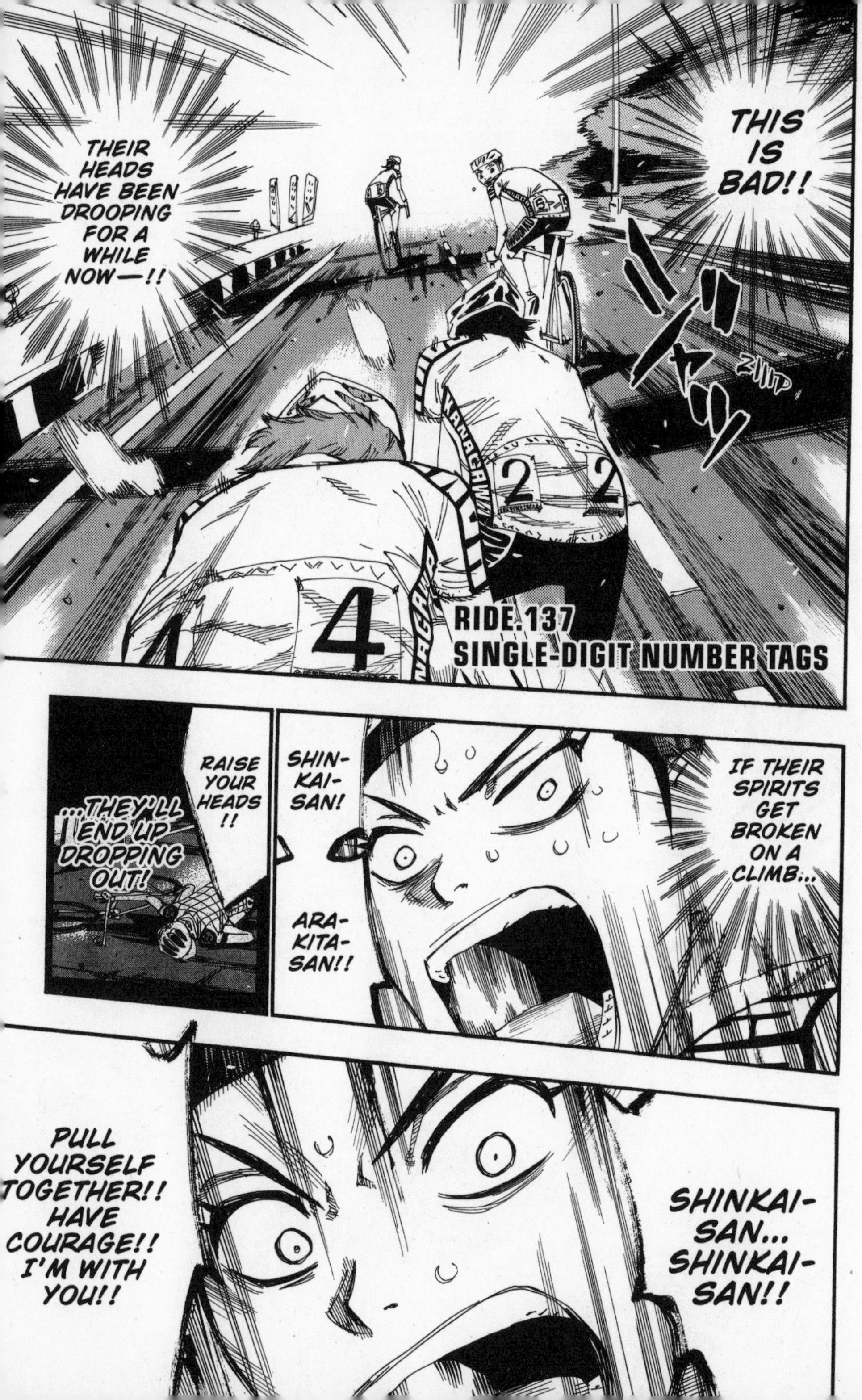
THIS IS BAD!!
ZIIIP
THEIR HEADS HAVE BEEN DROOPING FOR A WHILE NOW—!!
RIDE.137 SINGLE-DIGIT NUMBER TAGS
IF THEIR SPIRITS GET BROKEN ON A CLIMB...
SHINKAI-SAN!
ARAKITA-SAN!!
RAISE YOUR HEADS!!
...THEY'LL END UP DROPPING OUT!
SHINKAI-SAN... SHINKAI-SAN!!
PULL YOURSELF TOGETHER!! HAVE COURAGE!! I'M WITH YOU!!

RIDE.137 SINGLE-DIGIT NUMBER TAGS

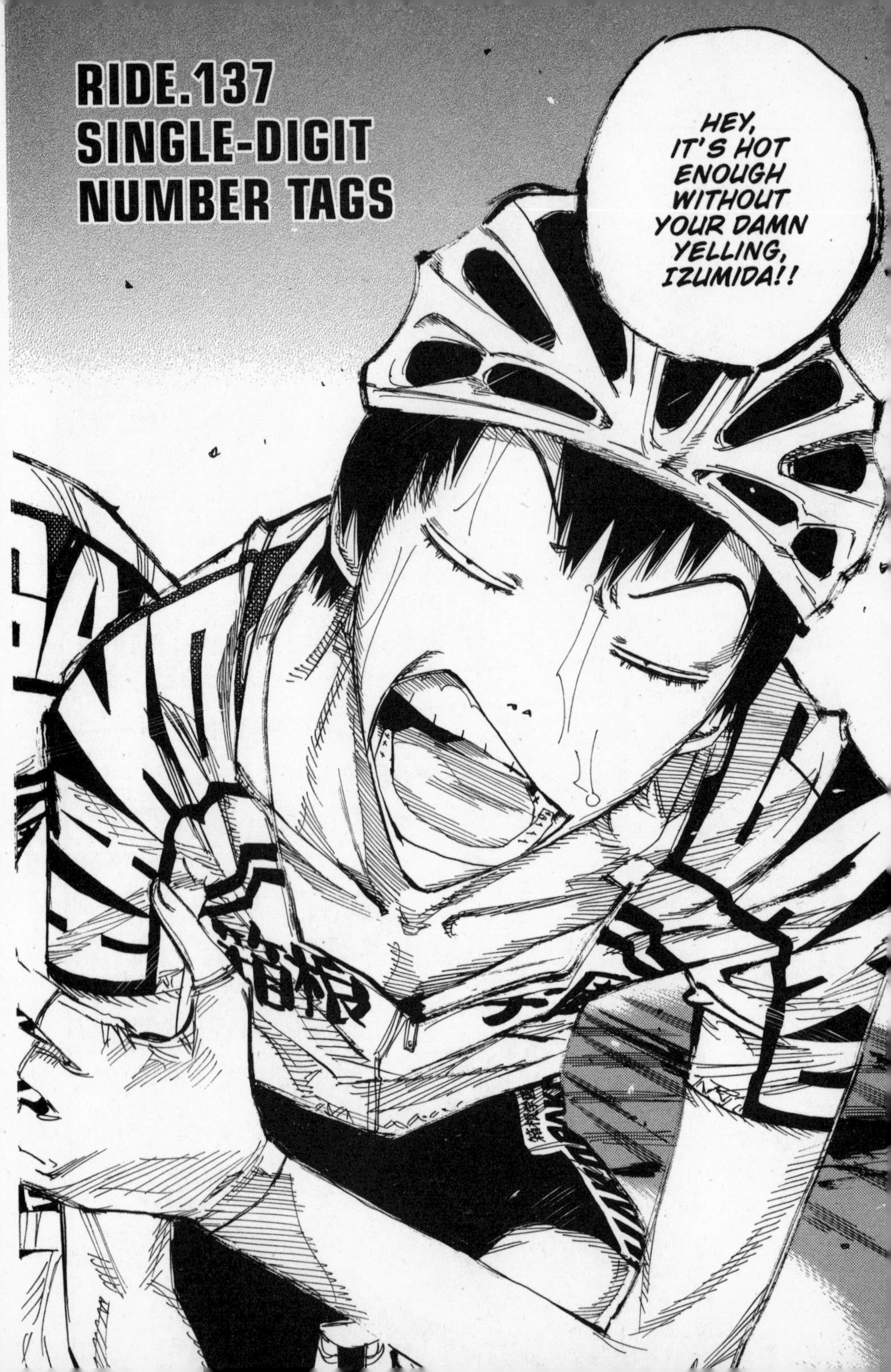
HEY, IT'S HOT ENOUGH WITHOUT YOUR DAMN YELLING, IZUMIDA!!

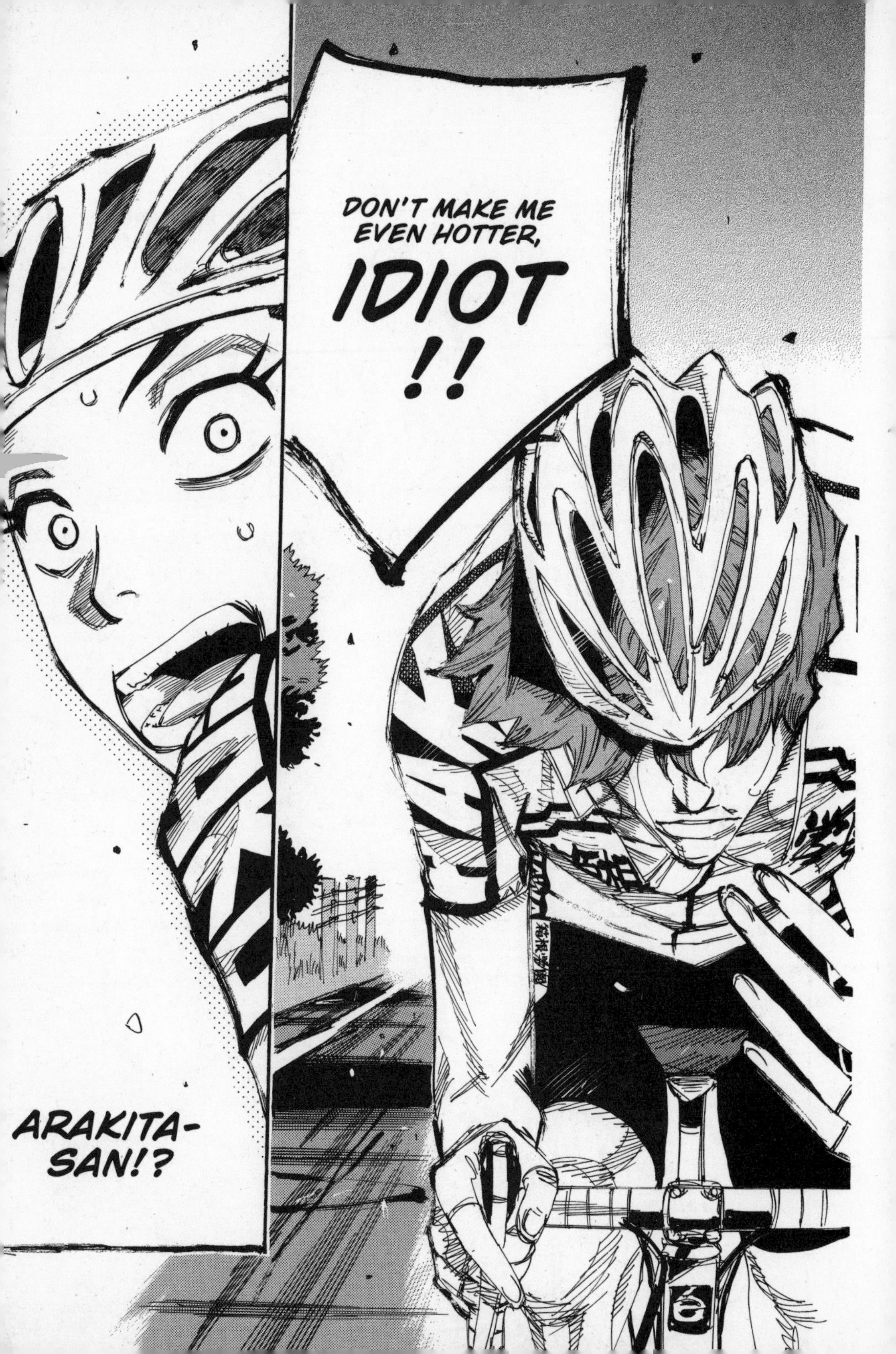
DON'T MAKE ME EVEN HOTTER, IDIOT!!
ARAKITA-SAN!?

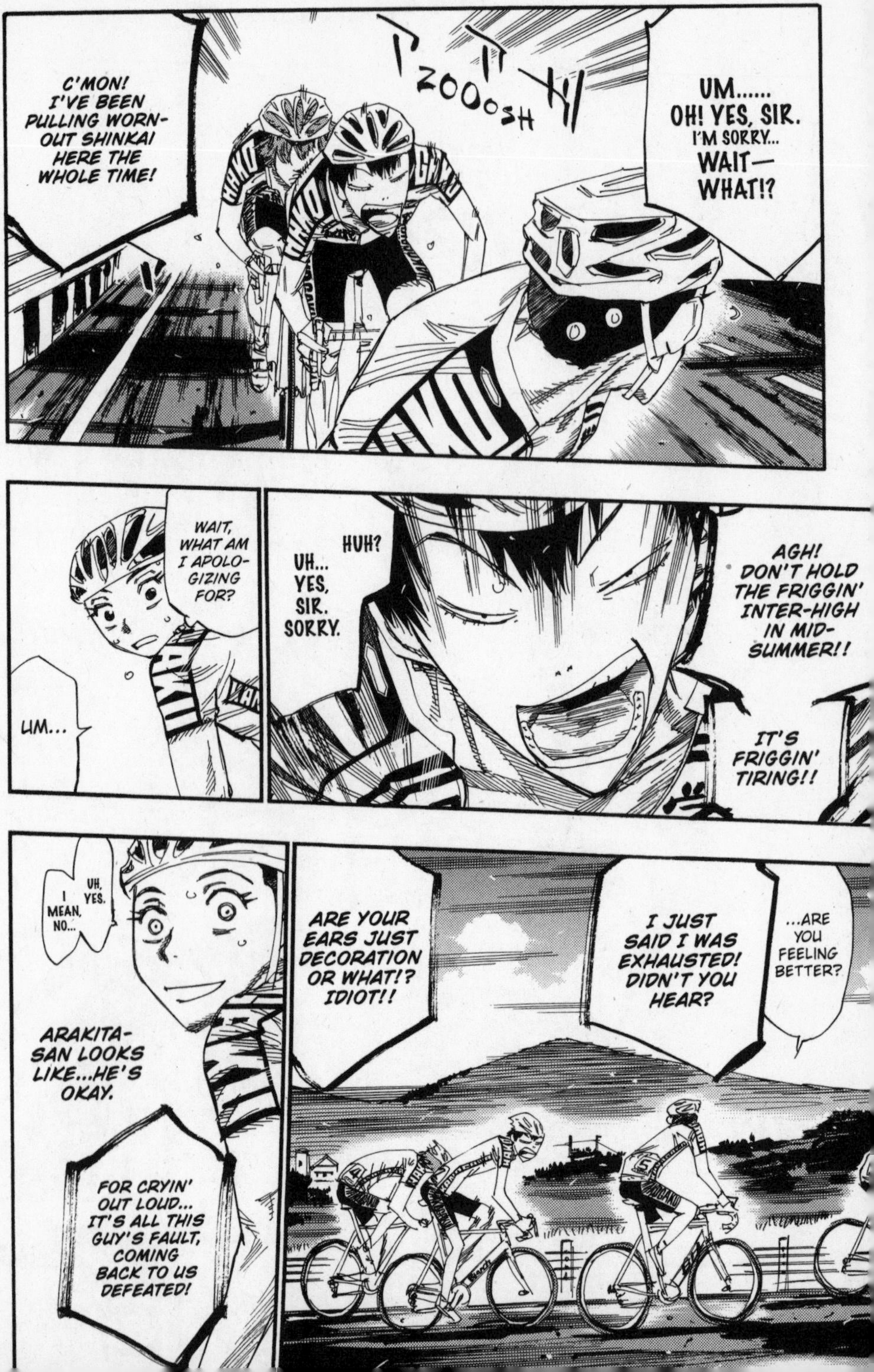
UM...... OH! YES, SIR. I'M SORRY... WAIT— WHAT!?
ZOOOOSH
C'MON! I'VE BEEN PULLING WORN-OUT SHINKAI HERE THE WHOLE TIME!
AGH! DON'T HOLD THE FRIGGIN' INTER-HIGH IN MID-SUMMER!!
IT'S FRIGGIN' TIRING!!
HUH?
UH... YES, SIR. SORRY.
WAIT, WHAT AM I APOLO-GIZING FOR?
UM...
...ARE YOU FEELING BETTER?
I JUST SAID I WAS EXHAUSTED! DIDN'T YOU HEAR?
ARE YOUR EARS JUST DECORATION OR WHAT!? IDIOT!!
UH, YES. I MEAN, NO...
ARAKITA-SAN LOOKS LIKE...HE'S OKAY.
FOR CRYIN' OUT LOUD... IT'S ALL THIS GUY'S FAULT, COMING BACK TO US DEFEATED!

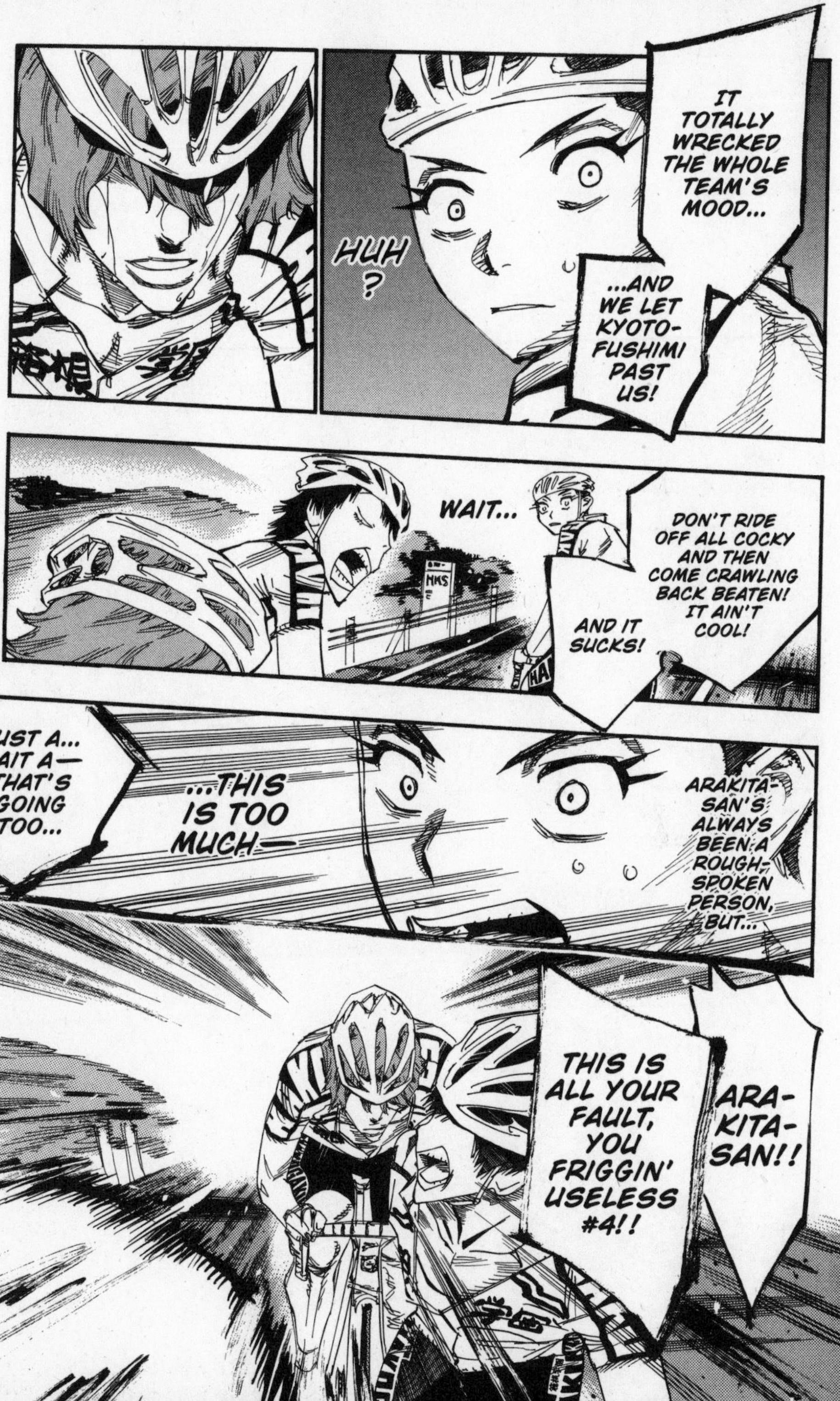
IT TOTALLY WRECKED THE WHOLE TEAM'S MOOD...
...AND WE LET KYOTO-FUSHIMI PAST US!
HUH ?
DON'T RIDE OFF ALL COCKY AND THEN COME CRAWLING BACK BEATEN! IT AIN'T COOL!
AND IT SUCKS!
WAIT...
ARAKITA-SAN'S ALWAYS BEEN A ROUGH-SPOKEN PERSON, BUT...
...THIS IS TOO MUCH—
JUST A... WAIT A— THAT'S GOING TOO...
ARA-KITA-SAN!!
THIS IS ALL YOUR FAULT, YOU FRIGGIN' USELESS #4!!

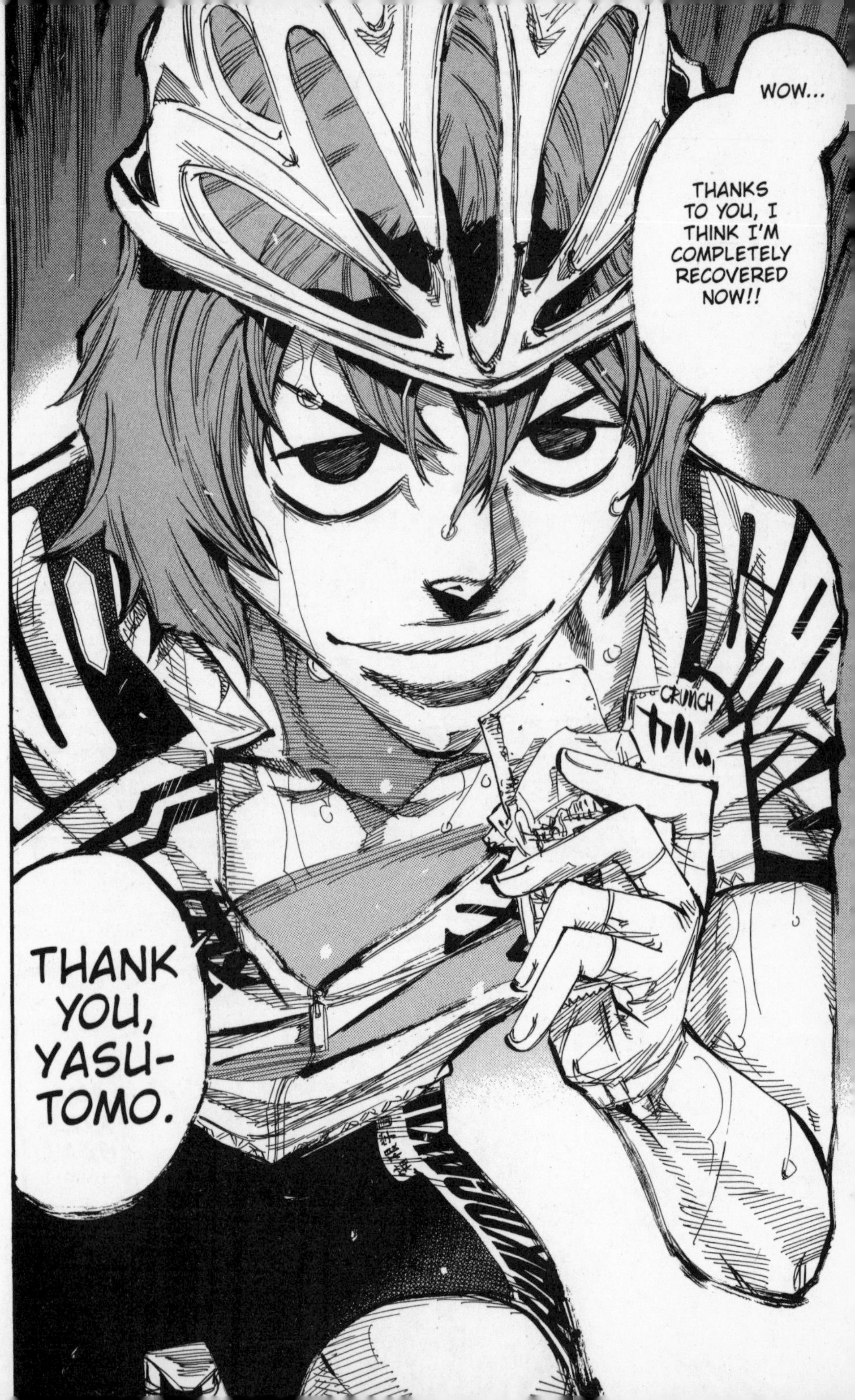
WOW...
THANKS TO YOU, I THINK I'M COMPLETELY RECOVERED NOW!!
CRUNCH
カリッ
THANK YOU, YASU-TOMO.

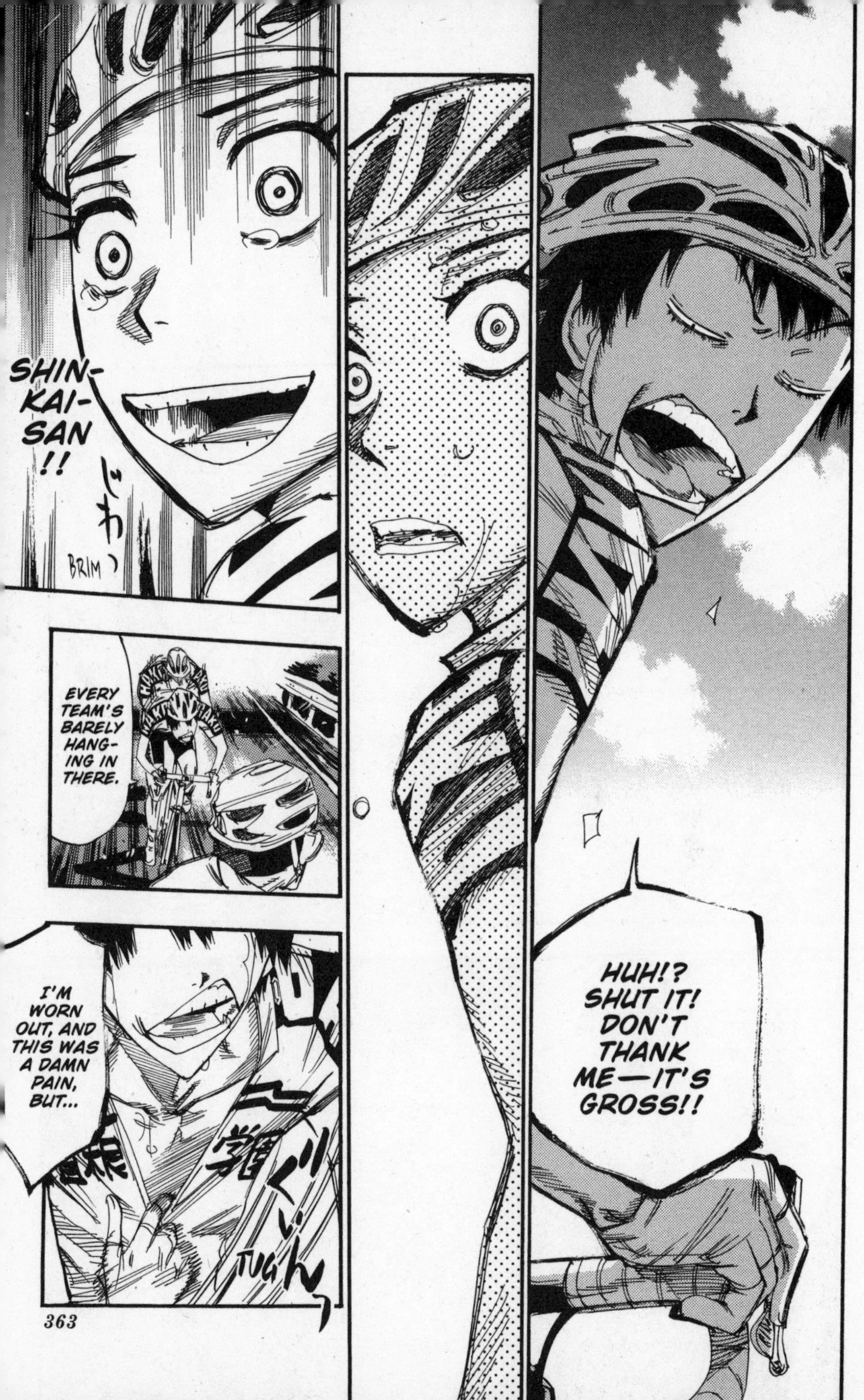
HUH!? SHUT IT! DON'T THANK ME—IT'S GROSS!!
SHIN-KAI-SAN!!
じわっ
BRIM
EVERY TEAM'S BARELY HANGING IN THERE.
I'M WORN OUT, AND THIS WAS A DAMN PAIN, BUT...
ぐいっ
TUG

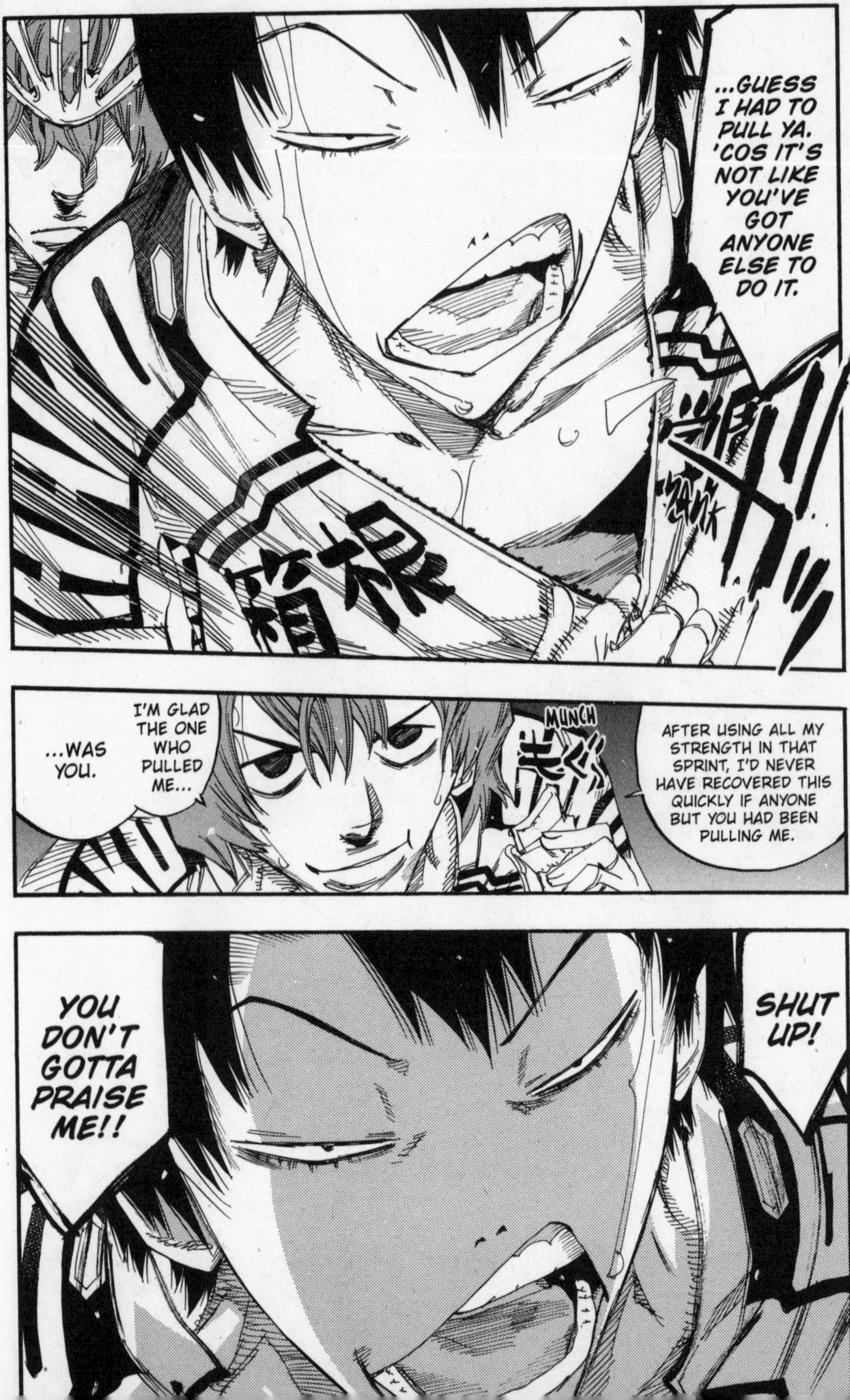
...GUESS I HAD TO PULL YA. 'COS IT'S NOT LIKE YOU'VE GOT ANYONE ELSE TO DO IT.
箱根
AFTER USING ALL MY STRENGTH IN THAT SPRINT, I'D NEVER HAVE RECOVERED THIS QUICKLY IF ANYONE BUT YOU HAD BEEN PULLING ME.
MUNCH
I'M GLAD THE ONE WHO PULLED ME...
...WAS YOU.
SHUT UP!
YOU DON'T GOTTA PRAISE ME!!

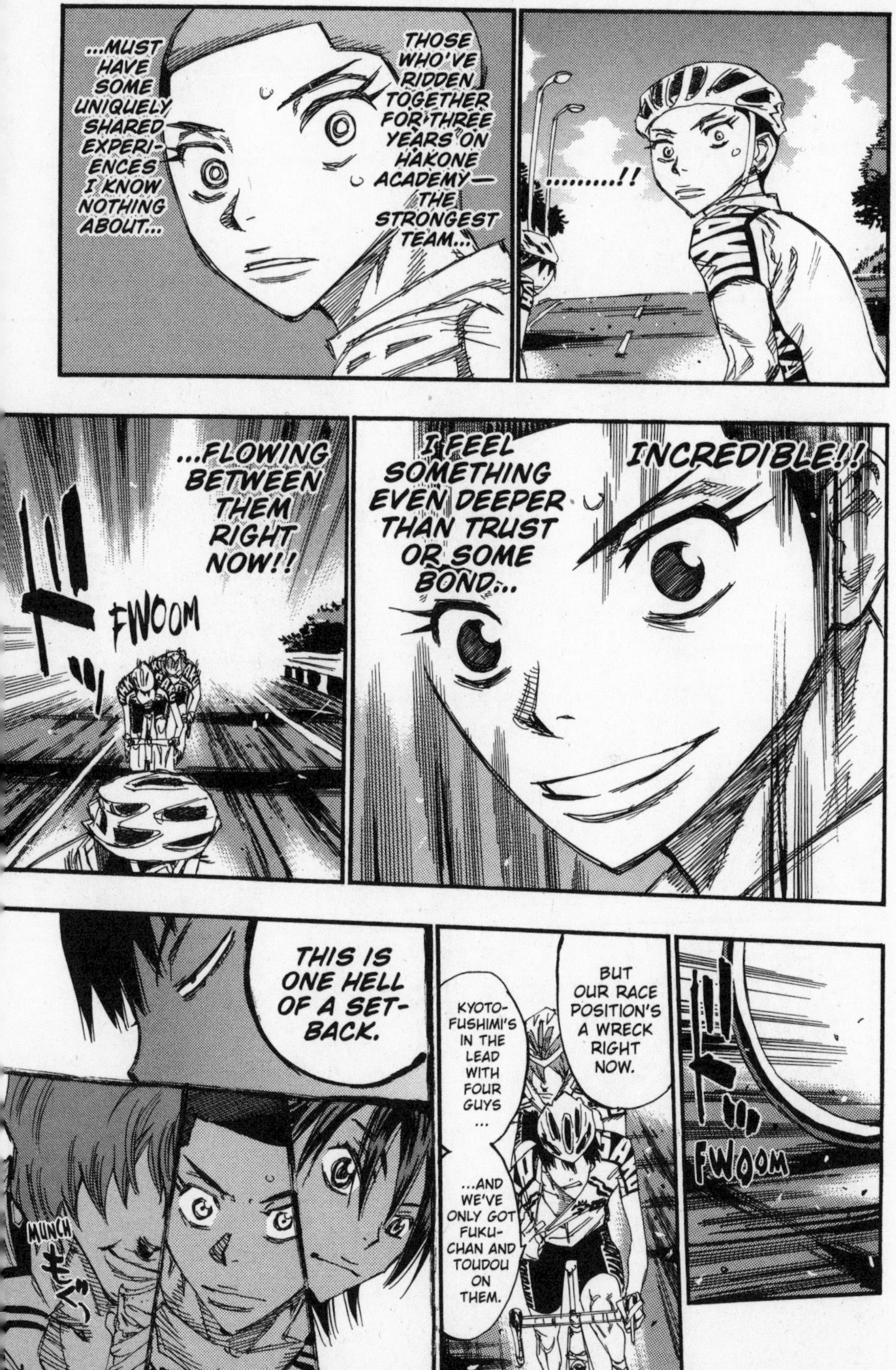
..........!!
THOSE WHO'VE RIDDEN TOGETHER FOR THREE YEARS ON HAKONE ACADEMY—THE STRONGEST TEAM...
...MUST HAVE SOME UNIQUELY SHARED EXPERI-ENCES I KNOW NOTHING ABOUT...
INCREDIBLE!!
I FEEL SOMETHING EVEN DEEPER THAN TRUST OR SOME BOND...
...FLOWING BETWEEN THEM RIGHT NOW!!
FWOOM
FWOOM
BUT OUR RACE POSITION'S A WRECK RIGHT NOW.
KYOTO-FUSHIMI'S IN THE LEAD WITH FOUR GUYS...
...AND WE'VE ONLY GOT FUKU-CHAN AND TOUDOU ON THEM.
THIS IS ONE HELL OF A SET-BACK.
MUNCH

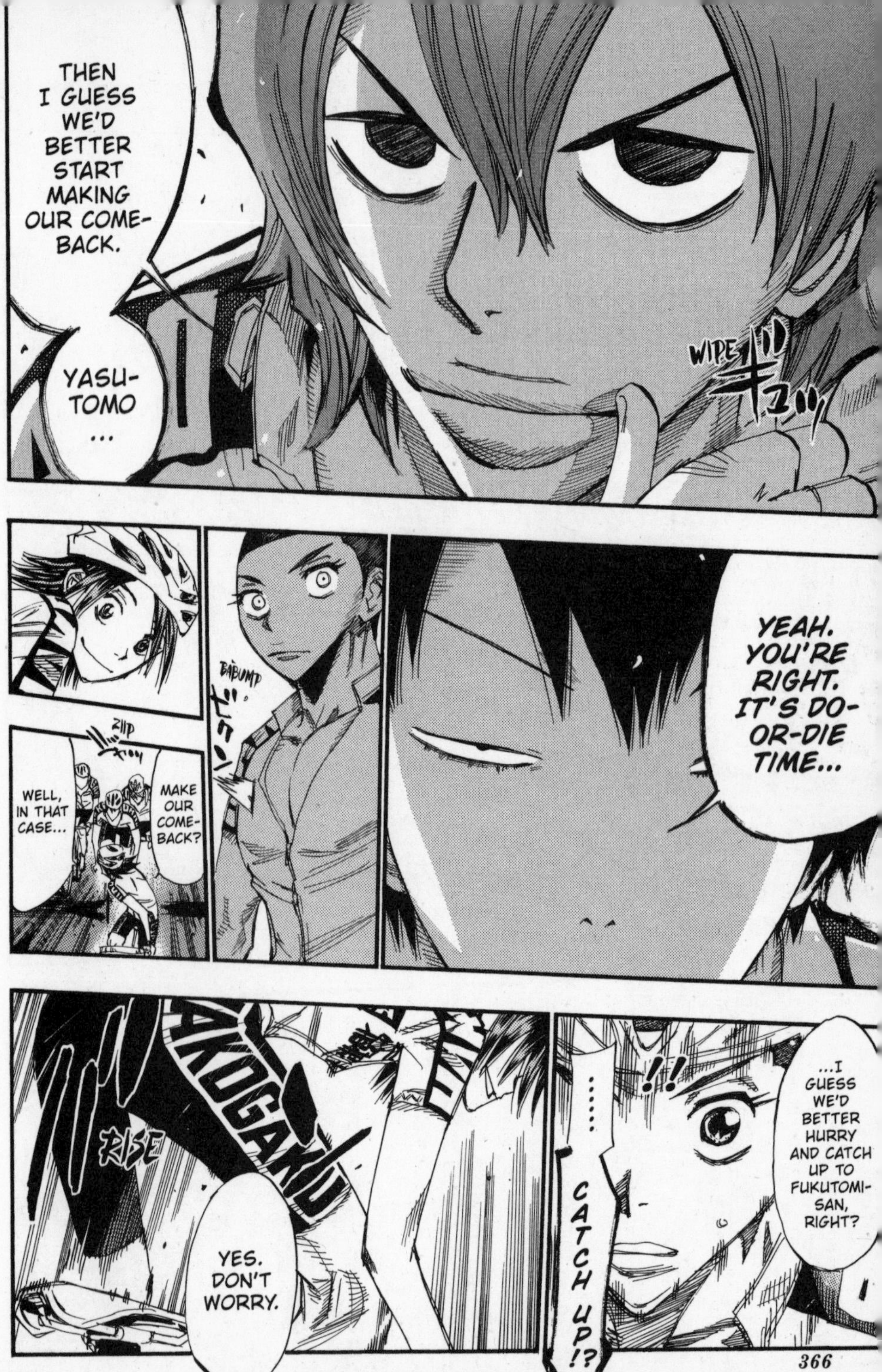

THEN I GUESS WE'D BETTER START MAKING OUR COME-BACK.
WIPE
YASU-TOMO ...
YEAH. YOU'RE RIGHT. IT'S DO-OR-DIE TIME...
BABUMP
ZIP
MAKE OUR COME-BACK?
WELL, IN THAT CASE...
...I GUESS WE'D BETTER HURRY AND CATCH UP TO FUKUTOMI-SAN, RIGHT?
!!
......
CATCH UP!?
AKOGAKU
RISE
YES. DON'T WORRY.

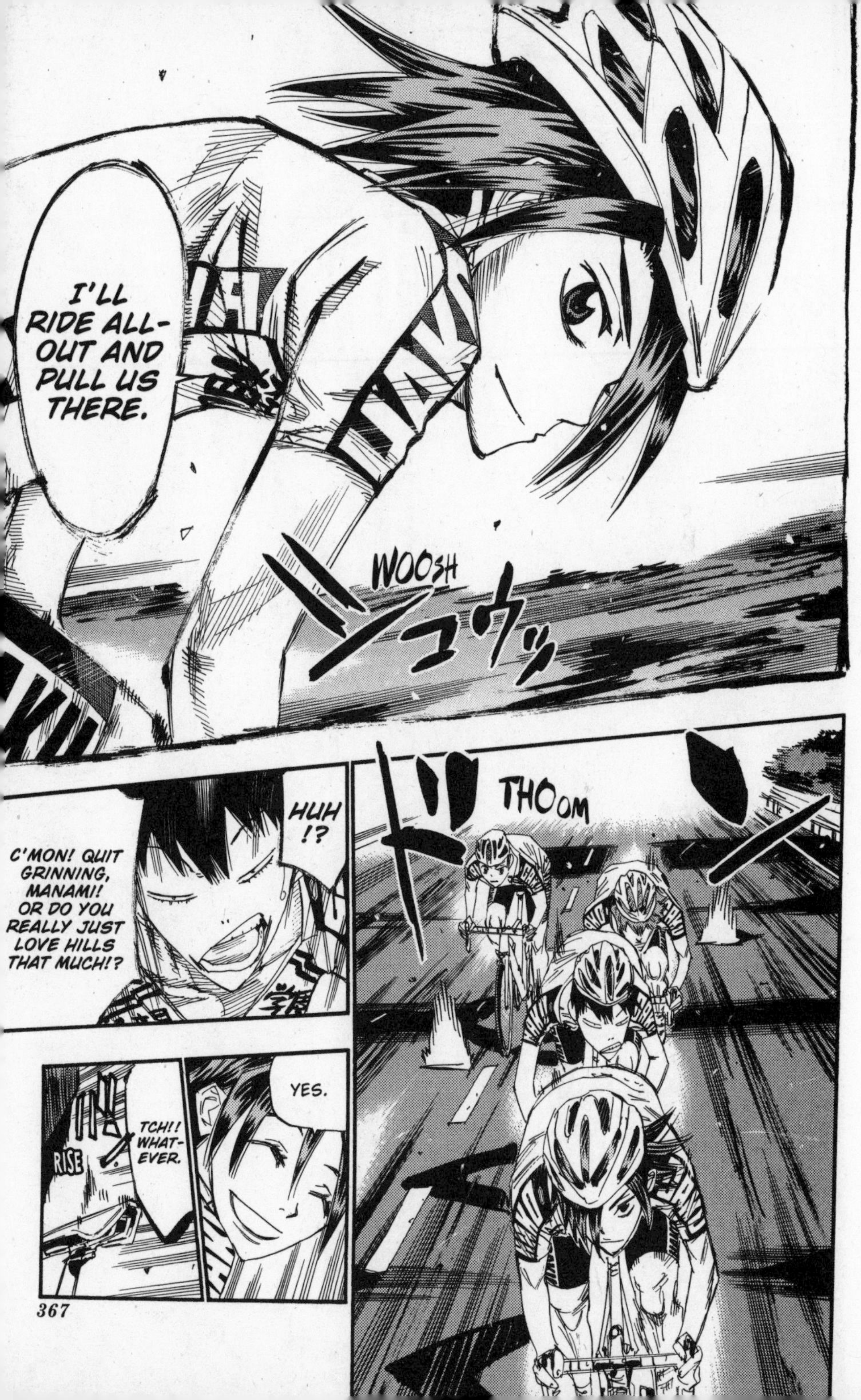
I'LL RIDE ALL-OUT AND PULL US THERE.
WOOSH
THOOM
HUH!?
C'MON! QUIT GRINNING, MANAMI! OR DO YOU REALLY JUST LOVE HILLS THAT MUCH!?
YES.
TCH!! WHATEVER.
RISE

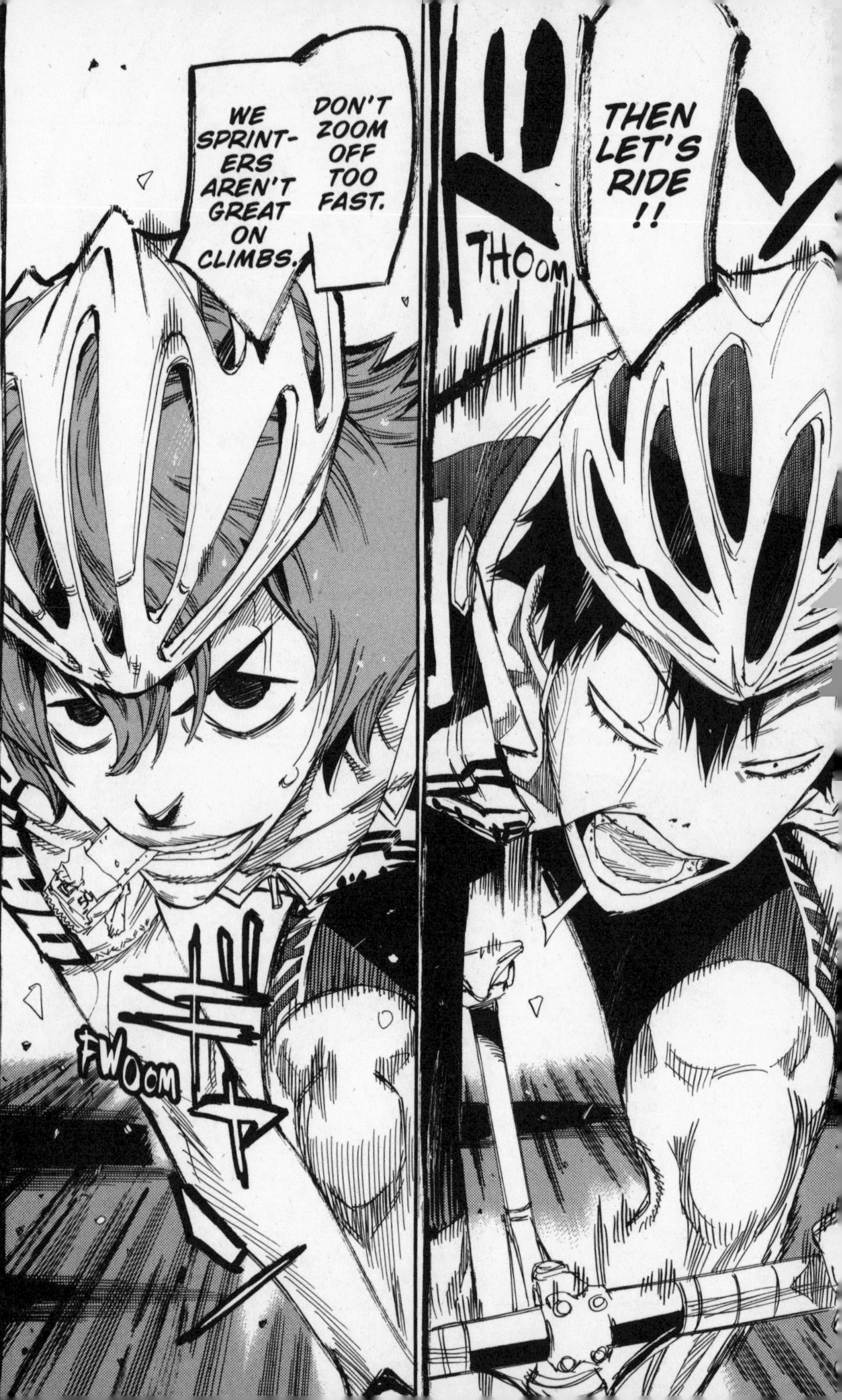
THEN LET'S RIDE !!
THOOM
DON'T ZOOM OFF TOO FAST.
WE SPRINTERS AREN'T GREAT ON CLIMBS.
FWOOM

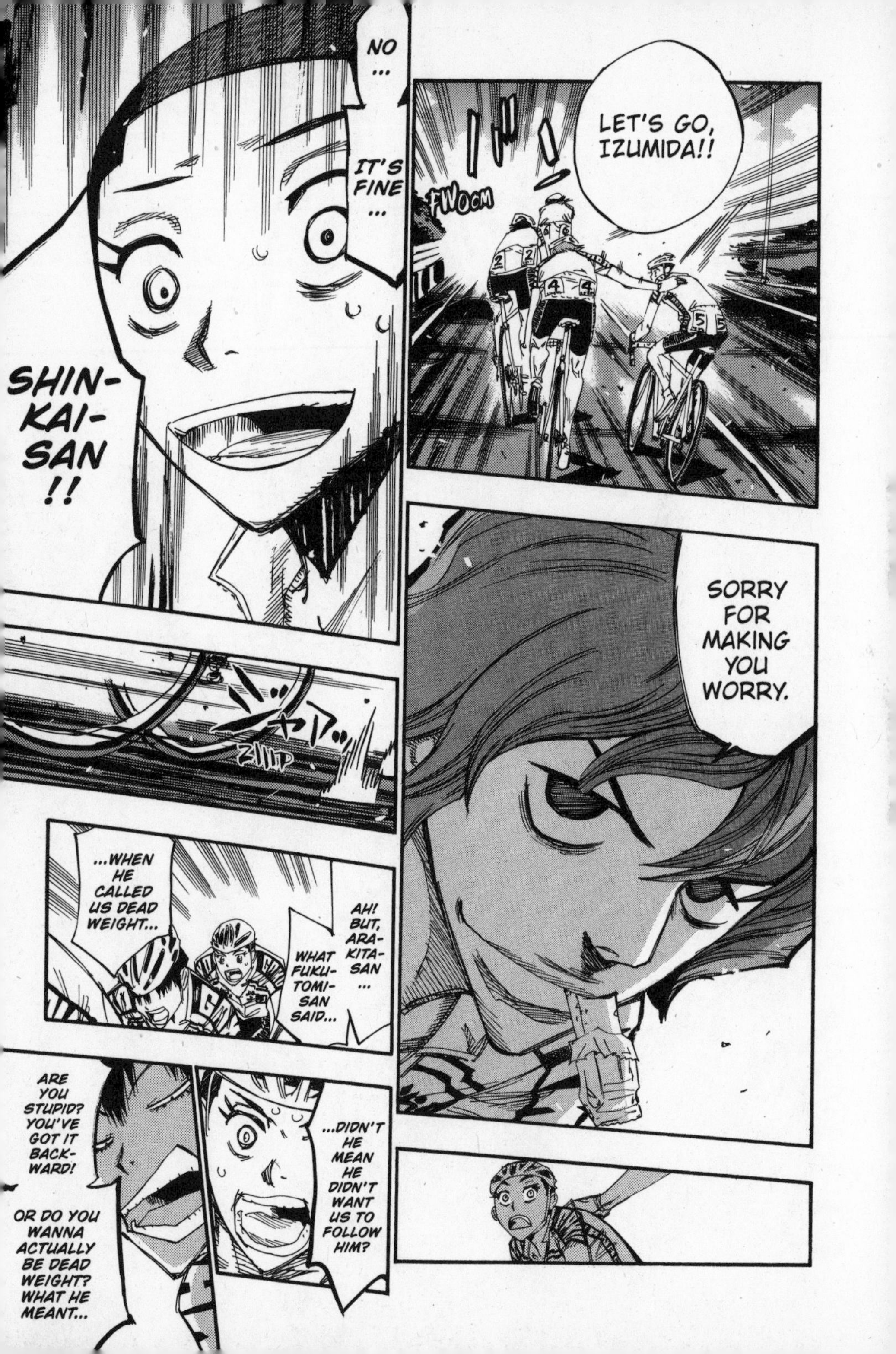
FWOOM
LET'S GO, IZUMIDA!!
NO ...
IT'S FINE ...
SHIN-KAI-SAN!!
SORRY FOR MAKING YOU WORRY.
ZIIIP
AH! BUT, ARAKITA-SAN ...
WHAT FUKUTOMI-SAN SAID...
...WHEN HE CALLED US DEAD WEIGHT...
...DIDN'T HE MEAN HE DIDN'T WANT US TO FOLLOW HIM?
ARE YOU STUPID? YOU'VE GOT IT BACKWARD!
OR DO YOU WANNA ACTUALLY BE DEAD WEIGHT? WHAT HE MEANT...

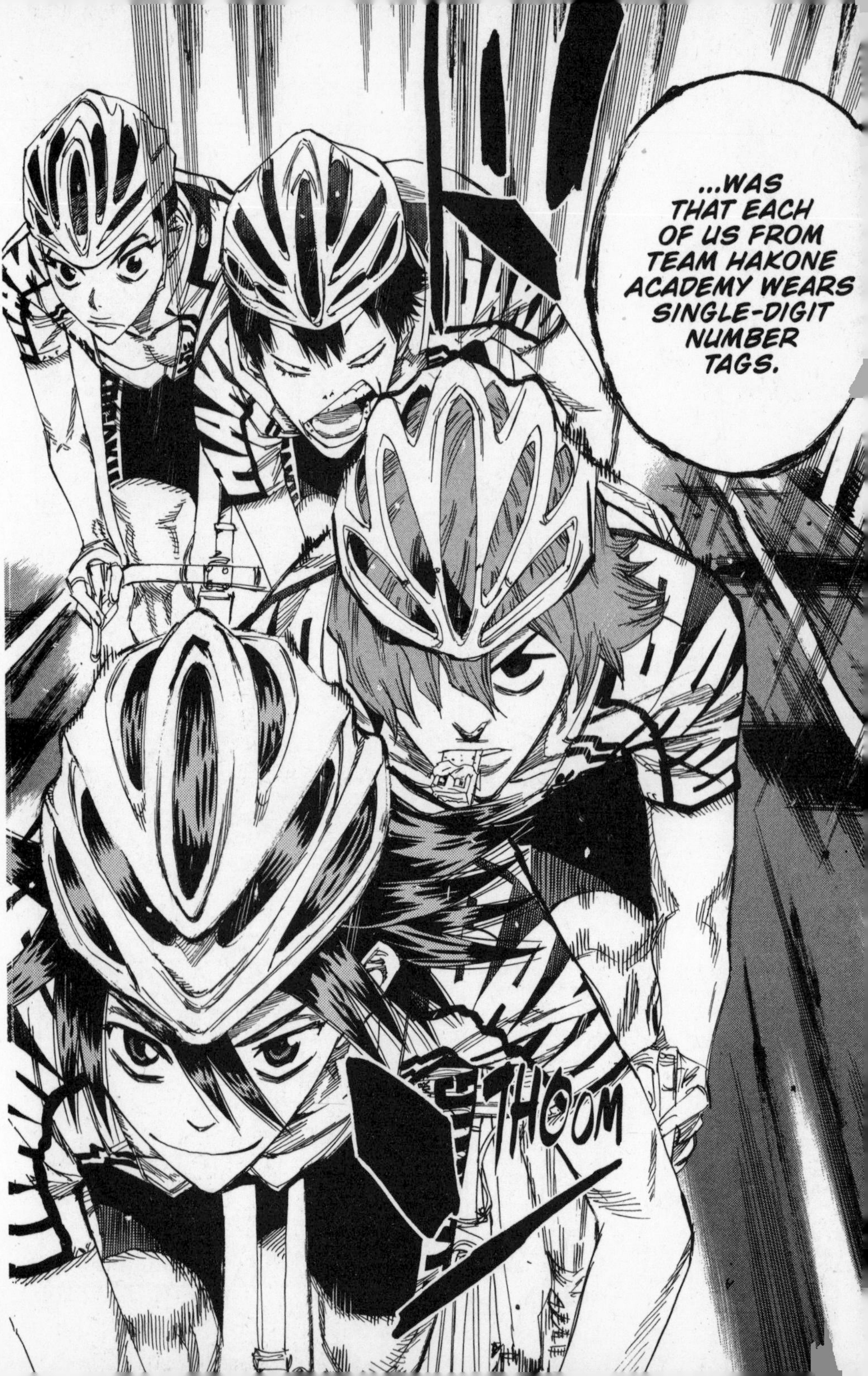
...WAS THAT EACH OF US FROM TEAM HAKONE ACADEMY WEARS SINGLE-DIGIT NUMBER TAGS.
THOOM

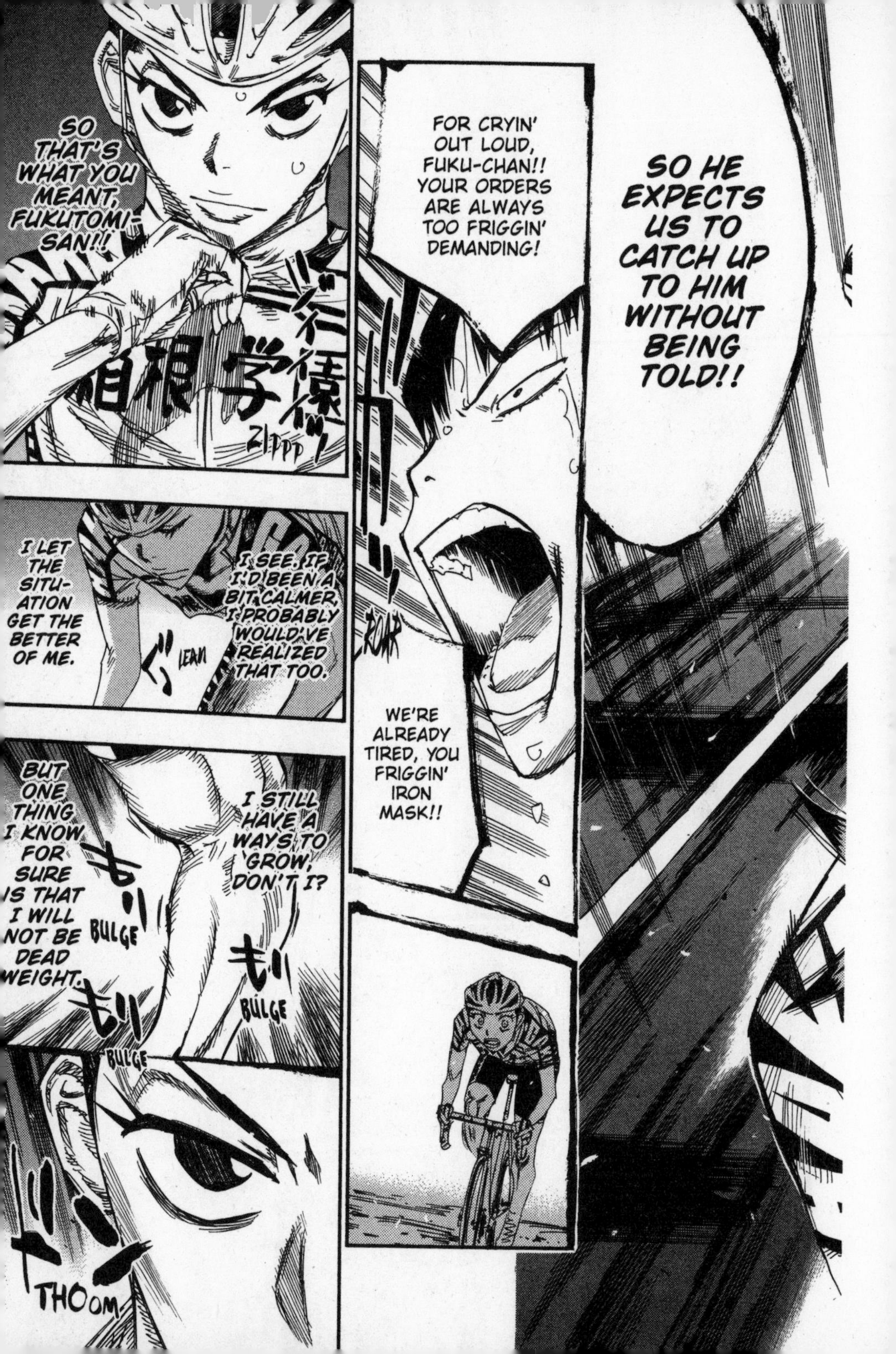
SO HE EXPECTS US TO CATCH UP TO HIM WITHOUT BEING TOLD!!
FOR CRYIN' OUT LOUD, FUKU-CHAN!! YOUR ORDERS ARE ALWAYS TOO FRIGGIN' DEMANDING!
ROAR
WE'RE ALREADY TIRED, YOU FRIGGIN' IRON MASK!!
SO THAT'S WHAT YOU MEANT, FUKUTOMI-SAN!!
ZIPPP
I SEE. IF I'D BEEN A BIT CALMER, I PROBABLY WOULD'VE REALIZED THAT TOO.
I LET THE SITU-ATION GET THE BETTER OF ME.
LEAN
I STILL HAVE A WAYS TO GROW, DON'T I?
BUT ONE THING I KNOW FOR SURE IS THAT I WILL NOT BE DEAD WEIGHT.
BULGE
BULGE
BULGE
THOOM

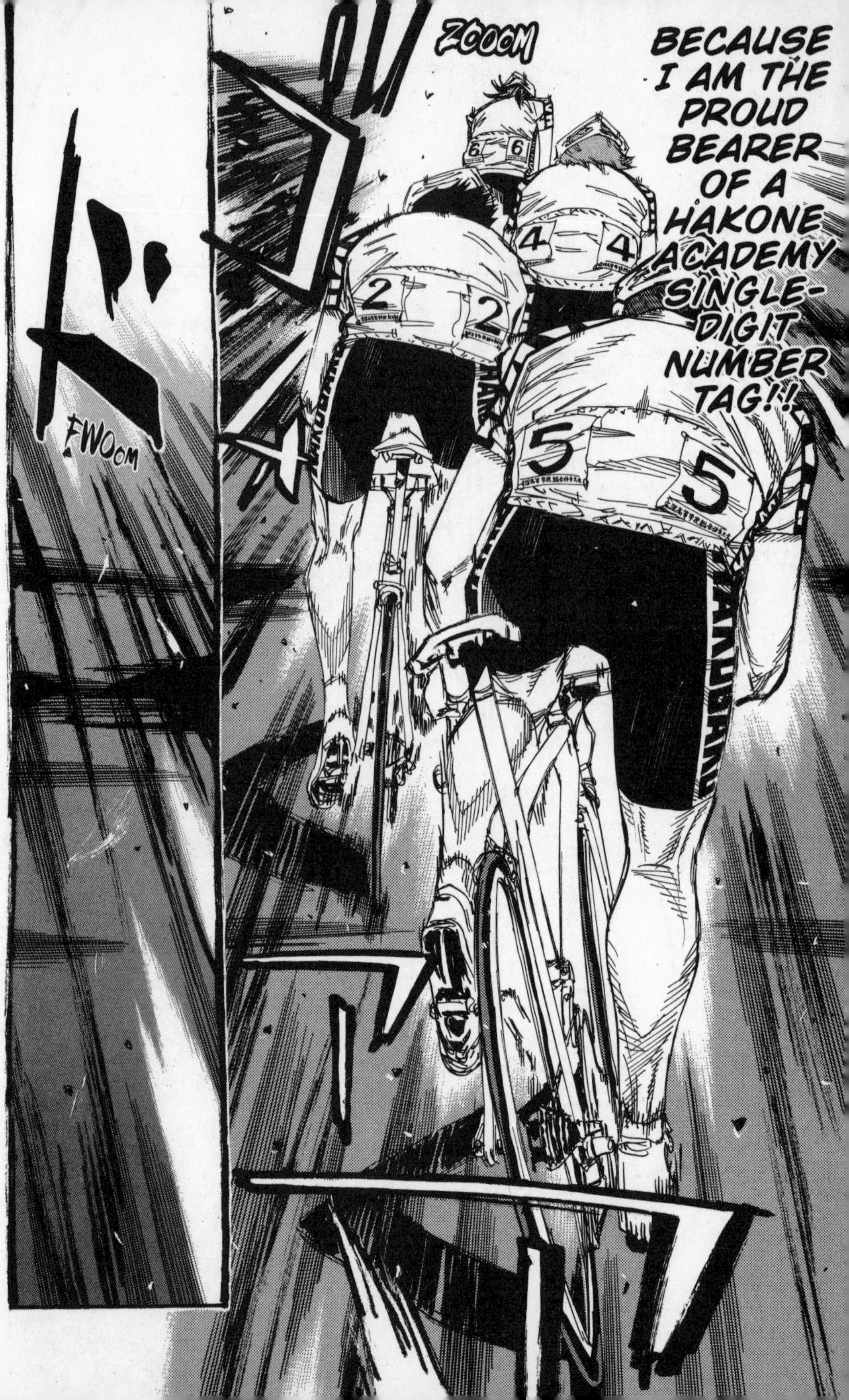
BECAUSE I AM THE PROUD BEARER OF A HAKONE ACADEMY SINGLE-DIGIT NUMBER TAG!!
ZOOOM
FWOOM

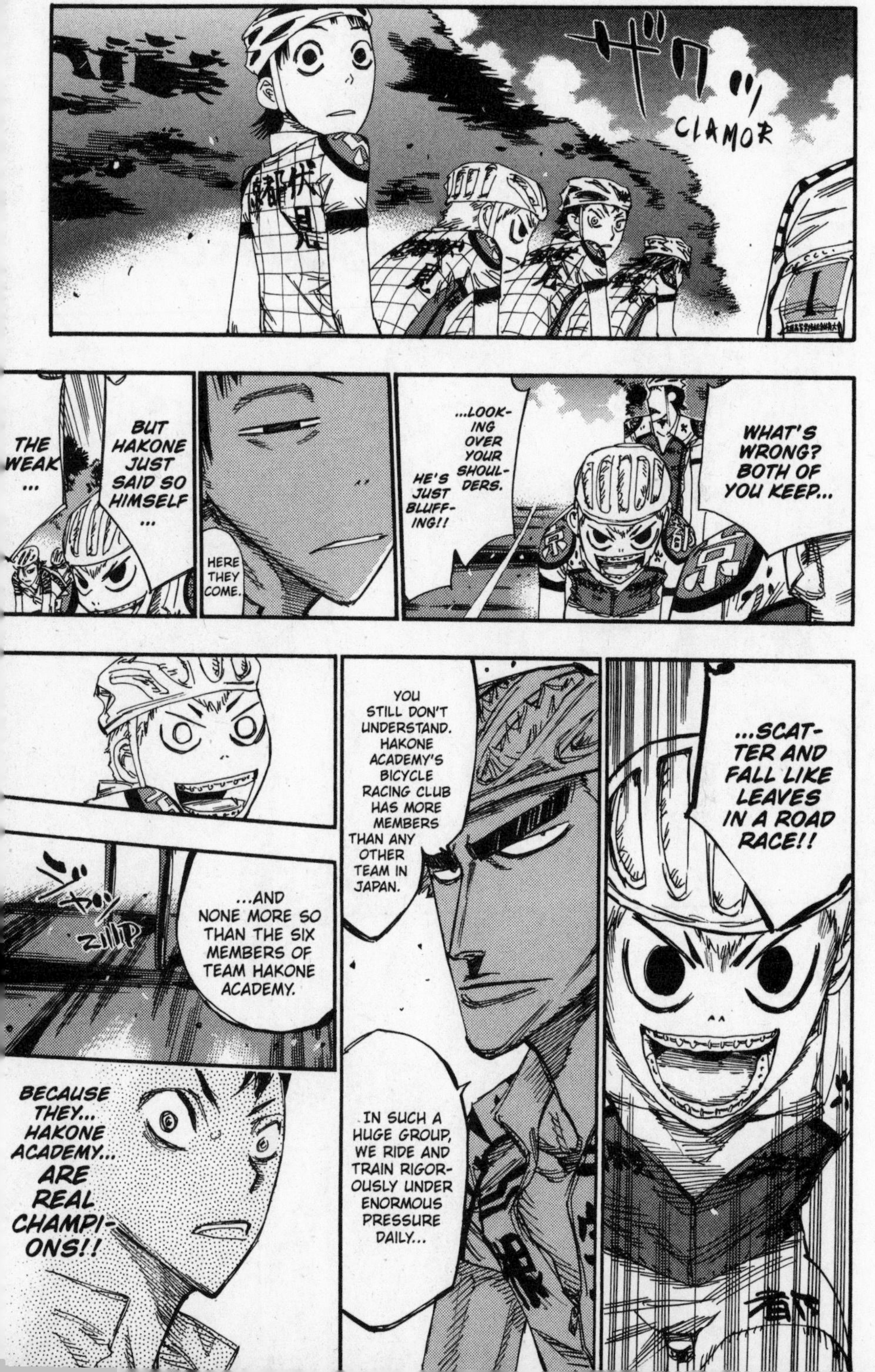

CLAMOR
WHAT'S WRONG? BOTH OF YOU KEEP...
...LOOKING OVER YOUR SHOULDERS.
HE'S JUST BLUFFING!!
HERE THEY COME.
BUT HAKONE JUST SAID SO HIMSELF...
THE WEAK...
...SCATTER AND FALL LIKE LEAVES IN A ROAD RACE!!
YOU STILL DON'T UNDERSTAND. HAKONE ACADEMY'S BICYCLE RACING CLUB HAS MORE MEMBERS THAN ANY OTHER TEAM IN JAPAN.
IN SUCH A HUGE GROUP, WE RIDE AND TRAIN RIGOROUSLY UNDER ENORMOUS PRESSURE DAILY...
...AND NONE MORE SO THAN THE SIX MEMBERS OF TEAM HAKONE ACADEMY.
ZIIIP
BECAUSE THEY... HAKONE ACADEMY... ARE REAL CHAMPIONS!!

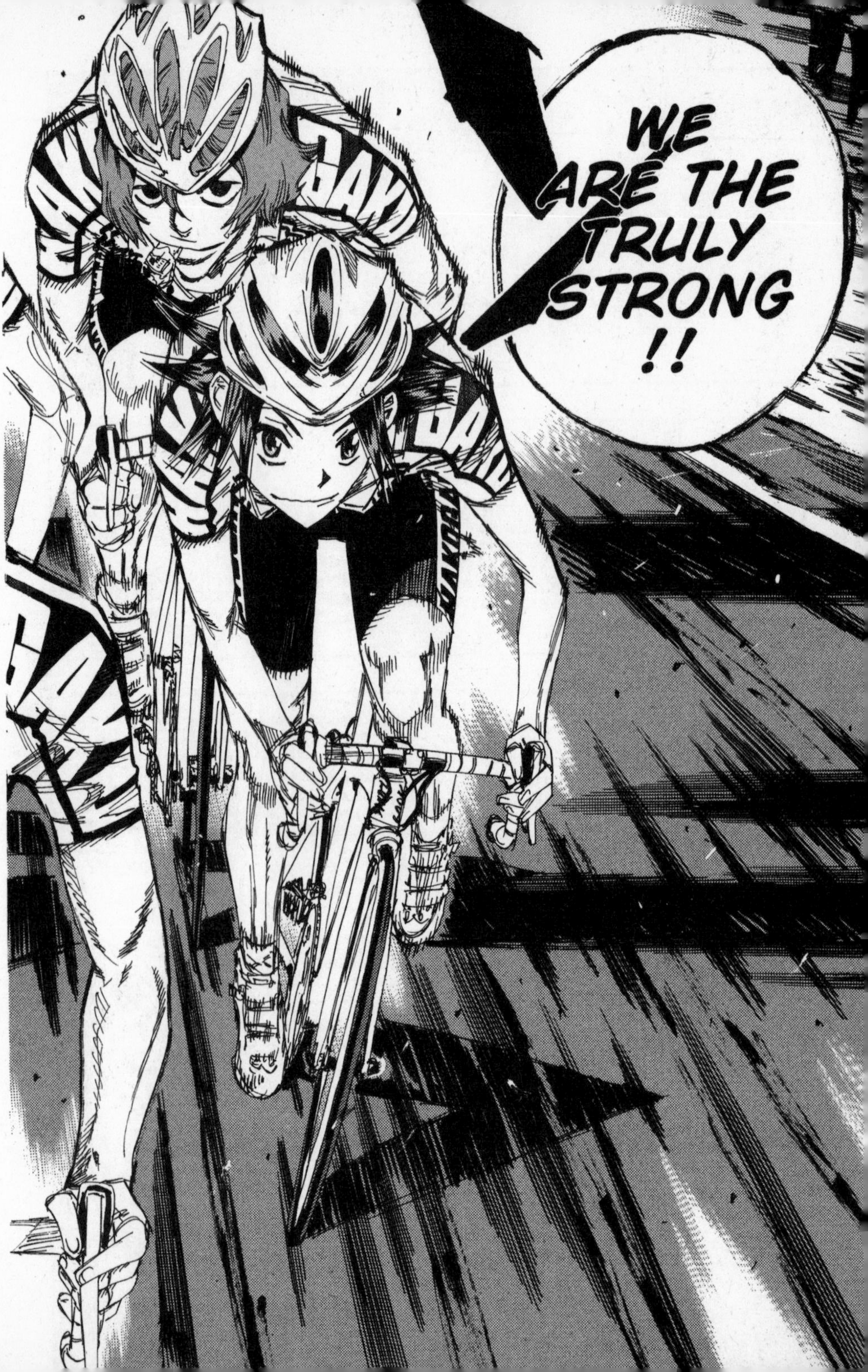
WE ARE THE TRULY STRONG!!

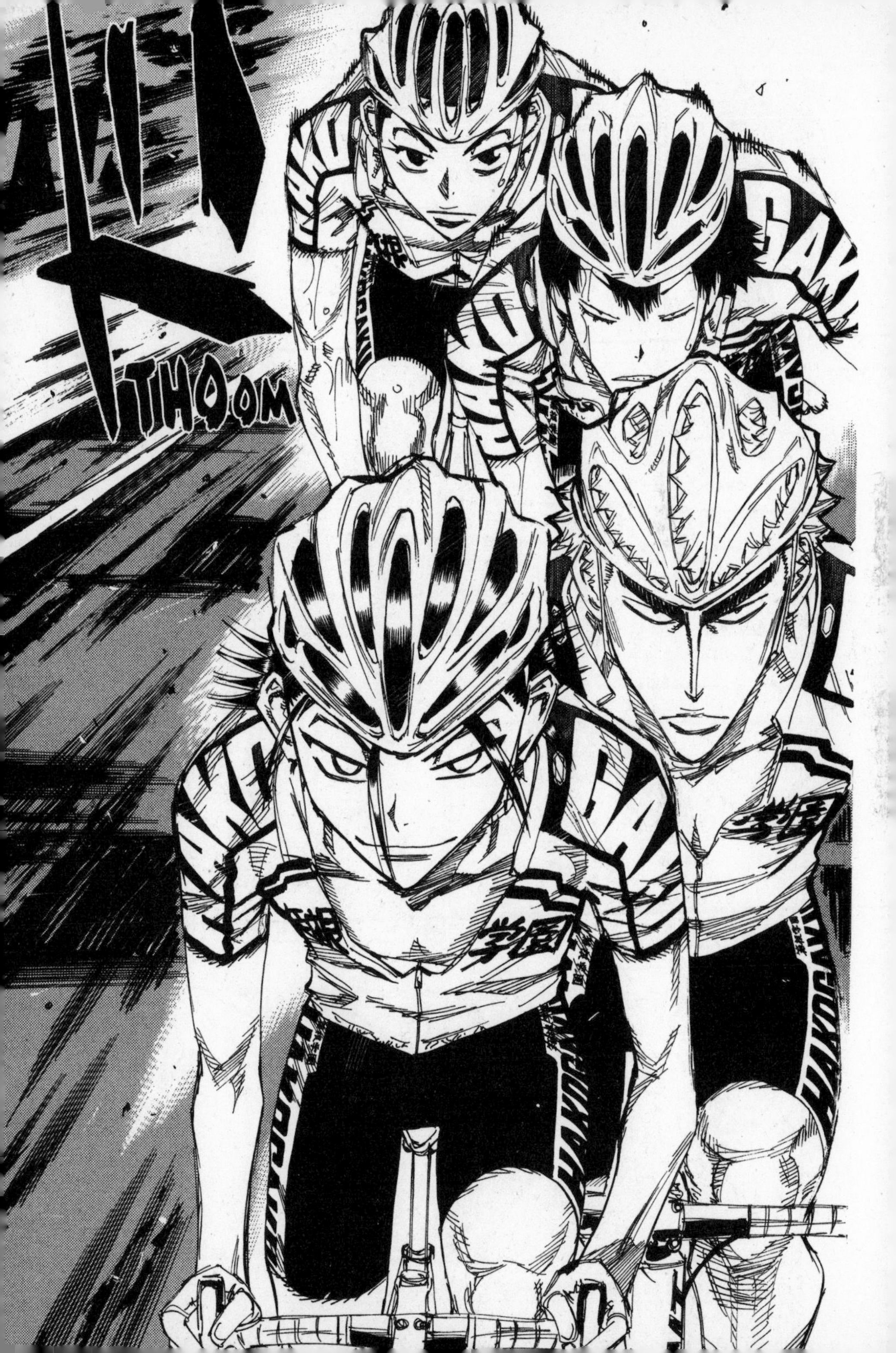
THOOM

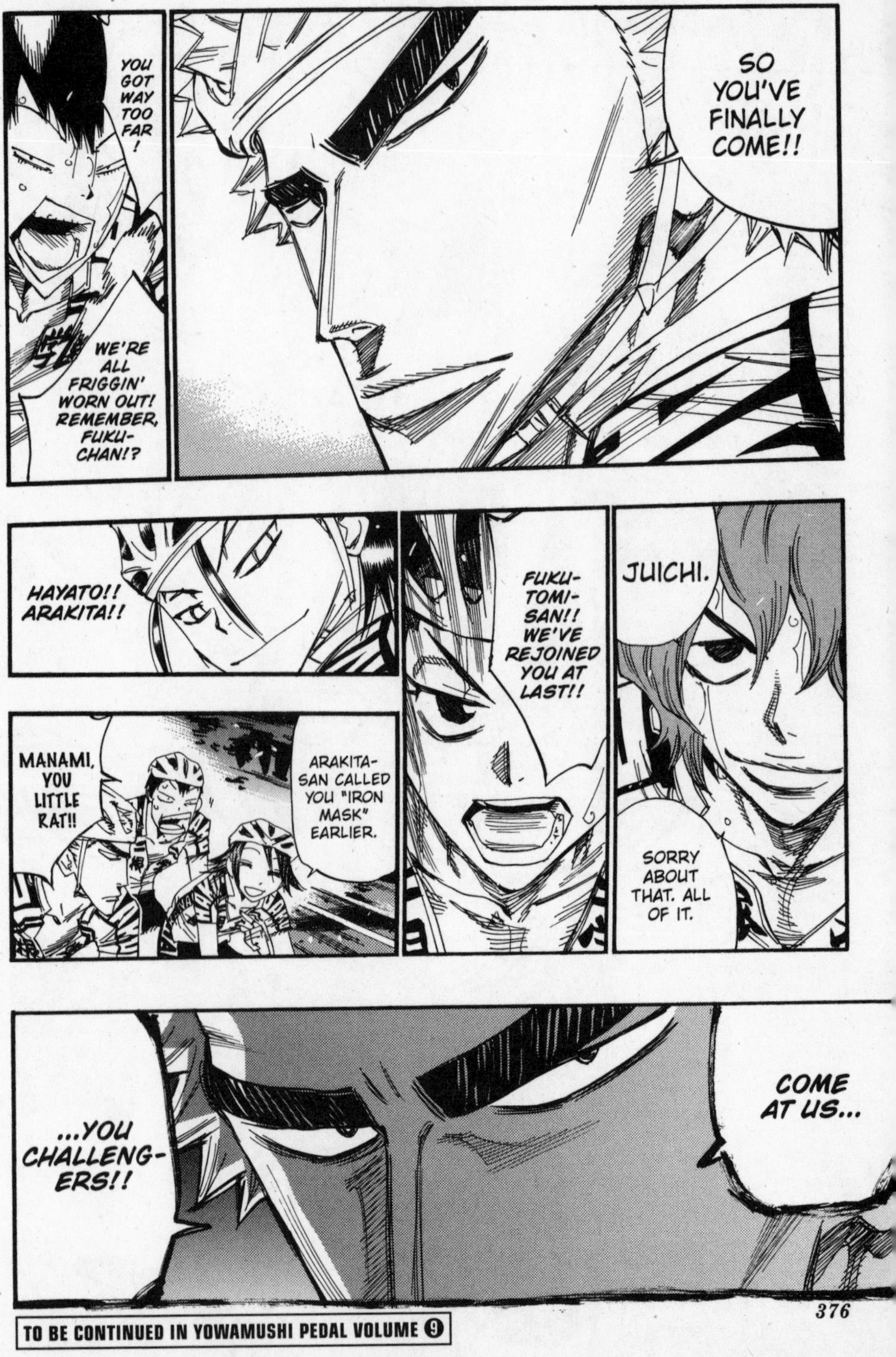
SO YOU'VE FINALLY COME!!
YOU GOT WAY TOO FAR!
WE'RE ALL FRIGGIN' WORN OUT! REMEMBER, FUKU-CHAN!?
JUICHI.
SORRY ABOUT THAT. ALL OF IT.
FUKU-TOMI-SAN!! WE'VE REJOINED YOU AT LAST!!
HAYATO!! ARAKITA!!
ARAKITA-SAN CALLED YOU "IRON MASK" EARLIER.
MANAMI, YOU LITTLE RAT!!
COME AT US...
...YOU CHALLENGERS!!

TO BE CONTINUED IN YOWAMUSHI PEDAL VOLUME 9

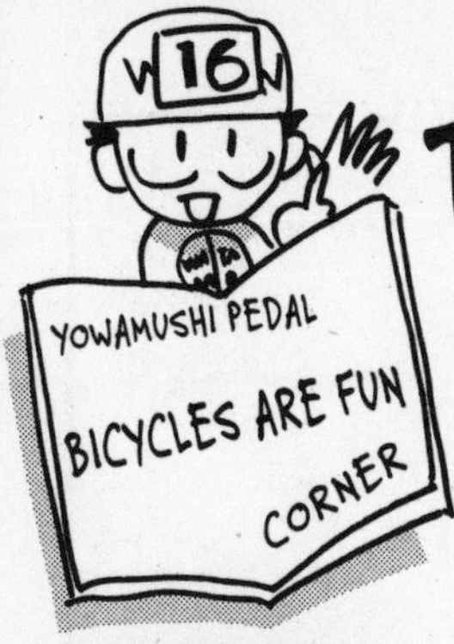
16
YOWAMUSHI PEDAL
BICYCLES ARE FUN
CORNER

THE ORIGINS OF *YOWAPEDA*

LATELY, A LOT OF PEOPLE HAVE BEEN COMING UP AND TELLING ME, "I'M READING *YOWAMUSHI PEDAL*!!" THANK YOU ALL SO MUCH!! ONCE WE START ON THE TOPIC, I TYPICALLY GET ASKED, "WHAT INSPIRED YOU TO START WRITING *YOWAPEDA* ANYWAY?" AHA, NOW I SEE...THIS IS CLEARLY A TOPIC THAT MANY OF YOU ARE PROBABLY WONDERING ABOUT AS WELL, SO I THOUGHT IN THIS VOLUME, I'D TELL YOU THE STORY OF *YOWAPEDA*'S ORIGINS (AT LEAST, AS FAR AS I KNOW!).

SPECIAL REPORT: BONUS MANGA

COINCIDENCES UPON COINCIDENCES!!

THIS WAS THE BIRTH OF *YOWAPEDA*!!

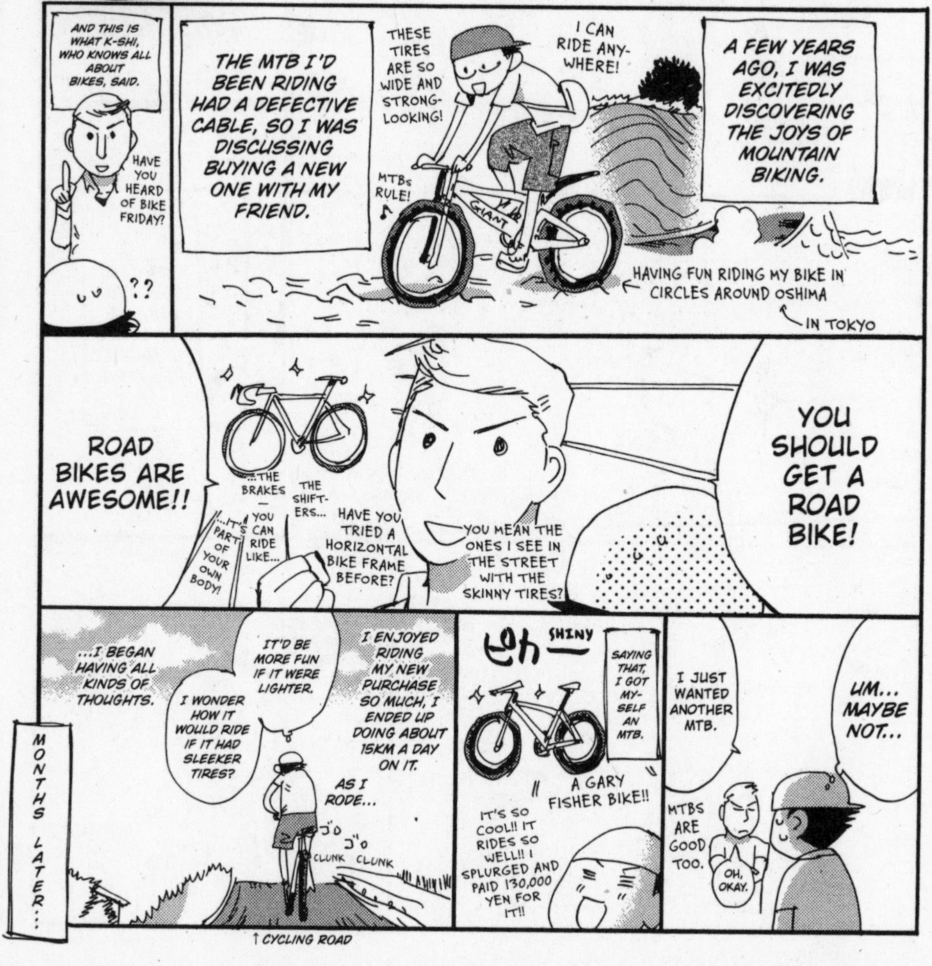
A FEW YEARS AGO, I WAS EXCITEDLY DISCOVERING THE JOYS OF MOUNTAIN BIKING.
I CAN RIDE ANY-WHERE!
THESE TIRES ARE SO WIDE AND STRONG-LOOKING!
MTBs RULE! ♪
GIANT
HAVING FUN RIDING MY BIKE IN CIRCLES AROUND OSHIMA
IN TOKYO
THE MTB I'D BEEN RIDING HAD A DEFECTIVE CABLE, SO I WAS DISCUSSING BUYING A NEW ONE WITH MY FRIEND.
AND THIS IS WHAT K-SHI, WHO KNOWS ALL ABOUT BIKES, SAID.
HAVE YOU HEARD OF BIKE FRIDAY?
??
YOU SHOULD GET A ROAD BIKE!
YOU MEAN THE ONES I SEE IN THE STREET WITH THE SKINNY TIRES?
HAVE YOU TRIED A HORIZONTAL BIKE FRAME BEFORE?
THE SHIFT-ERS...
...THE BRAKES — YOU CAN RIDE LIKE...
...IT'S PART OF YOUR OWN BODY!
ROAD BIKES ARE AWESOME!!
UM... MAYBE NOT...
I JUST WANTED ANOTHER MTB.
MTBS ARE GOOD TOO.
OH, OKAY.
SAYING THAT, I GOT MY-SELF AN MTB.
ピカー SHINY
A GARY FISHER BIKE!!
IT'S SO COOL!! IT RIDES SO WELL!! I SPLURGED AND PAID 130,000 YEN FOR IT!!
MONTHS LATER...
I ENJOYED RIDING MY NEW PURCHASE SO MUCH, I ENDED UP DOING ABOUT 15KM A DAY ON IT.
AS I RODE...
ゴロ ゴロ CLUNK CLUNK
IT'D BE MORE FUN IF IT WERE LIGHTER.
I WONDER HOW IT WOULD RIDE IF IT HAD SLEEKER TIRES?
...I BEGAN HAVING ALL KINDS OF THOUGHTS.
↑CYCLING ROAD

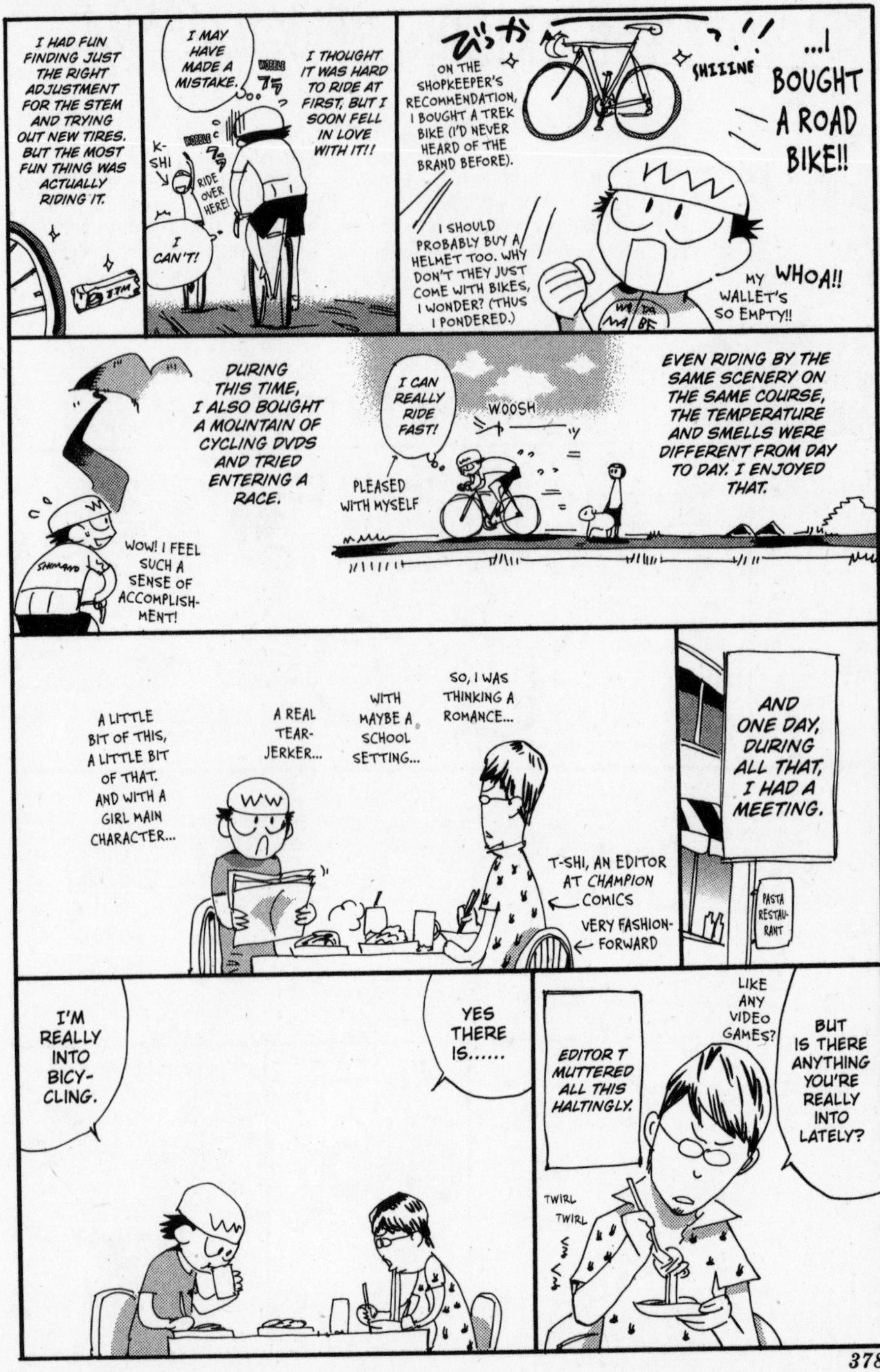

...I BOUGHT A ROAD BIKE!!
SHIIINE
ON THE SHOPKEEPER'S RECOMMENDATION, I BOUGHT A TREK BIKE (I'D NEVER HEARD OF THE BRAND BEFORE).
I SHOULD PROBABLY BUY A HELMET TOO. WHY DON'T THEY JUST COME WITH BIKES, I WONDER? (THUS I PONDERED.)
WHOA!!
MY WALLET'S SO EMPTY!!
I THOUGHT IT WAS HARD TO RIDE AT FIRST, BUT I SOON FELL IN LOVE WITH IT!!
I MAY HAVE MADE A MISTAKE.
WOBBLE
WOBBLE
K-SHI
RIDE OVER HERE!
I CAN'T!
I HAD FUN FINDING JUST THE RIGHT ADJUSTMENT FOR THE STEM AND TRYING OUT NEW TIRES. BUT THE MOST FUN THING WAS ACTUALLY RIDING IT.
EVEN RIDING BY THE SAME SCENERY ON THE SAME COURSE, THE TEMPERATURE AND SMELLS WERE DIFFERENT FROM DAY TO DAY. I ENJOYED THAT.
WOOSH
I CAN REALLY RIDE FAST!
PLEASED WITH MYSELF
DURING THIS TIME, I ALSO BOUGHT A MOUNTAIN OF CYCLING DVDS AND TRIED ENTERING A RACE.
WOW! I FEEL SUCH A SENSE OF ACCOMPLISHMENT!
AND ONE DAY, DURING ALL THAT, I HAD A MEETING.
PASTA RESTAURANT
SO, I WAS THINKING A ROMANCE...
WITH MAYBE A SCHOOL SETTING...
A REAL TEAR-JERKER...
A LITTLE BIT OF THIS, A LITTLE BIT OF THAT. AND WITH A GIRL MAIN CHARACTER...
T-SHI, AN EDITOR AT CHAMPION COMICS
VERY FASHION-FORWARD
BUT IS THERE ANYTHING YOU'RE REALLY INTO LATELY?
LIKE ANY VIDEO GAMES?
EDITOR T MUTTERED ALL THIS HALTINGLY.
TWIRL TWIRL
YES THERE IS......
I'M REALLY INTO BICYCLING.

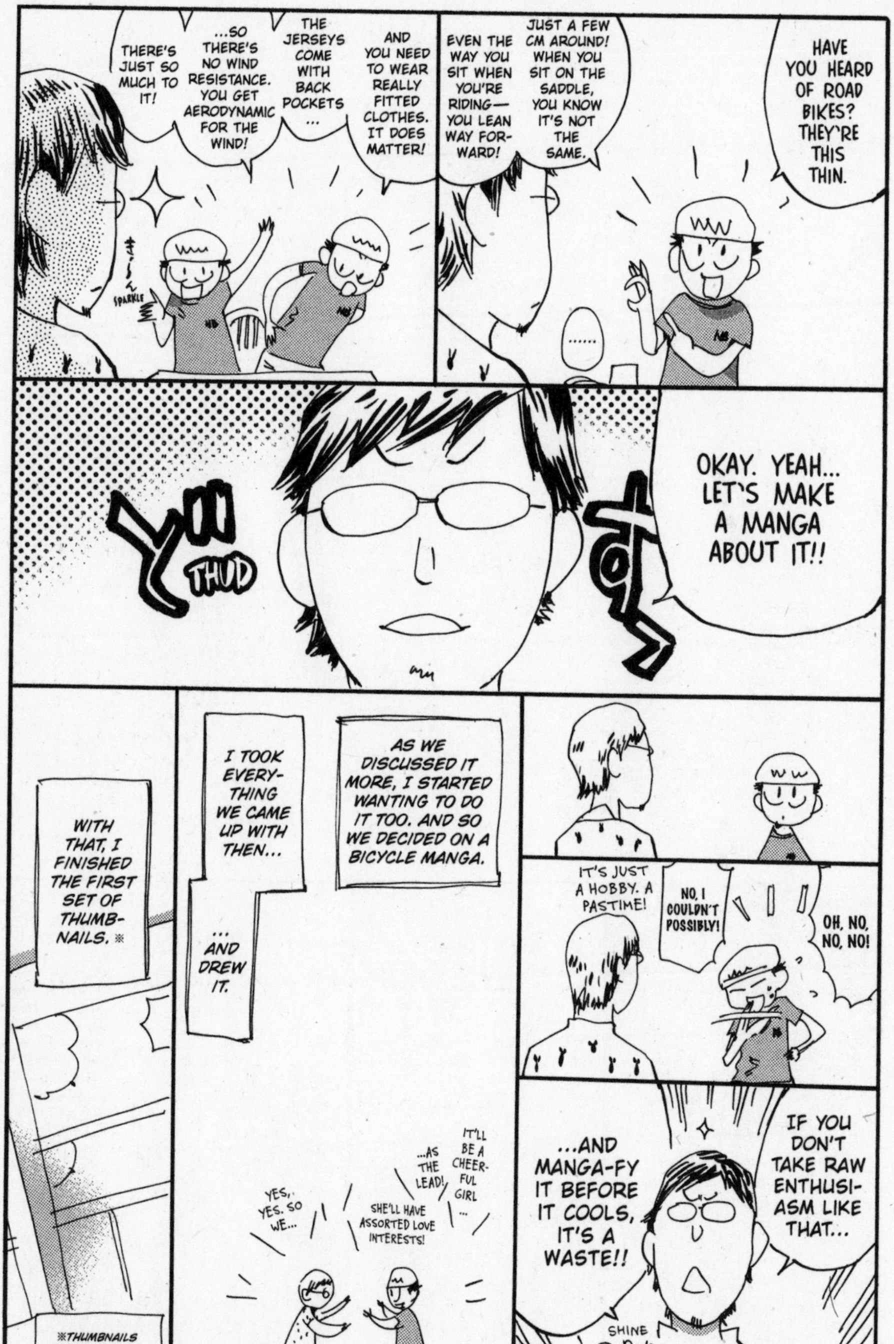
HAVE YOU HEARD OF ROAD BIKES? THEY'RE THIS THIN.
JUST A FEW CM AROUND! WHEN YOU SIT ON THE SADDLE, YOU KNOW IT'S NOT THE SAME.
EVEN THE WAY YOU SIT WHEN YOU'RE RIDING—YOU LEAN WAY FORWARD!
......
AND YOU NEED TO WEAR REALLY FITTED CLOTHES. IT DOES MATTER!
THE JERSEYS COME WITH BACK POCKETS ...
...SO THERE'S NO WIND RESISTANCE. YOU GET AERODYNAMIC FOR THE WIND!
THERE'S JUST SO MUCH TO IT!
SPARKLE
OKAY. YEAH... LET'S MAKE A MANGA ABOUT IT!!
THUD
OH, NO, NO, NO!
NO, I COULDN'T POSSIBLY!
IT'S JUST A HOBBY. A PASTIME!
IF YOU DON'T TAKE RAW ENTHUSIASM LIKE THAT...
...AND MANGA-FY IT BEFORE IT COOLS, IT'S A WASTE!!
SHINE
AS WE DISCUSSED IT MORE, I STARTED WANTING TO DO IT TOO. AND SO WE DECIDED ON A BICYCLE MANGA.
I TOOK EVERYTHING WE CAME UP WITH THEN...
...AND DREW IT.
IT'LL BE A CHEERFUL GIRL...
...AS THE LEAD!
SHE'LL HAVE ASSORTED LOVE INTERESTS!
YES, YES. SO WE...
WITH THAT, I FINISHED THE FIRST SET OF THUMBNAILS. ※

※THUMBNAILS ARE THE PENCIL-DRAWN ROUGH DRAFT OF A MANGA THAT SHOWS THE LAYOUT AND STORY.

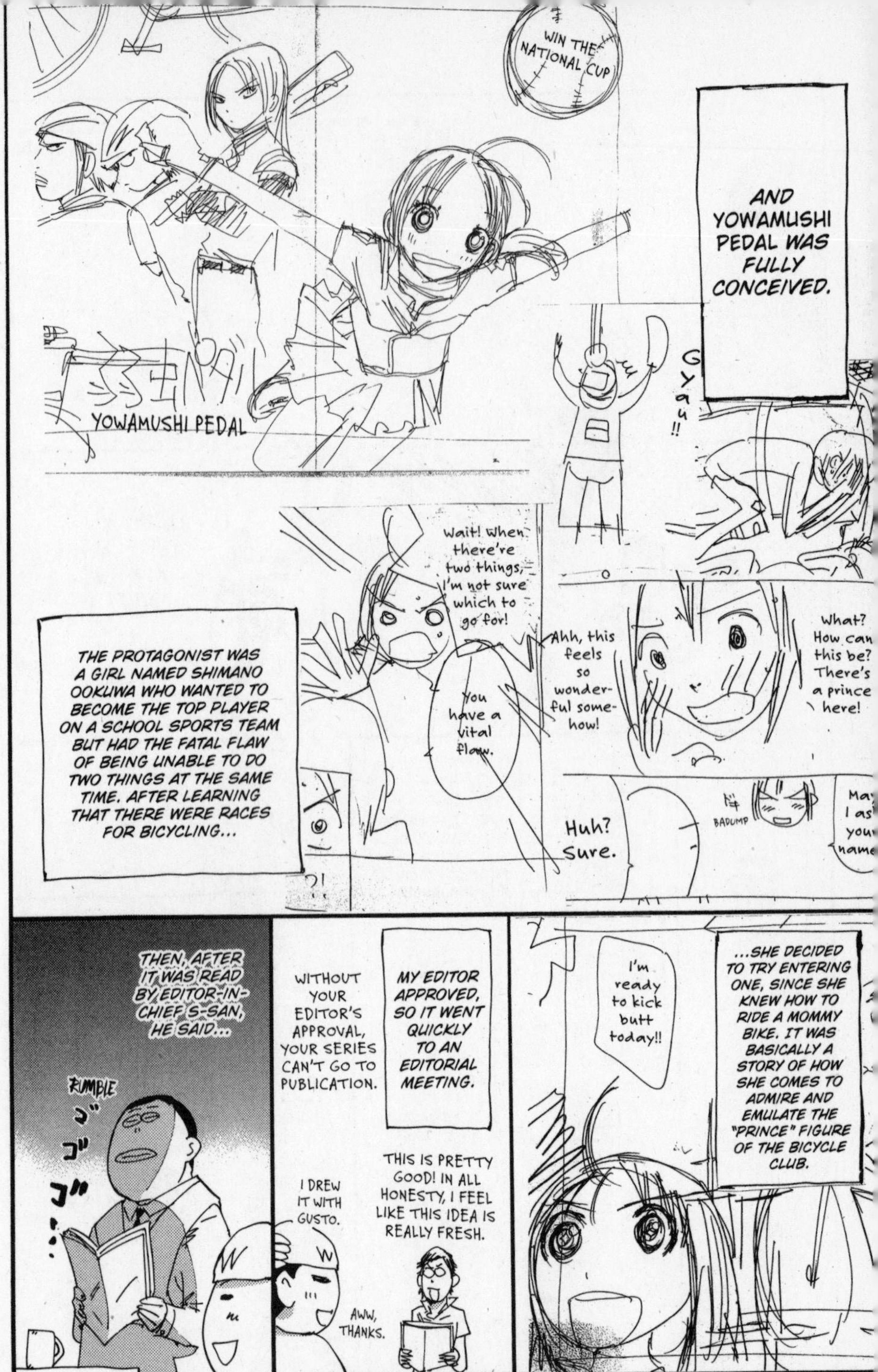
AND YOWAMUSHI PEDAL WAS FULLY CONCEIVED.
WIN THE NATIONAL CUP
YOWAMUSHI PEDAL
GYau!!
What? How can this be? There's a prince here!
Ahh, this feels so wonderful somehow!
Wait! When there're two things, I'm not sure which to go for!
You have a vital flaw.
BADUMP
Huh? Sure.
?!
THE PROTAGONIST WAS A GIRL NAMED SHIMANO OOKUWA WHO WANTED TO BECOME THE TOP PLAYER ON A SCHOOL SPORTS TEAM BUT HAD THE FATAL FLAW OF BEING UNABLE TO DO TWO THINGS AT THE SAME TIME. AFTER LEARNING THAT THERE WERE RACES FOR BICYCLING...
...SHE DECIDED TO TRY ENTERING ONE, SINCE SHE KNEW HOW TO RIDE A MOMMY BIKE. IT WAS BASICALLY A STORY OF HOW SHE COMES TO ADMIRE AND EMULATE THE "PRINCE" FIGURE OF THE BICYCLE CLUB.
I'm ready to kick butt today!!
MY EDITOR APPROVED, SO IT WENT QUICKLY TO AN EDITORIAL MEETING.
WITHOUT YOUR EDITOR'S APPROVAL, YOUR SERIES CAN'T GO TO PUBLICATION.
THIS IS PRETTY GOOD! IN ALL HONESTY, I FEEL LIKE THIS IDEA IS REALLY FRESH.
I DREW IT WITH GUSTO.
AWW, THANKS.
THEN, AFTER IT WAS READ BY EDITOR-IN-CHIEF S-SAN, HE SAID...
RUMBLE

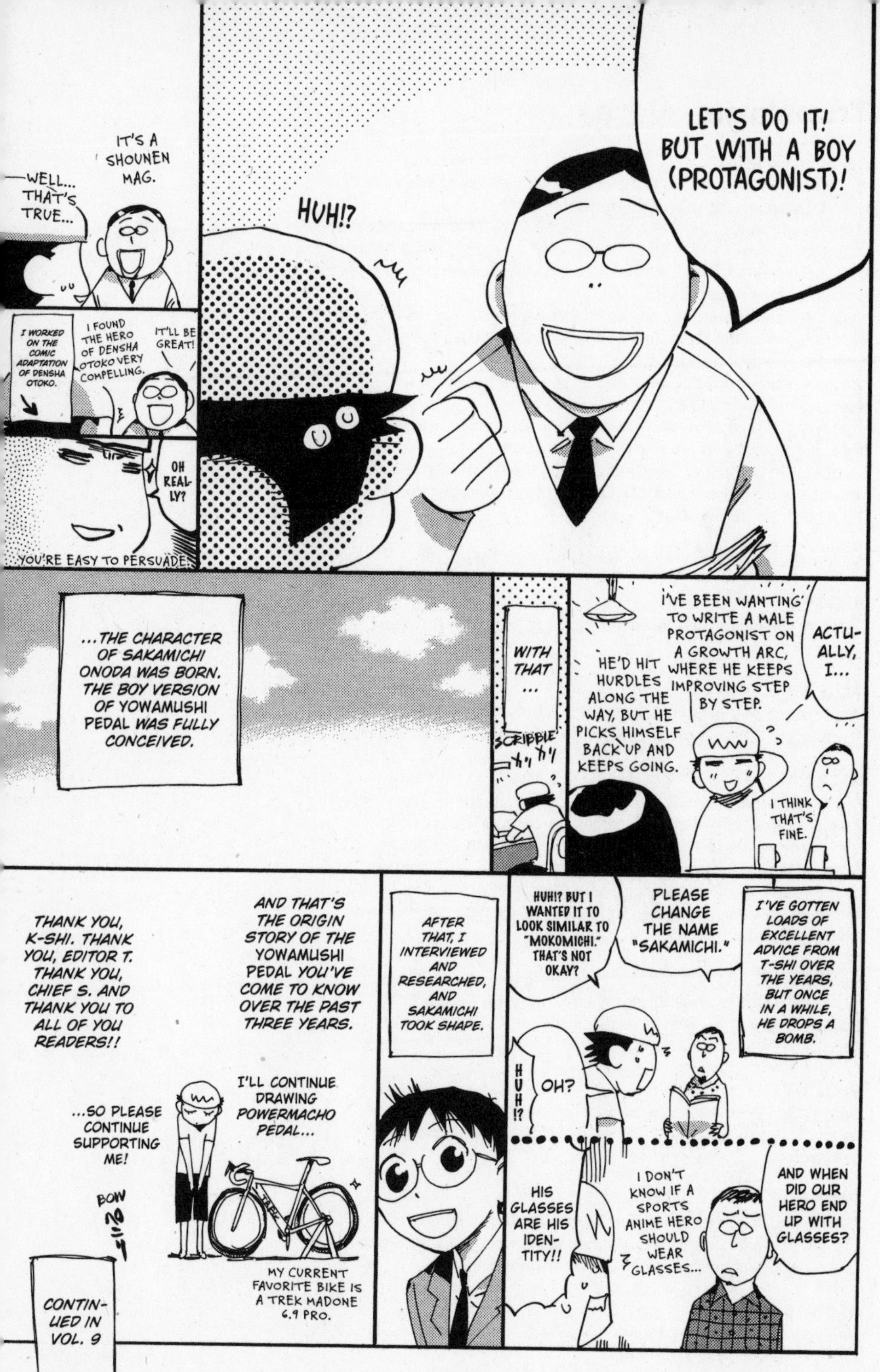
LET'S DO IT! BUT WITH A BOY (PROTAGONIST)!
HUH!?
IT'S A SHOUNEN MAG.
WELL... THAT'S TRUE...
IT'LL BE GREAT!
I FOUND THE HERO OF DENSHA OTOKO VERY COMPELLING.
I WORKED ON THE COMIC ADAPTATION OF DENSHA OTOKO.
OH REAL-LY?
YOU'RE EASY TO PERSUADE.
ACTU-ALLY, I...
I'VE BEEN WANTING TO WRITE A MALE PROTAGONIST ON A GROWTH ARC, WHERE HE KEEPS IMPROVING STEP BY STEP.
HE'D HIT HURDLES ALONG THE WAY, BUT HE PICKS HIMSELF BACK UP AND KEEPS GOING.
I THINK THAT'S FINE.
WITH THAT...
SCRIBBLE
...THE CHARACTER OF SAKAMICHI ONODA WAS BORN. THE BOY VERSION OF YOWAMUSHI PEDAL WAS FULLY CONCEIVED.
I'VE GOTTEN LOADS OF EXCELLENT ADVICE FROM T-SHI OVER THE YEARS, BUT ONCE IN A WHILE, HE DROPS A BOMB.
PLEASE CHANGE THE NAME "SAKAMICHI."
HUH!? BUT I WANTED IT TO LOOK SIMILAR TO "MOKOMICHI." THAT'S NOT OKAY?
OH?
HUH!?
AFTER THAT, I INTERVIEWED AND RESEARCHED, AND SAKAMICHI TOOK SHAPE.
AND WHEN DID OUR HERO END UP WITH GLASSES?
I DON'T KNOW IF A SPORTS ANIME HERO SHOULD WEAR GLASSES...
HIS GLASSES ARE HIS IDEN-TITY!!
AND THAT'S THE ORIGIN STORY OF THE YOWAMUSHI PEDAL YOU'VE COME TO KNOW OVER THE PAST THREE YEARS.
THANK YOU, K-SHI. THANK YOU, EDITOR T. THANK YOU, CHIEF S. AND THANK YOU TO ALL OF YOU READERS!!
I'LL CONTINUE DRAWING POWERMACHO PEDAL...
...SO PLEASE CONTINUE SUPPORTING ME!
BOW
MY CURRENT FAVORITE BIKE IS A TREK MADONE 6.9 PRO.
CONTIN-UED IN VOL. 9

Translation Notes

Common Honorifics
-*san*: The Japanese equivalent of Mr./Mrs./Miss. If a situation calls for politeness, this is the fail-safe honorific.
-*kun*: Used most often when referring to boys, this indicates affection or familiarity. Occasionally used by older men among their peers, but it may also be used by anyone referring to a person of lower standing.
-*chan*: An affectionate honorific indicating familiarity used mostly in reference to girls; also used in reference to cute persons or animals of either gender.
-*senpai*: A suffix used to address upperclassmen or more experienced co-workers.
-*shi*: A more formal version of *san* common to written Japanese, it's the default honorific used in newspapers.
no honorific: Indicates familiarity or closeness; if used without permission or reason, addressing someone in this manner would constitute an insult.

A kilometer is approximately .6 of a mile.

PAGE 12
Peloton: A cycling term for the "pack," or the main group of riders in a race.

PAGE 13
Wussyzumi: In the Japanese version, Midousuji calls Imaizumi "Yowaizumi," playing off of the Japanese word for weak (*yowai*).

PAGE 21
Goofs: Midousuji uses the term *zaku* in the Japanese version, which means "assorted vegetables for *sukiyaki* hot pot," but is also the name of the common enemy robot in the anime *Mobile Suit Gundam*. The former meaning refers to the rest of Kyoto-Fushimi being there to serve Midousuji, while the latter refers to how Midousuji treats his teammates as generic and interchangeable.

PAGE 25
Hakogaku: This phrase, present on all Hakone Academy uniforms, is a shortened version of the school's name in Japanese (*Hakone Gakuen*).

PAGE 51
Domestique: A cyclist in a competitive team who focuses on helping the team and the ace rather than winning the race themselves.

PAGE 90
Kumamoto: The capital of Kumamoto Prefecture in Kyushu, known for its frequent rain and being the home of Kumamoto Castle—the largest complete castle in Japan.

PAGE 165
Usakichi: *Usagi* is Japanese for "rabbit," so this name is akin to something like "Mr. Rabbiton."

PAGE 322
Pocari: Pocari Sweat is a popular electrolyte-replenishing sports drink in Japan.

PAGE 377
Bike Friday: A brand of high-performance bicycles and bicycle parts, especially for travel and commuter use.

130,000 yen: Approximately $1,300 USD.

PAGE 381
Mokomichi: *Densha Otoko* actor Mokomichi Hayami's highly unusual name is said to mean "straightforward path" and a piece of Japanese pop culture trivia in the 2000s.

ENJOY EVERYTHING.

YOU SHOULD COME PLAY WITH YOTSUBA TOO!

Join Yotsuba as she delights in the things many of us take for granted in this Eisner-nominated series.

VOLUMES 1-13 AVAILABLE NOW!

Hello! This is YOTSUBA!

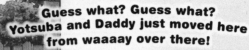

Guess what? Guess what? Yotsuba and Daddy just moved here from waaaay over there!

And Yotsuba met these nice people next door and made new friends to play with!

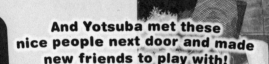

The pretty one took Yotsuba on a bike ride!
(Whoooa! There was a big hill!)

And Ena's a good drawer!
(Almost as good as Yotsuba!)

And their mom always gives Yotsuba ice cream!
(Yummy!)

And...
And...
OHHHH!

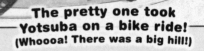

YOWAMUSHI PEDAL 8

WATARU WATANABE

Translation: Su Mon Han

Lettering: Lys Blakeslee, Brndn Blakeslee

This book is a work of fiction. Names, characters, places, and incidents are the product of the author's imagination or are used fictitiously. Any resemblance to actual events, locales, or persons, living or dead, is coincidental.

First published in Japan in 2010, 2011 by Akita Publishing Co., Ltd., Tokyo.
English translation rights arranged with Akita Publishing Co., Ltd. through Tuttle-Mori Agency, Inc., Tokyo.

Yen Press
1290 Avenue of the Americas
New York, NY 10104

Visit us at yenpress.com
facebook.com/yenpress
twitter.com/yenpress
yenpress.tumblr.com
instagram.com/yenpress

First Yen Press Edition: April 2018

Yen Press is an imprint of Yen Press, LLC.
The Yen Press name and logo are trademarks of Yen Press, LLC.

The publisher is not responsible for websites (or their content) that are not owned by the publisher.

Library of Congress Control Number: 2015960124

ISBNs: 978-0-316-52078-2 (paperback)
978-0-316-52079-9 (ebook)

10 9 8 7 6 5 4 3 2 1

WOR

Printed in the United States of America